CHAUCER AND MIDDLE ENGLISH STUDIES

ROSSELL HOPE ROBBINS

CHAUCER AND MIDDLE ENGLISH STUDIES

in honour of
Rossell Hope Robbins

EDITED BY
BERYL ROWLAND

THE KENT STATE UNIVERSITY PRESS

© George Allen & Unwin Ltd 1974

Published in the United States of America
by The Kent State University Press

LC 73-78046

ISBN 087338-141-6

Printed in Great Britain
in 11pt Baskerville type
by W & J Mackay Limited, Chatham

PREFACE

This volume has been written to honour Rossell Hope Robbins on his sixtieth birthday. It is a tribute to a scholar of international repute, a recognition of the high regard in which he is held in universities in many parts of the world. His achievements have been prodigious: *The Index of Middle English Verse* (with Carleton Brown), *Secular Lyrics of the XIV and XV Centuries*, *Historical Poems of the XIV and XV Centuries*, *The Encyclopedia of Witchcraft and Demonology*, *Early English Carols*, and numerous other writings of permanent value are monuments to his indefatigable and productive research. In addition, he is a humanist with a warm response to life which has been quickened, not diminished, by years among manuscripts. To read a manuscript, as he himself observes, is a liberal education, providing new insights and a kind of pleasure which may be called mirth:

> I have got a lot of fun out of life. From personal knowledge, I think the researcher in manuscripts experiences very intensely this kind of mirth. Such is my conviction; it cannot be proved, it can only be shared.

The existence of a scholar can be a lonely one: too often he must sit, hermit-like, at his books "also domb as any stoon." An irrepressible zest for life and the ability to communicate it are rare qualities. As the possessor of both, in addition to all his other talents, Rossell Hope Robbins has given hours of enjoyment not only to readers but to innumerable listeners in classrooms and lecturehalls who are proud to be included among his friends, and among the friends of his wife, Helen Ann Robbins—*dux femina facti*.

Not all those who wished to write an essay for this volume were able to do so. Time and other factors affected some contributions from distant places such as Japan and elsewhere. But if this book owes its genesis to the affection as well as esteem which Rossell Hope Robbins has inspired in his many friends, the thirty-six essays here assembled do, I think, provide some indication of the measure of appreciation due to him.

BERYL ROWLAND, YORK UNIVERSITY, TORONTO

9

CONTENTS

ROSSELL HOPE ROBBINS: A CANADIAN VIEW

BY LLOYD A. DUCHEMIN

Perhaps it was pure chance that I met Rossell Hope Robbins and his remarkable and gracious wife Helen Ann in London in the fall of 1961. In retrospect this brief encounter seems as inevitable as fate. My wife and I were drawn immediately into a friendship which has endured and strengthened over twelve years of academic vicissitudes and turbulences. Nobody, of course, who knows them will be surprised at their capacity for making friends quickly, and keeping them.

The first impression is of a short, rubicund, close-cropped, friendly presence, whose personality leaps out and captures you instantly with its curious combination of humility and confidence. One is drawn immediately by the eyes: they always impress one with their amiable mixture of intelligence and good humour. Often conveying a hurt quality when they survey an audience or a friend, they seem to apologize for summing you up in a glance. Young people were always attracted to him. Young scholars from Canada, especially, found him an encouraging confidant, who shared their enthusiasms and their delight in literary discoveries. I have never met anybody who could vicariously so enjoy the triumphs and the satisfactions of others.

In 1965 we invited Rossell to be Visiting Professor at Mount Allison University, with the blessing of the Canada Council. The Robbins made the trip from New York to New Brunswick in about ten hours' driving. They brought with them gaiety, good humour, an enormous amiability and desire to participate in our unknown northern world. It was a turning point. Not only was it their first visit to Canada, it was the first year since 1953 (save for his semester at Chapel Hill) that Ross had resumed active teaching. He derived great satisfaction from this renewal of contact with young students, which he has continued down to the present. Those twelve years of intense scholarship and writing had produced a rich harvest of published books, and had made him famous, but had satisfied only one part of his very complex nature. That term was a great triumph for the Robbins, taken as they were into the very heart of our community, while he lectured happily away on one or other of his great specialities, the history of witchcraft, or secular lyrics, or Chaucer, or medieval music.

Every great scholar has his idiosyncrasy. Everyone knows the Robbins hobby horse, which he still rides with endearing zest. It is, of course, visiting universities: meeting their faculties, lecturing to their students, savouring briefly their individual rhythms, inspecting their literary treasures, exchanging courtesies with their administrations. This obsession with collecting universities, as somebody has unfairly called it, for it is more than that—it is an aesthetic participation in the ongoing movement of scholarship and the pursuit of truth —has actually acquainted him with, and endeared him to, hundreds of scholars in both the new world and the old. He has literally crisscrossed this continent, from the Pacific to Atlantic Canada. It has been with a sense of relief, perhaps, that his best friends have seen him come to rest at last in the embrace of the State University of New York at Albany.

As I have learned to appreciate over the years, the most enduring traits of Rossell Hope Robbins are his continuous and loving pursuit of knowledge, his passionate enjoyment of good fellowship, his humane and civilized desire to communicate with other scholars, especially the young. He has lived a happy and useful life, which has now reached a kind of climax, though there will be many more achievements ahead. Perhaps a paraphrase of Shakespeare sums him up best: he is not only scholarly in himself, but the cause that scholarship is in other men.

MOUNT ALLISON UNIVERSITY, NEW BRUNSWICK

VITA

Born at Wallasey, Cheshire, 22 July 1912, son of Rossell Casson Robbins of Liverpool, England, and Alice Eveline Hope of Kirkudbright, Scotland.

Married on 9 June 1939 to Helen Ann Mins, daughter of Henry Felix Mins of New York and Elizabeth Lafell of New York, by the Rev. Carleton Brown in the Offices of the Modern Language Association of America.

Naturalized American citizen, 6 March 1944, Supreme Court, Eastern District of Virginia.

Military Service in Army of the United States, 8 March 1943 to 20 January 1946, First Lieutenant, War Department Special Staff, Pentagon and SHAEF.

Educated at
The Wallasey Grammar School, England, 1921–30.
The University of Liverpool, 1930–33, B.A. First Class Honours, School of English Language and Literature. Student of J. H. G. Grattan, 1933. School of Education, Liverpool, 1933–34. Diploma of Education, 1934.
The Matthay School of Music, Liverpool Branch, 1930–36. Licentiate of the Guildhall School of Music, London, 1932. Full member, The London Verse Speaking Choir (Marjorie Gullan), 1935–37.
Cambridge University: Emmanuel College, 1934–37. Ph.D., 1937. Open External Studentship; Wallasey Borough Research Scholarships, 1934, 1935; University of Liverpool Graduate Scholarships, 1934–36. Student of G. G. Coulton.

Fellow of the Royal Society of Literature, 1958.

Cambridge University, England, Director of Studies, 1935–37.
Brooklyn College, Instructor in English, 1941–42.
National Institute of Social Relations, Washington, D.C., Section Head, Youth and Educational Policies, 1946.

Polytechnic Institute of Brooklyn, Assistant Professor of English, 1946–49; Associate Professor, 1949–54.

University of North Carolina, Chapel Hill, Advanced Visiting Professor, 1958.

Mount Allison University, New Brunswick, Canada Council Professor, 1965.

Duke University, Cooperative Program in the Humanities Professor, 1965.

University of California, Berkeley, Mrs William Beckman Professor, 1966.

Sir George Williams University, Montreal, English Summer Institute, Professor, 1968.

University of California, Riverside, Regents' Professor, 1968–69.

State University of New York at Albany, International Professor, 1969– .

Guest lecturer at universities: 1957—Northwestern; 1962— Amsterdam, Berlin, Bonn, Leyden, Utrecht; 1964—Birmingham, Chicago, Kentucky, Leeds, Liverpool, London, Nottingham; 1965—Acadia, Dalhousie, McMaster, New Brunswick, New York Upstate Medical Center, North Carolina, Toronto; 1966—Chapman, Claremont, UC Davis, Longwood, McMaster, Richmond, Richmond Polytechnic, UC Riverside, St Paul's, Virginia, Virginia Military Institute, Wake Forest, William and Mary, York; 1967—Amsterdam, Connecticut, Erlangen, Frankfurt, Groningen, Heidelberg, Helsinki, Jyväskylä, Kiel, Leyden, Munich, Nijmegen, Salzburg, Würzburg; 1968—Huron, New York Mount Sinai Hospital; 1969—Sir George Williams, Southern California, UCLA; 1970—Connecticut, Missouri; 1971—Haverford, SUNY Cortland, SUNY New Paltz; 1973—St Joseph, SUNY Binghamton, UT Austin.

Commonwealth Fund of America Fellow, 1937–39 (at New York University); University of Liverpool, Noble Fellow, 1939–40 (in absentia); Modern Language Association of America Grant-in-aid, 1954–55; Simon Guggenheim Memorial Fellow, 1955–56; Ford Foundation Visiting Scholar, Dunster House, Harvard University, 1958, 1959; Overseas Speaker, British University Teachers of English, Hull, 1962; American Council of Learned Societies Grantee, 1963, 1969; Honorary Associate, University Seminar in Medieval Studies, Columbia University, 1956–

59, 1960–66; Overseas Speaker, British Association for the Advancement of Science, Aberdeen, 1963; Visiting Scholar, University Center of Virginia, 1966; Guest Speaker, Humanities Association of Canada, 1966, 1969; Speaker, International Musicological Congress, Ljubljana, Yugoslavia, 1967; Fellows Lecturer, Huron College, Ontario, 1968; H. E. W. Visiting Lecturer, California State College, Pennsylvania, 1969; Speaker, International Federation for Modern Languages and Literatures Congress, Islamabad, Pakistan, 1969; Speaker, American Library Association, Chicago, 1972.

Member of the Modern Language Association of America (Chairman, English II Bibliography Committee, 1959–); Mediaeval Academy; Modern Humanities Research Association; International Association of University Professors of English; Humanities Association of Canada; American Association of University Professors.

LIST OF PUBLICATIONS

BOOKS

The Index of Middle English Verse (jointly with Carleton Brown). The Index Society. New York: Columbia University Press, 1943, pp. xix, 785.

> *Papers of Bibliographical Society of America*, 37 (1943), pp. 161–5 (Curt Bühler); *Neuphilologische Mitteilungen*, 49 (1948), pp. 126–33 (Tauno Mustanoja); *New York Herald Tribune*, Section VIII, 21 March 1943, p. 22 (Lawrence C. Wroth); *Speculum*, 20 (1945). pp. 105–11 (F. L. Utley).

Christopher Marlowe: Dr Faustus. Great Neck, New York: Barron's Educational Series, Inc., 1948, pp. xii, 52. 2nd edn., 1967.

The T. S. Eliot Myth. New York: Henry Schuman, Inc., 1951, pp. 226. Repr. Ann Arbor, Michigan: University Reprints, 1965.

> *America*, 16 Feb. 1952 (Michael F. Moloney); *American Literature*, 24 (1952), 400–1 (Irving Howe); *Birmingham News*, 30 Nov. 1951 (Richard C. Pettigrew); *Books Abroad*, Autumn 1951 (Karl D. Uitti); *Books on Trial*, Jan.–Feb. 1952 (Daniel. T. Mitchell); *Brooklyn Eagle*, 3 Feb 1952 (Philip Shaw); *Calvin Forum*, April 1952 (Henry Zylstra); *Chicago Tribune*, 18 Nov. 1951 (John Frederick Nims); *Christian Century*, 69 (6 Feb. 1952), 161 (Haver C. Currie); *Congress Weekly*, 18 Feb. 1952 (Ward Moore); *Dallas Times-Herald*, 16 Dec. 1951 (Alfred Kreymborg); *Educational Theatre Journal*, 11 Dec. 1951, pp. 346–66 (E. J. West); *English Studies*, 36 (1955), 90–1 (Irène Simon); *Harvard Crimson*, 30 Nov. 1951 (Aloysius B. McCabe); *Hufvudstadsblatt*, 4 Feb. 1952, Nr. 33 (Harry Jarv); *Idea* [Roma], 3, No. 51, 23 Dec. 1951 (Giuseppe Prezzolini); *Library Journal*, 1 Nov. 1952 (Gerald P. McDonald); *Masses and Mainstream*, 5, No. 3 (1952), 58–61 (Sidney Finkelstein); *National Jewish Post*, 4 Jan. 1952 (Harold U. Ribalow); *New England Quarterly*, 25 (1952), 104–6 (Thomas Moser); *New York Times*, Book Review Section, 18 Nov. 1951 (Randall Jarrell); *Paideia*, 6 (1952), Nr. 6 (N. Orsini); *San Francisco Chronicle*, 6 Jan. 1952, p. 20; *Saturday Review of Literature*, 2 Feb. 1952, p. 19 (Ben Ray Redman); *Science and Society*, 16 (1952), 179–80 (Edwin Berry Burgum);

Southwest Review, Spring 1952 (W. M. Frohock); *Stockholms-Tidningen*, 21 March 1952 (Anders Osterling); *Yale Review*, NS 41 (1952), 458 (Martin Price); *Wings*, Spring 1952 (Stanton A. Coblentz).

Secular Lyrics of the XIVth and XVth Centuries. Oxford: Clarendon Press, 1952, pp. lviii, 331. 2nd rev. edn. 1955.

Anglia, 71 (1953), 335–6 (R. J. Schoeck); *Archiv*, 190 (1953), 236–7 (Hermann Heuder); *Blackfriars*, June 1952 (J. V. Curran); *Cambridge Review*, 11 Oct. 1952; *Durham University Journal*, NS 13 (1952), 109; *English Studies*, 34 (1953), 32–3 (A. A. Prins); *Etudes anglaises*, 6 (1953), 354 (Ferdinand Mossé); *Manchester Guardian Weekly*, 66, No. 22 (22 April 1952) (Ifor B. Evans); *Modern Language Notes*, 68 (1953), 571–2 (A. K. Moore); *Modern Language Quarterly*, 15 (1954), 372–3 (Kenneth Wilson); *Modern Language Review*, 48 (1953), 329–30 (Phyllis Hodgson); *Modern Language Review*, 53 (1957), 408–9 (A. C. Cawley); *Nation*, 12 July 1952 (Rolf Humphries); *Neuphilologische Mitteilungen*, 53 (1954), 488–93 (Tauno Mustanoja); *New Statesman and Nation*, 10 May 1952; *New York Herald Tribune*, 31 Aug. 1952 (G. F. Whicher); *Nieuwe Rotterdamse Courant*, 24 Feb. 1953; *Poetry*, Jan. 1953 (Betty Miller Davis); *Review of English Studies*, NS 4 (1953), 154–5 (R. M. Wilson); *Spectator*, 11 April 1952 (J. M. Cohen); *Studia Neophilologica*, 24 (1952), 216–17 (S. B. Liljegren); *Time and Tide*, 2 May 1952 (Philip Inman); *Times Literary Supplement*, 25 July 1952, pp. 477–8; *Virginia Quarterly Review*, Winter 1953.

Historical Poems of the XIVth and XVth Centuries. New York: Columbia University Press, 1959, pp. xxvii, 440.

Anglia, 80 (1962), 335–6 (Bogislav von Lindheim); *Catholic Historical Review*, 45 (1960), 519–20 (Thaddeus V. Tuleja); *Dalhousie Review*, 40 (1960), 108–10 (A. M. Kinghorn); *English Studies*, 45 (1964), 53–4 (A. A. Prins); *Journal English Germanic Philology*, 59 (1960), 273–5 (Merle Fifield); *Kwartalnik Neofilologiczny*, 7 (1960), 236–7 (Margaret Schlauch); *Medium Aevum*, 30 (1960), 57–9 (K. B. McFarlane); *Modern Language Notes*, 75 (1960), 606–9 (R. L. Greene); *Modern Language Review*, 55 (1960), 429 (R. M. Wilson); *Modern Philology*, 60 (1962–3), 56–8 (E. Talbot Donaldson); *Review of English Studies*, NS 13 (1962), 400–1 (Ethel Seaton); *Studia Neophilogica*, 32 (1960), 188–90 (Lucia Glanville).

The Encyclopedia of Witchcraft and Demonology. New York: Crown Publishers, Inc., 1959, pp. 571. 2nd rev. printing, 1960; 3rd printing, 1963; 4th printing, 1965; 5th printing, 1966; 6th printing, 1968; 7th printing, 1970; 8th printing, 1970. London: Peter Nevill, 1959.

Augumenty [Warsaw], Nr. 14 (147), April 1961, p. 9 (Margaret Schlauch); *Humanist* [London], March 1960, pp. 87–9 (Victor Purcell); *Journal American Folklore*, 73 (1960), 172–4 (Arthur Freeman); *Journal English Germanic Philology*, 59 (1960), 559–60 (G. Blackmore Evans); *Modern Philology*, 57 (1960), 128–30 (F. L. Utley); *New York Herald Tribune*, 22 Nov 1959 (John T. Winterich); *Renaissance News*, 13 (1960), 179–80 (E. E. Ericson); *Spectator*, 4 Dec 1959 (Alan Brien); *Speculum*, 35 (1960), 479–80 (A. B. Friedman); *Springfield Republican*, Mass., 15 Nov. 1959 (Richard McLaughton); *Western Folklore*, 20 (1961), 140–1 (Ray B. Browne).

The Hundred Tales: Les cent nouvelles nouvelles. New York: Crown Publishers, Inc., 1960, pp. xxi, 390. 2nd printing, New York: Bonanza Books, 1962. London: W. H. Allen, 1962.

Atlantic, Feb. 1961; *Moderna Sprak*, 55 (1961), 384–6 (Alain Renoir); *New York Sunday Times*, 4 Dec. 1960 (Henri Peyre); *Renaissance News*, 14 (1961), 197–9 (Huntington Brown); *Saturday Review*, 3 Dec. 1960 (Otis Fellows); *Times Literary Supplement*, 5 Oct. 1962, p. 782.

Early English Christmas Carols. New York and London: Columbia University Press, 1961, pp. 87

Anglia, 81 (1963). 233–6 (Imogen Birkholz); *Archiv*, 201 (1964), 136–7 (Theo Stemmler); *English Studies*, 64 (1963), 364–7 (Winifred Maynard); *Library Journal*, 15 Dec. 1961 (Catharine Keyes Miller); *Neuphilologische Mitteilungen*, 63 (1962) 203–4 (Tauno Mustanoja); *New York Herald Tribune*, 10 Dec. 1961; *Notes and Queries*, 208 (1962), 431–2 (Douglas Gray); *Renaissance News*, 15 (1962), 224–47 (R. L. Greene); *Western Folklore*, 21 (1962), 130 (Henry H. Malone).

Supplement to the Index of Middle English Verse (jointly with John L. Cutler). Lexington, Kentucky: University of Kentucky Press, 1965, pp. xxix, 551.

American Notes and Queries, 4 (1966), 138–140 (V. M. Bonnell); *Bulletin des bibliothèques de France*, 12 (1967), No. 2851 (Marie-José Imbert); *Notes and Queries*, 211 (1966), 309–10 (E. G. Stanley); *Review of English Studies*, NS 18 (1967), 444–8 (Norman Davis); *Speculum*, 42 (1967), 548–50 (Morton W. Bloomfield); *Studia Neophilologica*, 38 (1966), 360–2 (Sylvia W. Holton).

ARTICLES AND REVIEWS

1938

The Earliest Carols and the Franciscans, *Modern Language Notes*, 53, 239–45.

Some Misgivings about Choral Speaking, *Speech*, 3, No. 2, 34–8.

A Further Justification of Choral Speaking, *Quarterly Journal of Speech*, 24, 437–43.

1939

Punctuation Poems, *Review of English Studies*, 15, 106–7.

Popular Prayers in Middle English Verse, *Modern Philology*, 36, 337–50.

The Gurney Series of Religious Lyrics, *PMLA*, 54, 369–90.

Private Prayers in Middle English Verse, *Studies in Philology*, 36, 466–75.

The "Arma Christi" Rolls, *Modern Language Review*, 34, 415–21.

English Almanacks of the XVth Century, *Philological Quarterly*, 18, 321–31.

The "Speculum Misericordie", *PMLA*, 54, 935–66.

The Middle English Religious Lyric, *Abstracts of Dissertations* 1937–8, Cambridge, 1939, p. 82.

Choral Speaking at the Oxford Festivals, *Quarterly Journal of Speech*, 25, 227–35.

The Choice of Poems for Choral Speaking, *Speech*, 3, No. 9, 56–8.

The Oxford Festivals and Standards, *Speech*, 3, No. 9, 53–5.

[reviews] *Quarterly Journal of Speech*, 25, 163–4; 25, 341; 25, 679.

1940

The Authors of the Middle English Religious Lyric, *Journal of English and Germanic Philology*, 39, 230–8.

Two Fourteenth-Century Mystical Poems, *Modern Language Review*, 35, 320–9.

A Checklist of Poems for Boys' Choirs, *Western Speech*, 4, No. 2, 12–13.

[reviews] *Quarterly Journal of Speech*, 26, 333–4.

1942

The Burden in Carols, *Modern Language Notes*, 57, 16–22.

Levation Prayers in Middle English Verse, *Modern Philology*, 40, 131–46.

Two Satirical Love Epistles, *Modern Language Review*, 37, 415–21.

1943

Two New Carols (Hunterian MS 83), *Modern Language Notes*, 58, 39–42.

A Gawain Epigone, *Modern Language Notes*, 58, 361–6.

Pre-School Education in Wartime England, *Harvard Educational Review*, 13, 240–5.

1949

Social Awareness and Semantic Change, *American Speech*, 24, 156–8.

A Sixteenth-Century English Mystery Fragment, *English Studies*, 30, 135–6.

[review] Liriche religiose Inglesi del secolo quattordicesimo (Obertello), *Speculum*, 24, 282–4.

1950

The Fraternity of Drinkers, *Studies in Philology*, 47, 35–41.

An English Mystery Fragment *c.* 1300, *Modern Language Notes*, 65, 30–5.

The T. S. Eliot Myth, *Science and Society*, 14, 1–28; *repr.* Il mito di T. S. Eliot (*trad.* G. Corsini), *Rinascita*, 7, 216–20.

The Poems of Humphrey Newton, Esquire, 1466–1536, *PMLA*, 65, 249–81.

Preservation of Old and Middle English Words in Modern Technology, *American Speech*, 25, 121.

Variable Meanings of Technical Terms, *American Speech*, 25, 149–50.

The Basis of Bop, *Harlem Quarterly*, 1, Nos. 3 & 4, 9–16; repr. *Jam Session*, ed. Ralph Gleason, New York: G. P. Putnam's Sons, 1958, pp. 186–94.

1951

Acronyms and Abbreviations from Aviation, *American Speech*, 26, 67–70.

Some Charles d'Orléans Fragments, *Modern Language Notes*, 66, 501–5.

[review] Early Middle English Texts (Dickins and Wilson). *Neuphilologische Mitteilungen*, 52, 283–5.

1953

A Possible Analogue to T. S. Eliot's "The Cocktail Party," *English Studies*, 34, 165–7.

[review] The Secular Lyric in Middle English (Moore), *Neuphilologische Mitteilungen*, 54, 89–92.

[review] The Background of Modern Poetry (Isaacs), *Science and Society*, 17, 281–2.

[review] Religious Lyrics of the XIVth Century (Brown-Smithers), *Speculum*, 28, 867–9.

1954

Five Middle English Verse Prayers from Lambeth MS 541, *Neophilologus*, 38, 36–41.

Middle English Versions of "Criste qui lux es," *Harvard Theological Review*, 47, 55–63.

A Late Fifteenth-Century Love Lyric, *Modern Language Notes*, 69, 153–60.

A Love Epistle by "Chaucer," *Modern Language Review*, 49, 289–92.

A Dramatic Fragment from a Caesar Augustus Play, *Anglia*, 72, 31–4.

The Findern Anthology, *PMLA*, 69, 610–42.

"Consilium domini in eternum manet" (Harley MS 2252), *Studia Neophilologica*, 26, 58–64.

Fire Terms: Additional Words and Definitions, *American Speech*, 29, 272–6.

An Unkind Mistress, *Modern Language Notes*, 69, 552–8.

A Song for Victory in France (1492), *Neuphilologische Mitteilungen*, 55, 289–93.

The World Upside Down: A Middle English Amphibole, *Anglia*, 72, 385–9.

[review] The Great Tradition (Rubinstein), *Science and Society*, 18, 283–5.

[review] John Lydgate: Ein Kulturbild aus dem 15 Jahrhundert (Schirmer), *Neuphilologische Mitteilungen*, 55, 228–30.

1955

God Amende Wykkyd Cownscell (1464), *Neuphilologische Mitteilungen*, 56, 94–102.

A Middle English Diatribe Against Philip of Burgundy, *Neophilologus*, 39, 131–46.

On Dating a Middle English Moral Poem, *Modern Language Notes*, 70, 473–6.

An Epitaph for Duke Humphrey (1477), *Neuphilologische Mitteilungen*, 56, 241–9.

1956

A Warning against Lechery, *Philological Quarterly*, 35, 90–5.

The Five Dogs of London, *PMLA*, 71, 264–8.

Spooner and Spoonerisms, *Word Study*, Feb., pp. 7–8.

A Political Action Poem, *Modern Language Notes*, 71, 245–8.

Transferred Techniques for Non-Majors, *College English*, 18, 166–7.

Program Notes: History of the English Carol, *Vanguard Recording*, VRS 499.

1957

Friar Herebert and the Carol, *Anglia*, 75, 194–8.

Geoffrey of Monmouth: An English Fragment, *English Studies*, 38, 259–62.

[review article] Deonise Hid Diuinite (Hodgson), *Speculum*, 32, 405–10.

1958

[review] Studies on Chaucer (Giffin), *Neuphilologische Mitteilungen*, 59, 282–5.

1959

An Early Rudimentary Carol, *Modern Language Review*, 54, 221–2.

The Middle English Carol Corpus: Some Additions, *Modern Language Notes*, 74, 198–208.

Middle English Carols as Processional Hymns, *Studies in Philology*, 56, 559–82.

1960

Middle English Poems of Protest, *Anglia*, 78, 193–203.

1961

Sex and Witchcraft, *Sexology*, 27, 388–93; repr. Sexo y Brujeria, *Luz*, 9, 388–94.

The Early English Carols, *The Choir*, 52, 126–8.

1962

Courts of Love, *Sexology*, 28, 392–6; repr. Cortes de Amor, *Luz*, 10, 397–402.

The Code of Adultery, *Sexology*, 28, 456–9; repr. El Codigo des Adulterio, *Luz*, 10, 466–70.

Amorous Tales of Medieval France, *Sexology*, 28, 602–8; repr. Cuentos Amorosos de la Francia Medieval, *Luz*, 10, 598–602.

[review] John Lydgate (Schirmer), *Anglia*, 80, 454–5.

1963

The Imposture of Witchcraft, *Folklore*, 74, 545–62.

Good Gossips Reunited, *British Museum Quarterly*, 27, 12–15.

Wall Verses at Launceston Priory, *Archiv*, 200, 338–43.

Isabel: A Riddling Mistress, *English Language Notes*, 1, 1–4.

[review] Pale Hecate's Team (Briggs), *Renaissance News*, 16, 28–30.

[review] A Razor for a Goat (Rose), *Speculum*, 38, 499–501.

[review] Science and the Renaissance (Wightman), *American Notes and Queries*, 2, 12–14.

[review] A Selection of English Carols (Greene), *Speculum*, 38, 484–7.

[review] A Dictionary of Middle English Musical Terms (Carter), *Journal American Musicological Society*, 16, 75–8.

1964

An English Nativity Song from a Latin Processional, *American Notes and Queries*, 2, 147–9.

Middle English Research in Progress: 1963–64, *Neuphilologische Mitteilungen*, 65, 360–9.

[review article] Die englischen Liebesgedichte des MS Harley 2253 (Stemmler), *Anglia*, 82, 505–13.

[review] Medieval English Lyrics (Davies), *Notes and Queries*, 209, 320.

1965

Middle English Lyrics: Handlist of New Texts, *Anglia*, 83, 35–47.

The Rochester Rappings, *Dalhousie Review*, 45, 153–64.

Middle English Research in Progress: 1964–65, *Neuphilologische Mitteilungen*, 66, 250–4.

[review] Medieval English Lyrics (Davies), *Speculum*, 60, 130–1.

[review] John Skelton (Pollet), *Archiv*, 202, 138–9.

1966

The Bradshaw Carols, *PMLA*, 81, 308–10.

Alchemical Texts in Middle English Verse: Corrigenda and Addenda, *Ambix*, 13, 62–73.

The Real Crime of Witchcraft, *California Monthly*, 76, 4–7.

The Heresy of Witchcraft, *South Atlantic Quarterly*, 65, 532–43.

The Warden's Wordplay: Toward a Definition of the Spoonerism, *Dalhousie Review*, 46, 457–65.

The Physician's Authorities, *Studies in Language and Literature in Honour of Margaret Schlauch*, ed. Mieczslaw Brahmer, Warsaw and Oxford, 1966, pp. 335–41.

Middle English Research in Progress: 1965–66, *Neuphilologische Mitteilungen*, 67, 205–13.

1967

A New Chaucer Analogue: The Legend of Ugolino, *Trivium*, 2, 1–16.

Middle English Misunderstood: Mr Speirs and the Goblins, *Anglia*, 85, 270–81.

A Late Sixteenth-Century Chaucerian Allusion (Douce MS 290), *Chaucer Review*, 2, 135–7.

Middle English Research in Progress: 1966–67, *Neuphilologische Mitteilungen*, 68, 208–12.

[review article] Education at Berkeley (Report of the Select Committee), *Dalhousie Review*, 47, 235–43.

1968

A Highly Critical Approach to the Middle English Lyric, *College English*, 30, 74–5.

A Middle English Prayer to St Mary Magdalen, *Traditio*, 24, 458–64.

Old Guard and Young Turks: The Problems of Reviewing, *Archiv*, 205, 177–88.

Muncy, Tumpha, Myfmaffemose, *American Notes and Queries*, 6, 101–2.

A New Lydgate Fragment, *English Language Notes*, 5, 243–7.

"Lawriol": *CT*, B 4153, *Chaucer Review*, 3, 68.

January's Caress, *Lockhaven Review*, 10, 3–6.

Mirth in Manuscripts, *Essays and Studies*, NS 21, 1–28.

Chaucer's Lyrics, *Companion to Chaucer Studies*, ed. Beryl Rowland, Toronto: Oxford University Press, 1968, pp. 313–28.

Middle English Research in Progress: 1967–68, *Neuphilologische Mitteilungen*, 69, 488–99.

[review] Bibliography of Chaucer 1954–63 (Crawford), *Archiv*, 205, 65–6.

[review] Chaucer and Chaucerians (Brewer), *Archiv*, 205, 67–8.

[review] Walter Hilton's Eight Chapters on Perfection (Kuriyagawa), *Speculum*, 43, 516–17.

[review] Art and Tradition in Sir Gawain (Benson), *Revue belge de philologie et d'histoire*, 46, 545–8.

[review] Early Middle English Verse and Prose (Bennett and Smithers), *Revue belge de philologie et d'histoire*, 46, 878–9.

1969

Refrain Poem from N. L. W. Peniarth MS 395, *Trivium*, 4, 43–9.

John Crophill's Ale-pots, *Review of English Studies*, NS 20, 182–9.

Middle English Research in Progress: 1968–69, *Neuphilologische Mitteilungen*, 70, 534–45.

[review article] English Medieval Literature (Schlauch), *Archiv*, 205, 489–94.

1970

A Note on the Singer Survey of Medical Manuscripts, *Chaucer Review*, 5, 66–70.

Signs of Death in Middle English, *Mediaeval Studies*, 32, 282–98.

Medical Manuscripts in Middle English, *Speculum*, 45, 393–415.

Yellow Cross and Green Fagot, *Cornell Library Journal*, 10, 2–33.

Victory at Whitby, A.D. 1451, *Studies in Philology*, 67, 495–504.

The English Fabliau Before and After Chaucer, *Moderna Sprak*, 64, 231–44.

Middle English Research in Progress: 1969–70, *Neuphilologische Mitteilungen*, 71, 501–4.

[review] Jack Upland (Heyworth), *Notes and Queries*, 215, 266–7.

[review] English Religious Lyric (Woolf), *Speculum*, 45, 337–8.

[review] Selections from John Gower (Bennett), *Archiv*, 207, 304–6.

[review] Vision of Piers Plowman (Oiji), *Neuphilologische Mitteilungen*, 71, 524–5.

1971

The Witchcraft Collection, *Cornell University Libraries Bulletin*, No. 171, 7–9.

Chaucer's "To Rosemounde," *Studies in the Literary Imagination*, 4, No. 2, pp. 73–81.

Middle English Research in Progress: 1970–71, *Neuphilologische Mitteilungen*, 72, 513–16.

[review] Thomas Hoccleve (Mitchell), *Archiv*, 207, 466–7.

[review] Witchcraft (Rosen), *Modern Language Review*, 66, 860–2.

[review] A Glastonbury Miscellany (Rigg), *Anglia*, 89, 140–3.

1972

"Conuertimini:" A Middle English Refrain Poem, *Neuphilologische Mitteilungen*, 73, 353–61.

Middle English Research in Progress: 1971–72, *Neuphilologische Mitteilungen*, 73, 705–7.

[review] Hymnar und Hymnen im englischen Mittelalter (Gneuss), *Speculum*, 47, 759–61.

[review] Oxford Book of Medieval English Verse (Sisam), *Notes and Queries*, 217, 387–8.

[review] Peterborough Chronicle 1070–1154 (Clark), *Archiv*, 209, 149–50.

I

THE ELIXIR OF YOUTH

BY CHARLES H. TALBOT

At a time when the eyes of the whole world are fixed on youth, what could be more heartening than the third reprint of the *Book of Quinte Essence*? It comes as balm to an afflicted soul. Not only to members of the Early English Text Society in particular, and to staffs of English Departments in general, but also to older people, who, like the writer, are now painfully decrepit, this text will bring comfort and consolation. For within its pages, written long ago, lie the secrets of the water of life, and with it the secrets of everlasting youth. "Þis breue tretis" tells

> how þat olde euangelik men, and feble in kynde, myȝte be restorid, and haue aȝen her firste strenkþis of ȝongþe in þe same degree þat is in al kynde, & be mad hool parfiȝtly, except þe strok of þe þundir blast, & violent brusuris, and oppressynge of to myche betyng / Also perilous fallyngis of hiȝ placis, to myche abstynence, & oþere yuel gouernaunce aȝens kynde.

Readers who have never dabbled in Alchemy may well stand aghast when they realize what they have been missing all these years, the simple methods, the cheap ingredients, the ineffable effects, all so vividly described in this manual of rejuvenation. They may well wonder why they allowed themselves to be dissuaded from pursuing the noble art of alchemy by their most cherished author, Chaucer, who in his *Canon Yeoman's Tale* propounded the theory that the quest was wasteful of time and money, and that the whole process was a fraud and a delusion.

It is quite obvious to us now that Chaucer said this out of pique. He was a disappointed man. Not only had he failed to discover the secret of making gold out of base metal, but he had never succeeded in distilling the elixir of life, which, judging by Hoccleve's experience, is absolutely essential to the man of letters:

> What man þat thre & twenti yeere and more
> In wryting hath continued, as haue I,

> I dar wel seyn it smerteth hym ful sore
> In euere veyne and place of his body.

We could well forgive Chaucer his chagrin at being thwarted in his search for this celestial liquor, but it is impossible to condone his baneful influence, exercised not only over his contemporaries, but also on all posterity. Instead of encouraging others to persevere where he had wilted, he used all his authority to bar the way to further exploration, supporting his pessimistic views by a quotation from Plato, that arch-creator of myths:

> "Tell me the roote, good sire" quod he tho
> "Of that water, if it be youre wil."
> "Nay, nay," quod Plato, "certein, that I nyl.
> The philosophres sworn were everychoon
> That they sholden discovere it unto noon,
> Ne in no book it write in no manere. . . ."

What could be more obscurantist than this? Where could you find a more discouraging statement? The result was that all Chaucer's contemporaries, despairing of Plato, ran off to Aristotle, hoping to find an answer in his book, *Secreta Secretorum*. They translated it into prose, they made poetic versions of it, they gave it fancy titles like *Confessio Amantis*, *The Secrees of Old Philosophres*, *The Regement of Princes*, and so on. But, sadly, there was not one word in it about making Quintessence. All they got from Aristotle was a set of rules for keeping fit, lists of what to eat and what to drink, times when to fast and abstain, where to build a house or sink a well, and lots of other useless and dreary information.

The outcome was catastrophic. Gower, disillusioned, devoted himself to the Seven Deadly Sins and went blind. William of Ockham, finding his razor unsuited to logic-chopping, emigrated to Bavaria and took up politics. Lydgate, confessing:

> I souhte leechys for a restoratiff
> In whom I fond no consolacioun

and realizing that "Aurum potabile for folk ferre ronne in age" was "Hard to be bouht for folk in poverte," became more doggerel as he got older and suffered at the end from chronic extrapolation. Hoccleve went mad:

> Witnes vppon the wyld infirmytie
> which that I had / as many a man well knewe,
> and whiche me owt of my selfe / cast and threw.

Wycliffe, transmuting the bible into muddle English, fell into clerical errors, whilst Trevisa, an even sadder case, was driven up the wall, where he spent his waking hours inscribing the Book of Revelation on the ceiling of Berkeley Castle chapel.

Now all this could have been averted if Chaucer had not been so obstructive. He must have known that Ramon Lull, the celebrated alchemist, had been invited to the court of Edward III and that he had given the King a recipe for the Elixir of Life. He must have known that Queen Isobel had availed herself of it with most gratifying results. And he must have been aware that even if the secret had been filched from the King whilst campaigning in Scotland, the secret existed somewhere. But Chaucer kept all this to himself.

That the friars and monks possessed this secret was beyond doubt, but cunning as they were, they prevented it from becoming known outside their cloisters. George Ripley, a Canon Regular of Bridlington, knew all about it and handed the art to another canon at Lichfield, who in turn passed it to Thomas Dalton, a monk in Gloucestershire. Ripley also communicated the secret to another monk, William Holleweye, *alias* Gibbes, who became Prior of Bath Abbey, and who, on the imminent dissolution of the monasteries, hid the elixir in one of the abbey walls. But apart from these no one could fathom the mysteries of the water of life. A few intrepid spirits, braving ecclesiastical censure, attempted to break down this monkish monopoly, and in 1456 John Fauceby was granted a royal licence to produce the Elixir on a large scale for the benefit of the kingdom. But whether he lacked the requisite competence or mixed the wrong ingredients we shall never know. His process was a complete failure, and as a consequence his royal patron, Henry VI, went out of his mind. No further proof for the concealment of Quintessence from the people can be found than the fate of the Duke of Clarence. He was drowned, it is said, in a butt of Malmesy wine. Had he been placed in a tun of Quintessence the result would have been far different, for, as our treatise testifies:

> it ʒeueth incorruptibilite, & kepiþ a þing fro corruptibilite & rotynge. Forwhi, what pece of fleisch, fisch, or deed brid be putt þerinne, it schal not corrumpe, ne rote whilis it is þerinne.

Towards the end of the fifteenth century the recipe, which had been given by Ramon Lull to Edward III and been used by Queen Isobel, somehow came to light and was recorded by John Argentine, physician to the Princes in the Tower:

> *Aqua miraculosa cum qua Regina Iezabella septuagenaria, decrepita, guttosa,*

et paralitica [sanata fuit]; et quia in ipsa totus fere spiritus erat mortuus, facta fuit in tantum sana et tanti uigoris, quod uiro quadragenario uoluit copulari.

But once again the process was hidden from people at large. Realizing that the water of life is more fitting for professors than for courtiers, Argentine took the recipe with him to the University of Cambridge, where it has remained in constant use ever since.

But rumour is bound to spread. The tradesmen in Cambridge, seeing the professors bouncing with energy and holding on to their chairs (a visible sign of stability), whispered that something was brewing in the colleges and monastic centres. When Henry VIII heard of this, he sent John Leland, the antiquary, round all the monasteries on the pretence of collecting books for the Royal Library. What he really wanted to find (and the history books are silent on this point) was the text that would not only cure his ulcered leg and "cool the membre," but would also give him that renewed vigour which Queen Isobel (of blessed memory) had so conspicuously enjoyed. Alas! All that Leland could find were a few miserable books on theology, several philosophical works, some histories and other rubbish of a like nature, which the King could not read out to his wives. Enraged at being hoodwinked by a mob of psalm-singing monks and learning that Prior Holleweye had hidden the Elixir in the walls of his abbey, Henry literally tore the monasteries apart. Anyone who has visited the venerable ruins that now litter the countryside of the British Isles can bear witness to the thoroughness of his search. However, nothing was found. So, deciding that if he could not have it, no one else should, he had all the manuscripts which he could lay his hands on, transported by the shipload to the Continent, where they were deservedly used by bakers for firing their ovens, or by fishmongers for wrapping up herrings.

Little did Henry suspect that the object of his dreams was lying on a shelf in one of the University Colleges, where the inmates gaily sang:

> *Poculis accenditur animi lucerna*
> *Cor imbutum nectare volat ad superna,*

which means, that after a couple of glasses of *aqua vitae* you are Flying High. These sounds of wassailing echoed as far as London, and Edward VI (Henry's sickly son) misled by the word *superna*, which his religious upbringing caused him to translate as "heaven," immediately set about Revising his Prayer Book. All to no avail. His heaven was totally different to the heaven cherished at Oxford, which, as our text tells us:

But vndirstonde þat oure quintessentia is nouȝt so incorruptible as is

heuene of oure lord god; but it is incorruptible in reward of com-
posicioun maad of þe 4 elementis; & it hath .iii. names by the philo-
sophoris, þat is to seie / brennynge water / þe soule in þe spirit of wyn,
& watir of lijf.

When Edward became aware that he had a wrong reading, he sent a
group of research scholars to Oxford to collate the manuscripts. But
the librarians, true to their watchword, *Secretum meum mihi*, which
they had read in Solomon's *Love Song*, gave nothing away. The research assistants (called Commissioners) were shown only texts with
intricate mathematical diagrams, treatises on dynamics and mech-
anics, theses by Duns Scotus on *esse* and *essentia*, problems on the
squaring of the circle and suchlike meanderings. There was absolutely
nothing suitable for the King's apparatus. The Commissioners'
frustration knew no bounds and they vented their anger by consign-
ing whole piles of manuscripts to the flames.

The suspicion that the Quintessence was circulating freely on the
campuses, whilst not one drop was allowed for general consumption,
had a devastating effect on the P.L.E.B.S. making them break out
into what has been called The English Sweat, a disease unknown at
that time on the Continent and not fully diagnosed since. The
sufferers complained bitterly to the King:

> Owre Englische nature cannot lyue by Rooatis
> by water herbys, or suche beggarye baggage,
> that may well serue for uile owtlandische Cooatis.

But getting no satisfaction, they naturally turned their minds towards
other substitutes. A contemporary observer reports:

> Euery cuntrey, citie, towne, village & other hath abundance of
> alehouses, tauernes & Innes, which are so fraughted with maultwormes,
> night & day, that you would wunder to se them. You shal haue them
> there sitting at the wine and goodale all the day long, yea all the night
> too, peraduenture a whole week togither, so long as any money is left;
> swilling, gulling & carowsing from one to another, til neuer a one can
> speak a ready word. Then when with the spirit of the buttery they are
> thus possessed, a world it is to consider their gestures' demenors, how
> they stut & stammer, stagger & reele too & fro like madmen: some
> uomiting, spewing, disgorging their filthie stomaks; other some pissing
> under the boord as they sit, & which is most horrible, some fall to
> swering, cursing & banning, interlacing their speeches with curious
> tearmes of blasphemie, to the great dishonor of God, & offence of the
> godlie eares present.

Edward VI, whose ears were very godly, packed most of them off to Calais to relieve the siege, and by mistake pressed into service Thomas Charnock, who was within an ace of discovering the heavenly liquor. Charnock was so incensed at being interrupted in his work that he took up an axe and, in his own words:

> With my worke made such a furious faire,
> That the Quintessence flew forth in the air.

The consequence was that by the end of Edward's reign the only thing that survived from his alchemical lucubrations was a Bloody Mary.

The yearning for the true Quintessence, however, did not abate. Witness this passionate outburst:

> Teach me, you sovereign skinker, how to take the German's upsy-freeze, the Danish rousa, the Switzer's stoop of rhenish, the Italian's parmizant, the Englishman's healths, his hoops, cans, half-cans, gloves, frolics and flapdragons, together with the most notorious qualities of the truest tosspots . . . Hide not a drop of thy moist mystery from me, thou plumpest swill-bowl; but like an honest red-nosed wine bibber, lay open all thy secrets, and the mystical hieroglypic o' the coals.

What more eloquent testimony could there be to the desire for the Elixir of Youth, and to the awareness that its secret was criminally hidden from the common gaze? But this cry from the heart brought forth no response.

People in certain parts of the Continent appeared to fare no better. Dürer and his nordic neighbours, surrounded by their alembics, crucibles, polyhedral stones, and seven-runged ladders, seemed steeped in Melencolia, whilst the Dutch were driven into a frenzy, which could have been produced only by the acceptance of substitutes. The series of paintings by Hieronymus Bosch, particularly the Paradise of Delights and the Hay Wain, which display naked figures turning into eggs, insects, fish, birds, and every abomination, have puzzled art connoisseurs for generations. But to interpret them, as some experts have, on the basis of religion, saying that Bosch belonged to the sect of Adamites, or that his metaphorical images are a system of hieroglyphs which conceal a secret religious revelation, is mistaken: it is Bols. What went wrong with Bosch and his confrères was that, instead of being satisfied, as our treatise recommends, "with eche tyme a walnote-schelle fulle," they drank by the pint pot, and so they not only regained their youth but went right back to the egg and even further back to earlier stages of evolution.

Meanwhile in Mediterranean lands the secret of making Quint-

essence had been imparted to certain privileged souls, and in particular to the Spaniards under their Catholic King. Well could Hilaire
Belloc write:

> But Catholic men, who live upon wine,
> Are deep in the water and frank and fine:
> Wherever I travel, I find it so:
> *Benedicamus Domino.*

Belloc, of course, meant "þe soule in þe spirit of wyn," which our
treatise describes, but he could not say it without spoiling his verse.
No wonder that Calderon de la Barca could write a whole play entitled *La Vida es Sueño*, a description possible only under the influence
of ichor, and that Lope de Vega, fresh from his trip with the Armada,
could sit down and scribble fifteen hundred *Autos Sacramentales*. But,
as every author knows, after a gulf of *aqua vitae*, writing comes easy.
And what of Fray Luis de Leon? After an absence of four years from
his chair at Salamanca he began his lecture with the words, *Como
deciamos por ayer* (As we were saying yesterday), surely the longest
hang-over in recorded history. I say nothing of the extraordinary
territorial conquests of the Spaniards, for the poet tells us that stout
Cortez and his men sat boozing on a peak in Darien, thus disclosing
the whole secret of their heady advance. Listen to our treatise:

> The 15 medicyn, to make a man þat is a coward, hardy and strong,
> and putte a-wey almaner of cowardise and drede . . . ȝeue it him to
> drinke. and aftir sodeynly, as it were by myracle, þe coward man schal
> lese al maner drede and feyntnes of herte, and he schal recouere strenkþe
> þat ys lost by drede, and take to him hardynesse, and he schal dispise
> deeþ; he schal drede no perelis, and passyngly he schal be maad hardy.
> þis is trewe, for it haþ ofte tymes by oolde philosophoris bene preued.
> þerfore it were a greet wisdom þat cristen princis, in bateilis aȝen
> heþene men, hadde wiþ hem in tonnes brennynge watir, þat þei myȝt
> take to euery fiȝtynge man half a riȝt litel cuppe ful þerof to drynke in
> þe bigynnynge of þe batel.

Herein lies the explanation of Philip II's decision to embark his men
at Jerez de la Frontera.

Queen Elizabeth, on the other hand, declared *incapax* by her
physicians, but determined to make Virginia accessible to Walter
Raleigh, despatched a fleet to the New World, for as our treatise says,
"riȝt fewe lechis snow lyuynge knowe þis priuytee." Fastening on to a
chance remark made by the Spanish ambassador about Quito and
Asuncion (which in her ignorance of Spanish she understood as

queynte essence) and wishing to rival the exploits of her synonym, Isobel, she waited impatiently for the medicine that would "make hym lyue, þat is almoost consumed in nature." Imagine her disgust when, a few years later, Walter turned up with a pipe of tobacco and a potato. Inevitably he was directed to the executioner's block, where, historians say, he was heard to murmur; "It is a sharp and fair medicine to cure me of all my diseases," a remark which could apply only to Quintessence, which was known to cure leprosy, gout, palsy, fever, ague, cramp, and the itch.

It will be recalled that when Edward III was campaigning in Scotland, he lost the recipe for Quintessentia. It so happened that the text was followed, as was common in medieval manuscripts, by a series of letters, which could easily be expanded into words by anyone understanding the text. For instance, in homiletic literature we find sermons ending like this: q v e r d p o s s a, which all readers immediately interpreted as: *qui vivit et regnat deus per omnia saecula saeculorum, Amen.* Now, Edward III's recipe had the following letters at the end: u s q u e b e a t h a, which any adept should have known meant: *Vita solum quintessentia eveniet beatifica: essentia affinis terribilis hominibus alienigenis,* in other words, only quintessence will make life worth living; any similar spirit will have terrible results on people living over the border. The Scots, ignorant of Latin, could not make head nor tail of this, and thought it was one complete word. Ever afterwards they employed this name for their version of the recipe, in which they substituted potatoes, wood, and oats for the real ingredients, and called their type of "water of life" USQUEBEATHA. I will refrain from listing the deleterious effects this mongrel imitation of quintessence had on the Scottish character, though we can see some of them in the person of James I, who is universally acknowledged to have been obstinate and pedantic, awkward and boorish, argumentative and given to unaccountable fits of falling. But I cannot curb my indiscretion from mentioning one far-reaching consequence. When the Scots discovered that tobacco and potatoes were cheaper in America, they uprooted themselves from their crofts, bothies, and bogs, and fled across the sea with their sporrans and usquebeatha. As a result, two centuries later, an ingenuous traveller happening upon those regions can traverse vast expanses of treeless plains, to say nothing of the dry and sultry deserts, without encountering one drop of genuine quintessence. Everywhere his thirst is slaked with icy waters in which lotions like bourbon, sour rye, root beer, and a poisonous venom called coke (from *coccum,* a scarlet dye) have been immersed. The disorders that can arise from this were seen long ago by Ruteboeuf:

Et boivent tant que ils s'entêtent,
Et a trois ou quatre, qui font
Quatre cents écoliers se battre
Et chomer l'université.

But I pass over this sorry state of affairs. It is Hoccleve, not I, who
said:

Euery man owiþ studien and muse
To teche his brothir what þing is to do,
And what be-houëly is to refuse.

As an honest ineffectual, however, I feel bound to draw attention
to the mental disturbance this has caused to black-collar workers.
As our treatise puts it:

Forwhi. þat humour of blak coler is so noyous, þat if it a-bounde and
a-sende up to þe heed, it troubliþ alle þe myȝtis of þe brayn, engen-
drynge noyous ymaginaciouns, bryngynge yn horrible thouȝtis boþe
wakynge and slepinge; and siche maner of men ben born undir þe con-
stillacioun of saturne, the wickede planete. Forsoþe, to siche men
deuelis wole gladly appere, & minister to hem her priuy temptaciouns
wiþinne þe cours of her þouȝtis; and þese men þus turmentid wiþ þe
passiouns of malencoly comouly speke wiþ hem, stryue and dispute
wiþ hem silfe whanne þei be a-loone, þat ofte tymes oþere folk may
heere it . . . and naturaly it plesiþ hem to dwelle in derk, & in blak,
orrible stynkynge placis, in heuynesse, wreche, & malencoly, & in þo
þingis þat pretende þe condicioun of helle.

This, strangely enough, has nothing to do with the witches of
Salem. It refers to those frustrated scribblers, whose particles have
been spurned by the Potatores Metropolitani Lactis Aquosi, and who
ever afterwards, their phrases livid with envy, besmirch in their refuse
the nobler writings of their compeers. What such wretches need to
study is not *Vander Hulpen des Ghebrecs des Wiins*, not *Die Clareit-und
Ypocrasrezepte* in Thomas van der Noots *Notabel Boecxken van Cokeryen*,
nor even the *Buchlein von den gebrannten Wässern*, but our golden
treasury, "Forwhi, it makiþ a man liȝt, iocunde, glad, and merie, and
puttiþ awey heuynesse, angre, melencoly, & wraþþe." Then, like
Aureolus Theophrastus Bombastus von Hohenheim, they can cast
their *Opera Omnia, particularia et universalia necnon paraphernalia* into the
flames, shake the dust of the university from their feet, and reel un-
steadily from state to state, babbling their thoughts in low German.
They might even find, like Galileo, that the earth revolves about
them, for did not he, when facing the four cardinal points, remark:

E pur se muove? Much better a fate to discard Chaucer, who always spoke of people, even in the most compromising situations, as being "bolt upright," and embrace those who (ineffable symbolism!) built their towers leaning.

Sorrowfully, we must turn from these serious matters to discuss the text put so generously into our hands by the Early English Text Society. Let it be said at once that the authorities have conspired to defraud readers of the complete secret. They have not published the text in full or, to put it another way, they have not taken care to see that it contains the truth, the whole truth and nothing but the truth. What they have printed is not merely a truncated and garbled version of the original text, but a version that robs the undoubted author of the credit he deserves. What is one to think of a text which claims to be written by

> Hermys þe prophete and kyng of Egipt, after the flood of Noe, fadir of philosophris, hadde by reuelacioun of an aungil of god to him sende,

when we know perfectly well that it was written by somebody else, at a long distance from Egypt, and at a much later period in time? This is what Cardinal Newman in his *Apologia* called "poisoning the wells." The real author was a Franciscan Friar, named John de Rupescissa, or, if you prefer it in Catalan (for that was his nationality), Juan de Pera-Tallada. Far from being king of Egypt, he was a professor of theology, and before that he had studied at Toulouse for five years. He was something of a prophet too. In 1345 he was put into prison at Figeac for saying things unpalatable to his superiors, and he appears to have served other sentences at Avignon and elsewhere even as late as 1356. It was whilst he was incarcerated that he wrote his book on Quintessence and was able to test the efficacy of his discovery.

> And when I was unjustly thrown into a dingy prison by my enemies, my body began to rot through the chafing of the iron fetters. But I managed, through the kindness of the gaoler, to get some brandy from a man of God, a friend of mine, and by simply smearing the affected parts with it, I was cured.

There were other hazards in a prison besides chafing fetters: the swarming lice. The quintessence was so effective that he included this experience in his book:

> The 7 medicyn for to heele ycche, & for to distrie lies þat ben engendrid of corrupt humouris. take oure essence bi him silf a-loone, and use to drynke þerof a litil quantite at oonys / and take also a litil quantite of

Mercurie, & mortifie it wiþ fastynge spotil, & medle it wiþ a good quantite of poudre of stafis-agre, & put it in to a greet quantite of brennynge watir, & thanne waische al his body, or ellis þe heed where þe ycche & þe lies ben. & use þis medicyn .2. or .3. & þe sijk man schal be hool.

Doubtless, other parts of the text reflect his own experiments, but we will leave these aside to concentrate on the distortions his book has suffered in translation. Not only has the prologue been shifted right to the end of the treatise, but whole passages have been omitted, some parts mistranslated, and the whole arrangement so jumbled up that patience is needed to fit the English to the Latin. If we take the 1561 edition printed at Basle as the basis of comparison, we find that the English version begins at page 14, takes one sentence from p. 17, makes a quotation of a few words from p. 16, moves on to p. 19 and then jumps from p. 23 to p. 28. Later on it omits seven pages from p. 33–40, returns to p. 35, omits the whole of pp. 36–52, selects some passages from 54–7, hops to pp. 111–12 and falls back on p. 55. It would be tedious to list examples of this nature which mar both the flow of ideas and the logical construction of the original treatise.

Added to this are the mistranslations of words and phrases. Where the English says, "riȝt so oure quinta essencia . . . wole be maad fair wiþ þe sunne *mineralle*," the Latin has *mirabili*. Where the English says, "And oure quinta essencia . . . is of þe nature & þe *colour* of heuene," the Latin has *calor*. Other examples of similar mistakes can be found on almost every page. For instance, "For sikirly þe philosophore seiþ, þat wiyn hath also þe propirtee to *restreyne* in it þe influence and vertues of gold," whereas the author's words mean quite the opposite: *vinum habet naturam recipiendi in se influentias & proprietates auri*. "wiþoute doute it wolde quenche anoon a brennynge sijknes clepid þe *fier of helle*," where the Latin has *ignem sacrum*.

I will not weary the reader with a catalogue of errors, but allow one final instance to suffice. In the list of remedies towards the end of the treatise the translator puts this sentence: "The .14. medicyn, to caste out venym fro mannys body / take oure 5 essence, and putte þerinne *fleisch of a cok*." What the author really recommended was *crocus*.

This makes it obvious that the conspiracy to mislead the public at large still continues. Were a man to make up this fourteenth medicine as directed, he would end up with *chair de poule*. All the same, in spite of blemishes, the book is valuable. It was written for "olde euangelik men," that is to say, for peripatetic professors who, in accordance with the scriptures, travel to the four corners of the earth dispensing their knowledge to the simple and the ignorant, and it was written in order that they might heal their bodily miseries and infirmities without notable expenses (*sine notabilibus expensis*). Let it not fall, as our author piously desires, into the hands of tyrants and reprobates, that is, into the clutches of those who force unwilling pupils to read the *Miller's Tale*, the *Reeve's Tale*, and other depressing examples of Chaucerian gloom, when they could be studying with profit the Book of Wisdom, Ecclesiastes, and Proverbs, all permeated with the Divine Spirit, but keep it rather for those who, welling over with the Water of Life, pour out copious libations at the scholar's feast. For such a Fest was this Schrift indited.

THE WELLCOME INSTITUTE OF THE HISTORY OF MEDICINE, LONDON

NOTE: As I have said in another book: To add footnotes would have overloaded the pages to such an extent that the text would have suffered. But the reader can rest assured that the references exist, and that nothing is said here which is not found in original texts or in manuscripts.

2

CHAUCER'S BLASPHEMOUS CHURL: A NEW INTERPRETATION OF THE *MILLER'S TALE*

BY BERYL ROWLAND

The *Miller's Tale*, as critics have rightly emphasized, is a requiting of the Knight's story of chivalry and romance. The situation, the wooing of a young woman by two young men, is basically similar. But in the one, the love triangle accommodates a larger philosophical purpose; in the other, the stock, farcical situation of low-life adultery is central, and the underlying intention, as distinct from the ostensible purpose of the teller, is oblique. Contrast in characterization, setting, tone, moral values, general style, as well as the judicious use of verbal echoes, enhances the burlesque. The Miller forecasts a "noble tale" (3126); the Reeve implies that it will be "lewed dronken harlotrye" (3145). What emerges is an ironic fusion of elegance and ribaldry.

Since E. M. W. Tillyard remarked that the tale displayed "a delicate mixing of the sacred and the obscene,"[1] many critics have noted parodies on biblical themes and phrases and have suggested that the deliberate, frequent reminders of the Church and the ironic misapplication of religious ideas form the backdrop against which to assess the action. But a re-examination of the ingredients which make up the "mixing" indicates that we have yet to recognize a particular kind of medieval humour which this tale contains: not only verbal blasphemy but blasphemy of situation and action. That an audience should recognize and appreciate such blasphemy is wholly likely. Throughout the Middle Ages scenes and incidents from the Vulgate Bible, the apocryphal books and various services of the Church were subject to merciless burlesque accompanied, as Haskins has observed, "by a degree of irreverence for which the modern reader is unprepared."[2]

The juxtaposition of the brutal or obscene and the spiritually beautiful is often seen in the miracle plays. In the Towneley pageant of the Crucifixion, for example, inept carpenters make comedy out

43

of the nailing of Christ to the Cross. In the Chester Shepherd's play the shepherds travesty the announcement of salvation by burlesquing the angel's song. And in the *Secunda Pastorum* of the Wakefield Master the central episode burlesques the Nativity and uses a prolific hard-drinking termagant and a long-snouted sheep as surrogates for the Virgin and Child. This kind of humour was proper to a churl, and Chaucer therefore uses it in his churl's tale. But whereas such humour may be inadequately controlled in the mystery pageants, obtruding on the main action in a way which seems incongruous or even offensive to modern taste, Chaucer holds it tightly within the central design, because he selects a minimum of items as the basis for the burlesque and restricts the equivalents.

He also uses it within the framework of the thoroughly profane story. He will not "falsen" his "matere." His disclaimer in the prologue to the *Miller's Tale*, ". . . every gentil wight I preye, / For Goddes love, demeth nat that I seye / Of yvel entente" (3171–3), and his final retraction of "the tales of Caunterbury, thilke that sownen into synne" (X, 1086) may reflect an awareness of the audacity to which his art had committed him, an audacity which went further than mere transgression of decorum.

The Miller specifies a particular kind of tale. He "wol telle a legende and a lyf / Bothe of a carpenter and of his wyf" (3141–2). It is to be a story about a saint. *Legende* is the regular title for the life of a saint. The use of the word here is suggestive: even without the recent allusion to the mystery plays (3124) and the other allusions to follow, the audience would probably identify the saint with the famous carpenter who played an important role in the mystery plays, St Joseph, the husband of the Virgin Mary. Both the anticipated action (3143) and the ostensible moral of the tale, "An housbonde shal nat be inquisityf / Of Goddes pryvetee, nor of his wyf" (3163–4), suggest that some ironic inversion is in store, and St Joseph was already a subject of burlesque.

Huizinga has aptly remarked that as the figure of the Virgin is exalted, "that of Joseph becomes more and more of a caricature. Art portrays him as a clown dressed in rags . . . Saint Joseph remained a comic type in spite of the very special reverence paid to him."[3] In the gospel version he was mentioned briefly: he learned of Mary's pregnancy and resolved to divorce her quietly, "being a just man and unwilling to put her to shame;" he changed his mind when an angel appeared and told him of Mary's conception by the Holy Ghost. In the Middle Ages there developed an expanding tradition called "Joseph's trouble with Mary." In some treatments the aged husband was a model of patience,[4] but in drama he became the caricature of the old husband with the young wife. The Chester cycle has a short "Old Man's Lament," telling of the folly of age marrying youth, and it has counterparts in other pageants, giving rise to dramatic development. Joseph becomes a cantankerous old rustic, dazed by the ways of the world yet too knowing to accept the truth:

> þanne se I wele youre menyng is
> þe Aungell has made hir with childe
> Nay, som man in aungellis liknesse
> With somkyn gawde has hir begiled.[5]

He is cast in a humorous cuckold frame, and argues that an old man should not marry a young woman lest he be betrayed. He appears in various pageants such as *The Betrothal of Mary*, *Joseph's Return*, *The Trial of Joseph and Mary*, *The Birth of Christ*, *The Purification*, *The Massacre of the Innocents*, *Christ and the Doctors*, taking a major role in several of them,[6] and in his most comic aspects he can be identified with the cuckolded elderly *jaloux* of the *fabliau*.

The opening lines of the *Miller's Tale* might seem to confirm the expectation that this is to be a tale about St Joseph. St Joseph, too, was "a riche gnof" and he was a carpenter. But before the analogy can be confirmed, the narrator, instead of making a full *effictio*, continues with a description of Nicholas, informing us immediately that there is nothing saint-like about the young clerk:

> Of deerne love he koude and of solas;
> And therto he was sleigh and ful privee
> And lyk a mayden meke for to see.
>
> (3200–2)

He has other attributes, a room strewn with aromatic herbs, a personal daintiness, an interest in astronomy and music, an ability to get his friends to support him, but it is in the description of his song that we have the clearest indication of his role in the story of St Joseph:

> And al above ther lay a gay sautrie,
> On which he made a-nyghtes melodie
> So swetely that all the chambre rong;
> And *Angelus ad virginem* he song;
> And after that he song the Kynges Noote.
> Ful often blessed was his myrie throte.
>
> (3213–18)

Chaucer's references to melody or harmony often contain symbolic undertones. The music here is, of course, picked up *passim*, and at the climax it is clearly figurative, "Withouten wordes mo they goon to bedde, / . . . Ther was the revel and the melodye" (3650–2). In addition, however, a particular implication is being made. Nicholas is proficient in the Old Dance but he sings the New Song, the angel's song of the Annunciation. To an audience familiar with the mystery plays, the title would recall one of the most dramatic situations in biblical history (such as was performed at York by the spicers) the Annunciation, in which an angel is sent by God to tell Mary of her conception. This young man Nicholas, angelic in appearance and smelling like a pomander "as sweete as is the roote / of lycorys, or any cetewale," is assuming the role of the Angel singing to the Virgin.[7]

He follows *Angelus ad virginem* with a song called the *King's Note*, the significance of which has never been satisfactorily explained. The title may refer to a specific song, but I would suggest that it contains one of the many puns which occur frequently throughout the tale in relation to singing and general noisemaking of the characters. Its importance is not in the musical note but in *note* (OE *notu*) meaning business, a word used by Chaucer in the *Reeve's Tale* (I, 4068). The angel in the pageant of the Annunciation is singing the business of the Heavenly King; Nicholas is also singing the *King's Note*, but it is business inspired by the Enemy.

The audience is again reminded of the carpenter of the mystery plays by the next reference to Nicholas' host:

> This carpenter hadde wedded newe a wyf,
> Which that he lovede moore than his lyf;
> Of eighteteene year she was of age.
> Jalous he was, and heeld hire narwe in cage,
> For she was wylde and yong, and he was old,
> And demed hymself been lik a cokewold.
>
> (3221–6)

St Joseph was old, jealous, newly wed, and devoted to his wife.

But Chaucer the pilgrim has already warned that this is to be a tale of "harlotrie" and that men should not "maken ernest of game." With the entry of Alison the nature of the game seems less equivocal:

> Fair was this yonge wyf, and therwithal
> As any wezele hir body gent and smal . . .
>
> (3233–70)

The most unusual image here is that of the weasel; an animal which, according to Rabanus Maurus "*est furti figura . . . Mustela vero eos per figuram demonstrat, qui ingenium naturale sub dolo malitiae polluunt et totam vitam suam in insidiis et fraudibus ducunt.*"[8] Details in the portrait suggest that Chaucer retains the animal image, giving his heroine distinctively weasel-like attributes known either in folklore or natural history. Huntsmen knew the weasel as a quarry of the second class, an animal of the "stingand fute,"[9] but its outstanding feature from a theological point of view and one which was constantly repeated in bestiaries and encyclopedias was that it conceived by the ear and gave birth through the mouth.[10] In like manner the Virgin conceived, and in illustrations of the Annunciation she was therefore often depicted with an angel or dove representing the Holy Ghost whispering in her ear.[11] The statement that the Word ($\lambda \acute{o} \gamma o \varsigma$) was made flesh was literally interpreted. Since the word entered the ear, it was understood that the incarnation of *Logos* was achieved in the same fashion. Hence the acknowledgment "*Gaude Virgo, mater Christi / Quae per aurem concepisti.*"[12]

The ensuing images not only parody those applied to a typical heroine of romance, but contain more covert comparisons. To the Dominicans, black and white were the colours of holiness, and Alison's appearance in them may remind us of the white weasel or ermine. But with her plucked eyebrows and "likerous ye" she plainly lacks the ermine's widely accredited symbolism of chastity.[13] The reference to her as a whole tree of potential, early-ripe fruit invites analogy, not to the single "white lylye flour" of the Virgin,[14] but to the still burgeoning vitality of that older Alison, the Wife of Bath, accustomed to bestow her "flour" on lovers as well as in "actes and in fruyt of mariage" (III, 114). Wool, the most famous of all symbols of the Virgin Mary,[15] here serves only to emphasize Alison's inviting animality. Not for her the tower of the highborn lady nor the phoenix metaphor of uniqueness;[16] Alison's only tower is where money is made, adumbrating the "meed" which Absolon, with his knowledge of town women, is to proffer her; her voice is like that of a swallow, a single, loud, excited, high-pitched 'tswee" sound, not dissimilar to her later outrageous "Tehee!" (3740); it may also reflect her sexual proclivities.[17] She is neither the *hortus conclusus* nor the roe skipping up the mountains,[18] but a flower of the woods for anyone's picking, a young animal looking only for sensual satisfaction or struggling in the trap of concupiscence (3282). She may smell fragrantly, but not of spices; she is the eternal Eve with her mouth as "sweete as bragot or the meeth, / Or hoord of apples leyd in hey or heeth," images which convey sweetness, fermentation, natural ripeness, and tell us that this is a country girl suitable for country pleasures.

We are thus prepared for the action which follows. The husband, like Joseph in the mystery plays, absents himself on account of his work, and Nicholas makes love to the wife:

> And prively he caughte hire by the queynte,
> And seyde, "Ywis, but if ich have my wille,
> For deerne love of thee, lemman, I spille."
>
> (3276-8)

The action in which he engages clearly conveys the iconographic idea of lechery, and is an undeniable travesty of the situation contained in *Angelus ad virginem*. His song, with its plea for "salvation," is secular and blasphemous; his love is secret not because it is divine, but because it is adulterous. The inversion continues when he smacks her "aboute the lendes weel," kisses her "sweete" and sings a fast tune on his psaltery. It is in the same spirit that one sees illustrated over and over in the visual arts of the Middle Ages. In the Arundel Psalter, for example, the grotesques make melody to the Devil's tune while above, in the initial for the text *Cantate domini canticum novum*, three figures sing the New Song.[19] Each incident has its counterpart: the figure of the angel speaking to Mary is in opposition to that of the Devil tempting Eve.[20]

The story now necessitates the introduction of Absolon, a second lover, whose connection with the parody is less direct. Much has been written on the way the total portrait of the fastidious barber-clerk, who is "somedeel squaymous of fartyng," not only provides striking contrast to that of the successful lover but contains all the threads for his ultimate humiliation. It also confirms the values that are being flouted. Presumably Absolon has religious aspirations, but he has worldy interests, and has a predilection for barmaids:

> In al the toun nas brewhous ne taverne[21]
> That he ne visited with his solas,
> Ther any gaylard tappestere was.
>
> (3334-6)

His biblical namesake, who shared his most distinctive attribute, the curled hair that as "gold it shoon, / And strouted as a fanne large and brode" (3314-15), signified the excesses of the flesh, concupiscence of the eyes and pride of life. Herod, whom Chaucer's Absolon played in the mystery plays "upon a scaffold hye" to show his "maistry," had a similar reputation.[22] As Absolon amusingly demonstrates his ineptness as a courtly lover, the pervasive theological references serve to remind us that he as well as Nicholas and Alison is thoroughly committed to the Old Dance and to prepare us for the final *significatio*.

As the plot develops, the blasphemous burlesque extends its dimension with a striking juxtaposition of the contemporary and the biblical. Oxford was noted for the activity of its astrologers.[23] The

great eclipse of 1345 gave rise to various predictions by John Ash-
enden and other astrologers, and in 1388 an earthen head was made
at Oxford by allegedly necromantical means which, at set times,
would utter, "*primo caput decidetur, secundo caput elevabitur, tertio pedes
elevabuntur super caput.*"[24] Oxford was the right place for predictions
such as those of Nicholas, and that the carpenter should have already
been exposed to prognostications of an astronomer-clerk (3457), is
altogether likely.

But the tale which Nicholas tells after he has feigned sickness and
aroused his host's concern and curiosity is made even more convincing
by acknowledgment of biblical precedent:

> "Hastow nat herd hou saved was Noe,
> When that oure Lord hadde warned hym biforn
> That al the world with water sholde be lorn?"
> "Yis," quod this Carpenter, "ful yoore ago."
> "Hastou nat herd," quod Nicholas, "also
> The sorwe of Noe with his felaweshipe,
> Er that he myghte gete his wyf to shipe?"
>
>   (3534–40)

Living in a centre for mystery plays, belonging to a guild likely to
have participated in them, and probably erecting the stages, John
might be expected to have such knowledge. In the mystery drama the
episode of Noah and his wife is a point of high comedy. It is based on
certain incidents in a lost apocrypha, the *Book of Noria*, and was widely
treated in literature and art in medieval Europe.[25] According to
popular legend, Noah, although enjoined to secrecy by God, revealed
to his wife that he was building an ark and she disclosed the secret to
the Devil. She later enabled the Devil to enter the ark because she
herself demurred until Noah angrily exclaimed, "Come in, you
devil!"

In one version of the mystery plays, God's angel, later to appear to
Mary at the Annunciation, comes to aged Noah and declares that "all
this wyde werd shall be dreynt with flood, / Saff thou and thi wyff
. . ."[26] In another, God himself appears to Noah. In the present
drama, John, who is to give Nicholas the salvation he is seeking, is
the surrogate for Noah who was said to prefigure Christ.[27] Nicholas
apes God, and even imposes on his dupe the same condition of
chastity.[28] But his real role is indicated by his offering his host "al
the world" (3582),[29] and is confirmed when he remarks that Noah
would have given all his "wetheres blake" to have his wife sail by herself. Noah's wife, unknown to her husband, was plotting with the
Devil; Alison, unknown to her husband, is in collusion with Nicholas.

As the dramatic situation moves to its climax, the blasphemy shifts to the other lover. Reasoning incorrectly about the carpenter's unusual absence from his labours, Absolon, with his lips itching for a kiss, presents himself at Alison's low casement window, kneeling (3723), as at an altar. There he addresses her in a parody of love songs from the Song of Songs, casting himself as the bridegroom (Christ or God) and Alison as the bride (Holy Virgin or Church).

Alison's brutal reply, besides conveying her anger at being disturbed in her love making, indicates that she recognizes the blasphemy:

> "Go fro the wyndow, Jakke fool," she sayde;
> "As help me God, it wol nat be 'com pa me.'
> I love another—and elles I were to blame—
> Wel bet than thee, by Jhesu, Absolon.
> Go forth thy wey, or I wol caste a ston,
> And lat me slepe, a twenty devel way!"
>
> (3708–13)

As the Wycliff Bible states: "Leed thow out the blasfeme (*blasphemum*) out of the tentis . . . and al the puple stone hym."[30] Death by stoning was the traditional punishment for blasphemy.

The rite in which Absolon then unwittingly engages was traditionally associated with the worship of the Devil. *Osculum in tergo* was the extremity of blasphemy attributed to heretics, and was one of the principal charges levelled against the Waldensians and the Catharists in the thirteenth and the Knight's Templars early in the fourteenth century.[31] Absolon acknowledges the sacrilege:

> Who rubbeth now, who froteth now his lippes
> With dust, with sond, with straw, with clooth, with chippes,
> But Absolon, that seith ful ofte, "Allas!"
> "My soule bitake I unto Sathanas,[32]
> But me were levere than al this toun," quod he,
> "Of this despit awroken for to be."
>
> (3747–52)

Cautery, to which he now resorts, is not only the logical expression of his own frustration, but a skill in which he must have been professionally accomplished. As parish clerk, he purified the wives by swinging a hot censer full of live coals (3340); as barber-surgeon he would have adopted more practical methods of purification. At Oxford barber-surgeons were incorporated as a guild in 1348 when they agreed to "maintayne a light befor our Ladie Chappell of St Frisworth,"[33] the healing saint whose aid John invoked for Nicholas earlier in the tale (3449), and a common surgical operation was cauterization *in ano*.[34] His desperate act also reminds us that fire, according to the exegetical writers, symbolized the Holy Ghost: the Holy Ghost impregnated the Virgin with inner fire and protected her from concupiscence.[35] Absolon now intends to purge Alison by fire, not with his *cauter* (ME cauterie), to be sure, but with something nearer at hand which would retain its heat—a coulter from Gervais, the smith. In the Chester cycle, *The Purification of the Virgin* was undertaken by the blacksmiths.

But Alison does not repent and Absolon is unable to *absoilen*.[36] With his gold hair, fine clothes and falchion he has the same insignia as Herod who, in the pageant of *The Massacre of the Innocents*, raged the streets in frustration.[37] The role adumbrates his failure.

Always ineffectual, he re-enacts his scene at the window and receives further insult before striking hot with his iron. Nicholas, exchanging places with Alison, "leet fle a fart, / As greet as it had been a thonder-dent, / That with the strooke he was almoost yblent" (3806–8).

It is true that Luther later used similar methods to expel the Devil[38] but the fart was the Devil's own. The Devil was "Goddes ape," and parodied the Holy Trinity.[39] The Holy Ghost could be symbolized by fire, vitalizing breath, or the Dove; the Devil's base equivalent was the fart.[40]

With Nicholas' gesture the blasphemous parody is once more acknowledged. Then it dissolves in the general comedy:

> Of gooth the skyn an hande-brede aboute,
> The hoote kultour brende so his toute,
> And for the smert he wende for to dye.
> As he were wood, for wo he gan to crye,
> "Help! water! water! help, for Goddes herte!"
>
> (3811–15)

The cry for water brings the old carpenter crashing down in his tub, thinking that the Flood has come. Everyone disbelieves his strange story and is persuaded by Nicholas and Alison that he is mad. The tale ends with a frank capitulation of the action, in laughter broadened by a recognition of the complicated weave of its humour. It is a humour which, if it makes no overt distinction between the sacred and the profane, nevertheless seems to offer another perspective. The Annunciation, perennially enacted, was too miraculous to be forgotten. Through the parody, the ephemeral world of trivial lust and vulgar jest is set against the cosmic and timeless background of divine ordinance.

YORK UNIVERSITY, TORONTO

NOTES

[1] E. M. W. Tillyard, *Poetry Direct and Oblique*, 2nd edn (1934; London: Chatto and Windus, 1945), p. 87. In the second edition "a delicate" has been substituted for "the wickedest" (p. 218, 1934 edn).

[2] Charles Homer Haskins, *The Renaissance of the Twelfth Century* (1927; rpt. New York: Meridian, 1957), p. 184.

[3] J. Huizinga, *The Waning of the Middle Ages* (1924; rpt. New York: Doubleday, 1954, pp. 169–70.

[4] R. Morris (ed.), *Cursor Mundi* (EETS, OS 59, 1874, pt. II, pp. 639–41; F. A. Foster (ed.), *Stanzaic Life of Christ* (EETS, OS 166, 1926), p. 10; Lawrence F. Powell (ed.), *Nicholas Love's Mirrour of the Blessed lyf of Jesu Christ* (Oxford: Clarendon Press, 1908), p. 41.

[5] Lucy Toulmin Smith (ed.), *York Plays* (1885; rpt. New York: Russell & Russell, 1963), p. 106.

[6] K. S. Block (ed.), *Ludus Coventriae* (EETS, ES 120, 1922), p. 110. See also H. Deimling, (ed.), *The Chester Plays* (EETS, ES 62, 1892), pt. I, *The Nativity* VI; *The Slaying of the Innocents* X; *The Purification of the Virgin* XI; George England and Alfred W. Pollard (eds), *The Towneley Plays* (EETS, ES 71, 1897), *The Annunciation* X; *The Flight into Egypt* XV; *The Purification of Mary* XVII; *The Play of the Doctors* XVIII; see also H. Craig (ed.), *Two Coventry Corpus Christi Plays* (EETS, ES 87, 1957), p. 47.

[7] On Satan's resemblance to an angel in medieval illustration and drama see A. N. Didron, *Christian Iconography* (1851; rpt. New York: Ungar, 1965), I, pp. 158–9; Irena Janicka, *The Comic Elements in the English Mystery Plays Against The Cultural Background* (Poznan: Posnanskie ser., 1962), pp. 52–3. See also Theodor Erbe (ed.), *Mirk's Festial* (EETS, ES 96, 1905), p. 106, stating that Mary was abashed at Gabriel's salutation because "þer was þat tyme in þat conre a man þat cowþe moch of wycchecraft, and so, by helpe of þe fende, he made hym lyke an angyll, and come to dyvers maydyns, and sayde he was send from God to hom on þys message." The legend first appeared in Josephus, and was later taken over in the *Disciplina Clericalis*, Boccaccio, followed by many an Italian novelle. For the version in *Les cent nouvelles nouvelles*, see Rossell Hope Robbins (tr.), *The Hundred Tales* (New York: Crown, 1960), pp. 52–7; analogues, p. 382.

[8] *PL*, CXI, 226.

[9] Juliana Berners, *The Book containing the Treatises of Hawking; Hunting; Coat-Armour; Fishing; and Blasing of Arms*, edited by J. Haslewood (London: White and Cochrane, 1810), p. 25.

[10] Charles Cahier and Arthur Martin, *Mélanges d'archéologie d'histoire et de littérature* (Paris, 1851), II, pp. 147–8; *Il Bestiaro d'amore di Ricardo di Fornival*, pub. by Giusto Grion in *Il Propugnatore* (1869), II, 159, 170–1; Edward B. Ham, "The Cambrai Bestiary," *MP*, 36 (1939), p. 233; Alfons Mayer (ed.), "*Der Waldensische Physiologus*," *RF*, 5 (1890), p. 408; but see also Pseudo-Hugo de Saint Victor, *De bestiis et aliis rebus*, *PL*, CLXXVII, 66; F. J. Carmody (ed.), "*Physiologus Latinus Versio Y*," Univ. of California Publications in Classical Philology, 12 (1941), p. 127, and for the history of this misconception and its subsequent modification see Florence McCulloch, *Mediaeval Latin and French Bestiaries*, 2nd edn (1960; Chapel Hill: Univ. of North Carolina Press, 1962), p. 187.

[11] S. Reinach, *Répertoire de Peintures du moyen âge et de la Renaissance, 1280–1580* (Paris: E. Leroux, 1905–23), II, 42, i, 43, 44, i, 47, 52, i, 53, ii, 55, 58, i, 60, i, 60,

ii, 63, i, etc.; Lilian M. C. Randall, *Images in the Margins of Gothic Manuscripts* (Berkeley: Univ. of California Press, 1966), fig. 675, [BM Addit. MS 42130, f. 86]; Jean Porcher, *French Miniatures from Illuminated Manuscripts* (London: Collins, 1960), p. 70, fig. 75 [Bibliothèque Mazarine MS 469, f. 13]; pl. lxxvi [Bibliothèque Nationale MS lat. 1161, f. 31]; Marcel Aubert et al., *Le Vitrail Français* (Paris: Edition 2 mondes, 1958), fig. 198. See also Didron, I, 507n; E. P. Evans, *Animal Symbolism in Ecclesiastical Architecture* (New York: Holt, 1896), pp. 98–9; Louis Réau, *Iconographie de l'art chrétien* (Paris: Presses Universitaires de France, 1955–9), I, p. 100; II, pp. 185, 190.

12 Clemens Blume and Guido M. Dreves (eds), *"De XIV gaudiis BMV,"* *Analecta Hymnica Medii Aevi* (Leipzig: Reisland, 1886–1922), XLII, p. 82; Konrad von Haimburg's *"Gaudia Beatae Mariae,"* in G. M. Dreves (ed.), *Ein Jahrtausend Lateinischer Hymnendichtung* (Leipzig: Reisland, 1909), I, p. 423 [*Anal. Hymn.*, III, p. 34]; see also *Anal. Hymn.*, XXXI, pp. 176, 180, 186, 197; XLII, p. 83, and St Augustine, *Sermo* ccxxv, *In die Paschae*, *Opera Omnia* XX, edited by D. A. B. Caillau (Paris: Parent-Desbarres, 1836–9), II, iv; St Gaudentius, *PL*, XX, 934; St Bernard, *PL*, CLXXXIII, 327.

13 Carl Appel (ed.), Petrarch *Trionfi*, *"Triumphus Mortis,"* *Die Triumphe Francesco Petrarcas in kritischen Texte* (Halle: Niemeyer, 1901) v, 19–20. The symbolism, stemming from a belief expressed by Aelian, II, xxvii, and others, was very persistent. See Guy de Tervarent, *Attributs et symboles dans l'art profane* (Geneva: Droz, 1958), cols. 212–14. For detailed comparison of Alison to a weasel, see Beryl Rowland, *Blind Beasts: Chaucer's Animal World* (Kent, Ohio; Kent State Univ. Press, 1971), pp. 27–9.

14 *CT*, VII, 461: for the use of this and other symbols for the Virgin Mary see F. J. E. Raby, *A History of Christian-Latin Poetry from the beginnings to the close of the Middle Ages* (Oxford: Clarendon Press, 1953), pp. 365ff. See also R. E. Kaske, "The *Canticum Canticorum* in the *Miller's Tale,*" *SP*, 59 (1962), 487–9, who remarks on the "tantalizing half-correspondences" between Alison and the *sponsa* of the *Canticum*. One suspects a pun in *pere-jonette*: see Rossell Hope Robbins (ed.), "Love in a Garden," *Secular Lyrics of the XIVth and XVth Centuries*, 2nd edn (1952, Oxford: Clarendon Press, 1955), pp. 15–16, no. 21, where, as Robbins remarks, p. 234, there is word play on *"per ienet"* and *"per robert."*

15 Raby, op. cit., p. 371.

16 Cf. *Anal. Hymn.*, LIV, p. 435; XXXXVIII, p. 443; Raby, op. cit., p. 445.

17 See "The Payne and Sorowe of Evyll maryage" in Thomas Wright (ed.) *The Latin Poems commonly attributed to Walter Mapes*, Camden Soc., 17 (1841), p. 297 "Wyves been bestes very unstable / in ther desires . . . / Like a swalowe, which is insaciable."

18 See Raby, op. cit., p. 366.

19 BM MS Arundel 83 f. 63v. See Robertson, *Preface to Chaucer* (Princeton: Princeton Univ. Press, 1963), p. 129, fig. 36.

20 For analogy between Mary and Eve, see Towneley pageant of *The Annunciation*, p. 87. Compare also Alison, her face transfigured as a result of Nicholas' "song" ["Hir forheed shoon as bright as any day"] as she goes to church "Cristes owene werkes for to wirche" (3308), with Mary whose face shines "as þe sonne with his bemys quan he is most bryth," Block, op. cit., p. 109.

21 Absolon would probably "clippe and shave" in taverns. Since soap was expensive in the Middle Ages, some barbers used ale froth and basted the face with it [see H. E. Salter (ed.), *Munimenta civitatis Oxonie* (Oxford: Hist. Soc., 1920), p. 110, n. 4]. In view of Absolon's marked conviviality—"with compaignye, hym to disporte

and pleye" (3660)—and his offer of money to Alison (3380), it is worth remarking
that barber-surgeons were often stewkeepers. See R. R. Sharpe (ed.), *Calendar of
Letter Books* (London: Corporation of the City Library, 1899–1912), I, p. 178;
K, p. 17; D'Arcy Power, *English Medicine and Surgery in the Fourteenth Century*, Har-
veian Lecture (1914), p. 16.

²² Robertson, op. cit., p. 385, n. 204, cites instances in which Herod signified
"vainglorious" and "glorying in clothing." The *York Plays* emphasizes his
vanity: "I am worthy, witty and wyse" (p. 124); *Lud. Cov.*, his beauty and fine
robes (p. 169). That the role of Herod is carried through the tale is further
suggested by the similarity of the reactions which both Herod and Absolon
provoke. As Martial Rose (ed.), *The Wakefield Plays* (1962, New York: Doubleday
Anchor Books, 1963), p. 310, observes, the frequent calls for silence indicate
that Herod (like other tyrants) was invariably greeted with a storm of jeers and
cat-calls. See also n. 32 below.

²³ John Gutch (ed.), *The History and Antiquities of the University of Oxford in two books
by Anthony à Wood* (Oxford: Clarendon Press, 1792), I, p. 481.

²⁴ J. R. Lumby (ed.), *Chronicon Henrici Knighton, Rerum Britannicarum Medii Aevi
Scriptores*, 92 (1889–95), II, p. 258.

²⁵ F. L. Utley, "The one hundred and three names of Noah's Wife," *Spec.*, 16 (1941),
pp. 426–52; Anna Jean Mills, "Noah's Wife Again," *PMLA*, 56 (1941), pp. 613–
26; Don Cameron Allen, *The Legend of Noah: Renaissance Rationalism in Art, Science
and Letters*, Illinois Studies in Language and Literature, 33 (1949), pp. 3–4. On
Noah's fame as an astrologer see John J. O'Connor, "The Astrological Background of the *Miller's Tale*," *Spec.*, 31 (1956), pp. 120–5.

²⁶ Block, op. cit., p. 39; cf. Toulmin Smith, op. cit., p. 41.

²⁷ Isidore, *PL*, LXXXIII, 102, 229. The mystery plays link the Flood with the
Nativity (Noel) because Noah prefigures Christ; "Nowelis flood" suggests a
similar association. On the prefigurations in the *Miller's Tale*, see B. Rowland,
"The Play of the *Miller's Tale*: A Game within a Game," *ChauR*, 5 (Fall, 1970),
pp. 140–6. It is worth noting that the adjective *sely* applied to the carpenter,
3404, 3423, 3509, 3601, 3614, could still mean *holy* as well as *hapless, pitiable*.
See Mary Brookbank Reid, "Chaucer's Sely Carpenter," *PQ*, 41 (1962), pp. 768–9.

²⁸ On the Flood as punishment for lechery see *Pars T*, X, 839.

²⁹ The Tempter, according to medieval exegesis, tried thus to persuade Christ—
"*Et ostendit omnia regia mundi . . .*" See Paul A. Olson, "The World: The
Pattern of Meaning and the Tradition," *CL*, 13 (1961), p. 28, n. 4.

³⁰ Lev. xxiv, 14. Alison's threat seems to have little relevance to John viii, 7.

³¹ Walter Map, *De Nugis Curialium in Anecdota Oxoniensia*, edited by M. R. James
(Oxford: Clarendon Press, 1914), dist. I, xxx; Pierre Dupuy, *Histoire de la con-
damnacion des Templiers* (Brussels, 1713), I, p. 141; *Alanus de Insulis, PL*, CCX,
366; Thomas Wright and James Orchard Halliwell (eds), *Reliquiae Antiquae*,
(London: Wm. Pickering, 1841–3; rpt. New York: AMS Press, 1966), I, p. 247;
see also Symphorien Champier, *Dyalogus in Magicarum Artium Destructionem*
(Lyons, ca. 1500), iii, 3, sig. bij.

³² Note the similarity between this speech and that of Herod (whom Absolom
portrayed "upon a scaffold hye") in the Chester *Slaying of the Innocents*, I, 202;
"I bequeath here in this place / my soule to be with Sathanas."

³³ The practical implication of Absolon's profession has not been suffici-
ently noted. Stith Thompson, "The Miller's Tale," in W. F. Bryan and Germaine
Dempster (eds), *Sources and Analogues of Chaucer's Canterbury Tales* (New York:
Humanities Press, 1958), p. 106, suggests that Chaucer "forgets that the duped

lover should appropriately be a smith;" Paul E. Beichner, "Absolon's Hair," *MS*, 12 (1950), p. 222, n.1, considers that Chaucer decided against the occupation of smith "lest he appear too much like the rough and ready carpenter," and made Absolon what he was to heighten the humour of his downfall. T. Craik, *The Comic Tales of Chaucer* (London: Methuen, 1964; New York: Barnes and Noble, 1965), p. 14, finds that such details as "wel koude he laten blood and clippe and shave" contribute to the general substance and conviction of the tale but are otherwise unnecessary. For the Oxford guild of barber-surgeons see H. E. Salter (ed.), *Munim. civit. Oxon.*, pp. 109–10. The profession included surgery, barbering and the making of church wafers; see also Wood's *Hist. and Antiquit.*, edited by Gutch, I, pp. 443, 444.

34 See John of Arderne. *Praxis Medica et Chirurgica*, BM MS Sloane 2002, f. 24 v; Lanfrank's *Science of cirurgie*, edited by R. Fleischacker (EETS, OS 102, 1894), p. 305; *Treatises of Fistula in ano* . . . by John Arderne, edited by D'Arcy Power (EETS, OS 139, 1910), p. 51. See also Loren Mackinney, *Medical Illustrations in Medieval Manuscripts* (Berkeley: Univ. of California Press, 1965), figs. 43, 44, 46, 51, 86, 87a, 87b.

35 Honorius "Augustodunensis," *PL*, CLXXII, 904; Bernard of Clairvaux, *PL* CLXXXIII, 63; Rabanus Maurus, *PL*, CLI, 513; Chaucer, *An ABC*, 89–96; see also E. Harris, "Mary in the Burning Bush," *JWCI*, 1 (1937–8), pp. 281–6.

36 One suspects a pun. See *MED*, sv. "absoilen" [Cf. ME assoilen and L. *absolvere*]. See also *CT*, VI 387, 913, 933, 939; I 661. The name Absolon was, however, not uncommon. See E. G. Withycombe (comp), *The Oxford Dictionary of English Christian Names* (Oxford: Clarendon Press, 1953), p. 2.

37 See H. Craig (ed.), *Two Cov. Corp. Christi Plays* (EETS, ES 87, 1902), p. 86. In the Chester cycle Herod seems to be the personification of rage, as he does, indeed, on the misericords. See M. D. Anderson, *Drama and Imagery in English Medieval Churches* (Cambridge: Cambridge Univ. Press, 1963), p. 156, pl. 22b; Janicka, op. cit., p. 86, fig. 39

08 J. Aurifaber (ed.), *Tischreden oder colloquia*, (Eisleben, 1566), II, 1557.

39 Tertullian, *PL*, I, 1313, 1879; II, 65; Dante, *Inferno*, xxxiv, l. 38; see also Didron, II, p. 22, fig. 34; p. 23, fig. 35; L. U. Lucken, *Antichrist and the prophets of Antichrist in the Chester Cycle* (Washington: Catholic Univ. of America Press, 1940), pp. 16–17.

40 See Block, op. cit., p. 27, l. 355; cf. St Augustine, *De anima, Opera Omnia* XXXIV, edited by Caillau, I, xviii.

3

NOTES ON SOME
MIDDLE ENGLISH CHARMS

BY DOUGLAS GRAY

In the course of the dinner-party at the house of Deiphebus in the
second book of *Troilus and Criseyde*, the conversation turns to the sickness of Troilus, and as might happen still, everyone becomes an
amateur doctor. But the suggestions made are not of pills or of new
drugs, but of charms:

> Compleyned ek Eleyne of his siknesse
> So feythfully, that pite was to here,
> And every wight gan waxen for accesse
> A leche anon, and seyde, "In this manere
> Men curen folk."—"This charme I wol yow leere."
> But ther sat oon, al list hire nought to teche,
> That thoughte, "Best koud I yet ben his leche."[1]

Later in the same poem, Troilus reproves Pandarus in his own colloquial manner, and uses against him a homely charm, which in fact
has survived into modern folk-tradition:

> But kanstow playen raket, to and fro,
> Nettle in, dok out, now this now that, Pandare?[2]

The Parson, like many moralists before and after, vehemently attacks
"thilke horrible sweryng of adjuracioun and conjuracioun, as doon
thise false enchauntours or nigromanciens in bacyns ful of water, or
in a bright swerd, in a cercle, or in a fir, or in a shulder-boon of a
sheep," and those "that beleeven on divynailes, as by flight or by
noyse of briddes, or of beestes, or by sort, by nigromancie, by dremes,
by chirkynge of dores, or crakkynge of houses, by gnawynge of rattes,
and swich manere wrecchednesse," and only grudgingly admits
"Charmes for woundes or maladie of men or of beestes, if they taken
any effect, it may be peraventure that God suffreth it, for folk sholden
yeve the moore feith and reverence to his name."[3] Very different,
however, is the reaction of the carpenter in the *Miller's Tale*, who

combines a distrust of intellectuals with an extreme credulity, when he thinks that his lodger has fallen in some "woodnesse or som agonye." He says a "nyght-spel" at the four corners of the house and at the threshold of the door.[4] Again, the "white pater-noster" which he uses in his magic ritual against the night-demons is another ubiquitous charm surviving into modern times.[5] All of these examples show that the greatest of our medieval poets knew, and made literary use of, the popular magical lore of his own day.

It is surprising, therefore, that students of medieval literature have paid so little attention to the charms scattered through the medical and pseudo-medical manuscripts. As in so many other areas, the basis for future work has been laid by the patient researches of Rossell Hope Robbins.[6] The following notes represent only a preliminary stage of what I hope will be a longer study.

The world which is implied by the popular medical manuscripts seems a very strange place to a modern reader. For him religion has retreated to the periphery of life, magic has become the preserve of an eccentric minority, and medicine that of an exclusive, and highly paid, professional group. In the popular medieval charms, however, the three are inseparably united. The carpenter—and no doubt many people of his time—is unlikely to have thought, as we do, of the "natural" and the "supernatural" as two quite distinct and exclusive spheres. In this, his attitude (which quite naturally leads him to invoke magical protection when danger threatens) is very similar to that of people in "primitive" societies the world over. The world was full of spirits and demons, some benevolent, but many malevolent, who could produce all manner of evil, danger, or disease.[7] Fairies, in spite of the Wife of Bath's sceptical opinion, not only existed, but could carry off mortals. The ancient demons of the night might be prevented by prayer (it seems likely that the Middle English versions of the hymn *Christus qui lux es et dies* would be used for this) or by magical means. A very interesting verse charm, "Seynt Iorge our lady knyghth" (which again survived into later times), is to be written in a "bylle" and hung in the mane of a horse to protect it against the nightly riding of the "nightmare."[8] In rural areas of England the idea that horses found running with sweat in the morning had been ridden by a demon during the night survived for centuries (cf. Thomas Hardy's *The Woodlanders*, ch. 28). The rubric which accompanies the charm also advocates the use of another magical object, familiar in later times, "a flynt stone that hath an hole thorow of hys owen growyng" hung over the stable door. (The notion that the nightmare would also "ride" people as well as animals survives in the word "hag-ridden.") The charm reproduces an ancient pattern, in which the saint/hero/god goes in search of the demon, meets her, beats and binds "that fowle wyghth," and extracts a promise that she will not come to bring danger or disease.

Medieval popular religion in some of its aspects was very close to magic, and it is not surprising to find the charms using devotional images or prayers, or the symbols and figures of orthodox religion. The saints presided over holy places (especially wells) or were regarded as specially efficacious in guarding against particular diseases or dangers. Around some of them all sorts of magical beliefs clustered. St John the Baptist presided over and gave his name to various potent herbs and plants—St John's Wort (*fuga daemonum*) which drove away evil spirits, vervain, fern, bracken, etc.[9] The pious and devout were protected by the ministrations of individual guardian angels— the Monk of Farne remembers that he would have been crushed by a wall, if his angel had not caught him up and carried him to a safe distance, and again that he was saved from falling from a plank into the Cherwell.[10] Angels played an even more important part in the magical tradition (especially the Jewish), so that it is not surprising to find them making an appearance in our manuscripts:

> At morne whan þou risist oute of þi bed haue Myȝel in þi mynde, and þou schal haue al þat dai glad to þe. ȝif it þondir haue Gabriel in þi mynde, and it schal not greue þe. ȝif þou spekist wiþ þi aduersary haue Vriel in þi mynde, and þou schalt ouyrcum hym. ȝif þou etist or drynkyst haue Raphael in mynde, and it schul do þe myche good. ȝif þou goist any iorney haue Raguel in þi mynde and nothing schal greue þe. ȝif þou standist bifore any domesman haue Rachel and Tobie in thi mynde, and þou schalt spede weel. ȝif þou comist in to any congregacioun of pepil haue (?) Fantuseronem in þi mynde and þe(i) schul ioie alle aȝens þe.[11]

The sign of the cross was, naturally enough, regarded as of great magical power. The carpenter uses it: "I crouche thee from elves and fro wightes," and it survived into modern folk-tradition (wicker crosses were hung over cow-sheds, for instance). The sign is found in many charms—one gives very elaborate instructions for the preparation of a large lead plate, large enough to cover the wound which is to be healed, with a cross made in each corner (the idea is that of a protecting *lorica*; cf. the carpenter's action in saying his nightspell in the four "halves" of his house), and a fifth in the centre. The accompanying charms include a mention of the five wounds of Christ.[12] We have also an English verse charm, "Helpe, crosse, fayrest of tymbris three,"[13] and a popular Latin charm "Crux Christi" which claims to have been sent by "Pope Leo" to Charlemagne.[14] (A well-known feature of traditional magical charms is to claim some special form of spiritual authority, e.g. by being sent directly from some great magician, saint, or God himself.) Again, the cults of the wounds of Christ or of the Precious Blood make their contribution—the intense veneration of the great wound in the side of Christ sometimes finds expression in devotional images which are crude representations of the gash, and purport to give its exact measurement. These are sometimes accompanied by a rubric claiming that an indulgence may be obtained by looking at it, or wearing it, or placing it in one's house, which effectively transforms it into a popular religious amulet.[15]

Naturally enough, there is much use of Christian formulae and prayers. As Singer says of Anglo-Saxon England, "paternosters accompany every conceivable medical process." These words and phrases (even *fiat, amen*—very important in Coptic magic) are words of power, of proved spiritual efficacy, and their potency was no doubt increased because they were in a mysterious and sacred language. Less well known is this charm for "fevers," which involves the use of three Hosts:

> Tak and write in thre hostys thre clausis. In the furst hoyst write in the compas aboute this pater + est + sanitas +, and a midde wryte + Alpha and O +. And in the secunde hoyst wryte in the same wise + filius + est vita + and a midde write + emanuel +. And on the thridde hoyst write + spiritus sanctus + est remedium + and a midde write + tetragramaton + And ȝeue the seke to ete hem thre daies a rewe, and þat or the sonne arise. And let hym say .v. pater noster and aue.[16]

The charms were the stock in trade of practising physicians, cunning men, charmers, and wise women, as well as being available for private use. It is important to remember that they are not part of an intellectually conceived system of magic or hermetic philosophy, but that they are practical recipes, meant to be used, and thus a small but interesting part of the social structure of medieval England. "Wise men" and "wise women" survived until very recent times in rustic England (J. C. Atkinson's *Forty Years in a Moorland Parish*, 1891, gives a vivid portrait of Yorkshire wise men at the beginning of the nineteenth century), and in Europe as well (the *sabia* or wise woman and the *curanderos* or healers still had an important role in the Southern Spanish village life studied by J. A. Pitt-Rivers).[17] Their functions would include the finding and recovery of lost property, various sorts of divination and oracular forecasting, midwifery, and healing.[18]

Certainly, some of the medicine thus practised was, to say the least, strange. It is not hard to find, in any manuscript, some spectacular concoctions, as

> To make an ointment for the gout:
>
> Take a moldwerp and sethe it wele in wax and wryng it thurgh a clathe and hell it in buystes, for euer þe langer it es halden þe better es it to many maner other þan to þe goute.

> To make a powder for "the cankre":
>
> Tak þe heued of a stork and þe fete and all þat es wyth in þe stork bot þe body ane. Do it all in a pot þat was neuer noted, and do it in a ouen and dri it swa þat þow mak poudre þar of.[19]

There were plenty of quacks, and much of the "honest" medicine was hopeful rather than scientific, or simply misguided—as the accepted treatment of wounds with oil, or the famous wonder medicine, "treacle"—but there was some genuine medicine, and some of the traditional herbal remedies have stood the test of modern science. Even the purely magical remedies, it might be claimed, are not totally despicable intellectually, since behind them lies a system, or at least the remains of a system, of intricate analogies, whether symbolic or astrological, between the components of the created universe. Magical medicine makes much more sense in its social setting (and here again there are valuable parallels in "primitive" societies). The power of suggestion and of faith in healing, which is not despised by modern physicians, is likely to be even more effective in rural societies where all the assumptions predispose the patient to expect at least some alleviation. Moreover, where the relationship between a modern doctor and his patient may be extremely tenuous, the medieval cunning man, like his counterparts in primitive societies, was aware of the past psychological history of his "patient" and of the social influences and pressures surrounding him, with the result that his non-scientific medicine might well have been successful.

The formal characteristics of the Middle English charms are similar to those of the many European charms recorded for centuries. There is the same liking for number and colour symbolism; the same reliance on the magic power of names—whether of God (e.g. tetragrammaton, etc.), or of angels, or of the Magi.[20] Sometimes the boundary between charm and prayer becomes rather blurred. It is usually held that the speaker of a magical charm speaks with authority, and commands, rather than humbly approaching the divinity as a suppliant—"*das religiöse Gebet gipfelt in der Bitte, das magische im Befehl*"[21]—but it is not always easy to maintain the distinction. On the one hand, for instance, the late medieval use of indulgences often seems to make certain prayers or devotions automatically efficacious, and some prayers use an imperative, "Jesu, make me . . . " (where much would depend on the intention of the speaker), while, on the other hand, some of the more pious charms make at least a gesture in the direction of the orthodox idea of prayer by adding the phrase "if it be Thy will." "Thilke horrible sweryng of adjuraccioun and conjuracioun," as the Parson calls it, is usually distinctive enough. The charmer, speaking with the authority of the divine powers, orders the disease or danger to obey his words, in a cumulative series of commands, which often invoke the source of his authority ("I conjure thee by the power of . . . "). Fairly common (cf. the examples quoted below) are the charms which conform to the ancient type in which a mythical narrative is rehearsed in the conviction that it is a perpetual source of power. This is a pattern of thought which is found in orthodox Christianity, as for instance in the *anamnesis* of the passion of Christ in the mass, or the expressive typological passage in the *Exultet* in the Easter liturgy. Often, in Christian prayers, the Deity is reminded by means of a series of relative clauses of the wondrous deeds he has done in the past; thus in the Middle English *Havelok* the author prays for Goldeboru in prison, and aptly recalls the "mythical" parallel of the freeing of Lazarus from the bonds of death:

> Jesu Crist, that Lazarun
> To live brouhte fro dede-bondes,
> He lese hire with his hondes . . .

But usually in the charms, where there is no explicit statement of a providential framework, it seems to be felt that the simple rehearsal of the mythical story will release magical power.

Charms have to be "performed"—whether this means simply repeating the words a specified number of times, or making signs on lead or parchment, or going to a church and saying the charm "before the croyce knelyng on thi kneis." This implies a symbolic action, a ritual which is both efficacious and expressive. In its humble way, it is, like the magic rituals of primitive societies, "the acting out of a situation, the expression of a desire in symbolic terms."[22] Often, the action implies a social desire for the re-establishment of order against the spiritual or physical disorder which threatens it.

Charms for stanching blood are an important group in our manuscripts. The practice of blood-charming (whether of humans or animals) went on in folk-tradition, and can still be found today.[23] The terror caused by wounds which cannot be stopped is eloquently expressed in the ballad, "The Twa Brothers." It was natural enough for pious charms to recall the Precious Blood of Christ which was shed on the cross. Here, to take one of many examples, is a charm which uses the legendary figure of Longinus, the centurion who inflicted the great wound in Christ's side:

> First byhoues þe ask þe name of man or of woman, for whan þow will say. Ga than in to þe kirke, and say thar þi charme, bot loke þat þow say it noght bot for man or woman.
> + *In nomine patris et filii et spiritus sancti. Amen.*

> Wen our lauerd was done on þe croyce, þan come Longyus þedir and smatym wyth his spere in þe syde. Water and blode come out at þe wounde. He wyped his eighen, and sagh als sone thurgh þe haly vertu of þat godhede. I coniure þe, blode, þat þow ne com out of þis cristen man or cristen woman (neuen þe name).
> *In nomine patris et filii et spiritus sancti. Amen.*

> Say þis charme thris; thare ye neuer reke whar þe man bee bot þow conne þe name.[24]

This is followed in the manuscript by an even more ubiquitous charm:

> Another.   Crist was born in Betlehem,
> and cristend in flom Iordane;
> and als þe flom stode als a stane,
> stand þi blode, N. (neuen his name)
> *In nomine patris et filii et spiritus sancti.*
>
> >   Amen.

which is in turn followed by a more abrupt and startling remedy:

> Another. Lay þi ballokes in aysell, or in cald water, and þe blode sall staunche.

The "flum Jordan" charm, or the "*Jordan-segen*" as it is known to German folklorists, appears again and again in various forms in Middle English manuscripts, goes into later manuscript collections, and survives in modern folk-tradition.[25] Ebermann finds the oldest Latin formula in the ninth and tenth centuries. It is based on the legend that the Jordan stood still during the baptism of Christ (it has presumably been influenced by the story in Joshua iii). An indication of the importance which the baptism of Christ had in the popular imagination is given by a couple of Epiphany carols which celebrate the event[26] (it was thought that the visit of the Magi, the baptism of Christ, and the marriage at Cana—all three events full of magical potential—took place on the same day of the week). The gospel narrative of the event itself, with its heavenly voice and mysterious dove, is supernatural enough, and would naturally become a base for further legend. The Baptist, the "last of the prophets," "more than a prophet," who comes down from the mountain, and is asked if he is the Messiah, is a potentially magical figure (cf. the fascination which his severed head on the platter seems to have exercised). In some Eastern charms his place is taken by his father Zacharias, whose blood was supposed to have turned to stone when he was slain in the temple. Dr A. A. Barb, in his interesting study of the background of these charms,[27] suggests that behind these figures lies an old Semitic god with a sickle, the equivalent of Kronos-Saturnus. A river itself (and especially the Jordan) is a source of spiritual power; the miraculous stopping has its antecedents in earlier demonstrations of power by Joshua and Elias (2 Kings ii, 7–8), and by Moses on the Red Sea—one charm for bleeding begins, "Stanche blood, stanche blood, / So dyd Moses flood."[28] So that the "mythical" narrative which is rehearsed is full of magical power.

Blood-charms were used for women in childbirth, a difficult and dangerous time both physically and spiritually, since they were especially prone to the attention of demons or fairies (hence women "in childbed" appear in the list of the mortals taken by the fairies in *Sir Orfeo*). Various magical amulets like the "eagle-stone" (*haematites*) were also used. An interesting section on childbirth in MS Sloane 962 includes some well-known Latin formulae ("*Maria peperit Christum*" and "*Sator arepo tenet opera rotas*") and a rather grim-sounding medical recipe: "Drynk ysope wit hote watur, and so che chal haue childe, þof it be dede or forroted."[29]

Another little group of charms is meant for a humbler but still painful ailment—toothache. "There never was yet philosopher," says Leonato in *Much Ado*, "that could endure the toothache patiently." The patience of our ancestors, whether philosophical or not, must certainly have been tried very grievously. Dentistry was very rudimentary—there were crude attempts at filling, scraping, binding loose teeth with wire, replacing lost teeth with bone substitutes, but the normal cure was extraction. For centuries itinerant tooth-drawers were familiar figures at markets and fairs. Our manuscripts record some herbal remedies, but naturally enough include magical attempts to "charm ache with air and agony with words." St Apollonia was the saint who took particular care of those suffering from toothache (because she had her teeth knocked out before she was martyred)— the messenger in More's *Dialogue* says sharply "Sainct Apoline we make a toth drawer, and may speke to her of nothing but of sore teth." So a Latin charm begins with *memoria* of her passion: "*Sancta Apollonia virgo fuit inclita, cuius pro Christi nomine dentes extracti fuerunt* . . . "[30] It is St Peter, however, who appears in a famous charm which recalls how he sat on a stone, was met by Christ, and told him that his teeth ached.[31] One folklorist found an example of it used as an amulet in Scotland last century: "the charm . . . was written on what seemed like an old fly-leaf, and was encased in a piece of green silk, sewn into the form of a Maltese cross." It seems to survive in the nursery rhyme "Peter stands at the gate waiting for a buttered cake." Again, its antecedents can be traced back to earlier apocryphal literature, possibly to the prayer of Adam's son Seth outside the gates of Paradise.[32] Two Middle English verse charms against toothache[33] address the disease as "laythely beste," "þou wikkyde worme." The loathly beast is probably both a spiritual and a physical creature—a demon of disease and also the worm which for centuries was thought to cause decay. It is said that later quacks used to extract a worm from their patients' mouths as a sign that the toothache was cured.

Charms were also used to protect household animals and property. The sections in the manuscripts dealing with the diseases of horses have some especially interesting examples. This one, after a nice familiar dialogue, uses the common mythical pattern of the angelic spirit seeking out and destroying the demons of disease (cf. "Saint George our Lady Knight" above). It has a particularly elaborate and emphatic version of a technique which is found in many charms (and which survives in children's games)—the "counting out" or "counting down" of the spirits of disease. From ancient times (cf. the famous Latin tonsils charm "*novem glandulae sorores*") it proved itself an effective and expressive symbolic pattern:

Aske þe mannes name þat owes þe hors and (þe) hew of þe hors, and sey þis charme.

Lord, als wissely as þis is þe first corne þat god let sow and setten on erthe, also stedfastliche, if þi wil be, deliuer þis hors of festre (and of worme) and of rankel. Michael in þe hel cam to his brother Raphael þe archangele and seyde to him, 'Raphael, wher astou ben þat I ne mith þe þis day sen?' 'I haue ben in þe land of wormes.' 'Turne ageyn, Raphael, and sle þe wormes, fro i tul ii, fro ii tul iii, fro iii til iiii, fro iiii til v, fro v til vi, fro vi til vii, fro vii til viii, fro viii til ix, fro ix til viii, fro viii til vii, fro vii til vi, fro vi til v, fro v tul iiii, fro iiii tul iii, fro iii til ii, fro ii til i, so þat þou let n(on) on on liue.' As Raphael delyuered þe ix wormes, als stedfastli, lorde, if þi wil be, delyuer þis hors fro farcioun and of þe rankel and of all wormes. And þis is preued for soth.[34]

The nine (or three) "worms" appear again in conjunction with the patriarch Job in other charms involving "counting down." This type is well known to German folklorists, but has not (I think) been noticed before in English manuscripts:[35]

for wormes and bottes:
Job lay on a dongehill and in a dongehill he lay and cride vppon oure
lord Jesu Crist, 'ix wormeʒ ete my fflesshe and my blode. iii ben white,
iii ben blak, and iii ben rede.' Oure lorde Jesu answerid and seide, 'Thei
ben dede, and dede shall be as many ben þerynne thorwe the vertu of
the ffadre, þe Sone and holy Gost, iii personys and on god in Trynyte.
. . .

for the botteʒ:
In the name of God and of oure ladi and Job. iii pater noster and
iii aueʒ.
Oure lorde god that sende vertu in word, ston, and gras, sende vertu
in to my worde.
Gode Job, downe he leide and criede oure lorde uppone, and seid,
'Thre wormes eten me. One is blak, another is white, the thridde is rede.
On etis my flesshe, another my bon, the thride my blod.' Thei were
dede, so mot theʒ ben, in vertu of the. *In nomine patris, etc.*

a charme for þe farsynes:
In nomine patris, etc. In þe honour of oure lord Jesu Crist, and oure
ladye seynt Marie, and seynt Jop, and seynt Jopes fader sowle, and his
modir sowle, and all his auncetris sowles, seye iii pater noster and iii
aues. Seynt Jop had ix wormes, had viii, he had vii wormes, he had vi
wormes, he had v wormes, he had iiii wormes, he had iii wormes, he
had ii wormes, he had þat hadde non hede. Sey þus abowte þe hors and
he shal be hole.[36]

Satan was allowed to afflict "good Job" with ulcers or boils (cf. *Job*
ii, 7 ff.; xvii, 14), which were thought to be caused by worms. The
striking description of the man sitting *in sterquilinio* obviously caught
the imagination, and is thought to have influenced the iconography
of the late medieval image of *Christus im Elend*, the figure of the Man
of Sorrows (of whom Job was a figure) sitting bound and covered with
many wounds.[37] But the indications are, as Dr A. A. Barb argues,
that the central figure in the charm was originally not Job but Christ.
A German charm with St Peter in place of Job has the saint lying in
the *grave*. Barb draws attention to a story in the Coptic "Book of the
Resurrection of Christ," in which Death and his six sons go into the
tomb of Christ to take possession of his body; the seven demons
wriggle like worms, and "were apparently imagined in the shape of
worms." Barb compares their possible prototype in the Babylonian
Ababu-demon and his six ministers, who can "creep like a snake on
their bellies."[38] It may well be that behind this charm lies a "mythical" narrative of the conquest of death by a god.

Of the charms for the protection of property, those against thieves have attracted some attention.[39] Like the blood-charms they often use images of "stopping" or "binding," as in this example in simple verse:

> *coniuracio bona pro latronibus venientibus ad domum:*
> I bitake þe, holy gost, þis place here ysette,
> And þe fadir and þe sone, þeues for to lette.
> If any þeues here come my good awey to fette,
> The holy gost be hem byfore, and do hem for to lette,
> And do hem for to abyde til ageyn I come,
> In þe vertu of þe holy gost and þe fadir and þe sone.
> This nyȝt I wil wende my wey, tide what bytide;
> If any þeues hider come, here þei schal abyde,
> þorow þe vertu of Mathew, Luke, Marke and Johan,
> The foure archangelis acorden in to one.
> I bynde þe þeues so fast, and do hem no sore,
> So dede seynt Bartholomew þe fende with his berd so hore.
> Stondeþ, þeues, in þe vertu of þe trinyte,
> and for þe passioun of Jesu Crist,
> and of his deþ and his vprist,
> Stylle þat ȝe stonde til I bydde ȝow gane.
> *In nomine Jesu. fiat. fiat. Amen.*[40]

In the margin there is written *"signum sali"* with three pentangles beneath it, which suggests that protective signs were to be made about the house, just as the carpenter said his nightspell at its four corners (the four evangelists seem in this version to have been made into the even more magical archangels).[41]

The magical command to ensure the "binding" of thieves is often found in the charms, and sometimes very emphatically expressed: that "they stond as stylle as eny ston / they haue no powere away to gon," or that "þei stande stille as eny stake as euer þer was any ybounde, and as euere was þe mulston." It is found in later charms, and in other societies—it is said that in some parts of Africa it is possible to buy a magical medicine which has the power to paralyse thieves.[42] The English charms are of course imitating the wonderful feats recorded of a number of saints, e.g. of St Edmund, who from his grave bound eight wretched thieves who were attempting to break into his sepulchre so that they were "frozen" there until morning, when "men wondered at this, how the thieves were hanging—one on the ladder, one bent over to dig, and each bound fast in his work." It is easy to be very scornful about this sort of charm, but the truth is probably that it would have some social value. The magical detection of thefts and the prevention of robbers was a traditional function of "cunning men," and the "effect" of these charms was probably psychological. The knowledge that they were used would induce fear into the minds of thieves, so that they might reveal themselves, or be compelled to return the goods. As Keith Thomas aptly says, the deterrent effect "was much like that of modern devices to shower burglars with indelible paint."[43]

The charms against thieves show considerable variety. From many examples one might mention the common adaptation of the "*Jordan-segen*"[44] (with words such as "þereinne was no þef, but god himself that was so lef"), a version of a popular Latin charm based on the differing fates which, according to legend, befell the two thieves who were crucified with Christ:

> On bowes of tre of gret myght
> Hengene thre bodys be day light;
> Jesus henge heme betwene,
> Dismas and Jesmas, and þat was sene.
> Dismas to Jesus he gane call,
> And Jesmas in wanhoppe anone gone fall.[45]

Another verse charm invokes three supernatural "stoppings"—God and the Red sea, Joshua and the sun and moon, Jesus and the tempest —and in it the charmer boldy states that the thieves shall stay bound

> Vntyll my stretched arme shall make
> a syne to them ther way to take.
> As Moses stretched the Red sea moved.[46]

The interest of all this material for the student of medieval religion or cultural history will, I hope, be evident, but I should like to suggest that the literary critic may find some of it useful. There are, for instance, a number of places in literary works, where for one reason or another, some of the typical rhythms and devices of incantations are echoed. Passages which immediately spring to mind include Horn's farewell to his boat in the romance *King Horn*, the owl's account of its wisdom and skill in divining the future in *The Owl and the Nightingale*, or later, in Spenser's *Epithalamium* the passage which forbids the dangers and noises of the night to disturb the newly-married pair. The magical use of language deserves further investigation. The charms are efficacious symbolic actions, and their language, with its urgent and expressive rhetoric and rhythmical patterns, often seems both to imitate and instigate the magical action. It is in a real sense "language as gesture." By way of illustration I end with two examples. The first, which is not well-known, is a long conjuration which generates its effect by cumulative rhetoric:

Thys is þe charme of seynt William þat Gabriel brout fro oure lorde for to charme of þe worm of þe canker, of þe festre, of þe goute meuande, and of all maner of goutes. First to syng a messe of þe Holy Gost, and after warde sey this charme:

Also veraly os God is and was and chal be, and als verali as þat he sayd was sothe. And als veraly as þat he did wel he did. And als veraly os þat he of þe virgyne Marie flesche and blod toke. And als veraly os he on his worthely body suffred v. woundes for all synful. And als veraly os he on þe holy croys hang. And als veraly os his body was on þe crosse don and dampned were, to thefes ihanged aboute hym, and in his rith syde with a spere of erne was stongen, and his handes and his feet were nayled thorow, and his hed wit a crowne of thorne was prikked. And als veraly os his holy body in þe sepulchre rested. And als veraly as he þe gates of hell brake, and his toke out. And als veraly os he on þe thryd day ros vp from ded to lyue, and afterward in heuen stey vp, and on þe ryth half his fader rested. And also verali as he at þe day of dome chal come, and ilk a man in flesche and blode, and in age of xxx wynter chal ryse. And als verali os oure lorde alle at his lykyng chal deme. And als verali as þat is sothe, and I in him trow, and in sothe it is and sothe chal be, and als veraly warysche þis man .N. of þe goute of þe canker, of þe goute in þe bon, of þe worme, of þe goute meuande, of þe goute arage, of þe goute ardaunt, and of al maner of goute. Dede is þe goute. Dede is þe cancre. Dede is þe festre. Dede is and dede be, if God wil, of þis man .N.

Pater noster. In nomine patris et filii et spiritus sancti.

Sey þis charme iii tymes be iii dayes ouer þe seek, and deffende him þat he ne do no noþer medicyne, ne for bere no maner of mete, and with help of God with in ix dayes he chal be hol for euer. And ley to þe sore a leef þat is calde hokkelef and non oþer thyng.[47]

The second is the early "Wen-charm," which has appeared in a number of anthologies but has hardly received the attention it deserves. Here the techniques are handled in a homely and witty way, with the offending wen being persuasively called by an affectionate name. Unlike most of the Middle English verse charms, it becomes an interesting poem in its own right:

> Wenne, wenne, wenchichenne,
> Her ne scealt þu timbrien, ne nenne tun habben;
> Ac þu scealt norþ heonene to þan nihgan berhge,
> þer þu havest, ermig, enne broþer.
> He þe sceal legge leaf et heafde.
> Under fot-volmes, under vether earnes,
> Under earnes clea, a þu geweornie!

Clinge þu alswa col on heorþe,
Scring þu alswa scerne a wage,
And weorne alswa weter on anbre!
Swa litel þu gewurþe alswa linset-corn,
And miccli lesse alswa anes hand-wurmes hupe-ban;
And alswa litel þu gewurþe þet þu nawiht gewurþe![48]

PEMBROKE COLLEGE, OXFORD

NOTES

[1] *TC* II, 1576–82. All citations to Chaucer from F. N. Robinson (ed.), *The Works of Geoffrey Chaucer*, 2nd edn (Boston: Houghton Mifflin, 1957).

[2] *TC* IV, 460–61.

[3] *CT* X, 605.

[4] *CT* I, 3477–86.

[5] Cf. A. A. Barb, "Animula Vagula Blandula," *Folklore*, 61 (1950), pp. 15–30.

[6] Notably (with Carleton Brown) in *The Index of Middle English Verse* (New York: Columbia Univ. Press, 1943) (hereafter *Index*), and (with John L. Cutler), *Supplement to The Index of Middle English Verse* (Lexington, Kentucky: Kentucky Univ. Press, 1965) (hereafter *Suppl.*); and "Medical Manuscripts in Middle English," *Spec.*, 45 (1970). pp. 393–415. *The Encyclopedia of Witchcraft and Demonology* (New York: Crown Publishers, 1959) also contains a vast amount of information on popular magic. Further MSS are listed in N. R. Ker, *Medieval Manuscripts in British Libraries* (Oxford: Clarendon Press, 1969), I. Curt Bühler, "Prayers and Charms in Certain Middle English Rolls," *Spec.*, 39 (1964), pp. 270–80 is a most valuable study. Some of the charms survive into later collections, e.g., MSS Bodleian e mus. 173, e mus. 243, Add. B 1, etc. The notes which follow give only minimal references to the vast quantity of comparative material available.

[7] Cf. the material collected by George Lyman Kittredge, *Witchcraft in Old and New England* (1929; rpt. New York: Russell & Russell, 1958); G. R. Owst, "*Sortilegium* in English Homiletic Literature of the Fourteenth Century," in J. Conway Davies (ed.), *Essays Presented to Sir Hilary Jenkinson* (London: Oxford Univ. Press, 1957), pp. 272–303; and Keith Thomas, *Religion and the Decline of Magic* (New York: Scribner's, 1971), rev. Rossell Hope Robbins, *Renaissance Quarterly*, 26 (1973), pp. 70–2.

[8] *Index* 2903; Rossell Hope Robbins (ed.), *Secular Lyrics of the XIVth and XVth Centuries*, 2nd edn (Oxford: Clarendon Press, 1955), p. 61. Cf. Kittredge, op. cit., p. 220. For the hymns, cf. Rossell Hope Robbins, "Middle English Versions of *Criste qui lux es et dies*," *Harvard Theological Review*, 47 (1954), pp. 55–63.

[9] Christian Hole, *Saints in Folklore* (New York: Barrows 1965), pp. 132–42.

[10] Hugh Farmer (ed.), *The Monk of Farne* (Baltimore: Helicon, 1961), pp. 127–37.

[11] MS Sloane 2584, f. 37.

[12] F. Holthausen, "*Rezepte, Segen und Zaubersprüche aus zwei Stockholmer Handschriften*," *Anglia*, 19 (1897), p. 81.

[13] *Index* 1182; Robbins, *Secular Lyrics*, op. cit., p. 58.

14 Carl Horstmann, *Yorkshire Writers* (London: Swan Sonnenschein, 1895), I, pp. 375–6. Cf. B. Bischoff, *"Ursprung und Geschichte eines Kreuzsegens," Volk und Volkstum*, 1 (1936), pp. 225–31.

15 Cf. L. Gougaud, *"La mesure de la plaie du côté," Revue d'histoire ecclésiastique*, 20 (1924), pp. 223ff.; Bühler, op. cit., pp. 273–7; Douglas Gray, "The Five Wounds of Our Lord," *N & Q*, 208 (1963), 50–9, 82–89, 127–34, 163–8; and Karl Josef Höltgen, *"Arbor, Scala und Fons Vitae,"* in Arno Esch (ed.), *Chaucer und Seine Zeit* (Tübingen: Niemeyer, 1968), pp. 355–91, with detailed bibliography.

16 MS Sloane 2457, f. 29.

17 Julian Alfred Pitt-Rivers, *The People of the Sierra* (London: Weidenfeld and Nicholson, 1954), pp. 189-95.

18 Cf. the account in Thomas, op. cit., pp. 177–279.

19 MS Royal 17. A. viii, ff. 28v, 35v.

20 On the Magi in charms cf. Douglas Gray, *Themes and Images in the Medieval English Religious Lyric* (London: Routledge, 1972), p. 118 and references; F. Hälsig, *Der Zauberspruch bei den Germanen* (Leipzig: Seele, 1910). pp. 98–9.

21 Angelicus M. Kropp, *Ausgewählte Koptische Zaubertexte* (Brussels: Edition de la Fondation égyptologique reine Elisabeth, 1931), III, p. 217ff.

22 John Beattie, *Other Cultures* (London: Cohen and West, 1964), p. 206.

23 Cf. O. Ebermann, *Blut- und Wundesegen, Palaestra*, 24 (1903); H. Bächtold-Stäubli, *Handwörterbuch des deutschen Aberglaubens* (Berlin and Leipzig, 1930–1), s.v. "Blutsegen." One example of the many books containing material from modern British folklore is Ruth E. St Leger Gordon, *The Witchcraft and Folklore of Dartmoor* (London: R. Hale, 1965), pp. 150, 168, 175.

24 MS Royal 17. A. viii, f. 48v. Cf. Ebermann, pp. 42—52; Hälsig, pp. 81–5; T. Oswald O. Cockayne, *Leechdoms, Wortcunning and Starcraft of Early England*, 3 vols., Rolls Series, 35 (London: Longman, 1864), I. p. 393; W. G. Black, *Folk-Medicine* (London: Folklore Soc. Publications, 1883), pp 79—80.

25 Ebermann, pp. 24–5; Hälsig, pp. 88–92; Black, p. 76; etc. *Suppl.* 624 lists 13 MSS.

26 Richard Leighton Greene (ed.), *Early English Carols* (Oxford: Clarendon Press, 1935), Nos. 130, 131.

27 A. A. Barb, "St Zacharias the Prophet and Martyr," *JWCI*, 11 (1948), pp. 35–67.

28 *Suppl.* 3209.5; MS Harley 665, f. 302. Cf. Ebermann, p. 30.

29 MS Sloane 962, f. 35v. Cf. Thomas R. Forbes, *The Midwife and the Witch* (New Haven: Yale Univ. Press, 1966), pp. 80–93.

30 Holthausen, op. cit, p. 84.

31 Cf. Kittredge, op, cit., pp. 389–93; Bächtold-Stäubli, op. cit., s.v. "Zahnsegen;" Black, op, cit., pp. 77–8; Moses Gaster, *Ilchester Lectures on Greeko-Slavonic Literature* (London: Trübner, 1887), pp. 85–6.

32 Barb, *"Animula Vagula Blandula,"* op. cit., p. 17; "The Survival of Magic Arts," in Arnaldo Momigliano (ed.), *The Conflict between Paganism and Christianity in the Fourth Century* (Oxford: Clarendon Press, 1963), p. 123.

33 *Index* 1292, 3709.

34 MS Sloane 962, f. 135. On "counting" charms, cf. Barb, *Animula Vagula Blandula*, op. cit.; Black, op. cit., pp. 122–3.

35 Bächtold-Stäubli, op. cit., s.v. "Hiob," "Wurmsegen;" Hälsig, op. cit., pp. 92–6; Kittredge, op. cit., pp. 40 (a later example from England), 395–6.

36 MS Royal 17. A. xxxii, ff. 120, 127v, 129v.

37 G. Van der Osten, "Job and Christ," *JWCI*, 16 (1953), pp. 153–8.

38 Barb, *Animula Vagula Blandula*, op. cit., pp. 19ff.

39 J. M. McBryde, Jr., "Charms for Thieves," *MLN*, 22 (1907), pp. 168–70; Curt

F. Bühler, "Middle English Verses against Thieves," *Spec.*, 33 (1958), pp. 371-2; and "Three ME Prose Charms from MS Harley 2389," *N & Q*, 207 (1962), p. 48.

[40] MS Sloane 2584, f. 74v. Cf. the later version in Bodl. MS e mus. 243, f. 36, of which the reading "yᵗ you theeves be bounde all so sore" is clearly closer to the original legend. Cf. the German practice, recorded by Bächtold-Stäubli, op. cit., s.v. "Bartholomäus," of smiths, who on the saint's day would strike several times an empty anvil, apparently to bind the devil's fetters.

[41] Cf. *Index* 3771: "So St Bartylmew bownd the Devyll / With his bearde so hoare." And cf. M. R. James, *The Apocryphal New Testament* (Oxford: Clarendon Press, 1924), pp. 467-8; Charlotte d'Evelyn and Anna J. Mill (eds), *South English Legendary*, EETS, OS 236, II, p. 379.

[42] The medicine is called *rukwa*. Cf. Michael Gelfand, *Witchdoctor* (London: Harvill Press, 1964), pp. 47, 72; and *The African Witch* (Edinburgh: E. and S. Livingstone, 1967), pp. 149ff. On later English magic against thieves, cf. Thomas, op. cit., pp. 212-22; an example of the many charms in Katherine Mary Briggs, *Pale Hecate's Team* (New York: Humanities Press, 1962), p. 260. Kittredge, op. cit., pp. 200-2, 513-14, lists much comparative material.

[43] Keith Thomas, *Religion and the Decline of Magic* (London: 1971), p. 222.

[44] E.g. MS Sloane 2584, f. 73v.

[45] Not in *Suppl*. MS Sloane 56, f. 100.

[46] *Suppl*. 412.5.

[47] MS Sloane 962, f. 72. Cf. Holthausen, p. 82.

[48] *Index* 3896; printed most recently in Celia and Kenneth Sisam, *The Oxford Book of Medieval English Verse* (Oxford: Clarendon Press, 1970), No. 2.

4

PIETY AND PROPAGANDA:
THE CULT OF KING HENRY VI

BY JOHN W. MCKENNA

Fifteenth-century England was distinguished for a series of royal governments which developed increasingly sophisticated methods of reinforcing their increasingly tenuous claims to the throne. Skilful publicists celebrated the Lancastrian usurpation of 1399, the Yorkist triumph of 1461 and the Tudor victory at Bosworth Field in 1485.[1] Court and popular poetry, the designs of coinage, and the trappings of state banquets and royal entries were altered to incorporate symbolic themes and motifs to bolster and enhance the failing regality. Posters and even billboards proclaimed political messages and drew political morals for the generality, and the royal coronations and crown wearings recovered their central importance as instruments of governance.[2] Other groups borrowed and improved upon these same devices as vehicles for the strident anti-royal propaganda of the age, arguing their own legitimacy at the expense of the reigning sovereign. Few of these techniques, however, rivalled the shrewd political manipulation by royal and anti-royal publicists of the popular or unofficial canonization of political heroes or political martyrs. And few political cults had as lengthy or important a role in English history as the posthumous cult of King Henry VI. Begun in opposition to the Yorkist Edward IV and nourished by popular distrust of Richard III, this sanctification of the unworldly and ineffectual Henry, the last and least of his dynasty, fed on the flourishing lay piety of the age and flourished in turn under the grateful aegis of the earlier Tudors who looked to sanctify their own origins by canonizing their ancestor.

The political manipulation of popular religiosity was hardly novel: Shrewd royal publicists had long exploited the Confessor as a sainted symbol of royalty, and Richard II had even sought to expunge the precedent of Edward II's deposition by securing the canonization of that unsaintly monarch. Enemies of the crown had venerated such diverse opponents of royal tyranny as Thomas Becket, Simon de

72

Montfort, Stephen Langton and Thomas of Lancaster, while the fifteenth century had already offered the spectacle of the martyred Archbishop Richard Scrope of York whose posthumous cult survived royal and ecclesiastical prohibitions for some six decades or more.[3] Nor was this exploitation of piety uniquely English: The rival kingdom of France had for centuries boasted the more substantial royal saint Louis IX; competition between the two realms having exhausted the rivalries of thaumaturgy and competing claims to a heaven-sent coronation oil,[4] a new post-Conquest royal saint could rival the French royal patron and serve the Lancastrian faction of the 1470s by undermining the prestige and the claims to legitimacy of Edward IV.

The object of this strenuous activity, Henry VI himself, was as poor a saint by modern standards as he was unkingly in the eyes of contemporaries. Too much a saint to be a proper king, he seems too bad a king to have been a useful political saint, and indeed with the death of his father the hero-King Henry V in 1422 there had commenced in England more than a half-century of political chaos and public confusion. As the joint heir to his father's kingdom of England and to the France of his maternal grandfather Charles VI the nine-month-old infant had inherited a sound claim to the two greatest of the western monarchies. But with that dual monarchy he had received as well the *damnosa hereditas* of his father's futile hope to recapture forever the French lands lost by England in the reign of John, and from his mother the French princess Catherine he carried the congenital madness of the later Valois kings. As a resurgence of French nationalism bore the Hundred Years War to its inglorious conclusion, a fifteen-year royal minority set the circumstances and the tone for nearly fifty years of internecine rivalry among the English baronage. The accession of a weak king in this age of personal government further undermined monarchical prestige, and thus the third and last of the Lancastrian Henrys, whose reign was one of the longest in European history, saw the nadir of the medieval English monarchy.

The government of Edward IV had foreseen the possibility of a posthumous cult of Henry VI and had attempted to preclude any such development. On 21 May 1471, scarcely two weeks after the Yorkist victory at Tewkesbury, it was announced that Henry had died in the Tower from "pure displeasure and melencoly" at the defeat of his cause,[5] though the Tudors would soon enough blame Richard III. Popular rumour held that Henry had been "stykked with a dagger, by the hands of the duke of Glouceter,"[6] and the very weapon was thereafter displayed in the Augustinian bridge chapel between Reading and Caversham.[7] This chapel and the tomb of the late King became

natural focal points for the pilgrimages which began shortly thereafter, despite all the efforts to deter them. In order to forestall any
rumours of his survival, Henry's corpse had been exhibited for a night
at St Paul's, escorted under close guard to Blackfriars, and then
finally rowed to Chertsey Abbey, where it was interred in the Lady
chapel. Soldiers from the Calais garrison were employed on this
mission, no doubt to ensure discretion,[8] and the isolated Chertsey
must have seemed likely to deter veneration of the remains or pilgrimages to the burial site.

But softened memories of the gentle Henry VI and growing dis-
illusionment with his successor soon foiled these precautions. Within
a year loyal adherents of the Lancastrians were establishing shrines to
the late King in country churches and in such major cathedrals as
Ripon and Durham.[9] York Minster, centre of the tenacious anti-
Lancastrian cult of Archbishop Scrope, openly welcomed the new
anti-Yorkist cult. The Dean of York was the Lancastrian Richard
Andrew, once private secretary to Henry VI, and the Great Screen
which he began building there about 1475 was designed to hold
statues of the English kings from William the Conqueror to Henry VI.
There was no niche and no statue for Edward IV, and this affront to
the reigning monarch was further compounded when pilgrims and
devotees of the dead Henry began decorating his effigy with flowers
and offerings.[10] Soon enough it became an altar and a shrine to the
Lancastrian martyr.[11] As the government of 1405 had moved quickly
to halt the cult of Scrope, so now the Yorkist officials persuaded the
time-serving Archbishop of York Lawrence Booth to ban this uncanonical veneration of Henry VI. In a letter of 27 October 1479 Booth
condemned those who brought offerings to the statue of Henry in
contempt of the universal church and in depreciation of King
Edward.[12] This archiepiscopal *monitio* seems, however, to have had
as little success as similar efforts in the past. Though the statue of
Henry VI did disappear from the Minster screen either then or
later,[13] an altar and shrine to that monarch remained in York until
the Reformation while others sprang up in such isolated areas as
rural Norfolk.[14] Meanwhile Henry's tomb at Chertsey had become
the site of numerous pilgrimages encouraged by growing rumours
miracles which had been performed by invocation of the new
saint.[15]

The popular veneration of Henry VI which had been so active
during the closing years of Edward IV's reign became all the more
intense when the congenial Edward was replaced by his unloved
brother Richard. Henry's cult took on new meaning in opposition to
the allegedly tyrannous and illegitimate regime of his supposed

murderer, and allegiance to the last Lancastrian became a quasi-religious touchstone of political opposition. Two of the many miracles attributed to Henry VI's intercession during Richard's brief reign involved cures of scrofula, the skin ailment which could only be healed by the miraculous touch of the rightful anointed monarch. In one of these incidents Margaret, the daughter of William Tryll, was reportedly cured of the King's Evil by vowing a pilgrimage to Chertsey,[16] while in 1484 the parents of nine-year-old Agnes Freeman rejected their neighbours' advice that young Agnes be brought to Richard III to be cured of the same affliction. Richard, they are supposed to have replied, was a usurper from whom they would ask no favours, and instead their daughter too was cured by a vow of pilgrimage to the tomb of the Blessed Henry, whose body had been moved that year to Windsor.[17] The Lancastrians were apparently advertising their martyred leader as the lawful and potent substitute for his supposed murderer and eventual successor, and the government could hardly ignore their success in this campaign. In August 1484 Henry's body was removed from Chertsey Abbey to the chapel at Windsor Castle, presumably because Richard hoped either to identify himself with the cult and so disarm its effect, or to bring it more closely under his control. In this he may well have consciously imitated Henry V who on his accession in 1413 had stilled critics of his dynasty by restoring the remains of Richard II to Westminster Abbey.

If indeed this was Richard III's intention his hopes were futile and his plans short-lived. St George's Chapel at Windsor became a more successful shrine to Henry than Chertsey had ever been. Rumours circulated that exhumation had discovered the corpse in a perfect state of preservation, which was taken as yet more evidence for the dead King's sanctity.[18] Craftsmen were commissioned to embellish the new shrine, and John Tresilian designed for it the splendid wrought-iron alms box with its elaborate motif of the letter "H" which can still be seen at Windsor.[19]

The priests at Windsor continued to collect the pilgrims' stories of Henry's miracles as the monks of Chertsey had done in years past, and as these stories multiplied yet more pilgrims thronged to pay homage to the popular new saint. One man testified at Chertsey to his miraculous escape from the Cambridge gallows upon invoking the name of St Henry, and this only a month before the body was removed to Windsor. Later, perhaps flushed with his new distinction, the man journeyed to Windsor and had his story recorded there also.[20] Henry's physical appearance seems to have been well known, since the sea captain Thomas Everingham claimed to have recognized an apparition from Henry VI dressed in his familiar blue gown and yellow cap. Everingham was planning to visit Chertsey when he heard that the body had been moved to Windsor, and so gave testimony there.[21] Yet another time Henry appeared to a man in his familiar coat of blue velvet but with rather drawn features.[22] The King who in life had been mocked for his habitual costume of a townsman's gown and cap and the square-toed boots of a farmer now carried those trademarks in death as badges of his humility and other-worldliness. That very cap itself, though mysteriously transformed into red velvet, was displayed to pilgrims at Windsor as late as 1534 as a "Sovereigne Medicine against the Headache," while Henry's spurs and a small chip of his bedstead were treated as precious relics to the disgust of sixteenth-century writers such as William Lambarde.[23] The late King's boots and other souvenirs of those long wanderings in the North during his exile in the 1460s were preserved by families with whom he had sought refuge, while *memoria* to Henry in contemporary books of hours add to the testimony of surviving shrines, statues and stained glass images in numerous country churches.[24] When Richard III met defeat at Bosworth in 1485 he was facing that Henry Tudor who according to legend had been singled out by Henry VI as his successor to the throne. The powerful cult of the last Lancastrian had proved a forceful weapon against the last Yorkist.

With the accession of Henry VII the followers of Henry VI were firmly in the ascendancy, and their cult could furnish the new regime with a sainted royal ancestor. Petitioners to the new government stressed their loyalty to "the most noble and blessed Prynce of most holy memory, King Henry the Sixt, your Uncle . . . "[25] whereas his reputed murderer now became "Richard late in dede and not in right King of England the IIId."[26] Henry Tudor's mother the Lady Margaret Beaufort, powerful and pious matriarch of the clan and source of the alternate Tudor claim to succeed from Edward III, was doubtless a strong adherent of the earlier Henry's claim to sanctification,[27] though the King's wife Elizabeth of York may well have begrudged her several offerings to the tomb at Windsor when she visited there some years later.[28] Soon enough all of the new King's followers and suitors learned to trade on his special relationship with his sainted ancestor and his preoccupation with monarchs named Henry. Upon his entry into the ciy of York in 1486 the King was greeted by pageant tableaux including a scene of the six previous Henrys,[29] and when he later visited Cambridge its then chancellor Bishop Blyth pointedly recalled Henry III's contribution to the University.[30]

As the first decade of Tudor hegemony drew to a close the tomb which Henry VII began to plan for himself at Windsor became an intended shrine to associate himself in perpetuity with Henry VI. By 4 October 1498 Henry had secured two papal bulls from Alexander VI, one annexing the lands of a suppressed Benedictine priory to the new royal chapel and the other granting to the foundation those powerful indulgences associated with the chapel of the Scala Coeli outside Rome.[31] Further indulgences were secured in March and October of 1496 and in January 1498.[32] The old chapel of Henry III at Windsor which had been refurbished and refounded by Edward III for the Order of the Garter was chosen as the foundation for this newest chapel. A new base was laid for the tomb of Henry VI, and by 1498 the artisans had already begun work on the sepulchre of Henry VII.[33]

As preparations went forward for the splendid new chapel to be erected at Windsor, efforts were also under way to secure full and formal canonization for Henry VI. English exertions at the Roman Curia were rewarded by a bull of Alexander VI issued in October 1494 which ordered the English hierarchy to inquire into the sanctity and the reported miracles of Henry,[34] while a later bull of Julius II ordered the appointment of a second commission of inquiry.[35] No doubt it was these orders and the impending canonical process that elicited the remarkable collection of miracles attributed to Henry VI, a compilation and translation into Latin of the vernacular testimony collected at Chertsey and at Windsor. There are two surviving manuscripts of these *miracula*, the earliest and more complete being the original compilation of AD 1500 against which the committee of inquiry checked its findings, indicating in the margin whether each story had been verified (*"probatum"*) or was insufficiently documented (*"non invenitur"*).[36] The steady collection of these tales and reports over the preceding fifteen years indicates some anticipation of an eventual canonical process but the Latin compilation itself is an invaluable witness to the extent and range of Henry's cult and its influence.

In expectation of Henry's canonization, but also because he had now passed into the realm of legend, those who had known the King in life were now recalling personal anecdotes and generating the apocryphal tales which inevitably surround the central figure of a popular cult. Among the most valuable reminiscences which have survived from his contemporaries is the memoir of his chaplain John Blacman, possibly written before Bosworth Field but first published in the reign of Henry VII.[37] C. L. Kingsford once dismissed Blacman's memoirs as "concerned only with [Henry VI's] piety and patience in adversity,"[38] but these unquestionably pietistic memoirs actually offer most revealing insights into the conduct of Henry and the standards of his age. Blacman describes the same gentle, befuddled King whom we know from other records and from the chronicles, a monarch who was too unworldly and indifferent to save his treasury or his throne. But what were exemplary virtues to his sometime chaplain in the rosy afterglow of Henry's posthumous reputation sometimes seem stern indictments against his kingly character by the secular standards of the day. The King who eschewed all oaths except for an habitual "forsooth and forsooth" showed less orthodoxy and more heresy to an age in which abhorrence of oaths was a clue to Lollardy.[39] Again Blacman praises Henry's careless indifference to possessions and his ready willingness to distribute his personal belongings, but the same recklessness lost crown lands and income at the expense of his patrimony.[40]

If the saintly Henry's attitude to matters of state was somewhat peculiar, so too was his much vaunted patronage of moral training for the young. As the founder of King's College at Cambridge and of Eton College he was famed for his interest in the moral training of the young boys who attended his foundations. In a famous statement he had even given instructions that he would rather see his boys somewhat ignorant of music than deficient in holy scripture.[41] Blacman, however, unwittingly casts doubt on the high moral tone of Henry's interest in the young courtiers by relating the method which Henry devised to assure himself that their chastity was being protected from the temptations of court life. Summoning a stonemason, the King had secretly caused small slits to be carved in the inner walls of the castle so that he could observe in private the dalliances of his courtiers.[42] He also showed an unusual preoccupation with nakedness, and we are told that the sight of the bathers at the spa in Bath caused him to flee the town entirely. Apparently his courtiers and nobles unwisely attempted to introduce a more worldly note into the palace activities by introducing a bevy of unclad dancers into a Christmas Ball. Predictably Henry fled the room, crying "fy, fy for shame! Forsooth ye be to blame."[43] On normal occasions the King had said little or nothing, sometimes for days on end, which sometimes led foreign ambassadors to inquire if he were ill. His insistence that every meal be adorned with representations of the five wounds of Christ must have made Henry's banquets rather more solemn than those of other medieval princes. If Blacman's accounts are to be believed, the King was a serious exponent of the new lay piety, but he brought to it a severe righteousness which must have influenced few and offended many.[44]

Any attempt to assess Henry's character and his suitability in the role of royal saint inevitably stops short against this curious mixture of charming indifference and exasperating incompetency. The gentle King who walked about in a kind of trance, often falling off his horse and absent-mindedly dropping his royal cap which the courtiers had to retrieve constantly, apparently spoke of visions of Christ in Glory and the Assumption of the Virgin, and claimed according to Blacman that he was guided by the voices of John the Baptist, the Virgin, St Dunstan and St Anselm. But the account of his chaplain deserts us entirely as an historical authority when it claims that Henry fed the Lancastrian army in the North by multiplying bread and fishes.[45] The problem is that Henry's voices, unlike those of his contemporary Joan of Arc, accomplished nothing of political significance, and any miracles he wrought for the Lancastrian troops came too few and too late to save that unfortunate band. Thus his posthumous reputation is all the more at variance with the testimony of contemporaries who had seen in him a dour, puritanical fellow who hated small talk, considered fiscal responsibility as avarice, and avowed his hatred of bloodshed while many died in his name and for his cause.[46] Surrounding himself with the trappings of piety and the mantle of righteousness, Henry met the two great crises of his long life with two bouts of certifiable (and certified) insanity. From a youth surrounded by ambitious and greedy magnates Henry had developed a remarkable unworldliness and an extraordinary disdain for the duties of a medieval king. In an age of magnates Henry was a poor feudal lord. In an age of rich and ambitious merchants Henry was an abominable businessman. This pitiable boy called upon to rule a tough and troubled realm would not even have been a good palatine bishop, for he had no political sense at all and not a shred of deceit. The terrible truth is that Henry was that rare phenomenon a True Christian, which is to say that he was meek, charitable, gentle, other-worldly, temperate, and extremely prudish. Like all living saints he was impossible to live with, and as a royal saint he was the greatest single disaster since the previous English royal saint Edward the Confessor.

These dubious virtues were no deterrent, however, to the new dynastic strength of his cult which under the aegis of Henry VII could now promise royal patronage as well as divine compensations. Contemporary clerics well knew the rewards of superintending a major shrine, and especially one under royal protection; the glory and riches of Becket's tomb at Canterbury served as a constant reminder to the vicars of rural churches and the chapter monks of great cathedrals that their establishments too might someday become famous objects of pilgrimage.[47] Piety and profit commingled as happily in the business of pilgrimage as they had in the Crusades, and the profits from a major cult were incentive alike to the proud, the pious and the merely greedy.

It was perhaps some combination of these motives which impelled the Abbot and Convent of Westminster to begrudge Windsor its new glory. In February 1498, when the new chapel and tomb had been well begun, the Westminster officials suddenly petitioned Henry VII to move his saintly ancestor's body once more and to reinter him at Westminster Abbey. Fears of losing their primacy as the royal mortuary undoubtedly spurred the appeal, though it was significantly at variance with the Abbey's silence when Henry was first buried at Chertsey by Edward IV or when he was reburied at Windsor by Richard III. But after the restoration of Edward IV in 1471 the Convent of Westminster had reaped the reward of having given sanctuary to Edward's queen and his heir, and at that time they would have had no desire to receive the corpse of their late King at the expense of forthcoming royal favours. Now matters were quite different and the Abbot and Convent of Chertsey also determined to press its claim for return of the body, while the Dean of Windsor naturally opposed both claims strenuously. These petitions were accordingly referred to the adjudication of the chancellor and a great council, and representatives of all three contending parties were summoned to appear at Westminster on 26 February to assist in determining the disputed claim. Most of the documents in this case have perished along with the council records for that period, but a memorandum of the proceedings fortunately survives among the muniments of Westminster Abbey. This narrative summary of the case, preserved as the Abbey's record of the ultimate decision, gives us the substance of the oral and written evidence which was submitted to the Great Council of the realm sitting in the Star Chamber at Westminster Palace on 26 February 1498.[48]

The debate began with a submission from the Abbot of Chertsey, who argued that Henry's corpse had been *"violenter exhumatum et extractum"* by Richard III who was King *"de facto et non de jure"*, this last phrase being the standard form for rejecting the legitimacy of an opposing dynasty. The rebuttal then came from Christopher Urswick, the Dean of Windsor, who along with two of the canons attached to that chapel testified that the Abbot of Chertsey had not only consented to the exhumation but indeed had broken ground for it with his own hands. They also argued that Henry VI had elected to be buried at Windsor, and that the council ought to take into account their present possession of the corpse and the undesirability of yet another exhumation. Finally, the Prior and the Bailiff of Westminster appeared on behalf of their community. Their argument, like that of the Dean of Windsor, was a tripartite one: contrary to other assertions, they contended, Henry VI had chosen the Abbey for his sepulchre. The monastery of Westminster was the traditional burying-place of English kings, and the ancestors of Henry VI "*ac pro sic vulgariter dicto nominato et reputato palam publice et notorie.*" Lastly, they argued that Henry VI had been a parishioner of the Abbey, for it was in Westminster that English kings lived out their public lives and celebrated the great public events of their reigns.[49] Having taken these submissions the council then postponed its decision until 5 March, when the matter could be considered by the King who would then be sitting in council at Greenwich.

When the hearing reconvened on the 5th the council accepted written evidence from all three contestants in the dispute. A considerable amount of written testimony was taken down for evidence, and the Westminster Steward's account records numerous expenses incurred in transcribing evidence,[50] including a fascinating series of anecdotes concerning the late King. Twelve workmen and artisans connected with the Abbey in the 1450s and 1460s recalled Henry VI's regular nocturnal rambles through the cathedral in search of a site for his tomb. Although recorded more than four decades after the events described, and from witnesses who by then were all described as in various stages of decrepitude and senility, these statements carry the ring of plausibility which is reinforced by the naïveté and imprecision of their recollections. Witnesses such as James Bromlay and Philip Ilstowe, falconer and lavender respectively of the Abbey, and Richard Herring, a Westminster weaver, recalled Henry's frequent visits in the years before the Battle of Wakefield. One evening sometime before 8 p.m. he had wandered over from Westminster Palace with his confessor Thomas Manning, and with Abbot Kirkton went around by torchlight to consider the alternative sites. On another occasion, accompanied by Prior Flete he rejected first one and then other possibilities as they were suggested to him. He apparently preferred to be buried near Henry V, but refused permission to move that tomb slightly so as to accommodate his own: "Nay, let him alone;" he said to Flete, "he lieth like a noble prince. I would not trouble him." Finally it was decided that the reliquary of Henry V's sepulchre could be moved back so that Henry VI could lie near his father and St Edward. The King borrowed Lord Cromwell's white staff to point out the spot, and Thirks the master-mason was set to laying it out. Forty groats had been paid out to begin the new tomb, with one groat to the common workmen, which they recalled so many years later.[51]

Convinced by this testimony, or perhaps swayed by political considerations and a desire to please the Londoners, the King and council ended their deliberations with a judgement in favour of the Abbey and appropriate orders that the decision be implemented.[52] The representatives of Windsor seem not to have accepted this seemingly final decision, however; apparently they persisted in attempts to have the decision overruled, for although no further documentation survives in the case the Windsor Steward's accounts show numerous entries for journeys made to London on this matter during April and May. Perhaps the Windsor officials were only assisting the Westminster chapter to facilitate removal of the tomb. But one suspects that the frequent trips and those expense-account dinners at Burgeys Tavern may well have dragged out the council hearings as late as mid-May.[53] In any case the King's mother, the Lady Margaret, was forced by the new decision to cancel her plans for a chantry chapel at Windsor, the royal licence for which had been issued on 1 March 1497, and formal permission from the Dean of Windsor granted on 18 July following.[54] Henry VII on his part affected a resigned annoyance at the decision of his council, though it is clear that he had participated in that decision. The new chapel which was to link him for all time with his saintly predecessor would now have to be built at Westminster, and the new tomb which was already begun would have to be moved there from Windsor. But the expense of this move was obviously repugnant to the notoriously parsimonious Henry, and he resolved that the Abbey of Westminster should contribute a substantial amount for the honour of housing his new chapel.

Henry's demands were high, but the £500 in "laufull mony of Englond" which he extracted from the Abbey was a small contribution towards the glorious new chapel which he proposed to build there, and a small price for the assurance of Westminster's continued primacy among the royal chapels. The agreement was sealed by an indenture of 26 June 1498 between the King and Abbot Fawcett of Westminster. This agreement related Henry's efforts at Windsor and his hope to be buried there with "his Uncle of blessid memory King Henry the vjth." But it goes on to relate the decision of his council that the body ought to be removed to Westminster where the late King might rest with his father Henry V and his mother Queen Catherine "and other his noble progenitours and auncestours sumtyme Kinges of this lond . . ." But because there would be "grete costes and charges" for the papal licence, and for transporting the body, and for the tomb, and for the other costs which this "chaunge and alteracion" would entail, the convent agreed to contribute to the project, and indeed the Sacrist's account for the year shows that it kept that promise.[55] In the meantime Henry apparently continued payments to the artisans working at Windsor until such time as the incomplete tomb could be moved to Westminster. Regular payments were made to John Esterfield, a canon of Windsor until 20 January 1503, when a final £10 was paid out for conveying the King's tomb from Windsor.[56] This removal of the tomb itself was probably intended to mark the inception of Henry VII's new chapel, which was begun with appropriate ceremonies for the cornerstone-laying by Abbot Islip and the architect Sir Reginald Bray at a quarter to three o'clock on 24 January 1503.[57]

By this time Henry had secured the requisite papal licences for his new endeavour, including a bull of Alexander VI issued in January 1500, transferring the properties of several suppressed monasteries to the new chapel.[58] This was followed by several bulls from Julius II dated 20 May 1503, confirming the foundation, transferring other properties to it, and honouring it with the prized indulgence which had previously been attached to the new chapel at Windsor.[59] The next step was to press for the formal canonization of Henry VI, using the documents and testimony of his miracles which had already been collected. But such matters were slow and costly at the renaissance curia and the proceedings dragged on throughout the remainder of Henry VII's reign, reportedly hampered by the King's unwillingness to contribute the necessary sums. According to the chronicler Edward Hall, it was more expensive to secure the canonization of a king than of a bishop, even if it were a bishop of Rome, and the thrifty Welsh monarch "thought it more necessary to kepe his money at home, for the profite of his realme and countrey, rather than to empoverish his kingdom, for the gaining of a new holy day of sainct Henry: . . ."[60]

It is surely true that Henry VII, who was on excellent terms with the papacy and frequently utilized papal bulls to publish his political proclamations, could easily have expedited the canonization of his uncle. Perhaps the death of the Lady Margaret had removed a family champion of that cause. But it is equally probable that the cult of Henry VI had simply lost much of its political vitality by the latter part of Henry VII's reign; with the strengthening of Tudor control over the realm, royal interest in a new royal saint was now more personal and less a matter of political expediency. In the will which he had drawn up on 31 March 1509, Henry VII expressed a determination "right shortely to translate . . . the bodie and reliquies of our Uncle . . .", but the will of his son and heir Henry VIII required that the tombs and altars at Windsor of his great uncle Henry VI and his maternal grandfather Edward IV "be made more princelie, in the same places where theie now be, at our charges."[61] The cult of the Blessed Henry, still uncanonical, was to continue through the Reformation and in the late 1520s the agents of Henry VII at the papal curia apparently attempted once more to revive proceedings for the canonization.[62] But by 1528 the English representatives at Rome were deeply embroiled in the King's Great Matter, and the royal divorce overshadowed the royal ancestor.

Other political cults of the age had ended on a strong note, assailed by state and Church or submerged by the waves of religious reform. But the cult of Henry VI, like the reign of that unhappy monarch himself, met a more shadowy end when its utility had been superseded. In the end that King who was almost the last of England's medieval sovereigns was almost the last of England's medieval saints; in death, as in life, things never went quite right for Henry VI.

HAVERFORD COLLEGE

NOTES

[1] The most important collection of the surviving poetry is, of course, Rossell Hope Robbins (ed.), *Historical Poems of the XIVth and XVth Centuries* (New York: Columbia Univ. Press, 1959).

[2] The manner in which these diverse activities could be made to reflect political themes is explored in J. W. McKenna, "Henry VI of England and the Dual Monarchy: Aspects of Royal Political Propaganda, 1422–1432," *JWCI*, 28 (1965), pp. 145–62 and pl. 26–29.

[3] On the earlier anti-royal cults see Josiah Cox Russell, "The Canonization of Opposition to the King in Angevin England," in C. H. Taylor and J. L. La Monte (eds), *Haskins Anniversary Essays in Medieval History* (Boston: Houghton, Mifflin, 1929), pp. 279–90. The cult of Richard Scrope is traced in J. W. McKenna, "Popular Canonization as Political Propaganda: The Cult of Archbishop Scrope," *Spec.*, 45 (1970), pp. 608–23.

[4] The traditional rivalry between the English and French kings over their competing claims to thaumaturgic or wonder-working powers was explored in Marc Bloch, *Les Rois Thaumaturges* (Strasbourg: Libriarie Istra, 1924; London: OUP). On the coronation oil as a subject for such rivalry see P. E. Schramm, *History of the English Coronation* (Oxford: Clarendon Press, 1937), pp. 131ff; J. W. McKenna, "The Coronation Oil of the Yorkist Kings," *EHR*, 322 (1967), pp. 102–4; Walter Ullmann, "Thomas Becket's Miraculous Oil," *JTS*, 8 (1957), p. 129ff. For a criticism of these last three opinions see T. A. Sandquist, "The Holy Oil of St Thomas of Canterbury," in T. A. Sandquist and M. R. Powicke (eds), *Essays in Medieval History presented to Bertie Wilkinson* (Toronto: Univ. of Toronto Press, 1969), pp. 330–44.

[5] John Bruce (ed.), *Historie of the Arrivall of Edward IV in England and the Finall Recouverye of his Kingdomes from Henry VI*, Camden Society, 1 (London, 1838), p.

38. This explanation for Henry's death was an ironic echo of the Lancastrian excuse for Richard II's disappearance.

6 Henry Ellis (ed.), *The New Chronicle of England and France by Rogert Fabyan* (London, 1811), p. 662. Yet another Tudor authority, Thomas More, claimed that this was common knowledge in his day: R. Sylvester (ed.), *The History of King Richard III by Thomas More* (New Haven: Yale Univ. Press, 1964), p. 8.

7 Thomas Wright (ed.), *Letters relating to the Suppression of the Monasteries*, Camden Society, 26 (London, 1843), p. 224; Ronald Knox and Shane Leslie (eds), *The Miracles of King Henry VI* (Cambridge, 1923), p. 6.

8 *Archaeologia* 60 (1908), p. 21, citing the Issue Rolls for Easter, II Edward IV, 505. I am indebted for this reference and for other assistance to Lawrence E. Tanner, Librarian and Keeper of the Muniments at Westminster Abbey.

9 James Raine (ed.), *The Fabric Rolls of York Minster*, Surtees Society, 35 (Durham, 1859), p. 209n.

10 Arthur Gardner, *English Medieval Sculpture* (Cambridge: Cambridge Univ. Press, 1951), p. 234.

11 The earliest York reference appears in the Fabric Roll for 1472–3 recording a payment of 40s: "*In retribucione data magistro Ricardo Latomer pro laboribus suis impositis circa scripturam deposicionum cetorum personarum coram ymagine regis Henrici sexti in Ecclesia Cath. Ebor. offerencium.*": *York Fabric Rolls* p. 82. Inventories made in the years 1500 and 1509 list objects which formed part of an altar to Henry VI, including "*unus pannus operis le arays*" and "*unus pannus operis le tapstrye*": Ibid., p. 227. Associated with these are such articles as "*iij le banqweres, unum album, aliud rubium, tercium blosium*" and "*iij panni cum armis Angliae.*"

12 There is a note on Booth's political vacillation in R. Davies (ed.), *Extracts from York Records* (London: J. R. Nichols & Son, 1843). The monitio itself is printed from Booth's episcopal register in *York Fabric Rolls*, pp. 208–10, and in James Raine (ed.), *Historians of the Church of York and its Archbishops*, Rolls Series, 71, 3 vols (London, 1879–94), iii, pp. 336–7.

13 There is no record showing when it was removed, but unlike the other statues in the screen from William I to Henry V which survive intact the statue of Henry VI has been missing for centuries: Gardner, op. cit., p. 234. In 1515–16 one John Painter of York was paid 20s. "*pro piccione j ymaginis Henrici regis*" (*York Fabric Rolls*, p. 97) which may, however, refer to a replacement which perished in the Reformation.

14 Notices and surviving evidence for the *cultus* have been collected by Knox and Leslie, Intro., *passim*, and in Cardinal Gasquet's *The Religious Life of King Henry VI* (London: G. Bell, 1923). Other evidence is cited in Leonard Smith, "The Canonization of King Henry VI," *Dublin Review*, 168 (1921), p. 48, and in Paul Grosjean (ed.), *Henrici VI Angliae Regis Miracula Postuma* (Brussels: Subsidia Hagiographica 22, 1935).

15 Contemporary Tudor manuscripts of the reported miracles are edited with a full apparatus in Grosjean, op. cit., while a partial translation is provided in Knox and Leslie, op. cit.

16 Grosjean, op. cit., p. 73. Knox and Leslie, op. cit., pp. 124–5.

17 Grosjean, op. cit., pp. 122–3; Knox and Leslie, op. cit., pp. 109–10.

18 The topographer John Rous, no devotee of Richard III, describes the corpse as perfectly preserved except that the remains were "*parum depressa cum macilentiori aspectu solito.*" Thomas Hearne (ed.), *Joannis Rossi Antiquarii Warwicensis Historia Regum Angliae* (Oxford: Univ. Press, 1716), p. 217.

19 See the notes on Tresilian's work in W. H. St John Hope, *Windsor Castle* (London:

Country Life, 1913), ii, p. 429. A similar almsbox which has not survived was constructed for the analogous tomb of Master John Shorn at Windsor: W. Bond (ed.), *Inventories of St George's Chapel, Windsor* (Windsor, 1944), p. 286.

[20] Grosjean, op. cit., pp. 106–12; Knox and Leslie, op. cit., p. 89ff.

[21] Grosjean, op. cit., pp. 98–9; Knox and Leslie, op. cit., pp. 77–9.

[22] Knox and Leslie, op. cit., p. 153. This appears to be a reflection of the same account which John Rous had heard. Evidence from the modern exhumation of Henry's remains suggests that the body was mutilated for relics during the move from Chertsey: W. H. St John Hope, "The Discovery of the Remains of King Henry VI in St George's Chapel, Windsor Castle," *Archaeologia*, 62 (1910), pp. 533–42; *Proceedings of the Society of Antiquaries of London*, 2nd ser., 23 (1909–11), pp. 451–3.

[23] William Lambarde, *Dictionarium Angliae Topographicum et Historicum* (London, 1730), p. 422, cited by Hope, *Windsor Castle*, op. cit., ii, p. 415. Writing *c.* 1577, Lambarde noted that a stained glass window near Henry's tomb in Windsor still carried the dead King's image: Ibid.

[24] There is an early miniature of Henry VI in Fitzwilliam Museum (Cambridge) MS 55, f. 141v, which is a Norfolk book of hours *c.* 1480. There are *memoria* to Henry there, and in Fitzwilliam Addit. MS 38–1950, the so-called Bohun Psalter (*c.* AD 1370), which was later owned by Henry VI and by Archbishop Stafford. An obit of Henry VI in a fifteenth-century hand is inserted into the Calendar on f. 240, and there are memoria to him on f. IVb. Several of the surviving hymns to Henry VI seem to have been written before the body was moved in 1484: Knox and Leslie, op. cit., p. 8; Grosjean, op. cit., p. 249; Gasquet, op. cit., pp. 122–32.

[25] *Rotuli Parliamentorum ut et Petitiones, et Placita in Parliamento*, n.p., n.d. [London, 1767–77], vi, p. 336a, from the important Act of Resumption of 1485.

[26] Ibid., vi, p. 313a.

[27] The famous oration delivered by Bishop Fisher at her funeral stressed the Lady Margaret's piety and her respect for her family, two of the principal factors in the royal patronage of ancestral tombs and shrines: cf. the "Morning Remembrance" in J. E. B. Mayor (ed.), *The English Works of John Fisher* (EETS, ES 27, 1876), i, pp. 290–1.

[28] Nicholas Harris Nicolas (ed.), *Privy Purse Expenses of Elizabeth of York* (London: W. Pickering, 1830), pp. 3, 29, 42. By 2 March 1506 Sir Thomas Derby, inhabitant of St Mary's Leicester, was being described as sometime keeper of King Henry's tomb at Windsor: 8th Report Hist. MSS Comm. (London: HMSO, 1881), pt. 1, p. 420b; Grosjean, op. cit., p. 21*, n.1.

[29] *York Civic Records*, i, pp. 156–7. The preoccupation with others of his name was also a characteristic of Henry VI and those who sought to please him; among the books dedicated to Henry VI was John Capgrave's *Liber de Illustribus Henricis*, edited by F. C. Hingeston, Rolls Series, 7 (London, 1858).

[30] James Gairdner (ed.), *Letters and Papers Illustrative of the Reigns of Richard III and Henry VII*, Rolls Series, 24 (London: Longman, Green, 1861–3), i, pp. 422–3, from MS Bodley 13.

[31] Thomas Rymer (ed.), *Foedera, conventiones . . .*, orig. edn (London, 1704), xii, pp. 563, 565; Hope, *Windsor Castle*, op. cit., ii, p. 478. The Chapel of Scala Coeli, near the Church of St Anastasius on the Ostian Road, had attached to it a plenary indulgence for 29 January. Exaggerated legends circulated in England concerning the efficacy of this particular indulgence: F. J. Furnivall (ed.), *The Stacyons of Rome* (EETS, OS 25, 1867), pp. ix, 5; see also W. H. Rossetti, "Notes

on the Stacyons of Rome" in F. J. Furnivall (ed.), *Political, Religious and Love Poems* (EETS, 1866), pp. xxvii–xxviii. Lord Rivers had secured the Scala Coeli indulgence for the Chapel of Our Lady of the Pew at Westminster: Cora L. Scofield, *The Life and Reign of Edward IV*, 2 vols (London: Longmans, 1923), ii, p. 451.

32 *Foedera*, op. cit., xii, pp. 591, 644, 672. These three bulls are dated respectively on 1 March 1495–6, 28 October 1496, and 21 January 1497–8; see on this Hope, *Windsor Castle*, op. cit., ii, p. 489, n. 3.

33 A. P. Stanley, *Historical Memorials of Westminster Abbey* (London: John Murray, 1896), p. 137; Hope, *Windsor Castle*, op. cit., ii, p. 478.

34 This bull is printed in David Wilkins (ed.), *Concilia Magnae Britanniae et Hiberniae* (London, 1737), iii, p. 640; cf. Edward Peacock, "King Henry VI: Proceedings relating to his Proposed Canonization," *The Antiquary*, 39 (1894), 18–20.

35 *Foedera*, op. cit., xiii, pp. 100, 97, 102.

36 Both manuscripts are in the British Museum; one is BM Royal 13. c. viii and the other is BM Harley 423, ff. 72–128. The latter is part of Foxe's collections, and is a copy of the first part of the former. On these see John Blacman, *Henry the Sixth: Collectarium mansuetudinum et bonorum morum Regis Henrici VI* edited by M. R. James (Cambridge: Cambridge Univ. Press, 1919), pp. 51–4. Royal 13. c. viii is dated AD 1500, and bears the ownership signatures of Lord Lumley and of Archbishop Cranmer. This is the central manuscript which is excerpted in Knox and Leslie and edited formally by Grosjean.

37 John Blacman, *De Virtutibus et Miraculis Henrici Sexti* in *Duo Rerum Anglicarum Scriptores*, edited by T. Hearne (Oxford, 1732); *Collectarium*, op. cit.

38 "Henry VI" by C. L. K[ingsford], *Encyclopaedia Britannica*, vol. 11.

39 Henry's successor Edward IV is supposed to have sworn a most virile and kingly oath "by God's mercy:" Scofield, i, p. 442; though Thomas More insisted that Edward swore "by Goddes blessed Ladie (that was ever his othe):" More, *History of Richard III*, pp. 13, 64. According to Blacman, however, Henry VI *"nulla unquam habere solebat alia juramenta, ad confirmanda dicta sua veredica, quam haec verba proferendo, 'Forsothe and forsothe'."* *Blacman's Memoir*, ed. James, p. 16.

40 *Blacman's Memoir*, pp. 9–11.

41 Ibid., p. 12.

42 Ibid., p. 8.

43 Ibid., p. 8.

44 Ibid., pp. 14–16. The consequences of Henry's innocence are explored in Albert Mackinson, "The Saintly Plantagenet Henry VI," *History Today*, February 1962, pp. 97–104.

45 Ibid., p. 20.

46 Henry often protested his hatred of bloodshed, but when a Yorkshire shipman named John Harris mocked the royal entourage at Stony Stratford by pretending to thresh its path with a flail he was led off for questioning at Northampton and then drawn and quartered: "John Piggot's Memoranda" in C. L. Kingsford, *English Historical Literature in the Fifteenth Century* (Oxford: Clarendon Press, 1913), p. 371.

47 McKenna, "Popular Canonization," op. cit., pp. 609–10.

48 Westminster Abbey Muniments MS 6389*. This and the other Abbey records of the dispute are printed with minor inaccuracies in the second appendix to the first three editions of Stanley, op. cit., pp. 609–12, but dropped from the numerous subsequent editions.

49 *"Et hoc quia fovebat in Westmonasterio antedicto principalem larem et edem palacium*

Regis dictum ac principale domicilium, ibidemque fuerint coronationes et unctiones Regum, parliamenta pariter, et consilia pro bono publico Regis et Regni sepissime ibidem celebrantur." W.A.M. MS 6389*; Stanley, op. cit., app. 2, p. 610.

[50] Ibid., pp. 612–15, printing W.A.M. MS 6389**.

[51] W.A.M. MS 6389***.

[52] W.A.M. MS 6389*.

[53] These entries from the Steward's accounts are in Stanley, op. cit., pp. 613–15.

[54] C. H. Cooper, *Memoir of Margaret, Countess of Richmond and Derby* (Cambridge: Cambridge Univ. Press, 1874), p. 59.

[55] W.A.M. MS 6389***, the Abbey copy of this indenture bearing the royal sign manual. Printed in Stanley, op. cit., app. 2, pp. 615–16, and (apparently) from there in Hope, *Windsor Castle*, op. cit., ii, p. 479, since Hope reprints the transcriptional errors in Stanley. The Westminster Sacrist's account for the year in question shows £500 paid "*pro removacione corporis Illustrissimi Regis Henrici Sexti a Wyndesore usque monasterium Beati Petri West.*" Stanley, op. cit., p. 616.

[56] BM Addit. MS 7099 in Hope, *Windsor Castle*, op. cit., ii, p. 481. Payments were made to Esterfield on 23 July and 18 November 1501, and on 27 January, 11 March and 29 April 1502. During this interim period the cult had continued active at Windsor, and it was there that Queen Elizabeth of York had made her offerings to the Blessed Henry in 1502: see above, n. 28. Similarly, a Cambridge will of AD 1500 left bequests to the shrines of John Shorn and King Henry at Windsor: Knox and Leslie, op. cit., p. 7.

[57] Henry Ellis (ed.), *Holinshed's Chronicle* (London: Rivington, Payne, 1808), 3, pp. 529–30.

[58] The monasteries in question were Mottisfont and Luffield: *Foedera*, op. cit., xii, p. 738.

[59] Ibid., xiii, pp. 100, 97, 102.

[60] Edward Hall, *The Union of the Two Illustrious and Noble Houses of Lancaster and York*, edited by Henry Ellis (London: Rivington, Payne, 1809), p. 304. For an account of characteristic expenses incurred in obtaining canonization see E. W. Kemp, *Canonization and Authority in the Western Church* (Oxford: Clarendon Press, 1948), pp. 118, 132–3, 138.

[61] Both are quoted in Hope, *Windsor Castle*, op. cit., ii, pp. 480, 415. The anonymous translator of Livius, writing in 1513, mentioned that Henry VI "nowe resteth intumelate at Windsor.": C. L. Kingsford (ed.), *The First English Life of King Henry the Fifth* (Oxford: Clarendon Press, 1911), p. 173, and the exhumation of AD 1910 (see above, n. 22) confirms this.

[62] Grosjean, op. cit., pp. 97* ff.; Knox and Leslie, op. cit., p. 5. It was in 1510, at the beginning of Henry VIII's reign, that Robert Coplande of London published the *editio princeps* of Blacman: James, *Blacman's Memoir*, Intro., p. vii.

5

DIRECTIONS FOR MAKING MANY SORTS OF LACES

BY E. G. STANLEY

Humphrey Wanley, in the *Catalogue of the Harleian Collection of Manuscripts*, 1759, II, sig. 4Z, describes article 4 of MS 2320 thus:

> 4. *Directions for making many Sorts of Laces, which were in Fashion in the times of K. Henry* VI. *and Edward* IV. *such as* Lace Bascon, Lace endented, Lace bordred on boþe sydes, yn o syde, þykke Lace bordred, Lace Condrak, Lace Dawns, Lace Piol, Lace couert, Lace couerte doble, Lace compon couerte, Lace maskel, Lace cheyne brode, Las Cheueron, Lace oundé, Grene dorge, Lace for Hattys, *&c. fol.* 52.
>
> *In the principal Letter, is a damaged figure of a Woman sitting, & making of Lace.*

Both *OED* and *MED* seem to have left these *Directions* alone, except for Henry Bradley's entry in *OED* (s.v. "Mascle," sb.[1], 2.b.), where he quotes Wanley's "Lace maskel" from the *Catalogue* entry; he regards it as an attributive use of "mascle" with the sense "*Mesh* of a net." Bradley refers to the folio number for the occurrence, a fact derived from the manuscript itself, not from Wanley. Since he thinks of a net he seems to have connected the *Directions* with lace such as pillow lace or point lace, not with laces, i.e. knotted strings.[1]

Wanley seems to have understood that, but, in the posthumously published *Catalogue*, there is confusion of laces with lace in the description of the "principal Letter;" that, as far as I can make out, shows a woman (probably) sitting, but not making lace or laces, though she may have some lengths of thread (or perhaps of knotted strings, except that I think they are too long for convenient manufacture) hanging down over her right knee; her left hand is raised as if to instruct, and her right hand seems to be clutching the outer frame of the "principal Letter."

The historians of lace proper, when they refer to the *Directions*, rightly dismiss them as irrelevant;[2] indeed, they confess that they

89

have not been able to understand them. Mrs Palliser refers to two seventeenth-century manuscripts, both in the British Museum, MS Addit. 6293 and Lansdowne Roll 22. The Roll is much damaged and difficult to read; according to the (handwritten) catalogue, it is of about the time of Charles I; MS Addit. 6293 bears the date 1651 on the vellum cover, and there is no reason for not accepting that date as the date of the manuscript. MS Addit. 6293 is very well preserved, and has stitched in position specimens of almost all the various kinds of strings, made of stranded silk, for which instructions are given.

Wanley's date for MS Harley 2320 is presumably the period when he says the laces were in fashion, 1423–83, but there is some linguistic evidence that the date of composition is earlier than that. Bradley seems to have set aside Wanley's dating in favour of "*a*1500" because he thought of lace, not laces, and knew that there was no lace in the middle of the fifteenth century. A. S. Cole too puts a late interpretation of Wanley's dating, "about 1471," the year of Henry VI's brief restoration.

The many errors in *Directions* prove that we are dealing with a copy, written at a time when final -*e* could be treated with indifference. That indifference extends also to final -*e* from the French participial -*é* in heraldic terms, e.g. "compon" (< *componé*), "dawns" or "downs" (see *OED*, s.v. "Dancy"), "piol" (< *piolé*). A single act of copying ignorantly from a nearly contemporary exemplar could account for frequent improper omission of -*é*; such errors would, however, be more easily explained by the assumption of an underlying earlier text, perhaps fifty years earlier, written at a time when perhaps unstressed -*e* was still in some use in Southern English. Loss of final -*e*, stressed as well as unstressed, in the Harley MS could be the result of a single late copying of such an earlier text or the result of a succession of increasingly faulty intermediate texts. The use of "hond" as a plural, e.g. f. 67r and v, when it is not immediately obvious that it is a plural, also fits in better with the assumption of a relatively early date of composition. The language of the text is, however, too mixed for me to feel that it can be used as evidence for date or provenance with any confidence.

The text preceding the *Directions* in the Harley MS is the poem *He þat wol herkyn*,[3] the composition of which is dated by Farnham on linguistic grounds as "very early fifteenth century," a date generally accepted. There is, of course, no evidence that MS Harley 2320 gets both these texts from the same source, but the date given by Wells as "at latest, very early 15th cent." for *He þat wol herkyn* would fit the *Directions* too.

Understanding of the *Directions* is obtained by reading MS Addit.

6293 and looking at the specimens. Before he rushes into print, the ideal editor of the *Directions* will work his way through them till he can point to nearly forty lengths of different strings made by him with the help of his fellow knotter; but I regret to have to confess that my wife and I had enough to do to make the first of the laces, the "brode lace of v bowes" of ff. 53v–54r, with her doing the knotting and me trying to explain the text. It worked, and that gives us confidence that when Ross and Helen Ann have a go at the other strings the making of which the *Directions* describe they will not fail, unless the text is faulty.

A few things may help by way of explanation. As a result of my not having worked through the *Directions* what follows is too theoretical to be anything more than very tentative. An interest in lexicography roused by seeing a cluster of Middle English rare words in Wanley's *Catalogue* entry is insufficient for a serious craft.

At least two people are needed for knotting strings. There is the "he" of f. 53r, the man who reads out the *Directions*, for the knotter is too busy with the actual working of the laces to be able to keep an eye on the *Directions* too. The principal knotter is throughout addressed in the second person singular. For some more complicated laces the knotter will require a fellow, and the *Directions* use the second person plural for the pair of knotters. The last sentence of the text (which breaks off suddenly) calls for three knotters. The Roll also calls for two people, a heading on the dorse says "Two ladies worke," and MS Addit. quite often goes up to four people (one of whom, however, could be the director).

No tool is used, except once in the making of "lace condrak departyd" (f. 57v) when a "turne," spindle, spool, bobbin (cf. *OED*, s.v. "Turn," sb., 7.b, quot. 1564; and *EDD*, s.v., 1.), is called for; how exactly the "turne" is to be used I cannot understand, and I believe the text is corrupt. The "bow(e)s"—the word is used variously spelt in all three manuscripts—are loops of (silk) thread, as Mrs Palliser says. They must be of equal length, and tied together in a knot at the bottom, as is implicit in the slightly more complicated knotting together described on f. 60v and, using whipcord for enlarging the string, f. 69v. These loops are set on the fingers, sometimes given a twist of half a turn ("reuersed"), sometimes put on straight ("vnreuersed").[4] The working of the laces consists in one finger taking the lace off another finger usually through one or occasionally more than one bow. The process of reversing is explained at ff. 53r and v. In order to make clearer the directions given, the fingers are provided with letters at the opening of the *Directions*, these letters serving also to identify the bows set on them. "High" and "low" are used to mean near to and away from the thumb; the verbs "hye" and "lowe" are used for changing a bow over to a finger on the same hand nearer to or further from the thumb; and, in reversing, "vp-ward" and "donward" similarly indicate the direction. The process of taking the bow "þorow(out)" one or more other bows is often expressed in a construction in which the named finger (the subject) takes, "þorow(out)" one or more named bows, the named bow (the object of the verb). When such directions as "aboue" and "beneþe" are given it is not always easy to be sure if the reference is to the top end (or bottom end) of the hand or to above and beneath on a single finger, as when more than one bow is set on a finger. The Roll at a much damaged place seems to refer to "doble boes," and so do the *Directions* when they refer to "ouer bow" or "forme bowe" and "hyndre bow" or "neþer bow." In a reversed bow the "ouer syde" must be the side of the bow that is crossed over the other side. MS Addit. uses "top" and "vp" much as the *Directions* use "ouer" and "aboue." The Roll uses high, middle and low to identify the fingers and bows. A "bow departed" (explained on f. 55r) is made up of two colours, presumably by knotting, where the loop is on the finger, two different-coloured pieces of thread into a single bow; MS Addit. has "boes linckt" [e.g.] "with red and whyte." When two knotters are sitting side by side the adjoining hands are the "next hond(es)" (the "in(ward) hands" of MS Addit. and Roll), as opposed to the "ferþer hond(es)" (the "out hands" of MS Addit. and Roll).

Some of the terms used to describe the strings are ordinary words given special applications not all of which are clear to me. Many are adjectives or past participles used adjectivally or nouns used attribu-tively and post-posited. Among ordinary words with special senses the following may be worth noting: "brode lace" (Roll uses "broad" similarly), "þykke" and "þynne lace" seem to refer simply to flatness, thickness ("gretnys," f. 60v) and thinness. "Round lace" (the damaged dorse of Roll appears to have "round string") is circular in cross-section; in fact, "round" is the opposite of "brode;" it is worthy of note that the specimens in MS Addit. in the case of some of the round strings had to be stitched on to the paper with one aspect on top, viz. the one with the figure or pattern central. "Comyn" (f. 70v) is common, ordinary, i.e. without any figure or pattern knotted into it. "Holow" has the special sense tubular, MS Addit. (f. 2), under the heading "To make 2 strings att once" has a specimen tubular string with another string inside it, and made at the same time; the inner, concealed lace is a "lace couert" (f. 59v); it is possible to produce a concealed hollow lace within a hollow lace, and the concealed lace can then have a round lace within it, and if made correctly each lace can be drawn freely out of its ensheathing lace, as is described (f. 60v) for "lace couerte doble." The meaning "open" appears to be "plaine, without colour"—meanings given by Cotgrave, ed. 1611, for Fr. "*Ouvert*."[5] "A lace for hattys" (twice, f. 70v—and similarly MS Addit.) is *MED*'s "hat las" (s.v. "hat," lc. (a), quot. 1471).

Many of the most interesting of the rare words in the text are heraldic terms. The word "baston" is written, at each of its two occurrences, "bascon" in error: "lace bascon" (ff. 55r, 57r), emended to "baston" by me in the printed text. The sense cannot be identical with that of the heraldic "ba(s)ton:" the word "staff(e)" comes often in MS Addit. (ff. 7, 8, 10, 28, and on the dorse of Roll), and the specimens show various strings with narrow edging; i.e. the centre is uninterrupted lengthwise. "Lace bend" (ff. 64r, 65r) presumably has its ornament going athwart. "Lace bordered" has, presumably, coloured edging either along both edges or along only one edge. "Lace cheyne brode" (f. 65r) has a knotted ornament rather like a chain in appearance, like the specimen called "chaine" in MS Addit., f. 1, a broad lace with a multiple chevron ornament.[6] "Lace cheueron" (or "chyueron") can be either broad or round, and has a succession of chevrons as ornament; in a round string the chevrons are not apparent unless the string is held with that side facing up, as is clear from the specimens in MS Addit., ff. 3 and 9, where the word is also used. "Lace compon" (f. 61r) should be "componé" (see *OED* s.v.); from the description given, it emerges that the string changes pattern halfway through the making, so that the first pattern made is inverted in the second half. The word seems to have been used early in heraldry (see Tobler-Lommatzsch, s.v. "*componer*").[7] I cannot explain "lace condrak departed" (f. 57v). "Lace dawns" (f. 59r), "downs" (f. 59v), is ultimately derived from "*denticatus*" (see Wartburg, *FEW*, s.v., and cf. *OED*, s.v. "Dancy"); final -*é* has been omitted. "Lace endented" is string with tooth ornaments running lengthwise in a different colour (see *OED*, s.v. "Indented," ppl. a.[1], and *MED*, s.v. "endenten," 3). The phrase "grene dorge" in "A grene dorge" (f. 70r) stands for Fr. "(*à*) *grain d'orge*" barleycorn, explained by Cotgrave (ed. 1611, s.v. "*Grain*") as "In a triangular forme" and (s.v. "*Orge*") as "In a triangle forme." Presumably the lace so called has an ornament in that form. "Lace maskel" (f. 62r), "masclen" (with *n*-abbreviation, probably erroneous, f. 63r) is, as Cotgrave explains (ed. 1611, s.v. "*Macle*"), "(in *Blason*) a Mascle, or short Lozenge, hauing a square hole in the middest" (see *OED*, s.v. "Mascle," sb.[1], for the etymology, and cf. Wartburg, *FEW*, 16, s.v. "**maskila*." Presumably the lace has knotted into it an ornament in the form of a lozenge with a lozenge-shaped opening. In "brode lace wᵗ cros and olyet" (f. 68v) and the similar round lace (f. 69r), "olyet" refers to an ornament consisting of a dot, knotted in to the string together with an ornament in the shape of a cross. The sense seems to exist in Old French (see Tobler-Lommatzsch, s.v. *"oillet" das Ringelchen am Buchstaben E*, but cf. Wartburg, *FEW*, 7 (s.v. *"oculus"*), 319/1 and fn. 63 (324/1), and *OED*, s.v. "Oillet"). MS Addit. (f. 6) has a specimen string under the heading "To make the Cross and Diamonde," corresponding to "lace wᵗ cros and olyet" except for the dot which is lozenge-shaped, inevitably since it consists of a single knot of stranded silk thread. "Lace ounde brode" and "rounde" (both f. 69v) is string characterized by a wavy ornament (in contrast, I presume, to the straight ornament of the "baston"); for the form "oundé" see *OED*, s.vv. "Oundy," a., "Undee," "Undy." The possible etymology of "pen-powerer" (ff. 67v–68r, "powerer" twice, once as catchword), viz. that of "*pin-pourer," is easier than the sense, whether the string is to be used as a pin-case or whether the green, red, black, and white (or blue) colours of the string merely give it some resemblance to a pin-cushion. (See *OED*, s.v. "Pin-case," for evidence that both senses are possible for words of this kind; so also Fr. *"pelote"* used both as a cushion and as a receptacle, see Wartburg, *FEW*, 8, 480, s.v. *"pila."*) Ff. 68r and v have two redundant additions of the *er* abbreviation to "ʒowr;" the possibility that the abbreviation was added similarly to "pen-power" has been considered, but no etymology at all suggests itself. The possibility that the first element is "pen" not "pin" has also been considered. "A lace pen-powerer," i.e. a case or a sheath for pens made of a single knotted string, seems even less likely than that such a string should hold pins. There is no reason why such a holder should be so elaborate; and that applies even more to the ribbons used, later at least, to tie penner to inkhorn. Final -*é* "piolé" must underlie "lace piol" (f. 59v); Cotgrave, ed. 1611, s.v. *"Piolé,"* gives the sense "Spotted, or speckled; whence . . . *Riolé Piolé*. Gaudie, or pide; also diuersified, or set out with sundrie colours;" (cf. Tobler-Lommatzsch, s.v. *"pïeler"*). Presumably a "lace piolé" is spotted, whereas a "lace party" (ff. 63v, 64r) is in halves of two colours; (cf. *OED*, s.v. "Party," a., 2., 3).

TEXT

I wish to express my gratitude to the Trustees of the British Museum for permission to print the text of these *Directions*.

Punctuation, capitalization, hyphenation, and word-division have been modernized; the paragraphing of the manuscript has been retained. Conjectural additions are indicated by ⟨ ⟩, probable lacunae by ⟨. . .⟩; other conjectural emendations are indicated in the footnotes. Italics are used for expansion of manuscript abbreviations, () for expansion of manuscript suspensions—except once at f. 67r where the manuscript itself has () round the Latin phrase; ʾ indicate intercalations, [] editorial addition of folio numbers. The abbreviation for -*us* in Latin has been expanded as -*es*, but -*ys* would have done as well. In some, especially cramped, positions final ʒ is used in the manuscript for -*es* or -*ys*: this has been printed as *z*.

IN þe maner of laces makyng þ^u schalt vndersto*n*d þat the furst fynger next þ^e thombe schal be called o [*f*. 52v] A, on þ^e s(e)c(un)de* fynger B, þ^e iij^e C, iiij^e D. Also sum tyme þ^u schalt take thy bowys reue*r*cyd and su*m* tyme vnreue*r*cyd. When þ^u schalt take þy bowe reue*r*cyd þ^u schalt take wyþ þyn one hand þ^e bowe of þ^e oþ*er* hond fro w^{t}owten, so þ^t þ^e syde þat was beneþen apon þyn one hond before þe takyng be aboue one þ^t oþ*er* hond after þ^e takyng. When hyt axith to be taken vnreue*r*cyd þ^u schalt take w^t þyn one hand þe bowe of þ^t oþ*er* hand fro w^{t}ynne so þ^t þ^e syde þ^t was aboue on þ^e one hond afore þ^e takyng be aboue on þ^t other hond aftur the takyng.

And sum tyme þ^u schalt reuers [*f*. 53r] þyn bowys vpward and sum tyme donward. When he bydd^t þ^e reue*r*s þy bowys þ^u schalt take þy neþ*er* syde of þy bowes and set hyt aboue, and þ^e syde þ^t was aboue set byneþ^e. And when he byddyþ þ^e reue*r*s thy bowes vpward yf þ^t þy bowe stond on B þ^u schalt take þ^e nether syde of þy bowes and set hyt aboue on A, and þ^t syde þ^t was betwene A and B schal dwell*e* stylle in hus stede. And when he byddyth þe reue*r*ce þy bowes donward, yf þ*er* be a bowe on A þ^u schalt take þe oue*r* syde of þe bowes and set hyt beneþ^e on B, and þ^t syde þ^t was betwene A and B schal be stylle. And su*m* tyme thow schalt [*f*. 53v] turne þy bowes. When þ^u schalt turne þy bowys þ^u scha⟨l⟩t† reue*r*ce þy bowez twyes, so þat þe syde þ^t was aboue before þe takyng ⟨be⟩ aboue aft*ur* þe takyng. And sum tyme thow schalt hy þy bowes, and su*m* tyme þ^u schalt lowen ham. When þ^u schaʾlʾt hyen hem þ^u schalt take þ^e bowe B and set on A, and þ^e bowe C set on B, and þe bowe D set on C. And when þ^u schalt lowen h*a*m þ^u schalt take þ^e bowe C and set on D, and þ^e bowe B set on C, & þ^e bowe A set on B.

FOR to make a brode lace of v bowes: Set ij bowes on B and C ryʒth, and iij bowys on A, B, C lyfte. Þen schal A ryʒth take [*f*. 54r] þorow þe bowe B of þe same hond þe bowe C of þe lyft hond reue*r*syd. Þe*n* lowe þy lyſt bowes. Þen schal A lyfte take þorowout B of þ^e same hond þe bowe C of þ^e ryʒth ho*n*d reue*r*ced. Þen lowe þy ryʒth bowes, and begynne aʒen.

* MS scdē.　　† MS schat.

FOR to make a round lace of v bowys: Do v bowys on þy fyngres as þᵘ dedyst in þe brode lace. Þen schal A ryȝht* take þorow B and C of þᵉ same hond þᵉ bowe C of þᵉ lyfte hond reuᵉrcyd. Þen lowe þy lyfte bowys. Þen schal A lyft take þorow B and C of þᵉ same hond þe bowe C of þe ryȝth hond reuᵉrcyd. Þen lowe þy ryȝth bowys, & begyn aȝen.†

[f. 54v] FOR to make a thynne lace of v bowys: Set a bowe on A lyfte hond, and ij sunder bowez on B lyft 'h'and, o bowe on C lyfte h(ond) and o bowe on B ryȝth hond. Þen schal A ryȝth take þorow B of þᵉ same hond þe bowe C of þe lyfte hond reuᵉrsyd; and B ryȝth schalle take the hyndre bowe of B lyft h(ond) þorowout þe bowe þat stondes before on B lyft vnreuᵉrcyd. Þen schal C ryȝth take bowe þat ys leuyd on B lyfte hond vnreuᵉrsyd þᵉ lowe bowe of A lyfte‡ vnto B lyfte. Þen schal A lyfte take þorow þᵉ bowe B of þe same hond þᵉ bowe C of§ þᵉ ryȝth hond vnreuᵉrcyd; and B lyfte [f. 55r] schal go þorow þe forme bowe of B ryȝth and take þe bowe þᵗ stondᵗ wᵗyn on B ryȝth vnreuᵉrcyd. Þenne lowe þe bowe of A ryȝt vnto B ryȝt, and begynne aȝene.

FOR to make a lace baston‖: Tak v bowes departed, þᵗ ys for to sey þat o syde of euᵉrych-a bowe be of o colour and þᵉ oþer syde of anoþer colour. Set hem on þyn hond as þow dedyst on þᵉ round lace, so þᵗ þᵉ colour þat ys abouen on þe ryȝt hond be byneþe on þy lyft hond, and þen werch in þe maner of þᵉ round lace.

FOR to make an open lace of v bowys: Set v bowez on þy fyngrys as yn þᵉ round lace [f. 55v] of v bowys and wyrke yn þe same manᵉre, saf þere þᵘ takest þᵉ bowys of boþᵉ þyn hond reuᵉrcyd, yn thys lace þᵘ schalt take þe bowes of bothe þyn hondys vnreuᵉrced.

FOR to make a lace endented: Take iij bowys of o colour and set on A and C of þe lyft h(ond) and also B of þe ryȝt hond, and ij bowys of anoþer colour, and set on B of þe lyfte hond & C of þe ryȝth hond, and wirke in þᵉ maner of þe round lace of v bowes.

FOR to make 'a' þyn lace bordred on boþe sydes: Þᵘ most take a ffelow and set hym on þy ryȝt hond, and set on hys hondes iij bo-[f. 56r] wes of o colour, one in B ryȝt and one A lyft and one in B lyft, and set on þyn hondes v bowys of another colour, as ys yn þe rounde lace. And þen schal þy felow take by þᵉ A ryȝt þorowout B and of þᵗ same hond þᵉ bowe B of þe lyft honde vnreuᵉrcyd. Þen lowe þy bowe of A ryȝt vnto B ryȝt, and so abyde vnto þe tyme ȝe haue changed twyes. And þen schalt þᵘ take wᵗ A ryȝt þorowout B and C of þᵉ same hond þe bowe C of þe lyft hond vnreuᵉrcyd. Þen lowe þy lyft bowes.

---

* MS ryght.
† *At the foot of the page an expunged proba pennae, the letters* a *to* p.
‡ MS lyste.   § MS oft.   ‖ MS bascon.

Þen schal A lyft take þorowout B of þe same hond þe bowe c of þe ryȝt hond reuerced donward. Þen schalt [f. 56v] þu lowe þy ryȝt bowes, and A ryȝt schal entre þe bowe B of þe same hond fro wᵗinne outwardes, and þe ouer syde of þe bowe of A lyfte of þy felow fro wᵗin, so þat þe syde þat was aboue afore be aboue aftur. And þenne lowe thy bowe of A ryȝth vnto B ryȝth, & change ȝowre bowes aȝen as ȝe dud beforetyme, so þat when ȝe haue changed tweys þᵗ þe colour dwelle stylle on ȝowre hondes as þey were at þe begynnyng, and begynne aȝenewardes.

FOR to make a lace bordred yn o syde: Set v bowys on þyn honde and iij bowys on þy [f. 57r] ffelowys hond, and wyrke and change as ȝe dudyn yn þe þyn lace bordred tofore, saue yn þˢ lace þy felow schal take þe bowys of boþe his hond reuercyd.

FOR to make a þykke lace bordred: Take x bowys departed, and set on þyn hond and on þy felowys hond in þe maner of a baston*, so þat ȝowre next hond acorde and eke ȝowre forþer hond. And þenne wyrke onys wyth ȝowre next hond and aftur wyth ȝowre ferþer hond yn þe maner of þe rounde lace of v bowys. Þen schal ȝe change þe ouer bowys of ȝoure next hond so þat þe colour þat was [f. 57v] furst aboue be alway aboue.

FOR to make a lace condrak departyd: ⟨Take⟩ vij bowys of ij colours, and do iiij on A, B, C, D ryȝth ⟨. . .⟩. And þen schal A ryȝth enter into B of þe self hond fro wytin outward, and vnder al þe bowys of boþe hond take þe ouer syde of A lyft reuerced. And þenne þu schalt hye þy lyft bowys, & D lyft schal take þe bowe. ⟨. . .⟩ þy ryȝt bowys, and begynne aȝen. And when þu schalt make þys lace loke þu knytte þe ende of þe lace to a turne þᵗ hyt may turne abowte.

FOR to make an holow lace of x bowys: Tak a felow, and set on hys hond v [f. 58r] bowys, and oþer v bowys on þyn hond. Þen schalt þu wyth A ryȝth take þorow B, c of þe same hond þe bowe c of þe lyft hond vnreuerced. Þen lowe þy lyft bowys, and A lyfte schal take þorowout B, c of þe same hond þe bowe c of þe ryȝt hond reuercyd. Þen schal þy felow wyrke in þe same maner, saue þen he schal take furst þe bowe of þe lyft hond reuerced and aftur þe bowe of þe ryȝt hond vnreuerced. Þen schal ȝe change þe ouer bowys of ȝowre next hond yn þe manere of þe þyn lace bordred, saue þer ȝe schal twyes and here but onis.

FOR to make an lace holow of [f. 58v] vij bowys: Set ij bowes on B & c in þy ryȝt hond and ij sunder bowys on A lyft h(ond), and ij on B lift, and on in c lyft. Þen schal A riȝt take þorow B, c of þe same hond þe forme bowe of B lyft vnreuerced; and B ryȝt schal take þe forme bowe of A lyft vnreuerced; and A ryȝt schal take þorow þe same þat

* MS bascon.

was on A lyft þe bowe C of þe lyft hond vnreuerced. Þen lowe þy lyft bowys. Þen schal A lyft take þorowout B, C lyft þe forme bowe of B ryȝt reuerced, and B lyft schal take þe forme bowe of A ryȝt vnreuerced, and A lyft schal take þorowout þe bowe þᵗ was [ƒ. 59r]on A ryȝt þe bow C ryȝt vnreuercyd. Þen lowe þy ryȝt bowys, and begyn aȝen.

FOR to make a lace dawns: Take iiij bowys of o colour, & set on A, B ryȝt and on A, B lyft; and iiij bowys of anoþer colour take and set* on C, D lyft and C, D ryȝt. Þen schal A of þe ryȝt hond go þorowout B, C, D of þe same hond and take þe bowe D of þe lyft hond vnreuersed. Þen lowe þy lyft bowes, and A lyft schal go þorow B, C, D of þe same hond and take þe† bowe D of þe ryȝt hond reuerced donward. Þen lowe þe bowys of C into D riȝt, and þen‡ lowe B to C, and þe bowe þᵗ [ƒ. 59v] is wᵗin on A schal go ouer þe forme bowe into B wᵗ help of þe other hond. And þe bowe þat stod wyþoute on A schal stond stylle on A. And begynne aȝen.

FOR to make a lace piol: Set foure bowys of o colour on þy ryȝt hond, and set§ iiij bowes of anoþer colour on þy lyft hond, and wyrke yn þe maner of þe lace downs.

FOR to make a lace couert: Take x bowes departed, and‖ set on ȝowre hondys in þe maner of þe þykke lace bordred, saue in þys lace þe o colour schal be aboue and þe oþer byneþen; and wyrke ones wyþ ȝowre ryȝt hondes & ones¶ [ƒ. 60r] wyth ȝowre lyft hondes yn þe maner of an open lace of v bowes. Þen change ȝe þe ouer bowes of ȝowre next hondes in þe maner of þe þyn lace bordred. Þenne reuerce þy bowe of A lyft donward so þat þe colour þat was beneþen be abouen; and þy felow yn þe same maner schal reuerce hys bow of A ryȝt. Þen schal ȝe change þe ouer bowes of ȝour ferþer hondes so þᵗ eyþer of ȝow take other bowys vnreuerced. Þen reuers þy bowe of A lyft vpward so þat þe colour þᵗ was aboue** be aboue; & þy felow schal wyrke in þe same maner wᵗ hys forþer hond. Þen schal ȝe begynne as ȝe dud before, and when [ƒ. 60v] ȝe begynne aȝen loke þᵗ þe colour þᵗ was aboue at begynnyng be aboue þen. And þen schalt þᵘ haue†† a lace of o colour wᵗin and anoþer of anoþer colour wᵗoute.

FOR to make a lace couerte doble: Tak a lace of þe gretnys of halfe þy bowys, and set x bowes on ȝowre hondes as ȝe dud before in þe lace couerte; & þᵗ one ende of þe lace schal be knyt wyth þe bowys, and þat oþer ende bytwene þe and þy felow. And þen schal ȝe wyrke in þe maner of þe lace couert; and ȝe schal change ȝowre next hondes

---

* MS sed, d *alt. fr.* o.   † MS þe þe.   ‡ *Foll. by letter (perh.* e) *expunged.*
§ MS set set.   ‖ MS and and.   ¶ *Catchword* wᵗ ȝowre.
** *Corr. fr.* abowe *by expuncting first downstroke of* w.   †† *Foll. by* of o *expuncted.*

beneþe þe lace and ȝowre ferþer hond*es* aboue. And þen schalt þ^u ha- [*f.* 61r] ue iij lac*es* ech*e* wythyn oþ*ere*, and eche may be draw out of other.

FOR to make a lace *com*pon cou*er*te: Take a felow, and wyrk as ȝe dud in þe lace cou*er*te; & when ȝe haue wroȝth as myche as ȝe wylle, torne al ȝowr bowys, and wyrke as mych as ȝe dud beforehond.

FOR to make a lace endented: Tak iiij bowes of o colo*ur*, and set hem on A, B, C, D ryȝt, and iiij bowes of anoþ*er* colo*ur*, and set h*em* on A, B, C, D lyft. Þen schal A lyft take þorow hys bowe on B, C, D lyft þe bowe of D ryȝt vnreu*er*sed; and þen schal D ryȝt take þ^e bowe [*f.* 61v] of D lyft vnreu*er*sed. And þen lowe þy lyft bowes so þat þe bowe þat was take of D ryȝt dwelle stylle on A lyft. Þen reu*er*ce al þy bowes, and þen schal A lyft take þorowout hys bowe on B, C, D lyft, and D ryȝt vnto C. Þen schal D ryȝt take þe bowe of D lyft vnreu*er*ced. Þen lowe þy lyft bowes as before, so þ^t þ^e bowe þat was take of C ryȝt dwelle on A lyft. Þen reu*er*s al þy bowes, and þen schal A lyft take þorowout hys bowe and B, C, D lyft and D, C ryȝt þe bowe B ryȝt vnreu*er*ced. Þen hye þy bowes of C, D ryȝt. Þen schal D ryȝt take þe bowe of D lyft. Þen lowe [*f.* 62r] þy lyft bowes as before. Þen reu*er*s alle þy bowes. Þen schal A lyft take þorowout hys bowe & B, C, D lyft and D, C, B ryȝt þe bowe of A ryȝt vnreu*er*ced. Þen hye þy ryȝt bowez, and D ryȝt schal take þe bowe of D lyft vnreu*er*ced. Þen lowe þy lyft bowes. Þen schal þ^u wyth þy ryȝt* hond do as þ^u dedyst wyth þy lyft hond, and at eu*er*y takyng reu*er*ce al þy bowes.

FOR† to make a lace maskel: Set iiij bowes of o colo*ur* on A, B ryȝt and on in A, B lyft. Þen schal A riȝt change w^t A lyft, so þat A ryȝt take þe bowe of A lyft þorowout hys bowe reu*er*cyd; and in þe same [*f.* 62v] maner schal B ryȝt change hys bowe wyth B lyft, and C ryȝt w^t C lyft, and D ryȝt w^t D lyft. In þe same man*er* þ^u schalt change al þy bowes aȝen. And when þ^u hast changed twyes, þ^t al þy bowes þat were on þy ryȝt hond be on þy ryȝt hond aȝen, þen schal A ryȝt change hys bowe w^t B lyft so þ^t A ryȝt take þoroȝ hys bowe þe bowe of B lyft reu*er*ced‡. In þe same man*er* schal B ryȝt change hys bowe w^t A lyft, and C ryȝt w^t D lyft, and D ryȝt w^t C lyft. Þen schal C ryȝt change hys bowe w^t B lyft, and B ryȝt w^t C lyft, and þen A ryȝt [*f.* 63r] w^t D lyft, and D ryȝt w^t A lyft. Þen begyn aȝen. And yf A, B be of o colo*ur* on boþe hondes then schal o mascl*en* be of o colo*ur* and þ^t oþ*er* of anoþ*er* colou*ur*.

FOR to make a brode lace of vij bowes: Set 7 bowes on þy fyngrys in þe man*er* of þe holow lace of 7 bowes and wyrke yn þe same maner of the holow lace; saue þ^t þ^u takyst in þe holow lace þe forme bowe B

---

* MS ryȝt ryȝt.　　† MS has cap. A *for* F.　　‡ MS reuer- [*new line*] reuerced.

of eyþer hond reu*er*ced, in þ^s lace þ^u schalt take þe bowe of B lyft reu*er*ced and þ^e bowe of B ryʒt vnreu*er*ced.

TO makc an open lace of 7 bowes: Set 7 bowes [*f.* 63v] on þy fyng*ri*s as yn þ^e holow lace, & wyrk yn þe same maner as þ^e holow lace, saue yn þ^s lace þ^u schalt haue al þy bowes vnreu*er*cyd; and yf þy bowes be dep*ar*ted þ^u schalt haue o lace of o colour* and þ^t oþ*er* of anoþ*er* colour*.

TO make a lace round party: Set 7 bowes dep*ar*ted on þyne hond yn þe maner of þ^e holow lace, so þ^t þ^e o colo*ur* be aboue and þ^e oþ*er* beneþe. Þen wyrke as þ^u dede yn þe open lace of 7 bowes; and what tyme þ^t þ^u hast but 2 bowes on þyn hondes þen þ^u schalt turne þe ou*er* bowes of þ^e same hond*e*, so þ^t þe colo*ur* þ^t was aboue afore [*f.* 64r] þe takyng be aboue aft*ur* þ^e takyng.

TO make a brode lace party: Do as yn þe rounde lace p*ar*ty; saue þere þ^u turnist in þe rounde lace þ^e ou*er* bowe of boþe þyn hond, in þ^s lace þ^u schalt t*ur*ne but þ^e ou*er* bowe of thyne on hond.

A lace bend brode of eyth bowes: Take iiij bowes of o colo*ur* & 4 of anoþ*er*, and worch as yn þ^e lace endented; saue þere þ^u worchyst furst w^t þy ryʒt hond and after w^t þy lyft hond, yn þ^s lace þ^u schalt do alwey w^t þy ryʒt hond.

A lace bend rounde of 8 bowes: Take iiij bowes of o colo*ur* and ⟨set⟩ on A, B, C, D ryʒt and 4 bowes of [*f.* 64v] anoþ*er* colo*ur* and set on þy lyft hond; and schal A ryʒt change hys bowe w^t D lyft, and B ryʒt wyth C lyft, and C ryʒt w^t B lyft, and D ryʒt w^t A lyft; and begyn aʒene. And loke alwey when þ^u change þy ryʒt bowes w^t þy lyft þ^u schalt take þorowe þy ryʒt bowes þe bowes of þy lyft hond reu*er*ced

A las bend on hys bowys: Take 8 bowes of o colo*ur* and set on þyn hondys and take 8 bowes of anoþ*er* colo*ur* and set on þy felowys hond*es*. Þen schal A lyft go ou*er* thy ryʒt hond and vnder þy felowys lyft hond, and take þe bowe D of h^s ryʒt hond reu*er*ced þorow hys bowe; [*f.* 65r] and yn þe same maner þy bowe B lyft schal take hys bowe C ryʒth, and þy C lyft hys B ryʒt, and þy D lyft hys A ryʒt. Þen schal ⟨A⟩ of þy ryʒt hond take backeward of þy felows hond þe bowe D lyft þorow hys bowe reu*er*ced, and yn þe same manere þy B ryʒt schal take hys C lyft, and þy C ryʒt hys B lyft, and þy D ryʒt hys A lyft.

TO make a lace cheyne brode: Take 8 bowes of ij colo*ur*s, & set on þyne hondes in þe man*er*e of þe lace bend. And þen schal A ryʒt change hys bowe w^t D lyft, so þat A ryʒt take þe bowe of D lyft þorow hys bowe reu*er*ced, & [*f.* 65v] in þe same maner schal A lyft þorow hys bow wyt D ryʒt, and B ryʒt wyt C lyft, a⟨nd⟩ B lyft w^t C ryʒt.

A las cheueron of 12 bowes: Set 3 bowes of o colo*ur* on A, B, C on þy ryʒt hond, and oþ*er* 3 bowes of þ^e self colo*ur* on þy felowys lyft

* MS colour*er*, *both occurrences.*

hond, & 3 bowes of anoþer colour on B, C, D on þy lyft hond, and 3
bowes of þe same colour on þy felows ry3t hond. Þen schal þow take
wyth A on þy lyft hond B of þe same hond reuerced, so þat þe syde þat
was bytwene A & B ⟨be⟩fore þe takyng* dewelle stylle. And þe syde
þᵗ was beneþᵉ ⟨on⟩ B ⟨be⟩fore þe takyng be aboue on A after þe takyng.
Þen schal B in same manere [f. 66r] take þe bow of C, and C of D;
schal D lyft take þe ouer syde of C ry3t reuerced, so þat þe syde þᵗ was
betwene C and B ry3t afore þe takyng be byneþe D lyft aftur þe takyng.
Þen schal C ryth take þe bowe of B lyft reuerced, so þᵗ þe syde þᵗ was
abouet on B be byneþe on C. In þe same maner schal B take þe bowe
of A reuerced. And loke alway when þᵘ schalt reuerce þy bowes þᵗ
eyþer hond help oþer. Þen schal A ry3t go þorow B, C of þe same hond
and enter B, C, D of þe lyft hond by þe ende of þy fyngrys and take þe
ouer syde of A lyft reuerced. And when þys ys in wyrkyng þy felow, þᵗ
syt- [f. 66v] typ on þy ry3t hond, schal wyrk wᵗ hys ry3t hond as þᵘ
dudyst wᵗ þy lyft hond and wᵗ hys lyft hond as þᵘ dudyst wᵗ þy ry3t
hond. And when 3e haue boþe ydone in þys maner 3e schal change
3owr ouer bowes of 3owre next hondes.

A brode lace cheueron of 8 bowes: Set 4 bowes of o colour on A, B
on boþe hondys, & 4 bowes of anoþer colour on C, D on boþe hondys.
Þen schal A ry3t take þoro3 D, C, B lyft þe bowe of A lyft vnreuerced.
Þen hye þy lyft bowys, and set þe same bowe on D lyft þat was taken
of A lyft. Þenne schal A lyft take þorow D, C, B [f. 67r] ry3t þe bowe of
A ry3t vnreuerced. Þen hey þy ry3t bowest, and set þe self bowe on
D þᵗ was taken of A. Þen schal D ry3t change hys bowe wᵗ D lyft. Þen
reuerce alle þy bowes and begyn a3en.

A round cheueron of 8 bowes: (Omnia sicut prius) saue whan þᵘ
hast changyd D ry3t wᵗ D lyft þu schalt change A ry3t wᵗ A lyft, and
reuersyng also. A cheueron of 16 bowes: Set 8 bowes of o colour on
3owre next hond on A, B and on C, D of 3owr ferþer hond, and 8 bowes
of anoþer colour set on A, B on 3owr ferþer hond and C, D on 3owr
next hond. Þen take boþe wyth A of 3our [f. 67v] next hond þorow alle
þe bowes of þe same hond and þe ferþer hond þe bowe A vnreuerced.
Þen hye þy bowes of þe ferþer hondys, and D of þe same hond schal
take D of þe next hond vnreuersed. Þen lowe 3owre bowes of 3owre
next hondys. Þen schal 3e change 3ouur neþur bowes of 3ouur next
hondys, and yn euery changyng reuerce al 3owre bowes. A cheueron
rounde of 16 bowes: wyrke as 3e dud yn þe chyueron brode of 16
bowes; and when 3e haue ychanged þe bowes of 3ouur next hondys
þen schal 3e change 3ouur bowes of 3ouur ferþer hondys. Þen reuerce
al þe bowes. A lace pen§- [f. 68r] powerer: Take 4 bowes of grene and

* t corr. fr. m.　　† MS a bowe.　　‡ hond expuncted before bowes.
§ Catchword powerer.

set on A, B on ʒowr* next hondys, & 4 rede bowes on C, D on ʒouur next hondys, and 4 blake bowes on A, B on ʒouur ferþer hond, and iiij whyte oþer blew on C, D on ʒouur ferþer hondys. And þenne wyrke as in þe cheueron brode of 16 bowes tyl þe grene bowes be on A, B on ʒouur ferþer hondys. Þen schal ʒe wyrke wᵗ ʒouur ferþer hondys as ʒe dud wᵗ ʒouur next hondys tyl þe grene bowes be aʒen on A, B on ʒouur next hondys, and þen begyn aʒen. & yf þᵘ wol make þᵉ lace round do in þe maner as aforand; & when ʒe haue changed þe ouer bowes of [*f.* 68v] ʒowr* next hondys ʒe schul change þe ouer bowes of ʒouur ferþer hondz, and begyn aʒen. **A** brode lace wᵗ cros and olyet: ⟨Take⟩ 12 ⟨bowes⟩ and set on þyne hondys and on þy felows hondys as in þᵉ lace cheueron of xij bowes, and wyrke boþe as in þᵉ selue lace, tyl þe iij tyme þᵗ þᵘ se alle þᵉ bowys be of o colour; and þen wyrke boþᵉ wᵗ ʒouur next hondys as ʒe dud wyth ʒour fe⟨r⟩-þer hondys, tyl ʒe se þᵗ þe colour be changed thryes. Þen schul ʒe boþe wyrke aʒene wyt ʒouur ferþer hondes as ʒe dud at þᵉ begynnyng; and loke þᵗ ʒouur next hondes acorde yn colour and yn worke, & ʒouur fer- [*f.* 69r] þer hondys also†. And when þᵘ hast changed iij wᵗ þy felow al þy bowes of þyne hond schulle be of o colouur; also when þᵘ and þy felow haue changed 9 tymes þe colouur of þyne one honde schal be changed iij, & þen schal ʒe change þe worchyng of ʒouur hond as hyt ys ywryte before.

   A round lace wyþ cros and olyet: Set 12 bowes on ʒouur hondys, & wyrke yn þe same maner of þe brode lace wᵗ cros and olyet. And when ʒe schul change ʒouur bowes of ʒouur next hondys ʒe schul change þᵉ ouer bowes of ʒouur ferþer hondys. And yf þᵘ wolt [*f.* 69v] þat þe lace be grete take a whyp-corde and knyt þᵗ o ende wᵗ þy bowes and þᵗ oþer ende bytwene þe and þy felow. And when ʒe schul change þe bowys of ʒouur next hondys ʒe schulle change beneþe þᵉ corde and ʒouur ferþer hondys aboue þe corde‡. **A** lace ounde brode of 16 bowes: Set 8 bowys of ⟨o⟩ colouur on A, B on ʒouur hondys, and 8 bowes of anoþer colour on C, D on ʒouur hondz, and wyrk as in þᵉ cheueron of 8 bowes; and þen schul ʒe change þᵉ ouer bowes of ʒowr next hondys. **A** lace ounde rounde of 16 bowys: Omnia ut supra, saue when ʒe haue changed þe ouer bowes of ʒour [*f.* 70r] next hondys ʒe schul change þe ouer bowes of ʒouur forþer hondys. **A** grene dorge of v⟨j⟩ bowes: Set 4 bowes of o colouur on B, C ryʒt and B, C lyft, and o bowe of anoþer colouur on D ryʒt, and o bowe of anoþer colouur on A lyft. Þen take wᵗ A riʒt þorow B, C ryʒt þe bowe of C lyft reuerced. Þen lowe þy bowe of B lift vnto C. Þen schal B lyft take þorow C lyft þe bowe C ryʒt reuerced. Þen lowe þy ryʒt bowes. Þen schal A lyft change wᵗ D ryʒt, &c(ete)ra.

---

* MS ʒowrer   † a corde yn colouur *expuncted before* also.
‡ *Corr. fr.* cordys.

A grene dorge of 12: Take a felow, and set on hys hondes v⟨j⟩ bowes, & set on þyne hondys yn þe maner of grene dorge of 6 bowes, & wyrke [*f.* 70v] as ȝe dud in þe same lace. Þen schul ȝe set þe ou*er* bowes of ȝou*ur* next hondys on A on ȝou*ur* ferþ*er* hondys, and change ȝou*ur* bowes B of ȝowr next hondes. Þen schul ȝe w*t* A of ȝou*ur* next hondz take the bowe A aȝen þat sytte on ȝoure ferþ*er* hondys, and begyn aȝen, &c(ete)*ra*. A lace for hattys: Take a felow, & wyrke as in þe lace comyn rounde of v bowes, and change þe ou*er* bowes of ȝou*ur* next hondys and þe ou*er* bowes of ȝou*ur* ferþ*er* hondys alle vnreu*er*ced. A lace for hattys: Take ij felows, and set on þy ryȝt hond one and on þy lyft hond another.

QUEEN MARY COLLEGE, UNIVERSITY OF LONDON

NOTES

[1] BM MS Addit. 6293, see infra, calls them "string(e)s."

[2] See especially Mrs F[anny] Bury Palliser, *History of Lace*, 3rd edn (London: Sampson Low, 1875), pp. 252–3; rev. M[argaret] Jourdain and Alice Dryden (London: Sampson Low, 1910), pp. 286–7; *Encyclopaedia Britannica*, 11th edn (1911), XVI, "Lace" by A. S. Cole, pp. 37–8.

[3] Carleton Brown and Rossell Hope Robbins, *The Index of Middle English Verse* (New York: Columbia Univ. Press, 1943), and Rossell Hope Robbins and John L. Cutler, *Supplement to The Index of Middle English Verse* (Lexington, Kentucky: Univ. of Kentucky Press, 1965), 1171; Willard E. Farnham (ed.), "The Dayes of the Mone," *SP*, 20 (1923), pp. 70–82. Cf. John Edwin Wells, *Second Supplement to A Manual of the Writings in Middle English 1050–1400* (New Haven, Conn.: Connecticut Academy, 1923), p. 1071; *MED*, Plan and Bibliography, p. 91. The connection of these verses with some by John Crophill (on whom see Rossell Hope Robbins, "John Crophill's Ale-Pots," *RES*, 44 (1969), pp. 182–9), is discussed by Farnham, and by M. Förster, *Anglia* 67 (1944), pp. 133–6.

[4] Except in the case of rare words, the etymology of which is discussed, spelling variants are not given in this introduction to the text.

[5] *OED*'s "Open," a., 7., and cf. the nineteenth-century term "Open-work," is not applicable. The "open lace of v bowys" of ff. 55r and v calls for no complication of any kind, and none of the strings in MS Addit. shows any interstices.

[6] Cf. *OED*, s.v. "Chain," sb., 19., "Chain-lace," quots. 1578, 1598, the former of which at least is wrongly explained.

[7] See J. Gwillim *Display of Heraldry*, (London, 1610), p. 198; and *OED*, s.v. "Counter-componed."

6

VERBAL RHYMING IN CHAUCER

BY TAUNO F. MUSTANOJA

In his admirable study of Chaucer's rhymes Michio Masui lists seven tendencies distinguishable in the way in which the poet builds up the ends of his lines.[1] One of these is a tendency to use verbs and particularly infinitives for this purpose. Is "verbal rhyming" a distinctive characteristic of Chaucer's poetic diction?

According to Masui, this inclination is "quite strong."[2] His authority on this point is Franz Beschorner, who published a special study of the subject some fifty years ago in much stronger terms.[3] Pointing out Chaucer's fondness for using infinitives as terminal elements of his lines, he claimed that the poet's predilection for verbal rhyming was uncommonly strong (*ausserordentlich stark*).[4] He arrived at this conclusion after calculating the ratio of verbal rhymes to non-verbal ones and to the verbal forms which occurred outside rhyme. He paid particular attention to the frequent occurrence of "gan" (the preterite of "gin") in connection with infinitives to form what might be called a periphrastic preterite (e.g., "What nedeth yow to tellen . . . How men gan hym with clothes for to lade," *TC* II, 1544) and to enable the poet to place the infinitive at the end of the line.[5] Beschorner also made some interesting observations concerning the chronology of Chaucer's works in the light of his verbal rhyming and his use of "gin."

In reading Middle English poetry I have often wondered whether the extensive use of verbs as terminal words of lines is really a Chaucerian peculiarity at all. I have had a strong impression that this aspect of Chaucer's versification is a reflection of a rather general trend, and it seems to me that for a full understanding of his art of rhyming it is necessary to look at the matter from a wider angle and try to have an idea of its occurrence in other poems of the period.

A convenient point of starting the discussion is a brief summary of *Anhang* 2 at the end of Beschorner's study, where he presents his findings in tabular form. The relevant parts of his tables are those columns which give the frequencies of the use of verbs and infinitives as rhyme words, calculated as percentages from the total number of the rhymes.[6]

	Verbal Rhymes per cent	Infinitive Rhymes per cent
Book of the Duchess	21.51	8.10
House of Fame	26.88	12.97
Legend of Good Women	31.27	15.39
Cant. Tales (couplet form)	22.89	10.21
Cant. Tales (stanzaic form)	30.24	14.42
Troilus and Criseyde	38.5	20.4
Minor stanzaic poems, excluding short ones	29.87–36.84	14.29–23.31

I have examined Beschorner's results in the light of samples taken from Middle English non-Chaucerian poetry, using the criteria he mentions at the beginning of his study.[7] Practically all the samples were from verse written in four-stress couplets. For the sake of comparison I also examined passages from two Old French texts written in octosyllabic couplets.

Even a superficial glance at some non-Chaucerian poems is enough to make one doubt whether a considerable use of verbs at the end of a line is a distinctive feature of Chaucer's verse. When I say this I am not thinking particularly of accumulations of verbal rhymes, such as the following one from *Cursor Mundi*:

> "Thoru þis prophet sal yee se
> To quam þe mai sal spused be.
> Sir Ysai, þat ald prophet,
> Wel lang siþen þat he yow hett
> Of rote of Iesse þar suld spring
> A wand þat suld a flur forth bring,
> Bath flur and frut suld þarof brest,
> þe hali gast þeron suld rest."
> Thoru þat voice þai þar cun here,
> þai said, "þis wand suld fluring bere
> þat suld o rote o Iesse spring."   (10717–27)

or this one from Gower's *Confessio Amantis*:

> "Florent be thi name,
> Thou hast on honde such a game,
> That bot thou be the betre avised,
> Thi deth is schapen and devised,
> That al the world ne mai the save,

Bot if that thou my conseil have."
  Florent, whan he this tale herde,
Unto this olde wyht answerde
And of hir conseil he hir preide.
And sche ayein to him thus seide:
"Florent, if I for the so schape,
That thou thurgh me thi deth ascape. . . ."

                                           (I, 1541-52)

or this from the same text:

    . . . and for Envie
Upon alle othre thei aspie;
And for hem lacketh that thei wolde,
Thei kepte that non other scholde
Touchende of love his cause spede:
Wherof a gret ensample I rede,
Which unto this matiere acordeth,
As Ovide in his bok recordeth,
How Poliphemus whilom wroghte,
Whan that he Galathee besoghte
Of love, which he mai noght lacche.
That made him forto waite and wacche
Be alle weies how it ferde,
Til ate laste he knew and herde. . . . (II, 99-112)

In the passages studied (in all 800 lines), *Confessio Amantis* had a noticeably higher percentage of verbal rhymes (41.1 per cent) than Chaucer's two original four-stress poems, *The Book of the Duchess* and *The House of Fame*, counting the total number of rhymes. The percentage of infinitives was 14.8. Gower's *In Praise of Peace*, written in rhyme royal, had practically the same frequency of verbal rhymes (39.1 per cent) as Chaucer's *Troilus and Criseyde*, but had fewer infinitives in rhyme (13.5 per cent). The fact that this poem of Gower's showed a lower percentage of infinitives (13.5) than of past participles (16.6) in rhyme, thus reversing the situation in *Confessio Amantis* (14.8 and 7.6), is clearly due to the difference between the types of poetry which these two poems represent.

In two other poems with four-stress meter the situation was roughly similar to that of *Confessio Amantis*, though verbal rhymes were slightly less numerous. In *Kyng Alisaunder* they amounted to 30.5 per cent, in *Cursor Mundi* to 35 per cent. The percentages of infinitives were 11.3 and 15, respectively. In one of the three early Middle English texts examined, *King Horn*, the proportions were practically the same: 34.5 per cent of all lines ended in a verb and 17.3 per cent in an infinitive. In *The Owl and the Nightingale* the figures were somewhat smaller, 28 per cent for all verbal rhymes and 9.3 per cent for infinitives. In *Genesis and Exodus* 32.3 per cent of the lines had a verb at the end. The proportion of past participles was considerable, 13.5 per cent, but for the infinitives the count (9.8 per cent) was no higher than it was for *The Owl and the Nightingale*, in spite of the fact that the author apparently made no conscious effort to avoid them:

> Ðo ne migte he non louerd ðhauen,
> Ðat him sulde ðhinge grauen.
> "Min fligt," he seide, "ic wile up-taken,
> Min sete norð on heuene maken,
> And ðor ic wile sitten and sen
> Al ðe ðhinges ðe in werde ben." (275–80)

My counts were made from a very limited number of texts, and naturally they can only claim to have suggestive value. The list of works included could have been made many times longer, but even admitting that the counts would have shown a certain amount of variation I doubt whether the overall picture would have been very much different. There do not seem to be sufficient reasons for believing that the extent to which Chaucer used verbs and infinitives at the ends of his lines is an individual trait in his art of versification.

Nor is there any ground for assuming that a tendency to use verbal rhymes occurred only in English poetry of the Middle Ages. It is common in Old French and Middle High German works. The counts I carried out in two octosyllabic thirteenth-century French poems, Huon le Roi's *Le vair palefroi* and Marie de France's *Le lai de Lanval* yielded the following data: total number of verbal rhymes, 36.5 and 43.5 per cent; infinitives in rhyme, 17 and 10.5 per cent; past participles, 13 and 14.5 per cent.

The tendency to favour verbs as rhyme words is obviously a rather general phenomenon and is not limited to medieval poetry. It is common in the Renaissance and can be illustrated by the following short passage from Marlowe's *Hero and Leander*:

> Her breath as fragrant as the morning rose,
> Her mind pure, and her tongue untaught to gloze;
> Yet proud she was, for lofty pride that dwells
> In towered courts is oft in shepherds' cells,
> And too too well the fair vermilion knew,
> And silver tincture of her cheeks, that drew
> The love of every swain. On her this god

Enamoured was, and with his snaky rod
Did charm her nimble feet, and made her stay,
The while upon a hillock down he lay,
And sweetly on his pipe began to play,
And with smooth speech her fancy to assay;
Till in his twining arms he locked her fast,
And then he wooed with kisses, and at last,
As shepherds do, her on the ground he laid,
And tumbling in the grass, he often strayed
Beyond the bounds of shame . . .

(First sestiad, 391–407)

and also by Ben Jonson's epigram *To my Bookseller*:

Thou that mak'st gain thy end, and wisely well
    Call'st a book good or bad as it doth sell,
Use mine so too, I give thee leave; but crave,
    For the luck's sake, it thus much favor have,
To lie upon thy stall till it be sought,
    Not offered, as it made suit to be bought;
Nor have my title-leaf on posts or walls,
    Or in cleft-sticks, advanced to make calls
For termers, or some clerk-like servingman
    Who scarce can spell th'hard names, whose knight less can.
If, without these vile arts, it will not sell,
    Send it to Bucklersbury, there 'twill well.

Just to get a numerical idea of Pope's use of verbal rhymes I counted them in the first two hundred lines of his *Essay on Man*. The result was: verbal rhymes, 35 per cent of all rhymes; infinitives, 10 per cent; past participles, 5.5 per cent. Pope uses relatively fewer infinitives in rhyme than Chaucer does; otherwise there is little difference.

It is difficult to account for this tendency to use verbs as the rhyming element of a line. Beschorner, referring to the elementary fact that in linguistic communication the advancing element is normally conveyed by the verb, believes that the reason for placing a verb at the end of the line is a desire to add to the vividness and concreteness of the narrative.[8] There is, perhaps, a kernel of truth in this; but it must be borne in mind that verbal forms differ considerably with respect to descriptive force. A finite form is normally a more forceful vehicle of the verbal idea than a non-finite one, and a non-finite form has normally a greater expressive force when it occurs in close combination with an auxiliary (e.g., *has made, is made, will go, is waiting, came riding*) than when the association with the finite verb is less close. And there are differences due to the form. The ending of the third person singular of the present indicative, -(*e*)*th*, for example, has little flexibility; it can usually rhyme only with itself—

> þe kyng þan wiþ his ost wendeþ;
> To many cite his sonde he sendeþ
>
> (*Kyng Alisaunder*, 2903–4)

and the same is often the case with the preterite form—

> Diverse folk diversely they seyde,
> But for the moore part they loughe and pleyde. (*CT*, I, 3857–8)

The most obvious reason for the relative popularity of the infinitive form as a rhyme word is its syntactical flexibility. It is usually attached to a short, monosyllabic, auxiliary verb, *shall, will, can, may, do, gin*, and the like, and this arrangement, which is more or less loose in character, provides a convenient means of placing the infinitive at the end of the line. This device of rhyme-making survived long after the Middle English period. Drayton, for example, makes frequent use of the combination of *do* and an infinitive, as a poetical convention, as shown by this passage from the thirteenth song of his *Poly-Olbion*:

> Here Arden of herself ceased any more to show
> And with her sylvan joys the muse along doth go.
> When Phoebus lifts his head out of the winter's wave,
> No sooner doth the earth her flowery bosom brave,
> At such time as the year brings on the pleasant spring,
> But Hunts-up to the morn the feathered sylvans sing . . . (39–44)

Another great advantage in building up a metrical line was that the infinitive could be used with or without *to* or *for to*, almost at will—

> Til that the belle of laudes gan to rynge,
> And freres in the chauncel gonne synge. (*CT*, I, 3655–6)

Beschorner's statement that Chaucer's tendency to use verbal rhymes was *ausserordentlich stark* is misleading, because it implies that he used them more extensively than did other poets of the time. This was not the case; he was only conforming his technique to established usage. I have the impression that he used this device with considerably greater flexibility than his predecessors had done, but the evidence on which my study was based was too limited to allow any definite statement on this point.[9]

UNIVERSITY OF HELSINKI

NOTES

1 Michio Masui, *The Structure of Chaucer's Rime Words* (Tokyo: Kenkyusha, 1964), p. 263.

2 Ibid., p. 138.

3 Franz Beschorner, *Verbale Reime bei Chaucer*, Studien zur englischen Philologie, 60 (Halle/Saale: Niemeyer, 1920).

4 Ibid., pp. 1 and 3.

5 Cf. my *Middle English Syntax*, Part I, Mémoires de la Société Néophilologique de Helsinki, 23 (Helsinki: Société Néophilologique, 1960), pp. 610–15, and H. M. Smyser, "Chaucer's Use of *Gin* and *Do*," *Spec.*, 42, 1967, pp. 68–83.

6 Beschorner gives no information concerning the ratio of verbal rhymes to verbal forms outside rhyme, apart from a passing mention that the *Physician's Tale* contains altogether 402 verbal forms, 74 of them (18.41 per cent) in rhyme. Accordingly, I have not counted this ratio in the texts which I have examined.

7 The following texts were examined: Gower's *Confessio Amantis*, edited by G. C. Macaulay (800 lines of Books I and II); Gower's *In Praise of Peace*, edited by Macaulay (the whole poem, 385 lines); *Kyng Alisaunder*, edited by G. V. Smithers, EETS 227 (400 lines); *Cursor Mundi*, MS Cotton, edited by R. Morris, EETS 59 (400 lines); *King Horn*, MS Camb. Gg. 4.27, edited by W. H. French and Ch. B. Hale, *Middle English Metrical Romances* (400 lines); *The Owl and the Nightingale*, MS Cotton, edited by E. G. Stanley (400 lines); *Genesis and Exodus*, edited by O. Arngart (400 lines); Huon le Roi, *Le vair palefroi*, edited by A. Långfors (200 lines); Marie de France, *Le lai de Lanval*, edited by J. Rychner (200 lines).

8 Beschorner, op. cit., pp. 1–2.

9 A graduate student of mine, Mrs Leena Poduschkin, is planning a comprehensive study of the subject.

7

AN INTERPRETATION OF *ALYSOUN*

BY THEO STEMMLER

This poem is preserved in the famous MS Harley 2253, which was written at Hereford *c.* 1340[1] and contains among other texts the most important love-lyrics before the time of Chaucer. Apart from *Sumer is icumen in, Alysoun* is certainly the best known Middle English lyric: it represents a standard item in anthologies used by specialized medievalists[2] as well as in collections of English lyrics intended for a larger reading public.[3] Since its first publication in 1790[4] it has attracted not only the interest of the philologist, but also the admiration of the general reader. The unanimous appreciation which the poem has found can be accounted for by aesthetic properties which so far have never been precisely analysed. The following quotation may serve as a typical example of the vagueness which has been so prominent in discussions of this poem:

> This is a poem of *delightful freshness* and *melody*. In particular, the burden or refrain *sings* itself, and, though there is need to *feel for* the rhythm at many points . . . the rhythm of the entire poem is *lyrical*.[5]

The following analysis constitutes an attempt to replace uncritical opinion by reasoned judgement.

The rhyme-scheme of *Alysoun* is: a b / a b / / b b b c DDDC. In other words: the poem consists of four tripartite stanzas with refrain. By repeating the b-rhyme the poet has established a close connection between parts 1/2 and 3. He has made use of a rhyme-scheme which on account of its difficulty was not at all usual among English poets of his time. The high artistic level of *Alysoun*—and of many other poems from the same manuscript—becomes apparent when we compare the Harleian poems with lyrics of the thirteenth century. The latter are predominantly written in rather simple stanza-forms, i.e.: a a a a, a a b b, a b a b, a a b c c b.[6] It is, moreover, remarkable that many poems of the thirteenth century are not composed in stanzaic form at all.[7] It is only in the poems of MS Harley 2253 that more difficult stanza-forms predominate.

Since rhyme-schemes similar to that used in *Alysoun* can be found in earlier lyrics of Old French and Provençal poets,[8] the existence of Continental influence may be assumed. The fact that c is, properly speaking, a "waif" and rhymes only with the last line of the refrain points in the same direction. It is not usual in Middle English lyrics, but characteristic of many Old French and Provençal poems that in all four stanzas line c ends with the same rhyme ("-oun"), thus connecting each stanza with the refrain.

In *Alysoun* the poet has succeeded, moreover, in connecting stanzas 2, 3, 4 more closely by repeating identical rhymes:

Stanza 2:	Stanza 3:	Stanza 4:
. . . .	wake	forwake
blake	. . . .	. . . .
. . . .	sake	make
ymake	. . . .	. . . .
take	. . . .	. . . .
make	. . . .	. . . .
forsake	. . . .	. . . .
. . . .	. . . .	. . . .

He has evidently tried to avoid a simple repetition of the same words rhyming on "-ake." He has made use of the various shades of meaning existing between the primary word and its prefixed derivation: *wake —forwake*. Etymological word-play such as in *forsake—sake*, *ymake —make* remind the reader of the many *adnominationes* found in medieval Latin and Romance lyrics. The poet has made a virtue of necessity, i.e. the relative scarcity of rhymes in the Germanic languages.

The number of stresses varies in each stanza and sometimes—as in many other Middle English poems—cannot be firmly ascertained. These metrical "irregularities" can be explained in two different ways. Either the textual state of the poem is corrupt[9] or the poet has tried to avoid monotony by modifying the basic metrical pattern.[10] The first theory is discredited by the observation that *Alysoun* does not contain any textual cruxes: the extant text of the poem seems to be correct. The second theory is corroborated by the fact that the metrical "irregularities" of the poem follow a clearly recognizable pattern. The corresponding lines of stanza 2 and 3 have the same number of stresses: 44/44//4443. Likewise the lines of stanza 1 and 4 (except lines 5 and 6) contain the same number of stresses: 43/43// 34 (?) 33 and 43/43//4333. If the metrical perfection of other lyrics from MS Harley 2253[11] is taken into account, one is inclined to regard the observed metrical symmetry of *Alysoun* as intended by the poet rather than as a casual phenomenon.

Though *Alysoun* shares essential features with the carol—stanzas with refrain—it is very far from being one of those generally simple carols whose usual rhyme-scheme was a a a b BB.[12] In contrast to many carols the refrain of *Alysoun* is metrically—and thematically (see below)—connected with the various stanzas. For this reason Degginger's contention[13] that the poem consists of "courtly" stanzas and a "popular," older refrain must be rejected. *Alysoun* cannot be compared with the carol *Blow, northerne wynd* from the same manuscript: indeed in that poem we observe only a loose thematic connection between stanzas and burden.

In *Alysoun* the thematic structure is also remarkable. This poem does not—unlike many other medieval poems—consist of a rather arbitrarily arranged sequence of motifs. It is, on the contrary, a well-constructed textual unit. There is a thematic caesura after every fourth line. Four different groups of motifs are recognizable and are presented in the typical order of medieval love-poems: *Natureingang* (motif A); praise of the beloved (motif B); description of the lover (motif C); prayer for the lady's indulgence (motif D). These motifs, however, do not follow one after another as isolated units; some of them are repeated in several passages of the poem. The *descriptio pulchritudinis* of stanza 2 (ll. 13–16) is continued in stanza 3 (ll. 26–9). The lover's condition is dealt with in stanza 3 (ll. 22–5) as well as in stanza 4 (ll. 31–4). These four groups of motifs are, moreover, separated by lyrical passages (motif x), where the lover complains of his "sweet suffering" (ll. 5–8, 17–20, 35–6). This may be summarized in the following diagram:

stanza 1:　　　　stanza 2:　　　stanza 3:　　　stanza 4:

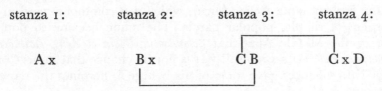

A x　　　　　　B x　　　　　C B　　　　C x D

It becomes apparent that stanzas 2, 3, 4 are closely connected by thematic repetition. Thus these three stanzas form a unit not only on account of the partial identity of their rhymes (see above), but also of their thematic connection.

In spite of the close coherence of stanzas 2, 3, 4 the spring opening is not isolated from the rest of the poem. At the time when *Alysoun* was written it had become fashionable to begin a poem with a spring opening. Very often such a *Natureingang* was prefixed to the poem proper without any apparent reason or connection. This is not the case in our poem. In *Alysoun* the spring opening is organically incorporated into the structure of the stanza. This close connection is achieved by two different formal techniques: rhyme and alliterative line-linking. The spring opening (ll. 1–4) and the lyrical effusion (ll.5–8) are linked by identical rhyme (b : b) and identical alliteration (*lud—libbe, loue—longinge*).

The spring opening itself is thoroughly conventional. More than two centuries before *Alysoun* William IX of Aquitaine had written:

> Ab la dolchor del *temps novel*
> *Foillo li bosc,* e *li aucel*
> *Chanton* chascus *en lor lati*
> Segon lo vers del novel chan . . .

Only the phrase "*sp*ray beginneþ to *sp*ringe" connects the spring opening of *Alysoun* with native poetic traditions. It is one of those numerous alliterative formulas which can often be traced back to Old English poetry.[14] The same phrase occurs in a carol of *c.* 1300:

> No[u] spri[nke]s the sprai,
> al for loue icche am so seeke
> that slepen i ne mai.[15]

The spring opening is followed by a lyrical passage where the lover describes his relation to his beloved in typically courtly diction: he is in her "power;" only the beloved can bring him "bliss," etc. The same hyperbolical language is used in the ensuing refrain: the beloved is his "destiny;" he will love only her, etc. Only the name Alysoun fails to fit into this courtly milieu. Alysoun is a continuation of the French name Aëliz (Alice), which was commonly used in the burdens of simple, popular carols. The name became so popular during the Middle Ages that "*chanter de Robin et Aéliz était devenu synonyme de chanter des rondes.*"[16] It is not by chance that in his *Canterbury Tales* Chaucer gave some of his bourgeois heroines the name of Alysoun or Alice.[17]

The second stanza begins with words of praise for the beloved. As in numerous other medieval love-poems the lady's beauty is described in detail. Following a long literary tradition, the poet proceeds in his description from head to foot. Some details, however, are unconventional: the lady's eyebrows are brown, her eyes black. The majority of medieval *descriptiones pulchritudinis* speak of black, curved eyebrows. Matthew of Vendôme writes:

Nigra supercilia via lactea separat, arcus dividui prohibent luxuriare pilos.[18]

In the Middle English love-lyric *Mosti ryden by Rybbesdale* from MS Harley 2253 we read:

> Heo haþ browes *bend* an heh,
> whyt bytuene ant nout to neh.[19]

In his *Miller's Tale* Chaucer praises the beauty of Alysoun:

> Ful smale ypulled were hire browes two,
> And tho were *bent* and *blake* as any sloo.[20]

In the colour of his lady's eyes the poet of *Alysoun* deviates from the medieval canon, too. In most Middle English poems the colour of eyes is "grey."[21] In *Mosti ryden by Rybbesdale* just mentioned we read:

> hyre eyȝen aren grete ant gray ynoh.

The other details of the *descriptio pulchritudinis* in *Alysoun*, however, are conventional: like countless other beautiful women in medieval literature Alysoun is provided with a slender waist and a swan-white neck.

The detailed praise of the beloved is summarized in several hyperbolical phrases. Alysoun is "semlokest of alle þynge" (l. 6), "feyrest may in toune" (l. 29) and "geynest vnder gore" (l. 37). In these three examples the poet has made use of a special kind of hyperbole—the hyperoche. The pattern of this rhetorical figure is:

> *Non est talis mulier super terram in aspecto, in pulchritudine, et in sensu verborum.*[22]

The phrase "feyrest may in toune" is very similar to the original statement of the formula that the beloved surpasses all other women on earth.[23]

Conventional is the so-called *Topos der Unsagbarkeit* (topos of ineffability) in ll. 26–7:

> In world nis non so wyter mon
> þat al hire bounte telle con.

The poet's hyperbolical statement that nobody can adequately praise the qualities of the beloved can be found in many medieval poems. Thibaut de Champagne writes in one of his poems:

> *Ses granz biautez, dont nus hons n'a pouoir qu'il en deist la cinquantisme part . . .*[24]

Chaucer uses the same *topos* in his *Miller's Tale*:

> There nys no man so wys that koude thenche
> So gay a popelote or swich a wench.[25]

At the beginning of stanzas 3 and 4 the poet depicts the lover's deplorable condition. The symptoms of the love-sickness as described in *Alysoun* are well known from other medieval love-lyrics: the lover is sleepless, wan, weary, etc. However, by representing these traditional details in strikingly new formulations the poet of *Alysoun* has succeeded in anglicizing old Continental commonplaces:

> 23   Nihtes when y *w*ende ant *w*ake—
>   forþi myn *w*onges *w*axeþ *w*on— . . .

> 31   Icham for *w*owyng al for*w*ake,
>   *w*ery so *w*ater in *w*ore . . .

In both these quotations the poet has again made use of the native technique of alliterative line-linking, as can be seen in the two lines containing the motif of the lover's sleeplessness which are formally linked by identical alliteration (w). The bold comparison with "water in wore" which occurs in *Maximion* from the same manuscript (l. 127)[26] would appear to represent another traditional alliterative formula.

The poem ends with an apostrophe: the lover prays the beloved to comply with his request. This motif is again commonplace, but appears in an anglicized form, combined, as it is, with a well-known alliterative formula:[27]

> 37   *g*eynest vnder *g*ore,
>   herkne to my roun.

In *Alysoun*, then, the conventions of the Continental courtly love-lyric are modified by means of native literary techniques and it is, above all, the use of the various possibilities offered by alliterative technique which play a central part in this process of anglicization. The poet's complete mastery of rhyme, metre and structure help to make *Alysoun* an exceptional example of Middle English poetry before Chaucer. Despite its formal perfection this poem conveys an unaffected and unpretentious impression.[28] This "simple complexity" is the reason why *Alysoun* has always been appreciated, but rarely understood.

UNIVERSITY OF BOCHUM

NOTES

1 On the localization and dating of MS Harley 2253 see N. R. Ker (ed.), *Facsimile of BM MS Harley 2253* (EETS, OS 255, 1965), pp. xxi–xxiii; Th. Stemmler, "*Zur Datierung des MS Harley 2253*," *Anglia*, 80 (1962), pp. 111–18.

2 Cf. Carleton Brown (ed.), *English Lyrics of the XIIIth Century* (Oxford: Clarendon Press, 1932), pp. 138–9; G. L. Brook, *The Harley Lyrics*, 3rd edn (Manchester: Manchester Univ. Press, 1964), p. 33; Rolf Kaiser, *Medieval English*, 3rd edn (Berlin: Rolf Kaiser, 1958), p. 466.

3 Cf. R. T. Davies (ed.), *Medieval English Lyrics* (London: Faber and Faber, 1963), pp. 67–8; Dieter Mehl (ed.), *English Poems—Englische Gedichte* (Munich: Langewiesche-Brandt, 1965), pp. 6–9; Celia and Kenneth Sisam, *Oxford Book of Medieval Verse* (Oxford: Clarendon Press, 1970), p. 107; Theodore Silverstein, *Medieval English Lyrics* (London: Arnold, 1971), pp. 85–7.

4 Joseph Ritson (ed.), *Ancient Songs from the Time of King Henry III to the Revolution* (London: J. Johnson, 1790), pp. 24–6.

5 Davies, op. cit., p. 313 (words italicized by author). Similarly vague are the statements of A. K. Moore, *The Secular Lyric in Middle English* (Lexington, Kentucky: Univ. of Kentucky Press, 1951), p. 68; M. T. C. Hogan, "A Critical Study of the English Lyrics of BM Harley 2253," Diss. Notre Dame, Indiana, 1962, p. 60.

6 About fifty out of seventy lyrics in Brown, op. cit., follow these rhyme-schemes.

7 Approximately twenty in Brown, op. cit.

8 It is used by Mestre Richart de Semilli: cf. Karl Bartsch, *Altfranzösische Romanzen und Pastourellen* (Leipzig: Vogel, 1870), III, p. 12; and Gaucelm Faidit: cf. H. J. Chaytor, *The Troubadours and England* (Cambridge: Cambridge Univ. Press, 1923), p. 137.

9 George Saintsbury is of this opinion; cf. his *History of English Prosody*, 3 vols. (London: Macmillan, 1906–10), I, p. 116; and his *Historical Manual of English Prosody* (London: Macmillan, 1910), p. 45.

10 View of Th. Stemmler, *Die englischen Liebesgedichte des MS Harley 2253* Diss. Bonn, 1961 (Bonn, 1962), p. 110; and Brook, op. cit., p. 18.

11 A good example of metrical subtlety is "In May hit murgeþ when hit dawes" (Brook, op. cit., pp. 44–5): the metre of the first stanza corresponds to that of the last, while the last parts of all four stanzas are metrically identical.

12 Cf. the collection of Richard Leighton Greene, *The Early English Carols* (Oxford: Clarendon Press, 1935). In "The Burden in Carols," *MLN*, 57 (1942), pp. 16–22, Rossell Hope Robbins shows that eighty-one per cent of all carols have burdens of two short lines.

13 Stuart H. L. Degginger, "The Earliest Middle English Lyrics, 1150–1325," Diss. Columbia 1953, p. 106.

14 Further examples of alliterative formulas in our poem are "blisse . . . bringe" (l. 7), "longe . . . lyuen" (l. 19), "feye . . . fallen" (l. 20).

15 Brown, op. cit., p. 119.

16 Alfred Jeanroy, *Les Origines de la poésie lyrique en France au moyen âge*, 3rd edn (Paris: Champion, 1924), p. 425.

17 Cf. the *Miller's Tale* and the *Wife of Bath's Prologue*.

18 I, Par. 56; Edmond Faral, *Les Arts poétiques du 12e et du 13e siècle* (Paris: Champion, 1924), p. 129.

19 Brook, op. cit., p. 37, ll. 25–6.

[20] F. N. Robinson (ed.), *The Complete Works of Geoffrey Chaucer*, 2nd edn (Boston: Houghton Mifflin, 1957), p. 49, ll. 3245–6.

[21] Cf. Stemmler, *Englischen Liebesgedichte*, op. cit., pp. 182–3.

[22] Judith, 11, 19; see Leonid Arbusow, *Colores Rhetorici*, 2nd edn (Göttingen: Vandenhoek & Ruprecht, 1963), p. 89.

[23] In this phrase "toune" does not mean "town," but "earth, world;" cf. Stemmler, *Englischen Liebesgedichte*, op. cit., pp. 135–8.

[24] Axel Wallensköld (ed.) (Paris: E. Champion, 1925), p. 19, ll. 33–4.

[25] Robinson, op. cit., p. 49, ll. 3253–54.

[26] Karl Boddeker (ed.), *Altenglische Dichtungen des Ms Harley 2253* (1878; rpt. Amsterdam: Rodopi, 1969), p. 249. Cf. another version in MS Digby 86 in Brown, op. cit., p. 97, l. 151.

[27] Cf. *Annot and John*, l. 16: "glad vnder gore" (Brook, op. cit., p. 31); *Maximion* (Digby 86), l. 149: "godlich ounder gore" (Brown, op. cit., p. 97).

[28] Cf. our poem with *Annot and John*, for instance (Brook, op. cit., pp. 31–2).

8

THE RHYTHM OF THE
ALLITERATIVE LONG LINE

BY CONSTANCE B. HIEATT

When George R. Stewart wrote in 1927 that an approach to the rhythm of the fourteenth-century alliterative line through Old English metrics was a case of *"ignotum per ignotius,"*[1] he had good grounds for such despair. The inadequacy of earlier metrical studies to explain the actual rhythm of Old English verse is amply documented in John C. Pope's *The Rhythm of Beowulf*,[2] which made a convincing rhythmic analysis of the older poetry possible. Now, thirty years after the publication of the original edition, Old English studies may have more to offer to students of Middle English alliterative poetry.

In her important book on the style and metre of *Sir Gawain and the Green Knight*,[3] Marie Borroff states that a system of musical annotation analogous to Pope's did not seem workable for *Gawain* (p. 272). Yet many of her findings suggest that the *Gawain*-line could be scanned in essentially the same way.[4] She demonstrates convincingly the four-stress basis of these lines, including those with three or more stressed syllables in the first half, and attributes the rhythmic effect to the reader's perception of the metrically stressed syllables as occurring at "regular—i.e., at formally equivalent—intervals in a continuum of time" (p. 191). Thus, while it may be impracticable to indicate the exact temporal relationships of syllables, a simpler version of the methods used in Old English prosodic studies might still be revealing. That is, we could proceed from Miss Borroff's identification of the "chief syllables" to indicate the boundaries of each metrical unit, or "measure."[5]

Thus, then, if we were to transpose a passage from *Gawain* as analysed by Miss Borroff, substituting for her *C* and *c* the symbols used in scanning Old English,[6] and then divide it into rhythmic measures with a bar before each primary stress, we would find lines 842–9 scanned as follows:

| Gawayn gly3t on þe | gome þat | godly hym | gret,

And | þu3t hit a | bolde burne þat þe | bur3 | a3te,

A | hoge haþel for þe | nonez, and of | hyghe | eldee;

Brode, | bry3t, watz his | berde, and al | beuer- | hwed, |

| Sturne, stif on þe | stryþþe on | stalworth | schonkez,

Felle | face as þe | fyre, and | fre of hys | speche;

And wel hym | semed for | soþe, as þe | segge | þu3t,

To lede a | lortschyp in | lee of | leudez ful | gode.[7]

However, such "measure" divisions show little about the rhythm of the passage. The "tendency toward isochrony" which Miss Borroff agrees is an essential element in the rhythmic principle (pp. 191–2) is not clarified by a system of notation that makes "bur3" roughly equivalent to "bolde burne þat þe." If this were an Old English line, most of us, following Pope,[8] would assume a "rest," that is, a pause, or its temporal equivalent in prolonged emphasis or syncopation, in the case of a one-syllable measure. Thus, in scanning a D or E verse, we would write *Beowulf* 194b "Higelāces | þegn ($\wedge$)," or 469a "bearn ($\wedge$) | Healfdenes,"[9] indicating the rest with a caret.

Various reasons might, of course, be advanced to argue that rests are a more dangerous concept in Middle English alliterative verse than in Old English.[10] One is that few critics would wish to maintain that Middle English narrative poetry was as closely associated with musical performance as Old English verse is thought to have been. Still, however it was read, recited, or sung, some rhythmical accommodation must also have been accomplished in Middle English, if only by a tendency to dwell on heavier syllables and hurry over light ones. And when we bear in mind the possibility of making use of pauses which arise naturally from the syntax,[11] some Middle English lines may lend themselves to a reading which, like that of many Old English verses, puts both the "chief syllables" of a two-stress half-line into one rhythmic measure: e.g., "And | þu3t hit a | bolde burne || þat þe | bur3 a3te."[12]

In fact, when we place a measure bar before each syllable which Miss Borroff identifies as a "major chief syllable" in the passages she annotates, all those which stand alone as filling a measure will be found to come at points where a pause indicated by the syntax may fill the function of rest in the method of Old English scansion cited above. In general, such single syllables are found in three positions: (1) part of a group following caesura plus some lighter syllables, as in

"‖ þat þe | burȝ aȝte;" (2) directly before caesura, as in such a line

as 740, "Bi a | mounte on þe | morne ‖ meryly he | rydes;" or (3) at

the end of an end-stopped line, such as 253, "Þe | hede of þis | ostel |

Arthour I | hat." But the use of the syntactic pause to postpone the first stressed syllable to another measure suggests a further complication.

The difficulty arises as soon as we go on to consider a sequence of verses, such as the first half of 845 in relation to the last of 844:

A | hoge haþel for þe | nonez, ‖ and of | hyghe eldee;

Brode, | bryȝt, watz his | berde . . .

That is, if both stressed syllables of 844b come in one measure, that measure still must include any syllables of anacrusis which precede the first lift of the next line, which, in this case, leaves us with a highly unlikely measure containing two half-lifts. This would seem to be extending the possible boundaries of a measure entirely too far. And, actually, would a prominent alliterating stressed word at the beginning of a line be so unimportant to that line as to be a rhythmic holdover from the last? The difficulty stems from a decision to stress the second adjective over the first; but that is not the only possibility here. We can surely reject "Brode, bryȝt, watz his | berde . . ." since such an intonation pattern bears no relation to the meaning and the normal prose rhythm for such a statement. Putting equal stress on *brode* and *bryȝt* would seem to lead back to the rhythmically dubious idea that such lines, especially when they show triple alliteration, have three equal stresses and are an "extended" line analogous to the Old English hypermetric.[13]

However, the editorial commas may suggest another way out of the difficulty: to treat such a half-line as we would an Old English

verse of Sievers' type D or E, or a variant thereof. "Brode, ‖ bryȝt,

watz his berde . . ." gives a verse of type D, comparable to such

verses as Beowulf 2774a, "eald | enta geweorc," and as a rough guide to stress gives as satisfactory a reading as subordinating the first adjective to the second. A good many of the lines with three clearly important syllables may be read with the D pattern: 98, "lede, ‖ lif for lyf, | leue vchon | oþer," for example. A great many lines with monosyllabic anacrusis fit this pattern: 8a, "Fro | riche | Romulus to Rome;" 61a, "Þat | day ‖ doubble on the dece;" 87a, "His | lif | liked hym lyȝt;" and so forth.

Others could be interpreted as D verses according to Old English standards only if the first lift were understood to be "resolved," that is, having two short syllables taking the place of a long one. In Middle English, of course, syllable length is no longer significant. But that may be all the more reason to suspect that such a pattern could have been developed from Old English verses of type D with resolution of the first lift, such as *Beowulf* 129a, "micel | morgenswēg." With the loss of attention to syllable length, such verses would become indistinguishable from certain types of A verses, e.g., *Beowulf* 408a, "mǣg ond | magoþegn."[14] Thus we might discern a Middle English type AD in such half-lines as 65a, "Nowel | nayted onewe;" 67a, "ȝeȝed | ȝeres-ȝiftes on hiȝ;" 112a, "Bischop | Bawdewyn abof;" and 162a, "Boþe þe | barres of his belt."

Some half-lines which may otherwise fit the D pattern, with or without anacrusis, have an extra lightly stressed syllable at the end of the rhythmic measure, as in 2, "Þe | borȝ | brittened and brent to | brondez and | askez;" 40, "With | rych | reuel oryȝt and | rechles | merþes;" and 76, "Smal | sendel bisides, a | selure hir | ouer." Such expansions of the pattern also have precedents in Old English type D with resolution; e.g., *Maldon* 284a, "Bærst | bordes lærig." Still others may vary from the older D type in that their anacrusis is more than monosyllabic, as is possible in the case of 70a, "And he þat | wan | watz not wrothe."

Of course, not all the lines with three important stressed syllables in the first half lend themselves to this rhythm. In some cases, the second stress should no doubt be subordinated to the first, as in l. 846, which was marked, following Miss Borroff's stress notation,

"Sturne, stif on þe | stryþþe on | stalworth | schonkez." Just as some lines discussed above seemed to have a rhythm like that of the Old English D verse, such lines as this suggest the pattern of Old English

type E. 73a, "Þe | best burne ay a | bof," is similar to the structure

of *Maldon* 113b, "wæl-reste ġe | ċēas," except that it has mono-syllabic anacrusis, which is rare (if not non-existent) before a type E in Old English. Like D types with more than one syllable of ana-crusis, these may be easily explained by the general prevalence of anacrusis in the Middle English line.

Less close to the E pattern are a number of half-lines which resemble it but have the initial sequence $/x\diagdown$ instead of $/\diagdown x$. Many

lines can be read this way, if we grant its possibility: 57a, "Dressed

on þe dere | des," for example, and 214, "Þe | stele of a stif | staf

þe | sturne hit bi | grypte." In the latter case, we have an extra light syllable—a situation similar to some of the lines designated AD above. Here again we have something which looks like a result of fusion with certain types of A verse, with a result resembling the structure of

Beowulf 943a, "efne swa hwylc | mægþa." Such lines might be classi-fied AE, a category in which we may find satisfactory readings of

846a and such others as 305a, "Bende his bresed | broȝez," and 181,

"Fayre fannand | fax vmbe | foldes his | schulderes."

It appears that all of the "extended" lines can be seen to follow a pattern identical to, or at least possibly influenced by, Old English typed D and E. But it is often uncertain which way suits the sense

and syntax. Should we read "With | rych | reuel oryȝt and |

rechles | merþes," as l. 40 was scanned above, or "With | rych reuel

o | ryȝt and | rechles | merþes"? Presumably such questions must be settled by the reader's judgement of the rhetorical and syntactical emphases; the guidelines for identifying stress patterns in Middle English cannot be very clearly laid down.[15] The point is that either of these patterns seems more satisfactory than taking the first of three stressed elements as anacrusis, if only because a stressed alliterating syllable is a prominent part of the verse it begins; yet it is sometimes not entirely clear whether an alliterating syllable in such a position is stressed. It seems probable that it is not in such cases as 1508, " 'I woled | wyt at yow, | wyʒe,' þat | worthy þer | sayde," but countless other cases may remain debatable, such as 344a, "Bid me | boʒe fro þis | benche," or "Bid me | boʒe fro þis benche," though we can no doubt rule out "Bid me boʒe fro þis | benche."

To re-scan the entire passage with which we started (842–9), then, according to these suggestions, we end up with something that may suggest more about the actual rhythm:

| Gawayn glyʒt on þe | gome þat | godly hym | gret,

And | þuʒt hit a | bolde burne | | þat þe | burʒ aʒte,

A | hoge haþel for þe | nonez, | | and of | hyghe eldee; |

| Brode, | | bryʒt, watz his berde, | | and al | beuer-hwed, |

Sturne, stif on þe | stryþþe on | stalworth | schonkez, |

| Felle | face as þe fyre, and | fre of hys | speche;

And | wel hym | semed for soþe, | | as þe | segge þuʒt,

To | lede a | lortschyp in lee of | leudez ful | gode.

The patterns of the half-lines, so scanned, have an amazing variety. There are clear examples of several of the Sievers' types: 848a is a B, 843b is a C, and 845a is an E, for example. If we presume that -e is generally not sounded,[16] then 848b is a C, but only with the following syllable of anacrusis to complete the pattern, while 843a does not appear to have any drop at all in the second measure and turns out to look like an A—it might be described as ABC in type. There are four plain A half-lines (842b, 846b, 847b, and 849b), but all but one depend on following anacrusis to complete the pattern. Most of the other lines are mixed types, but we can see that the dominant A rhythm is reinforced by the tendency toward an A structure in these mixed types (such as 844a, AE, and 849a, AD, and several verses here scanned as one or the other but for which the alternative possibility exists).

Miss Borroff has characterized the metrical patterns of this passage as "unusually emphatic," due to the cluster of lines with three stressed syllables in the first half, "in a number of cases made still more conspicuous by being juxtaposed" (p. 207). It can be noted that if the rhythmic presumptions here are correct, this emphasis is achieved without an effect of monotony in the rhythm because of variation not only in the patterns of relationship between lift and half-lift, but also in the use of caesural pause and anacrusis. For example, if we scan the first half of 842 as an AE and the second as A, it is still not the same construction as 846, which starts with what is probably an AE and ends with a different kind of A, one with a half-lift in place of one "drop" or "dip." It may be the same combination as 847, but 847 probably begins with an AD. 849 resembles 847, but differs in that it begins with anacrusis.

Such constant modulations, pleasing to the ear and contributing to the meaning of the whole, are just what we expect of a first-rate poet. However, if such analysis works at all, we should find some of the same variations in other poems written in the same verse line— and indeed we can. To take, for example, a few lines from the B-Prologue of *Piers Plowman*, we can find there, too, lines that work well rhythmically with similar scansion:

Þanne | loked vp a | lunatik . a | lene þing with- | alle,

And | kneling to þe | kyng | . | clergealy he | seyde; |

| "Crist | kepe þe, sire kyng | . | and þi | kyngriche,

And | leue þe | lede þi londe . so | leute þe | louye,

And for þe | riȝtful | rewlyng . be re | warded in | heuene!"[17]

As we might expect, the lines of *Piers Plowman* are not so richly varied as those of *Gawain*, though they are by no means all the same in rhythm. Other fourteenth-century alliterative works provide other sorts of examples. The opening lines of the *Morte Arthure* follow some of the patterns:

Now | grett glorious | Godde, thurgh | grace of hym | selven

And the | precyous | prayere | | of hys | prys modyr, |

| Schelde us fro | schamesdede and | synfull | werkes

And | gyffe us | grace to gye and | governe us | here . . .[18]

as do also the opening lines of a somewhat later poem, *Death and Liffe*:

| Christ, Christen | King, | | that on the | crosse tholed,

hadd | paines & | passyons to def | fend our | soules, |

| giue vs | grace on the ground the | greatlye to | serve

for that | royall | red blood that | rann ffrom thy | side;

& take a | way of thy | winne word | | as the | world asketh . . .[19]

Of course, the use made of rhythmic variation will be found to differ significantly from one poem to another. Lesser poets are, predictably, less skilful in their effects than the *Gawain*-poet. It may be fair enough to compare the passage from *Gawain* scanned above with a description of a similarly outstanding individual in *Death and Liffe*, 151–8:

I there | saye a | sight was | sorrowfull to be | hold,

one of the | vglyest | ghosts that | on the | earth gone.

There was | no man of this | sight but | hee was af | frayd,

soe | grislye & | great & | grim to be | hold.

& a | quintful | queene came | quaking be | fore,

with a | carued | crowne on her head, | | all of | pure gold,

& shee the | ffoulest | ffreake that | formed was | euer,

both of | hide & | hew & | heare al | so.

The poet somehow manages to be irregular and monotonous at the same time. Even if we try to scan the lines as patterns other than A when possible—and many lines certainly admit of doubts—we still find A half-lines overwhelmingly predominant. Nor do other effects combat monotony: almost every line is clearly run-on,[20] and little if any use is made of the possibilities of caesural pause. The only factor that saves the passage from jog-trot regularity is the eccentricity (or textual corruption, as the case may be)[21] of the alliterative pattern, which collapses so badly in 153 and 156b that the stress pattern is quite unclear.

Whether we look at a great poem or an obviously minor one, the general rhythmic pattern may still be seen as the same, fitting a scansion predicated on the survival of features widely held to be essential to understanding the rhythm of Old English verse, such as the rest and the three-stress (but not three-measure) half-line, arranged in the general pattern of Sievers' types D or E. To make such a claim, however, seems to fly in the face of the conclusions of all the scholars who have previously discussed the relationship between the Middle English line and the Old English types, since they all agree that the D and E types are not represented in Middle English.[22] The half-lines which obviously have three stresses appear to be thought of as deriving from Old English hypermetric verses,[23] although many statements on the subject agree that one of the three stresses can be subordinated to the others. Norman Davis makes a statement to this effect (p. 149), but accompanies it with a scansion showing three identical stresses (e.g., "smál séndal bisídes"), and goes on to state that "the OE. types (D and E) which depend on secondary stress do not appear."[24] Yet if we are to treat these as four-stress lines, one of the stresses must be secondary, and the result will inevitably be a pattern resembling that of the D or E verse.

Any true analogy with the hypermetric lines of Old English is bound to break down when we look at the second half of the line. If we are not deterred by rhythmic arguments, it is theoretically possible to scan a few such lines with three measures in every half-line, as I believe to be proper with the Old English hypermetric; for example,

118, "Nwe | nakryn | noyse || with þe | noble | pipes." But the effect is as unnecessary as it is in this context unpleasant, when it is

possible to scan the line as "Nwe nakryn | noyse with þe | noble |

pipes." And the great majority of second half-lines will not adapt themselves to such a treatment in any case: 13b, "Felix Brutus," is one of many that simply cannot be tortured into more than two measures.

The three-stress half-lines are comparable to the many quasi-hypermetric Old English verses which appear in isolation, without a hypermetric completing verse; these are especially frequent in later Old English poetry. *Christ III*, for example, has many verses which seem overloaded for a normal verse but are still not clearly hypermetric.[25] When not the result of scribal error, etc., such verses are probably not hypermetric, but, rather, slightly expanded or mixed patterns, such as the BC verse, exemplified in a context of normal Old English

verses by 102a of *The Dream of the Rood*, "mid his | miclan meahte." We find second half-lines resembling this in Middle English often enough, though usually the first light syllables are rhythmically required to complete the last measure of the first half, and thus fall into the pattern Tolkien and Gordon call AB (in Davis's revision, BA).

It would appear that all the Old English type patterns *except* the hypermetric can be observed in Middle English, even if the extra burden of lightly stressed syllables, together with other factors, tends to blur distinctions between the variants and the dominant A type. This is a logical enough development since, after all, variants are just that. It may be more notable that a number of the observations commonplace in discussions of the metre of the long line are, according to the scansion demonstrated here, of dubious validity. Caesura is by no means a constant feature;[26] rather, it occurs in less than half the lines here scanned from various poems. While true enjambment is indeed more rare than in Old English,[27] a large proportion of the lines are not end-stopped in rhythmic effect because of the frequent use of anacrusis. D and E verses have not disappeared, but provide a more satisfactory explanation of the lines with more than four principal stresses than does the theory that they derive from the hypermetric.

It is, however, possible that Old English hypermetric verses did have some influence on the alliterative patterns of these lines. The noticeable tendency to use double, triple, multiple, crossed, transverse, mixed, or just supplementary alliterative patterns is reminiscent of the practice of earlier poets in hypermetric lines. It may be that men of the transitional period were as confused as later readers in regard to what was or was not hypermetric. The distinction would seem to have been lost, logically enough, as the length of the normal lines was extended beyond the permissible limits of Old English classical standards.

THE UNIVERSITY OF WESTERN ONTARIO

NOTES

1 "The Meter of *Piers Plowman*," *PMLA*, 42 (1927), p. 119.
2 J. C. Pope, *The Rhythm of Beowulf*, rev. edn (New Haven: Yale Univ. Press, 1966).
3 M. Borroff, *Sir Gawain and the Green Knight: a Stylistic and Metrical Study* (New Haven: Yale Univ. Press, 1962).
4 Pp. 172–82 and 193–8.
5 Borroff prefers not to use the term *measure* because "its use might seem to imply that metrical rhythm is held to be identical with musical rhythm," though in using the phrase "metrical unit" she means what William Thomson defines as a "measure" in verse: "A portion of rhythm beginning with one strong accent and lasting up to, but not including, the next;" see n. 10, p. 259. This is what is meant by *measure* in discussion of Old English rhythms (cf. John C. Pope, *Seven Old English Poems* (Indianapolis: Bobbs-Merrill, 1966), 117–18), and the term is here used in this sense.

6 ['] or [/] for *C*, a *lift*, or "major chief syllable," and ['] or [\] for *c*, a *half-lift*, or "minor chief syllable." Cf., e.g., Pope, *Seven Old English Poems*, op. cit., pp. 109–16; Robert P. Creed, "A New Approach to the Rhythm of *Beowulf*," *PMLA*, 81 (1966), 23–33; C. B. Hieatt, "Prosodic Analysis of Old English Poetry: a Suggested Working Approach with Sample Applications," *Revue de l'Université d'Ottawa*, 42 (1972), 72–82. In his fully worked out scansions, Pope usually discriminates between four grades of chief syllable rather than two, using double accents to indicate the most important, as in "Nú scùlon hérià̀n héofon-rìces Wéard" (*Seven Old English Poems*, op. cit., p. 119), but this does not change the basic pattern, which he indicates with single accents on the page before.

7 See Borroff, op. cit., pp. 207–8. I have used the 2nd edn of Tolkien and Gordon's, rev. Norman Davis (Oxford: Clarendon Press, 1968); thus spelling and punctuation will vary slightly from Borroff's text.

8 Pope, *Seven Old English Poems*, op. cit., p. 118 ff., and *Rhythm of Beowulf*, op. cit., esp. pp. 38–95.

9 I follow Pope in using the 3rd edn of *Beowulf* edited by Fr. Klaeber (New York: Heath, 1936), and when referring to lines from one of the poems included in *Seven Old English Poems*, will use his spelling and punctuation.

10 Here too the concept has not gone unchallenged. Cf. the various objections and proposals reported, and replied to, in Pope's preface to the 1966 edn of *Rhythm of Beowulf*, op. cit.; and, more recently, Robert D. Stevick, *Suprasegmentals, Meter, and the Manuscript of Beowulf* (The Hague: Mouton, 1968) and Samuel Jay Keyser, "Old English Prosody," *College English*, 30 (1969), pp. 331–56.

11 Which is, of course, one of the procedures Borroff takes for granted; see p. 192.

12 I shall use a double bar rather than a caret in indicating such pauses since I avoid assuming "rest," in the sense of pause, unless it is syntactically justifiable, assuming prolongation or something of the sort elsewhere.

13 I support the idea that the Old English hypermetric verses have three measures rather than two; see "A New Theory of Triple Rhythm in the Hypermetric Lines of Old English Verse," *MP*, 66 (1969), pp. 1–8, and "Alliterative Patterns in the Hypermetric Lines of Old English Verse," *MP*, forthcoming. But the "extended" lines of Middle English alliterative poetry are a different question, one difference is further discussed below.

14 Even in Old English, it is frequently difficult to distinguish between certain types of A and D. Cf. Pope, preface to 1966 edn of *Rhythm of Beowulf*, op. cit., pp. xx–xxiii.

15 Cf. Borroff, op. cit., 164–71, 193–8.

16 Ibid., pp. 157, 182–3, 187–9.

17 Ll. 123–7, Walter W. Skeat (ed.) (EETS, OS 38, 1869).

18 John Finlayson (ed.) (London: Arnold, 1967).

19 James Holly Hanford and John M. Steadman, "Death and Life: An Alliterative Poem." *SP*, 15 (1918), pp. 225 ff.

20 Despite some indications to the contrary in the editorial punctuation; not surprisingly, rhythmic analysis may throw some editorial punctuation into question. *Gawain* 845–9, as scanned above, demands some changes in this respect.

21 See Hanford and Steadman's introduction, op. cit., p. 257.

22 See, e.g., J. P. Oakden, *Alliterative Poetry in Middle English* (1930, 1935; rpt. Sherman, Conn.: Archon, 1968), I, p. 149. It may, however, be recalled that C. S. Lewis claimed the D and E patterns to be the key to the rhythm of fifteenth-century verse in "The Fifteenth Century Heroic Lines," *E & S*, 24 (1938), pp. 28–41, esp. pp. 33 and 39.

[23] Oakden, op. cit., I, 131.

[24] Davis, op. cit., p. 151; but concentration on the second half-lines would naturally lead to this conclusion since few of them have three stresses. See Borroff, op. cit., p. 183.

[25] Cf. Pope, *Rhythm of Beowulf*, op. cit., p. 101.

[26] Cf. Davis, op. cit., p. 148: "The long line is divided by a natural pause, or caesura, into two half-lines each of which normally contains two lifts."

[27] See, e.g., Robert J. Menner, preface to *Purity* (New Haven: Yale Univ. Press, 1920), p. liv.

9

NUMERICAL STRUCTURE IN FITT III
OF *SIR GAWAIN AND THE GREEN KNIGHT*

BY HANS KÄSMANN

Sir Gawain and the Green Knight consists, like *Pearl*, of 101 stanzas. In *Pearl* this number is one aspect of a complex numerical pattern that determines the structure of the poem as a whole.[1] In *SGGK* it has been regarded as an isolated phenomenon, interesting because of the obvious parallel to *Pearl*, but without any function in the structure of the work.[2] Recently, however, Professor A. Kent Hieatt has argued that the formal proportions of *SGGK*, too, can be explained in numerological terms.[3] He starts from the fact that in *SGGK* as in *Pearl* the opening line is echoed at the end of the poem. In *Pearl* l. 1212, the very last line ("Ande precious perleȝ vnto his pay"),[4] contains an allusion to l. 1. In *SGGK* the echoing occurs at l. 2525, the last alliterative long line before the final bob and wheel ("After þe segge and þe asaute watz sesed at Troye"),[5] which, apart from "after," is identical with l. 1. This similarity can scarcely be accounted mere chance. The number 2525 cannot, like 1212, be explained as the inevitable product of 101 and a set number of lines per stanza. There is, in addition, in both cases a relationship between the number and the content of the poem.[6] The number 12 is prominent in those passages in *Pearl* that are based on *Revelation*. In *SGGK* the number 2525 directs us to the pentangle, which is of central importance as a symbol of Gawain's *trawþe* and indicates that he is "ay faythful in fyue and sere fyue syþez" (l. 632).

If these observations are correct, we must reckon with the possibility of the poet's having used a technique of numerical composition elsewhere in *SGGK*. Hieatt has drawn attention to two series of numerical parallelisms, the first of which occurs in Fitt i and Fitt iv:

(A) In Stanza 10 of Fitt i, the first axe and its *lace* make their appearance (ll. 208–17). (B) In Stanza 20 of Fitt i, Bertilak as the Green Knight departs. . . . (C) In Stanza 21, the axe, undoubtedly with its green *lace*, reaches its ultimate destination. It is hung against the wall-tapestry above the dais in Arthur's hall. That is the end of Fitt i. (A) In Stanza 10 of Fitt iv (the second half of the Beheading Test), an axe, with yet another gleaming *lace*, again appears (ll. 2222–6). (B) In Stanza 20 of this fitt, Bertilak again departs. . . . (C) In Stanze 21 of the same fitt, the *luf-lace* (knotted this time around a man, not an axe) reaches its ultimate destination in the poem. Wearing it over the pentangle and the red cloth of his coat-armour (ll. 2485–9), Gawain reaches Arthur's court (l. 2489).[7]

That in both cases the axe and its *lace* appear in Stanza 10 is of course striking. It is, however, doubtful whether Stanza 20 was equally deliberately chosen since the departure of Bertilak (in Fitt iv it is rather the departure of Gawain) must be related shortly before the end of each section. The evidence for (C) appears to me particularly weak, and it is very doubtful indeed if one can speak at this point of the use of parallelism. But even if we assume that the suspension of the axe with its *lace* in Fitt i is comparable to Gawain's wearing the *luf-lace* that he has received from the lady, we are left with the difficulty that though Gawain dons the *luf-lace* for his return journey in Stanza 21 (ll. 2485–8) he decides only in Stanza 22 (ll. 2509–10) to wear this "token of vntrawþe" for the rest of his life.

Hieatt proposes a second series of numerical parallelisms in Fitt iii. Each of the three days on which Gawain is subjected to the temptations of the Lady of the Castle is depicted in eleven stanzas that admit of a consistent fivefold division:

I   First stages of hunt.

II   The happenings in Gawain's bed chamber to departure of lady.

III Gawain's rising, religious observance, recreation with the two ladies of the castle.

IV   Conclusion of hunt; dressing or skinning of deer, boar, fox; return to castle.

V   Events of the evening: exchange of what has been gained during the day, entertainment; in eleventh stanza of each series: mention (1) of retirement of company for night; (2) of early activities of next morning; (3) of pledge(s).[8]

The crucial point is that on each day the reaching of an agreement, which gives renewed emphasis to the main theme of *trawþe*, occurs in the eleventh stanza (Stanzas 11, 22, 33). Hieatt assumes that the sequences of eleven stanzas, like the sequences of twenty-one stanzas in Fitt i and Fitt iv, have a symbolic and not merely a structural function: "What such an arithmetical conceit would signify is that, as the *luf-lace*, with its knot, adds an element which ruins the perfection signified by the knotless pentangle, so 5 plus 1, or a multiple of 5 to which 1 unit is added, signifies imperfection."[9]

This analysis, too, can be objected to on a number of scores. The third sequence of eleven stanzas can only be maintained by the device of excluding Stanza 34, which Hieatt describes as "super-numerary," despite the fact that there is no break in the continuity of the narrative between Stanzas 33 and 34. In this way, the account of Gawain's taking leave of the ladies would have to be interrupted after the first two lines (ll. 1977–8), and the remaining four lines (ll. 1979–82) would be left out of the numerological scheme. Hieatt's argument in respect of the three agreements is equally difficult to accept. It is true that there are three agreements about the exchange of winnings, but the first of these arrangements is already made at the end of Fitt ii. In Stanza 33 Bertilak promises to provide Gawain with a guide on the following morning. This is something entirely different and has nothing to do with *trawþe* as the main concern of the poem. And finally, Hieatt's attempt to pinpoint the end of the account of each day at the close of a stanza clearly brings him into conflict with the text. When he speaks of "mention of early activities of next morning" (V. 2) he in fact refers to what belongs to the following day. This applies to ll. 1412–20 and 1688–9 which according to Hieatt are parts of the depiction of the first and second days respectively.

In the light of these considerations we may well be sceptical about the presence of numerical patterns in *SGGK*. It would, however, be unfortunate if we were now to conclude that numerological elements in *SGGK* are confined to two or three details reminiscent of *Pearl*. For Fitt iii, if examined from a different angle, provides strong evidence that the poet made use of numerological patterns, though mainly as a method of composition and, as it seems, without any symbolic signi-ficance. Hieatt's insistence on the stanza as the constitutive element of his three sequences together with his attempt to read the symbolic 5 into the account of each of the three days (rather than drawing on the accepted fourfold division) made it impossible for him to recognize these patterns.

In what follows I proceed from the assumption that in Fitt iii a principle of structural arrangement can be detected apart from the stanzas and, so to speak, in contrapuntal relation to them. This principle works through a system of formal signals which mark most of the transitions from one unit to the next and enable us to establish the compositional pattern with something approaching objective accuracy. These formal criteria will help us to resist the temptation to impose preconceived and illusory patterns on the text.

The reporting of the events of each of the three days is structured through changes of scene: from the hunt to the castle, from there back to the hunt, and from the hunt again to the castle. Fitt iii does not, however, begin immediately with the first day's hunt but with seven lines that describe the departure of a number of the guests (ll. 1126–32). These lines can be regarded as an introductory or bridge passage. The first hunting scene is introduced through a formula ("Þe leue lorde of þe londe," l. 1133) that occurs with little variation on a number of occasions later in the text and always marks the beginning of a new section.

At the end of Fitt iii, we learn in l. 1990 that Gawain has been escorted to bed. Seven lines follow (including bob and wheel) in which the narrator appears in the first person singular that has previously occurred only once in Fitt iii (in the formulaic "as I haf herde telle," l. 1144). He makes an observation on Gawain's sleep before addressing his audience: "And ʒe wyl a whyle be stylle I schal telle yow how þay wroʒt" (ll. 1996–7). Neither of the two previous days ends in such a way. It seems as if the poet has at this point, after concluding his account of the day's events, added a passage that carries us over into Fitt iv. It has the same number of lines as the bridge passage as the beginning of Fitt iii. But there is no clearly marked caesura in the contents here. Nor is it certain that the use of the first person singular can be regarded as a sufficient formal criterion. It is with this reservation in mind that we regard ll. 1991–7 as an equivalent to ll. 1126–32 in that they are a transitional passage outside the main compositional pattern of Fitt iii.

The report of the first day's hunt begins, as we have seen, with mention of the "leue lorde of þe londe" (l. 1133). The beginning of the boar-hunt on the second day and of the fox-hunt on the third day can without difficulty be placed at l. 1412 and l. 1688 respectively. Both passages make reference to "þe lorde:"

> Bi þat þe coke hade crowen and cakled bot þryse,
> Þe lorde watz lopen of his bedde, þe leudez vchone. (ll. 1412–13).

> Þe lorde þat his craftez kepes,
> Ful erly he watz diʒt. (ll. 1688–9)

The transition from the first part of the description of the hunt to Gawain's experiences in the castle is effected for each of the three days in the middle of a sentence:

> Þus laykez þis lorde by lynde-wodez euez,
> And Gawayn þe god mon in gay bed lygez. (ll. 1178–9)[10]

> Þis day wyth þis ilk dede þay dryuen on þis wyse,
> Whyle oure luflych lede lys in his bedde. (ll. 1468–9)

And ȝe he lad hem bi lagmon, þe lorde and his meyny,
On þis maner bi þe mountes quyle myd-ouer-vnder,
Whyle þe hende knyȝt at home holsumly slepes. (ll. 1729–31)

The obvious parallels between ll. 1179, 1469 and 1731 can be regarded as a formal indication of the beginning of the second scene,
which can thus be placed with certainty.

The caesura suggested by Hieatt as occurring between the temptation scenes proper and the later events in Gawain's day in the castle
is in no way formally marked. The lady's departure from Gawain is
referred to in different words and without any stylistic echoings on
each occasion. In the case of the second day, only three verses occur
after this point and before the description of the hunt is taken up
again. The very brevity of this passage is surely evidence for its not
being a distinctive unit.

The transition from the castle to the second part of the description
of the hunt is very clearly marked, and in each case the alliterative
formula of l. 1133 appears again:

And ay þe lorde of þe londe is lent on his gamnez. (l. 1319)

Bot þe lorde ouer þe londez launced ful ofte. (l. 1561)

Ȝet is þe lorde on þe launde ledande his gomnes. (l. 1894)

The exact point of the change of scene from the hunt to the events
of the evening in the castle can be determined on the basis of formal
criteria only for the first and third day. Bertilak returns with his
retainers:

Strakande ful stoutly mony stif motez. (l. 1364)

Strakande ful stoutly in hor store hornez. (l. 1923)

With the next verse we are already in the castle itself:

Bi þat þe daylyȝt watz done þe douthe watz al wonen
Into þe comly castel. (ll. 1365–6)

Þe lorde is lyȝt at þe laste at hys lef home. (l. 1924)

The point at which the hunting scene ends on the second day is more
difficult to identify:

Þe bores hed watz borne bifore þe burnes seluen
Þat him forferde in þe forþe þurȝ forse of his honde
    so stronge.
    Til he seȝ Sir Gawayne
    In halle hym þoȝt ful longe;
    He calde, and he com gayn
    His feez þer for to fonge. (ll. 1616–22)

The main difficulty here is located in ll. 1619–20. These two lines can mean either that it seems to Bertilak, on his way home, a long time before he meets Gawain in the hall;[11] or that it seems to Bertilak, when he is already in the hall, a long time before he meets Gawain. The second interpretation is more convincing, since the "he calde" of l. 1621 presupposes that Bertilak has at that moment already reached the hall. We therefore assume that the fourth section of the second day begins at l. 1619.

Only one of the transitions we have discussed occurs at the beginning of a stanza (l. 1319).[12] In the majority of cases the scene changes shortly before the end or shortly after the beginning of a stanza. This is remarkable in a poem in which the demarcation of stanzas is very strongly emphasized by the bob and the wheel. One may surmise that this technique is comparable in its functional aim to the precise and carefully synchronized time-scheme of Fitt iii, which, in spite of the linearity of the narrative, creates the impression of events overlapping or occurring simultaneously.[13]

We can sum up our discussion of the structural elements of Fitt iii in the following table:

bridge passage		ll. 1126–32	7 lines	
first day	hunt	1133–78	46	
	castle	1179–1318	140	279 lines
	hunt	1319–64	46	
	castle	1365–1411	47	
second day	hunt	1412–68	57	
	castle	1469–1560	92	
	hunt	1561–1618	58	276
	castle	1619–87	69	
third day	hunt	1688–1730	43	
	castle	1731–1893	163	
	hunt	1894–1923	30	303
	castle	1924–90	67	
bridge passage		1991–7	7	

The symmetrical balance of Fitt iii is of course well known. On occasion even numbers have been mentioned, for example by J. A. Burrow, who maintains that "the poet's account of the events of the second day is almost the same length as his account of the first (276 lines to 286)."[14] He also remarks that the two sections on the boarhunt are somewhat longer than the corresponding passages on the deer-hunt, while the second temptation scene is considerably shorter than the first. A glance at our table will show that, for the first day, the interrelation of the four sections can scarcely be explained as a mere attempt to create an impression of compositional balance. The poet must have been counting his lines. Of this there can be no doubt, even though the sum does not always appear to be exact. It is not only that the two sections on the hunt are of identical length. The account of the evening in the castle is only one line longer. If one adds these three units together one arrives at a total of 139 lines, as opposed to 140 for the temptation scene. From the beginning of the hunt to the end of the temptation scene we have, on the other hand, 186 lines. The remaining two sections, taken together, give 93 lines. The proportion is exactly two to one.

In the case of the second day, the numerical pattern is not quite so obvious, but it is not difficult to find. The two parts of the description of the hunt (57 and 58 lines) differ by only one line. As this is the second time that such a balance has been established, there can be no question of coincidence. The evening in the castle is depicted at greater length (69 lines). At first glance a specific numerical relationship to the two hunting scenes cannot be discerned. But, taken together, these three sections give 184 lines and therewith exactly twice the number of the lines of the second temptation scene (92 lines).[15] In the case of the first day we have noticed an approximate relation of one to one in the corresponding parts; now it is a proportion of exactly two to one, a relation which we have also found for the first day by applying a different principle of division. It should further be observed that the first and the second day together take up 555 lines. It is tempting to see here a further pointer to the pentangle. But this temptation is perhaps best resisted so long as no evidence has been discovered in *SGGK* that would rule out the possibility of coincidence. Such evidence ought also to provide an explanation of why a symbolically meaningful number should play a role in only the first two days of the three-day sequence.

If a similar overall principle of numerical composition underlies the description of the third day, I have not been able to detect it. This part of Fitt iii is distinctly longer than each of the two preceding ones, and there does not seem to be a relationship between 303 and 279 or 276. The two parts of the account of the hunt and the concluding scene in the castle differ very considerably in respect of number of lines, and there is no discernible evidence of an underlying regularity. It is however noteworthy that, taken together, these three sections add up to 140 lines. The three parallel episodes of the first day take up 139 lines and the first temptation scene is 140 lines long. The equivalence or approximate equivalence of these sections may be an indication of an underlying pattern, but as there appears to be no explanation for the 163 lines given to Gawain's experiences during Bertilak's absence on the third day[16] it is probably safer to regard it as coincidental. Under these circumstances, it may be justifiable to try an alternative approach even though it obliges us to go back on an earlier decision which, however, we made only with considerable reservation. If we add the concluding seven lines of Fitt iii (ll. 1991–7), which we have regarded as a bridge passage, to the preceding castle scene we arrive at a total of 74 (67 + 7) lines. Now the description of the fox-hunt consists of 73 (43 + 30) lines, again a difference of only one line. On the other hand, if we repeat the method used in considering the first day and take the first and the second and then the third and the fourth sections together, we arrive at a relationship of 206 : 104, which is very close to 2 : 1. But here again there is only an approximate equivalence. It is difficult to opt for one of these approaches since conceivably both could be wrong.

The third day remains then a problem, although here, too, there are clues that point to the presence of numerical relations as a structural principle. Perhaps an examination of the other three fitts of *SGGK* will provide new vantage points from which a pattern may be discerned.

The present argument would of course be much more conclusive if it could offer a satisfactory analysis for the third day. The result of our examination of the first two days does, however, show with considerable certainty that the author of *SGGK* has availed himself of the techniques of numerical composition though not, as Hieatt suggested, through the use of symbolic numbers that stand in relation to the content of the poem. The poet's purpose was primarily aesthetic. He aimed at giving the narrative of Fitt iii a compositional symmetry based on simple numerical proportions. It remains to be seen whether similar techniques were made use of in other parts of the poem.[17]

UNIVERSITY OF HEIDELBERG

NOTES

[1] P. M. Kean, "Numerical Composition in 'Pearl'," *N&Q*, 210 (1965), pp. 49–51.

[2] Ibid., p. 51, n. 11, assumed that the irregular length of the stanzas precluded the possibility of numerical structuring in the poem.

[3] "*Sir Gawain*: pentangle, *luf-lace*, numerical structure," in *Silent Poetry, Essays in numerological analysis*, Alastair Fowler (ed.) (London: Routledge, 1970), pp. 116–40. It is an indication of the increasing interest in number symbolism and numerical composition that two further books on these subjects were published in England in 1970: Christopher Butler, *Number Symbolism* (London: Rout-

ledge, 1970), and Alastair Fowler, *Triumphal Forms* (Cambridge: Cambridge Univ. Press, 1970).

Numerological analysis of English poetry has centred on the sixteenth and seventeenth centuries. In the last twenty years, since E. R. Curtius published his Excursus XV on *"Zahlenkomposition"* in *Europäische Literatur und lateinisches Mittelalter*, 2nd edn (Bern: Francke, 1954), pp. 491–8, Willard R. Trask (tr.), *European Literature and the Latin Middle Ages* (New York: Pantheon, 1953), pp. 501–9, many numerological investigations on medieval German and French texts have appeared. In work on Old and Middle English poetry this approach has, however, not been greatly in evidence.

4 E. V. Gordon (ed.), *Pearl* (Oxford: Clarendon Press, 1953).

5 All quotations are from J. R. R. Tolkien and E. V. Gordon (eds), *Sir Gawain and the Green Knight*, 2nd edn rev. by Norman Davis (Oxford: Clarendon Press, 1968).

6 It must of course be assumed that *SGGK* has been preserved in its original length. Such an assumption is not difficult to make. For all the textual difficulties that have been accounted for in terms of the loss of one or more lines, there are in fact other and at least equally satisfactory explanations. There is no evidence that additions were made to the text after its original composition.

7 Hieatt, op. cit., p. 126.

8 Quoted from Hieatt's table on p. 128 where the number of stanzas and lines for the various sections of Fitt iii are given.

9 Ibid., p. 131.

10 *And* in l. 1179 can without difficulty be replaced by *whyle*.

11 This is clearly how Hieatt interprets the passage (p. 128); he places the end of the hunting scene at line 1620.

12 In one instance this occurs in the penultimate line of a wheel (l. 1688, the point at which the third day begins); in two instances (ll. 1179, 1894) in the second line of a stanza.

13 Cf. J. A. Burrow, *A Reading of "Sir Gawain and the Green Knight"* (London: Routledge, 1965), p. 73 f.

14 Burrow (op. cit., p. 89) has included the introductory seven lines in the account of the first day. It is probably for this reason that he did not detect the compositional pattern of this part of Fitt iii.

15 If one takes the two hunting scenes together, their relation to the other two sections is 115:92:69 or 5:4:3.

16 If one divides this scene as Hieatt does, the number of lines up to the departure of the lady (ll. 1731–1871) is 141. This number is, however, irrelevant to our purposes because it is the result of a division for which there is no useful parallel in Fitt iii.

17 There are no basic units of a particular length, such as have been discovered in Middle High German and Old French; cf. for units of 120 lines Hans Eggers, *Symmetrie und Proportion epischen Erzählens. Studien zur Kunstform Hartmanns von Aue* (Stuttgart: Klett, 1956), pp. 14 ff.; for units of about 30 lines (or multiples of + 30) which can be traced to the practice of medieval copyists, C. A. Robson, "The Technique of Symmetrical Composition in Medieval Narrative Poetry," in *Studies in Medieval French Presented to Alfred Ewert in honour of his seventieth birthday* (Oxford: Clarendon Press, 1961), pp. 26–75.

10

CHAUCER'S CLERKS

BY J. BURKE SEVERS

To begin by definition, a clerk was a student who had received the tonsure—that is, he had had the top of his head shaven as a sign of dedication to special service in the Church. The chief practical effect of receiving the tonsure was to put the individual under ecclesiastical jurisdiction rather than secular jurisdiction, and this was important because it conferred certain clerical privileges and immunities. For instance, it gave the individual the right to be tried in an ecclesiastical rather than a civil court; and in an age when college factional brawls sometimes turned into armed battles in the streets of Oxford, Cambridge, or London, ecclesiastical immunity meant that a man might have his first murder free—or at any rate without too unpleasantly restrictive consequences. Receiving the tonsure and so putting oneself under ecclesiastical jurisdiction did not necessarily imply that a student was in even the lowest grade of minor orders, though of course many clerks did take orders—either minor orders, which qualified a man for a minor post, such as parish clerk or assistant priest; or major orders, which qualified a man for any post which a priest could fill.[1]

Chaucer gives us six or seven clerks in the *Canterbury Tales*. There is Nicholas of the *Miller's Tale*, and possibly also Absalon, who are at Oxford. There are Alan and John of the *Reeve's Tale*, who are Cambridge college boys. There is the nameless clerk of the University of Orleans who performs the astrological magic in the *Franklin's Tale*. There is the Clerk of Oxenford himself, who tells the tale of Griseldis. And there is the Wife of Bath's fifth husband Jankyn, another Oxford man—no doubt the most unhappy of the lot.

Nicholas was the Oxford student in the *Miller's Tale* who predicted a second Noah's flood to his landlord, old John the carpenter, and so gained access to old John's young wife Alison. Nicholas is lodging in the house of a townsman: that is, he is a "chamberdeacon," as such students were called. By the late fourteenth century, both at Oxford and Cambridge, such students were in a small minority. Historically, the first students who lived together in groups, in the twelfth century, lived in boarding-houses called inns, or hospices, headed (when they came to have heads) by one of the students themselves, who was charged with the responsibility of collecting and paying the rent to the landlord. "By the close of the century [that is, by 1300] it had become the general practice in both universities for masters to rent premises to serve as boarding-houses where undergraduates or young graduates could lodge and be under tuition."[2] Later, in the middle of the thirteenth century, the first colleges were founded by benefactions which set up funds for the maintenance of students living under college regulations; and by Chaucer's day eight such colleges existed at Oxford, eight also at Cambridge. These colleges existed side by side with the older inns, or hospices; and only a small minority of students roomed separately in town, as chamber-deacons. Indeed, "at Oxford, lodging in the houses of townsmen was forbidden by statute c. 1410 [shortly after Chaucer's death] owing to the indiscipline of chamber-deacons."[3]

Chaucer devotes about thirty lines right at the beginning of the tale to a rather full portrait of Nicholas, his lodgings, his character, and his scholarly interests. In Chaucer's account of Nicholas' studies, there are interesting reflections of the curriculum at Oxford in the late fourteenth century. The curriculum consisted basically of the Trivium (Grammar, Rhetoric, and Logic) and the Quadrivium (Arithmetic, Geometry, Astronomy, and Music). These were called the Seven Liberal Arts; but the term "art" was sometimes used separately to denote the Trivium. Chaucer uses it so to tell us that Nicholas "Hadde lerned art, but al his fantasye / Was turned for to lerne astrologye" (I, 3191–2). Astrology in the Middle Ages was inseparable, of course, from astronomy, one of the subjects of the Quadrivium. Chaucer devotes most of the portrait to Nicholas' interest in it, telling us how the shelves at his bed-head contained Ptolemy's *Almagest*, the standard textbook of astrology, and an astrolabe, that medieval instrument for observing the positions of the stars, now superseded by the sextant. But the other subjects in the Quadrivium are not neglected, either. Nicholas also has on his shelf "augrym stones," that is, an abacus, the lightning calculator to serve as handmaiden to astrology; and of course the abacus represents a second subject of the Quadrivium—Arithmetic. Also prominent on his shelf is "a gay sautrie," a psaltery or kind of harp, representing another subject of the Quadrivium, Music. As Coffman has suggested, the account of Nicholas' studies, when one considers the use to which he puts them in the tale to follow, constitutes a kind of burlesque of the Seven Liberal Arts of the medieval curriculum.[4]

To what use does Chaucer put the details of Nicholas' portrait in the tale which follows? For, though the plot of the *Miller's Tale* is not original with Chaucer, the characters which he fits to it *are* original with him. Over and over again, as one compares Chaucer's tales with his sources or analogues, one is struck by his creative originality in imagining and portraying precisely the kind of character to bring the story alive and make it compellingly credible. None of the analogues to the *Miller's Tale* has a college student in the role corresponding to Nicholas: usually the lover is a priest, in the common fabliau triangle of husband-wife-priest.[5] In none of the analogues is the young lover a boarder in the house of the old man and the young wife—a chamber-deacon. Obviously Chaucer is working on the principle that proximity gives opportunity: what more likely than that youth will call to youth when both are constantly in the house together? Chaucer makes the point explicit for us when he contrasts Nicholas' appeal to the wife with Absalon's, the parish clerk's:

> Bycause that he [Absalon] fer was from hire sight,
> This nye Nicholas stood in his light. (I, 3395–6)

But more importantly Chaucer makes Nicholas a college student because, as a student studying the Quadrivium, he may realistically be portrayed as having interest and skill in astrology. And Chaucer gives him a primary interest in one special branch of astrology, prognosticative; gives him also especial skill and reputation in one special application of prognosticative astrology, that of foretelling the weather. Obviously Chaucer is preparing us here for the trick which Nicholas plays on old John in predicting the flood. The preparation is double, for Nicholas' known skill in foretelling the weather not only makes his use of the trick credible; it also makes the old man's credulity credible. For almost everybody believed in astrology in the Middle Ages; moreover, there was a well-known tradition, which old John must have heard, that Noah himself had been skilled in astrology and that Noah not only was told by God that the flood was coming but also foresaw it in the stars.[6] Therefore, how could the old man fail to be impressed by the prognostication of this college man whose special study was astrology and whom everybody in the neighbourhood came to for weather predictions?

Old John's credulity, then, is readily accepted by the reader; but, to make it seem even more likely, Chaucer portrays the old man as ignorant, uneducated, and simple-minded—characteristics which in general make him an easy gull for the clever Nicholas. He has the typical ignorant man's attitude toward learning—the typical attitude of the man who works with his hands toward the man who works with his head: disparaging, patronizing, but nevertheless impressed. Nicholas for his part has the superior attitude of the educated man: it'll be a cold day when a college man can't fool a carpenter, he tells Alison. Chaucer makes use of this typical antipathy between educated and uneducated to motivate his plot and render it credible.

Whether Absalon, the parish clerk, is also a student at the University is uncertain. Chaucer does not say that he is; he does tell us that he was a youth of numerous accomplishments. Obviously he was in minor orders, for he was assistant to the parish priest, participating appropriately in the church service. In addition, he earned extra fees as a barber-surgeon, and he knew enough Latin to draw up certain legal documents in proper form. Coulton suggests that Absalon may also have been a student at the University, paying for his education out of these various fees and hoping to proceed some-day to major orders and the priesthood.[7] Living at Oxford, as he did, he certainly had opportunity to attend the University lectures. Apparently he had neglected to maintain his tonsure, for he parted his golden hair carefully and curled it into the shape of a fan in the latest fashion; and if he was a University student, he was one who violated the college regulations (as many did). For instance, in addition to his long hair, Chaucer tells us that he wore shoes which had Paul's windows carved in them, and he went fashionably in red hose; and in the regulations of New College, Oxford, "eccentricities in dress, peaked shoes, red and green hose, long hair and beards, were severely discouraged."[8] Chaucer also tells us that Absalon could trip and dance and cast his legs to and fro in twenty different ways, after the school of Oxford, which apparently was an unusually energetic mode of dancing, for the authorities at New College, in order to protect the College property, found it necessary to prohibit dancing or jumping either in the chapel or in the adjoining hall.[9]

Absalon, you will recall, is the butt of the rump-kissing joke and retaliates with the hot coulter. Whereas in the analogues he is usually a blacksmith, Chaucer makes him a parish clerk-student-barber, stylish, dainty, effeminate, fastidious, squeamish, associated with sweet smells, whether censing the young wives in church, or chewing liquorice to sweeten his breath for his nocturnal love-making. Why Chaucer transforms him thus I have explored elsewhere;[10] here I may merely summarize by observing that Absalon is the very type whose sensibilities would be most revolted by Alison's and Nicholas' unsavoury and foul-smelling jests. By the contrast between the nature of the jests and the nature of the character who suffers them, Chaucer heightens the effect of the whole episode and gives us another striking example of how skilfully he fits character to plot.

Our next two college students are Alan and John of the *Reeve's Tale*, who first are befooled by the Miller when he steals their college's grain, and then, *en revanche*, befool the Miller and his whole family when they "swyve" both wife and daughter and retrieve their stolen property. Alan and John are Cambridge men, in contrast to Nicholas and Absalon of the *Miller's Tale*, who were Oxford men. Thus Chaucer balances one tale off against the other—a kind of reinforcing of the balancing off achieved by the quarrel between the Miller and the Reeve and their telling their fabliaux at each other's expense.

More specifically, Alan and John are fellows in a definitely named Cambridge college: King's Hall (now incorporated in Trinity College). In Chaucer's day the colleges at both Cambridge and Oxford were very small, most of them housing from twelve to twenty fellows;[11] King's Hall, one of the largest, seems to have consisted of thirty-two.[12] Alan and John, therefore, were members of a small fraternal group with whom they lived on terms of friendly intimacy. Thus again they are contrasted with Nicholas, of Oxford, who was a chamber-deacon, living alone, without any company. And just as Chaucer made Nicholas a chamber-deacon to fit the needs of his plot, so he has made Alan and John fellows of King's Hall to fit the differing needs of this tale.

Indeed, the motivation of John and Alan throughout the tale, and even much of the Miller's motivation too, turns upon the fact that Alan and John are college fellows. They personally bring the college's grain for grinding because they know that the Miller is thieving more outrageously than ever now that the Manciple of the college is ill. The Miller, in his turn, is quite aware of why they have come, and professional thief as he is, he is motivated to outwit these college boys by pride in his ability at thievery. And here enters into the story the same antipathy between the uneducated and the educated, between those who work with their hands and those who work with their heads, which we observed in the *Miller's Tale* between John the Carpenter and Nicholas the Oxford college student. Here in the *Reeve's Tale* the Miller sets out to show up these bright college boys who think they can outwit him. "The greatest scholars aren't the wisest men," he says; "I'll fool them for all their fine philosophy and brains" (see I, 4049–54). So here is an added motivation for the Miller to deceive Alan and John. And, of course, he succeeds. The boys bring their grain in an effort to catch up the Miller; instead they are ironically caught up themselves. But the Miller cannot stop here; he rubs it in. He makes fun of them for being college men. When they are forced to share his narrow accommodations, he mockingly says to them, "You college men with your philosophy and arguments can make things seem the opposite of what they are; I'm sure you can argue the bedroom into being bigger and more comfortable than it really is!" (see I, 4122–6.) This is literally adding insult to injury. Their knowledge that the Miller has succeeded in robbing them is motivation enough for attempting retaliation; these insults to their status as students are added motivation. When Alan takes direct action to avenge himself by ravishing the Miller's daughter, John is thereby motivated to rape the wife by a trick, lest he seem like a dolt in the eyes of the fellows at the college if he cannot report a conquest like that of Alan's (I, 4201–10). It is this thought which directly motivates his clever trick of relocating the cradle; and in this act he not only gets back at the Miller by leading the Miller's wife to get into bed with him; he also more than evens things up with Alan, for Alan is subsequently misled by the relocated cradle into getting into bed with the perilous Miller. And so, when the whole story is told back at King's Hall, John's share in the events will be even more worthy than Alan's of the approving laughter of their colleagues.

Thus far, in dealing with Nicholas and Absalon of Oxford and Alan and John of Cambridge, we have been analysing somewhat frivolous extra-curricular activities of fourteenth-century college men. All four share one general characteristic of college men of the period, namely, a predilection for rather violent expedients,[13] such as Absalon's laying on of the hot coulter, or the beating up of the Miller. Records of the period tell repeatedly of violent physical brawls among the students: brawls erupting into civil war sometimes causing deaths on both sides, whether the war was between town and gown, like the "Great Slaughter" at Oxford in 1354, in which over thirty men died, or between regional factions of the students, northern v. southern, such as is attested to in the Oxford Coroner's Rolls of 1314 detailing the deaths of two students: the jury (read the Coroner's Rolls) "say upon their oath that, on the Saturday aforesaid, after the hour of noon, the Northern clerks on the one part, and the Southern and Western clerks on the other, came to St John's Street and Grope Lane with swords, bucklers, bows, arrows and other arms, and there they fought together."[14] It is noteworthy that Chaucer takes pains to tell us that Alan and John, who beat up the Miller, were from Strother in the North; and Chaucer depicts them as speaking in a pronounced northern dialect. Perhaps they learned their violent ways in some of these factional wars. There is some reason for believing that these frays were somewhat more common at Oxford than at Cambridge; at any rate, Hastings Rashdall, himself an Oxford man, comments that, because of ecclesiastical immunities, the worst that could happen to an Oxford culprit usually was to be compelled to go to Cambridge to finish his studies.[15]

Chaucer also depicts for us three less frivolous clerks, three who at any rate are engaged in intellectual activities which should be more characteristic of university men: the clerk of Orleans in the *Franklin's Tale*, the Clerk of Oxenford who tells the tale of Griseldis, and the Wife of Bath's fifth husband.

With the *Franklin's Tale* we turn from fabliau to romance. Yet even in his romances, where the happenings and people are wondrous or supernatural, Chaucer is concerned with making his characters and their actions as credible as possible. In a recent essay I analysed in detail how Chaucer fitted the character of his clerk of Orleans to the demands of the plot and thus rendered the clerk's part in the story believable.[16] Here I would merely like to demonstrate Chaucer's realistic reporting of details about the University of Orleans, details which, well known to Chaucer's audience, would have made his account of the clerk seem true to them.

In the *Franklin's Tale*, when Aurelius was set the task of removing the rocks from the shore, it was Aurelius' brother who thought of going to Orleans for astrological help. The brother had formerly been a student at Orleans, and he recalled from his college days that one of his Orleans college mates, though studying to become a lawyer, had devoted a great deal of his time to books of natural magic and had acquired great proficiency therein. Though this had been years ago, the brother still hoped that some clerk at Orleans might have the learning in magic that would enable him to achieve the impossible task that had been set Aurelius. And indeed it did turn out so.

In all this Chaucer was reflecting two well-known facts concerning the University of Orleans. The first was that students there would normally be studying law. Indeed, in the fourteenth century, there was no faculty in arts at Orleans, only a faculty in law, both canon and civil.[17] Thus it was a realistic touch that the student whom the brother remembered had been studying law. The other fact was that the University of Orleans was a hotbed of astrological and magical studies, not formally, but informally. There is an interesting passage in the earliest extant French conversation manual entitled *La Maniere de Language . . . de France*, written in 1396, just four years before Chaucer died, which illustrates the reputation of Orleans for both legal and necromantic studies:

[Q.] *Est Aurilians une beau ville?*

[R.] *Oil, sire, si Dieu m'ait, le plus belle que soit ou roialme de France apres Paris. Et aussi il en y a une grande estude des loys, car les plus vaillanz et les plus gentilx clers qui sont ou cristiantee y repairent pour estudier en civil et canonn.*

[Q.] *Mon tresdoulz amy, je vous encroy bien, mais toutes voies j'oy dire que l'anemy y apprent ses desciples de nigromancie en une teste.*

There is also a poem in Hazlitt's *Early Popular Poetry* (III, 79) entitled "A Mery Geste of the Frere and the Boye" in which occur the lines,

> He is a grete nigromancere,
> In all Orlyannce is not his pere.[18]

Thus we see Chaucer enhancing the credibility of his story by using realistic details concerning the University of Orleans and his Orleans clerk.

If the clerk of Orleans was engaged in studies which in some quarters were considered allied to the devil, no hint of such alliance attaches to the exemplary studies of the Clerk of Oxenford who tells the tale of Griseldis. On the contrary, he is all devoutness and orthodoxy. With him, as with the clerk of Orleans, I shall not attempt any thorough critical analysis, but rather deal with a few interesting features of his life as a student.

In the first place there can be no doubt that Chaucer intended a contrast between the Clerk of Oxenford and that other Oxford clerk, hende Nicholas of the *Miller's Tale*. Whereas the Clerk of Oxenford has only a literary, religious interest in ideal, obedient women of the past such as Griseldis, Nicholas hotly makes love to and enjoys that delicious morsel Alison, another man's wife. Students both, they both have books at their bed's head: the Clerk of Oxenford's are of Aristotle and abstract philosophy, Nicholas' of astrology and its practical applications; and whereas the Clerk's shelves are filled entirely with his twenty books which he studies with most care and most heed, there is plenty of room on Nicholas' shelves for his gay psaltery, with which he makes music as he sings his songs of love and carries on his conquests. Clearly Oxford produced both kinds of students: the virtuous and scholarly, like the Clerk, and the amorous "lusty for to pleye," like Nicholas. Chaucer gives us no clear indication of the Clerk of Oxenford's affiliations at the University; but it was long ago plausibly suggested by H. S. V. Jones that he might have been a fellow of Merton College,[19] for an early historian of that college recorded that Merton was especially distinguished as "an example of industry and order" and harboured "young men of gentle nature and studious habits."[20] It may be added that "philosophical Strode," to whom Chaucer dedicated his *Troilus and Criseyde*, was also a fellow of Merton.

Professor Baum conjectures that the Clerk and the Squire must have been the youngest of the Canterbury pilgrims. He reasons thus:

Most boys entered the University at the age of thirteen to sixteen. It took four years to become a Bachelor of Arts, three more to win the M.A. Assuming, apparently, that the Clerk was just about to receive his M.A., Professor Baum concludes: "The Clerk would have been, if he went up at the age of thirteen—which is likely, considering his eagerness for learning—at the most twenty."[21]

Now (Professor Baum further reasons), if the pilgrimage, as is generally agreed, took place in 1387, and if the Clerk were twenty in that year, he must have been born in 1367. He tells us, in the introduction to his tale, that he learned the story of Griseldis from Petrarch, who translated it from Boccaccio's *Decameron* in 1373, then died a year later in 1374.[22] Had the Clerk been born in 1367 and learned the tale from Petrarch as late as 1374, you see the conclusion to which Professor Baum is reduced: the Clerk was only seven years old when he visited Petrarch!

Now Chaucer knew when Petrarch died: he had visited Italy in 1373, just the year before Petrarch's death, and again in 1378, just a few years after it; and the Clerk himself, speaking on the pilgrimage in 1387, comments that Petrarch is now dead and nailed in his chest. Whatever slips in chronological realism an artist may excusably be guilty of, he would hardly have had a boy of twenty claim to have learned a story from the lips of a famous literary man who had died a generation before.

Nor, indeed, is it necessary to accuse Chaucer of such an absurdity. As stated above, a university student required seven years to become M.A. If he wanted to do graduate work in theology, the supreme science, he had to work nine to twelve years more to win his doctorate.[23] No doubt the Clerk of Oxenford, who was unworldly and ascetic, and whose special study was moral virtue, was a graduate student in theology—a course that would have taken no less than sixteen to nineteen years after entrance at the university; and even if a boy entered college at the early age of thirteen he could not emerge a doctor of theology under twenty-nine to thirty-two; and if he entered at the age of sixteen, as many students did (the actual ages on entrance being from thirteen to sixteen), he would have been thirty-two to thirty-five by the time he became doctor of theology. Indeed, "a theologian's training lasted nearly half an ordinary lifetime."[24] I suggest, therefore, that our Clerk of Oxenford was a graduate student in theology nearing the end of his course, that he was in his early thirties, and that therefore there was no absurdity in his claiming that thirteen years before, when he was eighteen or nineteen, he had visited the famous Petrarch and learned from him the tale of Griseldis. And does this age not fit better the total picture we have of the Clerk? He is an obviously learned and mature man.[25] He had been at the University a long time. He "unto logyk hadde longe y-go" (IV, 286). And as a graduate student, he had been teaching as well as studying: "And gladly wolde he lerne and gladly teche" (IV, 308).

That story of Griseldis which the Clerk learned form Petrarch was the story of an ideal wife, patient and obedient to her husband under repeated intolerable demands which he made of her. She is the antithesis of the Wife of Bath, who, when she told her tale earlier, preached the heretical doctrine that a wife should be sovereign over her husband. Clearly the Clerk was answering the Wife of Bath's heretical views about sovereignty in marriage. But the orthodox Clerk was offended too by other attitudes which the Wife of Bath had expressed: her fleshliness, and her insistence against the teaching of the Church that marriage was as acceptable to God as virginity. Celibacy was the one basic requirement which the Church laid upon clerks in holy orders and upon its religious, the monks and nuns; and the Clerk of Oxenford, himself a celibate, was of course scandalized by the carnal, free thinking, crass-speaking Wife of Bath. The Wife further had said that no clerk can speak well of women; and though the Clerk of Oxenford had at first seemed to gainsay her by speaking well of Griseldis, he finally illustrated the truth of her remark by declaring that no real wife existed in that day who was like Griseldis and by ironically advising all wives to be like the Wife of Bath. Thus the Clerk clearly aligns himself with the antifeminist movement, and the line of battle is clearly drawn between the antifeminist Clerk and the anti-antifeminist Wife of Bath.

The last clerk to be dealt with was also a clerk of Oxenford: he was Jankyn, the fifth husband of this same Wife of Bath. Jankyn, too, was steeped in antifeminist propaganda. Only half the Wife of Bath's forty years, he had just come down from the University when Alice's fourth husband died; and within a month she had snared him into marriage. Soon disillusioned, he found what solace and delight he could in reading and quoting aloud to his wife from a large volume of antifeminist, antimatrimonial propaganda entitled *The Book of Wicked Wives*. The self-assertive Wife of Bath could stand this only so long; finally she grabbed three leaves and tore them out of the book right while he was reading it, and simultaneously fetched him a blow on the cheek with her fist, so that he fell backward into the fireplace. Angrily he picked himself up and knocked her down, where she lay as if dead. Frightened now, he knelt beside her and begged forgiveness; and the upshot was that she gained entire submission from him and he consented to burn the whole book right then and there.

The Wife tells us in some detail what the burnt book contained: chief among its contents were Valerius, and Theophrastus, and St Jerome. The first of these, Valerius, was a long letter written by the great twelfth-century figure Walter Map, Archdeacon of Oxford, to his friend Rufinus, urging him not to get married, with reasons. The second item, Theophrastus, misnamed "The Golden Book of Marriage," paints marriage as anything but golden and concludes that no wise man should ever marry. The third item, by St Jerome, consists of excerpts from a massive epistle against the fourth-century heretic Jovinian who had argued that a virgin is not better than a wife in the sight of God. Jerome lists scores of classical women who chose to die rather than give up virginity, and then lists an infamous group of wicked wives—all arguments against marriage.

The interesting fact is that numerous manuscript volumes like that described by the Wife actually exist. These manuscripts no doubt were read appreciatively by thirteenth- and fourteenth-century clerics pledged to celibacy, and no doubt served to resign them to their bachelorhood, if not rejoice in it. The manuscripts were cherished and studied seriously, for some of them contain long commentaries by later medieval scholars which explicate and develop the ideas contained in the original items. For instance, there are three commentaries on Walter Map's Valerius: one by John Walleys, who became Doctor of Divinity at Oxford around 1260; a second by Nicholas Trevet, a Dominican who studied at Paris and Oxford and who lectured at Oxford; a third by John Ridewall, a Franciscan, who was divinity reader of his order at Oxford. The commentaries by Trevet and Ridewall were both current at Oxford in the early fourteenth century and may be considered rival interpretations available to the Oxford students. Thus the fact that two of Chaucer's Oxford clerks—the teller of the tale of Griseldis, and Jankyn the Wife of Bath's fifth husband who owned *The Book of Wicked Wives*—have strong antimatrimonial views takes on new significance. Since more of these manuscripts are associated with Oxford than with any other place, it is not too much to say that antimatrimonialism constituted "a sort of fourteenth-century Oxford movement" of which Chaucer was aware and which he reflects in the characters of the Clerk of Oxenford and Jankyn.[26]

In summary, one or two generalizations may help to tie loose ends together. Over half of Chaucer's clerks are from Oxford—four out of the seven; and I suppose that it is natural that he should thus favour the older and more famous of the two English universities. He is aware that both frivolous and serious students attend the universities; possibly the fact that he records only the frivolous from Cambridge may reflect some lesser esteem for that institution. His depiction of his college men reveals considerable detailed knowledge of the curriculum, of the extra-curricular reading, of the living and social conditions both at Cambridge and at Oxford, and indeed at Orleans, too; moreover, he makes use of this knowledge to create realistic college characters who fit the specific demands of the action in their plots and so contribute to the overall credibility of the stories in which they occur. Thus he turns his realistic detail to artistic profit and once again demonstrates his simultaneous mastery as creator of character and teller of tales.

LEHIGH UNIVERSITY

NOTES

[1] Hastings Rashdall, *The Universities of Europe in the Middle Ages*, edited by F. M. Powicke and A. B. Emden (1895; rpt. Oxford: Clarendon Press, 1936), III, pp. 393–5.

[2] Austin L. Poole, *Medieval England* (Oxford: Clarendon Press, 1958), II, p. 526. See also Rashdall, op. cit., III, pp. 355–7, for this whole paragraph.

[3] Poole, op. cit., II, p. 526.

[4] George R. Coffman, "The *Miller's Tale*: 3187–3215: Chaucer and the Seven Liberal Arts in the Burlesque Vein," *MLN*, 67 (1952), pp. 329–31.

[5] Stith Thompson, "The Miller's Tale," in W. F. Bryan and Germaine Dempster (eds), *Sources and Analogues of Chaucer's Canterbury Tales* (Chicago: Univ. of Chicago Press, 1941), pp. 106–23.

[6] John J. O'Connor, "The Astrological Background of the *Miller's Tale*," *Spec.*, 31 (1956), pp. 120–5.

[7] G. G. Coulton, *Medieval Panorama* (Cambridge: Cambridge Univ. Press, 1938), p. 146.

[8] C. E. Mallet, *A History of the University of Oxford* (1924; rpt. New York: Barnes and Noble, 1968), I, p. 291.

[9] Rashdall, op. cit., III, p. 422.

[10] See my essay, "Appropriateness of Character to Plot in the *Franklin's Tale*," in M. Brahmer, S. Helsztyński, and J. Krzyżanowski (eds), *Studies in Language and Literature in Honour of Margaret Schlauch* (Warsaw: PWN—Polish Scientific Publishers, 1966), p. 386.

[11] Astrik L. Gabriel, "The College System in the Fourteenth-Century Universities," in F. L. Utley (ed.), *The Forward Movement of the Fourteenth Century* (Columbus: Ohio State Univ. Press, 1961), p. 92.

[12] Rashdall, op. cit., III, p. 300; see also Derek S. Brewer, "The *Reeve's Tale* and the King's Hall, Cambridge," *ChauR*, 5 (1971), p. 311.

[13] Rashdall, op. cit., III, pp. 427–35.

[14] G. G. Coulton, *Life in the Middle Ages* (Cambridge: Cambridge Univ. Press, 1930), II, p. 76.

[15] Rashdall, op. cit., III, p. 432. Cambridge did not relish receiving Oxford's castoffs, witness her statute, "A scholar coming here who is known . . . to have

been expelled from the university of Oxford as an evildoer is never to be admitted." M. B. Hackett, *The Original Statutes of Cambridge University* (Cambridge: Cambridge Univ. Press, 1970), p. 210.

[16] See my essay cited in footnote 10 above, pp. 394–6.

[17] Rashdall, op. cit., II, p. 151.

[18] James F. Royster, "Chaucer's 'Colle Tregetour,'" *SP*, 23 (1926), pp. 380–4. Royster gives both quotations, with bibliographical information.

[19] H. S. V. Jones, "The Clerk of Oxenford," *PMLA*, 27 (1912), pp. 112–15.

[20] George C. Brodrick, *Memorials of Merton College* (Oxford: Clarendon Press, 1885), Oxford Historical Society, IV, pp. 19–20.

[21] Paull F. Baum, *Chaucer, A Critical Appreciation* (Durham, N. C.: Duke Univ. Press, 1958), p. 139.

[22] See my book, *The Literary Relationships of Chaucer's Clerkes Tale* (New Haven: Yale Univ. Press, 1942), pp. 7–9.

[23] Mallet, op. cit., I, pp. 188–96; and L. J. Daly, *The Medieval University* 1200–1400 (New York: Sheed and Ward, 1961), pp. 144–51. For requirements for the various degrees at Oxford, see Rashdall, op. cit., III, pp. 153–60.

[24] Rashdall, op. cit., III, p. 411. The University of Paris did not permit one to take the doctorate in theology before he was 35 (Daly, op. cit., p. 145).

[25] Cf. Huling E. Ussery, "How Old Is Chaucer's Clerk?" *TSE*, 15 (1967), pp. 1–18. Professor Ussery argues interestingly that he is even more mature, "an eminent middle-aged logician." My own conclusions were reached before I read Professor Ussery's article: this paper on Chaucer's clerks was originally delivered as an invited address before the Pennsylvania College English Association in April 1967.

[26] Robert A. Pratt, "Jankyn's Book of Wikked Wyves: Medieval Antimatrimonial Propaganda in the Universities," *AM*, 3 (1962), pp. 5–27.

I I

SOME FIFTEENTH-CENTURY MANUSCRIPTS OF THE *CANTERBURY TALES*

BY DANIEL S. SILVIA

It has been customary to measure the popularity and circulation of medieval literary works by counting the surviving MSS. R. W. Ackerman commenced his discussion of the *Canterbury Tales* with such a count: "Including fragments, *The Canterbury Tales* is preserved to us in approximately 90 MSS, the discrepancies among which are directly responsible for a vast amount of scholarly activity."[1] Rossell Hope Robbins, however, counted fewer: "It exists in 64 MSS, second only to the *Pricke of Conscience* in 115 MSS."[2] And again, the two principal editions of the *Tales* (Manly and Rickert; Robinson) number eighty-two extant MSS or fragments that date from the fifteenth century.[3]

The present paper proposes to examine this discrepancy, its causes and some of the implications that can be drawn from the evidence. To begin with, all extant MSS containing any portion of the *Tales* do not represent MSS of once-complete versions of the *Tales*. While Professor Robbins has limited himself to counting MSS representing the complete work, others have generally counted any MS containing any part of the work. Whatever the final count, the *Tales* do in fact survive in more MSS than all other works but one. That is nothing new. What has not been sufficiently investigated is the group of MSS that contain some portion of the *Tales*, that never in fact contained more of the work than they now do, that are in fact not fragments of the complete *Tales*. These *other* MSS have minor interest for the textual critic, more interest for those who are concerned with questions of Chaucer's popularity and the reading tastes of the fifteenth century. Indeed, anyone concerned with literary interpretation should be concerned with the various contexts in which Chaucer's works were read, and a selected few of the *Tales* were read in contexts other than that of the complete *Tales*.

For convenience, it is useful to divide the extant MSS into three groups so that certain principal features and variations among MS types may more clearly emerge.

Fifty-five MSS have survived with reasonably complete texts of the *Tales*. Of these, nine originally contained the *Tales* along with works by other authors, while forty-six contained only the *Tales*.[4] These forty-six MSS peak between 1450 and 1480, when they start to slacken off with Caxton's printings in *c.* 1478 and *c.* 1484.

Most of the remaining nine MSS that contain "complete" texts of the whole of the *Tales* have about them a notable likeness of organization; seven possess the further similarity of containing, in addition to Chaucer's poetry, only works by his most prolific admirer, John Lydgate.[5] Of the remaining two MSS, one (Ha³) is a "library" of secular literature assembled by a religious house,[6] and the other (Dl) a collection of the *Tales* and selections from the *Confessio Amantis* prepared for a patron.

In the entire group of MSS that contain complete versions of the *Tales*, then, Lydgate alone figures prominently as a writer (essentially of secular compositions) whose works appear with the *Tales*. And the work by Lydgate that appears most often, the *Siege*, was taken to be by Chaucer. Selections of Gower appear only in two MSS.

In every instance in which the complete *Tales* appears in a MS, the *Tales* dominates that MS. Indeed, only two MSS (Gg, Ha³) contain extensive material in addition and these do not commence with the *Tales*. The important point about this large group of MSS, then, is how remarkably similar to each other fifty-three of these fifty-five MSS are.

In addition to these fifty-five MSS that, by fifteenth-century standards, contain complete versions, there exist still twenty-seven MSS that contain some part of the *Tales*. Of these twenty-seven, eight are fragments—mostly stray leaves—surviving from an earlier state that *may* have constituted a complete version of the *Tales*. These fragments, five certainly[7] and three possibly,[8] added to the fifty-five complete texts, produce a grand total of between sixty and sixty-three MSS now extant that are either complete or survivors of once-complete fifteenth-century texts of the *Tales*.[9] I would suggest that in the future writers speak about "roughly sixty" MSS of the *Tales* being extant. Though that is still an impressive figure, it is considerably smaller than the ones generally encountered.

While the remaining nineteen MSS should not be included in any count of "manuscripts of the *Tales*," it would be ill-advised, nevertheless, to exclude them from all consideration. Though they have little value in determining the text of the *Tales* and no value in assessing the extent of circulation of the *Tales*, they can provide information about the workings of the literary consciousness of their scribes and readers.

Three of these nineteen MSS are the products of certain easily understood procedures that will require little investigation:

1410   Ad⁴   Additional 10340
1470   Ha¹   Harley 1239
1490   Si   Sion College, Arch. L. 40. 2. E

Written very early, Ad⁴ is nevertheless insignificant: it contains only the *General Prologue* description of the Parson, quoted from memory, and written on a flyleaf. In the case of Ha¹ the scribe was selective, adding certain tales to the second half of a MS begun by the *Troilus*: the tales of the Knight, Man of Law (with Prologue), Wife of Bath, Clerk, and Franklin. All of these similar (because courtly) pieces would have been of interest to a homogeneous (courtly) audience; the compiler obviously knew Chaucer's work well enough to select only what he wanted. The final MS of the three, Si, is almost certainly complete as it now stands: the *Clerk's Tale* followed by Group D of the *Tales*, at the end of which is the first line of the *Clerk's Headlink* (did the scribe discover late that the *Clerk's Tale* followed Group D?). There is no other manuscript that presents similar contents; in a selection, it makes little sense simply to prepare a contiguous passage of such a sort. None of these three MSS is the fragment of a once-complete *Tales*. Neither can Ad⁴ or Si be considered anthologies.

The sixteen MSS that remain are anthologies. They present a context (and milieu) in which some of the *Tales* were read quite apart from the *Tales* complete; these MSS represent collections of various sorts, in which a piece or two from the *Tales* has a place within the whole, often with no mention of Chaucer at all. (Context and environment can here provide a kind of near-contemporary evidence concerning attitudes toward those tales excerpted at least as important as that accumulated in the later recorded opinions and Chaucer allusions.)

On the basis of their Chaucerian contents—and despite one overlap—these sixteen MS collections can be divided into two groups; those containing "courtly" works (*Man of Law's Tale, Knight's Tale, Clerk's Tale*—five MSS)[10] and those containing one or more of Chaucer's "moral pieces" (*Prioress's Tale, Second Nun's Tale, Monk's Tale, Melibeus, Parson's Tale, Retraction*—twelve MSS). In the courtly group, the *Clerk's Tale* appears in four MSS, while the other two tales appear once each only; taken together with its appearance in Ha¹ and Si, the *Clerk's Tale* represents the most frequently copied work among the *Tales*. Among the moral pieces, both the *Prioress's Tale* and *Melibeus* are represented in five MSS each, no other piece appearing more than twice. With the exception of the *Knight's Tale*, these are not among the pieces for which Chaucer is today principally esteemed; nor are they among the ones typically anthologized today. Indeed, it is unlikely that in the fifteenth century they were anthologized as being "Chaucer's Best;" quite to the contrary. Such literary considerations for this group were irrelevant. The sixteen MSS had various purposes, none apparently belletristic; like the other works present, Chaucer's pieces simply fitted into a larger plan for the various scribes. These sixteen MSS are

1430	Ll^2	Longleat 29
1460	Ar	Arundel 140
	Np	Naples xiii. B. 29
	St	Stonyhurst B. xxiii
1470	Hl^1	Harley 1704
	Hl^2	Harley 2251
	Ll^1	Longleat 257
1480	Ph^4	Phillipps 8299 (HM 140)
1490	Ct	Chetham 6709
	Tc^3	Trinity College Cambridge, R. 3. 19
1500	Ee	Cambridge Ee. 2. 15
	Hl^3	Harley 2382
	Hn	Huntington (HM 144)
	Pp	Pepys 2006
	Ra^4	Rawlinson C. 86
	Sl^3	Sloane 1009

Of the eight MSS to which Manly assigns a 1500 *terminus*, six appear in this group. With but one exception, all these MSS date from the latter half of the century. Within the sixteen MSS will be found nine different pieces from the *Canterbury Tales: Knight's Tale, Man of Law's Tale, Prioress's Tale, Melibeus, Monk's Tale, Clerk's Tale, Second Nun's Tale, Parson's Tale*, and the *Retraction*. The table on p. 157 is meant as a visual aid for examining the distribution of the pieces.

By their size and range of contents, these MS anthologies that contain only a tale or two of Chaucer's demonstrate that the Canterbury pieces were included for reasons quite apart from any relationship with Chaucer: there is generally no mention of Chaucer as author of his tales, even. Thus at least these certain ones of the *Tales* were read for reasons quite apart from considerations of Chaucer or any Canterbury sequence.

All in all, it appears that none of the MSS that exhibit the *Tales* complete can provide the kind of information to be found in these anthologies. That is so because all the MSS devoted to the complete *Tales* (except for Ha^3) were dominated by the work. As a corollary, it may be noted that today the *Tales*, complete, will not appear in any text anthology: the work is simply too extensive in itself. Those nine

"Courtly"			"Moral"					
MLT	KnT	ClT	PrT	SNT	MkT	Mel	PsT	Retr
Ee								
	Ll¹	Ll¹						
		Np						
		Ph⁴						
		Ra⁴	Ra⁴					
			Hl¹					
			Hl²					
			Ct	Ct				
			Hl³	Hl³				
					Hn	Hn		
					Tc³			
						Ar		
						Sl³		
						St		
						Pp	Pp	Pp
						Ll²		

MSS that contain works in addition to the complete *Tales* have been shown to be remarkably similar to each other; indeed, the group might be useful for study principally as a means of providing information concerning how Lydgate was viewed in relation to Chaucer—and whether the later poet's works were taken to be by the earlier one, or vice-versa.

These sixteen MSS make a small and fairly homogeneous group of Chaucer pieces. Except for the *Knight's Tale*, moreover, all the works that have been separated from the complete *Tales* could be grouped among those works of Chaucer's that "sownen into vertue." In a real sense all the other pieces are "moral." That in itself is significant. No other part of the *Tales* was divorced and presented in any extant MS anthology. None of the fabliaux were so anthologized. A kind of negative evidence, if you will, can be adduced for the works omitted from consideration by the anthologizers. For example, it can be inferred that no one viewed any of the fabliaux as appropriate companions, literally or allegorically, for the explicitly moral pieces.

Study of these sixteen MS anthologies might well reveal certain attitudes toward those tales by Chaucer that are included—attitudes as to purpose of the tale, attitudes as to how the tale should be read—to be adduced through the MS context in which the tales are set. Further, a certain negative evidence can be accumulated concerning works omitted from the anthologies. In view of the difficulties involved in knowing how works of earlier periods are to be read, the careful study of extant MSS can be helpful. I believe that from these MS anthologies one can deduce certain fifteenth-century notions about the works included. One regrets the vacuum in which, say, *Beowulf* has reached the present: one MS, dating from a time far removed from the date of composition of the poem. Unlike a work that has come to us in a solitary form, in the case of some of the *Tales* there is some slight variety. The context for a work provided by its inclusion in an anthology can provide a useful adjunct to the naked text in helping to determine meaning, intent, and significance.

While it lies beyond the intent and scope of the present study to exhaust the implications to be found in all the kinds of analyses that could be made, it is nevertheless to the point to illustrate what further study could develop. Two MSS of the group that will admirably serve are housed at the Henry E. Huntington Library: Huntington MS 144 (Hn) and Huntington MS 140 (Ph⁴—after its previous Phillipps MS 8299 classification).

In its present form, MS Ph⁴ contains sixteen items. Two or three originally separate books were brought together to constitute the present manuscript. The first book contains eight pieces, all by Lydgate or Chaucer (ff. 1–92); it was written by five scribes over some period of time (Manly dates it 1450–80). The remainder of the MS (ff. 93–169) may possibly be the result of two separate books (ff. 92–124 and 125–69). In it there are seven pieces, all of religious or moral nature and in English, save for *Apollonius of Tyre* in Latin.[11] The only part of the MS germane to the present study, the first part, is a Lydgate-Chaucer anthology, but one that is quite different from MSS of the complete *Tales*.

Here it is Lydgate's, not Chaucer's, work that predominates. Works by Chaucer are the *Clerk's Tale*, "Truth," and "Anelida's Complaint;" they occupy nineteen and a half folios. Lydgate's work consists of his *Life of St Alban and St Amphibal*, "Prayer upon the Cross," "Midsummer Rose," "Song of Virtue," and "Testament;" they occupy seventy-four and a half folios. The *Life of St Alban and St Amphibal*, which commences the MS, ends with an elaborate *explicit* in red:

> Here endith the glorious lyf and passyoun of the blessid
> martir / Seint Albone and seint Amphiball which glorious
> livis / were translatid oute of ffrenssh and latyn by
> dane John / lydgate Monke of Bury at þe request and
> prayer of Master / John whethamstede the yere of our lord

M¹ CCCC xxxix / and of the said Master John whethamstede
of his Abisse xix /

The *Clerk's Tale*, which follows it after a single blank page, is
written without any sort of division into stanzas. Indeed, the ballade
"Truth" follows immediately upon the last line of ClT without any
indication at all that another work has commenced, thus:

> And let hym curs wepe wryng and wayle
> ffle from the prees and dwell with sothfastnesse.

There is no mention of Chaucer. "Truth" ends with a large "Explicit,"
nothing more; the same sort of "Explicit" appears after the following
short works in the MS. Beyond the *explicit* there is only a blank half-
page after the poem. The Lydgate section at the beginning of the
MS is treated with a certain attention by the scribe that is not given
to the following Chaucer piece. "Anelida's Complaint" again makes
no mention of Chaucer; there appears the text of ll. 211–350 of
Anelida and Arcite, after which there is a space and then "Here endeth
the compleynt of Anelida the Quene of hermenye vpon fals Arcite of
Thebees."[12]

Lydgate's *Testament*, which is the final piece of the first book, is
incomplete. It may be fragmentary, but also it is possible that the
book today is missing additional leaves at its end. If more poems were
once present in those possibly missing leaves, it is likely they would
follow the pattern already set; namely, they would most likely be by
Lydgate.

Manly records a will, dated 16 January 1458/9 of one Sir Thomas
Chaworth, bequeathing three English books by title: *Policronicon,
Grace de Dieu,* and *Orilogium Sapiencie.* A fourth book, untitled, is
described in the bequest: "a newe boke of Inglisse ye which begynnyth
with ye lyffe of Seynt Albon and Amphiabell and other mony dyvers
lyfez and thynges in ye same boke." MS Ph⁴, Manly asserts, alone
among extant MSS answers the description (Manly, p. 609). If it is
the same MS, it should be noted that the will ignores, is ignorant of,
or seems not to recognize either Lydgate or Chaucer.

A religious MS, Hn has a more varied content than does Ph⁴ (see
Manly, 289; Manly's foliation disagrees at many points with the MS
itself). One hand wrote the entire MS, which is something of a religious anthology of fifteen pieces. The two contributions by Chaucer
stand together with no indication that their authorship was either
known or relevant. *Melibeus* appears with the running title "Prouerbis;"[13] at its conclusion the scribe wrote: "They that this present &
forseyde tale / haue or shal Reede: Remembyr the no/ble prouerbis.
that rebukyth Couetise / and Vengeaunse takyng. in truste of / For-

tune. which hathe causyd many / a noble Prince to falle. as we may rede / of them here folluyng."

Under the next MS heading, "The falle of Princis," commences the *Monk's Tale*:

> I wil biwaile in maner of tregede
> The harme of hem þat stod in heigh degre.

Manly demonstrates that the *Monk's Tale* was written down before the *Melibeus* (see p. 292). Even so, both of Chaucer's pieces derive from the same textual tradition (Manly, p. 291) and appear in proper tale order. Nevertheless, though the tales appear in proper Canterbury sequence and derive from the same textual tradition, the manuscript's physical make-up and the works' context imply that neither scribe nor patron for whom the MS was made knew that the tales were Chaucer's. The two Chaucer pieces occupy approximately thirty-one folios, more than the works of any other author; Benedict Burgh's *Cato* occupies twenty-two folios, and various pieces by Lydgate taken together fill twenty-three folios. Burgh's work is properly labelled by the scribe ("*Hic Incipit Paruus Catho*" and "*Hic Incipit magnus Catho*"). So is some of Lydgate's (e.g., "Here begynnyth the Tale of the Chorle and the Byrde" and "Thus endeth the hors, the Goos & þe Sheep"). On the other hand, Lydgate's *Life of Our Lady* (item 2 in MS) seems not to have been recognized even by Manly. The fashion of writing down portions of longer works is to be found especially toward the end of the MS, and the *Magnificat* from Lydgate's *Life of Our Lady* appears, inserted within the text of "The Pilgrymage and the wayes of Ierusalem." Clearly, the earlier medieval tradition of the anonymous author was not dead by the end of the fifteenth century.

In the case of both MSS examined, one secular and one religious, the name and fame of Chaucer are either irrelevant or lost to the MS maker. While it is possible to argue that Chaucer's name would not have to be attached for his work to be recognized, the evidence particularly of MS Hn argues against such a possibility: the heading "Prouerbis" for the *Melibeus* can hardly be the product of literary awareness.

These two MSS provide but two illustrations—and I suggest not eccentric—of a few of the facts that an examination of the MSS can reveal. Some years ago Robert A. Pratt argued the importance of MS study for knowledge about medieval education; it was his position that specific text and context cannot be ignored.[14] I suggest that a similar case can be made for studying the MSS that contain any part of Chaucer's works.

From the present study it should be clear that in the fifteenth century the *Canterbury Tales* appeared in one format: a complete version of the *Tales* that with only rare and notable exception dominated the MS in which it appeared, if indeed it were not the sole item (which was far more generally the case). Practically no other authors' works ever appeared in these MSS; Gower and Lydgate's works alone appeared more than once, with only Lydgate's being at all extensive. There are some MS fragments that derive from MSS that formerly were of the sort here described. In addition, there is a second fifteenth-century format: that of individual tales from the *Canterbury Tales*, appearing in anthologies. In these anthologies two kinds only of Chaucer's tales ever appear apart from the complete *Tales*: certain "courtly" tales and the "moral pieces." The basis for inclusion in the sixteen MS anthologies is similarity to each other of those works included; there is virtually no mixing of works with differing aims. The only possible exception to such a "rule" is MS Ra[4], a very large miscellany that contains both the *Clerk's Tale* (courtly) and the *Prioress's Tale* (moral). But it is likely that MS Ra[4] is the result of bringing together 4 or 5 originally separate books (see Manly, p. 473); if such is the case, the two Chaucer pieces appeared originally in different books entirely, and it is only by chance that they are now bound together.[15]

The *Canterbury Tales* does not travel from the poet's day to ours in a single, simple form. Nor does it assume a heterogeneous gaggle of formats. There are sixty to sixty-three MSS now extant that are either complete or survivors of once complete fifteenth-century texts of the *Tales*. With the exception of one eccentric compilation (MS Si) and one irrelevant bit of scribble (MS Ad[4]), the remaining MSS contain tales anthologized because of their appeal to a religious, moral, or courtly interest (I include in this group MS Ha[1]). There appear to be no exceptions.

UNIVERSITY OF CALIFORNIA AT DAVIS

NOTES

[1] "Middle English Literature to 1400," in John H. Fisher (ed.), *The Medieval Literature of Western Europe* (New York: New York Univ. Press for the Modern Language Association of America, 1966), p. 116.

[2] "The English Fabliau: Before and After Chaucer," *MSpr*, 64 (1970), p. 232. MSS listed in Carleton Brown and Rossell Hope Robbins, *The Index of Middle English Verse* (New York: Columbia Univ. Press, 1943), no. 4019; unlike the present study, the *Index* lists MS Ha[1] as a "fragmentary text:" thus Robbins' total of 64, as opposed to the present study's 63.

[3] Eighty-three, if the Oxford MS, which exists in two separated sections, is

counted now as two distinct authorities; eighty-four, if in addition the fragment of the *Pardoner's Tale* found in MS Morgan 249 is counted separately from the main text of that manuscript (of which it is a duplicate page made in error).

In preparing the present study I have relied on two principal sources: John M. Manly and Edith Rickert, *The Text of the Canterbury Tales*, 8 vols. (Chicago, 1940), and microfilms of all the manuscripts of the *Tales*, which I have been able to obtain through the generosity of the University of California Committee on Research and the graciousness of those libraries possessing the manuscripts. In addition, I am particularly indebted to the trustees of the Henry E. Huntington Library and Art Gallery for permission to examine and discuss in my study two manuscripts in their collection: MSS HM 140 and 144. Throughout my study the MS sigla adopted are those used by Manly and Rickert; volume I of their work is used extensively and will be referred to throughout as *Manly*. Unless otherwise noted, Manly records the contents of all the manuscripts of the *Tales*. The other principal text of the *Tales* is F. N. Robinson (ed.), *The Works of Geoffrey Chaucer*, 2nd edn (Boston: Houghton Mifflin, 1957), whose discussion of the manuscripts (q.v.) appears on pp. 886 ff.

[4] Forty-six MSS, arranged by decade, according to terminal dates for completion in Manly, II, 48; 1410—El (Ellesmere); Ha⁴ (Harley 7334); Hg (Hengwyrt); 1420—Cp (Corpus Christi 198); Dd (Cambridge Dd. 4. 24); La (Lansdowne 851); 1430—He (Helmingham [vellum]; see below and Manly, 259 f.); Pw (Petworth); 1440—Ps (Paris); 1450—Ad² (Additional 25718); Ad³ (Additional 35286); En¹ (Egerton 2726); En² (Egerton 2863); Hk (Holkham); Ii (Cambridge Ii. 3. 26); Lc (Lichfield 2); Ld¹ (Laud 600); Ln (Lincoln 110); Ph³ (Phillipps 8137); Ry² (Royal 18. C. ii); Sl¹ (Sloane 1685); 1460—Ha² (Harley 1758); He (Helmingham [paper]; see above and Manly, 259 f.); Ht (Hatton Donat 1); Mc (McCormick); Mg (Morgan 249); Mm (Cambridge Mm. 2. 5); Ra¹ (Rawlinson Poetry 141); Ra³ (Rawlinson Poetry 223); Tc¹ (Trinity College, Cambridge, R. 3. 3); 1470—Fi (Fitzwilliam McClean, 181); Ha⁵ (Harley 7335); Ne (New College, Oxford, D. 314); Nl (Northumberland); Ph² (Phillipps 8136); Ra² (Rawlinson Poetry 149); Ry¹ (Royal 17. D. XV); Se (Arch. Selden B. 14); 1480—Bo¹ (Bodley 414); Bw (Barlow 20); Gl (Glasgow); Py (Royal College of Physicians 13); 1490—Ld² (Laud 739); Ma (Manchester Rylands English 113); Sl² (Sloane 1686); To (Trinity College, Oxford, Arch. 49); 1500—Tc² (Trinity College, Cambridge, R. 3. 15). In their present state four of these MSS (Gl, Ii, Ma, and Tc²) contain non-Chaucerian materials that are excrescences—filler for blank leaves of a quire. To attach any significance to such material in the present analysis would be misleading. The tales of *Gamelyn* and *Beryn* I count as part of the *Canterbury Tales* because they do not exist apart from the *Tales* and were considered to be by Chaucer; other insertions of works taken to be by Chaucer will be discussed as appropriate. This study is concerned with the fifteenth-century MS state and ignores those additions that date clearly from the sixteenth century. In its present state MS Ra³ is the result of two dissimilar MSS being put together at some later date than that of writing: a fragment of Lydgate's *Troy Book* (paper, of smaller size, and different hand) and the *Tales* (vellum). Today MS Ry¹ consists of the *Tales* plus four fifteenth-century pieces that seem to have been attached, when written down, to the already-completed MS of the *Tales*; it cannot be said when the materials were brought together, though in an earlier state the non-Chaucerian pieces preceded the *Tales*, which they now follow (see Manly, 476, 481).

[5] MSS containing *only* Lydgate works in addition to Chaucer: 1440—Bo²

(Bodley 686); Gg (Camb Univ. Gg. 4.27); 1450—Cn (Cardigan): 1460—Ds (Devonshire): 1470—Ch (Christ Church, Oxford, 152); 1480—En³ (Egerton 2864); 1500—Ad¹ (Additional 5140). For Gg, see Manly, pp. 178–9; also Robert A. Caldwell, "Peculiarities of the Cambridge University Library MS, Gg. 4. 27," Diss. University of Chicago 1938; and idem, "The Scribe of the Chaucer MS, Cambridge University Library Gg. 4 27," *MLQ*, 5 (1944), pp. 33–44.

6 For Ha³ see Eleanor P. Hammond, *Chaucer: A Bibliographical Manual* (1908; rpt. New York: Peter Smith, 1933), pp. 176–7; see also Manly, pp. 207, 209, 214.

7 MSS 1410—Me (Merthyr); 1450—Ox (Oxford: Manchester Rylands Eng. 63 and Rosenbach); Pl (Plimpton); 1470—Do (Douce d. 4); Ph¹ (Philipps 6570). MS Do exists as a single leaf that was most likely used in the binding of a book (Manly, 125); it contains lines A 298–368 of the *General Prologue*, hardly a piece to be quoted at such length apart from a complete text of the *Tales*. Somewhat similarly, MS Me, a fragment of 3 leaves, could hardly represent anything short of a complete text, as it contains part of the *Nun's Priest's Tale* preceded by the *Nun's Priest's Link*: only in a full work would there be need—or justification—for the link. MS Ox exists as two fragments now separated but properly treated as a single manuscript; taken together, the 13 leaves represent snippets from various sections of what could only be a once-complete *Tales*. So also MS Pl, which contains on its double leaf a continuous passage, from the *Merchant's Endlink* to *Squire's Headlink* (changed here to *Franklin's Headlink*), followed by the *Franklin's Prologue* (on one of the 2 leaves) and a passage from the *Franklin's Tale* (on the other half of the double leaf): although the manuscript apparently omitted the *Squire's Tale*, still the framework present is appropriate only to the complete *Tales*. The fifth fragment, MS Ph¹, consists of 2 fragments of 12 folios each (one runs from C 831 to B 2543 [tale order C–B²], the other from I 587–1092); *prima facie*, two such sections can come only from a complete version; Manly (pp. 416–17) believes the manuscript was originally a large anthology.

8 MSS 1450—Ds² (Devonshire fragment) [cf. Ee]; Hl⁴ (Harley 5908 [cf. Ll¹, Np, Ph⁴, Ra⁴]; Kk (Camb. Univ. Kk. 1.3 [cf. Ct, Hl¹, Hl², Hl³, Ra⁴]. The two leaves of MS Ds² contain *Man of Law's Tale*, B 850–924, 1076–1144; the single leaf of MS Hl⁴ presents *Clerk's Tale*, E 808–91; MS Kk today has one vellum leaf bound in it containing *Prioress's Tale*, B 1650–1719.

9 For an explanation of Robbins' count of 64 MSS, see n. 2 above.

10 I use the term "courtly" with some reservations, inasmuch as ClT and MLT could both perhaps better be labelled "moral-courtly."

11 For full description of MS see Manly, p. 433. Manly's foliation consistently varies by one from my own examination of the MS.

12 Three other MSS contain the "Complaint" extracted from the longer work. Robbins discusses the practice of extrapolating from longer poems in "A New Lydgate Fragment," *ELN*, 5 (1968), pp. 243–7.

13 In a later hand, identified as John Stowe's, is written at the beginning "Chawsers talle of melebe."

14 "The Importance of Manuscripts for the Study of Medieval Education as Revealed by the Learning of Chaucer," *Progress of Medieval and Renaissance Studies*, Bull. no. 20 (1949), pp. 43–51.

15 Even if MS Ra⁴ was from the beginning intended as a single book (though most unlikely), the instance would prove exceptional only if my manufactured two categories are taken as definitive and rigid: Griselda's story is not that far distant in story and structure from the *Prioress's Tale*: it is something of a secular saint's life.

12

THE INTERLUDES OF THE MARRIAGE
GROUP IN THE *CANTERBURY TALES*

BY †CLAIR C. OLSON

Of all the dramatic devices used by Chaucer in his *Canterbury Tales*, the so-called Marriage Group is doubtless the most vividly dynamic. As to speculations that it may not exist, I leave all such "to divynys." The pro and con and final compromise of the principal tales of the group, as well as the Clerk of Oxford's song in honour of the Wife of Bath, the Merchant's passing reference to

> The Wife of Bath if ye han vnderstonde
> Of mariage which we haue on honde,

Harry Bailey's rueful reflections on his own married state, the Merchant's dramatic catching up and adaptation of the last line of the song to the Wife of Bath and his avowed purpose to talk of experiences in marriage, to say nothing of the detailed and explicit exposition by the Franklin of the relations between love and "maistrye" in married couples and his allusions to the ideas on marriage expressed by the Wife, the Clerk, and the Merchant—all these seem to me, as they have to others, conclusive evidence that Chaucer intended to have a group of his Canterbury pilgrims conduct a species of dramatized "debate" on the conditions necessary to produce happiness in marriage.

One of the finest aspects of Chaucer's dramatic art is the skill with which he employs a pattern that had been used in a somewhat obvious fashion by others but makes it more life-like by saturating it with the complexities of ordinary life. The mature Chaucer who wrote the best of the *Canterbury Tales* would certainly not use a baldly schematic device, whereby one character would present one side of a case, a second, the opposite side, and a third, the necessary compromise. That would not represent real life any more accurately than did the one, two, three of an old-fashioned high school debate. Such a plan might underlie one of Chaucer's beautifully detailed dramatic sketches; but the bare essentials—the rafters, beams, and girders—must be concealed from sight by a skilfully designed facade of details taken straight from the dramatic interplay of life as we all live it every day.[1]

Chaucer has done this with great effectiveness in all the principal tales of the Marriage Group except the Wife of Bath's, in which it is not needed. The Clerk of Oxford tells a story purporting to show that men should dominate their wives; but, as he is a cleric, he applies the principle of the story to the relations between God and man. The Merchant opens his tale with a long passage in praise of marriage, stressing among other thing its economic advantages, but the whole passage is highly ironical in the light of the final outcome of the story. In the *Franklin's Tale*, the idea of magnanimity between husband and wife is introduced in an abstract passage of forty-one lines near the beginning (V, 761–802), but is not emphasized at the end. To avoid too mechanical a scheme, Chaucer, in true medieval fashion, ends the story with the question of a three-point *demande d'amour* as to which was "the moste fre:" the knight, the squire, or the clerk.

For this reason the interludes of the Marriage Group deserve closer analysis than they have hitherto received. There are, of course, two: the comic interlude of the Friar's and the Summoner's tales, and the realistic-romantic interlude composed of the Merchant's and the Squire's tales. They are much more than mere interruptions, as they have been called. The relations they bear to the three principal tales of the group and to each other are one of the best illustrations we have of Chaucer's seemingly casual yet penetratingly realistic depiction of life.

Reduced to its simplest form, the Marriage Group consists of the three stories which present the woman's side, the man's side, and the compromise view of marital relations, with an interlude of two stories between the first and the second, and another interlude of two stories between the second and the third:

I. *Wife of Bath's Tale:* Women should dominate their husbands. [First Interlude: Coarse and humorous realistic tales by the Friar and the Summoner against each other; appropriate in atmosphere, but having no subject-matter connection with the theme of the Marriage Group.]

II. *Clerk's Tale:* Men should dominate their wives. [Second Interlude: Realistic tale by the Merchant balancing romantic exotic tale of adventure and love by the Squire, having no direct bearing on the theme under discussion, but serving as a transition from the cynicism of the *Merchant's Tale* to the idealism of the Franklin's.]

III. *Franklin's Tale:* Happiness in marriage is obtainable only if neither the husband nor the wife tries to dominate.

It is possible, however, to consider the *Merchant's Tale*, because of its emphasis on "the wo that is in mariage" as one of the principal stories. Indeed, several critics have done so,[2] restricting the second interlude to the *Squire's Tale*. According to this plan, the Marriage Group would be constructed as follows :

I. *Wife of Bath's Tale.*
[First Interlude: *Friar's Tale; Summoner's Tale.*]
II. *Clerk's Tale.*
III. *Merchant's Tale.* Women are deceitful, and marriage can be happy only if men are foolish and blind.
[Second Interlude: *Squire's Tale.*]
IV. *Franklin's Tale.*

By this view, the *Merchant's Tale* may seem to be raised in importance, and the overall plan of the Group may appear somewhat more complex. But, although very closely tied into the theme of the Marriage Group, and thus differing from the other three tales of the interludes, it is not part of the pro, con, and compromise structure of the Group, because the real object of its bitter sarcasm is not May's inadequacy but January's, and by the same token the Merchant's foolish and short-sighted reasons not only for marrying but for choosing an incompatible wife.[3] Therefore it seems more logical to consider it as part of the second interlude than as one of the principal tales of the Group.

No matter which plan is followed in the analysis of the Marriage Group, the important element lies in the nature of the tales comprising the interludes and their relations to the tales they follow and precede, as will become clear.

The first shot in the Marriage Group is fired by the Wife of Bath in her *Prologue* and *Tale*, a strongly emotional and vividly dramatic presentation of the theory that women should rule in marriage. The tremendous ending of the Wife's tale clinches her point:

> And Jesu Crist us sende
> Housbondes meeke, yonge, fressh a-bedde,
> And grace toverbyde hem that we wedde;
> And eek, I praye, Jesu shorte hir lyves
> That noght wol be governed by hir wyves;
> And olde and angry nygardes of dispence,
> God sende hem soone verray pestilence! (III, 1258–64)

Here is no pious and perfunctory ending such as we find on many of the tales. We know exactly how the Wife of Bath feels, and that her feelings are not only individualized but strongly held. It is the most dramatically appropriate ending in the *Canterbury Tales*.

Instead of passing at once to the opposite view, Chaucer seems to drop the matter. The Friar speaks up, not so much to comment upon the Wife's tale, although he does so, as to vent his pent-up spleen against the Summoner. After what might be called a token remonstrance by Harry Bailey, the Friar tells his clever fabliau directed at the Summoner, who, when it is finished,

> in his styropes hye stood;
> Upon this Frere his herte was so wood
> That lyk an aspen leef he quook for ire. (III, 1665–7)

retorts that "Freres and feendes been but lyte asonder," and proceeds to tell a most unsavoury double-barrelled tale against friars. Quite in the manner of the Pardoner, who preaches on the text *Radix malorum est Cupiditas*, the Summoner has the friar in his tale harangue poor Thomas at great length on the sin of anger, with the result that "This sike man wex wel neigh wood for ire," and bestowed upon the friar the gift which makes the point of the story.

Neither of these stories has any subject matter connection with the *Wife of Bath's Tale* nor with the general topic of the Marriage Group. They are based on the traditional animosity between the regular and the secular clergy, and are the best illustration of the quarrels between the Pilgrims which enliven the *Canterbury Tales*.[4] Their appropriateness is atmospheric rather than factual. Being realistic and in one case vulgar, they follow nicely after the long harangue of the Wife of Bath, who was doubtless not one of the gentils who protested against the Pardoner's telling a tale of "ribaudye." Chaucer skilfully prepares the way for the Friar-Summoner interlude with the Friar's laughing comment on the Wife's Tale, "Now, dame, . . . this is a long preamble to a tale," (III, 830–1) which causes the Summoner to rebuke him with the sarcastic remark that ". . . a flye and eek a frere / Wol falle in every dish and eek matere," (III, 835–6) and with the Wife's fling at friars, who, she says, have replaced the incubus of the old fairy tales, merely dishonouring women instead of carrying them off to fariyland (III, 864–81).

The Summoner's intense story against friars, coming after the Friar's cleverly humorous but not off-colour story about summoners, gives the first interlude an emotional climax. This differentiates it from the second interlude, in which the two stories are entirely unlike, not only from those of the first interlude but also from each other. In the first interlude there is growing emotional tension, not only because of the professional enmity of the Friar and the Summoner, but also because of the Summoner's angry promise to tell a story against friars and limitours. This feature is similar to the Cook's warning to the Host that he will tell a tale against hostelers later on (I, 4358–62), and ties the Summoner's remarks into Chaucer's plan to have each pilgrim tell more than one story.

As Professor Lumiansky has said,[5] Chaucer often arranges the *Canterbury Tales* so that both in type and content they are contrasted in accordance with differences in the personalities of their tellers as indicated in the *General Prologue*. Thus the Friar tells a clever but not off-colour story, at least on this occasion; whereas the Summoner, corresponding to his portrait in the *General Prologue*, and because of his anger at the Friar, tells a most disagreeably vulgar fabliau. There is a greater difference between the tales of the second interlude as the characters of their tellers are entirely different from each other, but in this latter case there is no leading up to a climax, as the disagreeable tale (the Merchant's) comes first, and the *Squire's Tale* is an appropriately smooth transition to that of the Franklin.

The change in point of view comes with the middle tale of the Marriage Group, the Clerk of Oxford's illustration of the idea that the woman should obey the man, even though he admits that his story goes further than he could expect any mortal woman to go. The Clerk, being a student of divinity, pretends to conceal his meaning behind a front of pious application:

> This storie is seyd, nat for that wyves sholde
> Folwen Griselda, as in humyltee;
> For it were inportable, though they wolde;
> But for that every wight, in his degree,
> Sholde be constant in adversitee,
> As was Griselda. Therfore Petrak writeth
> This storie, which with heigh stile he enditeth.
>   For sith a woman was so pacient
> Unto a mortal man, wel moore us oghte
> Receyven al in gree that God us sent;
> . . . .
> He preeveth folk al day, it is no drede. (IV, 1142–55)

But the Clerk's real purpose in telling the story of Griselda comes out in the biting sarcasm of the song which he says he has just composed in honour of the Wife of Bath; and here he comes as near to matching the stormy emotionalism of the Wife as his quiet, scholarly nature will permit:

Ye archiwyves, stondeth at defense!
Syn ye be strong as is a greet camaille,
Ne suffreth nat that men yow doon offense.
And sklendre wyves, fieble as in bataille,
Beth egre as is a tygre yond in Ynde!
Ay clappeth as a mille, I yow consaille.

. . . .

Be ay of chiere as light as leef on lynde,
And lat hym care, and wepe, and wryng, and waille!

(IV, 1195–1212)

In lines which many scholars have thought Chaucer originally intended to link the *Clerk's Tale* to the Merchant's, Harry Bailey is spurred to the remark that "Me were levere than a barel ale, / My wyf at home had herd this legend ones," (IV, 1214–15) but quickly subsides, as though it would not be judicious to say exactly why. In lines IV, 2419–40, however, which follow the *Merchant's Tale*, he bursts forth again in greater detail, saying that his wife, even though "trewe as any steel," is "of hir tonge, a labbyng shrewe" and "hath an heep of vices mo." He tries to stop—"Therof no fors! lat alle swich thynges go"—but his feelings drive him on:

But wyte ye what? In conseil be it seyd,
Me reweth soore I am unto hir teyd.
For, and I sholde rekenen every vice
Which that she hath, ywis I were to nyce.

Finally the thought that some of the Pilgrims will give him away when the party returns to the Tabard Inn brings him to a halt.

His longest confession (VII, 3081–3113; B[2], 1891–1923), in which he goes into picturesque and dramatic detail, comes later in the Ellesmere order, as if to show that his previous attempt to bottle up his feelings gave way after the *Tale of Melibeus* in a torrent of emotion as he tells what often happened at the Tabard Inn and the Bailey household. It is tempting to think that Chaucer may have intended these passages to be climactic; yet he seems to have cancelled the first, and if Professor Pratt's suggested order of the tales is correct (*PMLA*, LXVI [1951], 1141–67), the great emotional outburst precedes lines IV, 2419–40. But, as Professor Manly wrote, "None of the extant MSS exhibits an arrangement which with any probability can be ascribed to Chaucer."[6] Yet whatever their order, these passages show that Chaucer intended Harry Bailey to have an important place in his treatment of marriage.[7]

The Merchant in his prologue catches up the Clerk's last words and applies them to himself:

"Wepyng and waylyng, care and oother sorwe,
I knowe ynogh, on even and a-morwe,"
Quod the Marchant, "and so doon othere mo
That wedded been."   (IV, 1213–16)

And so we come to the second interlude, which is directly connected
in subject matter with the theme of the Marriage Group. This second
interlude is not, as was the first, merely for variation and to avoid too
consecutive and schematic a treatment of the theme. The drama has
moved on now to a higher point; two views have been strongly contrasted; and furthermore, Chaucer is too much of an artist to use the
same device twice. If there appears to be repetition, there must also
be variation to correspond with the state of development of the
material. And so the tales which compose this second interlude are
not merely tied into the topic under discussion, but are strongly contrasted with each other—as strikingly as were the tales of the Wife of
Bath and the Clerk.

The *Merchant's Tale* is a bitterly cynical and realistic picture of
some marriages, seen through the eyes of the Merchant and based
upon his own experience. Its function may be to get away from the
extreme position of the *Clerk's Tale* to a more human, though undesir-
able, attitude toward marriage. The Merchant's resemblance to
January in his tale helps tie the story into the Marriage Group,
whether as one of the principal aspects of the discussion, illustrating
"the wo that is in mariage," or as part of the second interlude, thus
making it entirely different from the first one. Chaucer has greatly
increased the contribution of the pear tree story to the Marriage
Group by making January an old man.[8] This also heightens the contrast to the *Squire's Tale*, which follows it. And, as Professor Huppé
has said, "The *Merchant's Tale* . . . extends the theme of the marriage debate by placing the primary responsibility for the Wife [of
Bath's] heresy where it belongs, on the husband. . . . As the reason
should control the will, the husband by right reason should control
his wife. . . . the husband is responsible for her actions as well as his
own."[9] The complexity of the Marriage Group and the human relations on which it is based are thus made clear, as there are reasons why
the *Merchant's Tale* could be one of the principal stories of the Group
or an important contribution to the second interlude.[10]

The *Squire's Tale* is exactly the opposite of the Merchant's: not a
story of marriage at all, at least if we may judge from what Harry
Bailey asks the Squire to tell, and from the incomplete portion of the
tale we have. It is a frame of picturesque and romantic adventure,
evidently designed as a vehicle for some account of pure and idyllic

love. So exactly opposite to each other are these two stories that it seems as though Chaucer must have designed them to show how one extreme might call forth its counterpart. In carrying out this pattern, if such it be, Chaucer has the cynical and sarcastic ending of the Clerk's Envoy lead naturally to the further development in the cynical tale of the Merchant, and the idyllic and other-worldly beauty of the *Squire's Tale* set the stage appropriately for the lofty idealism and compromise which pervade the *Franklin's Tale*. The latter's admiration for the Squire's story, which Chaucer evidently intended to finish, is an appropriate introduction to his tale.

We thus come naturally to the third of the principal tales of the Marriage Group: that of the Franklin, which not only illustrates the theory that a happy marriage can be founded only on unselfish compromise, but contains a long passage of abstract theory (V, 761–82) which makes it the logical conclusion of the debate.

Fully to appreciate Chaucer's skill in constructing the Marriage Group, reverse the two interludes and see how beautifully they fit where they are, and how much less appropriate they would be if interchanged. As the Group is arranged, there is a definite climax, emotional as well as intellectual, which is aided by the two interludes. The first is merely time out, but the effect is produced with atmospheric appropriateness, as in a comic relief interlude in a Shakespearean play; whereas the second interlude, by means of two strongly contrasted tales, leads directly from the Envoy of the *Clerk's Tale* to the Franklin's, yet gives the effect of relief from too direct a schematic plan.

How Chaucer thought of the interrelations among these seven tales we cannot say, except to point out that he has woven together with great skill several different points of view on the topic of marital happiness, and has done it in a completely natural and lifelike manner, typical of his maturest art.

UNIVERSITY OF THE PACIFIC

NOTES

[1] Professor Baugh has called "the interludes of dialogue and action" between many of the tales, as well as "the juxtaposition of stories, as when the Clerk replies to the Wife of Bath with the tale of the patient Griselda or when the Friar and the Summoner tell stories uncomplimentary to each other . . . Chaucer's great contribution to the technique of the literary device of the framed tale." A. C. Baugh (ed.), *Chaucer's Major Poetry* (New York: Appleton, 1963), p. 235.

2 Kittredge essentially interprets the *Merchant's Tale* as one of the main stories of the Marriage Group, as it is "in substance another reply [following the Clerk's] to the Wife of Bath and her heresies," in which "May, the young wife, is not so much its object as the dotard January." George Lyman Kittredge, *Chaucer and His Poetry* (Cambridge, Mass: Harvard Univ. Press, 1915), p. 202; also his "Chaucer's Discussion of Marriage," (1912; rpt. by Richard J. Schoeck and Jerome Taylor (eds), in *Chaucer Criticism, The Canterbury Tales*, Notre Dame: Notre Dame Univ. Press, 1960), pp. 144–5. Root stresses the connection between the *Clerk's Tale* and the Merchant's by his statement that the latter "restores the balance of actuality" after the account of Griselda's almost incredible patience, in Robert Kilburn Root, *The Poetry of Chaucer*, rev. edn, (Boston: Houghton Mifflin, 1922), pp. 262–6; Germaine C. Dempster, *Dramatic Irony in Chaucer* (1932; rpt. New York: Humanities Press, 1959), pp. 46, 292; W. H. Clawson, "The Framework of the *Canterbury Tales*," (1951; rpt. in Edward Wagenknecht (ed.), *Chaucer, Modern Essays in Criticism*, New York: Oxford Univ. Press, 1959), p. 16; David Holbrook, *The Quest for Love* (London: Methuen, 1964), p. 91.

3 Robert M. Lumiansky, *Of Sondry Folk* (Austin: Univ. of Texas Press, 1955), pp. 171–2; Dempster, op. cit., p. 46.

4 Frederick Tupper, "The Quarrels of the Canterbury Pilgrims," *JEGP*, 14 (1915), p. 270.

5 Lumiansky, op. cit., pp. 8–9, 129–36.

6 John M. Manly and Edith Rickert, *The Text of the Canterbury Tales* (Chicago: Univ. of Chicago Press, 1940), II, p. 489.

7 Lumiansky, op. cit., p. 175.

8 Root, op. cit., pp. 263–6.

9 Bernard F. Huppé, *A Reading of the Canterbury Tales* (Albany: State Univ. of New York Press, 1964), pp. 161–2.

10 Cf. Holbrook, op. cit., pp. 102–3; W. H. Clawson, op. cit., p. 16.

13

THE AUDIENCE OF CHAUCER'S
TROILUS AND CRISEYDE

BY DIETER MEHL

When we talk about Chaucer's audience we can mean very different things. We usually think of the poet reading his latest tale to a courtly circle of aristocratic men and women, including, perhaps, the king himself, as on the charming *Troilus* frontispiece of the Corpus Christi Manuscript.[1] Many recent critics have rightly insisted on the fact that Chaucer's poetry was written for a live performance, not for the study, and that this must have very definite consequences for our way of understanding these poems. There is no doubt that Chaucer belongs to a tradition of oral poetry, that he is essentially pre-Gutenberg, and that serious critical distortions result if we read him with the kind of expectation that the European novel from Richardson to James Joyce has helped to create. But it has also been observed that this particular audience at the court of Richard II is, for us, only a piece of historical fiction.[2] Whatever reality it may have had for Chaucer, for us it can never be more than an abstract reconstruction which does not really affect our experience when we read Chaucer.

There is, however, another, less specific kind of audience: Chaucer himself often mentions the more solitary and bookish reader who, like the Clerk of Oxenford, has a few manuscripts "at his beddes heed," and at the outset of *The Book of the Duchess* he pictures himself as a person who, troubled by insomnia, picks up a book, which then promptly sends him to sleep. I do not suggest that the poet wrote his works for that particular purpose, but I am sure that we take too limited a view of the kind of poetry he intended if we think of his audience only in terms of a well-defined group on one or two particular occasions. Chaucer, as is evident from every one of his major works, was deeply concerned with the function of literature within our experience of reality and our desire for wisdom and reliable authority. The ending of *Troilus* suggests very strongly that he saw himself, among other things, as a potential classic or at least as an author whose appeal would reach beyond the limits of his immediate surroundings and—more importantly—beyond the sphere of his personal control. When, in the Prologue to the *Canterbury Tales*, he warns the reader of what is to come and asks him to skip a story if he does not approve of it, he is obviously not talking to the courtiers listening at his feet, but rather to the anonymous reader of one of the many manuscripts that were soon to circulate. It is this audience he has in mind when at the end of *Troilus* he expresses his anxiety about the formal integrity of his book and its transmission for the benefit of future generations. It is an audience that is, almost by definition, undefinable, unpredictable and independent of time and place; but it is not necessarily out of the author's reach. On the contrary—Chaucer seems to have been well aware of the challenge presented to his poetry by this consideration for such a wider appeal and he must have wondered, as many poets did before and after him, how he could extend his own influence beyond the personal recital. One of the obvious and traditional means of doing this is to incorporate into the text the idea of a close relationship between the author and his public, a relationship that would thus not depend on the actual presence of the author.

In a simpler form this problem applies to many of the so-called "popular" romances, many of which are, as Richard L. Greene once said of carols, only "popular by destination," not "by origin." The thirteenth-century romance of *Havelok the Dane* provides a good example. It is told by a lively entertainer who is evidently anxious to establish a friendly and sociable contact with his audience. Before launching into his tale he wants to make sure of a relaxed atmosphere and, like Chaucer's Pardoner, asks for a drink:

> At the biginning of ure tale
> Fil me cuppe of ful god ale;
> And y wile drinken, er y spelle,
> That Crist us shilde alle fro helle![3]

The usual interpretation of these lines is that the poem was composed by a minstrel who would often recite it in some public place. This may of course be true of the first performances, but the work as we have it is a carefully constructed, highly rhetorical poem, neatly copied into a manuscript that could hardly be called a minstrel's book. It is a distinctly literary product and this means that the social occasion has become, as it were, fossilized; it has been turned into a literary motif designed to give to the poem an air of convivial spontaneity which survives even when we read *Havelok* in the study, far from any available "cuppe of ful good ale."

Spontaneity, as many modern theatre productions designed in

the name of spontaneity have proved, is as a rule unique and not repeatable; but poetry, as Keats knew and demonstrated, can preserve this spontaneity and give an impression of fresh and transitory uniqueness at every reading. Every time we read *Havelok* we are included in an audience that is independent of the particular occasion and we are, at least to a certain point, persuaded to react to the poem in the same way as its first audience. In this sense, what Geoffrey Shepherd says of *Troilus* is true of *Havelok* and many less sophisticated poems as well: "Chaucer has convincingly stylized in permanent form the ephemeralness of a living entertainment and the mobility of actual delivery."[4] This is a very good description of one important aspect of poetry that is at the same time oral and literary, composed for a live performance, but also meant to be preserved for an unlimited number of future performances.

More sophisticated poets have used subtler and less conspicuous means of controlling the reader's response, often in a way that openly admits the artificial and contrived character of such a relationship. In this respect, the English novelists of the eighteenth century are not as original as is sometimes assumed: Fielding's officious, patronizing and yet deferential concern for the good will of his reader can, I believe, teach us a good deal about the practice of earlier writers like Chaucer. Sterne is perhaps an even better example because his grotesque exaggerations of some of the traditional formulas adopted by sociable narrators can startle even the most innocent reader into an awareness of the author's method: "How could you, Madam," exclaims the author at the beginning of a new chapter, "be so inattentive in reading the last chapter?"[5] Why "Madam"? Surely, the novel is not just addressed to ladies? In fact, there are several places in the book where exactly the opposite is implied; but at this particular point, it is obviously the ladies' attention that is more important or more likely, and when we realize the extremely delicate nature of the question at issue, the author's comic intention becomes very clear.

Chaucer, in his rather more subdued way, achieves very similar effects. Like Sterne and like Gottfried von Straßburg with his insistence on the "*edele herzen*" before him, he does not treat his imaginary audience as an amorphous assembly of identical minds, but he makes pointed discriminations when it suits his purpose. He creates the illusion of a lively and mutual relationship between the fictional narrator, who has been singled out so often and so out of proportion in recent criticism, and the fictional audience with which we are asked to identify ourselves.

That this fictional audience has its own very definite kind of reality will be felt by most readers because as we follow the poet through his narrative there emerges a clear picture of the sort of listeners this story is addressed to and of the response that is expected of them. It is not a static picture and it is by its very nature not to be confused with the actual court circle to which the poem was perhaps first read. Even if we did not know anything at all about Chaucer's real audience, the poem would still give us a very lively and precise idea of the quality of mind it wants to appeal to and of a personal relationship it seeks to establish between narrator and listener or reader. The poem, as it were, creates its own audience and it implies a set of expectations which it partly fulfils and partly disappoints. Taken in this sense, the term "fictional audience" describes a very important aspect of the poem's rhetoric and can be useful in approaching many problems of interpretation.[6]

At the outset of *Troilus*, Chaucer, developing a hint from Boccaccio, addresses himself to the lovers among his audience, but not, as Boccaccio did, to ask for their personal sympathy and pity, but to appeal to their superior experience. Only they can really appreciate what is to come and only they can therefore react in the right way, which is, not to judge, but feel sympathetic compassion for the characters in the story and for all who are in similar pain. To move his audience to such pity is the poet's chief object:

> For so hope I my sowle best avaunce,
> To prey for hem that Loves servauntz be,
> And write hir wo, and lyve in charite,
> And for to have of hem compassioun,
> As though I were hire owne brother dere. (47–51)

By suggesting this distinction among his audience, the poet sets up a standard by which we are to judge ourselves and our response to the story. There is a challenge in the poet's claim that only certain members of his audience can really understand his poem. Again *Tristram Shandy* can illustrate this technique in its more extreme form: "I told the Christian reader—I say Christian—hoping he is one— and if he is not, I am sorry for it—and only beg he will consider the matter with himself, and lay not the blame entirely upon this book,— I told him, Sir—" (VI, 33) Chaucer does not, of course, carry the trick as far as Sterne, but the effect is not entirely different. He forces us into a reflection on how far we ourselves qualify for inclusion in his audience. The point is not so much that, as one critic says, "the poem is addressed to lovers, not to theologians,"[7] but that there is a provocative tension between the ideal audience the poet seems to envisage and our own particular and necessarily limited reading. Once alerted to the poet's claims, the reader will become more self-conscious and more aware of the variety of possible responses.

In the course of the poem the lovers among the audience are several times singled out as the only people whose understanding and experience can make up for the shortcomings of the poet. This is, of course, a fairly conventional rhetorical device, but Chaucer often elaborates it in a way that makes us more conscious of the fact that we are part of an audience and that more than passive submission to the poet's spell is expected of us. Both the conventional and the more personal touch come out in the appeal to the experienced lovers to imagine the intensity of Troilus' experience:

> Of hire delit, or joies oon the leeste,
> Were impossible to my wit to seye;
> But juggeth ye that han ben at the feste
> Of swich gladnesse, if that hem liste pleye!
> I kan namore, but thus thise ilke tweye,
> That nyght, bitwixen drede and sikernesse,
> Felten in love the grete worthynesse. (III, 1310–16)

Boccaccio is far more conventional at this point.

At other points in the poem, however, it is not the lovers to whom the story is specifically addressed. Troilus' conversion to love in the first book is presented as a warning to "Ye wise, proude, and worthi folkes alle," (I, 233) and at the end of the poem it is the "yonge, fresshe folkes, he or she" (V, 1835) who are the particular object of the poet's concern. The function of these varying appeals is again a sharpening of our awareness of the poem's different levels of meaning and our active response.

More interesting and provocative is the poet's appeal to the audience's judgement in questions concerning the characters of the story. We are sometimes told by historically-minded critics that medieval poets, including Chaucer, were not interested in drawing psychologically consistent characters. This is true to a point, but only to a point, because at certain stages of the story Chaucer does invite us to form our own judgement of a character in terms that go beyond the stereotyped situation and can only be defined by the psychology of human behaviour. The most elaborate instance is Chaucer's ambiguous statement about Criseyde's complicity in the lover's meeting arranged so resourcefully by Pandarus. When he asks her to dinner at his house it is, in view of his previous strategy, only natural that she suspects a plot:

> Soone after this, she gan to hym to rowne,
> And axed hym if Troilus were there.

> He swor hire nay, for he was out of towne,
> And seyde, "Nece, I pose that he were;
> Yow thurste nevere han the more fere;
> For rather than men myghte hym ther aspie,
> Me were levere a thousand fold to dye." (III, 568–74)

This is not completely reassuring and Criseyde has every reason to remain unconvinced, but Chaucer, in one of his most brilliant auctorial interventions, leaves the situation open:

> Nought list myn auctour fully to declare
> What that she thoughte whan he seyde so,
> That Troilus was out of towne yfare,
> As if he seyde therof soth or no;
> But that, withowten await, with hym to go,
> She graunted hym, sith he hire that bisoughte,
> And, as his nece, obeyed as hire oughte. (III, 575–81)

That Criseyde is not, in fact, reassured becomes clear from the following stanza where she asks him to be discreet whatever he may do with her.

In view of this deliberately unexplicit treatment of Criseyde's state of mind, the attempt of some critics to leap to her defence and prove her complete ignorance of Pandarus' scheme seems to me rather touching and, at any rate, to miss the point, because it is obvious that the audience is not given a piece of precise information, but an incomplete and therefore ambiguous statement that demands an active effort of imagination and judgement.[8] Each reader has to make up his own mind about Criseyde at this point, as at many other points of the story, and attempts by critics to make up his mind for him or to prove that Chaucer does, in fact, suggest a clear-cut answer to his question, should be regarded with suspicion. What the poet asks, as Fielding does so frequently in *Tom Jones*, is simply this: "What would you think if a living person into whose mind you cannot penetrate behaved like Criseyde?" The poet wants to present us with the same kind of uncertainty, pleasure and provocation that we meet in our daily relationship with complex and unpredictable human beings. He makes us aware that a poetic characterization is but an outline that has to be filled in by every member of the audience according to his own experience and knowledge of human nature.

Chaucer's use of direct intervention by the narrator to draw the reader's attention to the artificial nature of his narrative can be seen in two other places in the second book, where two possible objections of the reader are answered before they even occur to most readers.

The first is the famous passage describing historical changes and their influence on our attitude towards stories of the past. There may be, says Chaucer, among his audience a lover who, while listening, thinks to himself that he would have gone about love-making in a very different way. Nowhere else in Middle English literature—as far as I know—do we find this acute consciousness of the problems of historical fiction. At first sight we may feel that what Chaucer says here does not really apply to his treatment of Troilus and Criseyde because in many ways he has made his characters contemporaries of his audience. At least it can hardly be said that he has deliberately removed them from the manners and the sensibility of the fourteenth century. This is obviously not an example of historical pastiche, like the Waverley novels, for Chaucer does not intend that: he wants to make clear that these differences between periods are not more surprising and no more relevant than differences between individual human beings. His intervention here is obviously an appeal to his audience to distinguish between the ephemeral literary form and the genuine matter that cannot be made obsolete by linguistic and cultural changes. The responsibility for a true appreciation of the story is thus again returned to the audience and any potential criticism of the poem's style on the grounds of simple realism is refuted in advance.

Later on in the book an even more surprising kind of objection is singled out and crushed, "with a fine show of indignation."[9] Again some particular members of the audience are separated from the rest and we are warned not to identify ourselves with them:

> Now might som envious jangle thus:
> "This was a sodeyn love; how might it be
> That she so lightly loved Troilus,
> Right for the firste syghte, ye, parde?"
> Now whoso seith so, mote he nevere ythe! (II, 666–70)

To reproach Criseyde for falling in love too hastily would be far more appropriate in the case of *Il Filostrato* where things do indeed develop rather rapidly. Chaucer, however, goes out of his way to avoid any impression of undue hurry so that his intervention at first sight seems humorously pointless. In fact, it is another effective appeal for the mental cooperation of the audience. Once more we are reminded that literary fiction and reality are two very different things. Reality, as a rule, has no structure and no clearly recognizable transitions, but the poet has to select and to confine himself to a limited number of crucial moments. This is a commonplace of literary theory, but it is anything but a commonplace to be explicitly reminded of it in the midst of a most engrossing part of the story. Chaucer obviously does not care to have his audience too much engrossed by the story alone and therefore ignorant of the problems of its presentation. He also seems to urge his listeners, as at the outset and at the end of the poem, not to judge the characters by standards that are—in view of the fictional nature of his narrative—totally irrelevant.

Chaucer, it has been said, thought he was reporting a story that had actually happened. Even if this is true, it does not alter the fact that for him, the distinction between any historical Criseyde that may once have enjoyed and betrayed the love of a Trojan prince and his stylized portrait of her mattered far more than any kind of supposed accuracy. The reader is not simply encouraged to picture Criseyde as a human being of flesh and blood, although Chaucer's ambiguous rhetoric makes him do so most effectively, but he is also invited to help the poet recreate a particular emotional experience that cannot be adequately defined by literary means. By suggesting an objection which many readers might never have thought of he makes us wonder whether there are not many other possible responses to this story, whether we have, in fact, been sufficiently attentive to the text. And this constant awareness of our duties as an intelligent audience seems to me far more important than any specific interpretation we would like to elicit from the narrative.

Several critics have claimed that Chaucer's professed refraining from judgement is, in truth, his most effective means of judging his characters. This is, I think, one of the errors that result from too simple and anachronistic a conception of Chaucer's narrator. Nothing is gained, but a good deal is lost by putting Chaucer's tale into the mouth of a naive narrator who does not understand the meaning of his own story or commits serious errors of judgement, a "narrator" who "would have been unhappy if he had realized the effect he was producing."[10] It seems to me far more appropriate to see him as a poet who assumes different parts in the course of the narrative, who intentionally withholds information to sharpen our critical awareness or who pronounces simple judgements in order to suggest to us how inadequate such judgements are.

The most uncomfortable character problem in *Troilus and Criseyde*, and one that still baffles critics, is, of course, Criseyde's sudden moral collapse in the fifth book. Even a very recent introduction to the works of Chaucer repeats the traditional opinion that Chaucer "minimizes Criseyde's guilt in every way possible."[11] In fact, he does no such thing, but it would not be true to say that he does the opposite. I am convinced that all attempts to discover in the earlier books character-traits that would provide sufficient motives for her behaviour are beside the point. What can be proved, however, with some cogency is that Chaucer, despite all his declarations of sympathy for Criseyde, altered the story in such a way as to make her betrayal much harder to explain. Although the contrast between Troilus and the "sodeyn" Diomede is heightened to the point of comedy, Criseyde is more easily persuaded to transfer her favours to Diomede than Boccaccio's Criseida. "Why," a critic asks, "has Chaucer created unnecessary difficulties for himself?"[12] It is a good question, and I am sure it is very important to realize that Chaucer has indeed created unnecessary difficulties for himself by stressing at the same time the sincerity and beauty of her love and the suddenness and meanness of her betrayal. It would have been easy enough for him to make Criseyde's behaviour more consistent either by portraying her as an untrustworthy character from the start, as Shakespeare did 200 years later, or by softening her betrayal and making her appear less guilty (as he is claimed to have done by many critics). In fact, both alternatives have been seriously advanced in many interpretations and this genuine difference of opinion points to a real problem in the text. Perhaps this much discussed question becomes a little clearer if we see it as an aspect of Chaucer's treatment of his audience.

The poet (or, if you like, the narrator), as Chaucer presents him, is faced with the problem of having to tell a story he does not like and he cannot even find consistent. His solution is to pass the problem on to the reader and to incorporate into his work the difficulties of its composition. In this part of the book, more than in any other, we are constantly reminded of the fact that this is not a faithful image of reality, but an attempt to recapture events that have long passed out of existence, with insufficient information and the limited means of the poet's craft. We are made to distinguish between the bare story-material, the efforts of the poet and the full truth that lies somewhere behind all this and can never be recovered. It can only be tentatively approached by the groping gestures of the poet and the reader's active imagination they try to stimulate. From other parts of the poem we know perfectly well that Chaucer did not, in principle, hesitate to alter his material by inventing new details or providing motives for his characters where it suited his purpose. This makes it fairly certain that his scrupulous adherence to his source at this particular point is a calculated attitude to ensure the cooperation of the audience. Giving the stark facts of the story, he claims to have added nothing because he does not want to appear to blame Criseyde. Whether we read into this an even more devastating condemnation of the heroine or take the narrator's innocent apologies at their face value, is our own responsibility, but any interpretation that simplifies the issue or denies the need for the audience's own effort reduces the haunting provocation of the text to the level of plain statement. This is not so much a case of poetic ambiguity, but a supreme example of the way good narrative can involve the reader in the process of deciding, inferring and evaluating. And it is precisely this quality that gives us such a strong sense of the reality of Chaucer's characters.[13]

At this point, the poet no longer appeals to the lovers alone. Every member of the audience is included and no particular knowledge is required to appreciate the pathos of Troilus' disillusion and Criseyde's guilt, but at the same time the poet keeps us at a rational distance from his characters by constantly reminding us of the limitations of the poetic medium and his own deficiencies.

His appeal to the audience is not, however, confined to our evaluation of the characters, but applies to nearly all aspects of the poem's structure. One of the most interesting examples is the poet's treatment of time at the end of Book II. Troilus, whose pretended illness has by now almost turned into a genuine disorder, is waiting in his sick-chamber while Pandarus is about to lead Criseyde to him. In the final stanza the poet makes another appeal to the lovers' sympathy and creates a moment of intensely dramatic suspense:

> But now to yow, ye loveres that ben here,
> Was Troilus nought in a kankedort,
> That lay, and myghte whisprynge of hem here,
> And thoughte, "O Lord, right now renneth my sort
> Fully to deye, or han anon comfort!"
> And was the firste tyme he shulde hire preye
> Of love; O myghty God, what shal he seye? (II, 1751–57)

The last line takes us right into Troilus' mind; it could be described as an early example of interior monologue or reported thought which hardly reappears in English fiction before Jane Austen. But at the same time the poem breaks off abruptly ("*Explicit Secundus Liber*"). "In performance" this might even have meant the end of a sitting. There is, at any rate, a lengthy invocation at the beginning of the following book before we hear again from Troilus. After forty-nine lines the story is resumed:

> Lay al this mene while Troilus
> Recordying his lesson . . . .   (III, 50–1)

"Al this mene while" obviously means the time it has taken us to read the invocation. This deliberate confusion of two time levels is again very like Sterne's "It is about an hour and a half's tolerable good reading since my Uncle Toby rung the bell. . . ." (II, 8) It makes us conscious of the poem's careful artistry and again encourages us to dissociate the story from the way it is told. Yet at the same time we are persuaded to identify ourselves with Troilus and to enter imaginatively into his state of mind. It is a very personal and surprising version of the traditional topos which asks the audience to make up the deficiencies of the poet's art by an effort of good will and imagination, to "piece out our imperfections with your thoughts."

Modern literary criticism often draws attention to the fact that a work of fiction has no complete existence of its own, but depends on contact with a reader's mind to be brought to life. It is, to use Saussure's almost suspiciously useful terms, on the level of *langue*, not *parole*, that is to say, it is not a complete, self-sufficient statement, but a kind of abstract matrix, suggesting and allowing for an indefinite number of potential statements.[14] Every narrative asks us, implicitly or explicitly, to read between the lines, to supply by our own experience, intelligence and imagination what the text has left out. Some poets, not usually the best ones, try to disguise this fact by being as explicit as possible on all important points of the story, thus leaving us very little room for independent mental co-operation; but it is in the very nature of fictional narrative that it must omit large portions of the story and it is most important for a critical understanding to recognize where these blanks occur and how the author makes use of them. What many lesser writers seem to be unaware of or try to pass over as an unavoidable failing, Chaucer deliberately exploits as a chief means of his narrative rhetoric. By directing the attention of the audience to gaps in his account at the most crucial points in the story, he makes sure that our imagination becomes active in the right direction. The simplest way of doing this is a demonstrative withholding of precise information. In some cases this may be a merely playful fussing over minor points, as in the question of Criseyde's age or the possible existence or non-existence of her children; but it becomes more disturbing when the poet confesses ignorance on such an important point as the time it took for Criseyde to give her heart (or at least the appearance of it) to Diomede. It is a very characteristic example of Chaucer's relationship with his audience:

> But trewely, how longe it was bytwene
> That she forsok hym for this Diomede,
> There is non auctour telleth it, I wene,
> Take every man now to his bokes heede;
> He shal no terme fynden, out of drede. (V, 1086–90)

Again, this is obviously a calculated effect. If we take up the author's suggestion to do some independent source-study we shall find that it would have been easy enough for Chaucer to get some idea of a possible time-scheme from his sources, especially from Benoit, or to make up his own time-scheme; but, like Jane Austen at the end of *Mansfield Park*, he "purposely abstain[s] from dates on this occasion, that everyone may be at liberty to fix their own, aware that the cure of unconquerable passions and the transfer of unchanging attachments, must vary very much as to time in different people." This auctorial statement seems to fit Criseyde hardly less well than Edmund Bertram, and the function of the author's reticence is very much the same in each case.

Chaucer does not withhold this information in order to excuse Criseyde, but to make us aware of the very imperfections of the story, of its many blank spaces, and this applies to all the other instances of the poet's appeals to his audience I have quoted. No narrative can give all the information any reader might require, but to deny us even information that most readers would consider essential and, in addition, draw our attention to this refusal, throws us back on our own mental resources, and this is precisely what Chaucer's poetry does.

Of course we also have to recognize the limits of this freedom the poet allows to his audience or, rather, to define the areas in which we are meant to exercise it. Most critics, without giving much thought to the problem, take for granted this lack of explicitness in Chaucer's poetry by expecting or persuading us to read between his lines to a considerable extent. But an important distinction has to be made here, for although Chaucer does leave a good many decisions to the reader, he is, as a rule, very clear about where these decisions lie and he does not encourage us to ask the wrong sort of question. Probably no two readers would quite agree on this, but I think it is important to keep in mind the difference between questions the poem really provokes and those it ignores.

To give a well-known example: one question which, I feel, we are not meant to ask, but many readers seem to like to ask, concerns the problem of marriage. From time to time it is claimed, even very recently, that this is, in fact, the crucial moral issue in the poem.[15] If this were so, Chaucer would indeed expect a great deal of mental co-operation from his reader, but to me, at least, the only thing the text suggests very strongly is that we are not invited to pursue this point any further than the poem does. The concept of marriage is only mentioned in a very few places and mostly in very conventional terms; it is never made a real issue. Criseyde, in her first soliloquy, refers to marriage in passing rather like the Wife of Bath as a form of power-game: "Shal noon housbonde seyn to me 'chek mat!'" (II, 754) and, in their last interview, Troilus expresses his fear that she might be conveniently married off to some Greek by her father.

The most important reference to marriage in the poem is, however, a non-reference, to be read by the learned reader between the lines of Troilus' ecstatic praise of love towards the end of the third book where he gives a fairly close paraphrase of Boece (II, Metrum 8). Several critics have noted that whereas Boece speaks of the "sacrement of mariages of chaste loves," Troilus means his own union with Criseyde. But does this really imply a criticism of Troilus's love? The argument that is used to support such an interpretation is one that turns precisely on the problem of the audience's participation: Chaucer's readers or listeners, it is said, would have noticed Troilus' misapplication of Boece. But would they really? Chaucer's way of handling his audience suggests, on the contrary, that his readers should not notice the discrepancy or else if they noticed, nothing should be made of it. There is nothing to alert us to the presence of a real problem here, nothing to draw our attention to any basic flaw in Troilus' attitude at this particular point or to a significant silence on the part of the poet.[16]

It is, of course, perfectly possible for a modern or medieval reader, taking a sinister view of any extra-marital affair and of courtly love in general, to raise the question Chaucer has left alone, but this is a different kind of literary criticism from the one I am concerned with here.

Chaucer's rhetorical involvement of his audience is not arbitrary and it does not include all aspects of his story, but it concentrates on a number of important points where central questions of interpreting the story are at stake. Moreover, the poet does not leave us without any help or at least a precise idea of how we are to exercise our critical faculties. The first lines of the poem set the tone and describe very clearly the spirit in which all the following story should be read. This spirit underlies all the poem's rhetoric and its provocative silences, and as most readers feel—unless they are obsessed by a very naive and narrow idea of medieval Christianity—it is a spirit of sympathy and compassion for the sufferings and shortcomings of others. Although the poem continually appeals to our judgement and imagination it does all along give indications as to the direction our own appraisal should take. In this sense, the poet was perfectly right and sincere when he claimed in the Prologue to the *Legend of Good Women* that— whatever the spirit of his source may have been—his own intention was to further truth and to teach people to avoid falseness and vice.

The most interesting thing about this passage to me is the emphasis it puts on the effect of Chaucer's poetry on his audience. This is not a question of didactic poetry. Chaucer does not portray himself as a straightforward moral teacher, but he is evidently worried about the reception of his poetry and the whole debate in the *Prologue* concerns not so much the subjects of Chaucer's actual writing, but the audience and its response. If Chaucer had any more specific or topical reason for writing this apology for his poetry it may well be that he felt his courtly audience had mistaken his intentions and he had to be more explicit about the impression he wished to create.

The theme of the poet's effect on his audience recurs again and again in Chaucer's poetry, especially, of course, in the *Canterbury Tales* where it is implied in the very structure of the work. The way the pilgrims react to the individual stories is sometimes nearly as interesting as the stories themselves and tells us a lot about Chaucer's poetic intentions.

The problem of the audience and the way it is affected by poetry also lies at the heart of Chaucer's much discussed retraction at the end of the *Canterbury Tales* and, we may gather, of his poetic career. I am sure it is not a sudden impulse of humourless puritanism or a righteous rejection of all art and his own poetic achievement, but an expression of a deep concern for the effect of his poetry on the reader and, perhaps, a last effort to guide our response. Chaucer does, of course, explicitly revoke *Troilus and Criseyde* in its entirety, but "revoke" in this context can only mean that he does not wish to be responsible for any unedifying influence his poem might have and that he deeply regrets the fact that this poem and the others he mentions could ever have encouraged the wrong kind of response on the part of the reader. The *Retraction*, if it is not just a private confession of faith, is surely a last earnest appeal to the reader to believe in the good intentions of the poet and to read all the poems in this spirit. In this, the *Retraction* is not unlike the ending of *Troilus* where, though perhaps more ambiguously, the audience is also forced to reconsider the implications of the story and its presentation.

Middle English narrative literature before Chaucer was for the most part written with the expressed aim of entertaining and educating a public unable to read French or Latin. Often the audience is addressed as the recipient of a particular favour and of wholesome instruction. That is, the relationship between poet and audience is strictly a one-way communication. The only kind of co-operation expected of the listeners is attention and belief. Chaucer's attitude to his reader, as we have seen, is completely different. Even where his purpose is purely educational as in the treatise on the Astrolabe, written for the benefit of a ten-year-old boy whose Latin is not yet up to the original texts, he presents himself as the unworthy transmitter of his material: "I n'am but a lewd compilator of the labour of olde astrologiens." He goes far beyond the traditional humility formula in disclaiming any merit his work might have, and he thus draws the reader's attention to the author in a way quite unprecedented in Middle English literature; and this is not a particular cunning and subtle method of self-praise, but rather an intentional *Verfremdungs-effekt* to make us a self-conscious and critical audience. The colourful diversity of Chaucer criticism shows that his poetry still achieves that aim, at least among a certain section of his audience.

To claim, as I have done, that Chaucer leaves many of the crucial questions raised by his story for the audience to decide, is not to confuse the poetry with our personal reaction to it or to return to a simple form of New Criticism, but merely to state that Chaucer's poetry consciously presupposes and depends on an intelligent and co-operative reader, more, perhaps, than any other Middle English poetry. To be one of his audience does not mean just to listen to what he tells us, but to encounter a fictional reality that is full of questions and provocative blanks and to be in mental contact with an author who makes us aware of the truly sociable character of narrative poetry. In a general sense this is, of course, true of most good poetry, but it is often forgotten or ignored by less interesting authors and not often exploited in such a deliberate way as in Chaucer's text. To pronounce on the "meaning" of his stories is nearly always the wrong kind of critical approach. It is not our business as readers and critics to discover what Chaucer "really meant," how he himself judges his characters or what he thought about courtly love, but to respond to his appeal and participate in the dialogue his poetry wants to pro-voke.

Again, a classic statement of this kind of relationship occurs in *Tristram Shandy*, and though the critical vocabulary is clearly dated, due to "chaunge in forme of speche," it describes a fundamental quality of Chaucer's writing:

> Writing, when properly managed, (as you may be sure I think mine is) is but a different name for conversation: As no one, who knows what he is about in good company, would venture to talk all;—so no author, who understands the just boundaries of decorum and good breeding, would presume to think all: The truest respect which you can pay to the reader's understanding, is to halve this matter amicably and leave him something to imagine, in his turn, as well as yourself. (II, 11)

In using the words of an eighteenth-century practitioner of the art of fiction I will not, I hope, appear to be blurring basic historical differences. It hardly needs saying that Sterne activates the reader's mind in a completely different direction and to completely different ends and that the audience Chaucer has in mind is very unlike the eighteenth-century reading public. And yet, the explicit appeal to its imagination and judgement, the teasing omission of information and unambiguous guidance reveal the same awareness of the limits and potentialities of poetic fiction. To say that "no author, who understands the just boundaries of decorum and good breeding, would presume to think all" seems to me a very Chaucerian statement— although Chaucer would have seen the problem as one of rhetoric and "curteisie" rather than of decorum and good breeding. Consciously or not, Chaucer seems to have realized that to engage the readers' minds in a process of imaginative exploration and sympathetic evaluation can be a more effective means of instruction than anything that can be achieved by over-explicit and unquestioningly didactic poetry.

UNIVERSITY OF BONN

NOTES

[1] On the significance of the frontispiece see the interesting but highly speculative article by Margaret Galway, "The 'Troilus' Frontispiece," *MLR*, 44 (1949), pp. 162–77.

[2] "Geoffrey Chaucer reading aloud to certain groups in the late fourteenth century is for us a fiction; what remains is Geoffrey Chaucer addressing us from the printed page." Paull F. Baum, *Chaucer: a Critical Appreciation* (Durham, N.C.: Duke Univ. Press, 1958), p. 204. A similar suggestion with regard to the *Troilus* frontispiece is made by Derek S. Brewer in his excellent interpretation of the poem in W. F. Bolton (ed.), *Sphere History of Literature in the English Language*, I, *The Middle Ages* (London: Sphere Books, 1970), pp. 195–228: "It (i.e. the frontispiece) might itself even be a product of the poem's power to create the sense of a listening group" (p. 196). Brewer's interpretation agrees with mine in a number of important points.

[3] I have slightly modernized the text by W. W. Skeat, 2nd edn, rev. by K. Sisam (Oxford: 1915). On the artistry of the poem see Judith Weiss, "Structure and Characterization in *Havelok the Dane*," *Spec.*, 44 (1969), pp. 247–57, and my *The Middle English Romances of the Thirteenth and Fourteenth Centuries* (London: Routledge, 1968), pp. 161–72.

[4] G. T. Shepherd, "Troilus and Criseyde," in *Chaucer and Chaucerians: Critical Studies in Middle English Literature* (London: Nelson, 1966), p. 72.

[5] *Tristram Shandy*, I, p. 20. I quote from the edition by Ian Watt (Boston: Houghton Mifflin, 1965).

[6] I am here, of course, indebted to a number of recent works on narrative theory.

One of the most interesting accounts of *Troilus and Criseyde* from this point of view is to be found in Robert M. Durling, *The Figure of the Poet in Renaissance Epic* (Cambridge, Mass.: Harvard Univ. Press, 1965), pp. 44–66. There are also some very interesting observations on the audience of *Troilus* in Robert O. Payne, *The Key of Remembrance: A Study of Chaucer's Poetics* (New Haven: Yale Univ. Press, 1963), pp. 228–32.

7 See Durling, op. cit., p. 48.

8 See the rather one-sided interpretation by Robert P. ap Roberts, "The Central Episode in Chaucer's *Troilus*," *PMLA*, 77 (1962), pp. 373–85.

9 See E. Talbot Donaldson, *Chaucer's Poetry: An Anthology for the Modern Reader* (New York: Ronald Press, 1958), p. 970.

10 See E. Talbot Donaldson, "Criseide and Her Narrator," in *Speaking of Chaucer* (London: Athlone Press, 1970), pp. 65–83; the quotation occurs p. 77.

11 See S. S. Hussey, *Chaucer: An Introduction* (London: Methuen, 1971), p. 76.

12 See Hans Käsmann, "'I wolde excuse hire yit for routhe.' Chaucers Einstellung zu *Criseyde*," in Arno Esch (ed.), *Chaucer und seine Zeit: Symposium für Walter F. Schirmer* (Tübingen: Max Niemeyer, 1968), pp. 97–122; the quotation occurs p. 110. Käsmann's essay gives a particularly clear and thorough account of the difficulties of interpretation.

13 See Payne, op. cit., p. 182: "a fair share of the illusion of reality comes not from the actual processes of characterization, but from the affective immediacy of the moral and emotional problems within which the existences of the characters are defined."

14 See the interesting discussion of these problems in Hans Robert Jauß, *Literaturgeschichte als Provokation* (Frankfurt: Suhrkamp, 1970), pp. 144–207.

15 I am largely in agreement with Derek S. Brewer on this point; see his "Love and Marriage in Chaucer's Poetry," *MLR*, 49 (1954), pp. 461–4. The question has been re-opened by Käsmann whose interpretation is rather different on this point than the one suggested here.

16 See T. P. Dunning, "God and Man in *Troilus and Criseyde*," in Norman Davis and C. L. Wrenn (eds), *English and Medieval Studies Presented to J. R. R. Tolkien on the Occasion of his Seventieth Birthday* (London: Allen & Unwin, 1962), pp. 164–82, especially pp. 175–6, and H. Käsmann, p. 118.

14

ASPECTS OF DUNBAR'S IMAGERY

BY PRISCILLA BAWCUTT

Dunbar handles imagery with a brilliance that is still insufficiently recognized. Some critics have limited themselves to the artificial, aureate images in his courtly poems such as "The Goldyn Targe" or "The Thrissil and the Rois;" some have neglected the subject entirely. Only recently have other critics looked more searchingly and more appreciatively at Dunbar's imagery.[1] Images of every type—symbol, personification, metaphor, and simile—abound in Dunbar; in this respect he contrasts strikingly with his Scottish contemporaries, Henryson and Gavin Douglas. Although his imagery is not outstanding for its intellectual subtlety, it has enormous zest and energy. Much of the visual impact, the wit, and the emotional vitality of Dunbar's poetry is effected by images, which Dunbar handles with versatility. Indeed, the interplay between image and theme may often structure the whole poem.

I propose chiefly to discuss here some of the more colloquial, humorous or satirical poems, whose imagery has been less studied than that of the religious poems or courtly allegories.[2] One reason for this neglect may lie in the occasional difficulties or ambiguities of their language. For example, in "Of ane Blak-Moir" (No. 37), the "blak lady" is described as "tute mowitt lyk ane aep / And lyk a gangarall onto graep."[3] Small glossed *gangarall* as "child beginning to walk," and noted that "the line represents her waddling mode of walking." Craigie glossed *gangarall* as "spider." Mackenzie and Kinsley, however, preferred "toad," an interpretation supported by other sixteenth-century Scottish writers (see *DOST* and *OED*). The image thus suggests a skin dark and rough to the touch ("onto graep"), possibly even scarred by smallpox. But there are still far too many lines in Dunbar where editors have provided not glosses but comically divergent guesses, as may be seen in the varying explanations of *fepillis* and *hogeart* in "The Tretis" (ll. 114, 272). Such differences arise in part from Dunbar's extreme colloquialism, his liking for the sort of word common enough in speech but rarely written down, because it is too technical, too low, too slangy, or too obscene. Unfortunately for modern readers, images which in his own day were crisp and definite become blurred.

My primary concern is not with the sources of Dunbar's images, but with their poetic use; *how* they work, rather than *whence* they derive. Nonetheless I am aware that the source of an image is relevant to its effect in a poem—its associations, sacred or secular, courtly or vulgar, naturalistic or non-naturalistic. Dunbar draws on an enormous variety of literary sources—the Bible and the liturgy, the lapidary, the bestiary, and heraldic lore—but in the colloquial and satirical poems it is perhaps to be expected that the naturalistic images derive mainly either from direct observation of everyday life or from popular tradition. Some of Dunbar's most arresting and apparently original images employ the homeliest objects found in house or street or farm: soap (No. 37); a tar-barrel (No. 37); a saffron bag (No. 6, l. 171); a chamber-pot ("jowrdane-hedit," No. 19); a harrow ("hippit as ane harrow," No. 6, l. 179; a mortar stone ("mell-hedit lyk ane mortar stane," No. 19); a smith's pincers ("lyk turkas birnand reid," No. 57). He confronts us with the more unpleasant realities of late medieval street life: bull baiting (No. 5); cock fighting (No. 47, l. 326); choked gutters:

> With goreis his tua grym ene ar gladderrit all about,
> And gorgeit lyk twa gutaris that war with glar stoppit.
> (No. 47, ll. 98–9)

or a man on the gallows:

> With hingit luik ay wallowand upone wry,
> Lyke to ane stark theif glowrand in ane tedder. (No. 6, ll. 175–6)

Such images are reinforced by others which, though not of the same imaginative order, stem ultimately from a similar realm of experience. These are the commonplace, semi-proverbial similes, which were the stock in trade of all medieval poets, and often linger in our speech today; swift as an arrow, brim as boars, green as grass, sad as lead, lean as trees, small as wands, white as whalebone. Dunbar disdained their use no more than did Chaucer. Sometimes they are merely metrical and alliterative conveniences; sometimes an ironical twist is given to a trite simile, as in the First Wife's remark about her husband in "The Tretis" (No. 47, l. 96), "Bot soft and soupill as the silk is his sary lume," or in "Of the Ladyis Solistaris at Court" (No. 48), where Dunbar clearly has tongue in cheek when he terms the ladies "trest as the steill."

Single images in Dunbar strike us first for their vividness and imaginative accuracy. Isabel Hyde has noted Dunbar's "wild delight in light and colour;"[4] Dunbar takes a similar pleasure in recording movement. The animals to which his victims are compared are frequently shown in motion or transfixed in a characteristic grotesque posture:

> He stackeret lyk ane strummall aver,
> That hopschackelit war aboin the kne.
> > (No. 32: "A Dance in the Quenis Chalmer")

> Than cam in the Maister Almaser,
> Ane hommiltye jommeltye juffler,
> Lyk a stirk stackarand in the ry. (Ibid.)

> Than Yre come in with sturt and stryfe;
> His hand wes ay upoun his knyfe,
> He brandeist lyk a beir.
> > (No. 57: "The Dance of the Sevin Deidly Synnis")

Dunbar's imagination was not simply visual; many of his images are tactile. "Gangarall," quoted above, is a case in point. But the most striking instance occurs in "The Tretis," where the First Wife complains of her husband:

> And with his hard hurcheone skyn sa heklis he my chekis,
> That as a glemand gleyd glowis my chaftis. (ll. 107–8)

The reader is made acutely aware both of the sensation of prickly roughness and of the Wife's sense of repulsion. The "heckle" was an instrument for combing flax or hemp.

Single images strike us also for their compression. Just as his poems tend to be short (his longest, "The Tretis," is barely over 500 lines), so Dunbar seems to prefer metaphors and short simple similes to the long, spacious similes of Chaucer's *Troilus and Criseyde*. He favours the succinct combination of two nouns, in which the first noun carries the metaphor: "catt nois;" "bledder cheikis" (No. 19), suggesting fat, white, pendulous cheeks; "hoppir hippis" (No. 19), an image used later by Wycherly (*Love in a Wood*, II. i: "she is bow-legged, hopper-hipped"). The line previously quoted—"And with his hard hurcheone skyn sa heklis he my chekis"—is remarkably compressed, far more than the comparable lines in Chaucer's *Merchant's Tale*:

> With thikke brustles of his berd unsofte,
> Lyk to the skyn of houndfyssh, sharp as brere—

> For he was shave al newe in his manere—
> He rubbeth hire aboute hir tendre face.[5]

Elsewhere Dunbar uses verbs in this vigorous, metaphorical way: "My panefull purs so priclis me" (No. 1), or "That fulle dismemberit hes my meter" (No. 5).

Dunbar also achieves economy by exploiting ambiguities in everyday speech: *gillot, gillet* = 1. a wanton woman, 2. a mare; *gammaldis* = 1. a horse's bounds or curvets, 2. leaps or springs in dancing; *brankand* = 1. prancing, tossing the head (of horses), 2. strutting, walking confidently (of humans); *fry* = 1. offspring, in general, 2. the offspring of fishes. The intertwined animal and human associations in these words are highly relevant:

> Quhy should not palfrayis thane be prowd,
> Quhen *gillettis* wil be schomd and schroud,
> That ridden are baith with lord and lawd? (No. 22)

> Quhen I was young and into ply,
> And wald cast *gammaldis* to the sky. (Ibid.)

> And yit he is als *brankand* with bonet one syde,
> And blenkand to the brichtest that in the burgh duellis.
> ("Tretis," ll. 180—1)

> I buskit up my barnis like baronis sonnis,
> And maid bot fulis of the *fry* of his first wif. (Ibid., ll. 402–3)

In some of Dunbar's shorter poems a single image serves as the organizing principle of the whole poem. "Quhone Mony Benefices Vakit" (No. 11), a short poem of fifteen lines, pleads with the King for a more just distribution of benefices. Apart from the presence of this word (*benefice*) in the first line, the argument is entirely metaphorical, proceeding in terms of the fair distribution of food at a banquet:

> Schir, quhiddir is it mereit mair
> To gif him drink that thristis sair,
> Or fill a fow man quhill he brist,
> And lat his fallow de a thirst,
> Quhilk wyne to drynk als worthie war?

The poem is virtually a parable. The tone is light, even jocular; the effect of the metaphor is to veil and tone down Dunbar's criticism of the King. Another poem (No. 12) employs the same image in its opening line, "Off benefice, Schir, at everie feist," but it is not sustained, and its tone is far more outspoken and bitter. Yet another poem, slight but amusing, is organized round one central image, springing from a pun on the name of the unfortunate Keeper of the Wardrobe, James Doig or Dog (No. 33). Each stanza presents a different and comic picture of the "Wardraippcr:" barking as if "hc war wirriand ane hog;" a surly house dog that needs a heavy clog; "ane midding tyk . . . chassand cattell throu a bog;" a huge mastiff far too large to be the Queen's *messan* or lap dog. Dunbar clearly enjoyed this word play because he used it in two other poems. In the refrain to No. 34, a sequel to No. 33, Dunbar has to eat his words: "He is na Dog; he is a Lam." "Of a Dance in the Quenis Chalmer" (No. 32) plays with a similar idea:

> The Quenis Dog begowthe to rax,
> And of his band he maid a bred . . .
> Quhou mastevlyk about yeid he!

Another punning image—Mackenzie observes that "Dunbar does not pun"—is the focus of "To a Ladye" (No. 49), a brief, witty but rather frigid love poem.[6] The first two stanzas draw a parallel between the Lady who possesses every virtue except mercy and a garden that lacks only rue:[7]

> In to your garthe this day I did persew,
> Thair saw I flowris that fresche wer of hew;
> Baith quhyte and reid moist lusty wer to seyne,
> And halsum herbis upone stalkis grene;
> Yit leif nor flour fynd could I nane of rew.

The last stanza, which opens "I dout that Merche, with his caild blastis keyne, / Hes slane this gentill herbe that I of mene," is allusive and enigmatic in tone. Far from exhausting the comparison, it teases the reader into speculating on its exact significance.[8]

It is more profitable, however, to consider Dunbar's frequent use of groups or clusters of images. The simplest kind of grouping is seen in the torrents of abusive images that occur in "The Flytyng," or in certain petitionary poems, such as the "Complaint to the King" (No. 19):

> Wyld haschbaldis, haggarbaldis, and hummellis;
> Druncartis, dysouris, dyvowris, drevillis,
> Mysgydit memberis of the devillis;
> Mismad mandragis of mastis strynd.

Such catalogues occur at climaxes, moments of high indignation, when—as Dunbar himself puts it—

> . . . owther man my hart to breik,
> Or with my pen I man me wreik;

> And sen the tane most nedis be,
> In to malancolie to de,
> Or lat the vennim ische all out,
> Be war, anone, for it will spout,
> Gif that the tryackill cum nocht tyt
> To swage the swalme of my dispyt!
>
>   ("Remonstrance to the King," No. 17)

What may at first seem a haphazard selection, in reality displays considerable art. "Complaint to the King" (No. 19) has a preponderance of images drawn chiefly from the world of the labourer, clearly appropriate in a poem attacking upstarts: "jowrdane-hedit," "club-facet," "bledder cheikis," "hoppir hippis," "mell-hedit lyk ane mortar-stane." They are designed ostensibly to ridicule physical appearance, but they also suggest the tasks for which such men are fitted.

A characteristically witty cluster of images occurs in "None May Assure in this Warld" (No. 21):

> Towngis now are maid of quhite quhale bone,
> And hartis ar maid of hard flynt stone,
> And eyn ar maid of blew asure,
> And handis of adament laithe to dispone;
> So in this warld may none assure.

The stanza has a cumulative effect; the repeated "maid" suggests a Midas-like transformation of warm human beings into insensate stony blocks.[9] The images are complex; eyes are not only as blue but as hard as lapis lazuli; hands are like adamant because their owners are both hard and reluctant to part with money. In its context the stanza is an *amplificatio* of the preceding, echoing it line by line: "Fra everie mouthe fair wordis procedis; / In everie harte deceptioun bredis." The images are similarly related to the following stanza: "Yit hart and handis and body all / Mon anser dethe, quhone he dois call." The rest of the poem is far less tightly integrated.[10]

Elsewhere in Dunbar, however, juxtaposition of images may inform the whole poem. "In Secreit Place this Hynder Nycht" (No. 28) has Dunbar making fun of the conventional language of endearment. Pet names, diminutives, baby talk, and above all images are used in such profusion that they jostle incongruously:

> Quod he, "My claver, and my curldodie,
> My huny soppis, my sweit possodie."

Later the girl replies:

> "Welcum! my golk of Marie land,
> My chirrie and my maikles munyoun,
> My sowklar sweit as ony unyoun,
> My strumill stirk, yit new to spane."

Comparison of the loved one to flowers, young animals, and even food has of course a long history, but Dunbar's boorish lovers reduce such imagery to absurdity. The trite "sweit as the hunye" is mockingly echoed by "sweit as ony unyoun." The flowers to which the lover compares his girl are not the courtly rose and lily, but clover (chiefly used for fodder) and the "curldodie," a name which seems to have been applied to various weeds with large round heads. Dunbar's technique partly recalls that of Chaucer in the *Miller's Tale*, but the images have been coarsened and degraded. In the *Miller's Tale* Alison is compared to a weasel,[11] a kid, a calf, and a colt; in context these images are not unpleasing. Dunbar's lovers compare each other not only to a kid and a calf but to a clumsy young stirk [ox] and— what is surely an indignity—a "tuchan," a calf's skin stuffed with straw to persuade the cow to give milk. The *Miller's Tale* emphasizes images of food: Alison's mouth is "sweete as bragot or the meeth, / Or hoord of apples" (I, 3261–2); Nicholas is "sweete as is the roote / Of lycorys, or any cetewale" (I, 3206–7). But Dunbar's lovers compare each other to "possodie" and "crowdie mowdie," which have been respectively interpreted as sheeps' head broth[12] and a gruel of milk and meal!

Particularly subtle is Dunbar's use of imagery in his most ambitious poem, "The Tretis of the Tua Mariit Wemen and the Wedo." On the surface its structure is deceptively simple, three monologues on marriage overheard by the hidden poet. Yet it is a carefully and intricately composed poem, in which the elaborately described garden setting and the recurrent bird and animal images are skilfully interwoven to reinforce and at times to anticipate some of the more explicit themes of the poem.

Most readers of "The Tretis" are struck by the abundance of animal imagery, particularly in the volley of abuse that explodes from the First Wife:

> I have ane wallidrag, ane worme, ane auld wobat carle,
> A waistit wolroun, na worth bot wourdis to clatter;
> And bumbart, ane dron bee, ane bag full of flewme. (ll. 89–91)

The vehemence suggests the outburst of pent up feelings expressed by the Second Wife in another image: "Now sall the byle all out brist, that beild has so lang; / For it to beir one my brist wes berdin our hevy" (ll. 164–5). All three women repeatedly compare their husbands to animals: a cat ("that lene gib," l. 120); a dog ("I hatit him like a hund," l. 273); a coward cock that will not fight (the "craudone" of ll. 215 and 326). Their skin is bristly as a hedgehog's (l. 107) or a boar's ("As birs of ane brym bair, his berd is als stif," l. 95). Most common of all is the image of an old cart horse; there are oblique hints either of this or of an ox in the First Wife's desire for a husband who is "Yaip, and ying, in the yok ane yeir for to draw . . . A forky fure, ay furthwart, and forsy in draucht" (ll. 79, 85). This is followed by the use of the particularly contemptuous term "aver:"[13]

> And quhen the smy one me smyrkis with his smake smolet,
> He fepillis like a farcy aver that flyrit one a gillot. (ll. 113–14)

The "aver" is one afflicted with "farcy," a disease which causes swellings and discharge of mucous matter from the nostrils. Such images cast an ugly light on both partners in the marriage. The Widow triumphs over her last husband:

> I wald haif ridden him to Rome with raip in his heid . . .
> "Se how I cabeld yone cout with a kene brydill!
> The cappill, that the crelis kest in the caf mydding,
> Sa curtasly the cart drawis, and kennis na plungeing,
> He is nought skeich, na yit sker, na scippis nought one syd."
>
> (ll. 331, 354–7)

The husbands are tamed, domesticated beasts of burden. Furthermore, they are often viewed as sick or humiliated animals: a "broddit" beast (l. 33), a plucked heron (l. 382), or a "dotit dog:"

> He dois as dotit dog that damys on all bussis,
> And liftis his leg apone loft, thoght he nought list pische. (ll. 186–7)

By contrast, the Wives compare themselves to powerful, cruel, predatory animals; the Widow advises them to model themselves on tigers, dragons, and adders (l. 261). Even more revealingly, they picture themselves as birds.[14] The Widow boasts that her last husband "payntit me as pako, proudest of fedderis" (l. 379), and "I thought my self a papingay and him a plukit herle" (l. 382). A few lines earlier she had applied to herself a verb used also of birds trimming their feathers (modern "preen" and "prune" are variants of it)—"I wald me prunya plesandly in precius wedis" (l. 374). The ostensible resemblance is to the beauty and bright plumage of such birds, and the poet in part endorses this. The Wives are indeed beautiful, "swanquhit of hewis" (l. 243). But there is more to the bird imagery than this. It connects with one of the leading themes, stated explicitly in the First Wife's denunciation of marriage:

> Birdis has ane better law na bernis be meikill,
> That ilk yeir, with new joy, joyis ane maik,
> And fangis thame ane fresche feyr, unfulyeit and constant,
> And lattis their fulyeit feiris flie quhair thai pleis.
> Cryst gif sic ane consuetude war in this kith haldin! (ll. 60–4)

The Second Wife returns to the theme:

> Ye speik of berids one bewch: of blise may thai sing,
> That, one Sanct Valentynis day, ar vacandis ilk yer;
> Hed I that plesand prevelege to part quhen me likit,
> To change, and ay to cheise agane, than, chastite, adew! (ll. 205–8)

The Wives aspire not only to the beauty of birds but to their whole way of life, with its apparent freedom and joy and total irresponsibility. Yet although they make some show of seeking love and praising the law of nature ("It is agane the law of luf, of kynd and of nature, / Togiddir hairtis to strene, that stryveis with uther," ll. 58–9), their picture of the world of nature is partial and distorted.[15] It is instructive to compare Langland's interpretation of the "law of Kynd," where Kynd shows the dreamer how "reason" informs all the activities of birds and beasts:

> I hadde wonder at whom and where the pye lerned
> To legge the stykkes in whiche she leyeth and bredeth . . .
> Ac that moste moeued me and my mode chaunged,
> That Reason rewarded and reuled alle bestes,
> Saue man and his make.[16]

The Widow's speech makes it clear that what she desires is not love but promiscuity, not freedom but a tyrannical power over others. Some of her images are highly revealing, since they suggest not a natural but a highly unnatural, perverted state of affairs. One remark about her late husband is rich in implications: "I crew abone that craudone, as cok that wer victour" (l. 326). It is not simply that marriage is seen as a cock fight or that the whole of the Widow's speech is characterized by the crowing boastfulness of a cock. The sex reversal implicit in the image—the assumption of the male role by the Widow, who later compares herself not to the peahen but to the peacock—foreshadows the more explicit degradation of the husband into a "wif carll:"

> I maid that wif carll to werk all womenis werkis,
> And laid all manly materies and mensk in this eird. (ll. 351–52)

It suggests, furthermore, the kind of sexual humiliation which is latent in her boast that she "that grome geldit had of gudis and of natur" (l. 392). The use of "geld" here is extremely forceful. Dunbar seems to have been the first user of the verb in the figurative sense, and we are clearly meant to think also of its literal sense. It both suggests the Widow's sexual preoccupations, and links with the other imagery of mutilated animals.

There are many other aspects of Dunbar's imagery that might be discussed: its cruelty and painfulness, clearly linked to its satirical function; the shock, when Dunbar speaks of Kennedie's "gule" snout and "giltin" hips ("The Flyting," ll. 52 and 99), of dignified aureate epithets incongruously applied. The versatility with which Dunbar uses animal imagery would also repay study; the symbolic and deliberately unnaturalistic picture of the nightingale, "quhois angell fedderis as the pacock schone" ("The Merle and the Nychtingaill," No. 63), contrasted with the sensuous and exact observation displayed in such phrases as "catt nois" and "hurcheone skyn;" the ordered correspondence between the human and animal hierarchies in a poem such as "The Thrissil and the Rois", contrasted with the disordered, topsy-turvy world of "The Flyting" and other comic poems, in which the animal analogies degrade and dehumanize. A poet's handling of images is of a piece with his handling of language in general, and Dunbar has a craftsman's care for the choice and placing of his words. A study of his imagery can consequently but strengthen one's admiration for Dunbar, the "makar."

UNIVERSITY OF LIVERPOOL

NOTES

1 Isabel Hyde, "Primary Sources and Associations of Dunbar's Aureate Imagery," *MLR*, 51 (1956), pp. 481–92; and "Poetic Imagery: a Point of Comparison between Henryson and Dunbar," *SSL*, 2 (1965), pp. 183–97; Tom Scott, *Dunbar: A Critical Exposition of the Poems* (Edinburgh: Oliver and Boyd, 1966).

2 Poems are identified by the titles and numberings of W. Mackay Mackenzie (ed.), *The Poems of William Dunbar*, 2nd edn (London: Faber and Faber, 1966). All quotations are taken from this edition. Other references include John Small (ed.), *The Poems of William Dunbar*, 3 vols., STS 1st series 2, 4, 21, 28, 29 (1884–93); William A. Craigie (ed.), *The Maitland Folio Manuscript*, 2 vols., STS 2nd series 7, 9 (1912–27); James Kinsley (ed.), *William Dunbar Poems* (Oxford: Clarendon Press, 1958).

3 I retain the MS reading *graep*, which Mackenzie emends unnecessarily to *gaep*.

4 Hyde, *SSL*, 2 (1965), p. 186.

5 Canterbury Tales, IV, 1824–7. All citations from F. N. Robinson (ed.), *The*

Works of Geoffrey Chaucer, 2nd edn (Boston: Houghton Mifflin, 1957).

6 Tom Scott regards it as "the tenderest of Dunbar's poems" (p. 59). J. W. Baxter interprets it as a petition to the Queen for advancement: *William Dunbar: A Biographical Study* (Edinburgh: Oliver and Boyd, 1952), p. 121.

7 *Rue* as the name of a herb and *rue* meaning "pity, regret" are apparently not connected etymologically, but similar puns occur in Scottish proverbs, e.g., "Rue in thyme should be a maiden's poesie." *The Lay of Sorrow* may anticipate Dunbar: "And forthir, In my garding quahre I sewe / All peiciens now fynd I nocht bot rewe" (ll. 51–2): K. G. Wilson, "The Lay of Sorrow and The Lufaris Complaynt: An Edition," *Spec.*, 29 (1954), pp. 708–26.

8 See also "The Petition of the Gray Horse" (No. 22), which revolves round a single image, comparing the poet to an old neglected horse.

9 Christine Brooke-Rose notes the fairy tale effect produced by metaphors of this type in *A Grammar of Metaphor* (London: Secker and Warburg, 1958), pp. 132 and 144.

10 Stanzas 2–6 of "To the King" (No. 20) contain an elaborate comparison between courtiers and different birds; it is then dropped abruptly, although the poem continues for eleven more stanzas. So also in "To the Quene" (No. 31).

11 Cf. Beryl Rowland, *Blind Beasts: Chaucer's Animal World* (Kent, Ohio: Kent State Univ. Press, 1971), pp. 25–9. See also E. Talbot Donaldson, "Idiom of Popular Poetry in the Miller's Tale," *English Institute Essays 1950* (1951); rpt. in his *Speaking of Chaucer* (London: Athlone Press, 1970), especially pp. 25–7.

12 Sir Walter Scott glossed "powsowdie" even more disparagingly as "a miscellaneous mess" (*The Antiquary*, chap. 35).

13 As a term for a cart horse, *aver* seems invariably pejorative in Middle Scots. Dunbar collocates it with *strummall*, "staggering," or *lob*, "clumsy." In proverbs it is a type of worthlessness: "an inch of a nag is worth a span of an aver." See further *DOST* and *OED*.

14 *Bird* is also used for "maiden, young woman." So "The Tretis," l. 238: "I trow that bird of my blis suld a bourd want."

15 I thus interpret such passages, and much else in the poem, quite differently from John Spiers, who sees "no essential contrast between the natural scene . . . and the gossips," and finds "the hawthorn, the birds and the gossips . . . filled with the same heady wine, the same exuberance of life; they are equally on the plane simply of nature and instinct." *The Scots Literary Tradition*, 2nd edn (London: Faber and Faber, 1962), p. 60.

16 Walter W. Skeat (ed.), *The Vision of Piers Plowman*, 2 vols. (London: Oxford Univ. Press, 1886), B XI, 388ff.

15

ON RE-READING WILLIAM DUNBAR

BY J. SWART

The period between Chaucer and the great Elizabethans has held a challenge for me ever since I first became acquainted with English Literature. In those days we worked methodically. On the death of Chaucer we carefully walked around some one hundred thousand lines of Lydgate, who was of course an English Chaucerian, and then marched across the border to find the Scottish Chaucerians. They in turn seemed succeeded by a few more English Chaucerians, and then, with Wyatt and Surrey came the English Renaissance. To serious readers I have to apologize for presenting this view. It was the impression left on the student mind by such handbooks as Snell's *Age of Transition*—and I am most painfully aware that that is not what Snell's or any other book said. In fact it will be easily seen that my own sense of chronology at the time must have been, to say the least, faulty.

The reason why I revive these memories is not to point to the dangers of presenting this form of History of English Literature to beginning students. One of our problems then would be that Snell of 1905 and Martin S. Day of 1963 are likely to create much the same impression. One marvels at the continuity of educational techniques.[1]

To the serious scholar that is not the point. Anyone who is sufficiently interested to read a little more will quickly find out the obvious errors and sooner or later will come to see the very difficult problems connected with any form of periodization. But the alternative of writing about a number of very different poets individually, with possible concessions to chronology, tends in its turn to obscure tone qualities that are very essential to a person who tries to read with what Trilling defined as "a sense of the past." It may suggest continuities of a different kind that are as much a danger to the serious reading of poetry as periodization. When Emrys Jones, in his challenging edition of Surrey[2] proposes Petrarch as the original instigator of the neo-classical movement, and Surrey as his prophet in English, we have arrived again at a distortion.

This is not to say, then, that either point of view is altogether nonsense, but that by handling both our "diachronic" and our "synchronic" interconnections rather more carefully, we might arrive at greater precision of definition, which in turn may improve cultural insight and critical discernment.

In order to make this problem a little less of a theoretical concern, and at the same time specify the sort of problem that arises, I would like to examine some of Dunbar's poetry, Dunbar being one of the transition poets to whom I find myself returning with pleasure as well as curiosity.

In general he is regarded as a highly individual poet, he is spoken of with respect, and his is a representative case of the poet whom one is inclined to classify as late medieval rather than renaissance. There is, of course, immediately the wide problem that can be generally indicated by the term "passport difficulties." The fact that this problem is approached from this particular angle may make it clear that I here prefer to indicate problems rather than solve them. The problem can be extended to such vast proportions as to include not only the "Scottishness" of Sir Walter,[3] or the "Irishness" of Sheridan or Shaw, but the "Englishness" of T. S. Eliot, and, if one prefers, the "Polishness" of Chopin or the "Dutchness" of Vermeer. What we seem to be talking about, apart from such matters as national pride, is the relative importance of certain cultural features and the amount of prominence that they assume in the work of a given artist.

When Scotland is an independent kingdom in the fourteenth century it does not seem to be culturally very important or independent, and few would hesitate to incorporate Barbour's *Bruce*, as a northern text, in a Middle English anthology. But just as a certain accent would be laid on the Pearl group in such an anthology, as indicative of a distinct cultural pattern, so it would seem that the court of James IV deserves separate mention. Even though James himself is rumoured to have been an indifferent patron of letters, this has certain consequences: it would seem recommendable to take Dunbar along with Douglas, align him with Henryson and James I on the one hand, and Lindsay on the other to see if a Scottish tradition of writers can be built up. The attempt is in part frustrated by our lack of insight into the interrelatedness of a good deal of lyrical material, and in part by their very individuality as writers. In so far as they can be brought into line, it is on the basis of features that they share with Skelton or Hawes, and it is then a period characteristic that we may be envisaging. In so far as they are distinct, it is difficult to assign to them a "Scottish" temper, and it would seem that their individuality as poets outweighs the tradition in which they are presumed to have worked.

To illustrate the first point we might take the lyric "Sweit rois of vertew and of gentilnes/Delytsum lyllie of everie lustynes."[4] We notice a similarity of tone with Skelton's lyrics. C. S. Lewis remarked, when referring to the small amount of love poetry attributable to Dunbar, that the poem is "neither better nor worse than the innumerable sonnets which were soon to drive its kind out of fashion." But the heyday of the sonnet is possibly a century later, and we are in fact noticing one of the overlapping elements that go back to a long and honourable lyric tradition. The poem is in fact as decent an indication of the tradition from which Wyatt and Surrey sprung as we could wish to have. The "rue" pun is used by Greene, and later still, and as for the lily and the rose, they are attested well into the seventeenth century, not to mention Tennyson.

Now, all joking apart, such a phrase as "Delytsum lyllie of everie lustynes" carries a time flavour not easily associated with the later periods. We might be inclined to say tentatively that the court lyric up to c. 1525 is characterized by a certain amount of aureation. After that there is certainly an attempt to arrive at a simpler vocabulary and a preoccupation with greater clarity and distinctness of form— though not necessarily syntax.

Oddly enough Lewis found for the "Sweit rois" ("To a Ladye") a variant which bears the subtitle "Quhone he list to feyne," which in the Bruce Dickins reissue of Mackenzie is given to a different poem, "My hartis tresure, and swete assured fo." This last phrase is almost sufficient by itself to prove the strong Petrarchan affiliations of this cry for mercy. Now this takes us to another aspect of the treatment of what wavers between "influence" and "tradition."

It needs no argument that Petrarch influenced Chaucer (the translation of a sonnet incorporated into *Troilus*, as well as far more subtle instances). We never emphasize this influence as strongly as in the case of Wyatt and Surrey, presumably because in the earlier poet this influence is incorporated into, and in fact manipulated in a far larger context. Chaucer as well as Wyatt occupied himself with experiments in terza rima. Yet it is the appearance of the formal characteristics of the sonnet that mainly causes us to emphasize Wyatt and Surrey as instigators of a new tradition. Obviously, then, it is the Elizabethan sonnet that causes us to hail these poets as representatives of the true English Renaissance. Are we not then forgetting that this type of poetry came to lead, as it were, a life of its own with Tottel's *Miscellany* about the accession of the reign of Elizabeth? Is there perhaps a case to be made for a succession of phases, say c. 1460–1525, c. 1525–60, and then onwards in rather smaller units than we have often been doing?

To start once more from Dunbar, we may notice how in his "derge" ("We that ar heir in hevins glory") he makes a comic use of the Office for the Dead to persuade the King to return from the relative purgatory of Stirling to Edinburgh. A possibly comparable use is found in Skelton's *Philip Sparrow*. Lewis links the latter poem with the mock-heroic and calls it "the lightest—the most like a bubble—of all the poems I know."[5] But he looks upon Skelton as a poet in whose work anything may happen. "That," he says, "is his charm; the charm of the amateur. But Dunbar," he continues, "is professional through and through; the accomplished master of one tradition that goes back to Beowulf and of another that goes back to the Troubadours." Courageous words, these, but as statements hardly illustrable. In the first place, when Lewis wrote this, he had far less experience than we have with the methods of a number of modern poets who illustrate to us what Skelton was doing as far less of an arbitrary process than it may have seemed shortly after the war. And certainly if we look at the second part of Skelton's poem we can hardly compare its solemn commendation with a bubble. Others have, like myself, postulated a more serious religious undertone for the poem,[6] one might in fact wonder whether Dunbar's "*Requiem Edinburgi dona eis*" is not far more playful than Skelton's "*Requiem aeternam*." On the other hand the "*libera nos*" of the Scottish poet is called upon with equal force in "Why come ye not to Court?" (l. 476). In neither Dunbar nor Skelton, however, is there complete parody. The tradition may go back to the Goliards, but both in Skelton and Dunbar the mocking use of the *Officio defunctorum* is given the humanly persuasive background of a concern with sin and repentance.

Now let us for a moment regard the use of exactly the same device in *Ralph Roister Doister* (III, iii). If it is at all functional it should have something to do with Ralph's subsequent defeat in his attempt to conquer Dame Custance, a connection that is never for a moment even implicitly present. It becomes impossible to see the passage in this more or less religious light because it is so utterly embedded in the essential Latinity of this English play. It is a play belonging to the pre-Elizabethan period, and as in Wyatt or Surrey we feel the call of the Golden Age rule over that of the medieval past.

The same play contains what we may call a "complaint" on the part of Dame Custance (V, iii). This is contextually a pure formality, for which there is no justification, dramatic or otherwise. The difference with the earlier period is seen at once when we compare Dunbar's "How sould I rewill me or in quhat wys." The theme of the inconstancy of worldly good is there properly concluded when the question of the refrain is turned into the positive statement "The gratious God mot governe me." And it needs only a reference to Henryson's *Testament of Criseyde* to show how a complaint can be made functional in a larger context.

It is here, of course, that our thoughts must turn to the *Mirror for Magistrates*. Its Lydgatian, and indeed earlier medieval backgrounds make it a prime example of a survival of older forms. And lo and behold the injustice of literary history: do we speak of the Elizabethan Chaucerians? But let us not be led astray by superficial likeness. Raymond Williams has shown that at any rate a case may be shown for the suggestion that the medieval concept of tragedy is a good deal closer to the Aristotelian than our traditions would have us think.[7] After all the past comes down to us not unaltered by the views of those who have looked at it before us.

Therefore in this case if we have a series of tragedies or complaints —the distinction being here of little account—let us look at what the book really purports to be. Its interest lies not in correcting vice, though that is quite often suggested, but in what happened. When there is divergence among the chronicles the authors deal with it in this wise: "Which matter sith it is more harde to decide, than nedefull to our purpose, which minde onely to dissuade from vices and exalte vertue, we referre to the determination of the Haroldes, or such as may cum by the recordes and registers of these doinges." The interest in historical rather than religious truth is such that later editions, on the authority of the "parliament rolle," suggest that the reader reverse the parts played by Bolingbroke and Mowbray in the preceding poem, which was itself left unchanged.[8] The book centres on statecraft, and the position of the Magistrate in a much more modern sense than the older tragedies, which are not interested in abstract human justice.

It is a change of temper of this nature that causes us to select from Wyatt and Surrey, and from the *Mirror*, features that form a prelude to the Elizabethan mode, rather than stress the older tradition. We note in Wyatt, Surrey, and Sackville the conscious use of archaic forms, the forward-looking form of the sonnet, and a certain reluctance to use overt religious expression other than in an appropriate religious context.

When we re-examine our so-called Chaucerians we find on the contrary an inclination towards aureate diction, and a mixture of both styles and forms within one and the same poem, as well as an almost pervasive sense of moral religious connotation. To this may be added a curious attitude towards literary and religious tradition. Since both Dunbar and Skelton were priests it is not surprising that they should have used liturgical texts. But it is as if to them the classics are not distinct from the religious background. To return for a moment to Skelton's "Philip Sparrow," its attitude gains in certainty when we assume instant recognition, as it were, of Catullus. Nor is it only the better known "*Lugete . . . passer mortuus est*," but rather the slighter "*Passer, deliciae meae puellae*", with its significant phrase "*tecum ludere sicut ipsa possem.*"

In Dunbar we come upon Martial, quite suddenly and almost inexplicably in a prayer, in the reproduction of which I ask the reader's indulgence for my italics:

> Salviour, suppois my sensualitie
> Subject to syn hes maid my saule of sys,
> Sum spark of lycht and spiritualite
> Walkynnis my witt, and ressoun biddis me rys,
> My corrupt conscience askis, clips, and cryis
> First grace, syn space, for to amend my mys,
> *Substance with honour doing none suppryis*
> *Freyndis, prosperite*, heir peax, syne hevynis blys.

Here are the "*res non parta labore*," the "*lis nunquam*" possibly linked with "*vires ingenuae*," the "*pares amici*," the "*quod sis esse velis*" of Martial's epigram (X, xlvii).

Now this is unlikely to happen in either Gower or Chaucer, who would cite their authorities with some emphasis unless they have a deeper purpose, nor again is it likely to happen in the generation of Wyatt and Surrey. It may in fact give us a clue to an essential feature of the period under discussion. While on the one hand the vigour of the art of Chaucer and his age has disappeared and the tendency towards aureation in all formal contexts takes its place, so also the culture represented by the great art of the past is, as it were, taken for granted. The art aspect of a culture in this stage of development can be expressed by the more general meaning of the term "mannerism." The important truths of the feudal period, both secular and religious, are suffering as it were a bourgeois invasion, and for want of a unified vision we are presented with a variegated scala of poems which may be individually powerful, but are lacking in the consistent expression of a point of view. That is why Dunbar is a good representative of the period: his poetic ability is never in doubt. But on great questions such as justice or loyalty, or the power of evil he can say only minor things. That this holds good for his contemporaries, is, I think, also true; Henryson's *Testament*, impressive as it may be, has a super-abundance of machinery. Douglas is chiefly a translator, but then also in the aureate tradition. Hawes has little more to say than that a man should get himself an education. Skelton again is a considerable poet, but he shares with Dunbar many of his eccentricities, and is as arrogant about his merits as Dunbar is concerned with the levity of his purse. And whatever Lumiansky and his friends[9] may have achieved about Malory, it is difficult to maintain that Malory presents a unified view, if only for his complete lack of coherence in detail.

To describe the literature of a period in such terms as these is obviously to do it some injustice. But if it is a simplification, it may still be regarded as an indication of a coherent set of characteristics that can help to describe the range of the poets of the end of the fuedal period. Perhaps "late feudal" is a good term to describe this type of poetry. It typifies to some extent the backward-looking attitude that is one of the chief characteristics that to us distinguishes them from their successors. I hasten to say that this term also implies unwarranted assumptions about the comparative vigour that they may display; they would hardly have regarded themselves in that light.

Still, an interpretation of this type of poetry as essentially manneristic brings a certain unity into the picture. It may help us to understand the extremes of crudity and verbose elegance, and also perhaps to see where the merits of this type of poetry are chiefly to be found. That is indeed in the use of contrasted style, and of apparently calculated ambiguity.

It is because of the use of contrasted styles that the apocalyptic vision called up by the abbot who was going to fly never becomes true satire. Opening with "Lucina schynnyng in silence of the nicht," the poet needs the apparition of Dame Fortune to tell him about the expected event, but the prophecy of the beginning of "Antechrystic impyre," occasioned by it, is introduced as follows:

> Under Saturnus fyrie regioun
> Symone Magus sall meit him, and Mahoun,
> And Merlyne at the mone sall him be bydand
> And Jonet the weido on ane bussome rydand,
> Of wichis with ane winder garesoun.

However great the fear of superstitions may have been, "Jonet the weido" does disturb the picture. The successes are in such a poem as the "Tua mariit wemen and the wedo," although it should again be noticed how (l. 443) the "perle of plesance" is introduced most unobtrusively and yet perhaps not without overtones of some quite imperfectly paradisical vision.

There is about Dunbar, even in his lighter moods, often a sense of the ominous. The inconstancy of love is a theme that has been dealt with throughout the ages, and usually with a sense of unconcern. Yet see how Dunbar's version ("Quha will behold of luve the chance") manages to bring in the moral note and the grisly dance:

> It is ane pount of ignorance
> To lufe in sic distemperance,
> Sen time mispendit may avance
>   No creature;
> In luve to keip allegance,
> It war als nys an ordinance,
> As quha wald bid ane deid man dance
>   In sepulture.

This sense of the approximation of the end of all things may be one of the ways in which Dunbar as a poet feels the temper of his time. Much that once was good and glorious is to disappear for ever, and his world is to crash about him. That was how his famous lament first struck me: as a rendering of the approaching march of explosions of a stick of bombs, the last of which one will not survive to hear out.

That, to return to my beginnings, was the first poem by Dunbar that I ever read, and it has never failed to impress me. But if the approaching doom is present to his mind, so also is the religious sincerity of his medieval past. It is remarkable that he summarizes much of it in an image that was later to be elaborated by Herbert, but it is equally characteristic that Herbert's poem should be called *Man*, and that Dunbar's is a vision of *The Passioun of Christ*. Herbert sang the harmony of a unified world picture. Dunbar epitomizes the reality, the terror and the awe of Christ's suffering and its meaning for mankind, as it was present throughout the Middle Ages.

Good Friday carries to him this message:

> "Ordane for Him ane resting place,
>   That is so werie wrocht for the:
>   That schort within thir dayis thre
> Sall law undir thy lyntell bow,
>   And in thy hous sall herbrit be
> Thy blissit Salvatour Chryst Jesu."

UNIVERSITY OF AMSTERDAM

NOTES

1 F. J. Snell, *The Age of Transition 1400–1580*, Handbooks of English Literature (London: George Bell, 1905); Martin S. Day, *History of English Literature to 1660*, A College Course Guide (New York: Doubleday, 1963).

2 Henry Howard, Earl of Surrey, *Poems*, edited by Emrys Jones (Oxford: Clarendon Press, 1964), p. xxi.

3 It is a little unfair here to refer to the later 1962 preface of John Speirs' meritorious *The Scots Literary Tradition* (London: Faber and Faber, 1940; 2nd edn, 1962), pp. 19–23, but it does illustrate a serious aspect of this type of problem. Speirs himself does not regard his book as a literary history.

4 I used W. Mackay Mackenzie (ed.), *The Poems of William Dunbar* (1932; London: Faber and Faber, 1966). The poems are readily identifiable in this edition, except the last which is taken from No. 80, p. 158.

5 C. S. Lewis, *English Literature in the Sixteenth Century excluding Drama*, OHEL 3 (Oxford: Clarendon Press, 1954), p. 138 and p. 97.

6 *Vide* J. Swart, "John Skelton's Philip Sparrow," *English Studies, Suppl.*, 45 (1964), p. 161.

7 Raymond Williams, *Modern Tragedy* (London: Chatto and Windus, 1966), p. 18.

8 Lily B. Campbell (ed.), *The Mirror for Magistrates* (1938; New York: Barnes and Noble, 1960), p. 110.

9 R. M. Lumiansky, *Malory's Originality* (Baltimore: Johns Hopkins Press, 1964).

16

CHAUCER, RICHARD II, HENRY IV, AND 13 OCTOBER

BY SUMNER FERRIS

Although our knowledge of Chaucer's life is greater than for any English poet before him and for most English poets for several centuries after him, it is a dispiriting fact that till now no thorough and scholarly biography of him has been written. Moreover, the absence of such a biography has often combined with a superficial and eclectic acquaintance with "the age of Chaucer" on the part of some critics to permit the wildest flights of what Rossell Hope Robbins has called "personalist criticism," that is, speculative and fantastic interpretations of Chaucer's poetry. Every Chaucerian has his favourite examples of such perversities. Let me call attention here only to the notion, born of a faulty estimate of the influence of Innocent III and fostered by a misreading of *The House of Fame*, that a single-minded *contemptus mundi* was the rule according to which not only Chaucer wrote his poetry but even his royal patrons conducted their lives. My purpose here cannot be to dispel such a notion entirely but only to illuminate, first, one episode in Chaucer's life that will reveal him as rather a shrewder courtier than we usually imagine him to have been and, second, some of the political scene in 1398–9, in which Chaucer had a small share. As many of Professor Robbins' writings teach us, the social and political historian can both teach and learn from the literary historian.

By means of letters patent dated 13 October 1398, Richard II granted Chaucer a tun of wine a year, and somewhat unusually, this grant was repeated (or apparently repeated) in letters patent dated two days later, on 15 October. After Henry IV had seized the throne in the following year, he granted Chaucer, in reply to the "Complaint to His Empty Purse," an annuity of forty marks, in letters patent dated on his coronation, 13 October 1399—exactly a year from the date of Richard's grant of the wine. This coincidence of dates has been remarked on from time to time, but it has always been considered merely fortuitous.[1] Recently, however, it has been shown that Henry's grant to Chaucer was actually made towards February of 1400 (which provides a new date for the "Complaint") and antedated to the previous October;[2] and here it will be shown that Richard's original grant was that of 15 October, which was superseded by that of 13 October, which was in fact antedated too. The demonstration is easy to make, but once made it leads to a consideration of the significance of 13 October to two successive kings of England and to Chaucer himself.

It has long been known that the given dates of letters patent and other medieval English governmental documents are not always trustworthy and that the location, for the patents, on the Patent Rolls can provide a more reliable indication of the actual dates of issue of patents, as opposed to their effective date. For present purposes, all that needs to be said is that when one entry on the Rolls physically precedes another, then the first entry was made before the second, irrespective of the dates the two may bear. In turn, the corresponding patents were actually issued in the same order as the entries were made on the rolls.[3]

Such is the case with Chaucer's patents of 1398. The one dated 15 October, D.N. (Document Number) 476 in the new *Chaucer Life-Records*,[4] appears in the Patent Rolls in 22 Richard II, Part I, Membrane 8. Thus it precedes the one dated 13 October, D.N. 474 (*L-R*, p. 117), in 22 Richard II, Part I, Membrane 5. (Because of the way the membranes were rolled and stitched together, they are numbered in an order the reverse of their compilation.) Therefore, the letters patent dated 15 October were issued before those dated 13 October; or, to put it another way, D.N. 474 actually superseded D.N. 476, and not the other way around, as is commonly believed.[5]

The history of the grants, then, may be reconstructed much as follows. According to D.N. 473 (*L-R*, pp. 116–17), in December of 1397 Richard II had promised Chaucer a barrel of wine a year, but by October of the following year the promise had not been fulfilled. It was probably exactly on 13 October (for reasons that will become apparent) that Chaucer presented a formal petition, D.N. 473, to the King for the wine; and at any rate, as the Latin heading to the French document shows, the petition was granted on that day. But, as a perpetual calendar will reveal, 13 October fell on Sunday in 1398; and of course then as now governmental offices were closed on Sunday and then as now it took even the most efficient staff a couple of days to finish a weekend's backlog of work. The approved petition therefore went to the Office of the Privy Seal on Monday 14 October or Tuesday 15 October, for the Privy Seal warrant permitting the issuing of letters patent (D.N. 475; *L-R*, p. 117) was not drawn up till 15 October. When the warrant was sent to the Chancery, the resulting patent was as a matter of course dated on that same day and so issued to Chaucer. But although the terms of the grant must have been pleasing to Chaucer, apparently the date it bore must not have been, for the dates of the two patents, to repeat, are the only significant difference between them. Consequently, we may assume, he discreetly drew the matter to the attention of Richard, who saw to it that a new patent (D.N. 474) was issued, on his own authority (*Per ipsum Regem*, the patent states), this time with the date of 13 October. Why one date should have been considered more significant or honorific to either donor or recipient is, however, a longer subject to pursue.

That religion in general and the cults of the saints in particular were important to Catholics of the later Middle Ages is such a commonplace that paradoxically we often tend to overlook some of their important manifestations. During this period, for familiar reasons, saints were venerated for historical or regional associations; events were often customarily dated according to saints' days they fell on or near (a practice still vestigially present, even for legal purposes, in the use of Michaelmas and a few other feasts); and, whenever possible, forthcoming events were arranged so as to fall on or near propitious feasts. Where royalty was concerned, the veneration of saints became a matter of political or even dynastic policy, for when a king made it known that his house was especially devoted to or associated with a particular saint, the effect was not only to demonstrate the piety of the king but to suggest the sanction of heaven itself for his actions.

Richard II was probably the most genuinely pious of the later medieval kings of England, and his devotion to the Blessed Virgin is particularly well known. The iconographic examination of the Wilton Diptych and its backgrounds in a recent study will suffice to show how almost every important event in his life is dated in contemporary records by its proximity to a saint's day.[6] (Incidentally, Chauntecleer's reference to the life of St Kenelm may have pleased Richard, who was crowned on the eve of the feast of that saint.) It is probably more than accidental that Richard was forced to renounce the throne on Michaelmas, 29 September 1399: Henry was probably pleased by the complex of religious and legal associations surrounding the day, which would suggest both the finality of Richard's abdication and the justice of the *coup d'état*.

Of all the saints except the Blessed Virgin, it was St Edward the Confessor (who figures as one of Richard's sponsors in the Wilton Diptych) whom Richard came most to venerate in the last decade of his life. Edward's feast day is, properly speaking, 5 January, the date of his death in 1066 and only a day before Richard's birthday, 6 January according to Froissart; and on 6 January 1066 St Edward was buried in Westminster Abbey, which he had built and which became not only a royal peculiar but in effect the parish church of the royal family. After the abbey was rebuilt, the feast of the translation of St Edward's body there, 13 October, came to be considered pre-eminently the feast of St Edward. Moreover, the three kings of England preceding Richard had been named Edward, as well as his father, the Black Prince; and as William the Conqueror had based his claim to the throne of England largely on his consanguinity to the Confessor,[7] succeeding kings therefore came to think of themselves as descendants, in the sense, of St Edward. At his coronation Richard swore to uphold, as his predecessors had long done, the ancient laws of England, in particular those believed to have been made or confirmed by St Edward; and some of the coronation regalia, most notably a ring that was the subject of the most famous legend about the saint, were said to have belonged to St Edward himself.[8] During his reign Richard's veneration was shown by such acts as his appropriation of money for the upkeep of the saint's shrine in the Abbey and his contribution of vestments depicting St Edward, among others, to the clergy of the Abbey.[9] By the 1390s Richard had even quartered the arms of St Edward (fancifully reconstructed, of course) with his own;[10] and in this form his arms appear on the back of the Wilton Diptych.

As an important government official, as an associate of the King, and simply as a medieval Catholic, Chaucer would certainly have known of Richard's devotion to St Edward the Confessor. And one episode in particular connects Chaucer, Richard II, and 13 October. In 1390, a year or so after he had asserted himself as King, Richard held the famous Tournament of the White Hart, to which nobility from all over Europe were invited; and as Clerk of the King's Works Chaucer was in charge of preparations for the event. According to the Monk of Evesham the tournament itself was held on 10, 11 and 12 October and concluded as follows:

> *Et ad demonstrandam suam regiam excellentiam extraneis praedictis, tenuit Rex festum S. Edwardi Confessoris apud Kenyngton, solenniter sedens in regalibus, tam ad missam quam ad mensam, coronatus.*[11]

Since Richard's devotion to St Edward is well attested from other sources, it is not by chance that the tournament ended with a feast on that saint's day.

Given this background, one may infer with some confidence the

reasons for Chaucer's having received two patents embodying essentially the same grant from Richard in 1398. In the first place, it is
clear that in the later 1390s Chaucer was somewhat less provident or
at least in more modest circumstances than his admirers have cared to
admit. Objectively considered, the long record of his petitions, loans,
grants, advances, and lawsuits indicate pretty certainly that he was
not very well off. It cannot be known, of course, whether the promise
of a grant of a tun of wine made in December of 1397 (cf. D.N. 473)
was due to Chaucer's request or to an unsolicited act of generosity on
the part of King Richard. (One thinks, perhaps irrelevantly, perhaps
irreverently, of promises made impulsively at Christmas parties.) But
at any rate when the promise remained unfulfilled, Chaucer must
have been disappointed if not anxious about it. Yet, one may assume,
he was tactful enough not to importune his king and waited instead
for a suitable time to remind his sovereign about the gift. This came
on 13 October 1398, a day not only sacred to the King because it was
the feast of St Edward the Confessor but one on which for that reason
the King was likely to be generous. Richard was probably pleased by
Chaucer's choice of such an appropriate day and, reminded of his
years of service to the crown, happy to grant the request immediately.
But, as has been seen, owing to normal delays in bureaucratic procedures, the grant was not officially recorded, in D.N. 476, till 15
October—a date indifferent to both king and subject. Probably
Chaucer himself called discreet attention to the fact that, magnani-
mous though the gift was, it would be even more so if dated on the
feast of one of Richard's patron saints. At any rate, the King himself
had a new patent issued, D.N. 474, with the more honorific date of
13 October; and so an amount of fame could accrue to the saint, the
sovereign, and the subject. Moreover, a short time later, on 28 October, Chaucer was permitted the further favour of a £10 loan on his
annuity (D.N. 478; L-R, p. 523).

When, in the following year, Henry IV usurped the throne, he had to
justify having done so in such a way as to suggest that, far from a
revolution's having taken place, the venerable traditions of the kingdom were continuing uninterrupted. First, he offered several justifi-
cations for his becoming King: Richard's supposedly voluntary
abdication before Parliament and the three others succinctly presented
by Chaucer in the Envoy to the "Complaint to His Empty Purse":

> O conqueror of Brutes Albyon,
> Which that by lyne and free eleccion
> Been verray kyng . . .[12]

Second, Henry appropriated several of Richard's practices. Richard was devoted to the Blessed Virgin; so Henry let it be known that he was similarly devoted. For example, Richard had been intending to be crowned again, in order to be consecrated this time with some recently discovered holy oil, which (according to legend) the Blessed Virgin had given St Thomas Becket. In Henry's coronation, this was the oil used.[13] As the Confessor's arms had been quartered with Richard's, so for a time they were with Henry's.[14] And Henry chose to be crowned on 13 October 1399, the feast of St Edward the Confessor, and for the next year or so the new King rewarded some of his followers with gifts dated on that day,[15] Chaucer being (for us, at least) the most famous.

Therefore, although both the letters patent dated 13 October 1398 and those dated 13 October 1399 were in fact antedated, in neither case was the date fortuitous or arbitrary, for in each case it was a date significant to the King and in each case allowed the King to show esteem for Chaucer. Moreover, it raises again the knotty problem of Chaucer's relations with the fading House of Plantagenet and the emerging House of Lancaster in the 1390s. By late 1391, Chaucer had retired from the King's service, although he continued to be the beneficiary of the King's favour (cf., e.g., D.N. 413; *L-R*, p. 120, and D.N. 424; *L-R*, p. 514). It is often said, however, that Henry's gifts to Chaucer in 1395–6 (D.N. 444 and 445; *L-R*, p. 275) indicate something of a change of allegiance on the part of the poet from King Richard to his cousin Henry during what is often called Richard's "second tyranny" (in much the same way as Gower's changing of the dedication of the *Confessio Amantis* from Richard to Henry is sometimes interpreted). Nevertheless not only Richard's gift of the wine to Chaucer in 1398 but also the unusual way in which the date of the grant was changed show that, as late as the last year of Richard's rule, Chaucer considered himself and was considered to be a loyal supporter of that King. If he changed his allegiance in 1399–1400, so did most other Englishmen; for when Henry showed himself undisposed to punish whoever swore loyalty to him, Chaucer like other men great and small became a Lancastrian. Chaucer may not have been the Laodicean that R.S. Loomis called him, but he did have something of the Vicar of Bray about him.

Finally, Chaucer's tact, born of years of service as a courtier and diplomat, are evidenced in his requests to Richard and to Henry. His petition for the earlier grant was made by the usual means of a formal application, his petition for the later by the somewhat unusual means of a poem; but the tactfulness of tone of the "Complaint to His

Empty Purse" is matched by the aptness of his choice of 13 October to present a petition to Richard II. In both cases he flattered his King, in both cases he allowed them to show largesse, and in both cases he was successful. Of course Chaucer lived at a time when it was customary to feel and to express contempt for the world's riches and vanities; but, as we do, he liked to, had to, eat and drink, and if an appeal to Richard on the feast of St Edward the Confessor happened to flatter the King's sense of his own piety and result in a publicly gracious act of generosity, Chaucer is thereby a less austere, more human, and even more modern person than some unhistorically minded critics have pictured him.

CALIFORNIA STATE COLLEGE, PENNSYLVANIA

NOTES

[1] E.g., by G. G. Coulton, *Chaucer and His England* (1908; rpt. New York: Barnes and Noble, 1963), p. 50.

[2] Sumner Ferris, "The Date of Chaucer's Final Annuity and of the 'Complaint to His Empty Purse,'" *MP*, 65 (1967), pp. 45–52.

[3] For a full discussion of antedating see H. C. Maxwell-Lyte, *Historical Notes on the Use of the Great Seal of England* (London: H.M.S.O., 1926), pp. 63–71 and 253–65, and the discussion and references in "The Date of Chaucer's Final Annuity."

[4] Martin M. Crow and Clair C. Olson (eds), *Chaucer Life-Records* (Austin: Univ. of Texas Press, 1966), pp. 117–18—hereafter "*L-R.*" The locations of the entries in the Patent Rolls may be found here too, "Pt." meaning "Part" and "m." "Membrane." The expression "D.N." for "Document Number(s)" is borrowed from the *English Historical Documents* series and is keyed to the number assigned by Crow and Olson in the "Appendix: Chronological Table of Chaucer Life-Records" (*L-R*, pp. 550–96). Its use is sometimes extended, if there is no possibility of confusion, to cover the actual letters patent, etc. that some of the enrolments record.

[5] The usual explanation of why D.N. 474 was supposedly superseded by D.N. 476 can easily be shown to be trivial and inconsistent with the other documents concerned. R. E. G. Kirk thought that the explanation lay in "the more ample words" of D.N. 476, whereby the "grant was to take effect from the 1st December last, 1397 . . . and the wine was to be received from the Chief Butler, 'or his deputy' in the Port of London"—two provisions not found in the supposedly earlier D.N. 474 (R. E. G. Kirk (ed.), *Life-Records of Chaucer*, Part IV, Chaucer Society, 2nd Ser., No. 32 (London, 1900), p. xlix). But a new patent would not have been necessary to make a grant retroactive: a memorandum from one government office to another would have sufficed (cf. D.N. 488; *L-R*, p. 530); and then as now a deputy could perform routine duties on behalf of a Minister of the Crown without special authority. Moreover, since D.N. 474 was issued on the authority of the King himself (*Per ipsum Regem*) and D.N. 476 on the authority of the Privy Seal (*Per breve de privato sigillo*), it is improbable that any

merely administrative circumstances would have required, or even allowed, a writ of the Privy Seal to supersede the instructions of the King. It is much easier to account for the King's superseding the instructions of the Privy Seal. Lastly, there are a Privy Seal warrant (D.N. 475; *L-R*, p. 117) authorizing letters patent for D.N. 476 but not for D.N. 474, and an order of October 16 (D.N. 477; *L-R*, p. 118), passing D.N. 474, without fee. A patent that was issued earlier might have entailed such a warrant and perhaps such an order, but a patent that was issued later to replace it would not have. In fact, the "more ample words" of D.N. 476 suggest that D.N. 474 was a quickly done replacement, enrolling only the essentials of the grant and the altered date.

[6] See "The Iconography of the Wilton Diptych," *Minn R*, 7 (1967), pp. 342–7.

[7] David G. Douglas, *William the Conqueror* (Berkeley: Univ. of California Press, 1964), esp. pp. 50–5.

[8] Percy Ernst Schramm, *A History of the English Coronation*, trans. Leopold G. Wickham Legg (Oxford: Clarendon Press, 1937), pp. 136–8; V. H. Galbraith (ed.), *Anonimalle Chronicle*, (1927; rpt. Manchester: Univ. of Manchester Press and New York: Barnes and Noble, 1970), pp. 110–11, 186.

[9] J. Wickham Legg, "On an Inventory of the Vestry in Westminster Abbey Taken in 1399," *Archaeologia*, 52 (1890), pp. 290–3.

[10] John H. Harvey, "The Wilton Diptych—A Re-Examination," *Archaeologia*, 98 (1961), pp. 1–20, text and notes, passim.

[11] Monk of Evesham, *Historia Vitae et Regni Ricardi II*, edited by Thomas Hearne (Oxford, 1729), p. 122. Froissart's much more circumstantial account—most conveniently available in Clair C. Olson and Martin M. Crow (eds), *Chaucer's World*, comp. Edith Rickert (New York: Columbia Univ. Press, 1948), pp. 211–14—gives different dates for the tournament, but Froissart was not present at it and the English account is just as likely to be correct.

[12] F. N. Robinson (ed.), *Works*, 2nd edn (Boston: Houghton Mifflin, 1957), p. 540.

[13] Thomas of Walsingham, *Chronicon Anglie*, edited by Edward Maunde Thompson, Rolls Series, 64 (London: Longman, 1874), p. 239.

[14] Alfred B. Wyon, "On the Great Seals of Henry IV, Henry V, and Henry VI . . .," *JBAA*, 39 (1883), pp. 143–4.

[15] Cf. E. F. Jacobs, *The Fifteenth Century, 1399–1485*, Oxford History of England, V (Oxford, 1961), p. 18, and *Calendar of Patent Rolls, 1399–1401*, passim.

17

MIDDLE ENGLISH IN
OLD ENGLISH MANUSCRIPTS

BY ANGUS F. CAMERON

For many years now, one of the commonplaces in our study of English language and literature has been that Old English passed out of use as a literary language about the year 1200, and that its study did not revive until the middle of the sixteenth century. In the controversy over the continuity of English prose and poetry, the arguments have emphasized the continuity of subject matter and style rather than text and manuscript.[1] No one has suggested that OE MSS were read continuously throughout the later Middle Ages. R. W. Chambers, in his well-known essay, "On the Continuity of English Prose from Alfred to More and his School," speaks of OE MSS in the later Middle Ages as "useless curiosities, which a competent monastic librarian would eject,"[2] while Wrenn mentions OE texts which "were being used and copied through the twelfth century, until their language ceased entirely to be comprehensible."[3] Yet despite these statements there are clear signs that OE MSS were being read and understood from the beginning of the thirteenth century through to the early sixteenth century.

The OE texts to which Wrenn refers are late copies of sermons by Ælfric in the Lambeth and Vespasian homiliaries.[4] There are a number of such copies of OE texts, all written in modernized forms of OE, if not in ME, and dating from the end of the twelfth or the beginning of the thirteenth centuries. They include the Winteney version of the English–Latin Benedictine Rule,[5] the Hatton Gospels,[6] medical texts such as the *Herbarium Apuleii*,[7] and a copy of Ælfric's Grammar from Worcester in the "tremulous" hand.[8]

These are by no means the last OE texts to be copied by medieval scribes. OE versions of *Cædmon's Hymn* and *Bede's Death Song* are found in fourteenth- and fifteenth-century MSS of Bede's History and Cuthbert's Letter,[9] although, as so often happens when short texts in one language are incorporated in long texts in another, the OE words may be garbled.

Another example of OE quoted in a Latin text, but this time accurately and to good purpose, comes in the *Historia Maior* of Thomas Rudborne.[10] Rudborne, a fifteenth-century monk of St Swithun's, Winchester, quoted from a copy of the OE translation of Bede's History from Southwick Priory in Hampshire to prove that St Albans had been martyred *"in habitu monachali."*

Throughout the Middle Ages charters in OE were recopied in English cartularies.[11] In many cases the language was modernized, and occasionally scribes provided the OE texts with accompanying ME translations. The most striking example occurs in the fourteenth-century *Liber Abbatiae* of Hyde Abbey,[12] where all the OE documents have ME and Latin translations. While these translations are not always accurate, they show familiarity with, and a considerable knowledge of OE.

Although these copies of OE texts in later MSS give some evidence of the use of the language from the thirteenth to sixteenth centuries, more can be had from the ME and Latin annotations in OE MSS. From all periods of the late Middle Ages there are readers' and users' marks in OE MSS which show that they were being read and their texts understood. Editors of OE texts have only recently taken an interest in such annotations and glosses,[13] and there is clearly much more work to be done on them. Most of what we presently know about later annotations in OE MSS has been gathered by N. R. Ker in his *Catalogue of Manuscripts containing Anglo-Saxon*,[14] and the section of his introduction entitled "Use before 1540"[15] is the best treatment of the subject.

While Ker shows that OE MSS were indeed used between 1200 and the dissolution of the monasteries, he approaches the subject cautiously: "There is evidence that manuscripts in OE were considered to be practically without value in the thirteenth and fourteenth centuries."[16] He gives four examples of neglect.

The first concerns OE MSS in the 1247 catalogue from Glastonbury listed as *vetusta et inutilia*.[17] The second and third concern Exeter MSS.[18] In the Exeter catalogue of 1327, however, at least three OE MSS are singled out as being of special value, while the ones listed at the end as worthless include French and Latin MSS as well as OE. Ker's fourth example is a homiliary whose provenance is unknown, Cambridge University Library MS Ii.1.33. At the top of f.29, in a hand of about 1300, there is a note *"Hoc uolumen continet multam copiam sermonum in anglico. non appreciatum propter ydioma incognitum."*[19] Yet the same MS contains glosses in Latin and ME to several of its texts in hands which Ker dates later in the fourteenth century.[20]

In this paper I wish to look at these thirteenth- to sixteenth-century annotations in OE MSS, paying special attention to MSS which have notes and glosses in ME. I hope to give a survey of the present state of our knowledge of them, including information on what kinds of annotation were made, on when and where they were made, on what kinds of texts attracted annotation, and whether or not they were understood.

Of the 189 major OE MSS described by Ker, 44 or nearly a quarter show signs of annotation from the period between 1200 and 1540,[21] ranging from the addition of titles and rubrics to the texts to batches of interlinear glosses in ME and Latin.

At pp. xlix–l of the introduction to his *Catalogue*, Ker briefly presents a list of MSS showing use between 1200 and 1540 arranged according to kind of annotation and date. I will present an expanded version of this list, adding a number of items and drawing together information from the individual MS entries in the *Catalogue*. My list follows Ker's in its layout. The primary arrangement is by kind of annotation. Within each category the examples are listed in rough chronological order; the dating follows Ker and is given in his form. Within each entry the following information is given, (1) Ker *Catalogue* number, (2) MS identified by library and call number, (3) kind of MS or text, (4) exact page or folio references for annotations where these are given by Ker, and (5) ownership (and likely place of annotation) during the Middle Ages. Where annotations have been edited and commented on, I have given references to these printed sources in footnotes to the individual items.

Text supplied
s.xv/xvi
Ker 280. MS London, Lambeth Palace 427. Interlinear gloss to the Psalter. f. 78, text supplied (Latin and ME) Psalms lxiv 8–lxv 7 from the Priory of Lanthony, Gloucester.[22]

Text alterations
s.xiii
Ker 56. MS Cambridge, Corpus Christi College 302. Homiliary. pp. 119, 157, 159, 161, 189. medieval home unknown.
Ker 245. MS London, British Museum, Royal 1 A.xiv. OE Gospels. f. 148. addition to text of John vii 22 from Christ Church, Canterbury.
s.xv
Ker 310. MS Oxford, Bodleian, Bodley 343. Homiliary. f. 71v. from somewhere in the West Midlands.

Glosses in English
s.xiii
Ker 240. MS London, British Museum, Harley 3376. Latin-OE glossary. f. 49 additional gloss. from the west of England on the evidence of linguistic forms in the ME poem copied on ff. 16–17.
s.xiii/xiv
Ker 57. MS Cambridge, Corpus Christi College 303. Homiliary. p. 220. from Rochester.
s.xiv/xv
Ker 216. MS London, British Museum, Cotton Vitellius A.xv. Marvels of the East. f. 102v.[23]
s.xv
Ker 310. MS Oxford, Bodleian, Bodley 343. Homiliary. ff.141v–143v. from somewhere in the West Midlands in the early Middle Ages.[24]
s.xv/xvi
Ker 199. MS London, British Museum, Cotton Tiberius C.vi. Ælfric's homily *De septiformi spiritu*. ff. 28v–29r. written at Winchester. medieval home unknown.[25]

Glosses in Latin and English
s.xiii in the 'tremulous' hand from Worcester[26]
Ker 23. MS Cambridge, Univ. Library, Kk. 3.18. OE Bede. from Worcester.
Ker 30. MS Cambridge, Corpus Christi College 12. OE Pastoral Care.
Ker 41. MS Cambridge, Corpus Christi College 178. Homiliary and Benedictine Rule.
Ker 48. MS Cambridge, Corpus Christi College 198. Homiliary.
Ker 67. MS Cambridge, Corpus Christi College 391. "Portiforium Oswaldi" liturgical texts.
Ker 73. MS Cambridge, Corpus Christi College 557. Legend of the Cross.
Ker 178. MS London, British Museum, Cotton Otho B.x. ff. 29, 30. Homilies.
Ker 182. MS London, British Museum, Cotton Otho C.i, vol. 2. OE Gregory's Dialogues.
Ker 225. MS London, British Museum, Harley 55. ff.1–4. Recipes and Laws.
Ker 324. MS Oxford, Bodleian, Hatton 20. OE Pastoral Care.
Ker 328. MS Oxford, Bodleian, Hatton 76. OE Gregory's Dialogues, Herbal, etc.
Ker 331. MS Oxford, Bodleian, Hatton 113, 114. Homiliary.

Ker 332. MS Oxford, Bodleian, Hatton 115. Homiliary.

Ker 333. MS Oxford, Bodleian, Hatton 116. Homiliary.

Ker 338. MS Oxford, Bodleian, Junius 121. Ecclesiastical Institutes and Homilies.

Ker 343. MS Oxford, Bodleian, Laud Misc. 482. Penitentials, etc.

s.xiii

Ker 231. MS London, British Museum, Harley 585. Herbal and *Lacnunga*. medieval home unknown.[27]

s.xiv

Ker 18. MS Cambridge, Univ. Library, Ii.1.33. Homiliary. ff. 37–43, 110–111, 189. medieval home unknown.

Glosses in Latin

s.xiii

Ker 19. MS Cambridge, Univ. Library, Ii.2.4. OE Pastoral Care. f. 30. written at Exeter. medieval home unknown.

Ker 23. MS Cambridge, Univ. Library, Kk. 3.18. OE Bede. ff. 8v, 67. from Worcester.

s.xiv

Ker 245. MS London, British Museum, Royal 1 A.xiv. OE Gospels. ff. 144–146v. from Christ Church, Canterbury.

Ker 309. MS Oxford, Bodleian, Bodley 340, 342. Homiliaries. MS 340 f. 1. MS 342 f. 46, etc. from Rochester.

Ker 351. MS Oxford, Bodelian, Tanner 10. OE Bede. ff. 1–7, 58v–60. from Thorney.

Notes and Marginalia

s.xiii

Ker 153. MS London, British Museum, Cotton Faustina A.ix. Homiliary. Latin notes on ff. 70–73, 103–109. medieval home unknown.

s.xiii/xiv

Ker 21. MS Cambridge, Univ. Library, Ii.4.6. Homiliary. ff. 132, 146rv. from Tavistock?

Ker 57. MS Cambridge, Corpus Christi College 303. Homiliary. pp. 220, 222. Latin notes on the deadly sins. from Rochester.

Ker 344. MS Oxford, Bodleian, Laud Misc. 509. OE Heptateuch. Latin marginalia and marks of omission. medieval home unknown.

Ker 346. MS Oxford, Bodleian, Laud Misc. 636. Peterborough Chronicle. Latin marginalia f. 18, etc. from Peterborough.

s.xiv

Ker 62. MS Cambridge, Corpus Christi College 367, pt. II. Ælfric's *De temporibus anni*. ff. 1v–2v. medieval home unknown.

Ker 351. MS Oxford, Bodleian, Tanner 10. OE Bede. Latin notes. from Thorney.

s.xv

Ker 148. MS London, British Museum, Cotton Domitian viii. Bi-lingual Chronicle. from Christ Church, Canterbury.

Tables of Contents (detailed listings of separate chapters or homilies)

s.xiii

Ker 30. MS Cambridge, Corpus Christi College 12. OE Pastoral Care. f. 8. from Worcester. (last six chapters in Latin)

Ker 41. MS Cambridge, Corpus Christi College 178. Homiliary. p. vii. from Worcester.

Ker 331. MS Oxford, Bodleian, Hatton 114. Homiliary. ff. 9v–10. from Worcester.

s.xiv

Ker 309. MS Oxford, Bodleian, Bodley 342. Homiliary. f. iv^v. from Rochester.

Titles (to whole manuscripts)

s.xiii

Ker 264. MS London, British Museum, Royal 12 D.xvii. Leech-book. written at Winchester. medieval home unknown.

Ker 331. MS Oxford, Bodleian, Hatton 113, 114. Homiliary. from Worcester.

Ker 336. MS Oxford, Bodleian, Junius 85, 86. Homiliary. title "*Pars psalterii greci.*" f. 1. medieval home unknown.

s.xiii/xiv

Ker 18. MS Cambridge, Univ. Library, Ii.1.33. Homiliary. medieval home unknown.

s.xiv

Ker 309. MS Oxford, Bodleian, Bodley 340, 342. Homiliary. from Rochester.

Ker 334. MS Oxford, Bodleian, Junius 11. The Cædmon manuscript of OE poetry. from Christ Church, Canterbury.

Ker 367. MS Paris, Bibliothèque Nationale, Lat. 8824. Paris Psalter. ff. 186v–187v. belonged to Jean, Duc de Berry in 1402.

Ker 373. MS Rochester Cathedral, *Textus Roffensis.* f. 1. from Rochester.

s.xv

Ker 160, MS London, British Museum, Cotton Julius A.vi. Hymnary with interlinear OE gloss. from Durham.

Ker 362. MS Oxford, St. John's College 154. Ælfric's Grammar. from Durham.

Running titles (to individual items in large manuscripts)
s.xiii
Ker 333. MS Oxford, Bodleian, Hatton 116. Homiliary. marked in upper margin of each page to p. 271. from Worcester.
s.xiii/xiv
Ker 344. MS Oxford, Bodleian, Laud Misc. 509. Old English Heptateuch. medieval home unknown.
s.xiv
Ker 18. MS Cambridge, Univ. Library, Ii.1.33. Homiliary. medieval home unknown.
Ker 309. MS Oxford, Bodleian, Bodley 340, 342. Homiliary. from Rochester.
Ker 351. MS Oxford, Bodleian, Tanner 10. OE Bede. from Thorney.

Rubrics (to selected items in large manuscripts)
s.xiii
Ker 48. MS Cambridge, Corpus Christi College 198. arts. 63, 65. Homiliary. from Worcester.
s.xiv
Ker 220. MS London, British Museum, Cotton Vitellius C.v Homiliary. ff. 102, 107. from Tavistock?

Incipits and Explicits
s.xiii
Ker 60. MS Cambridge, Corpus Christi College 322. OE Gregory's Dialogues. Latin incipits and explicits to each book. medieval home unknown.

In this list there are sixty-two separate annotations in forty-four MSS. Of these thirty-three can be dated in the thirteenth century, seven at the turn of the thirteenth and fourteenth centuries, twelve in the fourteenth century, eight in the fifteenth century and two at the turn of the fifteenth and sixteenth centuries.

The big collections of homilies were clearly the most often read and annotated of all the OE texts. Annotations are found in seventeen homiliaries, in three MSS of the OE Pastoral Care, in three of the OE Gregory's Dialogues, in two each of the OE Bede, the Psalter, medical texts, the Anglo-Saxon Chronicle, and collections of legal texts, and in one each of the OE Gospels, the OE Heptateuch, Latin–OE glossary, the Cædmon MS of OE poetry, the Marvels of the East, liturgical texts, Ælfric's Grammar, Ælfric's *De temporibus anni*, the hymnal, penitentials, and Ecclesiastical Institutes.

Fourteen of the annotated MSS have no known medieval ownership, although it is possible that further study of their annotations will enable us to place them. Seventeen come from Worcester, and all show the work of the scribe with the "tremulous" hand, as well as some other hands. Three are from Christ Church, Canterbury, and three from Rochester, two from Durham, two possibly from Tavistock, one from Lanthony, one from Thorney, one from Peterborough, and one (the Paris Psalter) belonged to Jean, Duc de Berry.

Of all these annotated MSS, the ones which give the most information are those with interlinear glosses, and especially those with glosses in later forms of English. We can look at several examples of these to see the varieties.

In all cases the glosses are found in batches on a single page or folio, or at the most, running over two or three folios. This indicates that they are probably readers' rather than teachers' glosses, for the teaching glosses found in the Anglo-Saxon Psalters and Aldhelm MSS are continuous, or are evenly spread throughout their MSS. It is hard to say whether the readers who annotated these OE texts in later forms of English glossed words they knew or words they had to look up in other sources. At any rate they used a variety of techniques.

The simplest form of glossing is to respell the Old English words in modernized form. This is done by the readers of the *Marvels of the East* on f. 102v of MS Cotton Vitellius A.xv.[28] They change the spellings of eighteen OE words on the page, and in only one case is there any question of lexical substitution. OE diphthongs are represented by front vowels, l.2 *heafdum—hefdum*, l.3 *breostum—brestum*, l.11 *beoð—beth*. The dative plural ending in *um* is retained, although other inflectional endings are levelled. In l.2 the verb *habbað* becomes *habbyt*.

The fifteenth-century reader of Bodleian MS Bodley 343 is much more ambitious, and on ff. 141v–143v, in a set of Wulfstan pieces,[29] substitutes over ninety obsolete OE words with their late ME equivalents. As Ker notes, "the glossator shows on the whole a remarkably good knowledge of OE."[30] Some examples are, *modignesse—pride, frofre—confort, oft ꝸ ilome—mony sythes, tunglan—sterres, edlean—mede*.[31] There is only one striking error. In the clause, "And ðeah þæt beo þæt fela manna Antecrist sylfne næfre his eagum ne geseo," *eagum* is glossed "drede."[32] While confusion between the two words is certainly possible in ME, it is a mistake which should not have occurred, had the glossator been paying attention to the immediate context. However, he seems specifically interested in single vocabulary items, and does not gloss continuously except in Wulfstan's catalogues of nouns.[33]

The late fifteenth- or early sixteenth-century glossator[34] of Ælfric's homily *De septiformi spiritu*, in the Tiberius Psalter, provides something much closer to a continuous interlinear gloss. He glosses over two hundred words on ff. 28v–29r. One sentence from f. 29r gives an example of his technique:

> godes fer is ye sevent of thes gostly   gyftes and
> Godes ege is seo seofoðe þissera gastlicra gyfa   7
> yt gyft is bygyneng of al wysdom
> seo gyfu is angin   ealles wisdomes.[35]

The glossing is competent throughout, and while few of the words glossed present the difficulties of the Wulfstan vocabulary in MS Bodley 343, the reader shows that he has a good working knowledge of OE. Some of the hard words glossed are *geþyldig—pacient, arfæstnysse —meknes*, and *god ingehyd—gud cunynge*.[36]

If the ability to read OE were strong and widespread during the later Middle Ages, then we would not expect to find any interlinear glosses or translations for OE texts. However, surely their presence, along with the quality of the glossing and translation, shows that those who were interested could and did read OE. The readers' traces from the thirteenth to the sixteenth centuries are less frequent than, but much the same in kind as those we get from the sixteenth- and seven-teenth-century Anglo-Saxonists, who we know made a study of the language. They are also similar in kind to the vernacular glosses and notes we find in Latin MSS read in England in the tenth and eleventh centuries.

The annotations from the later Middle Ages show that while the greatest number of thirteenth-century glosses come from Worcester and are in the "tremulous" hand, other scribes were also at work there. And OE was being read at this time at Winchester, Canterbury, Rochester, Gloucester, Durham, and Peterborough, in monasteries and cathedral schools all over England.

In conclusion we can say that the ability to read OE never died out completely in England. Of the fifteenth-century glosses to Wulfstan in MS Bodley 343, Bethurum observes, "the concern with them confirms what is known from other sources, that interest in Old English in the West Midlands was not spasmodic antiquarianism but must have run a steady course to the end of the Middle Ages."[37] On the basis of a wider survey, we can extend this observation to cover much more of England. The use of OE texts as working documents merges directly into their use as antiquarian sources. Our study of this merger has only just begun.[38]

UNIVERSITY OF TORONTO

NOTES

[1] This controversy has a large literature. Some of the principal contributions are: G. P. Krapp, *The Rise of English Literary Prose* (1915; rpt. New York: Ungar, 1963); R. W. Chambers, *On the Continuity of English Prose from Alfred to More and his School* (EETS, OS 191A, 1932); Dorothy Bethurum, "The Connection of the *Katherine Group* with Old English Prose," *JEGP*, 34 (1935), pp. 553–64; A. A. Prins, *French Influence on English Phrasing* (Leyden: Universitaire Pers Leiden, 1952); C. L. Wrenn, "On the Continuity of English Poetry," *Anglia*, 76 (1958), pp. 41–59, rpt. in *Word and Symbol: Studies in English Language* (London: Longmans, 1967), pp. 78–94, and, slightly revised, in *A Study of Old English Literature* (London: Harrap, 1967), pp. 17–34; R. M. Wilson, "On the Continuity of English Prose," in *Mélanges de linguistique et de philologie, Fernand Mossé in memoriam* (Paris: Didier, 1959), pp. 486–94; N. Davis, "Styles in English Prose of the Late Middle and Early Modern Period," *Les Congrès et Colloques de l'Université de Liège*, 21 (1961), pp. 165–84; I. A. Gordon, *The Movement of English Prose* (London: Longmans, 1966); P. J. C. Field, *Romance and Chronicle* (London: Barrie and Jenkins, 1971), Ch. II, Background.

[2] Chambers, op. cit., p. lxvi.

[3] Wrenn, op. cit., p. 261.

[4] MS Lambeth Palace 487. R. Morris (ed.), *Old English Homilies and Homiletic Treatises First Series* (EETS, OS 29, 1868), pp. 2–159. MS Cotton Vespasian A.xxii, Morris, pp. 216–45.

[5] MS Cotton Claudius D.iii. A. Schröer (ed.), *Die Winteney-Version der Regula S. Benedicti* (Halle: Max Niemeyer, 1888).

[6] MS Bodleian, Hatton 38. W. W. Skeat (ed.), *The Four Gospels in Anglo-Saxon, Northumbrian and Old Mercian Versions* (Cambridge: Cambridge Univ. Press, 1871–87; rpt. Darmstadt: Wissenschaftliche Buchgesellschaft, 1970).

[7] MS Harley 6258B. H. Berberich (ed.), *Das Herbarium Apuleii nach einer frühmittelenglischen Fassung*, AF, 5 (1902); J. Delcourt, *Medicina de Quadrupedibus*, AF, 40 (1914).

[8] MS Worcester Cathedral F.174. Collated as W in J. Zupitza, *Ælfrics Grammatik und Glossar, Sammlung englischer Denkmäler 1* (Berlin: Weidmann, 1880), rpt. with foreword by H. Gneuss (Berlin: Weidmann, 1966).

[9] E. V. K. Dobbie, *The Manuscripts of Cædmon's Hymn and Bede's Death Song*, Columbia University Studies in English and Comparative Literature 128 (New York: Columbia Univ. Press, 1937).

[10] H. Wharton (ed.), *Anglia Sacra* (London, 1691) I, p. 183. The reference is given by N. R. Ker, *Catalogue of Manuscripts containing Anglo-Saxon* (Oxford: Clarendon Press, 1957), p. xlix.

[11] See P. H. Sawyer, *Anglo-Saxon Charters: an annotated List and Bibliography*, Royal Historical Society Guides and Handbooks, 8 (London: Royal Historical Society, 1968).

[12] MS Shirburn Castle, Oxon., Earl of Macclesfield, *Liber Abbatiae*. Edward Edwards (ed.), *Liber Monasterii de Hyda*, Rolls Series, 45 (London: Longmans, Green, 1866). Another example from Canterbury in the fifteenth century is in MS Canterbury, Reg. C, f.148v. W. de G. Birch (ed.), *Cartularium Saxonicum* 3 vols. (London: Whiting, 1885–99; rpt. New York: Johnson, 1964), nos. 529, 530.

[13] For examples see J. H. G. Grattan and Charles Singer, *Anglo-Saxon Magic and Medicine: illustrated specially from the Semi-Pagan text "Lacnunga,"* Publications of the Wellcome Historical Medical Museum, NS 3 (London: Oxford Univ.

Press, 1952); Dorothy Bethurum, *The Homilies of Wulfstan* (Oxford: Clarendon Press, 1957), pp. 104–6; J. C. Pope, *Homilies of Ælfric, A Supplementary Collection*, 2 vols (EETS, OS 259, 260, 1967–8), pp. 185–8.

[14] My debts to Dr Ker's work are apparent everywhere. I have followed his dating of the annotations.

[15] Ker, op. cit., pp. xlviii–l.

[16] Ibid., p. xlix.

[17] Ibid., p. xlvii.

[18] Ibid., p. xlvi.

[19] Ibid., p. 23.

[20] Ibid., p. 23. These can be seen on ff.37–40, 43, 110–11.

[21] There are of course many later additions in English, Latin, and French which have nothing to do with the original texts. Especially interesting are the English verses in MSS Cambridge, Corpus Christi College 188, p. 408 (Ker 43); Cambridge, Pembroke College 82, binding leaf (Ker 75); London, Harley 3376, ff.16–17 (Ker 240); Oxford, Bodleian, Hatton 20, f.55 (Ker 324); and Salisbury Cathedral 150, f. (iv) flyleaf (Ker 379).

[22] This folio is omitted in the edition by U. Lindelöf, *Der Lambeth-Psalter*, Acta Societatis Scientiarum Fennicae, 35, i and 43, iii (Helsinki: Societatis litterariae fennicae, 1909–14) vol. i, p. 100 f.4.

[23] These glosses or interlineations are noticed and partly printed by S. Rypins, *Three Old English Prose Texts* (EETS, OS 161, 1924), p. 59, and more fully by Jane A. Leake, "ME Glosses in the Beowulf Codex," *MLQ*, 23 (1962), pp. 229–32, and by Kemp Malone, *The Nowell Codex*, *EEMF*, 12 (Copenhagen: Rosenkilde and Bagger, 1963). They have been dated by L. E. Boyle of the Pontifical Institute of Mediaeval Studies.

[24] The glosses are printed by Bethurum, *Wulfstan*, op. cit., as part of the textual apparatus for homilies, Ib, pp. 116–18, IV, pp. 128–33, and V, pp. 134–41. They are marked by the siglum H.

[25] Text and interlinear gloss are both printed by H. Logeman, "Ango-Saxon Minora," *Anglia*, 11 (1889), pp. 106–10.

[26] There has been a considerable amount of work done on the Worcester scribe of the 'tremulous' hand. See W. Keller, *Die litterarischen Bestrebungen von Worcester in angelsächsischer Zeit*, Quellen und Forschungen, 84 (1900); S. J. Crawford, "The Worcester Marks and Glosses of the Old English Manuscripts in the Bodleian . . .," *Anglia* 52 (1928), pp. 1–25; N. R. Ker, "The Date of the 'Tremulous' Worcester Hand," *Leeds SE*, 6 (1937), pp. 28–9; Ker, *Catalogue*, op. cit., p. lvii, and the individual entries for the manuscripts listed there; Bethurum, *Wulfstan*, op. cit., pp. 104–6; Pope, *Ælfric*, pp. 185–8. A full study of these glosses is being prepared by John Bromwich of the University of Cambridge.

[27] The glosses and Latin notes for *Lacnunga* are printed by Grattan and Singer, op. cit., pp. 96–205 textual notes.

[28] For facsimile, see Malone, op. cit., f.102v and commentary on p. 37.

[29] Bethurum, *Wulfstan*, op. cit., nos. Ib, IV, and V.

[30] Ker, *Catalogue*, op. cit., p. 368.

[31] Bethurum, *Wulfstan*, op. cit., p. 135 gloss to l.20 note, p. 136 gloss to l.33 note, p. 137 gloss to l.54 note, p. 140 gloss to l.106, p. 141 gloss to l.117.

[32] Ibid., p. 116 homily Ib, ll.12–13.

[33] Ibid., p. 140 homily V, ll.103–4.

[34] Logeman, op. cit., p. 107 dates the glosses as sixteenth century and Wrenn, *Study*, op. cit., p. 237 assumes an Elizabethan glossator, but Ker, *Catalogue*, op.

cit., p. 262 speaks for an earlier date, around the beginning of the century.

[35] Logeman, op. cit., p. 108, ll.27–8.

[36] Ibid., p. 107, l.7; p. 108, ll.20, 24.

[37] Bethurum, *Wulfstan*, op. cit., p. 106.

[38] Work for this paper has been mainly done with the collection of microfilms of manuscripts containing Old English texts being assembled at the Centre for Medieval Studies, University of Toronto, as part of the *Dictionary of Old English* project. I wish to thank Christopher Ball, Leonard Boyle, Roberta Frank, John Leyerle and George Rigg for their helpful suggestions.

18

THE ENGLISH VERSES IN THE
FASCICULUS MORUM

BY SIEGFRIED WENZEL

For over half a century the *Fasciculus morum* has aroused the curiosity of many, and has received the attention of several. This handbook for preachers in Latin, written probably in the 1320s by either John Spicer or Robert Silk, exists today in twenty-seven manuscripts dating from the late fourteenth to the late fifteenth century.[1] Friar John dedicated the work to an unnamed "frater," at whose petition he claims to have collected this "small bundle of vices and virtues" for the use of the unlettered (*simpliciores*). Since by the rule of St Francis, as he says, "we are held to denounce to the people and to preach the vices and virtues, punishment and glory," he will describe the seven capital vices and their opposite virtues. This he does indeed, beginning with Pride and ending with Lechery and following each sin with the appropriate remedy, which is one of the standard seven theological and cardinal virtues. In dealing with these subjects he also collects much homiletic material, *exempla*, similes, and *narrationes* from a number of areas including contemporary hearsay, destined to drive home a point more forcefully. Due to the inclusion of much illustrative as well as doctrinal material, his clearly constructed book thus becomes a veritable *summa* of late medieval preaching and devotion.

The work was first brought to the attention of a wider audience by A. G. Little in 1917,[2] and since then a number of scholars have worked on it or scanned it for background information. The particular value which the treatise has for students of Middle English are the more than fifty English poems or "tags" that appear in it. Frances A. Foster, who studied the text for many years in order to make an edition, published a list of English words found in the manual.[3] More recently, Rosemary Woolf, in her monumental study of the Middle English religious lyric, drew extensively on the *Fasciculus morum* and published a number of its English verses.[4] Yet the main work still remains to be done: Besides an edition of the whole treatise, "the 55 entries of the *Fasciculus morum* demand extended study," as a reviewer of the *Supplement to the Index of Middle English Verse* declared a few years ago.[5] Here is a preachers' handbook which incorporated a proportionately large number of metrical items in the vernacular—a work, in other words, which like Friar Grimstone's "Commonplace Book" can shed much light on the origins, nature, and use of the simple religious "lyric" in Middle English.

The vernacular material contained in the *Fasciculus morum* is of various kinds: individual words, phrases or short sentences, un-rhymed tags which sum up the main points of a topic, and poems of at least one couplet and ranging to as many as fourteen lines. In this paper I am exclusively concerned with the latter. About fifty such metric items appear in the *Fasciculus morum* and in the sermon outlines which accompany the manual in several manuscripts. Foster assigned to these poems numbers, which appear in the *Index* and the *Supplement* as well as in the *Middle-English Dictionary*.[6] Since her list was made, new items have turned up in manuscripts not fully examined by her, so that the original list and the numbering as well as the entries in *Index* and *Supplement* need some correction.[7]

The particular question I wish to pursue in this paper concerns the *modus existendi* of these English poems. Precisely what is their relation in the manuscripts to their Latin context? Physically, the Middle English poems appear regularly as part of the text, i.e., not marginally. They are written either continuously or as verse, and in many manu-scripts especially marked by underlining or by brackets that link the rhyming lines. Their syntactic connection with the Latin context is, however, not uniform. Some are introduced with a transitional phrase, others are simply juxtaposed, and occasionally manuscripts vary in presenting the same item, so that no clear pattern can be discerned. But as to their logical relation to the Latin text they can be easily grouped into a number of types, which may be summarized as follows:

1. Middle English verses which translate the preceding Latin passage, which is either verse or prose.
2. Middle English verses which are suggested by the preceding Latin passage.
3-4. Middle English verses which are neither translated nor suggested.
   3. They are "tagged on," i.e., they can be dispensed with.
   4. They are an integral part of the context, i.e., indispensable.

In the following I shall illustrate these types by selected examples and comment on the various relations. Although these types cover all

English verses contained in the *Fasciculus morum*, I shall not attempt to classify and discuss each item here. I shall refer to them by the numbers originally given by Foster and the numbers under which they appear in the *Index/Supplement*.

1. *Middle English verses that translate a Latin passage*

At least twenty-nine items belong in this group. About two-thirds of these are based on a metrical text in Latin, which is usually in hexameters (often leonine) or less frequently a distich. A very simple example is No. 2 (*Index* 3339). The chapter on *superbia cordis* begins with the warning not to let proud thoughts rise in our hearts, because they are the devil's emissaries:

> *Et ideo, si eius suggestionibus adquiescamus, tanquam leo rugiens irruit in nos;*
> *sed si ei resistamus, tanquam muscam ipsum effugare possumus et in omnibus*
> *actibus vincere, iuxta illud metrice dictum:*
> *Hostis non ledit nisi cum temptatus obedit.*
> *Est leo si cedit; si non, quasi musca recedit.*
>   Þe fende oure foe ne may vs dere
>   But ȝyffe we bowen hym for fere.
>   He is a lyon, bote þou with-stonde,
>   And ferde as a flye, ȝyf þou ne wonde.
> *Et ideo faciamus sicut bonus miles. . . .*[8]

The technique here used is typical: The point of the discussion is expressed or summarized in Latin verses, which are then rendered into English verses. In this particular case, the two hexameters exist in a work other than the *Fasciculus morum*,[9] while the Middle English lines are unique to this handbook. This entire technique is often found in other sermon handbooks, collections of *exempla* (notably the *Gesta Romanorum*), and similar Latin treatises designed to help preachers in their work of instructing the laity.[10] Also, the rendering of a Latin hexameter into a Middle English couplet of four stresses is normal and apparently the favourite form, although occasionally longer lines and tail-rhyme stanzas are used.

No. 2 is rhetorically fairly simple. But in other examples one finds that the syntactic ingenuity of the hexameter has been imitated in the Middle English couplet, often by using different devices more in keeping with the vernacular language and meter. The following two items show this very clearly. No. 7 (*Index* 2298), on *oratio clamorosa*, sums up that "*Deus non verborum sed cordis est auditor, iuxta illud—*"

> *Non vox sed votum, non musica cordula sed cor,*
> *Non clamor sed amor sonat in aure Dei.*[11]

Anglice sic:

> Ne monnes steuen but gode wylle,
> No murthe of mouth but herte stylle,
> No cry but love ne oþer bere
> Nys murthe ny song God to here.[12]
>> (*Var.*: Thys murth soundes in Godys here[13]).

The distich is unusually rich in the use of rhetorical figures: threefold *antithesis* combined with two cases of *traductio* (*vox—votum, cordula—cor*) and *similiter desinens* or *homoeoteleuton* (*clamor—amor*). While the *traductio* is lost in the English, the translation preserves the antitheses and replaces the sound effect of *clamor—amor* with its end rhyme. In addition, the first two lines are linked by alliteration (*monnes—murthe—mouth*).

A similar instance of rhetorical "wit" appears in No. 25 (*Index* 1321), where Christ speaks from the Cross:

> *In cruce sum pro te; qui peccas, desine pro me.*
> *Desine, do veniam; dic culpam, retraho penam.*

Anglice sic:

> I honge on cros for loue of the,
> Lef þy synne for loue of me.
> Mercy aske, amende þe sone,
> And I forȝyf þe þat is mysdone.[14]

Here the antithesis of the first hexameter is taken over and expanded into "for loue of the—for loue of me." But the twofold sequence of second-person imperative—first-person statement of the second hexameter is changed into a different, to my feeling more successful pattern of the English verses, where the first-person statements in lines 1 and 4 surround the imperatives of lines 2–3. It is evident that these simple English verses, despite their closeness to the Latin models, show a feeling and desire for poetic form on the part of their translator that is quite remarkable.[15] This is especially clear where a word play in Latin could not be simply translated into English but had to be replaced with different linguistic means. One more example will demonstrate this. In No. 31A (*Index* 142) the false judge Gayus, being carried off by devils, is said to have exclaimed in what can be read as a hexameter:

> *Heu, heu, prodolor, sicut iudicavi sic iudicor!*

The crisp pun of *iudicavi—iudicor* can, of course, not be rendered with English verb forms as succinctly as it appears in Latin. The translator solved the problem, quite successfully, by using nouns:

> Alas, alas, þat I was boren,
> For dome with dome I am forloren.[16]

Besides items based on Latin hexameters, the *Fasciculus* also contains a number of Middle English verses that have been translated from Latin prose. Most of the original passages are biblical quotations, although quotations from St Jerome, St Gregory, St Bernard, and the *Gesta Romanorum* are similarly treated. No. 13 (*Index* 2058) follows the biblical text of Job xiv, 1–2 very closely:

> *Memorare novissima tua*, iuxta consilium Sapientis . . . quam breve est tempus [et] incertum, et quam vile est corpus mortuum, quia iuxta Iob: *Homo natus de muliere*, etc. [i.e., *brevi vivens tempore, repletur multis miseriis. Qui quasi flos egreditur et conteritur, et fugit velut umbra, et nunquam in eodem statu permanet*]. Anglice:
>
> > Mon iboren of wommon ne lyueth but a stounde.
> > In wrechednes and in wo ben his dayes iwounde.
> > He springus out as blossome and sone falles to grounde,
> > And wendes away as schadewe þat no wey is ifounde.[17]

2. *Middle English verses that are suggested by the Latin context*

In contrast to the preceding examples the items in this group do not render a Latin text more or less *verbatim* but were merely suggested by the prose exposition that precedes them. The context furnishes the idea and some of the actual wording, but the Middle English verse then adds substantial material of its own. No. 21B (*Index* 2001B) still is a borderline case between groups 1 and 2. The text speaks of true love, which is found in four kinds:

> *Si quis ergo cupit invenire amorem fidelem unde sibi coronam tanquam floribus pretiosissimis et mellifluis sibi* [sic] *parare voluerit, vadat ad cor suum; et si ibi ista quatuor invenerit sine fictione vel falsitate, certe illum lucratus est: Si diligat Deum super omnia, secundo animam* [suam] *sine peccato, postea si tertio proximum amicum in Deo, et quarto inimicum propter Deum.*
>
> > [Thou] loue God ouer alle þynge,
> > Sethen þyselfe withouten synnynge,
> > Sethen þi frend as kynde þe teches,
> > After þy fo withouten wreche.[18]

The four kinds of love (*quadrifolium amoris*) are taken literally from the Latin exposition (which is very traditional teaching), but the qualifications of types 3 and 4 ("as kynde þe teches," etc.) abandon the traditional *in Deo . . . propter Deum.*

No. 14 (*Index* 2283), based on a saying attributed to St Bernard, obviously received its two opening lines verbally from parts of the context (which I emphasize), but the remainder of the tail-rhyme stanza is a free expansion:

Unde Bernardus: "Cum homo," inquit, "moritur, nasus frigescit, facies pallescit, nervi atque vene rumpuntur, cor in duas partes dividitur. Nichil est horribilius cadavere *illius: In domo non dimittitur ne familia moriatur; in aqua non proicitur ne inficiatur; in aere non suspenditur ne ille corrumpatur; sed tanquam venenum pestiferum in fovea proicitur ne amplius appareat, terra circumdatur ne fetor ascendat, firmissime calcatur ne iterum assurgat, sed ut terra in terra maneat et amplius visus hominis illud non aspiciat." Unde Anglice dicitur:*

> Was þer neuer caren so lothe   *cadaver*
> As mon when he to put goth,   *pit*
>   And deth has layde so lowe.
> For when deth drawes mon from oþur,
> þe suster nul not se þe brother,
>   Ne fader þe sone iknawe.[19]

Even less of a basis for the English poem is provided by the context of No. 18 (*Index* 2002). The passage explains that God should be loved in triple fashion, with one's whole heart, soul, and mind; and these three aspects of man's love for God are linked to parallel aspects in Christ's love for man:

Hiis ergo tribus modis illum pre ceteris diligere debemus et tenemur ex precepto Evangelii, primo toto corde *considerando quomodo cor suum permisit pro nobis perforari; secundo* in anima *considerando quomodo suam [animam] pro suis amicis Deo Patri commendavit; tertio* in mente *considerando quomodo sua mentali intentione omnes salvare peroptavit.*

> Loue God [þu] þat loued the,
> þat for þe tholed deth on tree
>   And broght þe oute of helle.
> Loue hym with hert, sowle, and þoght
> þat þe now has wel derre boght   *more dearly*
>   þen any tonge con telle.[20]

Here only the fourth line rests verbally on part of the Latin passage; the rest follow it in thought alone.

3. *Middle English verses that are tagged on*

In this and the following group I include vernacular verses that are neither translated from nor verbally suggested by the preceding Latin text. They are of course related to the context thematically, at least to some extent, but they have very little or no actual verbal basis in the Latin. The preceding example, No. 18, approaches this state, with only one line echoing three Latin phrases. The following case is similar to it: No. 46 (*Index* 2077) follows upon another English item which is verbally based on the context. I present both with their context, a discussion of the value of almsgiving:

Tetio comparatur elemosina semini, quia sicut semen ante oculos seminantis seminatur et non a tergo, sic homo ante oculos suos elemosinas dat et non a tergo confidendo nimis in parentibus, relictis, et executoribus. Tales enim ut communiter morientes a tergo decipiunt, et citius frequenter domestici quam ignoti. Quia unusquisque, puta uxor, filius, filia, neptis et nepta, et huiusmodi, sibi appropriant bona defuncti, et sic anima a bonis meritoriis relinquitur supervacua. Et iuste, quia noluit seipsum iuvare quando potuit. Et ideo vulgariter dicitur:

[No. 45]   Who-so woll noȝt when he may,
                 He schall noȝt when he woll.[21]

[Et] ideo bene dicitur in Anglico:

[No. 46]   When þou þy lyfe vp-holdyste,
                 Þynke wan þou arte oldyste[22]
                    And do gode at þe ȝate.
                 When þou with deth vnboldeste,   *grow feeble*
                 Þou schal noȝt yf þou woldist,
                 For þan is al to late.[23]

No. 46 was evidently suggested by No. 45. They both echo the Latin *noluit seipsum iuvare quando potuit* in their second and fifth line respectively, and No. 46 repeats the gist of the Latin discussion, the warning to do good with one's worldly possessions while one has the chance.

But the next example, while still containing a slight verbal echo of the Latin, expresses a thought and uses imagery which are not suggested by the context. In the Rawlinson MS, from which I have so far quoted, No. 22 (*Index* 3802) follows very shortly upon No. 21B, quoted earlier, with only two short Latin sentences intervening:[24]

Et certe sic faciens inveniet quadrifolium illud amoris veri. Sed timeo quod dicere possum:

                 Trewe loue among menn þat most is of lette
                 In hattes, in hodes, in porses is sette.
                 Trewe loue in herbers[25] spryngeth in May.
                 Bote trewe loue of herte went is away.[26]

At best one can say that the English verses (for which no independent tradition outside the *Fasciculus* is known) were suggested by *amoris veri*: but the opposition between love of material goods and sensual love on one hand and "true love of heart" on the other, as well as the entire complaint at the absence of genuine "true love," is not found in the context. The verses are clearly tagged on.

4. *Middle English verses that are integral to the context*

Like Group 3, the final group consists of items that are not directly translated or substantially suggested by the preceding Latin text. But in contrast to Group 3 they are an integral part of the paragraph or the story in which they appear. All examples so far discussed, whether translated or tagged on, could be omitted from the text without loss to the point made or the story told. The items of Group 4, however, are logically indispensable or functional in the development of the context. There are five such cases, which need detailed discussion.

Before dealing with these cases one may ask what happens in manuscripts that do not contain these particular English items. For the present discussion it will suffice to give only a few illustrations of the various situations that occur. Two manuscripts are of particular interest in this respect. The Madrid MS,[27] which contains no English verses at all, was perhaps copied by a Spanish or Portuguese scribe and evidently intended for an Iberic audience, because it replaces a reference to London and Coventry with Lisbon. The Morgan MS[28] was made by a German Franciscan, Friar Johannes Sintram of Würzburg, who copied the *Fasciculus* at Oxford about 1412. It is clear from several references in his book that his exemplar contained English verses. He omitted all of them,[29] but recognizing their usefulness in preaching added in several places such marginal remarks as *"Hic deficiunt rikme in anglico scripte"* (fol. 83v) or *"Hic potes addere vulgare rikmas"* (fol. 97r). Moreover, he (or someone else) frequently made his own German verse translations of corresponding Latin pieces.

The first English item in this group is No. 20 (*Index* 2329), which occurs in the discussion of love of one's neighbour. Feigned love is likened to the action of those who diligently guard an orchard at harvest time, but abandon it unheeded as soon as they have picked its fruit:

> *Et ideo est de talibus sicut de pomerio fructuoso, quod tempore fructus diligenter custoditur et frequenter visitatur, sed ablatis fructibus sine custodia relinquitur. Revera sic est de ficta caritate. Dum enim aliquis talis mundanus fictus amicus ab aliquo [aliquid] desiderat, dilectionem simulat, blanditur, adulatur. Sed habito [et] obtento, dicunt illud Anglicum:*
>
> > Now ich haue þat I wyle,
> > Goddus grame on þy byle.
>
> *Sed certe ista non est perfecta caritas.*[30]

The English lines, which were proverbial (see below), do not repeat a thought already expressed in Latin but are an indispensable part of the *similitudo*. The two manuscripts made for non-English readers simply put the proverbial saying into Latin:

> Morgan: ". . . *dicunt: 'Nunc habeo quod volui. Valeas cum Deo!'*" (fol. 24r).
> Madrid: ". . . *dicit illud proverbium: 'Ex quo habeo quod desiderabam, de cetero maledicto* [read *maledico*] *tuam barbam'*" (fol. 37r).

MS Madrid is especially instructive because the scribe recognized the proverbial nature of the saying and because he translated it literally into Latin.

Similar in nature is the next item, No. 33 (*Index* 3408), which is actually presented by the texts as "an old proverb." The verses occur at the end of a long story in which a *ioculator* called Ulfridus is sent by Lady Fortune to King Attrides (?), from whom he receives a magic cloak that furnishes wealth but is taken from him as soon as he prides himself in his glory. The moralization of this story concludes with:

> *Revera quando magis de mundi clamide gloriantur, omnia in momento aufert ab illis et nudos, sicut prius invenit illos, delinquit, sicut de illo Ulfrido actum est, de quo sic metrice dicitur:*
> > *Ulfridus clamidem quam susceperat per Attridem*
> > *Servavit pridem; casus dedit, abstulit idem.*

[No. 32]   Þat mantel þe kyng*e* to Ulfride lente,
             Wi*th* hap hit come, wi*th* hap hit wente.[31]

> *Unde de illa domina Fortuna est antiquum proverbium sic canens:*

[No. 33]   The lade dame fortune   is bothe frende *and* foo.
             Of pore hoe maketh riche,   and ryche of pore also.
             Hee t*u*rneth woo to wele and   wele also to woo.
             Ne trust noght to his word,   þe whele t*u*rneth so.[32]

The Morgan MS is somewhat confused here: After the Ulfrid verse, given in Latin only, the sentence "*Unde de illa . . .*" is marked to be inserted but written in the lower margin of the folio. Instead of "The lade dame Fortune" the scribe then used the Latin equivalent of No. 34 (*Index* 1822), which normally appears a few lines after the passage quoted above (fol. 44r). The Madrid MS is clearer: Its scribe followed the same technique demonstrated earlier and translated the English verses into fairly rough Latin (fol. 63v).

Our next instance also partakes of the proverbial, or better gnomic, nature of the two preceding items. No. 48 (*Index* 3282) occurs in the discussion of fornication, the first species of *luxuria*. It heads a series of biblical injunctions and exemplary figures connected with this sin:

> *Et ideo, ut mihi videtur, iam propter illud peccatum tam commune verificantur quatuor contradictoria, scilicet:*
> > That lawe hath noo ry3te, /
> > þat trewþe hath no my3t,
> > þat wysdom is foly,
> > And holynysse is trechery.[33]
> *Primum patet de lege et precepto Dei . . .*

Each line is then shown to be true by reference to the sixth commandment (line 1), to Samson (line 2), to Solomon (line 3), and to David (line 4). The later references to lines 2–4, which appear at some distance from the original quatrain, actually repeat the English line within the Latin text. This particular item is, therefore, not so much a poem as a rhymed saying which approaches the function of a *divisio textus*, a technique occasionally found in other sermon manuscripts.[34] The two non-English manuscripts, in place of the English verses, give the *quatuor contradictoria* in Latin.

In contrast to the preceding three integral or functional verses, which were all proverbial in nature, the final two items are integral parts of a story.[35] The first of them, No. 31B (*Index* 142), occurs in the discussion of the evils that arise when confession is postponed. The two English lines were reportedly uttered by a woman whose voice was heard by her confessor after her death:

> *Narratur de quadam virgine devota in reputatione hominum et sancta, que tamen infirmitate preventa moriebatur. Post cuius sepulturam accidit cito post quod iacente sacerdote confessore eius in ecclesia vocem horribiliter audivit in hiis verbis lugentem sic:*
>
> > Alas, alas, þat I was born*e*,
> > Boþe lyf *and* sowle Y am for-lorn*e*.[36]

The story continues with the priest hearing the same lament in the two following nights. In the third night he sees two "horrible black demons" carry the girl off. When asked why she is damned, she replies that she used to murmur against her mother, but did not think that it was a grave sin.

The English lines are very widespread: They occur in seventeen of the twenty-seven manuscripts. Where no English is used, the girl's words are given in Latin, in a variety of forms. I offer three examples:

> MS Madrid: *"in hiis verbis: 'Heu, heu, quod fui nata, quia corpore et anima sum dampnata'"* (f. 95r).
> MS Morgan: *"in hiis verbis sic: 'Ve, ve, quod unquam fui natus* [sic], *quia contradixi patri et matri sum dampnatus'"* (f. 66v).
> MS Cambridge University Library Dd. 10.15: *"in hiis verbis: 'Heu, heu, quod unquam mater mea produxit me in hunc mundum'"* (f. 93v).

Our final item, No. 40 (*Index* 1935), forms part of a story about a tavern-haunting, negligent priest who used to "syncopate" his prayers. An "anchoress of holy life," who reportedly told this story to the Bishop of Worcester, had observed the priest for some time and had asked God in her prayers to show her whether the priest's service pleased Him.

Unde quadam die [var. *nocte*], *dum se orationi dedisset, audivit vocem venientem et ei sic Anglice dicentem:*

> Longe-slepers and ouer-lepers,
> For-skyppers *and* ouer-hyppers
> I holde luþer hyne.   bad servants
> I am noȝt heren ne þey ben myne.   theirs
> But þey sone amende thay shullen to helle pyne.[37]

The Madrid MS lacks this story altogether. Johannes Sintram, however, followed his usual procedure and put the English into Latin, this time rather elegantly, incorporating at the same time material from the story itself (as he had done in the preceding case, No. 31B):

> . . . *et ei sic dicentem:* "*De mane longe dormientes et sero tarde potantes, in orationibus verba sincopantes, de ecclesia ad tabernam festinantes, non in Dei laude sed in crapulis delectantes, istorum verbaque facta non Deo sed dyabolo sunt accepta; et in orationibus ut putant peccata eorum non diminuant* [sic] *sed augmentant.*"

In the margin he or some reader then added: "*Hec verba potes ad rigmam componere brevius*" (f. 55r). Another manuscript cites the divine answer to the anchoress' question more briefly: "*Non placet mihi obsequium illius potatoris et gulosi, quia non est speciosa laus in ore peccatoris*" [cf. Eccli. xv, 9].[38]

The appearance of English verses in a Latin manual and the variation in their relationships to the Latin context raise a number of questions about their origin and their purpose. Although a full answer would go far beyond the scope of this paper, a number of suggestions may be offered which are based on the material so far examined. First, there is a very strong probability that the English verses—or at least some of them—were present in the archetype of the *Fasciculus morum*. It is of course possible that metrical translations of Latin hexameters or of prose, as well as "tagged-on" items, were slipped into the text at a later stage of its transmission, as seems to be the case with the Latin text of the *Gesta Romanorum* or Latin sermon collections. But the existence of the English items which are integral to the text (Group 4 above), together with the variety of ways in which manuscripts without English verses substitute them, suggests strongly that at least these verses were incorporated by the author of the handbook himself.

What function do the Middle English verses have? For what purposes were they incorporated in a Latin preachers' manual? Here one should first of all remember that works like the *Fasciculus*, though written in Latin, were destined for the use of preachers who would normally address their congregations in the vernacular. Hence, the important thing is not that these items are in English, but that they are in verse. It is well known that medieval authors in general, and authors of handbooks in particular, took a very great delight in expressing the gist of a prose passage, or in summarizing its main points, in verse. This practice was widespread in all fields of medieval science,[39] history,[40] and theology, both speculative[41] and practical.[42] The impressive collection of such Latin "proverbs and sentences" in five volumes by Walther[43] is ample testimony to the richness and ubiquity of this tendency, and any reader who has some familiarity with later medieval manuscripts could easily increase that collection.

Perusal of works which make extensive use of such verses quickly reveals their primary function: They were an easy aid to memory, summarizing in succinct and memorable form the information needed in the pulpit or in the confessional or in private devotion. Even more important, especially in preaching, was their rhetorical purpose: Interrupting the flow of a prose sermon with a pithy saying that stood out by its marked rhythm and perhaps rhyme would undoubtedly break the monotony and add persuasive force to the speaker's words. This would be true of the written text as well, and Lhotsky has suggested that metrical inserts in late medieval historical works may well have been used to provide a welcome relief from the heavy chronistic subject matter compiled.[44] Finally, we should not overlook the rhetorical ingenuity displayed by a good number of these verses, which I believe reveal a strong aesthetic sensitivity, a delight in the artistic use of language on the part of the authors. Hans Walther has shown what a rich variety of often quite complicated verbal play and tricks can be found in mnemonic verses.[45] While not all share such metrical and rhetorical refinement, the best among them may indeed be considered a type of *Kleinkunst* where the desire to instruct is welded to the urge to create artistic pleasure.

These various functions apply to verses in Middle English as well. I have shown evidence of their maker's delight in form and word play in at least some of the *Fasciculus* verses. Several items in the handbook are also strongly mnemonic in purpose, such as No. 21B quoted above, on the four kinds of love, or the versifications of the Ten Commandments[46] and of the six (physical) qualities of the Host.[47] Most of the items, however, seem to have been included for some rhetorical purpose: to prove a point, to furnish wisdom, to warn and exhort sinners, to formulate a prayer, or to appeal for the audience's love of God.

Why were these particular English verses translated or included, and not others? And further, when the author of the manual included an item, did he draw on an existing stock of material or did he, rather, create the verse himself? These questions need further investigation of all Middle English items and of their "analogues" (beyond what separate occurrences outside the *Fasciculus* the *Index* reveals). Yet the analysis of the relation between Middle English verse and Latin context already furnishes several insights that may be significant not only for the *Fasciculus* but for Middle English lyrics in general.

The transitional phrases which link the English verses to their context suggest that some verses were current while others were made up by the author *ad hoc*. A large number of Middle English verses appear without any transitional phrase or have a simple *Anglice*, *Anglice sic*, or *sic Anglice dicitur*. But two items are introduced with *sic Anglice possum dicere* and *timeo quod dicere possum*,[48] and while *possum* indeed offers only scant proof that these verses may have been created by the author of the manual, the slight possibility is strengthened by the fact that no occurrence of these English verses outside the *Fasciculus* is known. On the other hand, the introduction of No. 33 (quoted above) as *proverbium antiquum* clearly points to an existing tradition, a fact substantiated by the appearance of these verses in at least three manuscripts outside the *Fasciculus* and their inclusion in a lullaby. Similarly, two items[49] are introduced with *quidam dixit Anglice* and *quidam Anglice sic dixit*, and although a *quidam* in a late medieval handbook may cover a multitude of sins, the distinction of these phrases from others more frequently employed in the *Fasciculus*, as well as the use of the perfect tense, are sufficient evidence that the respective English verses they introduce had been current before the manual was composed, a suggestion again substantiated in the second case (No. 51, the Signs of Death) by a rich tradition extant outside the *Fasciculus*.[50] A similar situation is found in No. 50 (quoted above), which is introduced with *quidam sic Anglice ait*.

The two last-mentioned items (Nos. 50 and 51) are both concerned with death, and throughout the *Fasciculus* one finds many more verses which, in several forms, express the warning of *Memento mori*. In fact, more than half of all English verses in the manual fall into half a dozen groups which deal with what may be called "favourite topics," such as *Memento mori* (Nos. 11–16 and 45–47), Christ's lament on the Cross (Nos. 23–27), true love (Nos. 18–22), warnings against Fortune (Nos. 32–35), and others. Rosemary Woolf has pointed to a number of such favourite topics and shown the genesis, expansion, and modifications of the Middle English lyrics that deal with them. Quite evidently, a favourite topic, or even more precisely a favourite devotional text in Latin, caused more than one English author to cast it into English verses. A good case in point is No. 25 (quoted earlier), rendering *In cruce sum pro te,* a text which appears in a different, closer translation in Grimestone's "Commonplace Book" and which inspired several poems of greater length.[51] In addition, one notices that in the *Fasciculus* each of the four favourite topics I have listed appears not in one isolated verse but in a number of successive items, all forming part of the same chapter. Evidently, certain "favourite topics" generated an outpouring of Middle English verses in the *Fasciculus,* whether these were taken over from tradition or made up by the writer. There are some other items in the handbook which do not occur in such groups, but whose inclusion I strongly suspect was also due to their dealing with "favourite topics" frequently versified elsewhere, such as the "Evils of the Time"[52] and the "Tutivillus verse."[53]

Another reason for the inclusion of certain English items derives from the nature of what I shall call "message verses."[54] These are metrical items which formulate such "messages" as the words of a dying sinner (for example, No. 31A, quoted above) or of a damned soul (No. 31B, above), a voice heard in prayer (No. 40, above), Christ's words from the Cross (No. 25, above), the climax of a dialogue in a story (No. 30, below), an actual message sent by a lover, or an inscription found on a statue or in a tomb. At least eighteen items can be thus considered. Obviously, the central importance which these "messages" hold in an illustrative story or for the doctrinal exposition in which they occur was primarily responsible for the author's choice of including at these points vernacular verses.

Finally, a number of the English verses are strongly proverbial in nature. Some of them are clearly variants of a well-known proverb, such as No. 20 (quoted above)[55] or No. 9 (*Index* 4156):

> Wo-so woneþ hy*m* no ʒt to goude furst all in hys/youth,
> *Unthewes* to leue were to hym in his elde wel vnkouþe.[56]

Others can be considered expansions of a proverb, a suggestion based on the fact that several times an English stanza is followed by a line which is attributed to "Hendyng" and found in medieval proverb collections that go under that name. A different example of expansion are Nos. 45–6 quoted earlier. No. 45, introduced as *vulgariter dicitur . . . in Anglico,* is a proverb attested in English from about AD 1000 on.[57] No. 46, which follows it immediately, incorporates the proverb and expands it. In the preacher's mouth, such proverbial sayings, which presumably were well known to his audience and recognized as wise old friends, must have been very effective in proving a point and moving the listeners' hearts. Indeed, the position of such proverbial verses (and of many others besides them) in the

Latin text reveals their function as "auctoritees," as proof texts of equal standing with biblical quotations. For example, the warning against talking too much (i.e., pride of the tongue) is made first by quoting Eccli. xx, 8, "He who uses many words injures his soul." This is followed by:

> *Et ideo dicitur Anglice:*
> [No. 4]   Who-so spekyth [oft]   of þyng þat is vnwrest,   *wicked* (?)
>   Þouh hit seme soft   when he spekyth mest,
>   He schal hit heren on l[o]ft when he wenyth lest.
> *Et ideo:* "Let þy tonge rest, *and* þe schall nouȝt rewe," quod Hendyng.[58]

This is in turn followed by a Latin quotation of Prov. xiii, 3 and another one from Cato's Distichs (I, 3, ed. M. Boas). This cloud of witnesses is further enlarged in two *Fasciculus* manuscripts by an added English proverb before "Who-so spekyth oft."[59]

It would therefore appear that many of the *Fasciculus* verses stand within a large tradition of proverbial sayings and of "favourite topics" which were again and again formulated in different ways. At the same time, it is most probable that the compiler of the handbook had a knack of making English verses, now casting a current saying into a new form, now making up a verse entirely of his own. One of his *narrationes* actually reflects how such verses may have come into being: A certain judge at Paris would often, for his greed, argue wrong cases against innocent persons. His name was Jean or Guillaume Malamort. (Sintram calls him "Hans Übelsterben," as one might have expected.) One day, as the judge cannot be found anywhere, his companions break into his chamber, only to find him strangled by a devil and reduced to dust. The shock of the scene does not prevent the bystanders from punning:

> [No. 30]   *Unde unus literatus de sociis metrice sic ait:*
>   *Morte cadunt subita Mala Mors simul et mala vita.*
> [Anglice:]   Þourgh ferly deth to-gedur arn falde
>   Bothe euel lyf *and* euel deth calde.
> *Cui alius metrice repondit sic:*
>   *Han[c] vitam vita, ne moriaris ita!*
> [Anglice:]   I rede such lyf þou forsake,
>   Wyth suche deth lest þou be take![60]

Surely, the verbal facility, moral stance, and ready wit displayed by the two Parisian *literati* must be claimed for the composer of *Fasciculus morum* as well.

UNIVERSITY OF NORTH CAROLINA

NOTES

1 It gives me great pleasure to offer this paper in honour and gratitude to Rossell Hope Robbins, who for years has fostered my interest in the *Fasciculus morum*. "God gif the blis quharevir thow bownes,/ And send the many Fraunce crownes,/ Hie liberall heart and handis not sweir!" (*Index* 2267). Dr Robbins transcribed these Middle English verses from Caius Coll. Camb. 71 and Caius Coll. Camb. 364 in "On the ME Religious Lyrics," Diss. Cambridge, 1937, II, pp. 603–17. He also included ninety-nine short verses from Friar Johan de Grimestone's MS, Advocates 18. 7. 21 (II, pp. 618–55), as well as preachers' tags from seventeen other manuscripts (II, pp. 584–602) and a complete Latin sermon, "*Amore langueo*," with Middle English verse from Magdalen Coll. Oxford 93 (I, pp. 514–48). Some discussion (I, pp. 72–6) partly included in his "The Authors of the ME Religious Lyrics," *JEGP*, 39 (1940), pp. 230–8. Some of the twenty-seven known manuscripts are incomplete and four are abbreviated versions of different kinds. In addition to these twenty-seven, three manuscripts contain short extracts from the *Fasciculus*, and a fourth has only the sermons. The manuscripts were listed by A. G. Little (*infra*, note 2). Corrections of his list were made by F. A. Foster, *Essays and Studies* (infra, note 3), p. 149, n.2. To her list should be added MS Canterbury Cathedral D.14.

2 A. G. Little, *Studies in English Franciscan History* (Manchester: Manchester Univ. Press, 1917), pp. 139–92.

3 F. A. Foster, "Some English Words from the *Fasciculus Morum*," in *Essays and Studies in Honor of Carleton Brown* (New York: New York Univ. Press, 1940), pp. 149–57.

4 R. Woolf, *The English Religious Lyric in the Middle Ages* (Oxford: Clarendon Press, 1968), passim.

5 V. M. Bonnell, in *American Notes and Queries*, 4 (1966), 139.

6 Carleton Brown and Rossell Hope Robbins, *The Index of Middle English Verse* (New York: Columbia Univ. Press, 1943) (hereafter *Index*); R. H. Robbins and J. L. Cutler, *Supplement to the Index of Middle English Verse* (Lexington, Ky.: Univ. of Kentucky Press, 1965) (hereafter *Suppl.*); Hans Kurath and Sherman M. Kuhn, *et al.*, *Middle English Dictionary* (Ann Arbor, Michigan: Univ. of Michigan Press, 1954ff.).

7 I am preparing a full edition of the English verses in the *Fasciculus morum*. Notice that the occurrence of the English verses varies considerably in the manuscripts. Only a few contain over fifty items, many contain fewer, down to only one or two, and several manuscripts contain no English verses at all.

8 MS Rawlinson C. 670, f. 8v. Not previously printed. Here and in the following quotations I present the Latin text in normalized form but preserve medieval *e* for classical *ae/oe*. The Middle English is reproduced as found in the manuscripts, with expansions marked by italics and capitals and punctuation added.

9 See H. Walther, *Proverbia sententiaeque latinitatis medii aevi* (Göttingen, 1963 ff.), No. 11,230c (from a fifteenth-century manuscript in Bern).

10 For example, S. Wenzel, "A Latin Miracle With Middle English Verses," *Neuphilologische Mitteilungen*, 72 (1971), pp. 77–85.

11 Walther, op. cit., No. 18,723; a rich tradition.

12 MS Rawl. C. 670, f. 13r. Printed from MS Worcester Cathedral F. 19 in Carleton Brown, *A Register of Middle English Religious and Didactic Verse*, Vol. I (Oxford: Bibliographical Soc., 1916), p. 450 (hereafter *Register*).

[13] The variant of the last line, here taken from MS Vatican Ottoboni 626, f. 4v, occurs also in MS Caius 71. It is a closer translation of *"sonat in aure Dei."*

[14] MS Rawl. C. 670, f. 45r, not previously printed. The Latin is not listed in Walther; but see the references in notes 15 and 51, *infra.*

[15] One should compare the much closer rendering of the Latin hexameters in Grimestone's Commonplace Book, printed in Carleton Brown, *Religious Lyrics of the Fourteenth Century*, 2nd edn rev. by G. V. Smithers (Oxford: Clarendon Press, 1952), p. 261.

[16] MS Rawl. C. 670, f. 69v, not previously printed.

[17] Ibid., f. 20v. The edition of the item (from another MS) by C. Brown, *Register*, I, 451, is incomplete.

[18] Ibid., f. 41v, not previously printed. The English verses are repeated on f. 128v. Other manuscripts give No. 21A in this context and 21B in the second passage.

[19] Ibid., f. 20v, not previously printed.

[20] Ibid., f. 37v–38r, not previously printed.

[21] No. 45 (*Index* 4151), not previously printed. This is obviously a proverb, further discussed below. See also *Suppl.*, p. 483.

[22] *arte oldyste*: var. *acoldyst*, "grow cold," in several manuscripts.

[23] MS Rawl. C. 670, f. 114r, previously printed by Foster, *Essays and Studies*, p. 157. The penultimate line is omitted in MS Rawl. and here supplied from MS Worcester Cath. F. 19, f. 211v.

[24] In other manuscripts the relation of 21B to 22 and of both to the Latin is different.

[25] *herbers*: var. *herbes* or *gresses*, in several manuscripts.

[26] MS Rawl. C. 670, f. 41v, not previously printed.

[27] MS Madrid Univ. Library, Faculty of Law, 116²⁰. 3.

[28] MS Morgan 298, at the Pierpont Morgan Library, New York.

[29] But he did not omit all English words or phrases, such as *tynkeler* (f. 19r), *eluenelond* (f. 78v), *a baly, mercy* (f. 85v), *ffor schamely it pokyt* (f. 91r), and others. Several of these as well as many other Latin words and phrases are translated into German.

[30] MS Rawl. C. 670, f. 40v, previously printed by Foster, op. cit., p. 151. Instead of *Goddus* several manuscripts read *Cristes*.

[31] No. 32 (*Index* 3287), not previously printed.

[32] MS Rawl. C. 670, f. 71v–72r. In the last line of No. 33, *his word* is apparently the *durior lectio*; other manuscripts read *hyr word* or *this world*. The final half-line also has several variants, *þe whele* being interpreted as *the while*. This poem has a tradition independent of the *Fasciculus* and has been printed a number of times; see *Index* and *Suppl.* 3408.

[33] MS Rawl. C. 670, f. 138v–139r. Previously printed from MS Corpus Christi Coll. Oxford 218, in *Register*, I, p. 525.

[34] A fine example is MS Lincoln Cath. Libr. 44, containing a number of Latin sermons. This manuscript is full of English tags and of verses not listed in *Index* or *Suppl.* An illustration of English sermon divisions in the Latin text is the following: The text *Congregabo super eos mala, et sagittas meas complebo in eis* (Deut. xxxii: 23) is translated in the margin as: "I sall gaderen hauel vpon hem/And myn arws i sall festen on hem." This is followed by "þe arwe of clepyng, [þe arwe] of motyng, [þe arwe] of fuldemyng," in schematic form, translating *sagitta vocationis* (i.e., calling the sheep, cf. Matt. xxv:31ff.), *disceptationis* (arguing the case of the sheep *versus* the rams), and *diffinitionis* (sending the damned into eternal fire), of the Latin text (f. 319r). A similar case is *Suppl.* No. 4094.8, also

in this manuscript (f. 334r) but not noted. For a parallel case in medieval French, see the sermons by Pierre d'Ailly, edited by E. Brayer, *Notices et Extraits*, 43 (1965), pp. 248–343.

35 A sixth item should be included in Group 4, viz., No. 28 (*Index* 1204). It is a joke about ferrymen who refuse to carry over a passenger who had answered their question as to who he was by saying that nobody knew him. Their answer, "Here is comen þat no mon wot," etc., is given only in English, MS Rawl. C. 670, f. 64v.

36 MS Rawl. C. 670, f. 104v. Previously printed from MS Lincoln Cath. Libr. 44, by G. R. Owst, *Preaching in Medieval England* (Cambridge: Cambridge Univ. Press, 1926), p. 273, n. 3. *Boþe lyfe*: var. *body* or *for body*.

37 MS Rawl. C. 670, f. 90r. Previously printed by Little, op. cit., p. 153 (not a good text, and not well edited), and by Foster, op. cit., p. 153.

38 MS Cambridge Univ. Libr., Dd.10.15, f. 78v.

39 L. Thorndike, "*Unde versus*," *Trad.*, 11 (1955), pp. 163–93.

40 A. Lhotsky, "*Über metrische Einlagen in spätmittelalterlichen Geschichtswerken*," *Festschrift Karl Pivec*, i.e., *Innsbrucker Beiträge zur Kulturwissenshaft*, 12 (1966), pp. 257–63.

41 For example, the notebook of John Lawerne, Benedictine monk and Doctor of Theology at Oxford in the 1440s, contains several Latin verses that summarize the contents of Peter Lombard's *Sentences*, such as the summary of Book III: "*Utrum parens generosa/ De spineto pura rosa/ Dei prolem peperit./ Mansit mater sine labe/ Sicut vitrum solis trabe/ Post partum cum genuerit.*" MS Bodl. 692, f. 7v.

42 A very good example is the *Summa brevis* ("*Qui bene presunt presbiteri*") by Richard Wetheringsett, Chancellor of Cambridge University, written probably between 1215 and 1222. See A. B. Emden, *A Biographical Register of the University of Cambridge to 1500* (Cambridge: Cambridge Univ. Press, 1963), pp. 367 and 679.

43 H. Walther, op. cit.

44 Lhotsky, op. cit.

45 H. Walther, "*Lateinische Verskünsteleien des Mittelalters*," *Zeitschrift für deutsches Altertum und deutsche Literatur*, 91 (1962), pp. 330–50. See also *Proverbia*, op. cit., Vol. I, pp. x ff.

46 No. 19 (*Index* 3254); printed in Little, op. cit., p. 150, n.1; and by J. M. Wilson, *The Library*, Fourth Series, 2 (1922), p. 263 f.

47 No. 39 (*Index* 2832); printed by Foster, op. cit., p. 156; and by Wilson, op. cit., p. 264.

48 Nos. 17 (*Index* 3147) and 22 (quoted above).

49 Nos. 36 (*Index* 3133) and 51 (*Index* 4035).

50 See Rossell Hope Robbins, "Signs of Death in Middle English," *MS*, 32 (1970), pp. 282–98.

51 See *supra*, note 15, and Woolf, op. cit., p. 219.

52 Nos. 36 (*Index* 3133) and 48 (*Index* 3282, printed in *Register*, I, 525). For the topic see Rossell Hope Robbins, *Historical Poems of the XIVth and XVth Centuries* (New York: Columbia Univ. Press, 1959), pp. 140–6, who prints No. 36 on pp. 145–6.

53 No. 40, on long-sleepers, quoted earlier. Latin verses on "syncopating" priests frequently incorporate a series of English nouns, such as "over-leapers," "for-skippers," etc. See *Suppl.* 707.5 (also in Bromyard, *Summa praedicantium*, "*Ordo clericalis*," II, xxvi), 1214.9, and 1655.5 (the last two are apparently the same). For Tutivillus, see S. Wenzel, *The Sin of Sloth* (Chapel Hill, N.C.: Univ. of

North Carolina Press, 1967), pp. 113, 153–4, and 245, nn. 50ff., to which should be added R. Wildhaber, *Das Sündenregister auf der Kuhhaut*, "F. F. Communications," 64, 163 (Helsinki, 1955).

54 They are sometimes called "*exemplum* verses:" see Woolf, op. cit., pp. 45 and 88. The term "message verse" allows me to include such items as Christ's lament on the Cross.

55 No. 20 is part of the proverb "When I woo, gold in my glove." See B. J. Whiting, *Proverbs, Sentences, and Proverbial Phrases From English Writings Mainly Before 1500* (Cambridge, Mass.: Harvard Univ. Press, 1968), G.317; *Suppl.* 4020.6. The beginning of this English proverb is also quoted in a Latin discussion of flattery and false promises, in a series of sermons on the Ten Commandments, MS Bodley 857 (SC. 2760), f. 98r.

56 MS Worcester Cath. F.19, f. 165v–166r, printed in *Register*, I, 451. *Unthewes* is corrected from the MS reading *Vn þys wise*. Cf. Whiting, op. cit., Y.29 and 32.

57 In the English translation of Alcuin's *De virtutibus et vitiis liber*. See Whiting, op. cit., W.275.

58 MS Rawl. C. 670, f. 10r, with emendations from other MSS, *Index* 4143. Previously printed from MS Worcester Cath. F.19, in *Register*, I, 451. The "Hendyng" proverb is apparently not attested outside the *Fasciculus*; cf. Whiting, op. cit., T.375.

59 "þe tonge brekyth bon and hath hymself non." MSS Oxford, Lincoln Coll. 52, f. 3r, and Cambridge, Caius 364, f. 3v (which should be added to *Suppl.* 3792.5). Cf. Whiting, op. cit., T.384, indicating a rich tradition.

60 No. 30 (*Index* 3716); MS Rawl. C. 760, f. 69v, not previously printed. Walther lists two variants of the Latin distich (Nos. 15,232 and 15,240), both with *mens* instead of *mors*.

19

"O JANKYN, BE YE THERE?"

BY DENNIS BIGGINS

At the time she went on the pilgrimage to Canterbury, was Alison's fifth husband alive or dead? Was Alison the married wife from St Michael's *juxta Bathon,* or was she a widow? On this puzzle much controversy has raged. Perhaps the reason why there is no unanimous consensus among the critics is that Chaucer deliberately leaves us uncertain about the degree of her sexual immorality and other related matters. Perhaps Chaucer uses her ambiguous marital standing as a means of arousing in us a complex response to the Wife.

That Alison had buried all five husbands is assumed by most commentators, including such well-known critics as Lounsbury, Kittredge, Root, Gerould, Curry, and Donaldson, to name but a few.[1] Robert A. Pratt, who acknowledges the "clashing inconsistencies" in the Wife of Bath's portraiture, suggests that this double-barrelled evocation of the Wife is due to Chaucer's having worked on it over a number of years.[2] The contradictory implications may have come about simply through the process of gradual accretion by which Chaucer built up her likeness. More recently, Bernard F. Huppé, who similarly cites the Wife's ambiguous references to her husbands, has suggested that Jankyn "has found the peace of his predecessors, but that the wife does not want to make clear her unprovided widowhood."[3]

Among the minority was consider Jankyn still living is Daniel S. Silvia, who suggests that Alison was on pilgrimage because of her habitual *purveiance of mariage,* or earmarking a successor during the lifetime of her current spouse.[4] Schmidt, on the other hand, points out that since her marriage to Jankyn was a happy relationship, after his concession of sovereignty and consequently fidelity to her, Alison had no reason to make such *purveiance* during his lifetime.[5] Only after his death, did she start looking for a sixth husband!

In light of the conflicting briefs for Alison as wife and Alison as widow, it is opportune to review the evidence (or hints) offered in their support. Despite Schmidt's dismissal of *purveiance,* the chief prop of Professor Silvia's argument, there are nevertheless other hints that Alison may not be a widow. Beryl Rowland, for example, is another who maintains that the evidence for Jankyn's death is inconclusive.[6]

Most obvious, of course, is the fact that Chaucer always refers to her as a *wife*. It is true that Chaucer refers to the unmarried hag as a "wyf" (*CT*, III, 998), but he usually distinguishes between spinsters, wives, and widows where the distinction is of some importance. The Wife herself remarks that the company of women assembled in Arthur's court to judge the erring knight's answer to the riddle comprised "Ful many a noble wyf, and many a mayde, / And many a wydwe" (*CT*, III, 1026–7). And she says a little later: "In al the court ne was ther wyf, ne mayde, / Ne wydwe, that contraried that he sayde" (1043–4). Similar distinctions are drawn elsewhere in Chaucer.[7] When Griselda is told by the Marquis that he is, with the Pope's permission, taking a new wife, she asserts that she will live with her father, "A wydwe clene in body, herte, and al" (*CT*, IV, 836).

Moreover, the Wife's flamboyant attire as described in the *General Prologue* hardly suggests a widow. Detailed information on the mourning etiquette of medieval England is hard to come by, but it would appear that by the late fourteenth century black or at least sober colours were an established feature of widow's weeds,[8] rigorously controlled by social protocol, with rings, gloves, or silks forbidden.[9] During the later medieval period certain articles of attire were established as tokens of widowhood. Le Roux de Lincy gives a description of representative middle-class mourning garb for widows, from the mid-fifteenth century; apart from the black dress, cloak and hood, the noteworthy articles were the white *guimpe*, or wimple, and *bandeau*, or chin-band, usually known in the later Middle Ages as a *barbe*.[10] The barbe was peculiar to widowhood as an article of secular attire in the fourteenth century, whereas the wimple was not.[11]

Chaucer's first mention of Criseyde describes her as a widow, dressed "in widewes habit large of samyt broun" (I, 109); the *samyt*, a kind of rich silk, which sorts rather oddly with Criseyde's otherwise impeccable deportment in widowhood, may perhaps be Chaucer's subtle opening hint of her instability. On the other hand, when Troilus first sees her in the temple, she is "In widewes habit blak" and "simple of atir" (I, 170, 181). In Book II, Pandarus urges Criseyde to dance in honour of May: "Do wey youre barbe, and shewe your face bare . . . / And cast youre widewes habit to mischaunce!" (110, 222). In view of the care Chaucer took to invest Criseyde with the appropriate external tokens of widowhood (especially the *barbe*), one would have expected him to describe the

Wife of Bath in similar terms, if he wished to make clear that she was a widow. Her portrait in the *General Prologue* (*CT*, I, 453–7), especially the reference to her red stockings and wimple, however, suggests quite the contrary. Scarlet, though favoured as a mourning colour by King Louis XI of France, has clearly no such significance for the Wife, since she herself tells us that in the days of her *purveiance* during her marriage to husband number four, she wore her "gaye scarlet gytes" (559) on divers but mainly festive social occasions. Chaucer says she was "Ywympled wel" under her large hat—that is, she wore the usual wimple, although the artist who painted her miniature in the margin of the Ellesmere MS gave her a gilt hairnet instead of wife's wimple—or widow's barbe.[12] After the death of her fourth husband, she was careful to observe all the public proprieties demanded of a widow, including (like Criseyde) veiling her face (*CT*, III, 587–90).

It also seems unlikely, at any rate uncertain, that the Wife is supposed to be a widow out of her period of mourning. As Professor Silvia points out, the Wife tells us that it is "her standard practice, out of her *purveiance*, to make sure that she should never be without mate,"[13] a point illustrated in her account of her preparations against the death of her fourth husband. The prescribed period of mourning for a deceased husband varied throughout the Middle Ages, but the tendency in later medieval times was to lengthen it. Aliénor de Poitiers, in her book of court etiquette (1485), laid down fifteen months as the period of mourning for a husband; the Vicomtesse de Furnes remarks of mourning attire in the mid-fifteenth century: "au temps passé, on ne le portoit qu'un an; mais il me semble que pour marits on le doit porter deux, si l'on ne se remarie."[14] The Wife might well wear mourning for a week or two, but hardly for a year or two, so that on this score alone we are free to doubt that she is in widowhood. She herself remarks that she married Jankyn at the end of the *month* in which she buried her fourth husband (*CT*, III, 627–91), and this would seem to be her usual pattern.

Apart from contemporary social custom, the medieval pulpit also offers us a normative ideal of widowhood against which to measure the Wife of Bath as a widow *in posse* or *in esse*. Owst quotes from a sermon on Judith's exemplary conduct as a widow; the behaviour expected is certainly not like what we hear of the Wife of Bath's:

> Also hit falleth to wedowes for to use symple and comune clothinge of mene colour and noght gay ne starynge, ne of queynte and sotil schap, and take ensample of the holy wedowe Judith, of whom holy writ maketh mynde . . . And to kepe hir wedowhode in chastite and

clennes, ffor sche was fayre and 30nge, sche used grete penaunce of fastynge and wered the heyre [*hair shirt*] nexte hir body. Right so schulde wedowes lyve.[15]

To such a formidable prescription the Wife's retort would perhaps simply be, "He spak to them that wolde lyve parfitly; / And lordynges, by your leve, that am nat I" (*CT*, III, 111–12).

The Wife's invocation of God's blessing on Jankyn's soul, it may be claimed, implies strongly that Jankyn is dead:

> Now of my fifth housbonde wol I telle.
> God lete his soule nevere come in helle!
>
> My fifthe housbonde, God his soule blesse!
>
> I preye to God, that sit in mageste,
> So blesse his soule for his mercy deere.
>
> (*CT*, III, 503–4, 525, 826–7)

While the Wife had piously dismissed her fourth husband in similar terms—"Lat hym fare wel, God yeve his soule reste!" (501)—her invocations on Jankyn's behalf do not in themselves necessarily imply that he too "is now in his grave and in his cheste" (502).

Unfortunately, none of these hints, suggestions, arguments is watertight, and the critic is forcibly thrown back on equivocation, doubts, and ambiguities. The Wife herself is no help. For example, her mingling of the pious and the profane early in her *Prologue* and at the conclusion of her *Tale* may plausibly be read either as wishful projections of her future, or as factual statements about her present matrimonial situation:

> Yblessed be God that I have wedded fyve!
> Welcome the sixte, what that evere he shal.
> . . . and Jhesu Crist us sende
> Housbondes meeke, yonge, and fressh abedde,
> And grace t'overbyde hem that we wedde.
>
> (*CT*, III, 44–5, 1258–60)

"Strange questions until one observes that it is not possible to determine with certainty whether 'Jankyn clerk' is alive or dead," concludes Huppé.[16]

This varied and discordant evidence provided both by Alison herself and by Chaucer as narrator, then, serves not so much to strengthen the case for the Wife of Bath's marital status being that not of widow, but of wife, or vice versa, but rather to help build up a set of conflicting impressions about her, as do so many other aspects of her *Prologue* and *Tale*. Notwithstanding the many compelling details that suggest inclusiveness, the Wife's portrait is not all of a piece; there are too many loose ends. Yet we seem to hear an individual voice speaking through her rambling discourse, and by it we are made aware of a distinct personality. It may well be that Chaucer's concern was not so much with the Wife as an individual as with the attitudes she represents. Yet it would seem that the ambiguity produced by the contradictory impressions Chaucer gives of her is designed to make the Wife both a sympathetic figure, and one that is critically "placed." Our response to her oscillates between repulsion and attraction: sexually promiscuous or not, widow or wife, she is an engagingly formidable creation. Just as we are puzzled by these minor biographical discrepancies, whereby "a man knows not where to have her," so the broader implications of her life and philosophy likewise divide us against ourselves. We are amused by her wiles, impressed by her energy, yet at the same time repelled by her pugnacity and bewildered by her deviousness. Her world is real and vital indeed; yet its dissonances may be Chaucer's way of putting us on our guard against too readily accepting it at face value.

UNIVERSITY OF NEWCASTLE, NEW SOUTH WALES

NOTES

[1] Thus Thomas Raynesford Lounsbury, *Studies in Chaucer* (1892; rpt. New York: Russell and Russell, 1962), II, pp. 525–6; George Lyman Kittredge, "Chaucer's Discussion of Marriage,' *MP*, 9 (1911–12), pp. 435–67; and *Chaucer and His Poetry* (Cambridge, Mass.: Harvard Univ. Press, 1915), p. 186; Henry Barrett Hinckley, "The Debate on Marriage in the *Canterbury Tales*," *PMLA*, 32 (1917), pp. 292–305; Robert Kilburn Root, *The Poetry of Chaucer* (1922; rpt. Gloucester, Mass.: Peter Smith, 1957), p. 236; Eugene E. Slaughter, "Clerk Jankyn's Motive," *MLN*, 65 (1950), p. 530; Gordon Hall Gerould, *Chaucerian Essays* (1952; rpt. New York: Russell and Russell, 1958), p. 77; E. T. Donaldson (ed.), *Chaucer's Poetry: An Anthology for the Modern Reader* (New York: Ronald Press, 1958), p. 894; Walter Clyde Curry, *Chaucer and the Mediaeval Sciences*, 2nd edn (1926; rpt. New York: Barnes and Noble, 1960), p. 112; Paul G. Ruggiers, *The Art of The Canterbury Tales* (Madison: Wisconsin Univ. Press, 1965), p. 200.

[2] Robert A. Pratt, "The Development of the Wife of Bath," in MacEdward Leach (ed.), *Studies in Medieval Literature in Honor of Professor Albert Croll Baugh* (Philadelphia: Univ. of Pennsylvania Press, 1961), p. 46.

[3] Bernard F. Huppé, *A Reading of The Canterbury Tales* (Albany: State Univ. of New York Press, 1964), p. 109.

[4] Daniel S. Silvia, "The Wife of Bath's Marital State," *N & Q*, 212 (1967), pp. 8–10.

[5] A. V. C. Schmidt, "Replies," *N & Q*, 212 (1967), pp. 230–1.

[6] Beryl Rowland, "Chaucer's Dame Alys: Critics in Blunderland?" *Studies*

Presented to Tauno F. Mustanoja on the Occasion of His Sixtieth Birthday, NM, 73 (1972), p. 390.

7 All citations from Chaucer from F. N. Robinson (ed.), *The Works of Geoffrey Chaucer,* 2nd edn (Boston: Houghton Mifflin, 1957). Cf. "Al be she mayde, or wydwe, or elles wyf" (*CT,* I, 1171); "Ne was I nevere er now, wydwe ne wyf" (*CT,* III, 1619); "How clene maydenes, and how trewe wyves, / How stedefaste widewes durynge alle here Iyves" (*LGW,* G 282–3).

8 Mrs Charles H. [Emily J.] Ashdown, *British Costumes During XIX Centuries* (London: T. C. and E. C. Jack, 1910; reissued 1929), p. 88. Cf. Also Joan Evans, *Dress in Medieval France* (Oxford: Clarendon Press, 1952), pp. 37, 43; Edith Rickert, comp., *Chaucer's World* (New York: Columbia Univ. Press, 1948), p. 419.

9 Paul Lacroix, *Moeurs, Usages et Costumes au moyen âge et à l'époque da la renaissance,* 3rd edn (Paris: Mesnil, 1873), p. 540; description of mourning customs and clothing at the Court of Burgundy in the mid-fifteenth century, given by the Vicomtesse de Furnes, cited by Louis Mercier, *Le Deuil: son observation dans tous les temps et dans tous les pays* (Londres: P. Douvet, 1877), p. 30.

10 Paul Lacroix, "*Vie privée dans les Chateaux, les villes et les campagnes,*" *Le Moyen Age et la Renaissance* [Paris, 1850], III, f. xxxv^r; cf. engraving f. xxx^v.

11 Blanche Payne, *History of Costume from the Ancient Egyptians to the Twentieth Century* (New York: Harper, 1965), pp. 194–5. Figure 220, from a memorial brass in Westminster Abbey, 1399, depicts Alianora de Bohun, Duchess of Gloucester, wearing a barbe as part of her widow's mourning.

12 But he was careful to give his miniature of the Prioress a wimple, or rather a barbe: "Ful semyly her wympul pynched was" (*CT,* I, 151) suggests a pleated barbe. Apparently, nuns as well as widows wore barbes; the Ellesmere miniature of the Secund Nun seems to show one, although in both figures the pleating is indistinct.

13 Silvia, op. cit., p. 8.

14 Jean de Glen, *Des Habits Moevrs, Certmonies* [sic], *Facons de Faire Anciennes & modernes du Monde* . . . Partie Premiere (Liège, 1601), f. 18^v; Evans, op. cit., p. 64; Mercier, op. cit., p. 25.

15 G. R. Owst, *Literature and Pulpit in Medieval England,* 2nd edn (1933; rpt. New York: Barnes and Noble, 1961), pp. 118–19. Cf. also W. Nelson Francis (ed.) *The Book of Vices and Virtues,* EETS, OS 217 (1942), pp. 250–1.

16 Huppé, op. cit., p. 109. For other examples in Middle English of prayers for the souls of living persons cf. Henry Barrett Hinckley, "The Date, Author, and Sources of the *Owl and the Nightingale,*" *PMLA,* 44 (1929), pp. 329–59; Kathryn Huganir, "Further Notes on the Date of *The Owl and the Nightingale,*" *Anglia,* 63 (1939), pp. 113–34.

20

CHAUCER AND CHRÉTIEN
AND ARTHURIAN ROMANCE

BY D. S. BREWER

Some evidence has already been noticed[1] that suggests that Chaucer had read Chrétien. The evidence is Chaucer's use of the word *vavasour* to describe the Franklin (*CT*, I, 360)—the only occurrence of that word in his writings. It is possible however to argue that two other references by Chaucer also reveal a knowledge of Chrétien's works. Consideration of these possible points of contact between two very different yet very medieval poets suggests some fruitful contrasts and comparisons.

The word *vavasor*, Frankis states, is not much more common in French than in English, and is also of somewhat vague significance as to social status in both languages. Chrétien uses the word in only two poems.[2] In each case *li vavasors* is a man notable for hospitality, and in *Erec et Enide* he has white hair and a good cook, which further associate him with Chaucer's description of the Franklin. Frankis suggests that Chaucer is saying that the Franklin was the sort of person whom Chrétien refers to as a *vavasor*, and one may emphasize that the unusual word occurs fairly frequently in Chrétien's two poems, and so might well stick in the mind. Chaucer may not have known *vavasor* as a legal term in English, since it is only so employed in Northern texts. The existence of the Middle English *Ywain and Gawain* witnesses to the availability of Chrétien's work in the fourteenth century in England, but it is notable that the romance, which is Northern in language, does not repeat the word *vavasor* from Chrétien. The translator uses the more general and colourless word "knight." Frankis also notes that there seems no other certain evidence that Chaucer knew Chrétien's work.

A reference to Chrétien may however lie behind the rather strangely pointed joking remark in *The Nun's Priest's Tale*:

> This storie is also trewe, I undertake,
> As is the book of Launcelot de Lake
> That wommen holde in ful greet reverence. (*CT*, VII, 3211–3)

This could be just a light-hearted antifeminist squib, possibly with some contemporary reference, and also an example of Chaucer's scepticism towards several aspects of contemporary chivalric ideals. Yet it is peculiar that it should be directed specifically against women because, as far as can be judged from what little evidence there is, men were quite as much interested in Arthurian story, and in Launcelot, as were women. The Order of the Garter was founded by Edward III on the Arthurian model about 1350, as is well known; Arthur had a firm place in British–English history; and there is nothing effeminate about the contemporary poems, the alliterative *Morte Arthure* and stanzaic *Le Morte d'Arthur*, both of which mention Launcelot. If Malory, writing about the middle of the fifteenth century, may be cited as circumstantial evidence, Launcelot is his great hero, and there is again nothing particularly feminine about Malory, his work, or, finally, his printer Caxton, and the "noble gentlemen" who asked Caxton to print Malory's *Morte Darthur*. It may be that there is some specific femininity associated with the vast body of French Arthurian romances, unknown to the present writer. But before hunting for that particular needle in the haystack it is worth noticing that the introductory remarks of Chrétien's own *Lancelot*, or *Le Chevalier de la Charrette*, pay very specific tribute to "my lady of Champagne's" interest in the story of Launcelot, since she provided the poet with the story and asked him to write the romance. Chrétien specifically says that her command has more to do with the work than any effort he himself may expend upon it:

> Puis que ma dame de Champaigne
> vialt que romans a feire anpraigne,
> je l'anprendrai molt volentiers . . .

[Praise of the lady]

> Mes tant dirai ge mialz oevre
> ses comandemanz an ceste oevre
> Del CHEVALIER DE LA CHARRETE
> comance Crestïens son livre
> matiere et san li done et livre
> la contesse, et il s'antremet
> de panser, que gueres ni met
> fors sa painne et s'antancïon. (ll. 1–29)

If we accept that Chaucer could have known this passage the point of his reference in *The Nun's Priest's Tale* at once becomes plain and sharp. He has read the beginning of Chrétien's *Lancelot*, has at least glanced at the rest, seen what a farrago of nonsense it is, and makes his passing joke for those in the know. We may also note that in his remarks there is no dramatic implication of the character of the Nun's Priest as ostensible narrator. The poet's own *persona* has taken over.

We may put this reference beside Chaucer's only other mention of Lancelot, also a light-heartedly sceptical dismissal; this time a joke at the expense of Lancelot's expertise in "deerne love" (as hende Nicholas would call it):

> Who koude telle yow the forme of daunces
> So unkouthe, and swiche fresshe contenaunces,
> Swich subtil lookynge and dissymulynges
> For drede of jalouse mennes aperceyvynges?
> No man but Launcelot, and he is deed. (*CT*, V, 283-7)

This is very much a flippancy by the poet in his own *persona*, as are the lines immediately preceding this passage, where the poet disqualifies himself from being just such a man as he has represented the Squire, the ostensible narrator, to be. The Squire's own character, were it "organically" presented, would surely be an enthusiast for Arthurian knighthood, just as surely as he is not the "dul man" (V, 279) who is at this stage the poet, in a favourite mock-modest *persona*, telling *The Squire's Tale*. Both references to Launcelot clearly hang together as characteristic of the narrating *poet* (*not* the Narrator), whom it is convenient to call Chaucer; who often likes to describe himself as "dull;" and who has a fresh, and cheerful scepticism about many of the fashionable sentiments of his day—love of sport, of animals (as Professor Rowland has recently shown us[3]), of adultery, and of Arthurian romance.

Indeed, one might almost go so far as to argue (broadening the issue when we recollect Chaucer's "realism" and his obvious pleasure in *fabliaux*) that Chaucer in his poetical character is decidedly anti-romantic. He could take his place in an Auerbachian procession towards ever greater realism, naturalism, and tragedy, whose ultimate historical climax might be found in the literary culture of our own age, which certainly sees itself very often as "realistic," "frank" and "tragic." *Troilus and Criseyde*, the first self-aware tragedy, so to speak, in English, being named as a tragedy within the text (V, 1786), would be an important stage in this progress. Chaucer's sarcasm about Arthurian romance, and about Chrétien's own *Lancelot*, would testify to the incompatibility of a great master of the realistic with Chrétien, the great master of symbolic fantasy. Chaucer's passing mockery of Chrétien might then be paralleled with the much more extensive and absolutely unquestionable mockery of the English romances which is found in *Sir Thopas*. The English romances are mocked, we may think, not only for their verbal incompetence and general silliness, but because they are *romances*, which to Chaucer means silliness.

Plausible as such an argument would be, and indeed partially true, it would be over-simple. The nature of the mockery in *Sir Thopas* itself witnesses to a deep engagement on the poet's part at an earlier formative time in his life with his later victims. I have shown elsewhere how Chaucer's own development is grafted on to the rough stock of earlier native English romance.[4] It may be argued that *Troilus and Criseyde*, for all its rejection of the supernatural and of the unmotivated events of much romance, nevertheless has the intrinsic quality of romance, though it is "tragic" or "ironic" romance. Chaucer's deep ambiguities and ambivalences are not easily resolved. Such thoughts may also be prompted by another possible reference to Chrétien's work. In his "retracciouns" Chaucer mentions "the book of the Leoun." The traditional speculation is that this lost work may have been a version of Machaut's *Dit dou Lyon*, though Deschamp's *La Fiction* (or *Le Dict*) *du Lyon* has also been mentioned. Chaucer probably knew the poem by Machaut, but doubt has reasonably been felt about the identification. It seems not to have been noticed that Chrétien's *Yvain* is primarily known in French as *Le Chevalier au Lion* and the beast plays a notable part in the poem. "The book of the Leoun" was probably an early work, since it has been lost. We know that *Yvain* was current in England in the fourteenth century as *Yvain and Gawain*, and we may imagine it popular. Chaucer's "Book of the Leoun" might have been a version of Chrétien's *Le Chevalier du Lion*.

Chaucer of course knew about Gawain, though he refers only once, and again flippantly, to "Gawain and his olde curteisye" (*The Squire's Tale*, V, 95);[5] just as he refers only once, and of course in flippant way, to King Arthur (*The Wife of Bath's Tale*, III, 857). In these two instances we again have evidence of the poet's poetical character, not of the so-called Narrator, nor of individual pilgrim-narrators, all casual two-dimensional masks to be raised or lowered as the poet feels inclined. Not Narrator nor narrators but Chaucer the poet derides Arthurian romance—it is one of his constant and notable though minor traits. And yet we must allow that Chaucer's derision for the English romances that preceded him is based on an earlier knowledge that was surely product of a youthful love. It would not be the only youthful infatuation repudiated in maturity yet always influential. These Arthurian references, derisory though they are, suggest that Chrétien's Arthurian stories may have been another passing attraction.

It would not be profitable to claim a deep or lasting affinity between Chaucer and Chrétien. But once some relationship is granted as a possibility, comparisons and contrasts may be fruitful. The two poets share some commonplaces, such as the detailed description of the beautiful heroine. A reading of *Troilus and Criseyde* in the light of *Cligès* gives further depth to some of Chaucer's unexpressed, or lightly expressed significances, most notably Criseyde's refusal to elope with Troilus (cf. *Cligès*, 5232 ff, where Fenice also says that Cligès will be her lord and her servant, as Aurelius is to Dorigen in *The Franklin's Tale*). Chrétien is more explicit than Chaucer on the topic of honour, the sentiment which underlies so much of Criseyde's behaviour.[6] Chrétien comments on the unreasonableness of love, yet finds in love his most fascinating subject-matter: here again is a parallel with the more enigmatic, less explicit Chaucer. In such cases Chrétien seems to express fully certain values which Chaucer takes for granted, or, for his own purposes, leaves under the surface.

EMMANUEL COLLEGE, CAMBRIDGE

NOTES

[1] P. J. Frankis, "Chaucer's 'Vavasour' and Chrétien de Troyes," *N & Q*, 204 (February, 1968), pp. 46–7.

[2] Mario Roques (ed.), *Érec et Enide*, CFMA 80 (Paris: Librairie Honoré Champion, 1952), and Mario Roques (ed.), *Le Chevalier au Lion* (Ywain), CFMA 89 (Paris: Librairie Honoré Champion, 1960).

[3] Beryl Rowland, *Blind Beasts* (Kent, Ohio: Kent State Univ. Press, 1971).

[4] D. S. Brewer, "The Relationship of Chaucer to the English and European Traditions," in *Chaucer and Chaucerians*, (London: Nelson, 1966). The point has recently been repeated by P. M. Kean, *Chaucer and the Making of English Poetry* (London: Routledge and Kegan Paul, 1972), II, p. 61.

[5] B. J. Whiting, "Gawain: His Reputation, His Courtesy," *MS*, 9 (1947), pp. 189–234, argues that Chaucer may have read *Sir Gawain and the Green Knight*. If so, he may well have thought poorly of it, as we may guess both from the flippancy of the reference to Gawain in *The Squire's Tale*, and the contempt for "rum, ram, ruf" of alliterative verse that is put into the Parson's mouth (*CT*, X, 43), though indeed he holds rhyme "but litel bettre."

[6] D. S. Brewer, "Honour in Chaucer," *E & S*, NS 28 (1973).

21

THE PRAYERS AND DEVOTIONS
IN THE *ANCRENE WISSE*

BY BARBARA RAW

The prayers and devotions in the first section of the *Ancrene Wisse* fall into two fairly well-defined groups. On the one hand, there is the office of the Virgin Mary, with the additions to the office which were normal from the tenth century, that is, matins and vespers of the dead, the litany, the seven penitential psalms and the fifteen gradual psalms.[1] To these official prayers the ancresses could, if they wished, add the hours of the Holy Ghost, a devotion which seems to have developed in the late twelfth or early thirteenth century.[2] In addition to these official prayers, there are groups of private prayers to be said at intervals during the day. The most important of these are the morning and night prayers, prayers to be said at the elevation of the Host, prayers to be recited before the crucifix, prayers in honour of the Virgin Mary, and groups of paternosters to be said for special intentions.

These private prayers, like the more official ones, include devotions already well-established in the late Anglo-Saxon period—for instance, devotion to the Cross—as well as more recent ones such as the recitation of five psalms in honour of the Virgin Mary, a practice which Talbot has shown to date from the very end of the twelfth century, or the prayers at the elevation of the Host, unlikely to have been known in England before 1207 and possibly not introduced until after 1215.[3]

Hitherto, discussion of these prayers has focussed on these later items to help determine the date of composition of the *Ancrene Wisse*. This article will discuss the older items and try to place these devotions within the English tradition.

Except for one or two items, the prayers and antiphons used in the *Ancrene Wisse* are drawn from the texts of the Mass and Office.[4] The prayers to the Virgin Mary, for instance, begin with a series of five brief meditations in English on the Five Joys. Each meditation is followed by a psalm and five complete recitations of the *Ave Maria*;[5]

then come five collects, each preceded by a versicle and followed by an antiphon. These texts are taken almost entirely from the liturgy for the feasts of the Annunciation and the Assumption.

Vers.   *Spiritus Sanctus superveniet in te.*
       Et virtus Altissimi obumbrabit tibi.[6]

Oremus   *Gratiam tuam quesumus Domine mentibus nostris infunde ut qui angelo nuntiante Christi filii tui incarnationem cognovimus per passionem eius et crucem ad resurrectionis gloriam perducamur.*[7]

Ant.   *Ave regina celorum,*
       Ave domina angelorum,
       Salve radix sancta
       Ex qua mundo lux est orta:
       Vale valde decora,
       Et pro nobis semper Christum exora.[8]

Vers.   *Egredietur virga de radice Jesse.*
       Et flos de radice eius ascendet.[9]

Oremus   *Deus qui virginalem aulam beate Marie in qua habitares eligere dignatus es: da quesumus, ut sua nos defensione munitos, iocundos faciat sue interesse festivitati.*[10]

Ant.   *Gaude Dei genitrix virgo immaculata.*
       Gaude que gaudium ab angelo suscepisti.
       Gaude que genuisti eterni luminis claritatem.
       Gaude mater.
       Gaude sancta Dei genitrix virgo, tu sola mater innupta, te laudat omnis filii tui creatura genitricem lucis, sis pro nobis pia interventrix.[11]

Vers.   *Ecce virgo concipiet et pariet filium.*
       Et vocabitur nomen eius Emmanuel.[12]

Oremus   *Deus qui de beate Marie virginis utero Verbum tuum, angelo annuntiante, carnem suscipere voluisti: presta supplicibus tuis, ut qui vere eam genetricem Dei credimus eius aput te intercessionibus adiuvemur.*[13]

Ant.   *Gaude virgo.*
       Gaude dei genitrix
       et gaude gaudium Maria omnium fidelium.
       Gaudeat ecclesia in tuis laudibus assidue
       et pia domina gaudere fac nos tecum ante dominum.[14]

Vers.   *Ecce concipies in utero et paries filium.*
       Et vocabis nomen eius Iesum.[15]

Oremus   *Deus qui salutis eterne beate Marie virginitate fecunda humano generi premia prestitisti: tribue, quesumus, ut ipsam pro nobis intercedere sentiamus, per quam meruimus auctorem vite suscipere: Dominum nostrum Iesum Christum Filium tuum.*[16]

Ant.   *Alma Redemptoris mater, quae pervia caeli*
          Porta manes, et stella maris, succurre cadenti,
          Surgere qui curat, populo: tu que genuisti,
          Natura mirante, tuum sanctum Genitorem,
          Virgo prius ac posterius, Gabrielis ab ore
          Sumens illud Ave, peccatorum miserere.[17]

At this point, there comes a group of fifty or a hundred Aves, followed by:

Vers.   *Ecce ancilla Domini.*
           Fiat mihi secundum verbum tuum.[18]
Oremus   *O sancta virgo virginum,*
           Que genuisti Filium,
           Triumphatorem zabuli.[19]

Apart from the final prayer, taken from a hymn by Marbod of Rennes, the only items not found in the official liturgy are the two antiphons beginning *Gaude virgo.* The second of these has not been identified; the first is found in a votive office of the Virgin Mary in a late Anglo-Saxon manuscript, Cotton Tiberius A. iii.

By the time the *Ancrene Wisse* was written, there must have been between four and five hundred prayers to the Virgin Mary, many of which, presumably, were widely known. A twelfth-century missal from Ghent, for instance, contains a number of private prayers, including a sequence of fifteen interspersed with the gradual psalms and recited in honour of the Virgin Mary. None of these prayers is found in the *Ancrene Wisse.*[20] The same feature is evident in the sets of paternosters, where the accompanying antiphons and collects are taken almost entirely from the liturgy for feasts appropriate to the various intentions.[21] For instance, in the prayers in honour of the Trinity, the antiphon and the collect are those normally used in the mass and office of the Trinity.[22] It is of interest that both items occur in the votive office of the Trinity in an eleventh-century Anglo-Saxon manuscript from Winchester, and in the memorial of the Trinity at matins in the votive office of the Virgin Mary already mentioned.[23]

It seems probable that the texts were taken from a familiar source in order that the devotions should be easily memorized. It is true, of course, that some of the devotions were written down for the ancresses. The author says, for instance, "Euchan segge hire ures as ha haueð iwriten ham" and "þe ureisuns þich nabbe buten ane i mearket. beoð iwriten ouer al wið ute þe leaste. leoteð writen on a scrowe hwet se ȝe ne kunnen."[24] But elsewhere he tends to imply that items are to be recited from memory: "Hwa se ne con þeos fiue. segge þe earste adoramus te. cneolinde fifsiðen," or "hwa se ne con þeos fif ureisuns. segge eauer an."[25] These remarks refer to the salutations to the Cross which would probably be among the most familiar prayers. The psalms, however, would certainly have been known by heart, and most of the collects and antiphons are very familiar. In the case of the hymn *Iuste Iudex* the author expresses doubts as to whether the ancresses would know it and gives an alternative.[26]

But these texts were not well known simply because they occurred in the liturgy. Many of them had been in use in collections of private prayers at least since the early eleventh century.

The main collections of private prayers from the late Anglo-Saxon period are found in four manuscripts: two from Winchester, one from Christ Church, Canterbury, and one from Worcester.[27] The devotions in these manuscripts include a number of individual prayers, but they generally consist of groups of psalms, antiphons, and collects, arranged either in the form of a votive office or in devotions of the kind which developed out of Alcuin's arrangement of the Psalter, and commonly found in Carolingian manuscripts. These devotions, like so much in tenth- and eleventh-century England, were borrowed from earlier continental practice. They have little in common either with the litany-like prayers found in the eighth-century Book of Cerne, or with the long meditative prayers added in the early eleventh century to the Vespasian Psalter, which in phraseology and tone anticipate the prayers of Anselm and his followers.[28]

The two Winchester manuscripts, Cotton Titus D. xxvi and xxvii, were written between 1023 and 1035 for the use of Ælfwine, deacon of New Minster. These books contain a number of prayers to individual saints, chapters and collects from parts of the office, prayers for the dead, prayers in reparation for one's sins and so on. But in addition to these they contain a number of more elaborate items. Titus D. xxvii, for instance, contains a group of three votive offices: in honour of the Trinity, the Cross, and the Virgin Mary.[29] The same manuscript contains three different sets of prayers to the Cross, and Titus D. xxvi contains a devotion based on the penitential psalms.[30] In addition, each manuscript includes a set of morning prayers.[31] Cotton Tiberius A. iii, a Canterbury manuscript, includes a votive office in honour of the Virgin Mary and devotions in honour of the Cross.[32] Similar devotions are found also in the *Portiforium Wulfstani*, at the end of a group of prayers to various saints.[33] In these manuscripts, the most frequently occurring and most fully developed of these semi-liturgical devotions are those to the Cross. Similarly, devotion to the Cross permeates the prayers of the *Ancrene Wisse*, being found not only in the prayers at midday but in the morning and night prayers and in the groups of paternosters. In the section on temptation, the author of the *Ancrene Wisse* recommends using Christ's passion as a shield, and in the section on love uses the image of the crucifix as a shield.[34]

The main prayers to the Cross in the *Ancrene Wisse* are arranged in five groups, each of which begins with the five antiphons to the Cross used as part of the morning prayers.[35] These antiphons are followed by a psalm, said with an antiphon, and followed by *Kyrie*, paternoster and collect. The psalm and collect are changed in each section, while the antiphons and *preces* remain the same. The form of each section then is as follows:

> *Adoramus te Christe et benedicimus tibi quia per sanctam crucem redemisti mundum.*[36]
>
> *Tuam crucem adoramus domine, tuam gloriosam recolimus passionem. Miserere nostri qui passus es pro nobis.*[37]
>
> *Salve crux sancta, arbor digna, cuius robur preciosum mundi tulit talentum.*[38]
>
> *Salve crux que in corpore Christi dedicata es et ex membris eius tanquam margaritis ornata.*[39]
>
> > *O crux, lignum triumphale,*
> > *Mundi vera salus, vale,*
> > *Inter ligna nullum tale*
> > > *Fronde, flore, germine.*
> >
> > *Medicina christiana,*
> > *Salva sanos, egros sana;*
> > *Quod non valet vis humana,*
> > > *Fit in tuo nomine.*[40]
>
> Ant.   *Salva nos Christe salvator per virtutem sancte crucis. (Psalm)*
> Ant.   *Salva nos Christe salvator per virtutem sancte crucis.*
>   *Qui salvasti Petrum in mare, miserere nobis.*[41]
>   *Christe audi nos, Iesu Christe audi nos.*
>   *Kyrie eleison, Christe eleison, Kyrie eleison.*
>   *Paternoster.*
> Vers.   *Protector noster aspice Deus,*
>   *Et respice in faciem Christi tui.*[42]
> *Oremus (Collect)*

The psalms and collects change at each repeat:

1. *Iubilate* (99); Deus qui sanctam crucem.[43]
2. *Ad te levavi* (122); Adesto quesumus Domine.[44]
3. *Qui confidunt* (124); Deus qui pro nobis filium tuum.[45]
4. *Domine non est exaltatum* (130); Deus qui unigeniti.[46]

5. *Laudate Dominum in sanctis eius* (150); Iuste Iudex and O beata et intemerata.[47]

Any ancress who thinks the devotion too long can omit the psalms.

Of the first five antiphons (said in the morning in honour of the five wounds and again at midday with the longer devotions to the Cross), three are found in Anglo-Saxon liturgical books. The first and second appear in the Friday office in honour of the Cross, and the fourth in Titus D.xxvi (f. 56v), among the collects after the litany. The fifth antiphon dates from the twelfth century. Of the collects used in the midday devotions, number three (*Deus qui pro nobis*) is used at vespers for the Invention of the Cross as well as at vespers on Wednesday of Holy Week, and number four (*Deus qui unigeniti*) as the collect in the Friday mass of the Cross. More importantly, many of these items occur in collections of private prayers in honour of the Cross.

Veneration of the Cross was associated primarily with the Good Friday ceremonies, and by the late Anglo-Saxon period a fully developed service of chants and psalms had long been established. The ceremony began with the chanting of the reproaches, or *Improperia*, followed by the chants *Ecce lignum crucis*, *Crucem tuam adoramus* and *Dum fabricator mundi*, together with psalms 66 and 118. This form of the ceremony is found, with minor variations, in Gregory's *Liber Antiphonarius*, in the tenth-century Leofric Missal, and in at least two eleventh-century Anglo-Saxon manuscripts.[48] The *Regularis Concordia*, however, prescribes a slightly different ceremony. The chants are the same, but the psalms are replaced by the seven penitential psalms, arranged in three groups and linked to three prayers.[49] The Good Friday prayers of the *Regularis Concordia* seem to have been used also on other occasions. The three prayers are found separated from the ceremony of psalms and chants in a number of manuscripts, and the ceremony itself is found with slight variations in the *Portiforium Wulfstani* and in Cotton Tiberius A. iii. The prayers in the Wulfstan manuscript are headed *Alia oratio ad deum deuote corde dicenda*; they consist of the penitential psalms, arranged in three groups, as in the *Regularis Concordia*, each group followed by one of the Concordia prayers. The one difference is that a group of *preces*, or short invocations, is inserted between each group of psalms and the following prayer. The devotion is followed by three collects, and then is repeated, partly in English and partly in Latin, with three additional collects, giving six in all.[50]

Tiberius A. iii has two sets of private devotions to the Cross which are similar to those in the *Regularis Concordia*. The first (ff. 58–9) is headed, "Sing þas sealmas swa oft swa þu oftust mæge þære halgan rode to lofe ꝺ to wyrþmynte." It is similar to the first of the Wulfstan sets of prayers, with psalm 85 added to the second group of psalms, and the first prayer divided into two and the second omitted. The second set (ff. 114v–115v) has one extra antiphon (*O crux splendidior cunctis astris*) and lacks the final blessing. In addition, both the *Portiforium Wulfstani* and Tiberius A. iii contain a third set of prayers to the Cross, preceded by the directions, "Gyf ðe ðince þæt ðine fynd þwirlice ymbe þe ðridian ðonne gang þu on gelimplicere stowe ꝺ þe ða halgan rode to gescyldnesse geciig ꝺ asete þe aðenedum earmum ꝺ cweð þus ærest."[51] Like the other ceremony, this consists of psalms, *preces*, and collects; here the psalms are numbers 7, 12, 16, 3 and 24.

In Titus D. xxvii the main prayers to the Cross are those on ff. 66–73v. They fall into three sections: prayers in front of the crucifix; a series of separate prayers to the Cross; morning prayers to the Cross. The prayers before the crucifix consist of a series of psalms, antiphons, and prayers which are to be recited in front of the different parts of the crucifix, beginning with the feet, then the hands, the mouth, breast and ears. After this set of seven psalms with their antiphons and petitions, comes a responsory based on the responsory for Maundy Thursday, and having the refrain, *Domine miserere nobis*. After the responsory a series of seven paternosters is recited, interspersed with antiphons; the sixth antiphon is replaced by a longer responsory with the refrain, *Dum supervenerit mihi mortis hora horibilis*. The devotions end with a final prayer to the Cross and an antiphon. In general, the structure of this devotion is like that of the ceremonies in Tiberius A. iii and the *Portiforium Wulfstani*, though more elaborate. The psalms, however, are quite different, even though they are seven in number.[52] What is noticeable about this ceremony is that the prayers are mostly petitions for mercy, particularly at the hour of death.

The Titus devotion, like that in the *Ancrene Wisse*, is sometimes claimed as an example of prayer in honour of the five wounds. Like the prayers in the much earlier Book of Nunnaminster, however, it probably commemorates Christ's sufferings as a whole.[53] Neither the prayers nor the antiphons are related to the parts of the crucifix before which they are recited, and the arrangement of the prayers in groups of seven, rather than five, is against this identification.[54]

If one compares the prayers and antiphons of the *Ancrene Wisse* with those in Anglo-Saxon collections of private prayers one finds that the *Adoramus te Christe* occurs in all three sets of private prayers in the *Portiforium Wulfstani*, and Tiberius A. iii.[55] It is also found in the night prayers to the Cross in the Durham Ritual and in the morning prayers to the Cross in Titus D. xxvii.[56] The antiphon *Tuam crucem* is found in the prayers of the Durham Ritual and possibly in the prayers in the *Portiforium Wulfstani*.[57] The antiphon *Salva nos Christe* is used in the prayers to the Cross for protection in the *Portiforium Wulfstani* and Tiberius A. iii, and in the votive office of the Cross in Titus D. xxvii.[58] Of the five prayers, the second and fourth (*Adesto quesumus* and *Deus qui unigeniti*) are found among the prayers to the Cross in the Durham Ritual.[59] The psalms, on the other hand, do not correspond to those used in any of the Anglo-Saxon devotions to the Cross. The reason is simple. The author points out that the psalms each contain five verses.[60] They are, in fact, the only psalms in the Vulgate text to do so, and it seems that someone, whether the author of the *Ancrene Wisse* or some other, noticed the fact that there were five psalms, each with five verses, and found this appropriate to a devotion to the five wounds. What seems clear from all this is that the author of the *Ancrene Wisse* was not devising these devotions himself nor, probably, was he taking them over direct from earlier devotions. He seems to have made use of a tradition of prayer to the Cross but to have adapted it, partly by the addition of a few fairly recent hymns and prayers, and partly by adapting it to more recent fashions.

One can perhaps see this question of fashion in the number symbolism of the *Ancrene Wisse* prayers. The groups of paternosters which are said for various intentions correspond in number to the intention for which they are said. For instance, three paternosters are said in honour of the Trinity, and twelve in honour of the twelve apostles. In the English prayer which precedes each set of paternosters the author groups together a number of items symbolized by the number with which he is dealing. For instance, under the number seven he includes not only the seven gifts of the Holy Ghost, but the seven hours of the office, the seven petitions of the paternoster, the seven capital sins and the seven beatitudes.[61] His favourite number, however, seems to be five. The morning prayers include five salutations to the Blessed Sacrament, five greetings to the crucifix in honour of the five wounds, and five Aves before the statue of the Virgin Mary. The prayers before the crucifix said at midday are arranged in five sections, each of the five psalms contains five verses, and each section begins with the five salutations used at morning prayers. The prayers to the Virgin Mary celebrate her five joys; each is celebrated by a meditation, a psalm and five Aves, and, as the author says, "the prayer about her five greatest joys runs in fives. If you count the greetings in the antiphons, you will find five in each."[62] Five paternosters are recited in honour of the five wounds, in order that man's wounds, caused by the five senses, may be healed. This idea, that Christ's five wounds atoned for sins committed through the five senses, is found also in the section on the custody of the senses.[63]

This interest in number symbolism is a commonplace in the early medieval period, but it is worth noting that whereas the author of the *Ancrene Wisse* has a preference for fives, the compiler of the prayers in Titus D. xxvii (ff. 66–73v) prefers sevens. His devotions include seven psalms, though they are not the usual penitential psalms; the group of antiphons interspersed with paternosters includes seven paternosters, and there is a prayer to the Cross with seven petitions. That this is not accidental can be seen from a note on f. 70: "*Hae sunt iiii causae quibus sancta crux adoratur. Prima causa est qui in una die septem cruces adit, aut septies unam crucem adorat, septem porte inferni clauduntur illi, et septem porte paradisi aperiuntur ei.*" A similar note is found in Tiberius A. iii (ff. 59v–60); it is followed, as in Titus D. xxvii, by the prayer with seven petitions (*Domine Ihesu Christe pro sancta cruce tua*), and the prayer *Per gloriam et virtutem sancte crucis*. It seems possible that we have here traces of a shift in emphasis which took place between the early eleventh century and the later twelfth century, by which devotions to the Cross which were originally penitential in character and related particularly to protection at the hour of death are replaced by devotion to the five wounds.

The prayers of the *Ancrene Wisse* bear witness to the strength of the Anglo-Saxon tradition in the South-west midlands in the early Middle English period. With the exception of one or two items, such as the salutations to the Blessed Sacrament and the collect which ends the prayers at the elevation, the texts are ones which had long been used in the official liturgy and in the private prayers of Anglo-Saxon monastic houses. The form of the devotions, with their psalms, antiphons, and groups of paternosters, resembles that found in a number of eleventh-century English manuscripts. The alternation of English and Latin texts is also characteristic of the devotions of the late Anglo-Saxon period.[64] The traditional element in these devotions is particularly evident if one compares them with prayers such as *On god ureisun of ure Lefdi* or *On lofsong of ure Louerde* which are found in the Nero manuscript of the *Ancrene Riwle*. The only trace in the *Ancrene Wisse* of this emotional, individual kind of prayer is the brief introduction to the Aves, beginning, "Leafdi swete leafdi swetest alre leafdi."[65] In this respect, the prayers provide a great contrast to the rest of the *Ancrene Wisse*, with its many borrowings from the writings of Anselm of Canterbury, Bernard of Clairvaux and their followers. They confirm what the author himself says about ways of praying, "Redunge is god bone. Redunge teacheð hu ⁊ hwet me bidde. ꝼ beode biȝet hit efter."[66]

KEELE UNIVERSITY

NOTES

[1] All references are to the edition by J. R. R. Tolkien, *The English Text of the Ancrene Riwle: Ancrene Wisse*, EETS, OS 249 (1962). For the addition of the Office of the Dead and the Gradual and Penitential Psalms to the monastic office see e.g. T. Symons (ed.), *The Regularis Concordia* (London: Nelson, 1953), pp. 12, 13, 15. The Little Office of Our Lady was in use at Verdun and Einsiedeln in the late tenth century, and was known in England from the eleventh century. For references see C. H. Talbot, "Some notes on the dating of the *Ancrene Riwle*," *Neophilologus*, 40 (1956), pp. 40–1.

[2] Talbot, op. cit., pp. 44–6.

[3] Tolkien, op. cit., pp. 22–4 and 20–1; Talbot, op. cit., pp. 42–3 and 46–50.

[4] The Latin texts have been expanded and the spelling normalized. Most of the texts have been identified: Josephine G. Cooper, "Latin elements of the *Ancrene Riwle*," Diss. Birmingham 1956; Glenys Magee, "The *Ancrene Wisse*: Part 1." Diss. Keele 1969.

[5] Tolkien, op. cit., pp. 22–6, Talbot, op. cit., pp. 42–3. This devotion was brought back from Beneventum by an archbishop of Canterbury. It is associated with a miracle at St Bertin some time between 1184 and 1203, and probably reached England in the late twelfth century.

[6] Responsory for the Annunciation, D. H. Turner, *The Missal of the New Minster, Winchester*, Henry Bradshaw Soc., 93 (1962), p. 84. Whenever possible, references are given to an Anglo-Saxon liturgical work.

[7] Postcommunion for the Annunciation, Turner, op. cit., p. 84; also used at Sext for the Annunciation, A. Hughes, *The Portiforium of Saint Wulfstan*, HBS, 89–90 (1958, 1960), Vol. 89. p. 99.

[8] Antiphon for the Nativity of the Virgin, Francis Proctor and Christopher Wordsworth, *Breviarium ad usum insignis ecclesiae Sarum* (Cambridge: Cambridge Univ. Press, 1882–6), III, p. 784.

[9] Chapter for Vespers of the second Sunday in Advent, Hughes, op. cit., 89, p. 2.

[10] Collect for the vigil of the Assumption, Turner, op. cit., p. 144, Hughes op. cit., 89, p. 105; see also U. Lindelöf (ed.), *Rituale Ecclesiae Dunelmensis*, Surtees Soc., 140 (Leeds: Whitehead, 1927), p. 66.

[11] Antiphon at Terce in the votive office of the Virgin Mary, Cotton MS Tiberius A. iii, f. 111; E. S. Dewick, *Facsimiles of Horae de Beata Maria Virgine*, HBS, 21 (1902), col. 29.

[12] Chapter for Vespers of the first Sunday in Advent, Hughes, op. cit., 89, p. 2: responsory for the Annunciation, Hughes, op. cit., 89, p. 98 and Turner, op. cit., p. 84.

[13] Collect for the Annunciation, Turner, op. cit., p. 83, Hughes, op. cit., 89, p. 98; Lindelöf, op. cit., p. 51; see also F. E. Warren, *The Leofric Missal* (Oxford: Clarendon Press, 1883), p. 71. Also used as the collect at Matins in the votive office of the Virgin Mary, Royal MS 2 B.v, f.2v; Dewick, op. cit., col. 6.

[14] Not identified.

[15] Versicle at Matins of the Annunciation, Proctor and Wordsworth, op. cit., III, 238.

[16] Collect for the Sunday after the Nativity, Warren op. cit., p. 65; collect at Terce in the votive office of the Virgin Mary, Cotton MS Tiberius A. iii, f. 111, and at Vespers, Royal MS 2 B.v, f. 5v; Dewick, op. cit., cols. 29, 16.

17 Antiphon for the Nativity of the Virgin Mary, Proctor and Wordsworth, op. cit., III. 784.

18 Antiphon at Lauds of the Annunciation, ibid., III, 245.

19 First three lines of Marbod of Rennes, *Oratio ad Sanctam Mariam*, C. Blume and G. M. Dreves, *Analecta Hymnica Medii Ævi* (Leipzig: Reisland, 1886-1922), L, 395, no. 306.

20 L. Gjerløw, *Adoratio Crucis* (Oslo: Norwegian Univ. Press, 1961), pp. 107–31. The only Marian prayer in the *Ancrene Wisse* which is not taken from the liturgy is the *O beata et intemerata*, Tolkien, op. cit., p. 22. For a discussion of Marian devotion up to the time of Anselm see H. Barré, *Prières anciennes de l'occident à la Mère du Sauveur* (Paris: Lethielleux, 1962).

21 Tolkien, op. cit., pp. 17–19.

22 Ibid., p. 17; A. Wilmart, *Precum Libelli quattuor aevi Karolini* (Rome: *Ephemerides Liturgicae*, 1940), p. 102; Lindelöf, op. cit., p. 158.

23 Cotton MS Titus D. xxvii, ff. 76v and 77; Cotton MS Tiberius A. iii, f. 110; Dewick, op. cit., col. 25.

24 Tolkien, op. cit., pp. 15, 25.

25 Ibid., pp. 14, 22.

26 Ibid., p. 17.

27 Cotton MS Titus D. xxvi and xxvii, Cotton MS Tiberius A. iii; Cambridge, Corpus Christi Coll MS 391.

28 A. B. Kuypers, *The Book of Cerne* (Cambridge Univ. Press, 1902); D. H. Wright, *The Vespasian Psalter*, Early English Manuscripts in Facsimile, 14 (Copenhagen: Rosenkilde and Bagger, 1967), pp. 32–3, ff. 155–60.

29 Cotton MS Titus D. xxvii, ff. 76–80, 80–81v, 81v–85.

30 Cotton MS Titus D. xxvii, ff. 64v, 66–72, 88v–89; Cotton MS Titus D. xxvi, ff. 46v–50.

31 Cotton MS Titus D. xxvii, ff. 72–73v; Cotton MS Titus D. xxvi, ff. 69v–71v.

32 Cotton MS Tiberius A. iii, ff. 107v–114v, ff. 58–59v and 114v–115v.

33 Hughes, op. cit., 90, pp. 1–24. Prayers in honour of the Cross are also found in Lindelöf, op. cit., pp. 93–4 and 149–51.

34 Tolkien, op. cit., pp. 151, 199, 200.

35 Ibid., pp. 21–22.

36 Versicle from Friday Office of the Cross, Hughes, op. cit., 90, p. 60; private prayers in honour of the Cross, ibid., 90, p. 20.

37 Responsory from Friday Office of the Cross, ibid., 90, p. 60; private prayers in honour of the Cross, ibid., 90, p. 22.

38 First two lines of the sequence from the votive mass of the Cross, Proctor and Wordsworth, op. cit., II, 507.

39 Part of an antiphon for Matins of St Andrew, ibid., III, 8; see also prayer 66 in Kuypers, op. cit., p. 161, and the opening of a prayer in Cotton MS Titus D. xxvii, f. 68v, *Salve crux pretiosa et inclita, cordi meo amantissima, que in sacro Christi corpore sublimiter es dedicata et ex membris eius tamquam margaritis ornata.*

40 Verses 18 and 19 of *Laudes crucis attollamus*, *Anal. Hymn.* LIV, 188, no. 120; see also the Mass for the Exaltation of the Cross, J. Wickham Legg, *The Sarum Missal* (1916; rpt Oxford: Clarendon Press, 1969), p. 321.

41 Prayers to the Cross, Cotton MS Titus D. xxvii, f. 80; private prayers, Hughes, op. cit., 90, p. 22; prayers to the Cross for protection, ibid., 90, p. 24, and Cotton MS Tiberius A. iii, f. 59.

42 Lindelöf, op. cit., p. 15.

43 Memorial of the Cross at Matins, Proctor and Wordsworth, op. cit., II, 92.

44 Prayers to the Cross, Lindelöf, op. cit., pp. 94, 150.
45 Collect for Passiontide, ibid., p. 23; Hughes, op. cit., 89, p. 45; Vespers of the Invention of the Cross, ibid, 89, p. 124.
46 Prayers to the Cross, Lindelöf, op. cit., p. 94; collect for the Exaltation of the Cross, Hughes, op. cit., 89, p. 108; collect for Friday Mass of the Cross, Turner, op. cit., p. 212; Warren, op. cit., p. 178; Cotton MS Titus D. xxvi, f. 56v.
47 Prayer of Berengarius of Tours, F. J. E. Raby, *A History of Christian-Latin Poetry*, 2nd edn (Oxford: Clarendon Press, 1953), p. 264; A. Wilmart, *Auteurs spirituels et textes dévots du moyen âge Latin* (Paris: Blond et Gay, 1932), pp. 474–504.
48 Gregory, *Liber Antiphonarius*, P. L. 78: 676; Warren, op. cit., p. 262; Cambridge, Corpus Christi Coll. MS 422, p. 316; Hughes, op. cit., 89, p. 48.
49 Symons, op. cit., pp. 42–4. These prayers have been discussed in detail by Gjerløw, op. cit.
50 Hughes, op. cit., 90, pp. 17–23. For other examples of the Concordia prayers see Gjerløw, op. cit., pp. 16–28.
51 Hughes, op. cit., 90, p. 24.
52 Psalms 3, 53, 66, 69, 85, 140, 76.
53 W. de Gray Birch, *An ancient manuscript of the eighth or ninth century formerly belonging to St Mary's Abbey, or Nunnaminster, Winchester*, Hampshire Record Society, 2 (London: Simpkin, 1889).
54 Devotion to the five wounds was known before the time of the *Ancrene Wisse*, however. A late eleventh-century manuscript from St Gall contains five prayers to be said in honour of the five wounds; see A. Wilmart, "L 'office du crucifix contre l'angoisse," *Ephemerides Liturgicae*, 46 (1932), 421–34. Cf. also Rossell Hope Robbins, "The 'Arma Christi' Rolls," *MLR*, 34 (1939), pp. 415–21.
55 Hughes, op. cit., 90, pp. 17–24; Cotton MS Tiberius A. iii, ff. 58–59, 114v–115v.
56 Lindelöf, op. cit., p. 150 and Cotton MS Titus D. xxvii, f. 72v.
57 Lindelöf, op. cit., p. 150.
58 Hughes, op. cit., 90, p. 24; Cotton MS Tiberius A. iii, f. 59; Cotton MS Titus D. xxvii, f. 80.
59 Lindelöf, op. cit., p. 94.
60 Tolkien, op. cit., p. 22.
61 Ibid., pp. 17–18.
62 Ibid., p. 25.
63 Ibid., p. 61.
64 Hughes, op. cit., 90, pp. 20–2.
65 Tolkien, op. cit., p. 25. For the prayers in Cotton MS Nero A. xiv see R. Morris, *Old English Homilies*, EETS, OS 29 and 34 (1868), pp. 190–217.
66 Tolkien, op. cit., p. 148.

22

CHAUCER'S TROILUS AND
ST PAUL'S CHARITY

BY FRANCIS LEE UTLEY

[Paul Elmer] More did not understand the fashion of literature, and I do not think very much the fashion of heroes either, in or out of literature. Prudent men and practical moralists seldom do; they want their heroes to purge them without themselves having anything to lose.[1]

Lotsa folks talk about heb'm ainta goin' there—Old Spiritual

Troilus has always had his defenders, which is as it should be, for he is surely to a man of common sense one of the most heart-warming and attractive of heroes. And the medieval audience must have contained plenty of men of common sense. Yet he has also had his modern impugners. Because he wept like Aeneas or Lancelot or any sensitive noble hero, he has often been called a milksop, an odd term for a man who fought like a lion. Now, by a double play from Jean de Meun to Sigmund Freud, he is sometimes called a narcissist. For very shame we will not say who the impugners are, but we wonder whether any of them could achieve half the measure of the fictive heroes they impugn for pusillanimity, for moral error, or for lack of charity.

Complex and stern as St Augustine's view of charity may be, it seems to me that to deprive Troilus of charity and burden him wholly with concupiscence is a serious misreading of Chaucer. Though Troilus is a fresh, lusty and virile gentleman, with some of the blemishes of that degree and others that are common to us all, one wonders what a charitable pagan would be if it were not Troilus. No doubt this is creeping modernism, spiritual blindness, and scholarly laxness, yet many of us, after a life of devotion to the understanding of both the Middle Ages and ourselves, are somewhat shaken by casual charges of modernism. Hence it has been a recent joy of mine to come across a fifteenth-century poem which defines the Sixteen Points of Charity with little attention to St Augustine but with ample attention to St Paul.

Before we discuss the poem in detail, and its striking correspond-
ences to *Troilus and Criseyde*, we must take a look at Troilus' official
virtues as set forth by Chaucer. This is no place for a full analysis of
Troilus' character;[2] we are interested at the moment in his virtues
rather than his vices. There are six major points in the poem in which
his heroic qualities are made clear to us, and they are well-distributed
throughout the poem: one in Book I, one in Book II, two in Book III,
and one each in Books IV and V.

The first represents the effects of Pandarus' assurance to him that
he may have hope of ultimately achieving his lady's love:[3]

> But Troilus lay tho no lenger down,
> But up anon upon his stede bay,
> And in the feld he pleyde the leoun;
> Wo was that Grek that with hym mette a day.
> And in the town his manere tho forth ay
> So goodly was, and gat hym so in grace,
> That ech hym loved that loked on his face.

> For hi bicome the frendlieste wight,
> The gentileste, and ek the moste fre,
> The thriftieste, and oon the beste knyght
> That in his tyme was, or myghte be;
> Dede were his japes and his cruelte,
> His hye port, and his manere estraunge;
> And ech of tho gan for a vertu chaunge. (I, 1072–85)

This may be misdirected love and misdirected hope, but the virtues
are positively enough described, and whatever a strict churchman
might say, no subtlety is needed to guess the appeal of this passage to
a gentleman or lady of the court of Richard II.

Since the second is a description of Troilus made by Pandarus to
Criseyde, it may be dramatically discounted:

> Now, nece myn, the kynges deere sone,
> The goode, wise, worthi, fresshe, and free,
> Which alwey for to don wel is his wone,
> The noble Troilus, so loveth the,
> That, but ye helpe, it wol his bane be.
> Lo, here is al. What sholde I moore seye?
> Do what yow list to make hym lyve or deye. (II, 316–22)

> Allas! he which that is my lord so deere,
> That trewe man, that noble, gentil knyght,
> That naught desireth but youre frendly cheere,
> I se hym deyen, ther he goth upryght. . . . (II, 330–34)

The rhetoric is that of a special pleader, but the actual virtues mentioned do not differ greatly from those mentioned in less suspicious passages. Pandarus at this point may be understating the specifics of Troilus' desire, but from what one has seen of Troilus one would declare him innocent of more than a kindly glance at this stage of the affair.

The Book of the Consummation twice pays tribute to its hero. In the first episode Criseyde explains why, after a stage of maidenly reserve, she has now accepted her lover:

> Lo, herte myn, as wolde the excellence
> Of love, ayeins the which that no man may,
> Ne oughte ek goodly, maken resistence,
> And ek bycause I felte wel and say
> Youre grete trouthe and servise every day,
> And that youre herte al myn was, soth to seyne,
> This drof me for to rewe upon youre peyne.
>
> And youre goodnesse have I founden alwey yit,
> Of which, my deere herte and al my knyght,
> I thonke it yow, as fer as I have wit,
> Al kan I nought so muche as it were right;
> And I emforth my connyng and my might,
> Have, and ay shal, how sore that me smerte,
> Ben to yow trewe and hool with al myn herte. (III, 988–1001)

Like Pandarus, Criseyde is a prejudiced witness, and the courtly rhetoric which asserts her own fidelity may be called dramatic irony and foreshadowing. Yet there is nothing to impugn the impression Troilus' virtue has made on her. Boccaccio's heroine is not impressed by her lover's moral qualities in this fashion, and thus the very mention of Troilus' goodness by Chaucer's Criseyde exalts his mistress. Even Dante is kind to lovers.

The second panegyric is the narrator's. Coming as it does after the consummation, it is the finest tribute of all, and it testifies to the ennobling effect of what we used to call courtly love:

> In suffisaunce, in blisse, and in singynges,
> This Troilus gan al his lif to lede;
> He spendeth, jousteth, maketh festeyinges;
> He yeveth frely ofte, and chaungeth wede,
> And held aboute hym ay, withouten drede,
> A world of folk, as com hym wel of kynde,
> The fressheste and the beste he koude fynde;

That swich a vois of hym was and a stevene
Thorughout the world, of honour and largesse,
That it up rong unto the yate of hevene.
And as in love he was in swich gladnesse,
That in his herte he demed, as I gesse,
That ther nys lovere in this world at ese
So wel as he; and thus love gan hym plese. (III, 1716–29)

Criseyde has caught him in her net, and in his rejoicing he sings a noble hymn of love taken from Boethius:

Love, that of erthe and se hath governaunce,
Love, that his hestes hath in hevenes hye,
Love, that with an holsom alliaunce
Halt peples joyned, as hym list hem gye,
Love, that enditeth lawe of compaignie,
And couples doth in vertu for to dwelle,
Bynd this acord that I have told and telle. (III, 1744–50)

Our strict moralists would no doubt call the mood one of hedonism, but one doubts whether the judgement of Chaucer's audience would have been universally so harsh. The four stanzas of the hymn are surely a testimony to Troilus' sobriety, and any ironic interpretation cannot cancel out their admiration. We may accept this highly serious poetry as pagan, since it does not mention Christ, and argue that it merely points to the greater revelation which will come in the epilogue to *Troilus and Criseyde*, with its similar cosmic strain. Yet there is surely a residue of the pagan in the divine. In any event the hymn reflects the highest courtly and pagan values, which Troilus reaffirms now that his hope of Book I has been fulfilled:

In alle nedes for the townes werre
He was, and ay, the first in armes dyght;
And certeynly, but if that bokes erre,
Save Ector, most ydred of any wight;
And this encres of hardynesse and myght
Com hym of love, his ladies thank to wynne,
That altered his spirit so withinne. (III, 1772–78)

So far I have found no allegorist who has suggested that the reason Troilus is always second to Hector is that his brother was a respectable married man, who had chosen not to burn. It is probably only a matter of time before I do.

But the narrator still has further tribute to pay to the new Troilus, ennobled by love. Like a proper soldier and knight he keeps in shape

in time of truce by hunting and hawking, and by greetings from his
lady in her window, which has so often framed her in the poem:

> And moost of love and vertu was his speche,
> And in despit hadde alle wrecchednesse;
> And, douteles, no nede was hym biseche
> To honouren hem that hadden worthynesse,
> And esen hem that weren in destresse,
> And glad was he if any wyght wel ferde,
> That lovere was, whan he it wiste or herde.
>
> For soth to seyn, he lost held every wyght
> But if he were in loves heigh servise,
> I mene folk that oughte it ben of right.
> And over al this, so wel koude he devyse
> Of sentement, and in so unkouth wise
> Al his array, that every lovere thoughte,
> That al was wel what so he seyde or wroughte.
>
> And though that he be come of blood roial,
> Hym liste of pride at no wight for to chace;
> Benigne he was to ech in general,
> For which he gat hym thank in every place.
> Thus wolde Love, yheried be his grace!
> That pride, envye, ire, and avarice
> He gan to fle, and everich other vice. (III, 1786–1806)

This tribute I find hard to discount, even by maligning the narrator-
persona.

In the next book Criseyde praises him, the fifth in our series of
tributes:

> For trusteth wel, that youre estat roial,
> Ne veyn delit, nor only worthinesse
> Of yow in werre or torney marcial,
> Ne pompe, array, nobleye, or ek richesse,
> Ne made me to rewe on youre destresse;
> But moral vertu, grounded upon trouthe,
> That was the cause I first hadde on yow routhe.
>
> Ek gentil herte and manhod that ye hadde,
> And that ye hadde, as me thought, in despit
> Every thyng that souned into badde,
> As rudenesse and poeplissh appetit,
> And that youre resoun bridlede youre delit,—
> This made, aboven any creature,
> That I was youre, and shal, whil I may dure. (IV, 1667–80)

Perhaps there is some dramatic irony here, since we know the outcome, and Criseyde's next lines are ominous:

> And this may lengthe of yeres naught fordo,
> Ne remuable Fortune deface. (IV, 1681–82)

Yet though Criseyde is seizing courage in the dark from her praise of
her noble lover, that praise leaves plentiful non-ironic residue. If
Chaucer here means us to take Troilus as a mere vessel of concupiscence, praised by the hypocritical and self-deluded Pandarus and
Criseyde and idiot narrator, he has failed as an artist.

There is no Augustinian obscurity in the praise of Troilus in the
last book. First we have the sixth tribute, the formal portrait borrowed
from Joseph of Exeter to give epic proportions to Troilus, Criseyde,
and Diomede in the sad time of their conflict. Chaucer's known
partiality assigns three stanzas to Criseyde, one to Diomede, and two
to Troilus:

> And Troilus wel woxen was in highte,
> And complet formed by proporcioun
> So wel that kynde it nought amenden myghte;
> Yong, fressch, strong, and hardy as lyoun;
> Trewe as steel in ech condicioun;
> Oon of the beste entecched creature,
> That is, or shal, whil that the world may dure.

> And certeynly in storye it is yfounde,
> That Troilus was nevere unto no wight,
> As in his tyme, in no degree secounde
> In duryng don that longeth to a knyght.
> Al myghte a geant passen hym of myght,
> His herte ay with the firste and with the beste
> Stood paregal, to durre don that hym leste. (V, 827–40)

Thus we are prepared for the finest tribute of all, that which allows
Troilus in death to envision a broader kind of charity than that which
is possible on earth, where he can hold

> al vanite
> To respect of the pleyn felicite
> That is in hevene above. . . . (V, 1817–19)

a felicity which nevertheless resembles in many ways the joy of Book
III, the human love which is not divine love but which is its simula-
crum. Of the ambiguities of this extraordinary epilogue I have
spoken at length elsewhere.[4] Chaucer is Christian enough to avoid

the dilemma of bringing Troilus, a pagan, to heaven, and Mercury no doubt could not have led him anywhere beyond Limbo, though the infernal and heavenly geography is intentionally left unclear. Though the epilogue brings us to a deeper knowledge of love and of the human condition, it in no way detracts from the moral stature of Troilus, a hero tragic enough, but therefore endowed with tragic vision, and with enough of Christian charity to be a righteous heathen of the kind which profoundly interested Langland, the *Pearl*-poet, and Chaucer.

To test our no doubt distorted modern views on so touchy a theological question we have a long-printed but much-neglected poem which its editor calls *The Sixtene Poyntis of Charite*, and prints from the text of MS Lambeth 853.[5] Brown and Robbins (2040) list another copy in MS Cambridge Univ. Library Ii. 6. 39 (f. 157r), the first three stanzas only, which I use for this paper, itself a tribute to our major guide to Middle English poetry, Rossell Hope Robbins.[6] Here our interest is only in its application to Troilus.

The two opening stanzas urge Man to consider the hereafter, and to act with charity that he may see the Blessed Face. God revealed these points of charity to St Paul in the third heaven, so that man could learn a just life:[7]

> Man among thi mirþe: þis haue in mynde
> Whennes þou cam and weder þou tendis.
> how felly þou fallist and filist thi kynde.
> Arise and make of mys amendis.
> þat þou mai here whan þou wendis.
> ouȝt of þis world þi god to see:
> Welkome my seruaunt þat þou me sendis:
> Mi chosen childe in charite
>
> þe litest lesson þat man may lere.
> wel to leue ȝif þou wolt loke.
> ȝif þou haue hap to holde and her:
> is primli printid in poulis boke
> god to poule þis lesson tooke.
> in þe þridde heuene on hiȝe
> Euery man to kunne and loke.
> þe propre partes of charite

Then follow two stanzas which paraphrase St Paul's resounding introduction to I Corinthians xiii:

> þowȝ I speke seiþ seint poule
> as aungel and with mannes tunge
> and haue not charite in my soule

I ham a brasen symbol sunge
þow priuy prophecie of me be sprunge
and mounteynes meue be feiþ of me
I ham not worþ to gon as longe
as me wantiþ charite   [End of Cambridge text]

Thou3 y to poore men 3eue al my good,   [Lambeth text]
And my bodi to brenne þere hoot fier ys,
And charite be not in my mood,
If profiteþ me not to heuen blis.'
But for god wolde it schulde not mys
To knowe in charite whanne we be,
He tau3te poul to teche al his
The .xvj. Poyntis of charite.

The numbered points follow, formularized in true medieval fashion. We shall take them up one by one, and see how they correspond to Chaucer's or his characters' words about Troilus.

> 1. 'Charite,' he seiþ, 'is pacient,
> Alle disesis meekli suffringe. . . .

No lover could be wholly patient, but Troilus promises Criseyde before she grants him the final favours:

> And I to ben youre verray, humble, trewe,
> Secret, and in my peynes pacient. . . .
> Lo, this mene I, myn owen swete herte. (III, 141–147)

At a very different time, in his letter after they are parted and she has missed the day of rendezvous, he perseveres in the virtue:

> For though to me youre absence is an helle,
> With pacience I wol my wo comporte. (V, 1396–7)

This is the language of courtly love rather than that of St Paul, but surely Troilus' own patience in wordly matters is no bar to his understanding of the same virtue on the cosmic level, when he learns of Christ's true meekness (V, 1847). It may well be that one lesson of *Troilus and Criseyde* is that transient human love can lead to the permanent love of God.

> 2. Benigne also in hir entent,
> Kindelid with fier of good lyuyng. . . .

In Chaucer's poem the word *benign* is generally applied to a divinity: to God by Chaucer (I. 40), to the God of Love by Troilus (I. 431), to Venus by Chaucer (III, 39), to Charity (III, 1261) and to his lady

(III, 1285) by Troilus, the last a clear case of the religion of love. The mystic "fier of good lyuyng" cannot be verbally located in Chaucer, but what we have called the fifth tribute to Troilus, including the hymn to Love at the end of Book III, is its secular counterpart. Despite his royal rank, which might have led him to the kind of pride which he did manifest before he was struck by Cupid's arrow, "Benigne he was to ech in general, For which he gat hym thank in every place" (III, 1802–3).

> 3. Neuere enuyose for ony þing
> To freend ne foo, wheþir it be,
> But euere glad to goddis pleing
> To cherische alle men in charitee.

Envy was one of the sins erased from Troilus' soul after the consummation (III, 1805). The lover's special envy, jealousy, is remarkably absent from the heart of this true blue lover. Horaste is but a fictitious rival inserted into the wooing by Pandarus (III, 796–812); when the real rival Diomede brings on jealousy, Troilus does not manifest an irascible spirit, but one of endurance, even despair:

> Therewith the wikked spirit, god us blesse,
> Which that men clepeth woode jalousie,
> Gan in hym crepe, in al his hevynesse;
> For which, by cause he wolde soone dye,
> He ne et ne drank, for his malencolye.
> And ek from every compaignye he fledde;
> This was the lif that al the tyme he ledde. (V, 1212–18)

Such a state precedes his dream, interpreted vainly by Cassandra, of the boar who was Diomede; Troilus rejects the interpretation as long as he possibly can. Though Criseyde uses the dread term of jealousy to him again and again in the Horaste episode (III, 837, 987, 1010, 1024, 1030), Troilus himself is an innocent lamb without gall, a man who resists envy and jealousy until the very last.

> 4. Charite dooþ neuere wickidli
> Bi purpos of wil, ne wickid dede, . . .

As the Authorized Version has it, charity "vaunteth not itself." After his youthful scorning folly, Troilus is the most modest of men; he is no boasting fellow who takes pride in his possessions, his rank, or his love; as a courtly lover he is the acme of secrecy. "Wickedness" is left to the "wicked tongues" who harass the lover, the demons of the code (I, 39, 1004; II, 785, 808, 837; V, 755, 1610). Criseyde speaks of "that wikked wyvere," jealousy (III, 1010; see V, 1212); and we have absolved Troilus of that in point three. Pandarus adapts the language of morality to that of courtly love:

> I thenke, sith that Love of his goodnesse
> Hath the converted out of wikkednesse,
> That thow shalt ben the beste post, I leve,
> Of alle his lay, and moste his foos greve. (I, 998–1001)

Troilus is no impossible prig, a paragon of all the virtues, and Chaucer seems to reserve the term of Cupid's Saints to the women of whom he tells the legends. His hero is truly rounded; he had been a proud scorner of love before his conversion, and jealousy, though held off as long as man can bear, did come to him in the final episodes of the poem, when there can be no doubt of Criseyde's infidelity. But if he was converted from his pride at the beginning of the poem, so is he finally provided with the vision which allows a second conversion or anagnorisis, though one which tragically cannot assure heaven to a pagan.

> 5. Ne blowen is with pride þouȝ sche be welþi,
> For to greue god is hir moost drede;
> For in helle depe schal be her meede,
> A low wiþ lucifir for to be
> þat for blynde pride wole take noon hede
> lowli to lyue in charite.

Charity "is not puffed up." Though Troilus had once been as proud as a peacock or a stallion feeling his oats (I, 210, 213, 218, 225, 230), pride is one of the first of his sins to go (III, 1805). Chaucer has brilliantly dramatized his role as a humble lover in the scene where Criseyde is brought by Pandarus to his bedside at Deiphebus's house. He tries to rise and kneel to his lady, and she embarrasses him by praying him for lordship and protection, for feudal aid:

> This Troilus, that herde his lady preye
> Of lordshipe hym, wex neither quyk ne dede,
> Ne myghte o word for shame to it seye,
> Although men sholde smyten of his hede;
> But, lord, so he wexeth sodeynliche rede,
> And, sire, his lessoun that he wende konne,
> To preyen hire, was thorugh his wit ironne. (III, 78–84)

His humility is no pose, no dissembling; he has abandoned the lesson Pandarus had taught him, and the roles of suitor are immediately reversed, with Troilus now the one making obeisance.

6. Charite is not coueitose toold
   Of worschipe ne of wronge wynnynge,
   For wiþ ypocritis sche may not holde,
   Ne consente with wrong getyng.

Avarice is another sin eschewed by Troilus after the consummation
(III, 1805). His foil is Calchas, Criseyde's inadequate father and an
antihero whose place in Criseyde's heart is taken by Troilus; Calchas
is the acme of avarice, since he has betrayed the Trojans for gain, and
Criseyde hopes to use this trait in gaining his permission to return to
Troy (IV, 1378, 1399). "Coueitose . . . Of worschipe" is of course
pride; of this Troilus already stands absolved. Another foil to Troilus
is Diomede, who may well be called a courtly hypocrite, a gallant
interested only in love as a leisure sport.

7. Sche sechiþ not hir owne þing
   For hindringe of neiȝboris þat myȝte be,
   For manye perels ben in pletynge
   þat acorden not with charitee.

The expansion of Paul's "seeketh not her own" by "thing" suggests
that the anonymous poet saw this vice in terms of the ubiquitous
medieval habit of litigation. As Calchas is a foil to Troilus' lack of
avarice, and Diomede a foil to his lack of hypocrisy, so Pandarus'
Poliphete with his patriotic loyalty suit is a foil to the charity which
loves her neighbour as herself (III, 1468–9). One can scarcely imagine
the sensitive nobleman Troilus engaged in a lawsuit; that is for
merchants and usurers, the enemies of aristocracy and *noblesse oblige*;
he is a man charitable to all lovers (III, 1791–1803) and to all mankind.

8. Charite wole no thing be wrooþ
   For harmes þat hir silf may hent,
   But for to synne, al oonli is hir looþ,
   Ayens goddis comaundement.

Ire is the fourth of the sins which Troilus abandoned (III, 1805);
even in the last wasteland of the book he "is not easily provoked,"
though of course he is a warrior and would appear therefore wrathful
to a non-militant cleric. Some provocation seems to have been acceptable; Chaucer's Parson, generally discreet and benign to sinners,
when he met an obstinate sinner "Hym wolde he snybben sharply
for the nonys" (*Canterbury Tales*, I, 515–23). The lion in battle (I,
1074; V, 830) was gentle enough in ordinary life; this contrast is
indeed the very nature of the gentleman. With Diomede he slips (V,
1800, 1751–64); but is not Diomede an obstinate sinner in love?

>   9. Charitee þenkiþ noon yuel in hir entent,
>   But stintiþ strijf, and stoondiþ free;
>   Al yuel wil, it wolde were went,
>   And chaungid al for charite.

This aspect of charity is Troilus the gentle wight, "and ek the moste fre" of Troilus in his first conversion (I, 1080). Between him and Criseyde there is no strife, and even after she has betrayed him his forebearance is heroic. To Pandarus he remains "The good, wise, worthi, fressh, and free." The word *free* is the special epithet of the nobleman, who is both generous and no bondsman, and thus it fits both Troilus and Paul's Charity.

>   10. Of wickidnes charite is not glad,
>   Bi lauȝter ne bi no likinge,
>   But euere sobre, soft, and sad,
>   In þouȝt, in word, and in worching.

Charity, which "rejoiceth not in iniquity," loves not wickedness, and has a serious view of life. Troilus never takes his love lightly, and there would not be the saving grace of humour in the poem if it were not for Pandarus, whom some call of the devil's party. Only when he views the earth from the eighth sphere does Troilus' laughter ring out at human folly and delusion; on earth both as lover and as warrior he retains his sober dignity. Even when elated by the news of possible success in love does he accept Pandarus' promise of aid "With sobre chere, although his herte pleyde" (I, 1013–14). Latcr, on his return from battle, when Criseyde sees him through her window and falls in love with him, he blushes at the plaudits of the people (II, 645; compare III, 453–4; V, 81–2):

>   That to byholde it was a noble game,
>   And sobreliche he caste adoun his eyen. (II, 647–48)

Constant are the softness and gentility of his words (IV, 540; V, 83). For some reason "sad," Chaucer's common synonym for "sober," is absent from the *Troilus*.

>   11. To riȝt and trouþe is her ioiyng,
>   To maynteine truþe where-euere sche be,
>   With feiþful and true folk Is hir dwelling,
>   For suche ben chosen in charite.

Criseyde's lack of truth is matched only by Troilus' fidelity; "true Troilus" is a proverbial phrase (II, 1082; III, 133, 992, 1229, 1297; IV, 1672; V, 1961). In her finest tribute Criseyde speaks of his "moral vertu, grounded upon trouthe" (IV, 1672).

12. Alle þingis sche beriþ vp meekeli,
    For al hir wronge schal turne to game;
    Sche falliþ not vnder for vilonye,
    For los, for sijknes, ne for schame.

Troilus is not only the epitome of truth, but his endurance (point six) we have already seen is likewise proverbial (I, 682, 785; II, 1645; III, 1043, 1491; IV, 1330; V, 48, 239). For impatient modernity he endures almost too much, but St Paul and Troilus' fellow courtiers would commend him.

13. Alle þingis sche trowiþ wiþ-out fame
    Þhat goddis lawe techiþ truþe to be,
    And bidiþ þerbi for ony blame,
    For suche ben children of charitee.

The truth of point eleven and faith are closely allied. In Pandarus' courtly parody of Christ's Church he says to Troilus "Thow shalt be saved by thi feyth in trouthe!" (II, 1503); only in the epilogue does he come upon a glimpse of Christian faith. Once more the fickle Criseyde is the antitype.

14. Alle þingis sche hopiþ to haue in blis;
    For suche sche suffriþ and serueþ heere;
    For of mercy sche may not mys
    þat þis lessoun wole loue and lere.

Though Troilus loses his long-established courtly hope in the dust and ashes of Book V, Troilus catches a glimpse once more of the Christian virtue in the epilogue, and this may be one reason for Chaucer's ambiguity about the place where Mercury "sorted hym to dwelle." The term often fits the lover: "But now of hope the kalendes biginne" (II, 7; see II, 1307, 1323, 1333, 1340; III, 426: V, 685); at times it is a false hope which blinds him (V, 1195). "Mercy" is the constant word of the lover to his lady: "Mercy, Emilye" were the last words of Arcite as he died (CT I, 2808), and the first words of Troilus as Criseyde lays her soft hands on him are "Mercy, mercy, swete herte!" (III, 98; see I, 585; II, 655; III, 1173, 1356, 1382; V, 168). Though Chaucer clearly knew that the grace and mercy of the courtly mistress were not the same as that of Christ (V, 1867-8, 1861), he also saw the similarity, and his use of the term was not parodic, but sober enough.

15. Sche abidiþ alle þingis with good chere
    þou3 sche þinke longe þe eende to se,
    For of reward sche haþ no were
    þat þus abidiþ in charite.

Endurance once more, aligned to Troilus' courtly hope and faith. In this context "were" means "doubt," and Charity has no doubt of reward in heaven, as Troilus at the height of his love has no doubt of reward on earth.

> 16. Charite falliþ neuere a-way
>   From him þat it in charite wole holde,
>   Bifore ne aftir domys day,
>   But encresiþ in blis an hundrid folde.
>   Whanne al tresour is tried and tolde,
>   Al help to blis is in þese þre,
>   Feiþ, hope, and charite, noþing colde;
>   Þe mooste of hem is charite.'

St Paul's stunning rhetorical climax with charity and its companion virtues fits Troilus like a metaphorical glove. The lover's pattern of development, from pride to sorrow and slow rise of faith and hope and love and noble qualities in the first book, his journey to bliss and ecstasy and even greater nobility in the second and third books, the setback and renewed hope in the fourth book, and the hope against hope in the fifth, with the discovery of a whole new law of faith, hope and love in the epilogue is a courtly paradigm of Pauline optimism. The poet goes on to expound the Pauline message:

> Bi charite, man, þou must loue more
> God þan silf, þe sooþ to say,
> For þis is þe lord-is owne lore,
> With al þi power him please and pay;
> Thi neiȝbore also, wiþ-oute nay,
> Loue as þi silf saaf to bee;
> To freend and fo holde faste þi fay,
> And chaunge þou neuere fro charite.
>
> If we þis lessoun we loue and leere,
> And take it truli to oure entent,
> We schulen haue knowinge good and cleere
> Who ben blamelees and who ben schent.
> God, þat hast us oure lijf lent,
> Graunte þat we may oure silf to enserche and se,
> As þou for us on roode were rent,
> þou chese us to þee for charite.

From Paul's sublimity we have moved down to good parish counsel, and to something of the modern view that charity is essentially good works and kindness to one's neighbour. Searching ourselves is good religion and good psychology, a task which Troilus in the end can be said to have accomplished. Searching him from the outside we find him the most virtuous of pagans and of Love's worshippers. Chaucer has not limited him to the rather forbidding classical virtues: Temperance, Fortitude, Prudence, and Justice; he has given him as much of Christian faith, hope, and charity as a noble pagan lover could receive.

Some have called all this a parody of Christianity; I should rather call it a poet's metaphorical tribute to the human love which is so much like divine love that it has often, as in the case of Mary Magdalene, led to divine love. What we have been doing, of course, is a *tour de force*, for the poem we are paralleling to *Troilus and Criseyde* was written half a century later, and it can be neither a derivative or a source. We all know that charity beyond Paul in the Middle Ages became a vastly complex matter, as Kaske shows it to be in *Piers Plowman*.[8] Augustine, discussing faith, hope, and charity, makes it plain enough that a love like that of Troilus for Criseyde is not the same as his view of Charity:

> Between temporal and eternal things there is this difference: a temporal thing is loved more before we have it, and it begins to grow worthless when we gain it, for it does not satisfy the soul, whose true and certain rest is eternity; but the eternal is more ardently loved when it is acquired than when it is merely desired.[9]

Or as Eliot puts it, "the torment of love unsatisfied, the greater torment of love satisfied." Yet do all those virtues of Troilus go for nought; is there no residue from them even after we have discounted all the wordly motives? In a little-known picture ascribed to Hieronymus Bosch the world contains a circle of the Seven Deadly Sins, with the lovers who are Lust on a high summit in the middle of the picture, clearly the worldly *summum bonum*. In the central axis beneath the lovers is a monk helping a fallen wayfarer, a symbol of charity to one's neighbours, and just above the lovers is Christ on the Cross.[10] The three actions are not the same, but are they not related? Would Troilus have come to his final vision if he had not experienced another kind of ecstasy?

OHIO STATE UNIVERSITY

NOTES

1 Richard Blackmur, *Anni Mirabiles 1921–1925: Reason in the Madness of Letters* (Washington, D. C.: Library of Congress, 1956), p. 50.

2 See, for instance, Alfred David, "The Hero of the *Troilus*," *Spec.*, 37 (1962), pp. 566–81.

3 Because of its variant readings I have used Robert Kilbourn Root's *The Book of Troilus and Criseyde*, by Geoffrey Chaucer (Princeton: Princeton Univ. Press, 1926), for the text cited. Other references are to F. N. Robinson (ed.), *The Complete Works of Geoffrey Chaucer*, 2nd edn (Boston: Houghton Mifflin, 1957).

4 "Stylistic Ambivalences in Chaucer, Yeats, and Lucretius—The Cresting Wave and its Undertow," *The University Review*, 35 (March, 1971), pp. 174–98.

5 Frederick J. Furnivall (ed.), *Hymns to the Virgin and Christ*, EETS, OS 24 (1867), pp. 114–17.

6 Carleton Brown and Rossell Hope Robbins. *The Index of Middle English Verse* (New York: Columbia Univ. Press, 1943) and Rossell Hope Robbins and John L. Cutler, *Supplement to the Index of Middle English Verse* (Lexington, Ky.: Univ. of Kentucky Press, 1965), No. 2040; see Carleton Brown, *A Register of Middle English Religious and Didactic Verse* (Oxford: Bibliographical Soc., 1916), I. pp. 442–4. There are no additions in Robbins and Cutler. Brown and Robbins list several related poems: a sixteen points of charity (593) and a fifteen points (3558); a number of short admonitions to charity (696, 740, 2060, 686); a counsel for alms-giving (4211); a long poem with the theme that God is charity (678); a poem on the abuses of the times which laments the loss of charity (4157), and a Treatise on Charity, Purity, and Hope (1093). Robbins and Cutler provide further information on 3558, and add 593.5, another abuses poem, and 1218.8 on almsgiving. Several of these are unpublished.

7 The basis of the poem is I Corinthians xiii, but in II Corinthians xii, 1–4 Paul speaks obliquely of being caught up to the third heaven. See Saint Gregory the Great, *Dialogues*, tr. Odo John Zimmerman (New York: Fathers of the Church, 1959), p. 147 (Dialogue Three), and Theodore Silverstein, *Visio Sancti Pauli* (London: Christophers, 1935).

8 R. E. Kaske, "'*Ex vi transicionis*' and Its Passage in *Piers Plowman*," in Robert J. Blanch (ed.), *Style and Symbolism in Piers Plowman* (Knoxville: Univ. of Tennessee Press, 1969), pp. 228–33. St Paul might reach a wider audience.

9 Saint Augustine, *On Christian Doctrine*, tr. D. W. Robertson, Jr. (Indianapolis: Bobbs-Merrill, 1958), p. 32.

10 Howard Daniel, *Hieronymus Bosch* (New York: Hyperion Press, 1947), p. 9 (not the Prado Sins, but a picture in the possession then of Tomas Harris, London). See F. L. Utley, "The Seven Deadly Sins—Then and Now," to appear in the May 1972 issue of *Indiana Social Studies Quarterly*.

23

CRESSEID'S DREAM
AND HENRYSON'S *TESTAMENT*

BY RALPH HANNA III

In terms of stylistic dexterity and thematic originality, few fifteenth-century poems can be compared with Robert Henryson's *Testament of Cresseid*. Yet because of its attractiveness and very obvious indebtedness to Chaucer's *Troilus and Criseyde*, this poem has always proved vexing to literary historians. For many readers, Henryson's creation proves most wanting in precisely those areas where Chaucer's is most impressive—the sympathetic response to the amatory experience created by Chaucer's manipulation of narrative point of view. In contrast, Henryson apparently depicts a world where planetary gods can harshly reward the heroine with a shameful death because of her blasphemy, a world where disease and suffering appear to be common.[1]

The disparity between the two poems has seemed so great that many critics would deny that Henryson merits the honorific epithet "Chaucerian." But the issues which emerge in reading past criticism of the *Testament* recall problems of the "sentence" of Chaucer's *Troilus* about the nature of human judgement. The critical debate over the interrelationship between heavenly and earthly judgements in Henryson's source surely is reflected in the central question asked by most critics of the *Testament*: Does Cresseid receive a just sentence and punishment for blaspheming Venus and Cupid? Depending upon the disposition of the critic in question, the answer to this question has usually been pushed toward an interpretation of the poem as an attack on or a defense of the justice of Henryson's cosmos.

Crucial to this understanding of the *Testament* as a cosmic drama is interpretation of Cresseid's dream, where the heroine is described receiving the punishment of disease and disfigurement. Here, past critics have found most to cavil about, for Cresseid is treated with what appears to be extreme vindictiveness. In stark contrast to Chaucer's ultimate refusal to judge his heroine, Cresseid's career in Henryson's poem begins with the most devastating of sentences: licensed destruction of the heroine.

288

But it should be pointed out that thematic similarities may exist only at the expense of distorting Henryson's more pervasive "Chaucerianism." The cosmic interpretations of the *Testament* ultimately depend on taking Cresseid's dream at face value. But since Henryson's knowledge of Chaucer's poetry is so obviously detailed, it seems unlikely that he could be unaware of Macrobian and Boethian *topoi* about the nature of dreams. In the light of these opinions, I find it difficult to view Cresseid's dream quite so uncritically as it has been in the past. And I would further suggest that, if the dream is viewed simply as a sleeping vision, the reader becomes aware of various clearly Chaucerian aspects of the narrative handling.

Cresseid's dream presents the heroine's disease as the result of action by the pagan gods in their planetary aspects; critics have implicitly assumed that the planets are to be treated as aspects of astrological government or ordering of the universe. Thus, Cresseid's fate is based upon a consensus judgement on her actions by universal powers. Such an interpretation rests on at least two assumptions about Cresseid's dream which require close examination. On the one hand, some critics assume that Cresseid's dream is scarcely a dream in any literal sense; they discuss this section of the poem as a straight-forward narrative which gives a definitive account of the causes for Cresseid's sickness and eventual death. A second group of critics sees the dream as less than literal truth, but implicitly suggests that because the actions of the dream seem to impinge on living reality the dream must be prophetic. As a corollary to this argument, they claim that because the dream is prophetic it somehow accounts in causal terms for Cresseid's sickness.[2]

The first of these arguments, that Cresseid is literally visited by the planets, may be dispensed with briefly, I think. Two passages are important in this regard:

> Quhen this was said, doun in ane extasie,
> Rauischit in spreit, intill ane dreame scho fell,
> And be apperance hard, quhair scho did ly,
> Cupide the king ringand ane siluer bell,
> Quhilk men micht heir fra heuin vnto hell . . .
>
> . . . . . .
> This doolie dreame, this vglye visioun
> Brocht to ane end, Cresseid fra it awoik. (141–5, 344–5)[3]

In both passages, Henryson is absolutely clear that what befalls his heroine is not waking reality, or in any sense a literal sequence of physical events. The word "dreame" appears at both the beginning and end of the event, on its second occurrence coupled with "visioun."

Further, the introduction to the dream precisely defines the heroine's state. Although the words "extasie" and "rauischit" may have slight overtones of mystical experiences, their primary reference here is almost surely physical. Together the words suggest physical collapse, a collapse brought on by heightened emotional confusion.[4] Our modern idiom "worried out of her mind" would be descriptive here, for Cresseid is no longer able to cope with the world rationally. This insistence upon her mental state is picked up forcefully in Henryson's striking mixed metaphor, "be apperance hard"; the noun, commonly used to describe magical "transmutations" of everyday reality, suggests definitively that what Cresseid will experience in the dream is not substance but only seeming. When Henryson returns to the verb "heir" in line 145, it is only to suggest that the dream has, from this moment, become an objective piece of reality for Cresseid.[5] But it is nonetheless still dream.

Critics who read the dream as literal narrative have probably been misled by certain aspects of Henryson's presentation. Within the dream, for example, the narrator intrudes abruptly to excoriate Saturn for the harshness of his judgement on the heroine (323-9). And at the end of the dream:

> . . . rais scho vp and tuik
> Ane poleist glas, and hir schaddow culd luik;
> And quhen scho saw hir face sa deformait,
> Gif scho in hart was wa aneuch, God wait!

> Weiping full sair, "Lo, quhat it is," quod sche,
> "With fraward langage for to mufe and steir
> Our craibit goddis . . ."   (347-53)

It seems to me overly credulous to base an interpretation of the heroine's state at this point solely on what she tells us about her situation and what the narrator tells us about it. That Cresseid herself is the first to draw the causal connection between the dream and her diseased situation should make one immediately suspicious. And one should be doubly suspicious when the narrator, whose major joy in the first half of the poem is protecting his heroine from any critical comment, strives to make her appear to us once more as a poor lonely woman put upon by forces outside her control. In fact, the narrator is merely playing the old Chaucerian game of protesting against received "auctorite" when it pleases him to do so; and Cresseid is playing the even older game of self-deception, refusing rather stead-fastly to see that responsibility for her fate may rest in herself and no-where else. These passages provide interpretations of Cresseid's experience which the reader must judge; Henryson does not intend to have them taken as statements about the existence of the pagan gods as actual actors in the story.

Even if Cresseid sees the pagan gods only within a dream, the possibility still remains that the dream, in coming true, has been somehow prophetic, and that it has described the causal mechanism by which Cresseid has succumbed to leprosy. To assess this possibility one should turn to the fount of most medieval dream lore, Macrobius' Commentary on the *Somnium Scipionis*. In Book I, Chapter III, Macrobius uses various principles of classification to distinguish five different varieties of dream.[6] For my purposes, the most relevant classification advanced is the distinction between dreams which may be used for divination or prophecy and those which are valueless in that regard. If Cresseid's dream is presented in terms which echo Macrobius' descriptions of prophetic visions, then one may reasonably expect that the action of the gods in the dream somehow shadows forth actions outside it, if not suggesting the causal structure behind these actions. If, however, Cresseid's dream is described in terms suggestive of Macrobius' non-prophetic dream-types, certain critical assumptions about the poem will have to be re-evaluated.

Macrobius describes the most frequent of the non-prophetic types, the *insomnium*, ἐνύπνιον, or nightmare, in these terms:

> *Est enim ἐνύπνιον quotiens cura oppressi animi corporisve sive fortunae, qualis vigilantem fatigaverat, talem se ingerit dormienti: animi, si amator deliciis suis aut fruentem se videat aut carentem, si metuens quis imminentem sibi vel insidiis vel potestate personam aut incurrisse hanc ex imagine cogitationum suaram aut effugisse videatur: corporis, si temeto ingurgitatus aut distentus cibo vel abundantia praefocari se aestimet vel gravantibus exonerari, aut contra si esuriens cibum aut potum sitiens desiderare, quarerere, vel etiam invenisse videatur: fortunae cum se quis aestimat vel potentia vel magistratu aut augeri pro desiderio aut exui pro timore.*[7]

Macrobius wishes to limit those dreams which are worth interpretation for purposes of foretelling the future. Dreams which arise as the result of definable natural phenomena have no value so far as the future is concerned; both a clear mind and a healthy body are necessary to receive a divinely sent forecast of future events.

The information which Henryson provides about Cresseid's state immediately before her dream shows that he intends the reader to recognize the appearance of the gods as part of an *insomnium*. Most particularly Macrobius' insistence on both *cura oppressi animi* and *cura fortunae* seems applicable to the dramatic situation. The detailed account of Cresseid's retirement to her father's temple is designed to present a preoccupied woman, one who carries her waking resentments into her sleep.

Cresseid has, of course, much to worry about, although, from the reader's point of view, her complaints often appear trivial. She is introduced by Henryson as an absolute paragon of beauty and grace; but so far as Cresseid is concerned, beauty resides primarily in use. It is valueless without masculine accompaniment, lovers who admire, adore, pay tribute to it. In her complaint against Venus she asks: "Quha sall me gyde? Quha sall me now conuoy?" (131); the only satisfactory experience Cresseid can visualize is one where she is an object of attention, where arrangements are ceaselessly made for her.

Cresseid's failure to find suitable masculine accompaniment limits her consciousness at this point in the poem. The heroine's utter loneliness, her inability to perform any act on her own behalf is recurrently suggested by the language of the poem. Without any masculine admirers, Cresseid is "desolait" (76), "destitute" (92), and "all forlane" (140). Being equipped by her creator for only one role, the lady who is loved, and being denied any opportunity to use that role, she goes to her father seeking the "comfort and consolatioun" (93) which experience has denied her.

Because Cresseid expects somehow to be accommodated by willing male admirers, she is incapable of facing the future directly. But her furtiveness and secrecy, in part a reflection of her belated interest in reputation, must be understood primarily as a mixture of injured pride and worry over where the next suitor will come from. She "disagysit passi[s]" (95) to her father's house, and she will make no appearance in the temple on the festival day for fear of revealing "hir expuls fra Diomeid the king" (119). Lest we need any further confirmation of her preoccupied state of mind, Henryson underscores it for us by implicitly comparing her with those who enjoy the feast of Apollo and Venus:

> . . . the pepill far and neir
> Befoir the none vnto the tempill went
> With sacrifice, deuoit in thair maneir;
> Bot still Cresseid, heuie in hir intent
> Into the kirk wald not hirself present.   (113–17)

For the worshippers, Henryson implies, a "deuoit *maneir*" is enough; whatever troubles may exist outside the religious context may be expelled for a time by the act of devotion. For Cresseid, unable to escape her sense of loss, no such detachment is possible.[8]

This careful, repeated insistence on Cresseid's dramatic situation is concluded by the spiteful complaint which the heroine makes before falling asleep. In her attack on the patrons of her shelter, Cresseid is oppressed by the prospect of decay and transience. Her sense of lost love is directly linked with the loss of beauty, the force which earlier made her "the flour and A per se/ Of Troy and Grece" (78–9). Against this background of frustration and worry about the possibility of continuing in the future, Henryson gives us the dream in which Cresseid's beauty is described as being wasted.

Clearly this careful and insistent attention to Cresseid's state is designed to have some impression on the reader. And at least one impression one should gain is that Cresseid is in no mental condition for a prophetic dream. Her condition resembles those dreamers of *insomnia* whom Chaucer describes in the *Parlement of Foules*:

> The wery huntere, slepynge in his bed,
> To wode ayeyn his mynde goth anon;
> The juge dremeth how his plees been sped;
> The cartere dremeth how his cartes gon;
> The riche, of gold; the knyght fyght with his fon;
> The syke met he drynketh of the tonne;
> The lovere met he hath his lady wonne.   (99–105)[9]

Cresseid's final thoughts before sleep are of the gods and their injustice, and these same thoughts fill her slumber. Although she resembles Macrobius' examples of *"cura oppressi animi"* and *"cura fortunae,"* her dream lacks the specific object Macrobius notes in his examples. Cresseid is interested in the male, not a single particular man, but the substance of the dream shows her clearly as *"amator deliciis suis . . . carens."* Of such dreams Macrobius comments, *"ultima ex his duo cum videntur, cura interpretationis indigna sunt, quia nihil divinationis adportant, ἐνύπνιον dico et φάντασμα."*

Yet it is necessary to face one further problem: the Macrobian dream-types are not mutually exclusive, and seem capable of appearing in combinations.[10] Thus Macrobius describes the dream of Scipio: *"Hoc ergo quod Scipio vidisse se rettulit et tria illa quae sola probabilia sunt genera principalitatis amplectitur."* Besides its clear relation to the *insomnium*, Cresseid's dream seems to reflect qualities of two prophetic varieties:

> *Et est oraculum quidem cum in somnis parens vel alia sancta gravisve persona seu sacerdos vel etiam deus aperte eventurum quid aut non eventurum, faciendum vitandumve denuntiat. Visio est autem cum id quis videt quod eodem modo quo apparuerat eveniet.*[11]

The appearance of the gods would seem to connect the dream with the *oraculum*, and the immediate discovery of leprosy would suggest that the prophecy is true, and the dream thus a *visio*.

This combination of two divergent dream types—the worthless *insomnium* and the prophetic *oraculum* or *visio*—creates some severe problems in interpretation. First, the dream clearly docs not fulfil all the criteria Macrobius establishes for the *oraculum*. Although Cresseid sees the planetary gods, they cannot be said to provide her with anything like the oracular knowledge which Macrobius suggests defines that type of dream. Cresseid is given quite direct information about *"eventurum quid aut non eventurum,"* but her dream does not *"faciendum vitandumve denuntiat."* She is offered no salutary advice about regulating her future action; indeed, within the context of the poem, evasion of her fate seems impossible. The discovery of her disease immediately upon waking suggests that no action on her part can undo the harsh necessity imposed by her accusers and judges.

Yet this same sense of necessity also typifies Cresseid's waking view of her state and is linked closely with the *insomnium* attributes of the dream. Cresseid's distinct inability to cope with her situation is powerfully and effectively mirrored within the dream. She sees herself as an absolutely passive figure, prone and senseless, in the power of baneful forces over which she has no control. As the dream progresses, the gods become more and more clearly vindictive; they destroy her beauty and grace, the major supports of her previous life style. By this action, the charge of malignity which Cresseid has made before falling asleep apparently becomes proven within her dream, and her suggestion that she has no active volition, no real responsibility for her fate, is depicted with great intensity.

But this sense of an utter necessity operating within the dream and thus influencing the reality outside it seems to violate certain canons of accepted dream lore. Before assuming that the actions within the dream are somehow directly responsible for the heroine's disfigurement, one should enquire further. The discussion of such matters in the Middle Ages is exceedingly complicated, inasmuch as problems of causality raise the question of man's freedom in the face of prior knowledge. In this regard, the prophetic dream probably should be looked upon just as any other prophecy. The material communicated by dream or prophecy is monitory, and the recipient of the prophecy bears full responsibility for the outcome of his actions. That assiduous collector of commonplaces, Vincent of Beauvais, in his discussion of revelations suggests such a point of view:

Dicimus ergo philosophis consentiendo: quod somnia non eueniunt de necessitate siue sint cause siue signa siue incursus futurorum accidentalis. At uero somnium Pharaonis et Nabuchodonosor et Danielis fuerunt prophecie secundum quod immobiles de futuro scilicet existentibus causis voluntariis simpliciter autem non.

Nam si merita voluntatis Egypciorum immutata fuissent non induxisset Deus famem. Similiter quod seculum est aureum, post-modum argenteum, et postea ferreum non aliter estimandum est quam propter dispositionem voluntatis eorum qui sunt in seculo, et non necessario.[12]

Although a vision may be sent by the divine, the responsibility for its effects within experience rests solely on the human agent. God may send revelations in sleep because he sees all experience whole, in an eternal present tense; but man's mode of cognition is inferior; he chooses his lot freely from moment to moment. Thus the working out of God's view of experience becomes dependent in human terms on the nature of human action, dependent upon the human faculty of choice.[13] In Nebuchadnezzar's dream, the silver age does not follow the golden because God has foreseen that it should. Rather, the nature of man declines, as a result of voluntary human acts, and to that form of historical decline one can give the name of "golden age," "silver age," and so forth. Dreams that come true do so because of human deeds, not because of some external predestination.

If Cresseid's dream has effect in this world, that effect is not due to the fact of the dream itself but due to Cresseid's own actions or choices. The cause of Cresseid's leprosy has to be sought in her own experience, in her descent toward harlotry, in her career not just as lady in love but as complaisant agent of lust. That leprosy was in the Middle Ages commonly assumed to be transmitted by sexual contact completes the causal chain; Cresseid's disfigurement ultimately stems from her own actions, her own dalliance.[14]

Henryson's version of the dream thus has to be taken with a certain degree of ironic detachment. In the dream, Cresseid sees mainly what she wants to, a kind of cosmic conspiracy which is devoted to reducing her to causeless ruin. She refuses to accept her disfigurement as being the result of her heedless actions but rather wishes to claim that it is a sign that all is not well in the cosmic fabric. But the reader should not be gulled by this special pleading; insofar as Cresseid's dream is at all prophetic, it reflects only the heroine's own prior choices and their natural results. Beyond seeing Cresseid as the creator of a spectacular *insomnium* resulting from *cura oppressi animi* and *cura fortunae*, the reader should be aware of the possibility that *cura oppressi corporis* causes the dream, as well as being dramatized in it.

UNIVERSITY OF CALIFORNIA AT RIVERSIDE

NOTES

1 For the view that Cresseid is justly punished and that her disease is a sign of the moral order of the universe, see E. M. W. Tillyard, *Poetry and Its Background: Illustrated by Five Poems 1470–1870* (London: Chatto and Windus, 1955), pp. 5–29; Denton Fox, *Testament of Cresseid* (London: Nelson, 1968), pp. 20–58; Del Chessell, "In the Dark Time: Henryson's *Testament of Cresseid*," *CR*, 12 (1969), pp. 61–72; John MacQueen, *Robert Henryson: A Study of the Major Narrative Poems* (Oxford: Clarendon Press, 1967), pp. 45–93; John Speirs, *The Scots Literary Tradition: An Essay in Criticism*, 2nd edn (London: Faber, 1962), p. 46; Kurt Wittig, *The Scottish Tradition in Literature* (Edinburgh: Oliver and Boyd, 1958), pp. 41–9. Harold Tolliver, "Robert Henryson: From *Moralitas* to Irony," *ES*, 46 (1965), pp. 300–9, argues that the gods are unjust but that the poem establishes clear moral orders. For the opposite view, see Douglas Duncan, "Henryson's *Testament of Cresseid*," *EIC*, 11 (1961), pp. 128–35; Sydney Harth, "Henryson Reinterpreted," *EIC*, 11 (1961), pp. 471–80; A. C. Spearing, "The *Testament of Cresseid* and the 'High Concise Style,' " *Spec.*, 37 (1962), pp. 208–25. E. Duncan Aswell, "The Role of Fortune in the *Testament of Cresseid*," *PQ*, 46 (1967), pp. 471–87, suggests that divine providence does not exist within the poem but that Cresseid is properly punished according to the laws of nature and time.

An uneasy middle ground is held by a large group of critics who find the poem too scrupulously moral. Although they admit the justice of Cresseid's fate, they suggest that Henryson, as a result of his dour Scottish school-teacher's mentality, shows too much interest in purely retributive chastisement; in effect, they argue that Cresseid should have been treated more sympathetically. Representative of this view are T. F. Henderson, *Scottish Vernacular Literature: A Succinct History*, 2nd edn (London: Nutt, 1900), pp. 123–4; A. M. Kinghorn, "The Mediaeval Makars," *TSLL*, 1 (1959), pp. 73–88; James Kinsley, "The Mediaeval Makars," in his casebook, *Scottish Poetry: A Critical Survey* (London: Cassell and Company, 1955), pp. 1–32; Tatyana Moran, "The *Testament of Cresseid* and *The Book of Troylus*," *Litera*, 6 (1959), pp. 18–24; Edwin Muir, "Robert Henryson," in *Essays on Literature and Society* (London: Hogarth Press, 1949), pp. 7–19.

2 Of all the critics cited above only Aswell, Chessell, MacQueen, and Spearing bother to reiterate that Cresseid's dream is a sleeping vision; only Chessell and MacQueen take the logical step of viewing the sequence within the conventions of medieval dream-vision.

3 All citations of the *Testament* are from Fox's edition.

4 Cf. other uses of "ecstasy" in Henryson, *Fables* 490 and *Orpheus* 399; for further examples, see *DOST*, and Harry's *Wallace* II, 427 and IX, 191. *MED* gives Chester *Ascension* 6 (where "longing" and "extasy" are implicitly connected) and the first Wycliffite translation of Acts iii, 10 (where the second translation has "stoniynge"). Gavin Douglas' use in "The translatar direkkis hys buk" 106 (at the end of the *Aeneid*) follows a modesty *topos* and refers to the translator's confusion in the face of Virgil's poetic complexity.

"Ravished (in spirit)" is a *hapax* in Henryson, and parallels are not abundant. But cf. Murdoch Nisbets' translation of one of the Wycliffite biblical texts into Scots (c. 1520) Acts x, 10 and xi, 5, 2 Cor. xii, 12-13. At Acts x, 10, Wycliffite version reads "An axcess of soule or rauysching of spirit fel on him" for Vulgate *"cecidit super eum excessus mentis"*; Nisbet omits the first phrase of the English. In the notes (*STS* 52,44) Nisbet's editor compares Nicholas de Lyra's definition, "*mentis excessus, id est raptus a sensus exterioribus,*" "Fell into a trance" or "lost awareness of her bodily surroundings" would seem to fit the context in Henryson. The citation from Nisbet may suggest explicit spiritual ravishment, as in *Pearl* 1088.

5 Line 145 intensifies the situation for the principal character; for a close parallel, see *Awntyrs off Arthure* 130–1.

6 James Willis, *Ambrosii Theodosii Macrobii Commentarii in Somnivm Scipionis* (Leipzig: Teubner, 1963).

7 Ibid., I, iii, Sect. 4.

8 The scene in the "secreit orature" (120) ironically echoes the temple scene in which Troilus is struck by the arrows of the God of Love (*TC*, I, 162–322). Like Troilus, Cresseid is converted from a state of prideful blasphemy against the deities of love.

9 F. N. Robinson, *The Works of Geoffrey Chaucer* 2nd edn, (Boston: Houghton-Mifflin, 1957), p. 311.

10 Cf. Troilus' dream of Diomede, in the form of a boar, embracing Criseyde *TC*, V, 1233–43, interpreted by Cassandra (V, 1443–1540). Considering Troilus' anguished despair and pain, one expects his dream to be an *insomnium*, but it also contains clear prophetic elements; I would view similarly the other major dream in *TC*, Criseyde's vision of the eagle (II, 918–31). This vision is probably as specific a Chaucerian source for Henryson's handling as one is apt to find.

11 Willis, op. cit., I, iii, 3; I, iii, 12; I, iii, 8–9.

12 *Speculum naturale, XXVII*, lvi ("*De reuelationibus que fiunt in somniis*"), Huntington Library copy (Strassburg: c. 1481). The chapter begins by distinguishing prophetic and nonprophetic dreams in a way which recalls Macrobius.

13 See especially *Consolatio Philosophiae*, v, pr. 4, 5, and 6, for Philosophy's argument that things are known according to the capacity of the knower and that, therefore, one can distinguish simple and conditional necessity. This distinction, for Boethius, allows man's free will to coexist with God's foreknowledge.

14 For discussion of pathology of Cresseid's illness, see Beryl Rowland, "The 'Sicknes Incurabill' in Henryson's *Testament of Cresseid*," *ELN*, 1 (1964), pp. 175–7; Fox, op. cit., pp. 23–41; Kathryn Hume, "Leprosy or Syphilis in Henryson's *Testament of Cresseid?*" *ELN*, 6 (1969), pp. 242–5.

24

A CAROL IN TRADITION

BY ALBERT B. FRIEDMAN

The "popularity" of the Early English carols is one of the more fascinating aspects of this genre. ("Popular" here means a position near the folksong end of a scale which has learned, sophisticated, courtly song at the opposite end.) Folklorists are reluctant to treat the carols canonized by Greene as popular songs because some of them evince the influence of intricate refrain songs; over a third contain Latin lines or tags; many of them had learned authors; and they are richly preserved in manuscripts and were copied from one manuscript to another.[1] For all that, several vital connections with folksong have been alleged. According to the conventional view, which Professor Robbins has combatted,[2] the prototypes of the extant carols were folk dance songs that no one bothered to record—such were the chances of medieval popular song and dance. Certain clerics, most likely Franciscans imbued with their founder's missionary injunction to become minstrels of God, took up the dance songs and fitted them with words of religious mirth, much in the manner of the religious parodies preserved in the Red Book of Ossory, whose complier, incidentally, was also a Franciscan. If we find folk themes, folk rhetoric, folklore, and phrases and cadences in these carols which remind us of later folksong, it is because the parodists appropriated the popular idiom along with the popular matrix and tunes. The purpose of the carol writers was to supplant the profane carols with more edifying fare. The carols of this type were then, if not true folksong (i.e. of folk creation or recreation), at least *volkstumlich*—popular by destination.[3]

But did they reach their destination? Four of the most important carol manuscripts set the verses to elaborate polyphonic music, and from this and other evidence it appears that most of the recorded carols were not meant for festive dancing or singing in halls or on the village green, but were composed rather for use—as processional hymns, Professor Robbins has argued[4]—in religious services, particularly services in monastic houses. In the early sixteenth century, the court took up the form, for we have amorous carols by Skelton, Henry VIII, and Wyatt. If the aim of the composers of religious carols was indeed to set them afloat in oral tradition, they seem to have had little success: merely a handful of carols found in medieval manuscripts has been discovered later.[5] The numerous carols bagged by folksong collectors during the nineteenth and early twentieth centuries do not have the distinct formal characteristics of the medieval carol, but are simply Christmas songs in hymn or ballad stanzas without independent danceable burdens, though often with elaborate refrains to stimulate choral participation.

In arguing that the medieval carols were popular songs, Professor Greene demonstrates from the variants of some of the simpler, more folk-like pieces that such carols were "passed orally from one singer to another." The texts are so stable, however, so free from the consequences of "lapses of memory and perversions of meaning," that it is clear they were not subjected to "uncontrolled oral tradition." Rather, singers who had committed the carols to memory had manuscripts available against which occasionally to compare their repertory. "This is exactly the type of transmission usual to song which is popular by destination." "True folk-song," on the other hand is perpetuated "by an oral tradition which, operating in an unlettered community and hence released from all control by written copies, in the course of time works profound changes in the wording of any song."[6]

Professor Greene's touchstone for the "true folk-song" is the Child ballad. If he had compared his carols with latter-day folk carols instead of the folk ballads, he would have found a folk genre tied to written texts in much the same way as, though on longer tether than, his popular-by-destination carols. For the folk carols in oral tradition were derived from, and competed with, versions printed on broadsides, in garlands, or recorded in personal "ballet" books. The presence of this written monitor doubtless inhibited the free operation of oral re-creation, comparison with the written text wiping out the changes—not necessarily corruptions—which the carol had accumlated during its brief tour in tradition. (Cecil J. Sharp, the greatest English folk-song collector, blithely patched defective oral carol texts with elements from broadside.[7]) The folk carols were even more subject to the tyranny of print than those folk ballads which had to compete with broadside versions because the carols were seasonal songs, unrehearsed during most of the year, and thus harder to fix in the memory.

To illustrate the conservativeness of folk carol transmission as a result of its control by writing and print, I offer two versions of the same carol which have never been brought into conjunction before. The older (A), from the Shanne MS.,[8] was recorded in Yorkshire in 1624 and may have been copied from a broadside, like many of its fellows in the manuscript; the other (B) was sung at a parish Christmas Eve service on the Isle of Man in 1860:[9]

A

1. We happie hirdes men heere
   maye singe and eke reioice,
   for Angells bright and cleare
   we sawe, and harde A voice.

2. Gladd tidings they vs toulde:
   "the kynge of all mankynde
   Newe borne and in clothes fould"
   (they saie) "we shall him fynde

3. "At Bethlem in A staull,
   And eke his mother free."
   Great comforth to vs all.
   Oh blissed maie he be:

4. Nowe let vs with much Joie
   in haist to Bethlem trudge,
   To se that blissed boie
   that once must be our Judge.

5. When we to Bethlem came,
   we sawe as it was saide:
   That child of glorious fame
   In maunger he was laide.

6. We sheperdes downe did fall,
   And songe with voice on hie.
   The Angells said, "we shall
   Singe glorie in excelsie."

7. All haile, O christ, O kynge,
   All haile, O virgins sonne;
   we praie the vs to bringe
   In heaven with the to woon;

8. Wheere we the father may
   See, with the holye goest;
   him magnifie all waie,
   with all the heavenlie hoste.

B

1. We happy hardmen here
   May sing and akere joyce
   For angles bright and clear
   We saw and heard there voice (3)

2. Glad tidings they have us told
   Of the King of all mankind
   Newborn and in Clettfould
   They say we shall him find.

3. In Bethelem is a stall
   Akewise his mother free
   Great comfort to us all
   And blessed may we be

4. Come let us with great joy
   Unto that bethelem drodge
   To see that Blessed Babe
   Who once must be our judge

5. When we to bethelem came
   As true as it was said
   A Babe of glorouis fame
   In a mainjer their was laid

6. All hail to Christ our King
   All to a virgins son
   We pray thee us to bring
   And heaven with thee to win.

7. When we the father may
   Thee with the holy Ghost
   And magnifi thy Name
   With all thy heavenly host

The Manx singer followed a copy of verses from a "carval-book" of 1793, and this was made the basis of the collector's text. The "akere joyce" of the second line of B1 indicates manuscript miscopying, as does "glorouis" of B5, line 3; elsewhere the changes indicate the workings of oral transmission, especially the unwillingness of the Manx carol to carry syntactical constructions across the stanza break (B2–B3; B6–B7). The garbles are all too obvious, notably the nonsense of Clettfould in B2 and the ruinous "Thee" for "See" in B7. The attempt to make sense of the archaism "to woon" (A7) in B6 would have been ingenious if it had not led to the awkwardly elliptical phrasing of the last two lines of that stanza. Stanza A6 dropped out in the later version probably because it was felt to be redundant, though the Latin may have had something to do with its loss. Altogether the Manx carol would be a bad text on which to argue that the changes wrought by oral transmission are not necessarily corruptions.[10]

CLAREMONT GRADUATE SCHOOL

NOTES

[1] See my *The Ballad Revival* (Chicago: Univ. of Chicago Press, 1961), p. 18.

[2] Rossell Hope Robbins, "Middle English Carols as Processional Hymns," *SP*, 51 (1959), pp. 559–82.

[3] Richard Leighton Greene (ed.), *The Early English Carols* (Oxford: Clarendon Press, 1925), pp. xciii–cx.

[4] See article cited above, n. 2, and rebuttal by Richard Leighton Greene in *A Selection of English Carols* (Oxford: Clarendon Press, 1962), pp. 32, 44–8. Cf. also review of Greene and Rossell Hope Robbins, *Early English Christmas Carols* (New York and London: Columbia Univ. Press, 1961), by Douglas Gray, *N & Q*, 208 (1963), pp. 431–2.

[5] "The Boar's Head Carol" (Greene *Early English Carols*, op. cit., No. 132); "Corpus Christi" (ibid., No. 332); "Sweet Jesus" and "Gloria Tibi, Domine" (Greene, "The Traditional Survival of Two Medieval Carols," *ELH*, 7 [1940], pp. 223–38); and "The Fox and the Goose" (cited by Robbins, "The Burden of Carols," *MLN* 57 [1952], p. 22; see R. H. Bowers, *JEGP*, 51 [1952], pp. 393–4, and Robbins, *Secular Lyrics of the XIVth and XVth Centuries* (Oxford: Clarendon Press, 1952, 2nd edn, 1955), No. 48; traditional features discussed by George Perkins, "A Medieval Carol Survival," *JAF*, 74 [1961], pp. 235–44).

[6] Greene, *Early English Carols*, op. cit., pp. xciii ff.

[7] *English Folk-Carols* (London: Novello, 1911), pp. 64–6.

[8] F. 136v; see Hyder E. Rollins, "Ballads from Additional MS 38,599," *PMLA*, 38 (1923), pp. 142–4.

[9] A.G. Gilchrist, "Songs Collected in the Isle of Man," *JFSS*, 7 (1926), pp. 281–3.

[10] As to the music, printed in both instances with the texts, Bertrand H. Bronson, who generously went over the sets with me, agrees that there is no resemblance between A and B. A is G dorian and has a strong modal flavor; B is in D major and very tonal. The tune of A is carried in the tenor, the two accompanying parts being worked in quite awkwardly. The much simpler melody of B emphasizes the tonic chord and is uninterestingly repetitious. (My colleague Roland Jackson also looked at the tunes with a view to tracing derivations—with the same negative results.)

25

MINOR CHANGES IN
CHAUCER'S *TROILUS AND CRISEYDE*

BY CHARLES A. OWEN, JR

The minor changes that Chaucer made in *Troilus and Criseyde*, changes of a word, revisions of a line or two, the shifting and cancellation of stanzas, present a special opportunity and a challenge to the critic. They bring him into intimate contact with the poet at work, as he scraped and rubbed at the mistakes of Adam and corrected or improved his own wording. Occasionally they point beyond the immediate detail, beyond the individual stanza to problems of characterization, to form and proportion, parallel and contrast, to questions of narrative technique as they relate to the communication of emotional intensity, in effect to the kind of concern revealed by the study of major additions to the poem. Such revisions I have discussed elsewhere.[1] That a poet like Chaucer revised his work should surprise no one. That evidence of the changes should have come down to us with the clarity Root's meticulous work on the manuscripts made manifest, this is the miracle.[2] We owe it, I suspect, to the evident popularity of the poem.

A fifteenth-century manuscript of the *Troilus* shows us in an illumination the poet reading his work to a distinguished group of auditors which included royalty. The eighteen complete and almost complete versions of the *Troilus* that derive from the manuscript tradition include not a single copy from the century of the poem's composition. The poem was not only read aloud by the poet, but the copies demanded by his auditors were in turn passed from hand to hand until they literally wore out. The complexity of the manuscript record, so baffling to the textual critic, bears witness to the dual impact of the poet's readings of his poem—first, the interest which led to a demand by some of its hearers for copies of their own; then, a desire in Chaucer, stimulated by his readings to keep on correcting and revising his personal copy, even while scribes were at work with it satisfying the demands of his auditors.

The revisions vary in importance. Many involve minor improve-

303

ments in language or rhythm.[3] In the bidding prayer that opens the poem, for instance, the injunction "preieth" of 1, 29, 32, and 36 is changed to the formal "biddeth" in β36, thus bringing it into agreement with I, 40 and 43. The change involves minor adjustments, principally the addition of an "And" that gives the five-stanza address to "ye loveres" a formal unity:[4]

> Praith for them that eke been disespeyred. α
> And biddeth ek for him that been despeired. β

A little later a change from a lame "them" to "love" in line 46 dictates a change from "loves" to "ladies" in the preceding line:

> And sende hem myght hire ladies so to plese,
> That it to love be worship and plesaunce.   (I, 46β)

Making clear to Criseyde the sleeping accommodations his house provides, in III, 668a, Pandarus refers again to the "litel closet" he had pointed to in the previous stanza as ideal for her:

> "And there I seyde shal youre selven be."

The change in β, less dramatic and rhythmically slack, reiterates the position of Criseyde, protected apparently by her women in the "myddel chaumbre" from any intrusion:

> "And all withinne shal youreselven be."

In IV, 1214, the change from "herte myn" to "lady myn" avoids a repetition of "herte myn" two lines later as the lovers greet one another, each of them returned as it were from near-death after Criseyde's swoon. A little more than a hundred lines further on the change Chaucer makes in 1322 eliminated the first of two that-clauses dependent on one another. Originally the line read:

> "That we shal evereme togedere dwelle."   (IV, 1322a)

Criseyde is imagining the joy of reunion after her return from the Greek camp. The β version in addition to the rephrasing of the middle line, has Criseyde (in her effort to persuade) escalate from "joie" to "blisse" in the third line:

> "And thanne at erst shal we be so fayn,
> So as we shul togideres evere dwelle,
> That al this world ne myghte oure blisse telle." (IV, 1323β)

The way a simple change can have its effect on other lines is illustrated in an earlier section of Book IV, in the account of Pandarus' visit to the grief-stricken Troilus after the "parlement." Apparently Chaucer first changed "For crewel smert," describing Troilus' condition, to "Neigh ded for smert" in IV, 373. Then he realized that he had described Pandarus as "Ny dede for wo" just fourteen lines earlier. Changing that to "For sorwe of this" required the alteration in the next line of "this sorweful Troilus" (IV, 360) to "this woful Troilus."

A more daring revision than any we have seen so far occurs when Chaucer changes a pallid line that comes at the end of a stanza:

> "Shal I never as in thys worlde have joye."   (IV, 1442 H₃)

The new line, which tries to express what Troilus will experience if Criseyde fails to keep her pledge to return, triples both the negatives and the values his life will no longer have:

> "Ne shal I nevere have hele, honour, ne joye." (IV, 1442β)

The strengthening of the final line of the stanza shows Chaucer's awareness of form on a small scale, an awareness that after some experiment had led him to the versatility of rhyme royal and the unobtrusiveness of the decasyllabic couplet as his preferred poetic measures. One of the most effective uses of the rhyme royal stanza, as explored in "Thy Drasty Rymyng . . . "[5] comes in the satirical description of Troilus' first letter to Criseyde. There the final line, that brings what was "endeles withouten ho" to a miraculous end, reads the letter over and folds it in the bargain, all without the slightest premonition in the preceding line—

> And seyde he wolde in trouthe alway hym holde,
> And radde it over, and gan the letter folde.   (II, 1085β)

—this ending did not apparently reach its consummate form without some initial fumbling. The "endeles" of 1083 was originally "infenit;" the sub-lexical "withouten ho" sent the scribes scrambling for plausible substitutes; and the final lines read:

> And how he wolde in trowth alwey hym holde,
> And his adieux made, and gan it folde.   (II, 1085)

Two less spectacular changes that show Chaucer's appreciation of rhyme royal structure are to be found in Book IV. One of them occurs as Pandarus finds Troilus at the Temple and chides him for his despairing inactivity. The first two stanzas of his speech consist originally almost entirely of rhetorical questions. The single exception is the fifth line of the first:

> "What, parde, yit is nat Criseyde ago!"   (IV, 1090)

The fifth line in rhyme royal is the line of quickened rhyme, where the stanza turns from the alternating quatrain to couplets. Originally the last three lines of the second stanza carried on the rhetorical questions:

"Kanstow nat thinken thus in thi disese:
That in the dees right as ther fallen chaunces
In love also ther com and gon pleasaunces?" (IV, 1099α)

In the revision the turn of the stanza that had in line 1090 stood as a single exception to the questions, in line 1097 marks the decisive end:

"Hastow nat lyved many a yer byforn
Withouten hire, and ferd ful wel at ese?
Artow for hire and for non other born?
Hath kynde the wrought al only hire to plese?
Lat be, and thynk right thus in thi disese:
That in the dees right as ther fallen chaunces,
Right so in love ther com and gon plesaunces." (IV, 1099β)

The second instance in Book IV involves the rearrangement of the seemingly unimportant words "in effect," "fynaly," and "now," as Criseyde offers her solution to the dilemma the lovers are in. Originally the stanza in which she stresses the tentativeness of her proposal had as its second line

"That in effect this thing that I shal seye"   (IV, 1290α)

and as its sixth line

"For fynaly what so ye me comaunde."   (IV, 1294α)

Whether the initial impulse for revision stemmed from the weakness rhythmically of "fynaly" or from the sense that "in effect" committed the stanza too soon, the two simple changes improved the "run" of the stanza:

"Makyng alwey a protestacioun,
That now thise wordes, which that I shal seye,
Nis but to shewen you my mocioun,
To fynde unto oure help the beste weye;
And taketh it non other wise, I preye.
For in effect what so ye me comaunde,
That wol I don, for that is no demaunde."   (IV, 1295β)

The changes studied so far have had almost no significance outside their immediate context. A few of the minor changes for which there is evidence in the manuscripts involve bigger questions of meaning. One of these occurs in the 142 lines of Book IV where a single manuscript, H[3], provides an interesting set of unique readings apparently attesting the very earliest state of Chaucer's text. Criseyde is developing for Troilus' reassurance the ways she can deceive her father into permitting her return. She will persuade him that it was his fear that made him misinterpret "the goddes text:"

> "Whan he from Delphos to the grekys sterte." (IV, 1411 H₃)

What the other manuscripts present at this point hardly seems an improvement:

> "Whan he for fered out of Delphos sterte." (IV, 1411)

Then we recall that it is only in Benoit that Calchas goes directly from Delphos to the Greeks. Book I of the *Troilus* makes clear that Calchas "stal anon" out of the city to the "Grekes oost." The revision that Chaucer made saves the line from being an explicit contradiction of what had occurred earlier in the poem. The earliest of the unique H₃ readings also involves meaning, though in a more restricted way. It occurs at line 1301 of Book IV, as Criseyde is developing her case for returning after an interval to Troy and not taking any immediate steps to resist the exchange. What Chaucer first wrote did not quite express his intentions:

> "And syn ther helpeth non avisement
> As in this cas, lat dryve it oute of mynde
> And lat us fonde a bettre wey to fynde." (IV, 1302 H₃)

"Avisement as in this cas" is precisely what Criseyde is pinning her hopes to. The substitution of "To letten it" for "As in this cas" made clear what Chaucer and Criseyde intended. The exchange cannot be "withstonde," but other ways can be found to insure continuance of their love. Two other changes affect the meaning in more subtle ways. For "lat dryve it oute of mynde" Chaucer substituted the much slacker "lat it passe out of mynde." Criseyde is in effect arguing against decisive action. The suggestion of violence, even if only in language, must give way to insinuation. Chaucer apparently felt the witty combination of "fonde" and "fynde" in line 1302 also inappropriate to the lovers' despairing colloquy and substituted "shape" for "fonde." A similar sensitivity to the connotations of language apparently led Chaucer to eliminate the single word "softe" from two places where it had originally appeared earlier in this final meeting between the two lovers. Their initial greeting originally included the line:

> But hem in armes hente and softe kiste. (IV, 1131a)

The revision desentimentalizes the line with the blunter "tok" for "hente" and the unemotional "after" for "softe:"

> But hem in armes tok and after kiste.   (IV, 1131β)

Then, as Criseyde emerges from her swoon, Chaucer had originally used "softe" in a context more unexpected and with the reinforcement of internal rhyme:

> For which hire goost, that flikered ay on lofte,
> Ayein into hir herte al softe wente.   (IV, 1222a)

The sentimental absurdity of her spirit's *soft* return into her heart is eliminated in the revision of IV, 1222:

> Into hire woful herte ayeyn it wente.

These changes and the many other changes of wording in *Troilus and Criseyde* provide an almost unique opportunity to watch a medieval poet at work. Repetitions are eliminated, rhythm improved, the idiom or the drama strengthened, clarity enhanced. Occasionally, as in the last revisions discussed, bigger issues of meaning and of the connotations of language are involved. Three instances, in which Chaucer cancelled or shifted stanzas, deserve special consideration. The cancellation of a single stanza in Book I is well-attested, for it appears in only three manuscripts, all of which present the earliest readings for that portion of the text. It occurs as the third stanza in the speech Pandarus makes after hearing from Troilus the name of the woman he loves. It reads as follows:

> "And for thi loke of good comfort thow be;
> For, certeinly, the firste poynt is this
> Of noble corage, and wele ordeyne,
> A man to have pees with hym self, ywis;
> So oghtist thow, for noght but good it is
> To loven wele, and in a worthy place;
> The oghte not to clepe hit hap but grace."   (I, 896)

Chaucer could hardly have cancelled the stanza out of a feeling that Pandarus is too long-winded, for the speech in which it occurs is only eight and a half stanzas long, by no means beyond the capacity of the speaker or out of keeping with the dramatic situation.

Root opined that the stanza "cannot escape the charge of digression," that both before and after Pandarus is speaking primarily of Criseyde, basing his hope for Troilus on the qualities of her character, and that the absence of the stanza "serves to unify the passage."[6] Detailed analysis of the speech and a full consideration of Pandarus' train of thought in this and his later speeches will confirm Root's diagnosis and reveal additional motivation for Chaucer's cancellation of the stanza.

The speech Pandarus makes in response to Troilus' confession centres on a relatively few themes. Chaucer emphasizes his relief that Criseyde is Troilus' love:

> And whan that Pandare herde hire name nevene,
> Lord, he was glad, and seyde: "frende so deere,
> Now fare aright, for Joves name in hevene,
> Love hath byset the wel. . . ."   (I, 879)

His rejoicing first takes the form of praising Criseyde and finding in her virtues hope for Troilus' plight. The cancelled stanza breaks this emphasis and centres on advice to Troilus on how to conduct himself, especially in the line, "A man to have pees with hym self, ywis." With the next stanza Pandarus returns to his original theme, stressing that among so many virtues pity will no doubt be present and warning Troilus against requiring of her anything "ayeyns hyre name."[7] The major transition then occurs: Pandarus expresses surprise that Troilus is "biset" in "so good a place" for he was "wont to chace / At love in scorn." Three stanzas follow in which Pandarus recalls the specific gibes Troilus made at lovers. He ends by advising Troilus to repent his follies against the god of love and pray for his grace. Without the cancelled stanza, the prevailing mood in the speech is one of light-hearted rejoicing and reassurance. The speech has even a certain elegance of form with three stanzas devoted to Criseyde's virtues, one to the transition, and three to Troilus' mockery of lovers. The control of the situation that Pandarus exercises beneath his casual manner, the skill with which he draws Troilus out and adjusts his conduct to the aberrations of his patient are slightly enhanced by the cancellation of the stanza in question.

Having celebrated the virtues of Criseyde, given Troilus grounds for hope, induced him to repent of his heresy against love, and expatiated on the likelihood that "joie is next the fyn of sorwe," Pandarus is ready to modulate to a more serious tone and instruct Troilus on the proper deportment of a lover. The subject mooted in the cancelled stanza now comes into its own:

> "Now loke that a-tempre be thi bridel,
> And, for the beste, ay suffre to the tyde; . . .   (954)
> Be diligent and trewe, and ay wel hide;
> Be lusty, fre; persevere in thy servyse; . . .   (958)
> But he that parted is in everi place
> Is nowher hool . . .   (961)

"And sith that god of love hath the bistowed
In place digne unto thi worthinesse,
Stond faste, for to good port hastow rowed;
And of thi self, for any hevynesse,
Hope alwey wel; for but if drerinesse,
Or over haste, oure bothe labour shende,
I hope of this to maken a good ende."   (973)

The cancellation occurs not so much because of the repetition, as because of the characterization of Pandarus. Even when he improvises, as in the present instance, he calculates his effects. He sends

. . . his hertes line out fro withinne
Aldirfirst his purpos for to wynne.   (I, 1069)

In his handling of the love-sick Troilus, as later in his even more successful manipulation of Criseyde, he has his wits fully about him, adapting his speech to the response he elicits and keeping his purpose always in mind. His aim in this scene is to help Troilus. In order to do this effectively he must bring him to confessing the name of his love and convince him that his despair is unfounded. He is still working on Troilus' despair in the speech with the cancelled stanza. His rejoicing over Criseyde's virtues modulates into the half-joking allusions to Troilus' former attitude. By requiring him to repent his heresies, Pandarus uses an old pedagogical technique for insuring his hold on Troilus' attention. The advice he then gives Troilus serves a double function. It works directly on the despair as being inappropriate to a lover and damaging to his suit. It envisages a time when his conduct will have an effect on Criseyde; it thus implies the intimate relationship that Troilus has despaired of attaining. By cancelling the stanza Chaucer has prevented Pandarus from telegraphing the punch that is to serve as climax in his attack on Troilus' inertia. He has strengthened the image of Pandarus as a man at ease and capable in delicate human relationships.

The cancellation is the kind of change one might expect the poet to make as a result of his public reading of the poem. Somewhat similar in its significance is the shift of a single stanza in Book IV from a position after stanza 105 (l. 735) to a position after stanza 107 (l. 749). This time Root finds the motive for the revision "not at all clear" and says "readers may well disagree as to which order . . . is preferable."[8] The stanza, which occurs during Criseyde's grief over her threatened separation from Troilus, reads in its final version, as follows:

> Therwith the teris from hire eyen two
> Down fille, as shoure in Aprille swithe;
> Hire white brest she bet, and for the wo
> After the deth she cryed a thousand sithe,
> Syn he that wont hire wo was for to lithe,
> She moot forgon; for which disaventure
> She held hire self a forlost creature. (IV, 756)

It is worth noting that in its original position the opening line read "The salte teeris from hir eyne [eyen?] tweyne," and that Chaucer changed "tweyne" to "two" (and the rhyme word "peyne" in the third line to "wo") in order to avoid repeating the rhyme (sound and words as well) from the final couplet of the preceding stanza.[9] As originally placed, the stanza opened the description of Criseyde's grief when she retired to her bedchamber after the departure of her friends. The new position follows a stanza of description and a stanza of lament, and precedes six more stanzas of lament. The intervening stanzas read as follows:

> Hire ownded heer, that sonnyssh was of hewe,
> She rente, and ek hire fyngeres longe and smale
> She wrong ful ofte, and bad god on hire rewe,
> And with the deth to doon boote on hire bale.
> Hire hewe, whilom bright, that tho was pale,
> Bar witnesse of hire wo and hire constreynte;
> And thus she spak, sobbyng in hire compleynte:
>
> "Allas," quod she, "out of this regioun
> I, woful wrecche and infortuned wight,
> And born in corsed constellacioun,
> Moot goon, and thus departen fro my knyght.
> Wo worth, allas, that ilke dayes light,
> On which I saugh hym first with eyen tweyne,
> That causeth me, and ich hym, al this peyne!" (IV, 749)

That Chaucer saw immediate advantages in the new position is apparent.[10] He avoids repetition of the death wish in two successive stanzas and more important he avoids the artificial separation of the description from the complaint. By interrupting Criseyde's words, he implies that the actions and words accompanied one another. Furthermore, the shifted stanza is stronger than the stanza that originally followed it. By postponing it he allows the grief to develop in intensity. That Criseyde tears her hair, wrings her fingers, turns pale, and laments her fate before bursting into tears and beating her breasts gives the scene a more dramatic reality, as if we were watching carefully and not just accumulating all the words and actions associated with a passionate outburst of sorrow.

The change helps to emphasize the already striking parallel between Troilus' response to the exchange and Criseyde's. The scale of the two is somewhat different and Criseyde's grief is gentler in its expression. But Troilus, once he had reached his room and shut himself off from interruption, first sat down on his bed "lik a ded image," then started throwing himself around the room, then burst into tears and sobs, with the result that three lines, in which he called on death and cursed the day he was born, were all that he could utter. Chaucer then explains in a single stanza that when time had somewhat assuaged the violent throes of grief, Troilus lay down on his bed weeping, and uttered a lament that goes on for eleven stanzas. The interspersing of description and direct quotation in both instances, though parallel in form, is by no means identical in meaning. The contrasts help to alert the reader to the comparison between the two expressions of grief.

The parallels go beyond the passages already noted. Troilus learns of the projected exchange at the "parlement," where he can neither speak out against the proposal for fear of compromising his lady's reputation nor express his feelings at the outcome of the debate. Criseyde similarly has the rumour she has heard confirmed by her friends' visit; their well-intentioned chatter serves only as a frustrating irritant, compelling her to observe the amenities and restrain herself from the full expression of her grief. The lovers retire to their chambers, where in both instances their lamentations are interrupted by Pandarus, who does what he can to rouse them from supine acceptance to consideration of alternatives. The parallels of the two sequences are the more effective for not being forced. Troilus would naturally hear of the exchange first. And Pandarus has shown throughout a greater concern for his friend than for his niece. Without his aid the lovers, prostrated by the sudden stroke of fortune, could hardly have arranged their final meeting. But his helpful intervention has the ironic effect of reviving their spirits somewhat and in particular of turning Criseyde's thoughts from the despair that might have incapacitated her for the exchange.

The contrasts in the two scenes of grief reflect to some extent the differences in the two sexes. We have already noted that Troilus' grief is the more violent; he throws himself against the walls and the floor of the room as well as beating his breast with his fists and weeping; for a time his grief chokes off all but the smallest utterance. When his fury has abated and he does speak, it is his own misfortune that he laments. He gives no thought to Criseyde's suffering. Possibly this failure to consider his mistress derives from the conventional relationship in courtly love, with the lady envisaged as an ideal above the reach of fortune, who herself grants or withholds her favour in accordance with her lover's deserts or her own feelings. But it also reflects his inability to think or act effectively in the difficulties that his love has brought him. In the beginning his love for Criseyde paralysed his energies. Even during the consummation scene his lady seemed inaccessible long after she had in effect offered herself to him. His respect for her continues to govern his actions when Pandarus comes to his room and, seeing his friend's state, improvises the suggestion, immediately rejected by Troilus, that he find solace with some other woman. For Troilus refuses to consider Pandarus' advice that he carry Criseyde off unless she herself assents to the plan. The power that love wields in his nature prevents him from seeing Criseyde's fatal dependence on others for the decisions that mould her life.

Criseyde, on the other hand, though overwhelmed by the sudden misfortune, thinks of his suffering in the midst of her own:

> "O deere herte ek, that I love so,
> Who shal that sorwe slen that ye ben inne?"   (IV, 760)

and again:

> "But how shul ye don in this sorwful cas,
> How shal youre tendre herte this sustene?"   (IV, 795)

She even goes so far as to hope he can get over his sorrow by forgetting her. Though the physical manifestations of her passion are not so great as to inhibit speech, she reveals the extent to which sorrow has taken possession of her in involuntary ways. For the first time she pays no attention to social propriety and appears before Pandarus with tearstained face and hair hanging "unbroiden" about her ears. Obviously shocked by the change in her, he warns her to moderate her grief lest it have a fatal effect on Troilus. And when Troilus comes to her, she finds it impossible to play the role Pandarus has asked her to, and faints in his arms. Though our view of Criseyde is interrupted by Troilus' thoughts on freedom of the will in the temple, it is clear that her suffering has intensified in the interval to the limits of her capacity. At the very beginning of his account of her sorrow, Chaucer by shifting a stanza of description gained the intrinsic interest of a more varied and carefully observed development and at the same time strengthened slightly the parallels and contrasts with the account of Troilus' grief. Though the formal complaint has lost a great deal of the appeal it had in the Middle Ages (Is the "blues" song its modern descendant or counterpart?), Chaucer's use of it in Book IV in his preparation for the climactic scene between the lovers helps to maintain the interest we have felt throughout in the subtle revelation of character.

A more drastic and significant shift occurred in Book III, where two stanzas that originally followed stanza 189 were shifted to a position after 200. As slightly revised for their new position,[11] they read as follows:

> But how although I kan not tellen al,
> As kan myn auctour of his excellence,
> Yit have I seyd. and god toforn, and shal,
> In every thing the gret of his sentence;
> And if that I at loves reverence,
> Have any thing in eched for the beste,
> Doth therwithal right as youre selven leste.
>
> For myne wordes, heere and every part,
> I speke hem alle under correccioun
> Of yow that felyng han in loves art,
> And putte hem hool in youre discrecioun,
> Tencresce or maken diminucioun
> Of my langage, and that I yow biseche;
> But now to purpos of my rather speche.   (III, 1414)

As originally placed these stanzas came at the climax of the first night of love Troilus and Criseyde experienced. They followed a stanza of apostrophe starting "O blisful nyght, of hem so long isought . . ." in which the poet asks why he hadn't sold his soul for the least of their joys. And they preceded a stanza, beginning "Thise ilke two, that ben in armes laft," which ended with the lovers questioning the reality of their experience:

> For which ful ofte ech of hem seyde: "O swete,
> Clippe ich yow thus, or elles I it meete?"   (III, 1330 (1344))

Though Chaucer's technique in describing this central scene so crucial for the meaning of the poem called for a series of wave-like intensifying movements and a series of rapid shifts in type of discourse, the drop in intensity in these two stanzas is clearly too sudden, too evenly flat, and too long.[12] The stanzas abruptly break the narrative mood, which with the following stanza returns to its previous intensity.

The new position for the stanzas comes at the end of the night, just before the cock, the morning star, and Fortuna Major call forth the lovers' aubade and lead to their parting. The intervening stanzas, eleven in number, lower the emotional pressure in two movements. Three stanzas of passionate conversation punctuated by kisses lead to two stanzas of narrative in which after an embrace Troilus' sighs are described and the lovers talk and exchange gifts. Three stanzas of contrast between the joy of lovers and the joy of misers drop the emotional level still further. Two stanzas of narrative in which the lovers reminisce raise the level slightly, but it falls in the final stanza as the author explains why he hasn't mentioned sleep. The fourteen lines in their new position mark the end of the love-making. They bring the wave-like movement of this most lyrical section of the poem to rest.

The improvement that Chaucer brought about in this shift of two stanzas is apparent. The rationale behind it points up the narrative devices Chaucer developed when faced with the problem of communicating to his audience the intensity of joy experienced by two very special lovers. Chaucer was not working with a purely abstract problem. The people in his story had a reality for him that he refused to violate.[13] They complicated the task he had set himself, and they contributed to its fulfilment. The ineptitude of Troilus as a lover, which reaches a climax in the comic swoon, gives the scene an atmosphere of authenticity. It also helps to define the quality of his love, to make clear his respect for Criseyde as a person. The presence of Pandarus, which turns out to be a necessary element in the consummation, suggests the unromantic circumstances that impinge on romance. Criseyde herself with her penchant for putting off decision helps to delay the consummation and to give it the increased emotional fulfilment that delayed resolution always involves. All three contribute to the mixed motivations, the deceptions and misunderstandings, the moments when forces below the level of consciousness and outside the control of the will compel the response of a person. They make the scene vivid, authentic, intricate. The consummation, when it comes, resolves a series of discords on many levels. The aesthetic fulfilment helps to convey the sexual.

The complexity of character and motivation provides the basis then for the gradually mounting emotional pressure of the scene, each psychological obstacle, as it is overcome, preparing for a new level. From the moment Pandarus appeared in Criseyde's bedchamber, the obstacles that delay or resist the consummation are entirely internal. At first it is Criseyde who tries to evade the issue, partly from a natural feminine modesty, partly from a conventional feeling that Troilus has not yet earned her final favour (see line 922), and partly from her own avoidance of decision. It is characteristic of her to yield when she does by leaving the decision to Pandarus. Yet when Troilus, "sodeynly avysed," takes her in his arms, she can truthfully say that she has long since made up her mind to yield. The certainty that she loves Troilus and will eventually become his mistress does not mean for her an immediate acceptance of him as a lover. Her love she has gradually discovered, as later she discovers the impossibility of keeping her promise to return to Troy. The consummation requires a decision and involves a moment of decisive change. Troilus on the other hand is blinded by his awe of Criseyde from perceiving that the time for possessing her has come. The situation is the more difficult because of the false position Pandarus has put him in with the story of his jealousy. His love for Criseyde reaches too deeply into his nature for him to be easily capable of falsehood in connection with it. Furthermore, as later with respect to Pandarus' plan of abduction, he will make no move that Criseyde herself has not assented to. The internal obstacles that thus delay the consummation make possible the wavelike intensification both we and the lovers experience in the scene. The high points of the successive waves are reached with Criseyde's blush as Troilus kneels at her bedside, with tears as she hides her head beneath the sheet, with the oaths she exacts from him when she allows him to remain in her bed after his swoon, with his straining her to him "sodeynly avysed," with his explicit caressing of her body, and with their final enjoyment of one another in sexual union. The troughs between these high points vary in depth. Between the last three there is hardly any lowering of intensity.

The building up to the final climax results in part from a quickening tempo of shifts in type of discourse. Throughout the *Troilus* Chaucer alternates between narrative, indirect discourse, and a fully dramatic presentation, interspersing occasional comments on the action. As the love scene moves toward its climax, shifts in the type of discourse occur more rapidly; similes from nature, some of them implicit, convey action or state of mind; dialogue, narrative, and authorial comment succeed one another; and the kinds of comment proliferate. When Troilus takes Criseyde in his arms, she is compared to the "sely larke" mute in the sperhawk's foot; Chaucer recognizes both the impossibility and inescapability of trying to convey to his audience the lovers' gladness, as he has already conveyed their "hevynesse;" Criseyde trembles in her lover's arms like an aspen leaf; Troilus in his happiness begins to thank the planetary gods. Chaucer comments on the way sundry torments bring people to heaven; Troilus bids Criseyde yield; and she makes her paradoxical response that reaches beneath the social and the rational to levels of being Troilus has awakened in her:

> "Ne hadde I or now, my swete herte deere,
> Ben yolde, iwys, I were now nat here."   (III, 1211)

Two stanzas of analogy from medicine and the sense of taste, with a line or two of admonition to women to emulate Criseyde, give way to narrative as we watch Criseyde briefly, and to a series of three similes, the first the woodbind, applying to both lovers, the nightingale to Criseyde, and the escape from death to Troilus. Then after the pious hope

With worse hap god late us nevere mete   (III, 1246)

we shift to direct narrative again as Troilus begins to caress appreciatively his mistress's body, to kiss her, to be at a loss what to do for joy; and finally to drama as Troilus addresses the Gods and then Criseyde. At this point we realize that their sexual union is yet to occur as Troilus says to Criseyde

"now wolde god I wiste
Myn herte sweete, how I you myghte plese."   (III, 1278)
"Ne I wol nat, certein, breken youre defence."   (III, 1299)

Criseyde's welcome to her lover is unequivocal and their union is celebrated in the two stanzas that originally preceded the shifted passage, two stanzas that present a kaleidoscope of authorial comment, apostrophe, implied narrative, and blasphemous question:

Of hire delit or joies oon the leeste
Were impossible to my wit to seye;
But juggeth, ye that han ben at the feste
Of swiche gladnesse, if that hem liste pleye!
I kan no more, but thus thise ilke tweye
That nyght, bitwixen drede and sikernesse,
They felte in love the grete worthynesse.

O blisful nyght, of hem so longe isought,
How blithe unto hem bothe two thou weere!
Why ne hadde I swich oon with my soule y bought,
Ye, or the leeste joie that was there?
Awey, thou foule daunger and thou feere,
And lat hem in this hevene blisse dwelle,
That is so heigh that no man kan it telle.   (III, 1323)

The stanzas that Chaucer moved to the end of the scene and that originally followed the two just quoted provided a drop in emotional intensity with their extended authorial comment that was much too sudden. In revising, the poet moved them to a more appropriate location at the end of the love-making, where they re-emphasize the historicity of what Chaucer has been describing and reaffirm his own willingness to submit whatever he has "eched" in to the critical judgement of those more experienced in love. He stresses in these two stanzas the uniqueness of his story, which happened once at a given time in a given place, and its universality, since each of us through his common humanity has some capacity for evaluating the story and contributing to it. He also implies the impenetrability of events to complete understanding or final judgement by men.

UNIVERSITY OF CONNECTICUT

NOTES

1 "The Significance of Chaucer's Revisions of *Troilus and Criseyde*," *MP*, 55 (1957), pp. 1–5.

2 See Robert Kilburn Root, *The Textual Tradition of Chaucer's Troilus* (Chaucer Society, First Series, 99, London, 1916), and *The Book of Troilus and Criseyde*, edited from all the known Manuscripts (Princeton: Princeton Univ. Press 1926). Root's conclusions have not been universally accepted, and editions other than his tend to give a mixture of readings based on the manuscripts rather than a text based throughout on Chaucer's final revisions or a reconstructed β text. As a result most students read the cancelled stanza (128, lines 890–6) in Book I, and the two stanzas in Book III (201, 2, lines 1401–14) in their unrevised position as lines 1324–37. Root's postulation of a single scribal copy, corrected and revised by Chaucer over a period of time, during which copies for readers were being made, accounts more simply than any other theory for the manuscript evidence as it has come down to us. Those who would ascribe the variants to scribal carelessness and tempering must explain (1) the uneven distribution over the text of the variations that are attributed by Root to authorial revision; (2) the numerous occasions where manuscripts have both readings; (3) the striking disparity between the variants that are obviously scribal and the others, which sometimes show an interdependence extending over several stanzas; (4) certain arbitrary shifts in manuscript affiliations, as for instance in Book IV, 1300–1442, where a single manuscript H3 has a set of unique readings. The external evidence, *Chaucers Wordes unto Adam, His Owne Scriveyn*, proves that Chaucer corrected the work of his scribe in the case of the *Troilus*. The two versions of the *Prologue to the Legend of Good Women* show us the poet revising his own work in precisely the ways Root concludes that he revised the *Troilus*, by adding, by cancelling, by shifting, and by revisions of the wording.

3 I am indebted to the work of a student, Meredith McMunn, whose study of scribal variants in *Troilus and Criseyde* stimulated my own thinking on these passages.

4 This is the third of the five stanzas, which begin in the revised form: But ye loveres, And preieth, And biddeth, And biddeth, And for to have. Quotations throughout will be from Root's edition of the poem, as "corrected" in 1945.

5 Charles A. Owen, Jr, "Thy Drasty Rymyng . . . ", *SP*, 53 (1966), p. 549.

6 Root op. cit., p.34.

7 Chaucer departs from his source, the *Filostrato* in having Pandarus find reason for hope in Criseyde's virtues. Boccaccio's Pandaro sees Criseida's virtue as the great obstacle but feels sure he can get around it with flattering words. Boccaccio's

Troilo is not nearly so much of a problem. Pandaro meets far less resistance in learning the lady's name and is able to arouse Troilo from his despair almost at once. He does not bring up Troilo's mockery of love, and includes in a single long speech the praise of Criseida and his instructions on how Troilo should behave. Cancellation of the stanza brings the first part of Pandarus' speech into closer relationship with its counterpart in the *Filostrato*, though this aspect of the change was not part of Chaucer's motivation, I think, in making it.

[8] Root, op. cit., p. 222.

[9] Chaucer also altered the first line of the following stanza in the new sequence to indicate that Criseyde was resuming her lament. "What shal he don what shal I do also?" becomes "She seyde: 'How shal he don, and ich also?'" The alterations to fit the stanza to its new context, the relationship to the source in Boccaccio (see footnote 7), and the manuscript affiliations in this passage assure both the direction of the shift and the authorial rather than scribal responsibility for it.

[10] Chaucer followed Boccaccio closely in the earliest version. In the stanza before the one shifted Chaucer has Criseyde fall on her bed "for dead" (instead of throw herself, as in Boccaccio). Weeping, beating her breast, calling on death now that she was forced to forsake her delight, and pulling at her hair and tearing it out, Chaucer found in Boccaccio. He filled out the second stanza by having Criseyde wring her fingers and by commenting on her pale colour. Then he translated fairly closely the first stanza of the complaint from Boccaccio.

[11] Originally the last lines of the preceding stanza and the first line of the shifted stanzas read as follows:

> And lat hem in this hevene blisse dwelle,
> That is so heigh that al ne kan I telle.

> But sooth is though I kan not tellen al.   (III, 1324*a*)

When the connection between the two stanzas was broken by the shift, Chaucer gave the preceding stanza greater finality by changing the last line to

> That is so heigh that no man kan it telle.   (III, 1323*β*)

It was also of course necessary to change the first line of the shifted stanza. At the end of the shifted stanzas in their new position Chaucer had two successive lines beginning "But." He changed the beginning of line 1415 from "But whan the cok" to "Whan that the cok."

[12] The consummation scene in the *Filostrato* is more quickly reached and much shorter. Pandaro is not present at all. Troilo comes to Criseida's house with the understanding that they will spend the night together, and when the coast is clear Criseida leads him to her bedchamber. Chaucer takes suggestions from Boccaccio's account in the *Filostrato* only towards the end of the scene. The suggestion for the second of the shifted stanzas and for most of the eleven stanzas between the two positions comes from the *Filostrato*. Of what went before only the two preceding stanzas ("Of hire delit . . ." and "O blisful nyght . . .") derive in part from Boccaccio's poem. For a more detailed discussion of the scene and the techniques involved, see "Mimetic Form in the Central Love Scene of *Troilus and Criseyde*," *MP*, LXVII (1969), p. 125ff.

[13] For a full discussion of this aspect of *Troilus and Criseyde*, see "The Problem of Free Will in Chaucer's Narratives," *PQ*, LXVI (1967), p. 439ff.

26

HOLY CHURCH'S SPEECH AND THE
STRUCTURE OF *PIERS PLOWMAN**

BY R. E. KASKE

One of the things that make *Piers Plowman* an unusually difficult poem is the fact that it seems organized in so many different ways at once. Most obviously, it is divided into a prologue and twenty passus.[1] Cutting across this format is a pattern of eight major dreams, the third and fifth of which contain a pair of "inner" dreams (XI, 4–396; XVI, 19–167). A broader principle of organization is the division into *Visio* (Pr.–VII) and *Vita* (VIII–XX); and the second of these two large parts is further divided into *Dowel* (IX–XIV), *Dobet* (XV–XVIII), and *Dobest* (XIX–XX). In addition, the poem is obviously organized around the three major appearances of Piers himself (V–VII, XVI, XIX), and apparently also around the development of Will. And finally, there is reason for suspecting that the whole of *Piers Plowman* may somehow reflect the structure of a liturgical year—beginning perhaps at the beginning of Advent and ending at the last Sundays before Advent, with for example the *De profundis* in the Offertory of the Mass[2] echoed in the final picture of Conscience: "And sitthe he gradde after grace . til I gan awake" (XX, 384).

In addition, *Piers Plowman* seems governed by at least one other large structural pattern, in its way perhaps more vital for the thematic unity of the poem than any of the others. After a Prologue affording a preliminary survey of worldly conditions as they are, the instructions of Lady Holy Church in Passus I present in outline the Christian principles that are to be applied to this raw material of human life. One noteworthy feature of her instructions is that they follow an orderly, almost wooden progression, quite unlike Langland's expository method in other parts of the poem. After a brief prefatory comment on the vision of the Prologue (I, 1–9), the first major section of Holy Church's speech (11–57) is devoted to the problems of *bona temporalia*, and is itself divided into two parts: a dis-

* This study was presented as a brief paper before the Middle English Group at the meeting of the Modern Language Association of America, 29 December 1972.

cussion of the natural goods—clothing, food, and drink (11–42), introduced by Will's question, "mercy, Madame . what is this to mene?" (11); and a discussion of artificially contrived goods or worldly wealth (43–57), introduced by Will's question,

> "Madame, mercy," quod I . "me liketh wel ӡowre wordes,
> Ac the moneye of this molde . that men so faste holdeth,
> Telle me to whom, Madame . that tresore appendeth?" (43–5)

The second major section of her speech (79–207) deals with the supreme spiritual values, and is also divided into two parts: a discussion of truth (79–135), introduced by Will's memorable question, "Teche me to no tresore . but tell me this ilke, / How I may saue my soule . that seynt art yholden?" (83–4); and a discussion of love (136–207), introduced by Will's questioning comment,

> "ӡet haue I no kynde knowing," quod I . "ӡet mote ӡe kenne me better,
> By what craft in my corps . it comseth and where." (136–7)

The instructions of Lady Holy Church, then, show a symmetry of arrangement as unmistakable as it is unusual in *Piers Plowman*— divided as they are into what might be called the problems of natural man and the problems of specifically Christian man, with each of these large sections again divided into two parts, and the beginning of each of the four parts clearly marked by a question of the dreamer. The two major sections are separated by the dreamer's questions and Holy Church's answers concerning the dungeon (hell) and the identity of Holy Church herself (58–78), which thus serve as a thematic transition between natural man and Christian man.

These four divisions of Holy Church's speech provide the basis for what I take to be an important structural principle in the poem as a whole.[3] Its method would be roughly analogous to that of the famous ninth-century hymn "*Ave, maris stella*," beginning with the stanza,

> *Ave, maris stella,*
> *Dei mater alma*
> *Atque semper virgo,*
> *Felix caeli porta.*

As Dreves pointed out long ago, the components of this opening stanza are picked up and developed successively in the stanzas that follow: "*Ave*" in the second stanza, "*maris stella*" in the third, "*Dei mater alma*" in the fourth, "*Atque semper virgo*" in the fifth, and "*Felix caeli porta*" in the sixth, before the closing doxology in the seventh.[4] In *Piers Plowman*, the two subjects dealt with in the first half of Holy Church's speech—natural goods and artificially contrived goods—are developed in the remainder of the *Visio*, which thus becomes recognizable as the part of the poem devoted primarily to the problems of natural man. The two subjects dealt with in the second half of her speech—truth and love—are developed in the *Vita*, which emerges as the part of the poem devoted to the problems of specifically Christian man.

In the *Visio*, the first subject to be developed after the end of Holy Church's speech is that of artificially contrived goods or worldly wealth, the uses and problems of which are elaborately dramatized in the allegory of Lady Meed (II–IV). Following the confession of the Deadly Sins and the announcement of the pilgrimage to Truth (V), the uses and problems of natural goods are dramatized with comparable fullness in the allegory of Piers' half-acre (VI), with its parallel to Holy Church's emphasis on clothing, food, and drink (VI, 13–21) and its expansion of her teachings on moderation in diet (I, 34–37; VI, 259–76). But if this is so, why are the confession of the Deadly Sins and the pilgrimage to Truth inserted between the two? And in particular, why is the order of the two subjects reversed from the order in which they have appeared in Holy Church's speech?

I would suggest that the answers to both these questions depend on the fact that whereas Holy Church's speech is organized according to the demands of straightforward exposition and so follows a logical pattern of ascending importance, Passus II–VI are organized dramatically around a continuing theme of attempted reform, and so follow a pattern of chronological narrative. In the Lady Meed episode, we are shown not only the problems created by the misuse of wealth, but also a king—surely reflecting at some level the good man or even the good Christian—trying to think his way through these problems with the help of Conscience and Reason; and the episode ends with a successful reform in the uses of wealth, and a picture of the king determined henceforth to rule by the dictates of Conscience and Reason (IV, 171–95). Presumably as a result of this partial reform, Reason preaches general repentance to the people (V, 9–62); we are then shown a means toward the elimination of sin in the confessions of the Deadly Sins (63–513), along with an attempt at a more positive programme in the proposed pilgrimage to Truth (514–651). This pilgrimage, we are told in the next passus, cannot be begun until Piers' half-acre has been plowed (VI, 3–6); and it is on the work of the half-acre that the reform eventually comes to grief, in the orgies produced by an abundance of natural goods (117ff., 304ff.). It would seem, then, that the pilgrimage to Truth (which I take to be the image for a specifically Christian perfection, and which does take place on an individual basis in the *Vita*) cannot begin until the problems of natural man have somehow been dealt with. Of these problems, the ones concerning artificially contrived goods (wealth) seem presented as not beyond solution; but those growing out of man's attachment to natural goods (food, drink, clothing) are shown as all but insoluble.

Now it is of course a commonplace of medieval thought that the most serious sins are those involving the least of physical appetite, while the slightest are those involving the most of physical appetite.[5] With this principle in mind, the inverted order of natural and artificial goods in Passus II–IV and VI can be explained with the help of a brilliant summarizing statement by John Freccero:

> Purely from the standpoint of human experience, and quite independently of any theological tradition, it is clear that the more prone one is toward sin, through no personal fault, the less is one's culpability for its commission. On the other hand, the further one progresses toward virtue, the less serious are the faults remaining to be purged, but the more difficult are they to overcome. The last step toward perfection, for those who believe in such moral progress, is always the most difficult to take.[6]

Within the theme of attempted reform that governs Passus II–VI, the reform in the uses of wealth can succeed because the abuses it is aimed at, though powerful, are still at one remove, so to speak, from man's most basic appetites; when the reform is confronted directly by these appetites on the half-acre, it fails.

This whole pattern, implying some order of descending seriousness in the sins portrayed in Passus II–IV and VI, can perhaps be supported obliquely from the order of the seven Deadly Sins in other parts of *Piers Plowman*. Though not absolutely consistent within the poem, this order is apparently intended to be somehow meaningful, approximating as it does the order of descending seriousness found in traditional enumerations of the Sins; for example pride, the most serious, appears consistently in first place in the most familiar medieval schematizations as well as in *Piers Plowman*.[7] A notable peculiarity in the treatment of the Deadly Sins in *Piers Plowman* is the continual close association of gluttony and sloth, explained by Siegfried Wenzel as probably resulting from "the fact that in late medieval popular literature *acedia* came to be reckoned among the sins of the flesh."[8] A closely related phenomenon is the fact that in all four passages where the Sins are enumerated completely, sloth is mentioned last; and that in three of the four, gluttony is mentioned second-last.[9] On the half-acre of Passus VI, it is precisely these two human failings upon which the reform finally founders. The point, I take it, is that gluttony and sloth are conceived of in *Piers Plowman* as the final sins in an order of descending seriousness; that, in accord with the principle expressed by Professor Freccero, they may be thought of also as the most basic and difficult to overcome; and that their triumphant emergence in Passus VI therefore speaks strongly for the pattern I have proposed—with the inversion of natural and artificial goods in Passus II–IV and VI dictated by the allegory of a reform which is successful up to a point, but which cannot succeed against the force of man's most instinctive and compelling appetites.[10]

Passus VI ends with the prediction of calamity and famine "But if god of his goodnesse . graunt vs a trewe" (332). Though this "truce" clearly refers in literal terms to an end of the time of famine, the social result of mishandling natural goods, it is followed immediately in Passus VII by the account of how Truth sends Piers a "pardon," which has been generally accepted as signifying the Atonement. I conclude that the end of Passus VI carries overtones also of the spiritual "starvation" that results from the misuse of earthly goods—in Augustinian terms, *enjoying* them instead of merely *using* them[11]—and that the "truce" mentioned in the final line is in this sense a hint of the Atonement. The attempted reform thus far, though presented in a Christian context and employing the more elementary Christian remedies, has been concerned almost entirely with the problems of natural man (or perhaps more accurately the problems common to all men, Christian or otherwise), and at this level it has failed. Clearly, something more is needed: the Atonement, seen not merely legalistically as a device setting up the machinery for salvation, but as the great actuating force of charity, creating the conditions under which true Christian perfection can be sought. This distinction, I believe, is the central theme of Passus VII; and it is in this way that Passus VII can serve as the transition between *Visio* and *Vita*, between the problems of natural man and those of specifically Christian man.

The second major section of Holy Church's speech (I, 79–207) has expounded the great spiritual values truth and love. In the *Vita*, Will's extended quest for Dowel, Dobet, and Dobest (VIIIff.) is easily enough understood as a search for truth—particularly in view of the abortive "pilgrimage to Truth" (V, 517ff.) of which it is surely a thematic continuation, and the substantial education that he does in fact receive from the personifications Thought, Witte, Studye, Clergye, Scripture, Resoun, and Ymaginatyf. It seems equally clear that at some point in Will's journey this quest for truth becomes, merges into, or is significantly combined with a quest for love or charity. Though there are of course repeated brief anticipations of the theme of love in Passus X–XII,[12] the major shift of emphasis from truth to love seems to occur somewhere between Passus XIII and XVI—whether in the symposium on Dowel, Dobet, and Dobest climaxed by Pacience's exposition of charity (XIII, 135ff.), in the application of charity and patient poverty to the problems of the Field of Folk in the person of Haukyn (XIV, 99ff.), or in Anima's eloquent description of charity (XV, 160ff.), with the account of the Tree of Charity in the following passus (XVI, 4ff.). If we are indeed to look for some such distinct transitional passage, I would be inclined to identify it as the speech of Pacience in XIII, 135–71, including the famous riddle of *ex vi transicionis*;[13] or it may be that we are to see the shift as a gradual one, extending from Pacience's speech through the vision of the Tree at the beginning of Passus XVI. In any case, Passus XVI–XVIII seem dominated by the theme of charity. The vision of the Tree is followed immediately by a swift resumé of the supreme work of charity, the Atonement (XVI, 90–166). The subsequent drama of Abraham, *Spes*, and the Samaritan (XVI, 172, to XVII, 123) certainly is to be understood at one level as an allegory of the three Theological Virtues, with emphasis on the supremacy of charity; and the long speech of the Samaritan explaining the Trinity (XVII, 131–348) seems particularly concerned with the Holy Ghost in His traditional role as charity itself (e.g., 215ff.). Passus XVIII is of course the full-scale dramatization of the Atonement, shot through, as might be expected, with references to love.[14]

Passus XIX–XX present the setting up of the Church and its growing corruption—again with significant references to love, climaxed by the final instructions of Kynde to Will:

> "Lerne to loue," quod Kynde . "and leue of alle othre.". . .
> "And thow loue lelly," quod he . "lakke shal the neure
> Mete ne worldly wede . whil thi lyf lasteth."   (XX, 207, 209–10)[15]

Perhaps a further implicit connection between this theme of charity and the eschatological context of Passus XX is to be found in a detail of Christ's famous prophecy concerning the final days: "*Et quoniam abundabit iniquitas, refrigescet charitas multorum*" (Matt. xxiv 12). It may be worth noticing that the Biblical context of this verse (Matt. xxiv 4–24) bears a general similarity of sorts to the events of Passus XX. In any case, the verse itself is a commonplace in medieval eschatology; for example a thirteenth-century *Liber de Antichristo et ejus ministris*, written in some form by William of Saint-Amour and presenting an antifraternal eschatology strongly resembling that of Passus XX, includes a sizeable chapter "*De refrigescentia charitatis*."[16]

Obviously, the structure I have been proposing cannot in itself account for the manifold complexities of *Piers Plowman*. To whatever extent it is convincing, however, it establishes Holy Church's speech as a kind of germinal statement of the broadest themes to be developed in the poem: the *bona temporalia* of natural goods and worldly wealth, and the great Christian "goods" of truth and love.

CORNELL UNIVERSITY

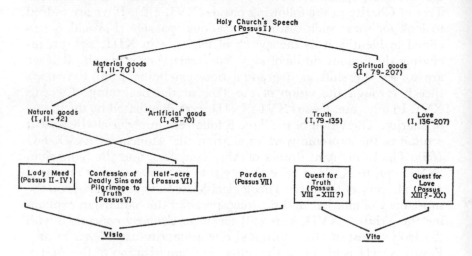

NOTES

[1] All references to *Piers Plowman* are to the B-text, edited by Walter W. Skeat (Oxford: Clarendon Press, 1886), I.

[2] J. Wickham Legg (ed.), *The Sarum Missal* (Oxford: Clarendon Press, 1916), pp. 194–5; *Missale ad usum percelebris ecclesiæ Herfordensis* (Leeds: McCorquodale, 1874), pp. 211–13; *Missale ad usum insignis ecclesiæ Eboracensis*, Publications of the Surtees Society, 59 (Durham: Andrews & Co. 1874), I, p. 253.

[3] Morton W. Bloomfield, *Piers Plowman as a Fourteenth-century Apocalypse* (New Brunswick, N.J.: Rutgers Univ. Press [1962]), p. 153, remarks that "the rest of the poem is a working out in detail, sometimes endless detail, of the speech of Lady Holy Church." A few elements of the present analysis are approximated by T. P. Dunning, C. M., "The Structure of the B-Text of *Piers Plowman*," *RES*, NS, 7 (1956), pp. 230–2.

[4] G. M. Dreves, S. J., "*Der Hymnus vom Meeresstern*," *Stimmen aus Maria-Laach: Katholische Blätter*, 50 (1896), pp. 558–69. The "*Ave, maris stella*" is edited by Clemens Blume, S. J., *Anal. Hymn.* (Leipzig: Reisland, 1886–1922), LI, p. 140, and appears in many anthologies.

[5] See for example Gregory, *Moralia in Iob*, XXXIII, xii, 25, on Job xl, 21 (*PL* 76, col. 688); Aquinas, *Summa Theologica*, I–II, q. 73, a. 5; and Dante's *Inferno*, XI, 25–6 and 83–4.

6 "Dante's Firm Foot and the Journey without a Guide," *Harvard Theological Review*, 52 (1959), p. 278.

7 Passus II, 79ff.; V, 63ff.; XIII, 276ff.; and XIV, 205ff. For medieval arrangements of the Deadly Sins, see Morton W. Bloomfield, *The Seven Deadly Sins: An Introduction to the History of a Religious Concept, with Special Reference to Medieval English Literature* (East Lansing, Mich.: Michigan State Coll. Press, 1952), particularly pp. 69–104.

8 *The Sin of Sloth: Acedia in Medieval Thought and Literature* (Chapel Hill, N.C.: Univ. of North Carolina Press, 1967), p. 140. See *Piers Plowman*, II, 92–100; V, 304–468; V, 366; XIII, 400–21; XIV, 234.

9 Passus II, 92–100; V, 304–468; XIII, 400–21; and XIV, 253ff. For orders of sins roughly approximating those in *Piers Plowman*, including the placing of *acedia* last, see Bloomfield, *Seven Deadly Sins*, op. cit., pp. 86–8, 106, 117.

10 For parallels to Langland's relatively early placements of lust—usually thought of as involving the strongest physical appetite and the slightest guilt of any of the Deadly Sins (as in Lady Meed's remark, III, 55–8)—see Bloomfield, *Seven Deadly Sins*, op. cit., pp. 86–8 and 106, on the rather uncommon order codified as *saligia*.

11 See for example Augustine, *De civitate Dei*, XI, 25, edited by Bernard Dombart and Alphons Kalb, *Corpus Christianorum Latinorum*, 48 (Turnhout: Brepols, 1955), XIV, ii, pp. 344–5; and Sermo CLXXVII, 8 (*PL* 38, col. 958).

12 For example X, 184–206; XI, 161–222; and XII, 141ff.

13 My interpretation of this difficult speech is presented in "*Ex vi transicionis* and Its Passage in *Piers Plowman*," *JEGP*, 62 (1963), pp. 32–60.

14 For example XVIII, 167, 180, 363, 412–14, 423.

15 Note also XIX, 244–9, 306–8.

16 I, xii, edited by E. Martène and U. Durand, *Veterum scriptorum . . . amplissima collectio* (Paris: Montalant, 1724–33), IX, cols. 1317–20 (mistakenly ascribed to Nicolas Oresme); according to M. M. Dufeil, "*Correction au 'Répertoire des maîtres en théologie de Paris au XIIIe siècle' de P. Glorieux* (*Paris, Vrin*, 1933) (à propos de Guillaume de Saint-Amour)," *Bulletin de la Société Internationale pour l'Étude de la philosophie médiévale*, IV (1962), p. 135, the work was revised by Nicolas of Lisieux. See also William of Saint-Amour, *De periculis novissimorum temporum*, VIII, *Opera omnia* (Constance: Alithophili, 1632), p. 40; and for an example of the usual interpretation of the verse outside the context of fraternal controversy, Ludolph of Saxony, *Vita Jesu Christi*, II, 39 (Paris: Victor Palmé, 1865), p. 534.

27

THE SHAPING OF THE VERNON
AND SIMEON MANUSCRIPTS

BY A. I. DOYLE

In his dissertation on the Middle English Lyric (1937) and in a number of his published articles Professor Robbins, developing the work of the late Carleton Brown and others, has shown how the selection of contents, the physical form and the subsequent alterations of manuscripts, especially anthologies of verse, may indicate the character and interests of the compilers and owners. In the *Index of Middle English Verse* and its *Supplement* he has provided the indispensable tools for tracing other copies and editions of particular items, and thereby the means of ascertaining not only the affiliations of those copies but also the recurrence together in the same manuscripts of groups of pieces, from which some notion may be had of the way an anthology was created and from what kinds of source.

Although there has not yet been published the fully comparable tool covering Middle English prose, for which Professor Robbins has recently argued,[1] the present writer, following the footsteps and example of Brown and Robbins, has been building up since 1945, an inventory of later Middle English religious and moral prose texts, copies, editions and studies, which can serve similar functions to those of the *Index* and *Supplement*. At the same time he has been exploring the circumstances of the production and use of all the manuscripts which contain Middle English verse and prose and those which are related to them in other languages. It seems therefore most appropriate to offer here some observations on the two largest Middle English anthologies of verse and prose, the Vernon and Simeon manuscripts (respectively Bodleian poet. a.1 and British Museum Addit. 22283), so frequently employed by editors, yet rarely discussed as a whole except incidentally and summarily. In this he is inevitably indebted to many of those editors and to other scholars, as it will appear.

The Vernon manuscript (hereafter called V) originally contained more than 420 leaves of vellum measuring at least twenty-two and a half by fifteen and a half inches, the pages ruled in three or two columns for normally eighty lines of text in each, written by one set English court-hand (*cursiva Anglicana formata*) of the later fourteenth century, apart from a preliminary quire and some rubrics in other hands, with much illuminated initial and border decoration and miniatures by two artists.[2] The Simeon manuscript (hereafter S), now far more defective than V, though uniform in most respects, possibly never ran to quite as many leaves, and its columns of normally eighty-five lines are written by at least four hands, of which the second is the same as the main one or V.[3] In comparison with contemporary jobs of copying, each leaf of V or S may have been one or two days' work for a single hand, and the whole of each volume thus must have taken more than one man-year, without allowing for interruptions or part-time engagement, or for preparation, decoration and binding, so probably in all it took several years, and cost between £50 and £100.[4]

According to Miss Serjeantson's numeration, V contained (before losses) 377 items, of which the last comprises 27 distinct poems, making a total of 404; but 113 constitute the Southern Legendary, 42 the miracles of Our Lady and 114 the *Northern Homilies*. Structurally, by the points at which the items end and begin at quire-changes, the volume is divisible into five very unequal portions, besides the single preliminary quire including the contents-table. Part 1 (as I shall call it) contained 104 leaves in the original foliation, with the Southern Legends in two columns and the smaller group peculiar to V in shorter lines and three columns (Serjeantson no. 1–122). Part 2 opens with the *Story of the Gospel*, followed by prayers and devotional exercises, the *Miracles of Our Lady* and more prayers, all in verse in three columns, 62 numbered leaves (Serjeantson 123–207). Part 3 begins with the *Northern Homilies* and continues with a large number of other long and short poems in three columns, for 152 numbered leaves (Serjeantson 208–354). Part 4, however, commences with a number of prose pieces and ends with three poems in long lines, all in two columns, 88 leaves, not all numbered originally (Serjeantson 355–76). Part 5 is only 6 un-numbered leaves of one quire, with short poems in three columns (Serjeantson 377).

The loss of the first 177 numbered leaves from S leaves it uncertain whether the contents ran precisely parallel with those of V, for they do not do so at three points later in the volume (so far as other losses allow one to tell), and there is an extra structural division at two of these. The discrepancy of foliation between copies of the same items in V and S, already established by the present beginning of the latter, may be the combined result of the larger number of lines per column in S, a different handwriting and perhaps the omission of pictures in S. It seems from the quire signatures that there may have been at least one division in the lost beginning of S, not necessarily coinciding with V, but the remainder of S is divisible in four.[5] Part 1 corresponds mostly with the first 96 leaves of V part 3, and part 2 with the next 40 (so far as gaps allow one to guess), but part 3 opens with a number of different prose pieces in two columns before reverting to three columns for the rest of the contents of V part 3 and those of V part 5 with a couple of additions. S part 4 corresponds with the contents of the first 50 leaves of V part 4, the rest lacking by loss or possibly non-completion.

The significance of these divisions, as should be remembered in any discussion, is that the consequent parts of each volume need not have been planned, begun or finished in the order in which they are now bound. It is plain from the separation for the most part of the verse and prose contents into distinct quires with different ruling that there was forethought, at least for economy, placing poems with short lines in three columns but the long lines of the Southern Legends and alliterative poems in two, like the prose. This grouping, however, also accords with stylistic and functional differences between the contents and it is clear from the changes in page-appropriation that it was of subordinate importance to the designers.

The very first quire of V, which gives the volume the title *Salus Anime* or *Sowlehele* before the table of contents,[6] must have been executed (like the prelims of many printed books) towards the end of the work as we now have it. The translation by Thomas N of Aelred of Rievaulx's *Informatio*[7] which follows the table might be regarded either as a preface to users of the anthology or as an appended afterthought to the similar prose treatises in its part 4, utilizing space left in the triple columns prepared for the table whose extent may not have been certain when it was started.

The first three parts of V contain several series and a number of separate instances of verse sermons for liturgical and other communal occasions, to judge from their predominant features, together with some longer poems of religious and moral doctrine meant for similar instalment use,[8] and a number of devotional exercises and prayers in verse varying in length and character. The oldest of the Southern Legends and *Northern Homilies* and the *Story of the Gospel* originated up to a century before their incorporation in V, while some of the other catechetic, moralizing and devotional pieces were of comparatively recent composition, but still with a strong public appeal,[9] At the same time the aim of some of the prayers is very personal, and the purpose of these parts of the anthology was not purely auditory edification, for the *Story of the Gospel* and the *Miracles of Our Lady* are both illustrated with sets of miniatures, the *Speculum Vitae* has an elaborate Latin and English diagram prefixed, and the *Prick of Conscience* another miniature.[10] In medieval conditions such provision for inspection and meditation by an individual or instruction of a small circle did not necessarily contradict more public exposition and exhortation from the same book, and the mixture of material with both emphases in V and S suggests that both were envisaged.[11] The development from an overwhelmingly oral mediation of vernacular literature, in the thirteenth and the earlier fourteenth century, to the larger share of private reading in the later fourteenth and the fifteenth centuries is naturally reflected in the contents, physical presentation and actual enterprise of creating these volumes, or virtual libraries, as they have been called. Their size and weight (V weighed more than fifty pounds when complete) were not meant for easy removal from one place (or even one room, as the Bodleian staff know only too well) to another: they were ledgers or couchers for a community or a household, in a church, refectory, hall, chapel, chamber or cell, where individuals could look and read for themselves or to others, few or many, according to circumstances.

Part 3, the largest, of V is such a miscellany of long and short poems, after the opening *Northern Homilies*, with no obvious thematic sequence, that it seems likely that they were simply copied consecutively as exemplars came to hand, either the whole contents or a selection from each manuscript.[12] The *Speculum Vitae* and the *Prick of Conscience* are each long enough to occur normally in separate manuscripts, sometimes with other pieces, though they are found together in one fourteenth-century volume with Yorkshire linguistic features.[13] Most of the other items are not long enough to have stood by themselves in bound volumes, but circulation and copying in wrappered quires was common. The inclusion of two different poetical renderings of St Edmund Rich's *Mirror of the Church* (and a prose one in part 4) may have been deliberate, but the repetition of the same text of the *Trental of St Gregory*, with merely a few variants of scribal inadvertence, demonstrates that either different sources with some of the same contents were employed at long enough intervals for the duplication not to be noticed, or else the same source was still available and its previous use forgotten, by the same scribe in each case.[14] It also confirms that the selection of contents was not entirely pre-determined, or that directions could be muddled or misinterpreted because of the number of exemplars involved. Of thirty-two items in this part of V, after the *Homilies*,[15] more than half survive in other copies, mostly later in date but varying enough to show that they are not derived from V or S or their exemplars, and in manuscripts sufficiently diverse in contents to suggest that the majority do not go back to one or two previous anthologies but to a considerable range of sources.

The prose of part 4 of V is mainly devotional and ascetical, again in no definite order, but falling into short groups, including works of Rolle and Hilton and versions of thirteenth-century compositions of both kinds in *A Talking of the Love of God* and the *Roule of Reclous*. The poems[16] which conclude part 4, *Piers Plowman* and *Joseph of Arimathea* in alliterative verse, and *Judas and Pilate* from the Southern Legendary, revert rather to the narrative and homiletic characteristics of the previous parts, and part 5 contains both moralizing and devotional poems resembling the strains of some found earlier.[17] While the contents of part 5 of V probably came from a single source (in view of their internal similarities and the addition of two more pieces with the same characteristics at the end of part 3 of S), those of part 4 of V were probably drawn from half-a-dozen to a dozen separate manuscripts, if one compares the occurrence and grouping of the items in other extant volumes, and their relationships.

When the contents of the whole volume are thus reviewed one may conclude that there was an intention of broad categorization of the material, better achieved in some parts than others, probably hampered by difficulties in obtaining exemplars for the most suitable things at the right time to fit them in the best place, and by the impossibility of complete consistency if the selection was partly made when the copying was already well advanced. In modern military terms, the logistics of the operation were formidable. Taking other surviving manuscripts, although mostly later, as representative of the range of likely sources for a single work, a group or a selection, and even allowing for the association in vanished volumes of more pieces that are now only found scattered, it is hard to imagine the total of separate sources utilized for V as less than a couple of dozen of various formats, and possibly a good many more. That was a large collection of vernacular manuscripts and it is unlikely that they were all assembled at one time or available at one spot. Whether borrowed or bought (and purchase would have added heavily to the expense of the task), procurement of exemplars for this purpose required a very wide knowledge of existing religious literature, old and new, for V and S contain a considerable proportion of what we know to have been written in the relevant genres up to that period; and, moreover, the connections and influence by which it could be acquired for transcription by a provincial team.[18] In fourteenth-century conditions, outside London and the universities, and even within, this was not always easy commercially, when only standard service-books, text-books and manuals in Latin might be kept in stock and most other books had to be individually commissioned or found second-hand. The pre-history of V and S is therefore no less remarkable than the end-products: the craftsmen had behind them a system of support, supply and command.

The range of supply regionally can be assessed to some extent from cognate copies and internal evidence. The *Prikke* or *Spore of Love*, for instance (one of the versions of St Edmund's *Mirror*), found only in V and S, refers its audience to the Newark College at Leicester and its founder Duke Henry of Lancaster (d. 1360) in such a way as to imply they were near enough in time and place to have seen both, but had not necessarily done so, remarks which would have most point in the North Midlands.[19] The *King of Tars* is only found apart from V and S in the Auchinleck Manuscript, a poetical anthology usually accepted as of London manufacture *c.* 1330–40, but the texts (like those of other pieces in common) are not directly related.[20] The pseudo-Bonaventuran *Stimulus Amoris* in English prose at the beginning of part 4 of V, ascribed elsewhere to Walter Hilton, and later the expositions of psalms 90 and 91 attributable to him, Book I of his *Scale of Perfection*, and his *Mixed Life*, may have been copied here before or not long after his death in 1396, and had probably all been written after 1375 in the East Midlands (Cambridge and Nottinghamshire).[21] That Book II of the *Scale*, composed later but not issued separately, is not in V may indicate the comparative date of its compilation or the time-lag in circulation of an augmented work, paralleled in the case of *Piers Plowman*, of which the A text is present, not B or C. Yet a much later copy from the same exemplar as served for V and S both in the *Scale* and *Mixed Life* includes Book II, which may therefore have been omitted as too difficult for the anticipated users, or possibly a subsequent addition to the exemplar.[22] The *Roule of Reclous*, V's version of the *Ancren Riwle* is most closely related to the West Midland thirteenth-century manuscript Nero A.xiv, but it is followed in V by a piece on the commandments and penalties of sin found with the other fourteenth-century volume with a *Reclous*, Pepys 2498, by a Central Midland scribe, to which the nearest thirteenth-century *Riwle* is in Titus D.xviii, also more eastern in language.[23] It is surely more than a coincidence that *A Talking of the Love of God*, which precedes the *Roule* in V (and in S, incompletely), is made up partly of matter from two thirteenth-century pieces in Nero and Titus.[24] We can discern the outlines of a common source of intermediate date and locality from such hints.

When a group of texts or a single text in V/S is so closely connected with copies in other manuscripts that editors have been convinced that they shared the same immediate exemplar, even if we must allow for the disappearance or re-appearance of virtual duplicates, the context of the cognate copies may be specific enough to suggest the channels and directions in which those exemplars were obtained. Whereas the V/S text of Rolle's *Commandment* (in part 4 of each) is abridged and of uncertain origin, the *Form of Living* and *Ego Dormio* are amalgamated in a peculiar version found only otherwise in Rawlinson A.389 and Bibliothèque Ste Geneviève 3390, closely related.[25] The Rawlinson manuscript is a leading authority for Rolle's epistles, made up of work by two contemporary scribes, the first of whom used a central West Midland orthography "with a strong Northern underlay" in this item, and the author's surname (an exceptional event), while the second gave an independent copy of *Ego Dormio* in purely Northern English as well as the *Commandment* in the same West Midland spelling with Northern traces.[26] There can be little doubt that the compilers of Rawl. A.389 drew direct on important Yorkshire sources: its copy of the very popular poem "Jesu thy sweetness" is the closest to that in MS Rawl. poet.175, the leading (Yorkshire) one, and the nearest again is in V (part 2).[27] There may have been a similar intermediary between the *Long Charter of Christ* at the end of part 3 of V and that in MS Rawl. poet.175, to which it is specially close, and the *Appeal of Christ from the Cross* preceding Rolle's epistles in part 4 of V and S and the text in Cambridge University Library MS Dd.v.64, the coeval Yorkshire manuscript which is the other chief authority for the epistles besides MS Rawl. A.389.[28] Rawlinson A.389 was at Lichfield Cathedral from at least 1470 to 1627, and most of its contents appear likely to have been written in that locality, perhaps during the episcopate of Richard Scrope (1386–98), of the Yorkshire family prominent in the cult of Rolle and vernacular devotion.[29] Another multiply-related manuscript indicative of the common source, although not apparently from the same exemplar, is British Museum MS Addit.37787, a collection of Latin, English, and French by John Northwood, a Cistercian of Bordesley (Worcestershire), made sometime after 1386–8. Of the 20 English verse and prose pieces in it, 14 are also in V (and S where not defective) and in all but one the texts agree against all other known copies, if any.[30] The shorter poems occur in part 2 of V, the longer in part 3, and the prose confession in part 4, so the source-volume must have been at hand during the work on each, unless some were drawn from a related source.

That the sources tapped for V/S were diverse professionally as well as regionally may be inferred, not only from the cases of MS Rawl. A.389 (cathedral clergy) and MS BM Addit.37787 (monks), but also from such things as the topical moralizing refrain poems in part 5 of V (part 3 of S), which would fit best into the mouth of a friar or of a secular priest like the somewhat later Shropshire one, John Audelay, some of whose poems seem to be based on other items of which copies are found in V/S.[31] It is only in V/S that so many of the refrain poems of this group, distinguished by style and ethos, occur together although (as Professor Robbins has recently pointed out) nine of the twenty-four occur in thirteen other manuscripts, none having more than three; and they are all later, dispersed as widely as the East Riding, East Anglia, the East Midlands and Somerset, varying textually as might be expected from this and their semi-oral character.[32] Carleton Brown came to a somewhat different conclusion, that "the scribe of the Vernon MS . . . was not merely their collector, for he took the liberty (which he used elsewhere in the manuscript) of editing his material . . . from a comparison with these independent texts we discover that in most cases the Vernon text has been 'edited,' sometimes by transposing stanzas, sometimes by adding new ones, most frequently by altering lines or phrases."[33] Whether he was right in these instances or not, since his time the testimony of editors and students of other texts in V/S, to which he refers, based on their collation of closely-related copies, is repetitive. In Beatrice Daw Brown's words, "the scribe of the Vernon Manuscript was addicted to tinkering with the texts that came into his hands."[34]

One must qualify this judgement (echoed a little too literally by those who have encountered the phenomenon) by saying that not all such alterations can sensibly be thought to have been made by the actual scribes (not always the same in S as in V) in the course of copying the present volumes. The translation of the texts of diverse origin into a consistent orthography may reasonably be attributed to them, and some current modernizations of older expressions, but the more substantial deliberate suppressions and substitutions must surely be referred to the preparatory selection and supervisory control of the contents of the anthologies, according to their purposes or sympathies, merely carried out by the copyists. The omissions of hortatory and expository passages from the Southern Passion, as described by B. D. Brown, seem to make it more suitable for reading than preaching. It is of course possible that the scribe of most of V and portions of S was also the director, or perhaps rather one of the others whose hands appear less, but more probably someone not deeply involved in the physical production. As some of the peculiarly-modified texts of V/S survive in single other copies[35] it may be that sometimes a preparatory transcript had to be made, to serve as a clear exemplar for the V/S scribes, and also because occasionally the antecedent could not be brought to them or they could not go conveniently to it; and the intermediary remained as a potential source for others. It is certain that for some items in V/S more than one exemplar was available, from which a conflation, combination or change could be made, by someone's decision or practical necessity.[36]

The parallels and differences between V and S afford a good deal of additional evidence about the processes of compilation and manufacture of both, despite the loss of very many leaves and quires in S (more than half the total) and also many in V. The list and order of the majority of the contents are identical, and editors have established that in most cases their copies were taken from the same exemplars, in some instances independently, in others possibly one from the other, which is not surprising if quires for the two were being written about the same time in the same place by the same people under the same guidance.[37] Although it may have been the first intention, S is not and was not, from a fairly early stage, a simple replica of V, nor can either be said to be consistently prior to the other in the common texts. The fact that V is more uniform in appearance and was perhaps always more complete need not mean that it was first to be started or finished but the divergences of S in contents and structure are more intelligible if V was regarded as the basis, rather than the other way round. We must, however, remember that there may have been another largely parallel volume (or more) made by the same team, which would affect the relationships and our hypotheses.[38] Copying for two or more such volumes, if planned from the outset, could have been controlled so that they were made up of inter-changeable parts or booklets, by beginning and ending short groups of contents to coincide with quire-divisions.[39] But most of the copying for V and S was done consecutively over long runs of quires, with rare coincident divisions forming the parts already listed, and not so that they were all interchangeable, except for part 4 of each and perhaps for what matched parts 1 and 2 of V in S, and the difference of page-ruling argues against that being effected. The packing in more matter to the page, the omission of pictures, and the changes of hand suggest that what we now have as S was separately conceived as a slightly cheaper stable-partner of V and the discrepancies of contents and structure were the result of after-thoughts, adapting it to different tastes and needs. The possibility that S was experimental and V perfected does not satisfactorily account for all the facts, particularly of codicology, which there is not room to discuss in full here.

The contents of S which are not now (or never apparently were) in V commence with a prose meditation on the five wounds of Christ at the end of part 1. This text can only be understood as an expedient to fill most of the last page, by the first scribe after a mistake concerning the *Prick of Conscience* (connected with the cancellation of the rest of the quire) before a new quire beginning part 2, with the *Prick* from a different exemplar than that of V, yet by the main hand of V.[40] At the beginning of part 3, the *Book of Vices and Virtues* (not in V), in comparison with two other copies otherwise close in text, has a longer opening exposition of the Decalogue substituted for the original and an extra short tract on the Lord's Prayer inserted later, besides lesser alterations.[41] Its conclusion is missing with the loss of a whole quire, and there follows the end of a treatise by Sir John Clanvowe (d. 1391) and four more prose meditations not to be found in V.[42] The meditation on the wounds, the same tract on the Lord's Prayer, and Clanvowe's treatise occur otherwise only in the earlier portion of University College, Oxford, MS 97, together with the exposition of the Decalogue, the other four meditations and another eight English prose pieces, most or all of which could have been contained in the leaves missing in S, besides the end of the *Book* and the beginning of Clanvowe. The pieces in common do not run in the same order in both volumes, except for three and allowing for the displacement of three to fill particular niches in S, so both manuscripts may have drawn on a common source, probably nearer in size and scope of MS Univ. Oxford 97 than to S. It is difficult to conceive that all the items in common could have been picked out of S to form the smaller collection, obscured as some were. The relevant portion of Univ. MS, a small volume, contains various authorship ascriptions and documentary precedents which suggest that it was written (possibly in London) for a clerk of predominantly West Midland links not long after 1401; and later fifteenth-century additions show that by then it was near the Staffordshire/Worcestershire boundary.[43]

The decision to insert the augmented *Book* and following prose pieces at the beginning of a new part 3 in S seems to have occasioned the displacement of its copy of the *King of Tars* from the corresponding point in V to near the end of the same part, which finishes with the group of refrain and other poems found in part 5 of V, though with the addition of two more poems.[44] Changes of hand here may be connected with changes of mind which remain to be studied.

S now ends thirty-odd leaves short of the final contents of part 4 of V, and it is uncertain if it ever contained them.[45] The rubrication, illumination and foliation show that it was regarded as complete, whether or not it had a contents-table like V, or any prefatory treatise. Its differences of content display a further shift towards recent prose literature as evinced in part 4 of both volumes. Who the compilers and users may have been, where and when the work may have been done, are questions that must be discussed elsewhere.[46]

UNIVERSITY COLLEGE, DURHAM

NOTES

[1] Rossell Hope Robbins, "Mirth in Manuscripts," *E & S*, NS 21 (1968), pp. 17–20. A check-list of Middle English prose writings of spiritual guidance, by Dr Peter S. Jolliffe, based on part of his thesis for the University of London, 1967, is shortly to be published by the Pontifical Institute of Mediaeval Studies, Toronto.

[2] Cf. Falconer Madan, *et al.*, *A Summary Catalogue of Western Manuscripts in the Bodleian Library at Oxford*, II, ii (Oxford: Clarendon Press, 1937), pp. 789–92, Nos. 3938–42; Mary S. Serjeantson, "The Index of the Vernon Manuscript," *MLR* 32 (1937), pp. 222–61. The fullest accounts previously published, which in various respects complement mine, with a few points of disagreement, are those by Kari Sajavaara, "The Relationship of the Vernon and Simeon MSS," *NM*, 68 (1967), pp. 428–39; and *Middle English Translations of Robert Grosseteste's Chateau d'Amour*, Mémoires de la Société Néophilologique de Helsinki, 32 (1967), pp. 103–27. I must acknowledge here correspondence with the late Hope Emily Allen, 1947–53, and copies of the late J. A. Herbert's notes on V and S done for her and kindly sent to me by Mrs N. S. Baugh, to whom I am also indebted for conversation on the subject, as to Dr R. W. Hunt for encouragement to pursue it.

[3] Cf. *Catalogue of Additions to the Manuscripts in the British Museum in the Years* 1854–60 (London, 1875), pp. 623–6. There are convenient (somewhat reduced) facsimiles of one S hand and the main V hand in A. Miskimin (ed.), *Susannah* (New Haven: Yale Univ. Press, 1969), and a more representative specimen of V in M. Salvina Westra (ed.), *A Talkying of the Loue of God* (The Hague: Nijhoff, 1950), pp. xiv–xv.

[4] The Great Cowcher Books of the Duchy of Lancaster written by Richard Frampton between 1402 and 1407, two volumes with smaller but more leaves than V and S, in a more formal script and with superior illumination and illustration, cost £118 7s. It does not seem to have been the scribe's sole occupation. See R. Somerville, "The Cowcher Books of the Duchy of Lancaster," *EHR* 51 (1936), pp. 598–616; cf. H. E. Bell, "The Price of Books in Medieval England," *The Library*, 4th Ser., 17 (1936–7), pp. 312–32; W. Wattenbach, *Das Schriftwesen im Mittelalter*, 3rd edn. (1896), rpt. Graz (1959), pp. 289–93, for time-rates.

[5] There is more than one series of early quire-signatures in V, but they do not reflect all the structural divisions, so far as they can be seen, nor those in S.

[6] Miss Serjeantson's notes on the "Index" (as she calls it) cite the incipits and editions of most items besides the opening leaf and other details, which it is unnecessary to repeat.

[7] See now the modernization by G. Webb and A. Walker, *A Letter to his Sister by Aelred of Rievaulx* (London: A. R. Mowbray, 1957).

[8] Cf. H. G. Pfander, *The Popular Sermon of the Medieval Friar in England* (New York: New York Univ. Press, 1937), pp. 26–32, 52.

[9] Cf. Margaret Deanesly, *The Lollard Bible* (Cambridge: Cambridge Univ. Press, 1920), pp. 148–9.

[10] See Bodleian colour transparencies, roll no. 150B. for the miniatures, and post-card C68X for one of the Nativity. The diagram is reproduced by M. P. Hussey, "The Petitions of the Paternoster in Medieval English Literature," *MÆ*, 27 (1958), pp. 8–16, facing p. 13.

[11] Cf. G. R. Owst, *Preaching in Medieval England* (Cambridge: Cambridge Univ. Press, 1926), pp. 277–8.

[12] Cf. Cambridge University Library MS Dd. i. 1, of the fifteenth century, written by R. Staundone, including not only the nearest version of the *Northern Homilies* to V but also a verse homily on Corpus Christi [Carleton Brown and Rossell Hope Robbins, *Index of Middle English Verse* (New York: Columbia Univ. Press, 1943), No. 4250 (hereafter *Index*)] the Lamentation of St Bernard and Our Lady (*Index* No. 1869), and the prose exposition of Psalms 90 and 91 found in V, though not immediately affiliated in any of these cases.

[13] BM Addit. 33995, belonging to the north-western corner of the county, according to Professor Angus McIntosh's mapping of the MSS of the *Prick* (unpublished).

[14] *Index* Nos. 1512, 974, 1653; C. Horstmann and F. J. Furnivall (eds.), *Minor Poems of the Vernon MS* (EETS, OS 98, 117, 1892, 1901), pp. 221–51, 268–97, 260–7, 747–50.

[15] Serjeantson, op. cit., Nos. 322–54.

[16] It is of interest that the prose life of Adam and Eve which precedes *Piers Plowman* is apparently adapted from verse, and that of *Joseph of Arimathea* is written at first as prose before falling into metrical lines, perhaps for reasons of space.

[17] Serjeantson, op. cit., No. 377 (i–xxvii).

[18] Its provincial character is indicated by the orthography and the illumination.

[19] Horstmann and Furnivall, op. cit., p. 273.

[20] F. Kraus, "*Kleine Publikationen aus der Auchinleck—HS.*, IX," *Englische Studien*, 11 (1888), pp. 33–62. The *Debate between the body and the soul* (*Index*, No. 351) and the *Sayings of St Bernard* (*Index*, Nos 2865, 3310) are in both; Horstmann and Furnivall, op. cit., pp. 551–22 for the latter.

[21] C. Kirchberger (ed.) *The Goad of Love* (modernized) (London: Faber, 1952), esp. pp. 19–20; Björn Wallner (ed.), *An Exposition of Qui Habitat and Bonum Est in English*, Lund Studies in English 23 (1954); A. B. Emden, *A Biographical Register of the University of Cambridge to 1500* (Cambridge: Cambridge Univ. Press, 1963), pp. 305–6.

[22] Cf. A. J. Bliss, "Two Hilton Manuscripts in Columbia University Library" (Plimpton 257 and 271), *MÆ*, 38 (1969), pp. 157–63, based on findings of Miss R. Birts, to whom I owe the textual relationship.

[23] E. J. Dobson, "The Affiliations of the Manuscripts of Ancrene Wisse" in *English and Medieval Studies presented to J. R. R. Tolkien* (London: Allen & Unwin, 1962), pp. 128–63; M. L. Samuels, "Some Applications of Middle English Dialectology," *ES*, 44 (1963), pp. 81–94, esp. p. 87 for the Pepys scribe.

[24] Westra, op. cit., pp. xvi–xxii, suggests that it may have been adapted for V and S.

[25] H. E. Allen, *Writings ascribed to Richard Rolle*, MLA Monograph Series, 3 (1927), p. 247; W. P. Cumming, "A Middle English Manuscript in Bibliothèque Ste Geneviève, Paris," *PMLA*, 42 (1927), pp. 862–4.

[26] I owe these distinctions to Professor Angus McIntosh. For the first scribe's work and locality, and the question of dialect translation and mixture, see his lecture, "A New Approach to Middle English Dialectology," *ES*, 44 (1963), pp. 1–11.

[27] *Index* No. 1781, and Rossell Hope Robbins and John L. Cutler, *Supplement to the Index of Middle English Verse* (Lexington: Univ. of Kentucky Press, 1965) (hereafter *Suppl.*); Carlton Brown (ed.), *Religious Lyrics of the XIVth Century*, 2nd edn rev. by G. V. Smithers (Oxford: Clarendon Press, 1952), pp. 61–5.

[28] *Index* No. 1718; M. C. Spalding (ed.), *The Middle English Charters of Christ*, Bryn Mawr College Monographs, 15 (1914), esp. pp. xcix–c; *Index* and *Suppl.* No. 3826; Brown, op. cit., p. 93; cf. Allen, op. cit., pp. 37, 294.

[29] N. R. Ker, "Patrick Young's Catalogue of the Manuscripts of Lichfield Cathedral," *MRS*, 2 (1950), pp. 166–7; Allen, op. cit., pp. 504–8.

[30] Nita Scudder Baugh, *A Worcestershire Miscellany* (Philadelphia: priv. ptd., 1956), esp. pp. 37–9.

[31] E. K. Whiting (ed.), *The Poems of John Audelay* (EETS, OS 184, 1931), pp. 235, 241. Not all the contents of Douce 302 are Audelay's own work. Amongst lost items from V (Serjeantson, op. cit., No. 203) was a prayer of Bede on the seven words of Christ on the Cross; judging from its place in part 2, probably a poem, of which Audelay had a specimen, *Index*, No. 2468.

[32] Rossell Hope Robbins, "A Refrain-Poem from N. L. W. Peniarth 395," *Triv.*, 4 (1969), pp. 43–9; the areas I mention are those of MSS BM Addit 31042, Sloane 2593, Caligula A. ii, Trinity Cambridge 0.9.38. and perhaps Garrett 143. See also Robbins, "*Conuertimini*," *NM*, 73 (1972), pp. 353–61.

[33] Brown, op. cit., pp. xx–xxi. His diagnosis of the original authorship of a number of the poems, in minimizing the share of mendicants, is also disputable.

[34] *Southern Passion* (EETS, OS 169, 1925), p. xxvi n., quoting Josephine D. Sutton, "Hitherto Unprinted Manuscripts of the Middle English *Ipotis*," *PMLA*, 31 (1916), pp. 114–60; cf. R. W. Tryon, "Miracles of Our Lady in Middle English Verse," *PMLA*, 38 (1923), p. 334; R. W. Chambers and J. H. G. Grattan, "The Text of *Piers Plowman*," *MLR*, 4 (1909), pp. 367–70; W. N. Francis (ed.), *Book of Vices and Virtues* (EETS, OS 217, 1942), pp. lxxv–vi; N. S. Baugh, op. cit., pp. 45, 50.

[35] Plimpton 257 & 271 for Hilton's *Scale* and *Mixed Life*, Harley 875 for *Piers Plowman*.

[36] T. F. Simmons (ed.), *Lay Folks Mass-Book* (EETS, OS 71, 1879), p. 362, notes the uses of two sources in V; Miss C. Kirchberger, op. cit., noticed the use by the V contents-table of a different list of chapters than for the actual text of the *Goad of Love*, p. 20 n.; and Professor A. McIntosh has found that V and S had different exemplars for the *Prick of Conscience*. It is obvious that some of the miscellanies used as sources must have overlapped in contents, with variant texts.

[37] E.g. R. F. Weymouth (ed.), *Castel off Loue* (London: Philological Soc., 1864), pp. iv–v; H. L. D. Ward, *Catalogue of Romances in the Department of Manuscripts of the British Museum*, I (London, 1883), pp. 763–4; Brown, op. cit., p. xx; cf. Horstmann and Furnivall, op. cit., pp. 205, 223, 446, 749, 751; Westra, op. cit., pp. xvi, 78; A. Miskimin, op. cit., pp. 29–30, 34.

[38] Miss Allen was led to this question by the occurrence of related contemporary notes in both V and S concerning the copying of poems from part 3 of S and of V, but it is not clear if they refer to another large volume or a shorter one.

[39] As, for instance, in the Auchinleck MS where there are twelve, in 334 leaves.

[40] The reasons for these changes will have to be explored elsewhere.

[41] Francis, op. cit., pp. li–ii.

[42] V. J. Scattergood (ed.), "The Two Ways: an Unpublished Religious Treatise by Sir John Clanvowe," *EPS*, 10 (1967), pp. 33–56; cf. E. P. Wilson, "A supplementary note," *EPS*, 11 (1968), pp. 55–6; C. Horstmann, *Yorkshire Writers*, II (London: Swan Sonnenschein, 1896), pp. 436–49. Only one other MS, Laud misc. 174, has as many as four of the pieces in S and Univ. 97.

[43] Cf. Pfander, op. cit., pp. 54–64, who is misled by a defective date into putting it after 1404.

[44] *Index*, No. 4135, 1369: Horstmann and Furnivall, op. cit., pp. 740–6.

[45] Westra, op. cit., p. xv, argues from a strip of a blank ruled leaf at the end that it was not finished.

[46] Eventually, I hope, in the publication of the Lyell Lectures, 1967, on English Scribes and Scriptoria of the Later Middle Ages.

28

THE DATING IN THE
CANTERBURY TALES

BY A. A. PRINS

The opening lines of the *Canterbury Tales*:[1]

> Whan that Aprill with his shoures soote
> The droghte of March hath perced to the roote   (I, 1–2)
> . . . and the yonge sonne
> Hath in the Ram his halve cours yronne   (I, 7–8)

have always been a stumbling-block in connection with the date in the Introduction to the *Man of Law's Tale*:

> He wiste it was the eightetethe day
> Of Aprill, that is messager to May,   (II, 5–6)

this eighteenth of April probably being the second day of the pilgrimage.

The natural interpretation of the lines in the *Prologue* would no doubt be that the sun had covered the first half, that is, the first fifteen degrees of the zodiacal sign of Aries (Ram). Now, in Chaucer's time, owing to the difference between the Julian Calendar of the time and our present Gregorian Calendar, the vernal equinox (that is the moment when the sun is in its ascending node or point of intersection between the ecliptic and equator) did not fall on 21 March as it does now, but on 12 March. The sun entered the zodiacal sign of Taurus one month later, on 11 or 12 April. The sun would therefore have covered the first half of Aries on 27 March and the second half on 12 April. Neither of these dates would fit in with the dating as given in the Introduction to the *Man of Law's Tale*.

Unless we assume a certain poetic licence or inconsistency on the part of Chaucer, we are therefore compelled to give a somewhat forced interpretation to "hath in the Ram his halve cours yronne," saying that Chaucer meant the second half of Aries; or rather that

342

the sun's course in April comprised twelve degrees in Aries and eighteen degrees in Taurus, and that the first half of its course during April (which was for the greater part in the sign of Aries) had been completed. But it cannot be denied that Chaucer's use of "half" in that case would not be quite correct, for by 15 April the sun was already three or four degrees in Taurus. Here also we can, of course, assume that this is a case of poetic licence, but Chaucer is generally fairly accurate in his astronomical and astrological data. Moreover, this interpretation is far from natural and only resorted to by commentators in their efforts to vindicate the text or Chaucer's consistency. For it seems somewhat unnatural, when referring to April in line 1, to speak of the sun's "halve cours" having been in the Ram in lines 7–8.[2]

There need, however, be no inconsistency at all if it is assumed that Chaucer does not here refer to the zodiacal sign but to the constellation of fixed stars, i.e. the stellar zodiac. Owing to the precession of the equinoxes, the vernal equinoctial point, which is the beginning of the mathematical or terrestrial (or astrological) zodiac and therefore corresponds to zero degrees Aries, moves backward with regard to the stellar (or solar) zodiac. Thus the vernal equinoctial point (0° Aries) corresponded with 0° Aries, or the beginning of the stellar constellation Aries, in the year 108 BC. In the year AD 2048[3] it will correspond with 0° Pisces of the stellar zodiac. Its retrogression is therefore 30° in 2156 years. In Chaucer's time (let us put the date at 1393 for convenience' sake[4]) the precession would be $\frac{1500}{2156} \times 30$ degrees or roughly 5/7 of 30° = 21°. This means that it corresponded with 30 minus 21 = 9° Pisces of the stellar zodiac. The sun would therefore still have to cover 21° to reach 0° Aries of the stellar zodiac. Since the sun travels 1° per day, it would reach this point twenty-one days after 12 March, that is on 2 April. By 17 April it would have covered fifteen degrees or half of the stellar zodiacal sign of Ram. Hence Chaucer could have said that on 16 or 17 April "the yonge sonne hath in the Ram his halve cours y-ronne."

There is one objection to this argument, namely that in European astrology all notations since the Middle Ages have been based on the mathematical (or terrestrial) zodiac and not on the stellar zodiac. But formerly astrologers always took the influence of the larger fixed stars into account and they were perfectly familiar with the difference between the two zodiacs and the precession of the equinoxes. Chaucer would probably have dealt with the subject in the *Astrolabe* if he had finished that treatise. He expressly refers to the difference in the *Franklin's Tale*:

> And by his eighte speere in his wirkyng
> He knew ful wel how fer Alnath was shove
> Fro the heed of thilke fixe Aries above,
> That in the ninthe speere considered is;
> Ful subtilly he kalkuled al this.   (V, 1280–4)

In Chaucer's time the terrestrial (or astrological) zodiac was supposed to be attached to the fixed ninth sphere; the fixed stars (the stellar constellations) and hence the stellar zodiac to the movable eighth sphere, and the sun and moon and the planets (Mercury, Venus, Mars, Jupiter, and Saturn) to seven other spheres, which were also movable. Hence the stellar constellations moved forwards with regard to the supposedly fixed terrestrial zodiac in the ninth sphere or *primum mobile*.[5] Alnath is the name for the bright star α Arietis, which in the year 108 BC corresponded roughly with 0° Aries of the terrestrial zodiac ("the heed of thilke fixe Aries above") and was very near it when Hipparchus discovered the precession more than a century before the Christian era.[6] In Chaucer's time it must, as we saw, have "shove" about twenty-one degrees. This proves that Chaucer, as might be expected, was not only familiar with the precession, but also took it into account.

Moreover, in the *Squire's Tale* he definitely locates a fixed star (Aldiran) in Leo:

> And yet ascendynge was the beest roial,
> The gentil Leon, with his Aldiran,
> Whan that this Tartre kyng, this Cambyuskan,
> Roos fro his bord, ther as he sat ful hye.   (V, 264–7)

This star Aldiran has been identified, though not with absolute certainty, as θ Hydrae, which rises just before the splendid star α Leonis.[7] This indicates that Chaucer here clearly does not indicate the ascendant by the zodiacal sign Leo, in his ninth sphere, but by the stellar constellation in sphere eight.

The traditional astrological indication is given in the *Squire's Tale*:

> Up riseth fresshe Canacee hirselve,
> As rody and bright as dooth the yonge sonne,
> That in the Ram is foure degrees up ronne.   (V, 384–6)

The time indicated is "The laste Idus of March" (F 47), i.e. 15 March, which corresponds exactly to the sun's position of 4° Aries (astrologically) in Chaucer's time in a leap year (16 March in other years).

There is one passage in the *Nun's Priest's Tale* which apparently seems to contradict the explanation given above with regard to the opening lines of the *Prologue*, namely:

Whan that the month in which the world bigan,
That highte March, whan God first maked man,
Was compleet, and passed were also,
Syn March bigan, tway monthes and dayes tuo,
Bifel that Chauntecleer in al his pryde,
His sevene wyves walkynge by his syde,
Caste up his eyen to the brighte sonne,
That in the signe of Taurus had yronne
Twenty degrees and oon, and somwhat moore,
And knew by kynde, and by noon oother loore,
That it was pryme, and crew with blisful stevene.

(VII, 3187–97)

Instead of "tway monthes and dayes tuo," which is the reading found in MS Harl[4] (Harley 7334), and adopted by me in this place for reasons which will soon become clear, the other manuscripts have "thritty dayes and two." Now, though Skeat says about this manuscript that it "requires very careful watching" and that "it is not the kind of MS that should be greatly trusted," he adds: "There is no doubt as to its early age and its frequent helpfulness in difficult passages."[8] I suggest that this might be a case in which MS Harley 7334 has the more natural and better reading. For it is generally accepted that the date meant is 3 May, which is confirmed by other indications, for which I refer the reader to Skeat's note on the passage.[9] It is obvious that if the date meant is 3 May, it can only be arrived at by giving a highly unnatural interpretation to "Syn March bigan" if we accept the reading "thritty dayes and two." It is then generally interpreted as being "parenthetical," but I fail to see that this solves the difficulty at all.[10]

Considering that the sun entered the zodiacal sign of Aries on 12 March, this implies that when it reached 21° in Taurus, "and somwhat moore," the date must indeed have been 3 May. To argue that Chaucer meant 3 April (apart from the reading in MS Harley 7334 and Skeat's note) would not help us to arrive at the correct degree, even if we interpreted the astronomical indication as referring to the stellar zodiac. For, in fact, 3 April would correspond with 21° Aries of the terrestrial zodiac and hence with 0° Aries of the stellar zodiac.

But we should not be entitled to do this in any case, for Chaucer explicitly says: the *signe* of Taurus, which clearly refers to the mathematical (or astrological) zodiacal sign. If we bear this in mind, this passage, instead of refuting our interpretation of the opening lines of the *Prologue*, might rather confirm it, for in the opening lines of the Prologue the word "sign" is not used. It could, however, be argued that this reasoning is a little too close, because Chaucer may have inserted or omitted the words "the sign of" as the metre required. This may indeed be the case and therefore its omission or insertion does not constitute irrefutable proof. But even so, the passage from the *Nun's Priest's Tale* cannot be quoted to disprove our contention. If it does not confirm it, it in no way refutes it.

So the evidence points to two things. First of all, Chaucer knew about the precession of the equinoxes and took it into account in the *Franklin's Tale*. Secondly, on one occasion (in the *Squire's Tale*) at least he definitely refers to the stellar zodiac and not to the terrestrial (astrological) zodiac. It seems therefore not unwarranted to assume that he may also have done so in the *Prologue* to the *Canterbury Tales*. If this is indeed the case, it would solve a seeming inconsistency between the dating as given in the *Prologue* and that given in the Introduction to the *Man of Law's Tale*.

UNIVERSITY OF LEYDEN

NOTES

[1] All citations from F. N. Robinson (ed.), *The Works of Geoffrey Chaucer*, 2nd edn (Boston: Houghton Mifflin, 1957).

[2] The only significant variant in line 8: half his (course) might perhaps be adduced in support of this interpretation, but even so the variant is found in MS Py (Royal College of Physicians), which dates, according to John M. Manly and Edith Rickert, *The Text of the Canterbury Tales* (Chicago: Chicago Univ. Press, 1940), I, p. 439, from 1460 to 1480, which is fairly late and therefore hardly authoritative in this respect.

[3] This is not quite correct, since between the year 1 BC and AD 1 there is only one year. The exact date would therefore be AD 2049. But in our case the difference is immaterial.

[4] Applying the correction in note 3, this gives 108 plus 1393 minus 1, which is 1500.

[5] Walter W. Skeat (ed.), *The Complete Works of Geoffrey Chaucer* (Oxford: Clarendon Press, 1899), V, p. 394.

[6] It is of course possible that "syn March bigan" is a corruption of "syn March bigon," i.e. since March past (cf. *MED* s.b. bī-gōn, 827b: past, gone by) or bē gōn: "is (was) over," in which case "thritty dayes and two" would indeed refer to 3 May. But the past participle is rare and the sense of be gone somewhat strained.

[7] Skeat, op. cit., V, p. 380; Robinson, op. cit., p. 719. It is true that whereas the twelve zodiac signs are exactly thirty degrees each, the constellations vary among themselves. Thus the constellation Aries is only twenty-five degrees in length, when measured along the ecliptic, and Taurus thirty-nine degrees. But it is quite probable that just as the terrestrial zodiac was divided into twelve signs of equal length, the stellar zodiac was also divided into twelve equal parts roughly corresponding with the constellations. This is at least the case in some

modern works on astrology which refer to the subject. Cf. Ir. C. J. Snijders, *Beginselen der Astrologie* (Amsterdam: Becht, 1940), p. 20; and especially A. E. Tiernens, *Cosmologie Elementen der Practische Astrologie* ('s-Gravenhage, 1941), p. 13, where the terrestrial and solar zodiacs are depicted, each being divided into twelve equal signs of thirty degrees each. That this division of the two zodiacs into twelve equal signs is an old one may be inferred from Prof. Dr E. Zinner, *Die Geschichte der Sternkunde von den ersten Anfängen bis zur Gegenwart* (Berlin: Springer, 1931). In the chapter entitled *"Die Sternkunde der Araber,"* the two zodiacs are mentioned: *"Der Aequator und der feste Tierkreis gehören dem obersten sternlosen Himmel der täglichen Bewegung an; der bewegliche Tierkreis ist aber mit dem 8. Himmel der Sterne verbunden"* (p. 293). In this view, as in Chaucer's, the terrestrial zodiac is considered as fixed, the solar zodiac as movable.

8 Skeat, op. cit., V, p. xx. Cf. J. B. Hinckley, *Notes on Chaucer* (1907; rpt. New York: Haskell House, 1964), for identification of Aldiran with Castor and Pollux (α and β of Gemini); and cf. Robinson, whose note to V, 263 cannot be correct, for there would at least be a complete sign (Cancer) between Gemini and Leo.

9 Skeat, op. cit., V, p. 250, note to l. 4045.

10 The date of MS Harley 7334 is given in Manly and Rickert, op. cit., I, 220, as 1410. The other variants are irrelevant.

29

VARIETIES OF MIDDLE ENGLISH
RELIGIOUS PROSE

BY NORMAN F. BLAKE

Accounts of Middle English prose, in any case relatively infrequent, have generally confined themselves to an outline of its historical development with occasional fuller comments on the more important texts. Style and tone are the usual criteria used to distinguish the historical development, though more recently the audience has been added.[1] So far we have had no survey of the various genres and types of Middle English prose; an approximation was the survey in *A Manual of the Writings in Middle English* by John Edwin Wells, now being rewritten.[2] In this manual, certain texts were grouped together for convenience, and no attempt was made to justify the arrangement. Yet the purpose and intention of seemingly similar works may well be different: although Rolle and Hilton are contemplatives, their works are strikingly different; even the works of Rolle are not all of the same type; or, to take a final example, not all sermons are comparable with one another since they were written for diverging purposes and follow different models. Indeed, we may limit our appreciation of individual sermons by regarding them as all belonging to a genre called "sermon."

The absence of a survey of the various types of Middle English prose with their characteristics has prevented a proper assessment of its contribution to the development of literature and has encouraged undue concentration upon certain texts and authors. Religious literature, however, is such an important part of that literature that we ought to start thinking of the literary contribution it made. This may perhaps best be accomplished within some kind of framework, and this article is an attempt to provide such a framework for the various types of Middle English prose. It will necessarily be incomplete and will doubtless have to be modified later, for not only are many Middle English prose texts as yet unedited or even undiscovered, but also the majority have not been properly assessed by modern scholars. My attempt to accommodate Middle English religious prose works into some schematized framework does not imply that all works can readily be fitted into a watertight system; a certain amount of overlap and uncertainty is inevitable. I hope, though, that it may provide a way of approaching the great mass of religious prose with more understanding and insight and that it may encourage further work in this area. It will certainly underline what is our greatest need in Middle English studies at the moment, so forcibly pointed out by Rossell Hope Robbins: we still have no index of Middle English prose to match that of the verse.[3]

Different criteria may be necessary for different genres, but in general I shall consider the purpose for which a particular text was written, since that purpose will often determine the form and approach, as its most important feature.

WORKS DESIGNED FOR INSTRUCTION

(a) Primary instruction: explanation and teaching

The author usually has a particular audience in mind, and his intention is straightforward and readily discernible: to explain some part of Christian teaching or to give rules for the conduct of life. Hence the material will be arranged in a catalogue or at least in an ordered progression—there would be no point in explaining something if the audience could not understand the explanation. The style will tend in most cases to simplicity and to the avoidance of emotive language and imagery. Within this group of primary instruction we may recognize several subgroups.

(1) Explanations of the tenets of Christian belief. Examples include at a simple level *Dan Gaytryge's Sermon* and in a fuller version *The Book of Vices and Virtues*.[4] The former arranges the various tenets in a simple catalogue so that each Christian may be aware of what he ought to believe; the latter tries to explain in greater detail what is implied by those various tenets. Both are schematic and follow an overall plan, though neither has any great pretensions to literary excellence.

(2) Translations of biblical texts and commentaries. Typical of this group is Rolle's prose Psalter with its commentary.[5] Apart from Rolle's work there are many translations and expansions of parts of the Bible, such as the Ten Commandments, and of Latin commentaries, such as the English version of the *Historia Scholastica*. Here belong those sermons based on a biblical text, but not those commentaries which are arranged more as meditations than as explanations of the Bible. The text of the Bible is explained as an end in itself in this group. Hence the arrangement of the works in it will usually

follow the part of the Bible they are translating, or in the case of the sermons they will follow the patterns of the *artes praedicandi*.

(3) Expositions of the services of the Church. A famous example is the *Mirror of Our Lady* written for the nuns at Syon Abbey.[6] This work sets out to explain the divine services in which the nuns take part so that they can participate with greater understanding and devotion. In arrangement the work follows the Latin of the service upon which it is a commentary. Besides this work there are extant explanations of the many movable and immovable feasts of the Church which may be regarded as part of the Temporale.

(4) Rules for conduct for a particular way of life. The essential feature of these texts is that they were written for a particular form of life or to give advice about a particular problem that arises during such a life, though naturally others could benefit in a more general way from this advice. These treatises include not only those with rules for a particular order, such as the *Rule of St Benedict* and the *Rule of St Saviour*,[7] but also more general recommendations to particular individuals or groups of people how they should regulate their lives. The difficulty in allocating texts to this group is that although some were written for specialized audiences, they were often read more widely as texts of general applicability. The *Ancren Riwle* is a typical example.[8] Written to advise three noble ladies on how to live as anchoresses, it was adapted for other audiences. Hilton's *Scala Perfectionis* was written for a recluse but contained much that was of a broader application;[9] so too the *Epistle of Discretion of Stirrings*. Many of the texts placed in this subgroup have been considered as mystical texts and have been treated as similar to Rolle's mystical texts. Such a procedure is justifiable if one is considering the development of English contemplation, but it can be unhelpful from a literary point of view. For Rolle's texts are descriptive and lyrical in tone, whereas the texts in this subgroup are more practical in purpose and restrained in tone. A comparison of the more mystical texts in this subgroup with the others in the subgroup, such as the *Rule of St Benedict*, still remains to be carried out; it could, I think, provide insights into the structure and organization of texts like the *Ancren Riwle*.

(b) Secondary instruction

The texts in this latter grouping were not, as far as we can tell, written for a particular person or persons to answer a particular need, but designed for general instruction and edification. This naturally presented an important problem of style and tone for the author. He had to make his material interesting for a whole range of people. Whereas the authors of primary instruction preserve an even tone because they know the person they are addressing and are sure of a hearing, those of secondary instruction are liable to fall into a more extravagant and strident style because they are afraid of losing their audience's attention. The purpose of these works will be to explain some part of accepted Christian belief or behaviour, and often they will deal with only one topic, like virginity or sin. The methods chosen to promote the subject vary widely, for each author will choose that method of presentation which suits his subjects best. Consequently this group will seem to have little formal unity, although the problems facing individual authors were similar. Some will use simple exposition, others allegory, and yet others the debate. Many will combine several types of presentation, for the need to keep the material lively and interesting is a demanding one.

Hali Meidenhad is a good example of the type. It is, like so many texts of this group, ostensibly an exposition of one Christian virtue, in this case virginity. But it is not addressed to any particular woman to help her lead her life in virginity; it is a general defence of that life. The treatise starts out as an allegorical exposition of a passage from Psalm 44. The more straightforward tone of allegorical exposition soon gives way to that of outraged disgust that anyone who was the bride of Christ could forgo that to become the bride of a human man. This leads to rather strident comparisons between the life of human marriage and that of spiritual marriage, in which exaggeration is a predominant feature. The tone can vary from the lyrical, as in the praise of virginity, to the coarse, as in the description of a human wife's condition. In this latter we see a tendency to the dramatic, a tendency characteristic of these texts which must force themselves on our attention. This tendency can also be seen in the use of personification allegory, which in this case takes the form of a contest between Virginity and Lechery. Finally the example of the virgin saints is held up as a model to be emulated.

This variety of approach is not uncommon in works of this category. It may be seen in such other works as *Abbey of the Holy Ghost*, which uses both allegory and drama, *Vices and Virtues*, composed predominantly in the debate form, *Treatise of Ghostly Battle*, a more straightforward allegory of a Christian knight's armour, and various types of exemplum literature such as the *Game of Chess*.[10]

WORKS OF A HISTORICAL AND LEGENDARY CHARACTER

Although their final aim, as with all religious literature, may be instruction, their starting point is different. These works do not deal with church services or with aspects of Christian behaviour, but they describe what has happened in human history, particularly the history of the Jews and of Christian peoples. Again one cannot distinguish a particular audience for whom such works were written since most were directed at a general public. The framework of each work is based round the narrative which provides the structure, though the narrative is often broken down into episodes. Each episode can then be used to illustrate the working of divine providence, and the desire to make this explicit often leads to the introduction of material of a legendary type. In one respect texts in this group resemble works of primary instruction since they both follow an external story or plan which is provided; but in another they resemble those of secondary instruction since the teaching takes second place to the vehicle of instruction. All the works have a narrative structure and often the instruction is either implicit or simply appended as a kind of moral.

If subgroups are to be set up, they will be based on the external form of the works themselves.

(a) *Saints' lives*
These are usually short, and are based on the biography of a person, as in the *Golden Legend*.

(b) *Longer historical works*
These works seek to show the exemplary nature of much that happened in the past, like the *Polychronicon*, translated by John Trevisa and printed by William Caxton.[11]

(c) *Historical romances*
Some might not wish to include this subgroup, shading off from the foregoing, as religious prose at all. A work like *Charles the Great*, printed by Caxton in 1483, was designed as history even though it can be distinguished only with difficulty from many romances.[12]

(d) *Apocryphal works*
Somewhat similar to the historical romances, these works are legendary and exotic, and attempt to fill in the historical record not covered by the Bible. They include legends of the Cross, stories about Adam and Eve, various accounts of Christ's life (particularly his childhood), and the *Gospel of Nicodemus*.

AFFECTIVE WORKS

This group, designed to stir up an emotional response from the audience, can be divided into four subgroups depending on their aim:

(a) To frighten the listener

Such works are usually descriptive, with a particular emphasis upon the horrific aspects of hell, the terror and suddenness of death, and the need for immediate repentance. The descriptions often amount to little more than a heaping up of one awesome detail upon another, and these catalogues are liberally interspersed with exempla of those who have failed to repent in time. Typical of this subgroup is the *Lambeth Sermon on Sunday*, which portrays Paul's visit to hell. When he gets there his guide, St Michael, shows him all the horrors of hell and the torments suffered by those who failed to repent on earth. The distress felt by Paul at the sights should be shared by us when we read the passage, for we must be made to repent through fear. Not very dissimilar are the various legendary accounts of visits to the other world such as *St Patrick's Purgatory* and the *Vision of the Monk of Eynsham*.[13]

(b) To entice the listener

In the foregoing works, however, there is also another element in so far as the visitor goes beyond hell to paradise, which is described in opposite terms. The terror of hell is thereby reinforced by the attraction of heaven. This approach is characteristic likewise of the many *Ars Moriendi* Pieces, which as the title implies are concerned with death. In *The Art of Dying*, for example, the Good Christian is urged to prepare himself for the next life by sending his soul out in advance to inspect the terrors of hell, the pains of purgatory, and the joys of heaven so that what he sees will encourage him to lead his life in a true Christian manner. In all these pieces there is little teaching as such, and the moral is quite simple and unambiguous: repent while you still have time. The bulk of such works is made up of descriptive passages which are arranged either in a catalogue or by means of contrast. The audience for such pieces was a very general one.

(c) To emphasize the emotional affinity for Christ or Mary felt by the listener

The imagery of the spiritual marriage recurs frequently in the works in this subgroup; best known are those in the English contemplative tradition associated with Rolle.[14] They share many characteristics with the second affective subgroup since description is more important than teaching. Hence the use of evocative imagery, lyrical phraseology, contrast and descriptive catalogues is common enough. The descriptions are often based on the human life of Christ and the life of Mary to underline how these ought to affect the Christian who considers them. Consequently these pieces draw heavily upon physical descriptions, the passion of Christ, and the sufferings and joys of Mary so that the conscience may be stirred and the heart wrung. The organization of the whole work is often less important than the evocative nature of its parts, and a certain amount of repetition is almost inevitable. The audience for this subgroup is more restricted than that for the other, since emotional attraction was clearly considered more suitable for religious than for lay people. Yet though these pieces may be addressed to an individual they are often more concerned with the author than the recipient, since the author's example will arouse the emotional responses of the reader.

(d) To assist the listener's devotions
Typical of these works are the prayers, some restrained, like the *Fifteen Oes* printed by Caxton in 1490,[15] others more lyrical and affective, like the so-called *Wooing*-group prayers. *The Wooing of Our Lord* itself might well be claimed for the affective group, but its purpose appears to be different. It was written as a prayer to be said by a religious as part of her devotions and it may in fact have fulfilled a liturgical purpose. Such prayers could be used in both private and public devotions, and inevitably brevity is necessary. Another type of work is that divided into passages suitable for meditation; usually the basic text was a part of the Bible (even if expanded) or a work describing someone's religious experience. Love's *Mirror of the Life of Christ* is a familiar example, but the prose life of Christ edited by Goates is in the same mould.[16] In the material they use, these works are similar to the legendary-historical works, but the intention behind them puts them into a different category and leads to their particular arrangement.

SPIRITUAL AUTOBIOGRAPHIES

Of the few texts, the best-known work is of course *The Book of Margery Kempe*, which describes Margery's life and religious experiences.[17] Such works are too individual to be easily categorized, though they will be planned round the life or visions which they are describing. They are intended more as a record than to influence or direct others.

POLEMICAL LITERATURE

This group includes many Wycliffite writings as well as the pieces which make up the controversy between Jack Upland and Friar Daw.[18] Here again it is difficult adequately to categorize the works because of their great differences. A biting tone and the use of satire are common enough. Teaching is not so important as the desire to score off an opponent. Religious and their way of life are frequently criticized, though such attacks are of a general nature. Thus in *The Perversion of the Works of Mercy* little attempt is made to encourage people to live virtuously, since the piece is more concerned to point out the shortcomings of others than to teach them how to live better lives. These shortcomings are described in a carping spirit and no allowance is made for the frailty of man, for these works are essentially polemical.

To attempt, as I have done, to arrange all Middle English religious prose in a few broad categories may well be regarded as a rash undertaking. I can only repeat what I have already said, that I hope it may lead to a greater understanding of religious prose. For those who disagree with my arrangement will no doubt indicate where I have gone wrong, and so promote a fuller appreciation of the purposes of the writers of Middle English religious prose and how this purpose influenced the way they set about their works. We have for too long been satisfied simply to edit the texts and trace their sources; it is time we moved on.

UNIVERSITY OF SHEFFIELD

NOTES

[1] N. F. Blake, "Middle English Prose and its Audience," *Anglia*, 90 (1972), 437–55.

[2] John Edwin Wells, *A Manual of the Writings in Middle English 1050–1400*, with nine supplements (New Haven, Conn.: Connecticut Academy, 1926–51); a completely new manual, which includes the fifteenth century, is now being edited by J. Burke Severs (1967), and Albert E. Hartung (1972).

[3] See R. H. Robbins, "Mirth in Manuscripts," *E&S*, NS 21 (1968), pp. 1–28; and earlier (1964) in the Introduction, p. xxiv, to his *Supplement to the Index of Middle English Verse*, with John L. Cutler (Lexington, Ky.: Univ. of Kentucky Press, 1965).

[4] *Gaytryge's Sermon* is edited in N. F. Blake, *Middle English Religious Prose* (London: Edward Arnold, 1972). Other works in this collection are not referred to in these footnotes. W. Nelson Francis (ed.), *The Book of Vices and Virtues* (EETS, OS 217, 1942).

[5] *Rolle's Psalter* is edited by Henry Ramsden Bramley (Oxford: Clarendon Press, 1884).

[6] J. H. Blunt, *The Myroure of Oure Ladye* (EETS, ES 19, 1873).

[7] M. M. Arnold Schröer, *Die Winteney-Version der Regula S Benedicti* (Halle, 1888), and E. A. Koch, *The Rule of St Benet* (EETS, OS 120, 1902). *The Rule of St Saviour* is unedited.

[8] The Early English Text Society is in the process of printing all the MS versions of the *Ancren Riwle*.

[9] Evelyn Underhill, *The Scale of Perfection* (London: J. M. Watkins, 1923); this text has modernized spelling.

[10] F. Holthausen, *Vices and Virtues* (EETS, OS 89, 159, 1888, 1921); the *Treatise of Ghostly Battle* is edited in C. Horstmann, *Yorkshire Writers* (London: Swan Sonnenschein, 1895–96), II, pp. 420–36; W. E. A. Axon, *Caxton's Game and Plays of the Chesse* (London: Elliot Stock, 1885).

[11] Churchill Babington and Joseph Rawson Lumby, *Polychronicon Ranulphi Higden*, Rolls Series 41, 9 vols (London: Eyre and Spottiswoode, 1865–86).

[12] S. J. H. Herrtage, *The Lyfe of the Noble and Crysten Prynce Charles the Grete* (EETS, ES 36, 37, 1880–1).

[13] C. Horstmann, *Altenglische Legenden* (Paderborn, 1875); and E. Arber, *The Vision of the Monk of Eynsham* (London: Constable, 1901).

[14] Hope Emily Allen, *English Writings of Richard Rolle Hermit of Hampole* (Oxford: Clarendon Press, 1931).

[15] Stephen Ayling, *The Fifteen O's and Other Prayers* (London: Griffith and Farran, 1869).

[16] Laurence Fitzroy Powell, *The Mirrour of the Blessed Lyf of Jesu Christ* (London: Henry Frowde, 1908); and M. Goates, *The Pepysian Gospel Harmony*, EETS, OS 157, 1922.

[17] Sanford Brown Meech and Hope Emily Allen (eds), *The Book of Marjory Kempe* (EETS, OS 212), 1940.

[18] P. L. Heyworth, *Jack Upland, Friar Daw's Reply* and *Upland's Rejoinder* (London: Oxford Univ. Press, 1968).

30

CAROLS IN TUDOR DRAMA

BY RICHARD LEIGHTON GREENE

Since the publication of my collection of the medieval English songs and verses in carol-form (*The Early English Carols*, Oxford, 1935) further research and indeed casual notice by myself and others have identified a considerable number of pieces in the true carol verse-form of initial burden plus stanza plus repeated burden which were written or at least published since the cut-off date of 1550 used for that edition. Some of them appear in unexpected places, and while, as a rule, no indication of a special manner of performance accompanies the texts, in a few cases there is some kind of context which shows that the old medieval method of singing a carol, the clear division into the stanzas as basically solo parts and the burden as basically a chorus part, is still understood. Sometimes it is preserved in the old style, and sometimes it is modified into a more complicated kind of performance which yet keeps alive the consciousness of the original burden and stanza structure.

One of the most charming as well as significant instances of this kind is that of the song which Izaak Walton introduces into the episode of the meeting with the beggars in *The Compleat Angler* (1653). He took it, as he acknowledges, from Francis Davison's anthology *A Poetical Rhapsody* (1602). It has the initial burden of the true carol, and, as is most frequent in earlier times, the burden is a simple couplet. It will be noted that Walton keeps the term "burthen." He writes:

> [One of the nine beggars] desired them to . . . draw cuts what song should be next sung and who should sing it. They all agreed to the motion; and the lot fell to her that was the youngest, and veriest virgin of the Company, and she sung *Frank Davisons* Song, which he made forty years ago, and all the others of the company joined to sing the burthen with her: the Ditty was this, but first the burthen.

> Bright shines the Sun, play beggars play,
> Here's scraps enough to serve to day.

What noise of viols is so sweet
As when our merry clappers ring?
What mirth doth want when beggars meet?
A beggar's life is for a King.
> Eat, drink and play, sleep when we list,
> Go where we will, so stocks be mist.
> Bright shines the Sun, play beggars play,
> here's scraps enough to serve to day.[1]

There are three stanzas in all.

The Compleat Angler has offered this example of a belated carol to many thousands of readers through three centuries, but a similar survival in the earlier Tudor drama has not had much notice. In providing his plays with incidental songs, some interwoven with the action, some presented as independent pieces standing on their own merits, Shakespeare is following a practice well established on the cruder English stage of the time of his youth and earlier. Among the forms which the writers of the earlier plays make use of is the old-fashioned medieval carol. Without attempting anything like a complete listing of songs in carol-form, we may notice a few of the plays which incorporate them. In none is there more extensive use of carols, or more explicit stage directions concerning their performance than in *Tom Tyler and His Wife*, which we know from the so-called "second impression" of 1661, which calls it "An Excellent Old Play, As it was Printed and Acted about a hundred Years ago."[2] It is a rough and ready comedy of no particular intellectual quality about marital strife—indeed Tom's spouse is named Strife—and in some of its situations and phrasing it quite startlingly resembles the group of medieval carols on henpecked husbands and struggles for dominance in marriage.

At the very beginning of the play, after a brief exchange between the moral abstractions Destinie and Desire, "Tom Tyler commeth in singing." What he sings is a true carol, complete with initial burden, a burden based, like the burdens of so many medieval carols, on a well-known proverb:

> The Proverb reporteth, no man can deny,
> That wedding and hanging is destiny.

The stanzas of the carol are made to carry the exposition of his identity which we expect from a character in drama of this elementary kind:

> I am a poor Tyler in simple aray,
> And get a poor living, but eight pence a day,

My wife as I get it, doth spend it away;
  And I cannot help it, she saith, wot ye why,
  For wedding and hanging is destiny.

I thought when I wed her, she had been a sheep,
At boord to be friendly, to sleep when I sleep.
She loves so unkindly. she makes me to weep;
  But I dare say nothing god wot, wot ye why?
  For wedding and hanging is destiny.

[Stza. 3 omitted]

The more that I please her, the worse she doth like me,
The more I forbear her, the more she doth strike me,
The more that I get her the more she doth glike me;
  Wo worth this ill Fortune that maketh me crie
  That wedding and hanging is destinie.

If I had been hanged when I had been married,
My torments had ended, though I had miscarried;
If I had been warned, then would I have tarried;
  But now all to lately I feel and crie,
  That wedding and hanging is destinie.[3]

There follows a scene of Strife with the other goodwives Sturdy and Tipple which strongly resembles the ale-house meeting of the medieval carol of the Good Gossips. As they imbibe their ale these stout shrews sing two genuine carols, the first one having its three stanzas designated for successive solo singing by the three women in turn: "Strife singeth this staff;" "Tipple singeth thiss staffe;" and so on: the burden is obviously sung by all three together:

Tom Tiler, Tom Tiler,
More morter for Tom Tiler.

As many as match themselves with shrowes,
May hap to carrie away the blowes,
  Tom Tiler, Tom Tiler.
As many a Tyde both ebs and flowes,
So many a misfortune comes and goes,
  Tom Tiler, Tom Tiler.
Though Tilers clime the house to tile,
They must come down another while,
  Tom Tiler, Tom Tiler.

Though many a one do seem to smile,
When Geese do wink, they mean some gile,

> Tom Tiler, Tom Tiler.
> Though Tom be stout, and Tom be strong,
> Though Tom be large, and Tom be long,
> Tom Tiler, Tom Tiler.
> Tom hath a wife will take no wrong,
> But teach her Tom another song.
> Tom Tiler, Tom Tiler.[4]

After a few lines of banter they all sing again, this time a carol which preserves the centuries-old dance-song device of rhyming the last line of each stanza with the burden. It also illustrates the survival of the medieval practice of borrowing a burden from another piece and using it even though its words have nothing to do with the sense of most of the stanzas. In this case the burden seems to have been taken from the long-lived and lively tradition of songs about lusty millers and their amorous opportunities and propensities:

> The Mill a, the Mill a,
> So merily goes the Mill a.

> Let us sip, and let it slip,
>   And go which way it will a,
> Let us trip and let us skip,
>   And let us drink our fill a.
> Take the cup, and drink all up,
>   Give me the can to fill a:
> Every sup, and every cup,
>   Hold here, and my good will a.
> Gossip mine and Gossip thine,
>   Now let us Gossip still a:
> Here is good wine, this Ale is fine,
>   Now drink of which you will a.
> Round about, till all be out,
>   I pray you let us swill a:
> This jelly grout, is jelly and stout;
>   I pray you stout it still a.
> Let us laugh, and let us quaff,
>   Good drinkers think none ill a:
> Here is your bab, here is your staffe,
>   Be packing to the mill a.[5]

There is a stage-direction immediately following: "Here they end singing, and *Tipple* speaketh first."

> *Tipple.* So merily goes the merie mill a;
> Hold, here is my can.

The carol is tied to the following action by Tipple's repetition in speech of the burden still running in her mind.

Tom Tiler continues to be afraid of his wife, but his friend Tom Tayler gives her a beating in the best morality-play style, and the two men celebrate her taming by singing a carol together, taking alternate stanzas in solo and joining in the burden. They call the piece "The tying of the Mare, that went out of square," and the stanzas are used to express the actual dramatic situation, while the burden is borrowed from an older carol in general circulation, "Tie the mare, Tom boy," which can be seen in Ritson's *Ancient Songs and Ballads*:

> Ty the mare, Tom boy, ty the mare, Tom boy,
>> Lest she stray
>> From the awaye.
> Now ty the mare, Tom boy.[6]

Prefixed is the stage-direction "Here they sing." Before each stanza is the appropriate direction: "Tom Tiler singeth" or "Tom Tailer singeth."

> Tom might be merrie, and well might fare,
> But for the haltering of his Mare,
> Which is so wicked to sling and flie,
>> *Go tie the mare Tomboy, tie the mare, tie.*
>
> Blame not Thomas if Tom be sick,
> His mare doth Praunce. his mare doth kick;
> She snorts and holds her head so hie,
>> *Go tie the mare Tomboy, tie the mare, tie.*
>
> If Tom crie hayt, or Tom crie hoe,
> His mare will straight give Tom a bloe.
> Where she doth bait, Tom shall abie.
>> *Go tie thy mare Tomboy, tie the mare, tie.*
>
> Tom if thy mare do make such sport,
> I give thee councel to keep her short.
> If she be coltish, make her to crie.
>> *Go tie the mare Tomboy, tie the mare, tie.*[7]

A very explicit stage-direction follows: "Here they end singing, and *Tom Tayler* first speaketh."

At the very end of the play when the character called Patience has reconciled the adversaries, there is a song not in carol-form (though Patience does suggest that all dance to it), which is then followed by a rather crude piece, labelled "The concluding Song," for which specific directions are given. The directions make it plain that the song is a true carol, with the burden repeated after every stanza. The unusual feature is that after all characters have left the stage, the soloist returns and sings the stanzas with instrumental accompaniment while the chorus remains off-stage: "Here they all go in, and one cometh out and singeth this Song following all alone with instruments, and all the rest within sing between every staffe, the first two lines."

> When sorrowes be great, and hap awry,   [burden]
> Let Reason intreat thee patiently.

> A Song
> Though pinching be a privie pain,
>   To want desire that is but vain.
> Though some be curst, and some be kind
>   Subdue the worst with patient mind.

> Who sits so hie, who sits so low?
>   Who feels such joy, that feels no wo?
> When bale is bad, good boot is ny
>   Take all adventures patiently.

> To marrie a sheep, to marrie a shrow,
>   To meet with a friend, to meet with a foe,
> These checks of chance can no man flie,
>   But God himself that rules the skie.

> Which God preserve our Noble Queen,
>   From perilous chance that hath been seen,
> And send her Subjects grace say I,
>   To serve her Highnesse patiently.
>   God save the Queen.[8]

No other play of Tudor times incorporates in its text as many carols as *Tom Tyler*, but there are a number which stop the dramatic action, sometimes quite surprisingly, in order to give the audience the change and refreshment of a choral song. In the rather solemn play of *Jacob and Esau* (1568) Abra, the housemaid of the family of Isaac and Rebecca, is presented as lightening her housework by singing a carol. A stage-direction reads: "Then let her sweepe with a brome, and while she doth it, sing this song, and when she hath song, let her say thus." The burden of her song is made, like that of many a fifteenth-century carol, by adding a line to a current proverb:

> It hath bene a prouerbe before I was borne,
> Yong doth it pricke that wyll be a thorne.

Who will be euill, or who will be good,
Who geuen to truth or who to falshood,
Eche bodies youth sheweth a great likelihood.
For yong doth it pricke that will be a thorne.

[Stzas. 2, 3 omitted. Stza. 4 and last:]

If a childe haue bene giuen to any vice,
Except he be guided by such as be wyse,
He will thereof all his lyfe haue a spice.
For yong doth it pricke that will be [a] thorne.
It hath bene a prouerbe. &c. [9]

What she "says thus" is:

Now haue I done, and as it should be for the nonce,
My sweeping and my song are ended both at once.

There are three carols in the play of *Apius and Virginia* by "R. B."
(1575) and two in *Damon and Pythias* by Richard Edwards (1571).
Those in the play of Apius may be left for the interested reader to
seek out, but the pair in *Damon and Pythias* show two points of
interesting adaptation of the old carol form to the uses of the stage.
One is introduced in a low-comedy scene of the shaving of Grimme
the collier. Both its burden, which goes:

With too nidden and todle todle doo nidden,
Is not Grimme the Colier most finely shauen?

and its stanzas are divided up among the three characters of Grimme
himself, Wyll, the lackey of Aristippus, and Iacke, the lackey of
Carisophus.[10] In the other Eubulus, the King's counsellor, sings the
stanzas, and the Muses, no less, sing the burden in chorus. The words
of the piece have obviously been written for this place in the drama,
and they show a sort of compromise between a heavy pastoral style
and the older carol rhetoric:

Alas what happe hast thou poore Pithias now
  to die,
Wo worth the [man which] for his death hath
  geuen vs cause to crie.

Evbvlvs
Me thinke I heare with yelow rented heares,
The Muses frame their notes my state to mone:
Among which sorte as one that morneth with harte,
In dolefull tunes, my selfe wyll beare a parte.[11]

[5 stzas. in all]

Other songs in true carol-form which are to be found in early Elizabethan plays are "I mun be married a Sunday" in *Ralph Roister Doister* (registered 1566–7), which Petruchio quotes in *The Taming of the Shrew* (II.i) just after saying, "Kiss me, Kate," and the two in *Common Conditions* (1576). The first of these is sung by the three tinkers, Shifte, Drifte, and Unthrifte, with this semi-proverbial burden:

> Hay tisty tosty tinkers good fellows they bee.
> In stopping of one hole they use to make three.

The second carol is sung by mariners and has for its burden:

> Lustely, lustely, lustely, let us sayle forth,
> The winde trim doth serve us, it blowes at
> the north.[12]

As in *Tom Tyler*, the association of carols with lower-class characters is maintained.

Finest of all is the classic drinking-song "Back and side go bare," which is often not recognized as the carol which it is, partly because of the propensity of modern editors to omit the initial burden, and which is almost universally known in the form in which it is sung to open the second act of *Gammer Gurton's Needle*. An earlier text is found in Victoria and Albert Museum MS Dyce 45 of about 1564, a miscellany of songs, medical prescriptions, and theological material very like the typical habitat of odd carols a century earlier. It continues the tone and tradition of the familiar "Bring us in good ale" (*The Early English Carols*, No. 422) with even greater art. The burden and first stanza of the longer and less familiar version run as follows (In this version "I cannot eate" etc. begins the *second* stanza):

> Backe and syde goo bare, goo bare,
> Bothe hande and foote goo colde;
> But belly, God send the good ale inowghe,
> Whether hyt be newe or olde.

> But yf that I
> Maye have trewly
> Goode ale my belly full,
> I shall looke lyke one,
> By swete Sainte John,
> Were shoron agaynste the woole.
> Thowthe I goo bare,
> Take yow no care,
> I am nothynge colde;
> I stuffe my skynne

So full within,
Of joly goode ale and olde.

It is interesting to see that the form of the medieval carol keeps about it in these late uses in drama an association in general with secular and colloquial language, with action which is indicated as accompanying the singing, and a strong tendency to keep the old division into chorus-burden and solo-stanzas.

WESLEYAN UNIVERSITY, CONNECTICUT

NOTES

[1] Izaak Walton, *The Compleat Angler*, edited by Richard Le Galliene (London, 1897), pp. 130–1.
[2] Edited by G. C. Moore Smith and W. W. Greg, The Malone Society Reprints, 1910.
[3] A_2^v, A_3^r.
[4] A_4^v, B_1^r.
[5] B_1^r, v.
[6] Ritson, *Ancient Songs and Ballads*, 3rd edn (London, 1877), pp. 175–7.
[7] B_4^r,^{v}.
[8] D_2^r,^{v}.
[9] *Jacob and Esau*, edited by John Crow and F. P. Wilson, The Malone Society Reprints, 1956, E_2^v.
[10] Richard Edwards, *Damon and Pythias*, edited by Arthur Brown and F. P. Wilson, The Malone Society Reprints, 1957, F_4^v, G_1^r.
[11] G_3^v.
[12] *Common Conditions*, edited by Tucker Brooke, Elizabethan Club Reprints (New Haven, 1925), A_4^v, B_1^r.

31

THE TWO VERSIONS OF CHESTER
PLAY V: *BALAAM AND BALAK*

BY DAVID MILLS

Writing of the English Corpus Christi Cycles, Glynne Wickham comments: "We know that it was a routine practice to rewrite old plays, to add new ones and withdraw others as local conditions suggested."[1] Unfortunately such changes can rarely be studied because plays in a cycle seldom survive in more than one version. The five extant "cyclic"[2] manuscripts of the Chester Cycle, however, contain two markedly different versions of Play V, which relate the giving of the Laws to Moses, the episode of Balaam and Balak, and either the Vengeance of Israel or the Prophet Sequence. It is my purpose in this essay to examine how the writers of these two versions have adapted the subject matter to meet different dramatic and thematic requirements.

At present, it is impossible to demonstrate which was the earlier version. One, the "Group-version," occurs in the four earliest manuscripts,[3] of which the first is Huntington MS 2 (HM) of 1591.[4] The other version is found in the latest MS, Harley 2124 (H) of 1607. The dates of the manuscripts are in themselves no guide to the date of composition, however, since all the manuscripts are later than the last recorded performance of the Cycle.[5]

Probably "local conditions" suggested the rewriting of Play V. The Group-version ends by urging the spectators to return the next day to see the Nativity of Christ. Since the Chester Cycle was performed in three sections on the Monday, Tuesday, and Wednesday of Whitsun week, this injunction implies that Play V is the last play with an Old Testament subject, and consequently concluded the Monday performances. A different division is provided by the play lists in the *Breviary of Chester History*, compiled after 1609 from the material of Archdeacon Robert Rogers of Chester Cathedral (d. 1595), and in MS Harley 2150,[6] which indicate that Plays I–IX (Creation—Oblation of the Magi) were performed on the Monday. The H-version, because of its variation from the Group-version, would better fit such a division, with Old Testament and New Testament plays both performed on the Monday.

The internal structure of a play must be related to its position in the complete Cycle. In Chester V, the immediate problem is its relationships to the preceding play of Abraham (IV) and the following play of the Nativity of Christ (VI), and the wider problems of its relationship to all the preceding Old Testament or following New Testament plays. Although at the end of the Group-version reference is made to the fulfilment of Balaam's prophecy at Christ's Nativity, the link between Plays V and VI is here weakened by the fact that Play VI was not performed immediately afterwards. On the other hand, in the last sixteen lines of Play IV in the Group, a Messenger rushes in to interrupt the action and demand room for the Balaam-Balak play (V), which evidently follows immediately. The H-version lacks this interruption as well as the preceding address of the Expositor of the Group-version praying the audience learn the example of obedience from Abraham (a recurrent theme of all the Old Testament plays). The Group dramatist clearly wished to raise the obedience theme to link Play IV to V, and to insure structurally that Play V followed immediately upon Play IV. He conceived his play as the conclusion of the Old Testament series, continuing from the preceding plays the organization of his material on a chronological basis, and stressing the story's exemplary potential, through which the obedience theme is conveyed. Moses is significant not as a historical leader, but as a man of unusual obedience who is rewarded; Balaam and Balak exemplify disobedience in contrast to Moses in his twin functions—servant of God and king among men. The conclusion shows the punishment of the disobedient by the obedient and hence the operation of divine justice through human agency.

The absence from H of the Messenger's end-link between Plays IV and V and the reference (in V) to the *next day's* performance may indicate that the H-dramatist wished to weaken the link between Play V and the preceding Old Testment plays and strengthen its link to Play VI (performed that same day). Such an indication is supported by the thematic emphasis of the H-version on the revelation of God's purpose to Man. This theme, it is true, is also to be found in the Old Testament plays, in such incidents as Adam's dream,[7] the covenant of the rainbow,[8] and even Balaam's Messianic prophecy in the Group-version, but nowhere does it attain the dominance which it has in the H-version (V) and nowhere else in the Old Testament plays does it so completely oust the obedience theme.

This theme of revelation is conveyed in the H-version in three episodes—the revelation of the Law to Moses, the revelation to

Baalam of the coming of Christ, and the detailed revelations by seven Jewish prophets of Christ's purpose and the coming of the Holy Spirit. Not only does H not have the narrative completion of the episode (the vengeance of Israel); it lacks even a chronological organization (e.g. the Balaam-Balak episode concludes after the procession of prophets). Moreover, H also does not convey its theme primarily by the exemplary nature of its material. It is evident that while these features of organization and conception represent a distinct break in continuity from the foregoing Old Testament plays, the inclusion of a line of prophets acknowledging the coming and purpose of Christ links the H-version of Play V closely to the following play of the Nativity of Christ (VI) and thereby to the whole of the New Testament series. While the Group-version is a fitting conclusion to a day of Old Testament plays, the H-version is perhaps better considered as an Advent play whose meaning will be fully understood in terms only of the New Testament plays still to come.

Corresponding to these differences in theme and organization are two different kinds of action. In the Group version, the theme is reinforced by using ridicule, in the comic episode of Balaam and his talking ass. The presentation indeed is substantially the same in both versions: Balaam has just confidently assured Balak's envoy that, once on his way, he will set God's will aside and work wondrous deeds. Now the man who has airily defied God cannot drive his ass onwards or even stay on its back; even the ass is wiser than he, for it can see the threatening angel, and so the ass has the right to rebuke the prophet. Finally, the once confident Balaam cringes in terror before the angel and begs for mercy. But in the Group version this comic reversal is only part of a larger comic action in which both Balaam and Balak are realized as ridiculously ineffectual figures. Balak is the unstable, choleric man miscast in the role of king, much as Herod is in the New Testament plays. Balaam is the avaricious soothsayer miscast in the role of unworldly prophet of God. Comic in themselves because each is unequal to the circumstances in which he is set, when they meet they serve as comic foils to each other, the rising anger of Balak at each blessing of the Israelites complementing the rising misery of Balaam as he sees his hopes of material gain disappearing. The result is a comic action in which ridicule rather than morality becomes a means of judgement. A more serious perspective is introduced through the contrast with the quiet obedience of Moses; and through the Doctor's stern reminder at the end of the play of the fatal consequences of this bungling mischief, which asserts a final moral frame of reference.

In the H-version, the comic episode of the ass serves a different function, a humiliation which not only teaches Balaam obedience, but marks the start of his rise to prophetic stature. Here Balak is a politic pagan who has decided to fight the Israelites' supernatural power with his own supernatural power, purchased from Balaam. Balak thus establishes a wordly, materialistic outlook which is shared by Balaam until his fall. When the two meet, however, Balak is comic in his anger and bewilderment at Balaam's conduct, but Balaam rises to heroic stature, sternly rebuking the pagan King and delivering not one but two Messianic prophecies. Comedy here becomes a means of assessing the rise of Balaam from uncomprehending soothsayer to prophet of God. His position is comparable to that of Moses in the first episode of the play, a figure above ordinary humanity which, in the first episode, is represented by a spokesman for the people called *Princeps Sinagogae*. The procession of seven prophets confirms Balaam's prophecy and his new exalted status to a courageous and dignified prophet from a comically blind and greedy profiteer, as well as an increasingly detailed revelation of God's purpose in the Incarnation. Here the Old Law gives place to the New, and here a Gentile assumes the role hitherto occupied exclusively by Jewish patriarchs. By such methods the H-dramatist has made Play V a key play in the total structure of the Cycle.

Although both versions have tripartite structures—Giving of the Law; Balaam and Balak; Vengeance of Israel (Group) or the Prophet Sequence (H)—these structures belong to different kinds of drama. The Group dramatist has created an action in which the audience must be able to identify with the characters and judge them as human beings. This effect is achieved partly by example, and partly by direct address. As Anne Righter has said: "There is much to be said for the subtlety of a theatre in which Moses can enjoin obedience to the commandments of God upon an audience of Israelites who lived before the birth of Christ and, at the same time, with all the force and directness of the original incident, upon medieval people who, at the conclusion of a day of pageants and processions, will make their way home through the streets of an English town."[9] The necessity in the Group version of enabling the audience to identify with the characters on stage is very different from the necessity of distancing the characters from ordinary humanity in order to stress their supernatural power which is characteristic of the H-version. The method used by H is closer to that described by V. A. Kolve in his discussion of the drama as play and game: "The *Expositor* figure (by whatever name) exists solely in order to speak for the dramatist—responsible for the design of the episode—and for God—responsible for the total historical and ethical design that the cycle imitates. . . . This convention fundamentally affects the kind of drama we see; characters conceived in this way demonstrate biblical history, but no attempt is made to sustain an illusion of being men caught up in that history."[10] Accordingly, the effect of the action would emphasize its unrealistic historical significance.

Since both versions have an Expositor ("Doctor" in the Group), it might seem that Kolve's remarks could apply equally to both, but although the Expositor necessarily stands outside the historical frame of action, a contemporary learned observer who is more knowledgeable than the audience, he nevertheless serves very different functions in the two versions. The Group Expositor is used to abridge the action by summarizing events, and as such is essential to the historical continuity of the action (ll. 41–64; 388–455). In doing so, he serves other functions. Thus his first speech divides the first episode into two parallel incidents, while the second asserts a moral perspective and then returns to contemporary reality by announcing the next performance. He does not stand between characters and audience; he takes over where the enacted action stops.

In contrast, the H-Expositor has nine speeches (65–88; and 305–12, 321–8, 337–44, 353–60, 369–76, 385–92; 401–32; 441–8). So far as continuity of historical action is concerned, the H-Expositor could be omitted, since all the prophecies are self-explanatory. Unlike the Group Expositor, he is a distancing device, talking to the audience while the action on stage is suspended. In the third episode (321–8) he intercedes between audience and prophets while the historical action of Balaam-Balak is suspended, turning the prophet-sequence into a kind of dramatic elaboration of Balaam's prophecy. Thus the H-Expositor is a presenter rather than an abridger, whose speeches serve to mark the structural divisions of the play and whose presence must have compelled the audience to shift its attention from the action on stage.

Much more could be said about the dramatic and thematic variations in the two versions, and the Giving of the Law in particular could be pursued further—the complexity of the H-version, the visual effect of the horned Moses on the hill as a God-like figure, or the alterations in the speeches of Expositor.

Any attempt to select the "better" version of Chester V must be based on subjective preference, for the two versions have different aims and succeed within their own terms. A medieval dramatist was potentially limited by many non-dramatic considerations, including the nature of his given subject, the division of the Cycle into episodes, and the changing fortunes and demands of guild and civic authorities. Yet in Chester V we have clear evidence that, despite all these difficulties, the dramatist remained in full control of his material and medium and could meet practical requirements without sacrificing his artistic integrity.

UNIVERSITY OF LIVERPOOL

NOTES

1 "Stage and Drama till 1660," in C. Ricks (ed.), *Sphere History of Literature in the English Language*, Vol. 3, *English Drama to 1710* (London: Sphere Books, 1971), p. 37.

2 "Cyclic" as opposed to the three extant "single-play" manuscripts for Chester.

3 MSS Huntington 2, Additional 10305, Harley 2013, Bodley 175.

4 This will form the base manuscript of the new *EETS* edition of the Chester Cycle by R. M. Lumiansky and myself.

5 Hermann Deimling, *The Chester Plays: Part I* (EETS, ES 62, 1892) took H as base manuscript. The text of H used for this essay is that which will appear as Appendix I.B of the new edition.

6 Quoted in "The Lists and Banns of the Plays," in *Chester Play Studies*, Malone Society (London: Oxford Univ. Press, 1935), pp. 121–71.

7 H.II. 441–72.

8 H.III. 313–72.

9 Anne Righter, *Shakespeare and the Idea of the Play* (1962; repr. Harmondsworth: Penguin Books, 1967), p. 24.

10 V. A. Kolve, *The Play Called Corpus Christi* (London: Edward Arnold, 1966), p. 28. For a different approach to the same material, see also L. M. Clopper, "The Structure of the Chester Cycle: Text, Theme and Theatre," Diss. Ohio State, 1969. This study was unfortunately not available to me when I was writing this article.

32

A POLISH ANALOGUE OF THE
MAN OF LAW'S TALE

BY MARGARET SCHLAUCH

In the sixteenth century, Polish translators and printers were busily occupied with the furnishing of vernacular prose texts, based on Western and general European originals, for the delight of the local public. The texts they issued took the form of *volksbücher* adorned with woodcut illustrations. The author of the learned and authoritative book on this subject, Professor Julian Krzyżanowski,[1] uses the term *romans* to apply to all types of narrative included in these fictional offerings. They ranged from pseudo-historical sources about Alexander of Macedon and the Trojan War to moral tales such as the famous *Seven Sages of Rome* and the *Gesta Romanorum* and comical ones derived from the cycles of Aesop, Marcholt and Eulenspiegel, as well as religious narratives, some of which were related to the Bible and the Apocrypha. A few stories classified as "humanistic" include three taken from Boccaccio's *Decameron* (those telling of Griselda, of Tito and Gisippo, and of Ghismonda: X, 10; X, 8; and IV, 1), and three love stories. One is the *Ethiopica* of Heliodorus (translated from the Latin into Polish as *Historya Murzyńska*), another the *Eurialus and Lucretia* of Eneas Silvius Piccolomini, and the third the *Isabella and Aurelio* of Juan de Flores. It may be added that the widely influential *Apollonius of Tyre* was also available in Polish. This romance, ultimately on the Greek model, is classified by Krzyżanowski among the moralistic. Morally edifying it may well have been, but it was surely entertaining as well.

Even these scattered examples will indicate that the reading public of the time in Poland had a wide range of inherited fiction at its disposal. The vogue of *volksbücher* may be compared to that prevalent in many Western European countries after the invention of printing.

A special category is labelled "Romans Rycerski" or Chivalric Romance. Krzyżanowski discusses four narratives: the story of Melusine, fabled ancestress of the Lusignan dynasty; the Provençal-originated romance of Magelonne; the edifying legend of Fortunatus;[2] and a tale about a non-historical personage designated as Emperor Oton of Rome: *Historia o Cesarzu Otone* (1569). This essay will discuss the latter item as an analogue to Chaucer's *Man of Law's Tale*.

The prose *volksbuch* about Emperor Oton goes back to a French romance concerning a fabled medieval Roman ruler, Octavian, and his family. It is called *Florent et Octavian* from the names of the Emperor's two sons, whose adventures take up the major part of the story. A shorter, more concise narrative also exists called *Octavian*,[3] on which two Middle English versions were based.[4] A lost twelfth-century *chanson de geste* has been suggested as ultimate source of the Octavian legend. Whenever it arose, the plot of the story represented a blending of themes already familiar in folklore, hagiography and courtly romance. It may be thus briefly summarized:

> A certain Emperor Octavian has a spouse Florence, who gives birth to twin boys. For some reason this infuriates Octavian's mother, and she accuses the Empress of adultery, claiming that no woman could bear twins unless two fathers had begot them. Moreover, she bribes a youth of the court to lie beside the Empress while she sleeps, and then leads her son triumphantly to witness the disgraceful sight. The youth is summarily killed without a chance to defend himself; the Empress is driven into exile. While she is resting by a fountain her two children are carried off by beasts. The first, named Florent, is taken by an ape (*un singe errant*, says the *Octavian*), rescued by a knight, kidnapped by robbers, but finally purchased and reared by a "villain," a butcher named Clement. The second child is carried off and nurtured by a lioness, then taken by sailors who restore him to his mother. She and the boy (named Octavian, like his father) and the faithful lion reach Jerusalem after several adventures. Meantime the Saracens invade France; the Emperor Octavian aids King Dagobert in resisting them. Young Florent, still unaware of his imperial ancestry, distinguishes himself in combat against the foe. He kills a gigantic champion of the enemy and wins the love of the Saracen princess to whom the giant had been betrothed. But he is captured along with his still unknown father, Octavian Senior. The younger Octavian has meantime learned about his origin from his mother. He now appears in France, fights the Saracens with the aid of his devoted lion, and makes the Sultan his captive. There follows a recognition scene when the two Octavians, Senior and Junior, tell their stories. Thereupon Florent is identified by his similarity to his brother, and the foster-father Clement confirms the relationship by his own account. The wicked mother-in-law is put to death, the family is reunited, and all ends happily.

It is obvious that this tale makes use of several widely disseminated themes: first of all that of the malignant mother-in-law, the false accusation of adultery based on the belief that twins must be the result of dual fatherhood (as in the celebrated *Lai le Fraisne* of Marie de France), the sufferings and peregrinations of the innocent persecuted queen, the separation of family members and their reunion thanks to techniques of recognition (autobiographies, tokens, family resemblances and the like). The devoted lion reminds us of both Androcles and Yvain. The general scheme is that of Greek romances, as adapted in the saints' lives of Eustachius and Placidus. The persecuting mother-in-law is at home in the realm of *märchen*. But her introduction of a suborned servant into the bed of the sleeping Empress represents a needless duplication, in view of the first accusation made. The device, taken from another sphere, is motivated by the Emperor's mildness in first dealing with the unhappy defendant.[5] The love of a Saracen princess for a Christian knight—leading of course to her conversion—was a stereotype to be found in other French verse romances, partly resembling the more military *chansons de geste*, composed in the thirteenth century. Repetition of such themes would indicate their popularity, at least in the circles for which such narratives were originally designed.

Florent et Octavian, the more elaborated version of the Octavian story, was the basis for a French prose romance, *L'histoire de Florent et Lyon, enfants de lempereur de Rome, Octavian*, printed early in the sixteenth century.[6] It was published in Paris (n.d.) by J. Bonfons and reprinted later several times (e.g. in Louvain by J. Bogard, 1592, etc.). The earliest German translation by Wilhelm Salzmann appeared in a folio edition (Strassburg: B. Grüninger, 1535), and this is the text used by the Polish translator. He did not follow the original slavishly, as is clear for example in his change of the Emperor's name and title from Keyser Octavianus to Cesarz Oton. The second son's name Leon, taken from the French, is due to the association with the hero's faithful attendant beast. In *Octavian* both father and son have the same name, which sometimes leads to confusion. Here it is avoided. The Polish translator has sometimes shortened his original, even at the expense of clarity, and sometimes expanded on it. He may have been no master of language, but he produced a text not without eloquence, especially in the direct speeches.

The adventures and misadventures of the long-suffering Empress (who remains nameless) furnish an analogue to Chaucer's Constance, but are only a framework to the story of her two sons, especially that of Florent (Florenc in Polish). Still, it is interesting to see what literary values were reflected in the saga of her patient sufferings as reported in this late prose treatment.

First of all, the dialogues and speeches are striking. The sinister mother-in-law, an analogue of Chaucer' Donegild, is endowed with considerable eloquence, and it is interesting that she observes all formalities of courtly discourse in addressing her son. This is her first, rather concise accusation:

> "Most illustrious Emperor and my lord, my son! Is it a thing possible or likely to be believed, that a woman might be able to give birth to two offspring at once, if she had to do with only one [begetter]?" (p. 2)

Later, her invective at the bedside of the Empress is more violent:

> "O thou wicked wife![7] Thine evil deed of a harlot has now become manifest, for thou, treacherously acting in relation to my son, and breeding [by way of] adultery, hast given birth to bastards [and] with these, according to my effort, thou must be publicly burnt to death!" (ibid.)

The attacks on the Empress continue, and the mother-in-law, called a malicious crone or *baba* (a term not easy to translate), even threatens to kill the twins because of the shame they have brought on the household of her son. The latter tries to appease her, in vain. The speeches addressed to the all too docile servant, asking him to feign adultery with the Empress, are strangely unconvincing. After an appeal to his sense of obedience, fortified by a bribe, the old woman continues:

> "Fear nothing, but just follow me!"—And taking him by the hand, quietly she led him to the bed of the Empress who, unwittingly asleep, knew nothing about this. (p. 5)

These are the instructions delivered to him:

> "Now then, having stripped thyself naked, lie down [variant reading: sneak in] by the Empress and when she wakens, do with her as may be pleasing to thee. For today, after she climbed out of her bed, she drank herself to tipsiness, and the Emperor is not at hand to satisfy her need, since he is praying in the church." (ibid.)

Foolishly convinced that he will be serving the Empress by his act, the youth complies.

Again there is a violent accusation when the old woman draws her son out of church to witness the shameful spectacle she has prepared. At first the Emperor almost loses his mind, but he makes a tolerant and rational reply, refusing to kill his sleeping consort without giving her a chance to defend herself.

"Gracious mother, though I have beheld what goes on here, nevertheless it does not befit an emperor to judge of one whose case has not been
heard, much less to kill one who is sleeping. Moreover I take heed of
the oath of my marriage, by which I pledged [her] good will as to my
own self; and since I took her under my defence and care, it is rather
proper to protect her welfare quite as well as my own. Wishing to
fulfil my vow, I must therefore remit this guilt of hers." (p. 7)

The scene that follows is fantastically unrealistic. The Empress,
awakened by a bad dream, sees her husband with his sword drawn
and also the naked youth beside her. Though surprised, she says
little in self-defence after a renewed attack by her mother-in-law.
Donegild's use of the Exchanged Letters, hackneyed though the
motif may be, was temporarily at least more convincing within the
framework of Chaucer's plot. This is the self-abasing speech of the
Polish heroine:

"Alas! Most illustrious Emperor, my gracious lord, where could it be
that Your Majesty should see fit to charge me with such ingratitude or
with such a deceit as this, of which I might now be rightly suspected?
Almighty God, from Whom nothing is concealed—to Him my innocence is most clearly known!" (p. 14)

After a short further interchange between husband and wife, during
which the suborned servitor continues to keep silence, the Emperor at
last strikes off the head of the supposed adulterer. At no point does the
Empress point out the unlikelihood of the situation. Would any
rational woman commit adultery under these circumstances? What
the lady obviously needed was a good lawyer, and the taciturn stooge
needed a bit of training in Roman rhetoric in order to defend himself.

Next day the Emperor makes a formal accusation before his
Council (*rada* in Polish) and asks whether his wife should not properly be burnt together with the children. The councillors hesitate,
and the oldest of them makes a valid point, already anticipated:
"Most illustrious Emperor, it befits us not to give judgement without
hearing the side of the aggrieved. . . ." (p. 10) They should listen
to her reply, he says. All of the others join in the plea, "and indeed
there was none who spoke evil of the Empress, or wished her ill, save
only the Emperor's mother, who was the cause of [all] this" (ibid.).
The debate in the Council continues on the third day, with the
mother-in-law insisting upon the execution by burning. The councillors are told, Do not dare to oppose the "mad old woman." One
wonders why—unless one thinks of analogous sinister characters in
märchen. As the persecuted heroine is led to the pyre with her children,

she gives voice to a prayer and then appeals directly to the Emperor, who now appears to have fallen entirely under his mother's influence. This is her discourse:

"Ah, my most kind lord! May Your Grace be pleased to exercise your wisdom in this, and weigh with yourself what your Imperial Grace promised when speaking to the Elders, and testified to the Lord God, claiming [to take] me under your care, namely that your Imperial Grace vowed to defend my health according to your best ability as if it were your own. Wherefore I ask in God's name, let not Your Grace infringe on this oath, for the Lord God is witness unto you, that I too have in no way broken my oath, nor have I been guilty of any deed for which I might be justly sentenced to death. Wherefore if I die, then it was an ill-starred envy that caused it, but like Christ my Lord I shall suffer that death of mine own will, praying the Lord God that He may absolve those who have been the cause of my death." (p. 13)

After this outburst there is much weeping, in which the Emperor joins, although his mother again urges a prompt execution. Especial emphasis is placed on the sorrow of "the poor folk" (*ubogich ludzi*), who had been fostered by her alms. Under such pressure, and again recalling his marriage vows, the Emperor changes the original sentence to exile from the realm. On her departure there is again much lamentation, "so that young maidens and ladies, also the common folk and especially the poor, having lost [hope of] rescue, bewept her exile with a mighty voice." (p. 14f.)

After this, the centre of attention is shifted (as in the sources) from the heroine to her two sons. Their adventures here again constitute the major part of the story, and they offer no parallel to the quiet life of the young Chaucerian Maurice, who had never been separated from his mother. But one incident during the exile of the Empress does somewhat resemble an episode in the *Man of Law's Tale*. It will be remembered that while Constance was adrift, her vessel was boarded by a recreant called "theef," who had been serving as steward in a heathen castle near by. This nasty person tried to force Constance to become his "lemman," but she resisted, she struggled with him, and with the aid of the Blessed Virgin she was able to pitch him into the sea. Somewhat similarly, our Empress, while en route to the Holy Land by ship, is subjected to the unwelcome advances of the boatswain (*bosman*). She rejects his first effort, made in the form of a persuasive speech. Then when he tries violence, she is saved by her son's devoted lioness, which tears him apart. Here is an effective earthly substitute for Chaucer's "blisful Marie." Besides, the Empress was not without friends aboard ship, for its owner (*patron*) had demonstrated his benevolence when he helped her to find her son and to take both of them along together with the lioness. Constance had no such human, earthly help in her situation of analogous peril.

The role of the Empress is played down even in the scene where she is recognized and restored to her former position. In the meantime the Emperor has learned the truth. This had not come about through the testimony of a disinterested third party (like the constable of King Alla), since the killing of the gullible servitor had eliminated the sole witness to the accused Empress' innocence. Instead, we are told that the furiously possessed mother-in-law had later conveniently re-covered sanity and herself revealed her own treachery. This is how Oton recalls the event in conversation with King Dagobert:

> "When I had done that, there was none from whom I could learn of this treachery, until from the sorrow of my mother, who now, having re-gained her reason, revealed the truth, herself testifying to the innocence of my lady, whom she had previously advised me to burn alive." (p. 56)

Thus Oton was able to avoid the matricide carried out by King Alla of Northumbria in Chaucer's tale, and by his prototype in the French verse romances.

By far the liveliest passages of the Polish romance are those depicting the youthful adventures of Florenc, the Emperor's son, reared by his worthy foster-father Klimunt. The latter tries to train him in humble occupations: first as a herdsman, then as assistant to his foster-brother (a money changer). Both times he shows his incompetence. He trades in two oxen (*woły*) for a sparrowhawk (*krogulec*) and parts with forty pounds of his foster-brother's money to buy himself a fine horse. He could have had it for thirty pounds, but he loftily gives the owner an additional ten. This impractical behaviour —supposedly aristocratic—makes Klimunt understandably angry, and he beats Florenc for it; but the foster-mother intervenes, protesting that the lad's tastes, and especially his skill with the horse, show that he must be of noble birth:

> ". . . thence it may be known, that he has that indeed by nature, which greatly draws him towards knighthood, for those things which he twice did—both of them show knightly desires." (p. 45)

There is no doubt that heredity is a more powerful factor than environment in such medieval romances about royal foundlings. Klimunt is finally convinced by his wife's arguments. He becomes a comic figure once again, contrasted with his imperial foundling, when he is brought into contact with the aristocracy of King Dagobert's court. His prosperous farm estate *(dwor* [sic]), said to be impressive for one of his rank, is within the area occupied by the King's army. There is a humorous account of Klimunt's boorish behaviour: he actually thinks he must pay for food served at a royal banquet, as is done in urban (i.e., bourgeois) circles.

These passages of condescending satire, interesting from the point of view of social history, go back to the French verse original. To only a limited degree can they be called realistic, because they too manifest conventional traits, but they do furnish a welcome antidote to the inflated discourses of the purely romantic sections.[8]

The succeeding versions in French, German, and Polish offer materials for an interesting study of evolving sixteenth-century prose style in Europe: the subject lends itself to a monograph which, hopefully, will be written by some trilingual expert who can have the appropriate texts at his disposal.

POLISH ACADEMY OF SCIENCES, WARSAW

NOTES

[1] J. Krzyżanowski, *Romans Polski Wieku XVI* (Warsaw: Polski Instytut Wydawniczy, 1962).

[2] The legend is best known by Dekker's treatment of it in his play *Old Fortunatus* (1600). A recent study by Witold Ostrowski emphasizes its relation to the ideology of merchant capitalism rather than medieval feudalism; hence the classification of "chivalric" may be questioned. See Ostrowski's chapter *"Romans i Dramat Wczesznego Kapitalizmu w Polskim i Angielskim* Fortunacie," in *Romans i Dramat* (Warsaw: Pax, 1970), pp. 37–73.

[3] Karl Vollmöller (ed.), *Octavian* (Heilbronn: Gebr. Henninger, 1883).

[4] Gregor Sarrazin (ed.), *Octavian: Zwei mittelenglische Bearbeitungen der Sage* (Heilbronn: Gebr. Henninger, 1885).

[5] I have dealt with some of these matters in my dissertation, *Chaucer's Constance and Accused Queens* (1927; rpt. New York: AMS Press, 1973), pp. 86ff.

[6] For this information and that which follows I am indebted to J. Krzyżanowski's edition of the *Historja o Cesarzu Otonie* (Kraków: Wydawnictwa Polskiej Akademii Umiejetności, 1928), Introduction. Passages quoted here in English translation are based on this text, with corresponding page references.

[7] In addressing the Empress, the mother-in-law shifts from the formal titled third person to the intimate—sometimes contemptuous—use of the second person singular. It is impossible to render these subtle distinctions in English, even in archaic English, which still used *thou.*

[8] Writing of the Middle English *Octavian,* Lillian Herlands Hornstein very justly says: "As in the French, the most striking scenes are those of good-hearted, realistic comedy with the bourgeois Clement, who beats Florentyn for his lordly tastes and plays jokes on the noble guests." See her chapter "Eustace-Constance-Florence-Griselda Legends" in J. Burke Severs (ed.), *A Manual of the Writings in*

Middle English, 1050–1500 (New Haven: The Connecticut Academy of Arts and Sciences, 1967), Fascicule I, p. 128. This is also true of the prose redactions. It may be noted that in the bibliography given on p. 286, the Krzyżanowski edition of the *Historja* is duly registered, but it is designated rather vaguely as a "Slavic" version. "Polish" would be more accurate and specific.—See also the appreciative remarks made by Albert C. Baugh on the comic role of Climent (both in the Old French and Middle English verse romances) in his article on "Convention and Individuality in the Middle English Romance," in Jerome Mandel and B. A. Rosenberg (eds), *Medieval Literature and Folklore Studies: Essays in Honor of Francis Lee Utley* (New Brunswick: Rutgers Univ. Press, 1970), pp. 140ff.

33

AN ANALOGUE (?) TO THE
REEVE'S TALE

BY THOMAS A. KIRBY

Traditionally, the closest analogue to Chaucer's *Reeve's Tale* is the French fabliau of the miller and the two clerks, *Le Meunier et les II Clers*.[1] There are, however, other versions in Latin, French, Italian, German, and Danish which also provide parallels of varying interest and importance. It is not the purpose of this note to add to this already abundant material but to call attention to a modern folk tale which, though not an analogue in the usual sense of the term, can hardly be heard or read without immediately bringing to mind the central situation in the *Reeve's Tale*.

This story is "Night Shift," one of *Playboy*'s "Ribald Classics," an Appalachian folk story retold by David Madden.[2] The locale is the mining company town of Cokeboro, and the six principals are Maud, from Hotchpot Holler, and Jack; Sue Charles, from Tater Hill, and Coker, her husband (the only one so labelled); and Tama, from "Lithuany," with Berk, who had "a caterpillar kind of mustache crawling on his lip." The incident centres around Maud's jealousy, occasioned by Jack's more than friendliness with other girls.

Every morning after the men go down into the mine to work, the three women gather on Maud's porch to talk. One day Coker is moved to the night shift, and the next morning Sue Charles rushes over to tell Maud about Jack's advances toward her during the night. She tells Maud that Jack is coming again the following night but that she will not let him in. To which Maud responds:

> "You will let him in. You'll leave the door open and be in bed when he gets there. Only it won't be you in bed, it'll be me. And I'll rip his eyes out! I'll tear the skin off his back and nail it to the wall of the company store!"

Events develop that night as planned—almost. Maud pretends to be asleep; Jack gets up and starts off for Sue Charles' house. Then Maud jumps out of bed and runs down the back way to reach the house before he does. She tells Sue Charles to go over to her (i.e., Maud's) house, and then she gets into Sue Charles's bed, after being assured that Tama is posted outside to serve as witness.

Things would doubtless have worked out as planned if Jack had been more eager, but he stopped at Lem Gaither's to have a drink ("a little nip of white lightning, aged in the ground two days"); one led to another, and he finally landed in Lem's cowshed "biled as an owl." Events now move rapidly to a climax. Sue Charles at Maud's house falls asleep, and Maud (at Sue Charles's) dozes also, but just before the first cock's crow, someone gets into the bed and is soon making love to her vigorously:

> "Jack?" she asked, but she was too sleepy to get mad again. Besides she was beginning to feel good. She forgot all about her plan to lock her legs around his waist and squeeze until he turned blue as a possum's ass.

At this point she feels a mustache that ought not to be there and realizes, of course, that it is Berk. Ultimately Jack sobers up, returns home, and goes to bed: "Maybe he noticed something different and maybe Sue Charles had a notion something was wrong, but neither of them let on until it was too late."

The anecdote ends hilariously when Tama sees husband Berk leaving Sue Charles' house by the back door:

> . . . she let out the loudest screech ever heard in these hills. Yelling something terrible in her own talk, she grabbed a stick and took out after Berk, with his pants half pulled up and his little mustache bobbing up and down. She chased him out of town, up the holler and over the mountain. All the way back to Lithuany. for all I know.

Benson and Anderson present in outline form (pp. 80–3) the points of resemblance and difference of the principal analogues to the *Reeve's Tale* under the following headings: setting, trip, lodging (and theft), entertainment, lovemaking with daughter, lovemaking with mother, the host apprised tussle, and the beating (or hoodwinking) of the host (and sequel). Quite obviously, "Night Shift" cannot be subjected to analysis based on these categories—it is barely a page in length and does not embody the basic details common to the principal analogues. Yet the element of mistaken identity, the planned and unplanned switching of the several bed partners, the essential role played by drink, and the earthy humour of it all make this short folk tale from the hills of Eastern Kentucky a striking reminder that the spirit and the technique of the fabliau are still very much alive.

LOUISIANA STATE UNIVERSITY

NOTES

[1] See W. A. Hart, "The Reeve's Tale," in W. F. Bryan and Germaine Dempster (eds), *Sources and Analogues of Chaucer's Canterbury Tales* (Chicago: Univ. of Chicago Press, 1941), pp. 124–47, and, more fully, Larry D. Benson and Theodore M. Anderson, *The Literary Context of Chaucer's Fabliaux: Texts and Translations* (Indianapolis: Bobbs-Merrill, 1971), pp. 79–201. The latter provide texts and translations not only of "Le Meunier, etc." but also of Jean Bodel's *"De Gombert et des II Clers,"* two German *Mären* (*c.* 1300), a sixteenth-century Latin prose tale, and an eighteenth-century ballad. To these should also be added Boccaccio's *Decameron*, 9, 6.

[2] *Playboy*, 18 (November, 1971), p. 177.

34

ENGLISH IMITATIONS OF THE
HOMELIA ORIGENIS DE MARIA MAGDALENA

BY ROSEMARY WOOLF

The *Homelia Origenis de Maria Magdalena*[1] or *Origenes upon the Maudeleyne* (to quote Chaucer's more familiar anglicization of the title) was long ago identified as the source of one German religious poem and as an influence upon two others, all written towards the close of the thirteenth century.[2] The English works indebted to it, however, are far more dispersed in time and divergent in form, and their debt to a common source has therefore remained less readily identifiable. The extant works are three in number: the play of the Resurrection of Christ in MS Bodley e Mus. 160; the late fifteenth-century "Lamentatyon of Mary Magdaleyne," which early editors of Chaucer included in the canon of his works; and a hundred years later *Marie Magdalen's Lamentations for the Losse of her Master* by Gervase Markham.[3] To these must be added Chaucer's own lost work to which he refers in the Prologue to *The Legend of Good Women* (A 428).

The *Homelia* itself has recently been described by John McCall and a long list of manuscripts enumerated.[4] At least twenty-three of these appear to be of English origin. The total number of extant manuscripts makes plain that the work was well known and highly esteemed. Moreover, quotation from it, once in the *Meditationes Vitae Christi* and extensively in the *Vita Jesu Christi* of Ludolf the Carthusian,[5] must also have served to diffuse the devotional tradition established by the work. Though the work is often labelled *Homelia*, and its attachment to the gospel for the Thursday after Easter indicated (John xx, 11–18),[6] it is in form and feeling a meditation rather than a homily. Its spiritual parents, as Saxer pointed out, are Anselm and Bernard,[7] and in particular Anselm since it is a rhetorical elaboration of his *Oratio ad sanctam Mariam Magdalenam*.[8] As in the latter, the meditator is half present in the scene, being there to act as a wise friend, urging discretion upon Mary Magdalene in the distraction of her grief or pleading with the risen Christ not to be offended by the blindness of her anguish. In its method and feeling the *Homelia* resembles some of the anonymous meditations of the twelfth and thirteenth centuries, and it is with works such as the *Liber de Passione Christi* (long attributed to St Bernard) that it is often associated in manuscripts.[9]

The popularity of the *Homelia* is also attested by the number of vernaculars into which it was translated at an early date: into German verse before the end of the thirteenth century and into French, Provençal, and Italian prose by the middle of the fourteenth century.[10] But in contrast to the quantity of manuscripts containing the Latin text and the frequency of its translation into western European vernaculars there stands out the mere handful of vernacular poems and plays to be actually influenced by it. The sum total of medieval works in western Europe at present known to have drawn upon it are two late thirteenth-century German biblical poems, one fifteenth-century English lyric and one English play of the same period. It seems to have been ignored by the almost innumerable writers who narrated or dramatized the events of the Sunday morning of the Resurrection.

It is not difficult to find the reason why so many authors who readily resorted to the *Liber de Passione* for their treatment of the Virgin's sorrow did not turn to the *Homelia* for an equally rhetorical and emotive expression of the grief of Mary Magdalene. The explanation is clearly that the *Homelia* would only have served to heighten an already awkward discrepancy between the account of the visit of the three Marys to the tomb as narrated in the Synoptic Gospels and that of Mary Magdalene's solitary visit to the tomb as narrated by John. Mark xvi, 1–10 (the appointed gospel for Easter Sunday) says that the women were too frightened to obey the angel's command to announce the Resurrection to the disciples. In Matthew and Luke, however, they hasten to give the good news to Peter and John, and such was the understanding of the Easter gospel established by the dramatic texts of the *Visitatio*, in which it is the duty of the Marys to proclaim the Resurrection, either to Peter and John or, less realistically, to the choir. So incapable are the gospels of harmonization that St Ambrose had made the conjecture that there were two Mary Magdalenes: one, a faithful witness who announced the Resurrection to the apostles; the other, one who lacked faith and told the apostles that the body of Christ had been stolen from the tomb.[11]

A study of Latin liturgical drama, vernacular mystery plays and verse biblical paraphrases shows the authors either not trying or trying unsuccessfully to reconcile these "two" Mary Magdalenes. Over and over again one finds Mary Magdalene in company with the other

Marys hearing the angel's revelation, "He is risen" (and sometimes even declaring this to the apostles), and then later replying to the angels who ask her why she weeps, "Because they have taken away my Lord and I know not where they have laid him." This kind of discontinuity in the behaviour of Mary Magdalene is more obtrusive in some works than others, but present to some extent in all. It was an almost inevitable discontinuity, but clearly to make the Mary Magdalene of the second episode so frantic with grief that she will not even pay attention to the angels (as happens in the *Homelia*) would only have accentuated the embarrassment of the already intractable material.

A further problem was the common theological tradition which saw in Mary Magdalene the chosen messenger of the Resurrection: as Eve had been the messenger of death so was Mary Magdalene the messenger of life. There was obviously a potential conflict between Mary Magdalene as the *apostolorum apostola* ("the apostles apostlesse" as Nicholas Love translated this common title)[12] who was given the special privilege of proclaiming the Resurrection, and Mary Magdalene as the *electa dilectrix et dilecta electrix dei* (as Anselm had called her),[13] who in her excess of love resolved to die of grief by the empty tomb. Indeed there was a danger that this second Mary might seem closer to Doubting Thomas than to a faithful apostle, and to counter this impression Gervase Markham, for instance, contrives that his distraught Magdalene should sometimes lapse into believing rationality, as when she considers that the spotless graveclothes could not have been ripped off the wound-marked body of Christ by hasty robbers come to steal the body from the tomb.

An understanding of the problems posed by the *Homelia* is not only useful in accounting for the rarity of its use in vernacular works but also in providing a frame of reference by which one can measure the ingenuity of the few authors who were not too timid to draw upon it. Each one within his limits has brought off a little *tour de force*.

The author of the play of the Resurrection[14] has boldly recast both the gospel narratives and the *Homelia* so that they are made to fit movingly and harmoniously. He does this by running together the two angelic appearances in that the angel first addresses the woman corporately, as in Mark, and then Mary Magdalene individually, as in John. He then turns Mary Magdalene's lament (deriving from the *Homelia*) that it was through negligence that she failed to keep watch by the tomb and so could not prevent the body from being stolen, into a lament that she did not keep watch by the tomb and so missed the sight of Christ's *uprisinge gloriose*. It is therefore not through despairing grief but through a loving desire to see the risen Christ that Mary

Magdalene is determined to remain by the tomb, and after her faithful love has been rewarded she can fittingly join the other women in announcing the Resurrection to the apostles in the dialogue of the "*Victimae paschali*," as in so many versions of the *Visitatio*.[15] Though in style much of this play may seem tedious and turgid, there are some delicate and tender moments in it, particularly in the lyrical passages (deriving immediately from the *Homelia* and ultimately from the Song of Songs), in which Mary expresses her passionate longing in the vocabulary and imagery of romantic love. But it is in his capacity for organization that the dramatist especially shows a thoughtful and sensitive imagination: indeed he is unique in reconciling two traditions that one would otherwise have accepted as irreconcilable, at least upon the stage.

"The Lamentatyon of Mary Magdaleyne,"[16] which early editors of Chaucer incorrectly thought to be his *Origenes upon the Maudeleyne*, but correctly recognized as deriving from the *Homelia* attributed to Origen, proceeds in an entirely different way. The author has divested himself of all narrative and theological problems by adapting only the *planctus* of Mary Magdalene, embedded in the *Homelia*. For the genre his vernacular model is clearly the many complaints of the Blessed Virgin which analogously derived from the *planctus* in the *Liber de Passione*. Nevertheless to extract the *planctus* from the *Homelia* was something of a conceit, for the audience is highly conscious that whilst in the poem Mary, on the point of dying for love, speaks her last words, "[*In manus tuas*] my spirite I commende," in the biblical and devotional world outside the poem the divine Gardener already stands behind her and is about to call her by her name.

This long complaint (it runs to more than seven hundred lines) preserves the distinguishing features of the *planctus* in the *Homelia*: Mary's conviction that Christ's body has been stolen and her self-reproach for not watching by the tomb; her resolve now to remain by the tomb and to die by it so that she may be buried therein; and the use of the erotic language from the Song of Songs to express her passionate longing and sense of loss. But various themes borrowed from other sources are interwoven with the material from the *Homelia*: a lamenting description of the Crucifixion, which owes quite a lot to the complaints of the Virgin including an apostrophe to the Jews rebuking them for their cruelty; a narrative summary of the seven sorrows of the Virgin ("These sorowes sevyn lyke swerdes every one"), a last will and testament in which, like Henryson's Criscyde, she makes appropriate bequests, and (to conclude) an adieu anaphora. In terms of apt adoption of traditional themes and of organization the poem is a well-contrived piece, but its manner is frigid, and the excess of emotion rhetorically expressed is without power to move. Furthermore, where the poet seems to be inventing, he lacks taste. Mary's appeal to the "virtuous women tender of nature" (i.e. the daughters of Jerusalem from the Song of Songs) to take her heart out of her breast when she is dead and, enclosing it in her box of ointment, offer it to Christ, gives an indecorously literal embodiment to a common religious metaphor. Such a gift recalls the savage action of Tancred, who in anger sends to his daughter Gismunda the heart of her murdered lover, rather than the bequest of a gentle lover to her beloved.

Though few readers nowadays find the poem pleasing, it seems to have had some reputation in its time. It is one of the rare religious lyrics to have been printed (by Wynkyn de Worde in 1520),[17] and it was presumably published on its own merits, as this edition does not attribute it to Chaucer. It is also worth noting that William Thynne's text in his edition of Chaucer's collected works in 1532 is not a reprinting of Wynkyn de Worde's: he obviously had access to a much better manuscript than that used for the earlier edition.[18] The divergencies between the two texts are so great that it is reasonable to infer a fairly long manuscript tradition behind them, and therefore that the poem had considerable manuscript circulation in the late fifteenth century, even though no manuscripts survive.

It would be interesting to know whether Gervase Markham was influenced by "The Lamentatyon of Mary Magdaleyne" as well as by the *Homelia* itself.[19] There do not seem to be any verbal echoes or very precise resemblances that are not explicable in terms of the common source. But there is sufficient similarity between the manner of recasting the *Homelia* in the two poems for it to be possible that Markham learnt something from the earlier work. Markham does not, like the anonymous author of "The Lamentatyon," confine himself to the *planctus*, but, though he includes all the matter of the *Homelia*, he presents it solely through a series of *planctus* spoken by Mary Magdalene. Obviously this elegant solution to the problems of turning the *Homelia* into a unified poem (as opposed to a vernacular paraphrase) could have been found independently; but "The Lamentatyon" had been printed in all the collected editions of Chaucer's works in the sixteenth century (including Speght's in 1598), and that Markham in adapting the *Homelia* should have borne in mind how Chaucer (as he would have supposed) had done it, seems an inherently likely assumption. Markham, incidentally, borrowed from the *Canterbury Tales* in his own framed collection of stories, *The Newe Metamorphosis*.[20]

This brief investigation of English imitations of the *Homelia* and of the problems involved in imitating it can finally serve as a frame of reference for some speculation about the nature of Chaucer's lost work. One thing is certain: Chaucer's *Origenes upon the Maudeleyne* kept very close to its original. To recast it as a narrative of the Resurrection or as a life of Mary Magdalene would have required a theological acuity entirely alien to Chaucer, whilst the device of extracting the *planctus* seems more characteristic of the decline and close of the Middle Ages when vernacular complaints of the Virgin were especially in vogue. Whether Chaucer translated the *Homelia* into verse or prose is uncertain. The context of the reference and the precise wording permit either interpretation, but general probability strongly suggests prose.

Two further tantalizing questions remain: why Chaucer made the translation in the first place and what are the precise implications of his singling it out for mention in the Prologue to *The Legend of Good Women*. Opinion on the first issue has ranged from Lounsbury's amazement that Chaucer should have concerned himself with so mean a work[21] to the recent and more ingenious arguments of John McCall that there was much in the Latin work to attract Chaucer in his youth.[22] It may, however, be conjectured that Chaucer translated the *Homelia* because he was asked to do so. A note in Speght's second edition of Chaucer's works observes that the "ABC" was "made, as some say, at the request of Blanche, Duchesse of Lancaster, as a praier for her privat use, being a woman in her religion very devout."[23] To make an extrapolation from this note of uncertain value is obviously a risky procedure. Nevertheless we may speculate that Chaucer made his translation at the request of a noble lady, though whether it was the wife of John of Gaunt depends upon its date of composition. This theory would also explain why the work has vanished. A work, undoubtedly written for a patron, namely *The Book of the Duchess*, survives in four manuscripts only and evidently never got into common manuscript circulation in the fifteenth century. *Origenes upon the Maudeleyne*, we may conjecture, perished in some manuscript of private devotions compiled for the personal use of some noble lady round about 1360–5.

Why Chaucer included a reference to this early work in his parody of a religious retraction (in the Prologue to *The Legend of Good Women*) is less speculative. The intention was undoubtedly witty. Mary Magdalene was a peculiar but striking example of enduring constancy in love: in an apostrophe to her the author of the *Homelia* had said: "*O mulier magna est fides tua: magna est constantia tua.*" Mary Magdalene's faithfulness to the point of death therefore enlarged the concept of the woman faithful in love, just as the *Second Nun's Tale* extends the concept of marriage in the *Canterbury Tales*. But there is the further possibility that by the time Chaucer wrote the Prologue, he had found out that he had not simply translated a work of devotion to please a patroness but that by chance he had translated a work of fashion. Two translations of the *Homelia* into Italian had been made by Dominicans of S. Maria Novella in Florence towards the middle of the fourteenth century;[24] and one (or both) was apparently current in Florence, for Boccaccio in the *Decameron* twice refers in an ironic context to the *lamento* (or *ramarrichio*) *della Maddalena*.[25] Despite present doubts to the contrary, it seems likely that Chaucer came across a copy of the *Decameron* when he went to Florence, and possibly he also observed that an Italian translation of the *Homelia* was popular reading amongst the wives of Florentine merchants. If so, it may have given him a special private amusement to put on record that he himself had translated this work. It would not be uncharacteristic of Chaucer to insert some tiny, subtle joke that only he could enjoy at the time and that remains for modern scholars laboriously to reconstruct.

SOMERVILLE COLLEGE, OXFORD

NOTES

[1] *Opera Origenis* (Paris, 1572), pp. cxxix–cxxxi.

[2] Cf. H. Hansel, "*Die Quelle der bayrischen Magdalenenklage*," *ZDP*, 62 (1937), pp. 363–88. *Von Maria Magdalena* is a translation of the *Homelia* into verse, *Gottes Zukunft* and *Der Saelden Hort* are respectively meditative and biblical poems, which draw upon the *Homelia* in their depiction of Mary Magdalene at the sepulchre.

[3] A poem that might seem to make a fourth, namely "The Lamentation of Mary Magdalen" by Lydgate, mentioned in some recent scholarly works, does not exist. Cf. J. B. Trapp, "Verses by Lydgate at Long Melford," *RES*, NS 6 (1955), pp. 1–5, and Derek Pearsall, *John Lydgate* (London: Routledge, 1970), pp. 182–3. "The Lamentation of Mary Magdalen" is a complaint of the Virgin.

[4] John McCall, "Chaucer and the Pseudo Origen *De Maria Magdalena*: A Preliminary Study," *Spec.*, 46 (1971), pp. 491–509.

[5] *Meditations on the Life of Christ*, trans. Isa Ragusa and Rosalie B. Green (Princeton: Princeton Univ. Press, 1961), pp. 361–2; L. M. Rigollot (ed.), *Vita Jesu Christi* (Paris, 1878), IV, pp. 191–5.

[6] For the attachment of the *Homelia* to feasts of the liturgical year see McCall, op. cit., p. 493.

[7] Victor Saxer, *Le Culte de Marie Madeleine en occident* (Paris: Clarveuil, 1959), pp. 346–8.

[8] Anselm, *Opera omnia*, edited by Francis S. Schmitt (Edinburgh: Thomas Nelson, 1946), III, pp. 64–7.

[9] English manuscripts combining the *Homelia* and the *Liber de Passione* are: Cambridge Univ. Library Ii. iii. 22; Pembroke Coll. Cambridge 265; Bodley 630; Rawlinson C. 61.

[10] For references see McCall, op. cit., p. 509.

[11] *PL*, xv, 1936; cf. Saxer, op. cit., p. 341.

[12] For the Latin phrase see Saxer, op. cit., p. 343, and Rossell Hope Robbins, "A Middle English Prayer to St Mary Magdalen," *Trad.*, 24 (1968), p. 458; and for the English, *The Mirrour of the Blessed Lyf of Jesu Christ* (London: Roxburghe Club, 1908), p. 277. The feminine form of apostle seems to have been coined specifically for Mary Magdalene.

[13] *Opera omnia*, III, 65.

[14] F. J. Furnivall (ed.), *The Digby Mysteries* (London: New Shakspere Society, 1882), pp. 201–26. I discuss this play more fully in Appendix A of *The English Mystery Plays* (Berkeley: Univ. of California Press, 1972), pp. 327–35.

[15] Cf. Karl Young, *The Drama of the Medieval Church* (Oxford: Clarendon Press, 1933), I, pp. 273–88, 336–8, 343, 672.

[16] Ed. Bertha Skeat (Cambridge: Fabb and Tyler, 1897).

[17] A. W. Pollard and G. R. Redgrave, *Short Title Catalogue of English Books, 1475–1640* (London, 1926), no. 17568. This work is hereafter referred to as *STC*.

[18] It was this text that Bertha Skeat printed. Among self-evidently better readings that a spot check has revealed in the 1536 text are: l. 30, "fonde;" 1520, "understande;" l. 30, "Alone;" 1520, "Alas." On the microfilm of the sole extant copy of the 1520 edition the last two pages before sig. B i are blank, ll. 337–92 being missing; the reason for this requires further investigation. Many works of scholarship refer to an edition of "The Lamentatyon" by Pynson in 1526. The ultimate origins of this lie in the Preface to Urry's Chaucer (1721), p.n. which refers to a collected edition of Chaucer's works (Pynson, 1526), which included this. This collected edition is in effect *STC*, 5086, 5096, 5088. Like the copy known to Dibdin (T. F. Dibdin, *Typographical Antiquities*, begun by Joseph Ames, augmented by William Herbert, II [London, 1812], p. 519), *STC* 5088 does not extend beyond *La Belle Dame sans Mercy*. As far as I know the Pynson edition either never existed or no longer exists now.

[19] A. B. Grosart (ed.), *Miscellanies of the Fuller Worthies' Library* II (London, 1871), pp. 536–96. Cf. F. N. L. Poynter, *A Bibliography of Gervase Markham 1568?–1637* (Oxford: Oxford Bibliographical Society, 1962), pp. 48–9.

[20] Cf. John H. H. Lyon, *A Study of The Newe Metamorphosis* (New York: Columbia Univ. Press, 1919), pp. 36–8.

[21] Thomas R. Lounsbury, *Studies in Chaucer: His Life and Writings* (1892; rpt. New York: Russell & Russell, 1962), II, p. 300.

[22] McCall, op. cit., pp. 501–4.

[23] Cf. Aage Brusendorff, *The Chaucer Tradition* (Oxford: Clarendon Press, 1925), p. 241.

[24] S. Orlandi, *Necrologio di S. Maria Novella* (Florence: Leo S. Olschki, 1955), I, pp. 470–2 (Jacopo Passavanti, though this attribution is not certain) and pp. 619–20 (Zanobi de' Guasconi).

[25] Vittore Branca (ed.) (Florence: Felice le Monnier, 1965), pp. 350 and 1243.

35

TWO THIRTEENTH-CENTURY
RELIGIOUS LYRICS

BY PETER DRONKE

In two songs, one Latin and one English, composed around 1250, we can observe poets working towards a new mode of organizing lyrical poetry. While this development implies a gain in imaginative freedom, the freedom is achieved in each instance through a particularly demanding virtuoso form. It is the form itself, shaped by echo and association, that seems to summon a content shaped by echo and association. The links of rhyme suggest new links of imagery; from echoes in the words further echoes in thought are generated. To study and compare this process in detail in the Latin and the English song, and to evaluate what each achieves, is the purpose of this essay.

Both the Latin song, *Furibundi*, and the English, *Somer is comen ond winter gon*, survive in unique manuscripts. Both present textual problems which, unless another manuscript were to be found, may never be fully soluble. The Latin text, with neums, is one of the later additions in the Codex Buranus, squeezed in at the foot of a page (f. 100v) by a mid-thirteenth century copyist.[1] It has never, to my knowledge, received any critical attention.[2] The lines themselves are scarcely legible in the manuscript, and in Schmeller's edition three lacunae remained. Two of these have now been filled in Schumann and Bischoff's text of the song. Only the opening phrase remains baffling: the legible letters, $O\ g\ldots\ldots ci$, with neums indicating an elaborate melisma over them, suggest that the song opened with a passionate apostrophe, two or three words at most, which must have been set off formally and melodically against the three strophes that follow.[3] These are clearly articulated in the manuscript, each beginning with a capital. They are freely constructed, nonetheless they have certain formal symmetries of their own. This is most immediately apparent in the way that the opening words of the three strophes echo one another.[4]

1. *Furibundi*	Raging,
cum aceto mixto felle	with vinegar mingled with gall
temptarunt te, tui velle	they goaded you, against your
contra: quodquod⁵ lacte, melle—	will: all those whom you—
de puella	born of a girl,
maris stella	a sea-star,
natus, alvo	mother with womb
tamen salvo	yet untouched—
matris—pascis tui oris	feed with the milk, the honey of your
et amoris.	and of your love. [mouth
2. *Letabundi—*	Rejoicing—
nam quos stravit	for these, whom a serpent's
morsus anguis,	bite laid low,
hos sanavit	your blood
tuus sanguis	has healed,
munda	pure
unda	wave,
et potavit;	and given drink;
recreavit	it has renewed them,
vivus	this living
divus	divine
panis iste,	bread—
o tu Christe,	you, Christ,
o benigne,	benign one,
digne	to be sung
odis,	in odes,
modis.	in melodies.
3. *Sitibundi,*	Thirsting
ut pax detur:	for the peace to be given:
"osculetur	"Let him kiss me
osculo me oris sui,	with the kiss of his mouth,
que de culpa nigra fui	who have been black with guilt,
sponsa pulchra, ut dilecta	a lovely bride, so that beloved
et perfecta,	and perfect,
simplex, recta	innocent, I may be
sim de bonis tuis, que te	ruled by the good things that are yours
placent."	and delight you."

Formally the song shows a virtuoso use of the *descort*, a "free" form that faces the poet with unusual challenges and dangers. In this form poetic control must be determined by intrinsic qualities of words, meaning and sound,[6] rather than by external formal criteria. If the poet can meet this challenge and establish an inner accord of meaning and expression far-reaching enough to dispense with outer regularities, the result can be a lyric exceptionally subtle in its imaginative organization, or capable of giving an impression of unpremeditated force and emotional flux. Among the Carmina Burana, *Dum Diane vitrea* (62) is an outstanding example of the first possibility,

Estas in exilium (69) of the second. Both significantly use a *descort* form. The dangers, when the regular parallelisms of strophic or sequence form are discarded, lie in loose or aimless organization, and in verbosity. These too can be found among *descorts* in the Codex Buranus.[7]

The first impression of *Furibundi* is one of breathless verve: the echoing rhymes follow one another so swiftly, there seems to be a headlong motion from start to finish. At the same time there is a complementary impression of complexity: the intelligence is caught back by the difficult syntax. Each strophe has its own demanding and refined syntactic pattern: the first, a sentence enclosing an involved parenthesis; the second juxtaposing two quite elaborate units; the third as if open-ended, one thought calling forth the next; at the close this sentence remains as if suspended at a great height.

I believe the poet has aimed at both kinds of effect, at arousing disparate but complementary responses in his listeners. On the one hand he achieves the momentum of the piece—perceptible both in the cascade of rhyme and in a motion of thought that can pass with such relentless speed from Christ's executioners at the opening to the celestial bride at the close. On the other he achieves an intellectually fascinating series of links in the sounds and in the images, which summon reflection long after the song itself is over. In considering these links more closely, it may be helpful to bear the two divergent but united kinds of poetic effect in mind.

The opening is dramatic and stark. Whatever words of outcry preceded, they could scarcely have diminished the shock of that word *Furibundi*, or the suddenness of *te*. We begin with the executioners at the cross, and then, without explanation, Christ is being addressed. Who is the speaker? A Christian meditating on the crucifixion? It might seem so, yet the next words (*quodquod lacte, melle* . . .) bring a second shock: those executioners are all, however many, who have been nurtured on the milk and honey of Christ's love. None is free from guilt; each becomes, at least for a time, one of the *furibundi*. The speaker is both accused and accuser; he is executioner and Everyman.

The words are chosen with deep care for their later reverberations in the song. This is most readily apparent with the first word. Indeed the three opening words—*Furibundi, Letabundi, Sitibundi*—could be seen as epitomizing the movement of thought in the poem: from the rage (leading to Christ's death) to the joy (of redemption) to the thirst (of the redeemed soul for the celestial love-union). The threefold movement is the dialectic of redemption in the macrocosm, the dialectic of conversion within the individual soul.

In the phrase about gall and vinegar the poet plays on and conflates several biblical associations. The wording itself is closer to Psalm lxviii, 22, in which this moment of Christ's humiliation was seen as prefigured, than to the Gospel narratives, where gall and vinegar are never mentioned together. From Matthew and Mark, however, we learn that the bitter drink was given "against his will," from Luke that it was offered in mockery. Only in John does Christ accept the drink, having said "I thirst."[8] The bitter taste of the gall and vinegar is thus associated not only with the contrasting sweet taste of the milk and honey—man offers God a bitter drink, God offers man a sweet one—but with the final stanza, *Sitibundi . . .* God was thirsty, but his thirst was mocked not quenched; man's thirst for God, his love-thirst, is quenched eternally.

The image of milk and honey links not only with that of gall and vinegar but points forward doubly. It was through the Exodus from Egypt that God led the Israelites to their land of milk and honey; but milk and honey are also the sweet taste of the mouth, the taste of love (*lacte, melle . . . tui oris | et amoris*), and so foreshadow the kiss of the divine Lover's mouth in the concluding stanza.

In the first stanza, only the words about Christ's nativity—*de puella | maris stella | natus, alvo | tamen salvo | matris*—are not given a further role in the growth of the song's imagery. This too seems to me deliberate: both syntactically and in terms of the poet's purpose they are subordinate. Lightly, parenthetically, almost playfully the poet calls to mind the other aspect of the redemption—the serene comfort of the incarnation as against the anguish of the passion. The theme and imagery of the incarnation are not taken up again; it is the note of serene comfort, first sounded here, which becomes fully orchestrated at the close.

Already the opening of the second strophe, however, brings the essential moment of reversal, from rage to joy. The *furibundi* become the *letabundi*: such is the liberating effect of the crucifixion. It is expressed in imagery dense with figural allusions. The Israelites in the desert became *furibundi* who "spoke against God" and were therefore afflicted by serpent bites (Numbers xxi, 4ff.); it was the bronze serpent set high on a pole at God's command who healed their bites. The ancient Christian figural interpretation of this episode[9]—the crucified Christ as the serpent on the pole healing the bites of that other serpent, Satan—is the dominant image here, yet with the words *tuus sanguis | munda | unda*[10] the poet enriches this image with a number of further associations. Christ's blood is a pure wave: Christ reverses the vengeful gesture of the Old Testament God who sullied the waters of Egypt by turning them into blood (Exodus vii). But *munda unda* is also a traditional expression for the water Moses struck from the rock during the Exodus (Exodus xvii), and this gesture itself a traditional figura for the healing water and blood which were struck by a lance from the side of the crucified Christ. The Good Friday liturgy contains a further variation on the theme: there in the *Improperium* Christ says to his people:

Ego te potavi aqua salutis de petra: et tu me potasti felle et aceto.[11]
I gave you the water of salvation to drink from the rock; you gave me gall and vinegar to drink.

Thus we can perceive not only the far-reaching connotations of the imagery at the opening of this strophe but also the structural relevance. Again the images link with what precedes and with what follows. The drinking of Christ's blood, *munda unda,* is a sweet potion, the reversal of the bitter drink, the gall and vinegar, of stanza 1. At the same time, this blood is drunk by Christians in the wine of the eucharist: that is why, in the second half of stanza 2, the vivifying effect of the blood-wine is conjoined with that of the "living divine bread," and in rhythm, rhyme and syntax *tuus sanguis | munda | unda | et potavit* is precisely counterbalanced by *recreavit | vivus | divus | panis iste.* This time it is at the close of the stanza—*o benigne, | digne | odis, | modis*—that the grace-notes, words which have no role in the pattern of imagery, come. The intellectual strenuousness resolves itself in a pure play of sound, expressing fervour and delight.

Once more the opening of the third stanza introduces a moment of dramatic unexpectedness. The first word, *Sitibundi,* seems to hark back to all the liquid images, bitter and sweet, that had gone before, the *pax* would seem to be the "kiss of peace" that precedes the moment of communion.[12] But suddenly a new dimension is introduced: the thirst is for a kiss of love, the peace is the consummation of love. Instead of continuing the communion imagery suggested by the previous stanza, the poet makes a brilliant transition to the erotic imagery of the Song of Songs.[13] The communion itself could indeed be seen as a foretaste of the complete love-union of the bride, the soul, to the divine Lover,[14] but poetically the effect is more splendid than this. The startling transition to direct speech transforms the *pax* from liturgical ceremony to an intimation of the bride's heavenly state of fulfilment. Her guilt in this life is not forgotten—she is still one of the thirsting—but the last lines open the heavenly vistas. She is both dark and beautiful (Cant. i. 5): again the poet's use of apposition is striking (*nigra fui | sponsa pulchra*), showing her beauty as it were emerging from her darkness. After the luxuriant play of rhymes, there is the beautiful withdrawn effect of the unrhymed last line. The preceding rhymes (*dilecta | perfecta | recta*) had created an intensification, and at the last, as no rhyme concludes the song, the effect seems almost that of a deliberate incompleteness: as if the bride's ardour for divine union, intensifying, is seen at the close as limitless.

What is new and exciting here is the extent to which the poetic meaning is enhanced—one might almost say created—by the poetic texture. It had been possible for some of the finest religious lyric poets of earlier centuries to develop subtle uses of associative imagery. They can be seen for instance in the twelfth century in the vivacious and unconventional language of Hildegard of Bingen's *Symphonia*[15]—but the echoes there are in the thought not in the rhyming; rhyme is extremely rare, and has no vital structural role. In the twelfth century too there are some intellectually remarkable uses of association in rhymed religious lyric. To give an illustration from a Christmas hymn by Walter of Châtillon,[16] which is particularly illuminating to compare and contrast with *Furibundi*:

Quos mortis scaturigine	Those whom, in the stream of death,
momordit pus vipereum,	the snake's purulence has bitten,
sanavit Christus oleum	were healed by Christ, oil
stillans de rosa virgine . . .	dropping from the maiden rose . . .
De rosa vite balsamum,	From that rose, the balm of life,
de rosa ros elicitur,	from that rose a dew comes forth
qui, si fide conficitur,	which, if aided by faith,
celestem donat thalamum.	brings heavenly nuptials.
Vera vitis ecclesie,	The true vine of the church,
succus eukaristie	the juice of communion,
prelo crucis exprimitur.	is pressed out in the winepress of the cross.[17]

As in *Furibundi*, the components include an allusion to the serpent-bites of the Exodus, to Christ as healer, to crucifixion, communion and celestial marriage. Here too the religious content is conveyed through images of liquid, first baneful then blessed. The differences lie in the poetic texture: in Walter's song the form is compact and compressed, in *Furibundi* it has a flowing movement. In Walter the imagery, finely controlled, approaches a set of cross-references; in *Furibundi* there is no less control, but it is less visible. The effect is spontaneous rather than calculated, as if the swift motion of the rhymes themselves were generating the associations.

These observations from the realm of Latin lyric are I think relevant also to understanding and evaluating the poetic processes in a Middle English song contemporary with *Furibundi*. The problems involved are nonetheless different in several ways. First, in Carleton Brown's words, "one must suppose that the existing text (*Somer is comen ond winter gon*) has suffered much from careless scribes." Unlike the Latin poem, the English has a regular strophic form, but like it, moves through a virtuoso scheme of echoes. This makes some corrections in the manuscript text fairly straightforward. Yet other passages raise a delicate question: how far did the poet's will to express certain things in a particular way override his will to formal flawlessness? How far does the flexibility so characteristic of his style also imply looseness of construction? It seems to me unlikely that we can attribute every "looseness" here to the negligence of a series of copyists, or to the faulty memory of a first recorder. Middle English lyric seldom aimed at, or achieved, the sheer effortless elegance of language and rhyme of the most polished contemporary Latin songs. So too the Middle English religious lyric often contains strong didactic elements, which do not always coalesce perfectly with the imaginative, however vivid these may be in themselves. This can entail artistic "looseness" of another kind. At all events decisions about possible flaws in particular lines of this song remain difficult. Let us first have the text before us.[18]

1. Somer is comen ond winter gon,	a 4	Summer has come and winter gone,
þis day biginniz to longe,	b 3	the day begins to grow long,
ond þis foules euerichon	a 4	and the birds, one and all,
ioye hem wit songe.	b 3	take their joy in singing.
So stronge	b 1	So fiercely
kare me bint,	c 2	sorrow binds me—
al wit ioye þat *me* fint	c 4	despite the joy that is found
in londe,	b 1	all around—
al for a child	d 2	all for a young knight
þat is so milde	d 2	who is so gentle
of honde.	b 1	of gesture.

2. Þat child þat is so milde ond wlong,
   ond eke of grete munde,
boþe in boskes ond in bonk
   isout me hauet astunde.
      Ifunde
   he heuede me
for an appel of a tre
      ibunde;
   he brac þe bond
   þat was so strong,
      wit wunde.

That young knight, so gentle and noble,
   and of great power too,
in the thickets and the hills
   has sought for me a while.
      He had found
   me bound
because of an apple
      from a tree;
   he broke the bond
   that was so strong,
      through his wounds.

3. Þat child þat was so wilde ond *bold*

   to me alute lowe.
Fram me to Giwes he was sold—
   ne cuþen hey him nout cnowe.

      "Do we,"[19]
   sayden he,
"naile we him opon a tre

That knight, who had been so defiant
                        and daring,
   bowed down low to me.
By me he was sold to Jews—
   they could not tell him for what he
                        was.

      "Let us,"
   they said,
"Let us nail him on a tree

a lowe.
Ac arst we sullen
him scumi*en*
a þrowe!"

up on the hill.
But first we must
make mock of him
a while!"

4. Ihesu is þe childes name,
    king of al⟨le⟩ londe.
  Of þe king he meden game
    ond s*mi*ten him wit honde.
      To fonden
      him opon a tre,
  he ȝeuen him wundes to ond þre
        mi⟨d⟩ honden;
      of bitter drinck
      he senden him
      a sonde.

Jesus is the young knight's name,
    king of every land.
  They made sport of the king
    and struck him with their hands.
      To test
      him on a tree,
  they gave him wounds, two and three,
        by hand;
      of bitter drink
      they sent him
      a feast.

5. Det he nom ho rode tre,
    þe lif of us alle,
  n⟨e miit⟩te it nowtt oþer be,
    bote we scolden *u*alle—
        ond wallen
        in helle dep
  nere neuere so swet
        wit alle:
      miitte us s*ocur*
      castel ⟨ne⟩ tur
      ne halle.

Death he accepted on the rood,
    he, life of us all;
  it could not be otherwise,
    unless we were to fall—
        and to boil
        in hell's depths
  would not be sweet in any way
        at all:
      nothing could aid us then,
      castle or tower
      or hall.

6. Mayde ond moder þar astod
    Marie ful of grace,
  hii let þe teres al of blod
    *u*allen in þe place.
      Þe trace
      ran of here blod,
  changed *h*ere fles ond blod
        ond face.
      He was todrawe
      so dur islawe
      in chace!

Maiden and mother stood there,
    Mary full of grace,
  she let her tears, all bloody,
    fall in that place.
      The trail
      of her blood ran,
  changed her flesh and blood
        and face;
      he was rent apart
      like a deer slain
      in the chase!

7. Det he n*o*m, þe suete m*o*n,
    wel heye opon þe rode:
  he wes hure sunnes euerichon
    mid is swete blode.
      Mid flode
      he lute adun
  ond bra*c* þe ȝates of þat presun
        þat stode,
      ond ches here
      out þat þere
      were gode.

Death he accepted, the sweet man,
    so high upon the rood:
  he washed away our sins, each one,
    with his sweet blood.
      With a torrent
      he bent down low
  and broke the gates of the prison,
        which had stood firm,
      and chose from out of them
      those there who had
      been good.

8. He ros him ene þe þridde day
 ond sette him on is trone;
 he wule come a domes day
  to dem us eueric*h* one.
    Grone
   he may ond wepen ay,
  þe m*o*n þat deiet witoute lay
    alone.
   Grante ous, Crist,
   wit þin uprist
    to g*o*ne.
     Amen.

By his own might he rose the third day
 and seated himself on his throne.
He will come on judgement-day
  to judge us, everyone.
    Groan
   he may and weep forever,
  the man who dies without faith,
    alone.
   Grant us, Christ,
   in your rising
    to rise with you.
     Amen.

1,7 is funde MS 2,3 bank MS 3,1 wlong MS 3,10 scumi him MS (*scumi* inserted from margin) 4,2 allonde MS 4,4 simten MS 4,8 mi MS 5,3 MS erasure illegible; 14th cent. hand in margin *ne mytte hit* 5,4 walle MS 5,9 ne miitte us saui MS; another possible correction: *ne miitte us saui* / *castel-wawe* / *ne halle* 6,3 thus 14th cent. hand in margin; MS erasure illegible. Brown reconstructs, *An⟨d of here eyen heo⟩ let blod*; but today, even with ultra-violet lamp, only the final *d* is legible with certainty. 6,7 changedere MS 7,1 nam, man MS 7,7 brace MS 8,4 euerichic one MS 8,7 man MS 8,11 gene MS For rhyme it would also be possible to regularize at 4,5: *fonde*; 4,8 *honde*; 5,5 *walle*.

The nature-opening is of a kind characteristic of love-lyric: the speaker, filled with longing, contrasts the joy of spring or summer, the joy of the birds and of the whole outer world, with his or her own inner grief, languishing for the beloved, unable to respond to the world's call to joy. Such an opening had often, a decade or two before this song was composed, been adapted to songs of divine love by the Flemish poetess Hadewijch: it is her most frequent and distinctive mode of opening a religious lyric:[20]

Men mach den nuwen tijt
Wel bekinnen overal:
Die voghele hebben delijt;
Die bloemen ontspringhen in berch in
    dal.

The new season
can be felt everywhere:
the birds have their delight,
flowers spring up over hill, over dale.

Waer so si staen,
Si sijn ontgaen
Den wreden winter diese qual.
Ic ben ontdaen,
Mij en troeste saen
Die minne jeghen mijn ongheval.

Wherever they are,
they have escaped
the torment of cruel winter.
I alone am lost,
if solace does not come
from Love to me in my wretchedness.

Hadewijch in her state of longing for divine love, which many times in her songs is evoked in chivalric terms, comes close in spirit to the opening of the English song. As Miss Woolf has pointed out, "child" is here used for "knight"—as so often in ballads and romances.[21] But I would venture to disagree with her on a point of emphasis. The *implicit* imaginative situation in the first two stanzas is not that of a man longing for a knight who will deliver him,[22] but rather of a woman—we could say, of Anima. Not only Hadewijch's lyrics, and all the religious poetry inspired by the Song of Songs, but also the world of romances, so rightly invoked here by Miss Woolf, would point in this direction. As in Chrétien, for instance,[23] Lunete, imprisoned and about to be burnt through no fault of hers, longs for Yvain to deliver her, Yvain who at last frees her from her bonds and from the fire (*au feu liiee*, 4323), so the soul, bound through the fault of her first parents, longs for her knight to break the bonds, that she should not *wallen | in helle dep*.

The associations of the romance world are again made poetically relevant later in the song. First, however, the poet establishes several contrasts with such a world. The heroic gesture itself—*he brac þe bond | þat was so strong*—is completed by *wit wunde*: *this* knight is hero in being victim, his triumph is his suffering. The paradox is further heightened by the poem's echoes. Twice this knight had been called *milde*; but if, as I believe with Carleton Brown (op. cit. p. 210), "we must read *wilde & bold*" at the opening of stanza 3, then the gentleness of Christ (*milde, wit wunde*) is counterbalanced by his champion's action, defiant and daring, of breaking the bonds that fettered the languishing soul—an action which later (7,7) merges with the breaking of the gates of hell's prison.

The words "wilde ond bold" are contrasted in their turn with the gentleness of "alute lowe"—a gesture of chivalric grace and, in the sacred context, an allusion to Christ's gracious *humilitas* (in both the courtly and the Christian sense) towards mankind. The God who had "bowed low" to man by descending to earth has inclined, wounded, *to me*. And suddenly the "I," the soul, accuses herself: "by me he was sold."[24] The shift in time, from that past moment when Christ was wounded, to any present in which a soul, meditating on Christ's passion, becomes aware of her complicity, is as dramatic as in *Furibundi*, where the soul identifies herself with the executioners. Anima is no longer a romance figure, a damsel awaiting her rescuer. She is a sinner, selling Christ as Judas sold him. She is responsible for Christ's ordeal, like the first stealers of the apple. The echo that links 2,7 to 3,7 ("for an appel of a tre—naile we him opon a tre") hints at the traditional identity of the tree of that apple and the tree of the cross.[25]

As the poet evokes Christ's executioners, the tone changes to bitter satire. Their mockery of Christ (3,5ff.) is conveyed in vivid direct speech. Only briefly, within this episode, the chivalric and divine aspects of Christ are recalled (4,1ff.). The five wounds ("wundes to ond þre")[26] inflicted on Christ are a "test" that the young knight must undergo; the bitter drink is a *sonde*, both senses of the word—gift and feast—being present, recalling the world of gracious behaviour by a grim irony. For the rest, the fourth and fifth stanzas are more directly didactic, alluding to moments of Christ's passion and reflecting on their meaning for mankind, for the process of redemption. The later part of the fifth stanza—"ond wallen / in helle dep / nere neuere so swet"—has again something of the sardonic tone first heard at the entry of the executioners. With its final words (difficult to reconstruct with certainty) the romance world, the world of *castel*, *tur* and *halle*, is decisively rejected—in its literal sense.

The sixth stanza is perhaps the most thrilling in the song, as well as the most problematic (so much so that a recent edition has omitted it altogether). Here the virtuoso form breaks down, as the poet appears both to rhyme *blod* (in the same meaning) with itself three times, and to confuse the "a" and "c" rhymes which in every other stanza he keeps distinct. A further difficulty is that in the illegible third line we must rely either on a fourteenth-century completion in the margin of the manuscript,[27] or else complete the line in our own way. With lines 5–7 the problems are different again. The first two, "þe trace / ran of here blod," seem to me moving and poetically flawless, even though the form should preclude an "a" rhyme here. We must reckon with the possibility that the break in form was the poet's deliberate decision, because of what he wished to say. Only in 7 "fles ond blod," a cliché that adds little to "changed here . . . face," seems suspect for reasons of sense as well as rhyme. Yet I do not know a way of correcting the line which would not be an arbitrary rewriting.

The stanza begins with the sufferings of Mary at the cross, and concludes with an astonishing image of the suffering of Christ. Already in the words used of Mary—"þe trace / ran of here blod"— the image of the chase may be implicit, her flowing tears of blood leaving a track or trail, like that of a wounded animal. The pitiful image of Mary disfigured by weeping is completed by that of Christ as the deer, slain and dismembered. The image of Christ as *cervus* is as old as Christian symbolism itself,[28] but for the concreteness and succinct savageness of its use here (a use that clearly has no literal counterpart in the passion) I know no parallel. The chase brings back the connotations of the chivalric world, whose sport is hunting, but in order to reverse them, as the knight's heroic gesture had been reversed before ("wit wunde"). The knight himself, the hunter, is the slain quarry. This is a paradox commonly developed in love-allegories of the chase, of which the earliest instances appear to be contemporary with this English song. The knight is a lover, hunting his lady's love, but doomed, because of her hardness, to be her quarry instead. Once more it may be an imagery already established in profane love-poetry that has here been transformed.[29]

In the last two stanzas the didactic element again predominates. The poet recalls to his listeners Christ's death and atonement, the harrowing of hell, the resurrection and the second coming, the judgement, with its ambiguous meaning for mankind: eternal weeping, or rising with Christ in joy. One moment, however, is filled with imaginative splendour: "Mid flode / he lute adun . . ." If we recall, as the poet almost certainly did, the lines in Fortunatus' hymn to the Cross:

> *mite corpus perforatur; sanguis, unda profluit,*
> *terra pontus astra mundus quo lavantur flumine.*
> The tender body is pierced; blood, water flow from it,
> a stream in which earth, sea, stars, universe are washed.

we realize that the flood, which can reach even to hell with such vehemence as to sweep open its gates, is no other than the blood and water which flowed from the side of Christ when he was pierced. Fortunatus had given the well-known biblical phrases—that Christ's blood washed away the sins of the world—a cosmic dimension. The English poet extends the daring image, to stress once more the Christian paradox: the knight's heroic moment is his moment of utter weakness and helplessness. The words "he lute adun" significantly echo his earlier, gracious and gentle motion: "to me alute lowe" (3,2).[30] As before the poet combined this with a seemingly discordant phrase—"so wilde ond bold"—so too there is a discord now between "lute" and "mid flode." But these discords are deliberate, the language itself helping to reaffirm the poet's central paradox. The champion smashing the gates of hell is the gentle wounded knight whose blood flows till it swells into a torrent.

In the English lyric as in the Latin, then, we can perceive a pattern of echoes in the movement of thought. Here the pattern is not as pervasive or as fully controlled as in *Furibundi*—at least as far as the surviving text can show—yet there are some unforgettable moments in which new bonds between images and expressions are forged. What the English and the Latin lyric share, and what is most unusual about them, is a poetic process in which the bonds of meaning are so largely determined by the texture of the verse, by the play of word and sound.[31]

CLARE HALL, CAMBRIDGE

NOTES

[1] *Carmina Burana* I, 3 (eds O. Schumann and B. Bischoff, 1970), no. 5*, pp. 117–18; *Carmina Burana* (ed. J. A. Schmeller, Stuttgart, 1847), no. CC, pp. 78–9. It should perhaps be recalled that the main body of the manuscript contains no religious lyrics, though there is a group of plays with sacred themes.

[2] The three references under *"Literatur"* (*CB* I, 3, 118) are to brief incidental allusions only; there is no mention of the song in surveys such as F. J. E. Raby's *Christian Latin Poetry* or J. Szövérffy's *Die Annalen der lateinischen Hymnendichtung*.

[3] Bernhard Bischoff has kindly informed me that even with the help of a powerful new ultra-violet lamp in the Bayerische Staatsbibliothek no further letters are decipherable. To the device of opening with a passionate apostrophe, formally set off from the rest of the lyric, I would see a certain parallel in *CB* 100, the beautiful lament of Dido, in which the rhythmic sequence form is preceded by an invocation in classical hexameters:

> *O decus, o Libye regnum, Carthaginis urbem!*
> *O lacerandas fratris opes, o Punica regna!*

Here, however, the invocation extends over into the first two lyrical lines, giving an effect of continuity as well as contrast.

[4] I give a plain prose translation facing the Latin and the Middle English texts, in case this should be helpful to readers of lyric coming from other languages and disciplines; it is also the most succinct means of indicating how I would construe the more problematic lines in each song.

[5] Adopting Schumann and Bischoff's suggestion (ad loc.), I take *quodquod* to be the manuscript spelling for *quotquot*.

[6] And of course melody (though in the case of *Furibundi* no attempt to conjecture this from the neums has yet been made).

[7] E.g. in *Bruma, veris emula* (57); *O Antioche* (97).

[8] Matt. xxvii, 34, 48; Mark xv, 23; Luke xxiii, 36; John xix, 28–30.

[9] Already in John iii, 14–15; more fully in the *Epistle of Barnabas* (130–140 AD), xii, 5ff.

[10] Schmeller printed *mundâ undâ*, construing the phrase ablativally; the new edition gives no indication. In view of the poet's fondness for apposition and asyndeton (cf. *lacte, melle*; *puella maris stella*; *odis, modis*), I prefer to construe *munda unda* in apposition to *sanguis*.

[11] *Liber Usualis Missae et Officii* (Paris–Tournai–Rome: Desclée, 1937), pp. 707–8.

[12] Already from the time of Gregory the Great the kiss of peace was seen as belonging to the preparation for communion—see J. A. Jungmann, *El Sacrificio de la Misa* (Spanish edn, Madrid: B.A.C., 1963), pp. 887ff.

[13] *Cant.* i, 1: *Osculetur me osculo oris sui*; for other echoes of the Song of Songs, see Schumann and Bischoff, ad loc.

[14] Cf. F. Ohly, *Hohelied-Studien* (Wiesbaden: Franz Steiner, 1958), pp. 41, 274.

[15] Cf. P. Dronke, "Hildegard of Bingen as Poetess and Dramatist," *Poetic Individuality in the Middle Ages* (Oxford: Clarendon Press, 1970), pp. 150–79.

[16] K. Strecker (ed.), *Die Lieder Walters von Châtillon in der Hs. 351 von St.-Omer* (Berlin: Weidmann, 1925), p. 2.

[17] Cf. Isaiah lxiii, 1–4: the winepress and vintner in this passage were interpreted figurally as the cross and the crucified Christ. For a recent account of this tradition (and of the related typology of Num. xiii), see R. Woolf, *English*

Religious Lyric in the Middle Ages (Oxford: Clarendon Press, 1970), pp. 199–202. I cannot agree with Miss Woolf, however, that the poem attributed to William Herebert, "What ys he, þys lordling"—to me the most memorable expression of these figurae—"is a clumsy slow-moving verse, of which the only interest is that the phrase *propugnator sum* has suggested to the author the Christ-knight image" (ibid., p. 200).

[18] My text follows the MS BM Egerton 613, f. IV except where noted; contractions have been expanded without comment. I have consulted the printed texts of Carleton Brown, *English Lyrics of the XIIIth Century* (Oxford: Clarendon Press, 1932), no. 54; Celia and Kenneth Sisam, *The Oxford Book of Medieval English Verse* (Oxford: Clarendon Press, 1970), no. 12 (fragm., omitting stanza 6); Theodore Silverstein, *Medieval English Lyrics* (London: Arnold, 1971), no. 12. As will be seen from the indications beside stanza 1, my analysis of the pattern of rhyme (or assonance) and stress differs in several points from that of Carleton Brown (p. 210). Neither he nor subsequent editors appear to have noticed the existence of a further "b" rhyme in the fifth line of each stanza, a line that is thus identical in form and rhyme with the eighth and eleventh. The editions hitherto have conflated this line with the following. Despite textual corruptions, the form is in my view sufficiently clearly discernible to justify a certain number of corrections for reasons of rhythm and rhyme. I have proposed corrections at 3,10; 5,4; 5,9–10; 7,1; 8,7; for the rest I adopt the suggestions of Carleton Brown, except at 1,7, where I rely on the Sisams.

[19] "Do we, . . . naile we him" appears to be a blend of two constructions: "do we þat we naile him" and "naile we him." The original text may have read "do we naile(n) him," ("let us have him nailed"). The Sisams' emendation of "Do we" to "Do wey" ("Have done!") seems to me unacceptable in that it destroys the expected "b" rhyme.

[20] Hadewijch, *Strofische Gedichten*, edited by E. Rombauts-N. De Paepe (Zwolle: Tjeenk Willink, 1961); I cite the opening of XVI (p. 122).

[21] Woolf, op. cit., p. 65; cf. also her valuable article, "The theme of Christ the lover-knight in Medieval English literature," *RES*, NS 13 (1962), pp. 1–16. As well as the knightly connotations of Middle English "child," the literal sense, "young man of noble birth" (contrasted with "churl") is relevant here (see *MED*, s.v. 6a), as it is in the other Middle English instances where "child" is used of Christ hanging on the cross (see *MED*, s.v. 2b). Christ is the noble "child" of the Father.

[22] Woolf, op. cit., p. 65; thus also Silverstein, op. cit., p. 25, speaks of "a captive knight sighing for a 'child.'"

[23] *Yvain*, 3563ff.

[24] Compare Christ's accusations that man has sold him, in the *Improperium* of the Good Friday liturgy (*Liber Usualis*, p. 707):

> *et tu me tradidisti principibus sacerdotum . . . et tu me duxisti ad praetorium Pilati.*

For the use of "fram," see *MED*, s.v. *from*, 6b.

[25] Cf. for instance, in Fortunatus' hymn *Pange, lingua*: *ipse lignum tunc notavit, damna ligni ut solveret.* For the wider ramifications of this theme, see esp. H. Rahner, "*Das Mysterium des Kreuzes,*" *Griechische Mythen in christlicher Deutung*, 2nd edn (1957: Zürich: Rhein-Verlag, 1966), pp. 55–73; E. C. Quinn, *The Quest of Seth for the Oil of Life* (Chicago: Univ. of Chicago Press, 1962).

[26] On the history of the five wounds in medieval religious lyric, see the fine discussion by Douglas Gray, "The Five Wounds of Our Lord," *N&Q*, 208 (1963), pp. 50–1, 82–9, 127–34, 163–8.

[27] As I have done; for the expression, cf. *King Horn*, 1405–6:

> Rymenhild was ful of mode,
> He wep teres of blode.

[28] Cf., for instance, St Ambrose, *De Interpellatione Job et David* II, 1 (*PL* XIV, 811).

[29] Cf. M. Thiébaux, "An Unpublished Allegory of the Hunt of Love: *Li dis dou cerf amoreus*," *SP*, 62 (1965), pp. 531–45; I. Glier, *Artes Amandi* (Munich: C. H. Beck, 1971), esp. pp. 156–78, and in the *Register* s.v. *Jagdallegorie, Jagdmotiv*.

[30] The sense "to move downwards (e.g. from heaven to earth)" for Middle English "lute" is not well documented in *OED*, but emerges clearly in OE (cf. King Alfred's *Boethius*, XXV, edited by Sedgefield, p. 57). The weak preterite is attested elsewhere in ME (e.g. *Ormulum* 8961). At 7,6 the Sisams (op. cit.) emend to *lighte*, but this would spoil the significant echo of 3,2.

[31] It would be an absorbing and worthwhile task to trace more fully the development of virtuoso "echo" forms in medieval European lyric, from the first major experiments of this kind in the late twelfth century (Arnaut Daniel, Raimbaut de Vaqueiras' *Kalenda maia*, Morungen's *Ich bôrt ûf der heide*) to those summits of thirteenth-century lyric where meaning and sound-play enhance each other (Cavalcanti's *Donna me prega*, King Alfonso's *Non me posso pagar tanto*), to the fourteenth-century decline into technical feats more playful than meaningful (the collection of Old French *estampies*, Heinrich Frauenlob).

36

LATIN HYMNS IN MEDIEVAL ENGLAND:
FUTURE RESEARCH

BY HELMUT GNEUSS

Among the various genres of religious and liturgical Latin poetry in the Middle Ages, the hymn undoubtedly occupied a leading position. We can gather this not only from the large number of hymns and the extent of their use, but also from the influence they exerted on vernacular literary forms such as the Middle English lyric. In the course of these pages I shall be attempting to trace very briefly what we know today of hymns in medieval England, and to outline some important questions which have, as yet, remained unanswered in this field. Admittedly there already exists an almost infinite number of books and articles on Latin hymnology; however, anyone searching for the possible Latin original of a Middle English poem, for instance, will soon discover that several important, even fundamental questions are still waiting to be answered: when and where in England were which particular hymns known? Which form or forms did their texts take? On what occasions were they used? This paper will address itself to the present state of scholarship and some tasks for future research.

It should be stressed, however, that this article is solely concerned with hymns in the more restricted sense of the word, that is to say, stanzaic compositions sung during the canonical hours of the Divine Office each day, whereas the expression "hymn" as such is often applied to the most diverse genres. Only the sequence will be mentioned in some detail in the final section.

The history of hymnology still has to be written. Certainly the subject dates back to the Middle Ages; the various versions of the *Expositio Hymnorum*, for example, were well known in England and on the Continent at the time.[1] A "hymnology" in the modern sense of the word, however, has only been in existence since the nineteenth century, when the newly emergent disciplines of literary history and textual criticism also made scholarly work on the hymns possible.[2] As a result, two kinds of hymnological work are particularly characteristic of the period of research which covers approximately the last 120 years: general surveys of the history of hymnography and critical editions of texts. There have been considerable achievements in both fields, but especially in the realm of comprehensive critical editions, first of all by Daniel and Mone, later by Dreves, Blume and Bannister in the fifty-five volumes of the *Analecta Hymnica*.[3] It has long been clear, however, that the *Analecta Hymnica*, admirable as they are, do not represent a definitive edition of the Latin hymns; many of the extant pieces have not been satisfactorily edited, others not at all, and many manuscripts (some of them very important ones) were unknown to the editors. The English tradition has not been properly taken into consideration either,[4] and the same is true of the only comprehensive critical edition to appear after the *Analecta Hymnica*, that of A. S. Walpole.[5] Works dealing with the history of hymnography are equally problematical; both here and in anthologies the poets and their biographies often play too large a part, in view of the fact that most of the commonly used hymns handed down to us are anonymous. Far more can be said about the history and tradition of individual hymns, however, if they are studied in their "natural surroundings," namely in the manuscripts, hymnals and breviaries. Much work remains to be done on these manuscripts, and new and important findings can be expected, together with answers to some of the questions posed above. For the reasons already given the following outline history of the hymns in England is based not so much on individual hymns or their authors, but rather on the hymnals, in other words hymn cycles used at a particular time and in a particular place for the Divine Office throughout the ecclesiastical year.

One of the most important results of the editorial work undertaken by Blume and Dreves for the *Analecta Hymnica* was the realization that, despite certain divergences, practically all the hymnals written since the tenth century are of a single type as far as their contents are concerned, whereas the few collections of hymns dating from earlier ages differ from the later type quite considerably. Blume believed that during the course of the ninth century a so-called "Old Benedictine" hymnal had been replaced by one coming from Ireland. In reality, however, the situation was rather different and more complicated, as I have shown in more detail elsewhere.[6] The solution suggested there to this problem forms the basis of what follows, though with a number of modifications which, in my opinion, have become necessary in the meantime.

Since the fifth century at the very latest a small cycle of about fifteen hymns, which I call the "Old Hymnal," had been spreading in Western Europe. This cycle can be reconstructed with some degree of certainty from the *Rule of St Benedict* (*c.* AD 540), the monastic Rules of the bishops Caesarius and Aurelianus of Arles (first half of the sixth century), from references in Cassiodorus' *Expositio Psalmorum* (sixth century), the Ambrosian hymnal (only handed down in the diocese of Milan from the ninth century onwards but in fact much older), from a Flemish manuscript, now missing (printed by Georg Cassander in the sixteenth century), from a lost Canterbury manuscript (extant there perhaps from *c.* AD 600), an extant Canterbury manuscript (BM Cotton Vespasian A.i., early eighth century) and from Bede's *De arte metrica* (*c.* AD 700).[7] The degree of conformity to be found in these sources—save for small discrepancies—is astonishing, and there is nowhere any evidence of a different type of hymnal until the middle of the eighth century. The form the texts took, on the other hand, is less certain; every edition to date (Blume,[8] Walpole, Bulst) makes use of some later manuscripts as well in reconstructing the text, but so far no one has taken into account the versions in Cassander's manuscript. A new edition of the Old Hymnal would therefore be welcome. Nothing is known of the origins of the Old Hymnal; some connection with the fourth-century hymnody of St Ambrose, however, is obvious since of about fifteen hymns contained in the Old Hymnal four can certainly be attributed to St Ambrose and a further six probably so. In Table I (p. 417 below) I have given a list of the hymns in the Old Hymnal, such as was found in the lost Canterbury manuscript.

How and when the Old Hymnal came to England, how commonly it was found there and how long it remained in use are questions which can hardly be answered, since no liturgical manuscripts have survived from this early period. I think it can be assumed that the Old Hymnal was introduced very early, at the time of St Augustine of Canterbury, and it is possible, though not certain, that it did not come directly from Rome but from the church of Gaul.[9] There is no evidence for the existence of a further type of hymnal in England besides the Old Hymnal before the tenth century. Whether hymns were used at all by secular clerics before that time we cannot tell, but the manuscripts from Canterbury and the references by Bede indicate their widespread presence in the monasteries. Exactly when the Old Hymnal was superseded depends on the question whether the Frankish Hymnal came to England and when the New Hymnal became known.

There is a small group of manuscripts dating from the second half of the eighth and the early ninth century which all originated in France and Southwest Germany and contain a hymnal (or parts of one) obviously different from the Old Hymnal.[10] I shall refer to it as the "Frankish Hymnal." Blume and hymnological literature to the present day have not clearly seen the dissimilarities between the Old and Frankish Hymnals, but have taken these to be one and the same work. However, I have pointed out that in the case of the Frankish Hymnal we are concerned with something new and different: a collection more comprehensive than the Old Hymnal (*c.* twenty-five hymns) and containing a number of pieces foreign to the earlier set of hymns. I therefore spoke some years ago of Type II of the Old Hymnal but now feel this term to be misleading for two reasons:

(1) The authentic Old Hymnal certainly dates back to the fifth century and was in general use until the eighth or ninth century.
(2) The so-called "New Hymnal" came into being only a few years after the Frankish Hymnal, namely in the early ninth century, and the earliest manuscripts of the New Hymnal were to be found in precisely the same monasteries in which, shortly beforehand, manuscripts of the Frankish Hymnal were still being written—in Corbie and Reichenau.[11]

In view of these facts we must consider the Frankish Hymnal to have been a first successful if short-lived attempt to replace the Old Hymnal by a fuller collection. Here it is worthy of note that the Frankish Hymnal provided for a different special hymn for lauds on the various days of the week, just as the New Hymnal did (while the latter also included special hymns for vespers and nocturn on each individual weekday), whereas the Old Hymnal made use of the same hymn at the same hour on different days.[12]

Several questions still remain, however. The Frankish Hymnal may well have originated in the west of the Frankish kingdom—perhaps in Northern France—in the eighth century; the fact that it was not in use for long is surely to be explained by the rapid and successful spread of the New Hymnal. But how common was the Frankish Hymnal? There are indications that this collection (or a related type) was in use in Spain. It is not certain whether it was known in Italy, but there is not the slightest evidence to suggest that the Frankish Hymnal reached the British Isles. This leaves two possibilities:

(1) The Frankish Hymnal came into use in some places in England, or even in the country in general, but every trace of it has disappeared. It must be remembered in this context that only very few manuscripts written in England before the tenth century have survived and that there are scarcely any liturgical manuscripts among them.

2. In England the Old Hymnal was directly replaced by the New Hymnal. This too can only be a hypothesis in view of the lack of liturgical hymns handed down in manuscript form or of other evidence in England between the early eighth and late tenth centuries. Perhaps an investigation of the relationship between the Churches of England and France in the eighth and ninth centuries could shed some light on our problem; but it would hardly provide a real solution.

In the ninth century something like a revolution took place in the history of Latin hymnody. At this time a new collection of hymns appeared, more comprehensive[13] than any older hymnal, and differently arranged, and within a century—if not within a few decades—this "New Hymnal" supplanted not only the Old Hymnal but also the Frankish Hymnal.[14] The New Hymnal has formed the basis of the hymns contained in the *Breviarum Romanum* and other breviaries to the present day. Where and why was this new collection originally introduced, where did its hymns come from and how is its remarkable success to be explained? It has not been possible to answer these questions adequately up to now, for we have to reconstruct the history of the hymnal from the liturgical MSS: there is no other direct evidence. Nevertheless it is to be hoped that competent church historians and liturgists will have more to say on these questions in the future.

There is no trace of the New Hymnal anywhere before the ninth century, but all its hymns—or at least many of them—are considerably older. Some had already been in the Old Hymnal and in the Frankish Hymnal, several others can be ascribed to well-known authors (Prudentius, Sedulius, Venantius Fortunatus); most, however, are anonymous and not found before the ninth century although, in part at least, they are thought to be more ancient.[15] Either therefore, purely by chance, they were not handed down in manuscript form before the compilation of the New Hymnal or else they are of more recent origin than has been assumed so far. Perhaps one day Medieval Latin Philology will be able to solve this problem.

Blume was of the opinion that the New Hymnal had originated in Ireland or other parts of the British Isles and had spread from there. Today this theory can be considered disproved, firstly because Blume has been mistaken about the origin of his two key manuscripts, secondly because the New Hymnal cannot be shown to have existed in the British Isles at all before the late tenth century. On the other hand, it is certain that the compiler of the New Hymnal used the Frankish Hymnal;[16] most important of all, however, the manuscript tradition—partly unknown to Blume—shows us where to look for the origin of the New Hymnal. The relevant manuscripts dating from the ninth century are:

Complete hymnals:
Düsseldorf, Landesbibliothek B. 3
   from Corbie, very early ninth century.
Manchester, John Rylands Library lat. 116 (Crawford 133)
   probably from Trier, first half of the ninth century, with numerous later additions and alterations.
Paris, B.N. lat. 13388
   from Tours, *c.* 850 or slightly earlier.
St Paul, Carinthia, Stiftsbibliothek 25.2.31b
and Karlsruhe, Landesbibliothek Aug. CXCV
   written by Irish scribes, possibly on the Continent (Reichenau?), middle of the ninth century.

Other early manuscripts, each with some hymns from the New Hymnal:
Köln, Dombibliothek 106
   from Werden? early ninth century.
St Gallen, Stiftsbibliothek 20
   probably from St Gall, first quarter of the ninth century.
Paris, B.N. lat. 14986
   from Paris, second half of the ninth century.
Bern, Stadtbibliothek 303
   hymns added in the third quarter of the ninth century to a manuscript written *c.* 836 at Orléans.
Verona, Biblioteca Capitolare XC (85)
   from Northern Italy, late ninth century.
Paris, Chambre des Députés 1 (A.20)
   from Lyon, ninth to tenth century.

Several of these manuscripts have apparently never been consulted by hymnologists; they now make a further examination of the earliest stage of development of the New Hymnal both possible and necessary.[17] It is clear at least that it originated in Frankish territory and spread in this area first of all; perhaps it was compiled in Northern France. In view of the quite tremendous success which this new collection enjoyed, however, it is difficult not to suspect that it had some connection with the reforms introduced by Benedict of Aniane.[18] This is also suggested by certain instructions on the use of hymns, almost completely ignored until now, which could have been compiled by him or one of his followers.[19]

All the relevant manuscripts of English origin dating from the tenth to the sixteenth century contain the New Hymnal. When, from where and in what form did it come to England? The oldest English manuscripts of the New Hymnal were written in the second half of the tenth century, perhaps around 970: the so-called Bosworth Psalter (MS BM Addit. 37517 with a complete hymnal) and the so-called Durham Ritual (MS Durham Cathedral A.IV.19, eleven hymns only). They therefore came into existence approximately 160 years after the Corbie Hymnal (Hs. Düsseldorf B.3). It is uncertain, and in fact rather unlikely—or so it seems to me—that the New Hymnal had already reached England in the ninth or early tenth century. This view is not only supported by the almost complete collapse of monastic life in England at this time, but also by the fact that most extant tenth- and eleventh-century hymnals are connected with the Benedictine reform introduced by Dunstan, Aethelwold and Oswald, while the most important document of this reform, the *Regularis Concordia* (*c.* AD 970), takes the use of the New Hymnal for granted.

What is certain is that in the earliest complete English manuscript, (BM Addit. 37517)—its hymns are listed in Table II at the end of this article—we no longer have before us the initial stages of the New Hymnal but a more fully developed form. It is certain too that, depending on their contents and their liturgical usage, the few English manuscripts and monastic rules up to the end of the eleventh century fall into two groups which can be traced back to two distinct centres of monastic reform: the Old Minster, Winchester (*Regularis Concordia*, Aelfric's *Letter to the Monks of Eynsham*, MSS CCCC 391, Cotton Julius A.vi) and Christ Church, Canterbury (MSS BM Addit. 37517, Cotton Vespasian D. xii, Durham Cathedral B.III.32).[20] There can be scarcely any doubt that this difference is indicative of certain continental sources of reform; connections between Winchester and Fleury, for example, have also been proved in the case of the sequences.[21] Three things are still missing, however, for a final solution to our problem:

(1) A catalogue of all manuscripts containing hymns written on the Continent up to the end of the eleventh century at least.
(2) An index of all the hymns contained in these manuscripts specifying the liturgical usage of each. We are therefore in urgent need of a completely revised edition of Mearns's book[22]—an admirable work at the time but nevertheless incomplete.
(3) An index of all the hymns which are mentioned in the *Consuetudines* of continental monasteries and churches, together with details about the use of these hymns.[23]

With the help of such aids it should be possible to answer the question about the origins of the New Hymnal in England more precisely than is feasible at the present moment, and many other questions may be solved at the same time. In addition to this, we still have no definitive critical edition of the New Hymnal. In view of the many hundred manuscripts and printed liturgical books this seems a hopeless task. Let it be remembered at this point, however, that in the Walpole and Blume–Dreves editions (especially *AH* 51) the New Hymnal has not been fully reliably printed, and that a large number of important ninth- to eleventh-century manuscripts have not been used. Critical editions utilizing all the manuscripts of this period—first of all perhaps for individual countries or regions—could be seen as useful groundwork for a comprehensive edition.[24] On the other hand it still remains doubtful whether conclusions could be drawn from the variant readings recorded in such editions as to the relationship between ecclesiastical centres in tenth-century France and England. The sheer number of texts, both extant and lost, and the daily singing of hymns (usually by heart) may well have led to extremely serious textual contamination.[25]

The small number of extant manuscripts makes it difficult to come to any decision about the general knowledge and use of hymns in Anglo-Saxon England; were, for example, hymns commonly known at all among clerics outside the great churches and monasteries? In the Middle English period from the twelfth to the sixteenth century the picture changes: manuscripts still extant and printed editions of hymnals and breviaries are numerous, despite the wholesale destruction of liturgical books at the time of the Reformation.[26] Verses from hymns were quoted in vernacular literature or used in macaronic poetry; hymns were translated into English—not for liturgical use, but as devotional literature, as religious songs or for use in sermons.[27] They were now not only familiar to almost all the clergy but to educated laymen as well, from the office of the Blessed Virgin in the Prymer, or Book of Hours.[28] What, however, do we know exactly about the corpus of Latin hymns in England from the twelfth to the sixteenth century? Here some problems have still to be solved which are similar to those posed by the continental manuscripts of the preceding period: there is no reliable, complete register of the manuscripts nor a corresponding index of the hymns and their usage; the compilation of a critical edition for the Middle English period too would be valuable, although it would certainly have to be based on a selection of the extant manuscripts and early printed books. Preliminary work for such a catalogue of manuscripts and hymns has already been carried out, but a great deal still remains to be done. Of those manuscripts which survive only very few have been used for printed editions in the last hundred years.[29]

With the state of research as it is at present, the situation in the Middle English period can be outlined approximately as follows: the basis for all the hymnals used by the secular clerics and most of the monastic orders was provided by the New Hymnal. The hymns for normal weekdays and Sundays were thus the same in the early sixteenth century as they had been in the late tenth century. In the case of the remaining hymns, however (for feast days and saints' days), divergences appear from the late eleventh century onwards: Temporale and Sanctorale nevertheless remain basically unchanged. A few old hymns disappear, some are put to different use, new ones are added—especially for recently introduced church festivals. These innovations, however, differ according to place and time; the contents of the Benedictine manuscripts from the various houses, for example, are by no means identical; some of them appear to be very conservative. Nevertheless, many of the changes and innovations are common to both the Benedictine manuscripts and those of the secular clergy.[30] But the most important development is doubtless the emergence of the "Use of Sarum" and the "Use of York." Probably from the twelfth century onwards the liturgical rite of Salisbury or Sarum spread over the whole of the British Isles with the exception of a small number of dioceses which predominantly followed the Use of York. The Use of Sarum was binding for secular clerics; it was therefore the most commonly found of all rites in England during the latter part of the Middle Ages, and anyone wishing to acquaint himself with the corpus of hymns and their texts at this time is therefore best advised to consult the Sarum Breviary. But this will not give him a complete inventory of Latin hymns in the Middle English period![31]

In Table II at the end of this article I have set out a list of the hymns in the Sarum Breviary and compared it with the content of the earliest New Hymnal in England (MS BM Addit. 37517). This comparison demonstrates the continuity of the New Hymnal throughout the centuries as well as certain changes since the twelfth century. How are the differences between the manuscripts of the Old and Middle English periods to be explained? This question in turn can only be answered authoritatively once the occurrence and use of hymns on the continent have been thoroughly recorded. But even now the tools of scholarship at our disposal, however imperfect, enable us to point out connections between the innovations in England and the usage of the monasteries in Normandy.[32] Nevertheless we cannot ignore the possibility that the hymnal in England might have developed along the same lines—perhaps under continental influence —even without the Norman conquest.

It has already been mentioned that the hymns only represent one genre of religious and liturgical poetry. Of the other forms the sequence—sung during Mass on Sundays and feast days between the Epistle and Gospel, immediately after the Gradual and Alleluia—is undoubtedly the most important.[33] The sequence, too, was important for the development of the Middle English lyric, especially the carols, but we are far less well informed about the texts and transmission of this particular Latin genre than we are in the case of the hymns. Blume mentions that some 4500 medieval sequences are edited in the *Analecta Hymnica*;[34] but which of them were known in England or even originated there? How did the corpus of sequences in England develop and change? Where and when did sequences appear in the English church for the first time and where did they come from? These and many other questions have not yet been answered satisfactorily—if at all. There is still no reliable and comprehensive textual edition of the sequence tradition in England; the individual texts are to be found scattered among the various volumes of the *Analecta Hymnica* or in some printed editions of English missals of the late medieval period.[35]

On the one hand work on the sequences is more difficult than on the hymns because here there was obviously not a clearly defined body of texts like the Old or New Hymnal; on the other hand the work is less difficult because sequences did not yet exist in the early Anglo-Saxon period (for which there are no extant liturgical manuscripts). The genesis of the sequence on the Continent is still a matter of dispute. The genre probably originated in Northern France in the ninth century and spread from there.[36] As Blume and Bannister have shown, however, there were basic differences between the collections of sequences to be found in the various countries from the very beginning; the early individual sequences were mostly (though not exclusively) either in use only in France, England and Spain, or only in German and Italian territory.[37] Thus we have an Anglo-French and a German-Italian tradition as far as the sequences are concerned. This tells us where we need to look for the source of the sequences in the English church. It is quite possible that the genre first came to England in the course of the tenth-century Benedictine reform.

In any event we have no evidence of any sequence texts being written in England before this time; the only Anglo-Saxon manuscripts containing complete collections of sequences are the two tropers from the Old Minster in Winchester, written in the eleventh century.[38] It has been proved conclusively that Fleury played an important part in transmitting sequences to England,[39] but in order to come to any detailed conclusions the whole French sequence tradition of the early period would have to be catalogued according to manuscripts and use—as in the case of the hymns. It is clear, however, that until the end of the eleventh century, sequences from the German–Italian camp, such as those written by Notker, were extremely rare in England. (On the other hand works composed in England itself did exist—though not before the end of the tenth century.)[40] This situation obviously continued even after the eleventh century, but the manuscripts of the Middle English period as well as additions to older manuscripts show that much had changed; new sequences were introduced, a number of older ones were dropped; again, the various rites of the Middle English period show considerable divergences one from another while having certain innovations in common—as for example in the case of the missals of York and Sarum. The Benedictine manuscripts,[41] too, agree in many respects from the twelfth century onwards with those of Sarum and York but not with the old Benedictine manuscripts in Winchester. The situation, therefore, is similar to that of the hymns, but as far as the sequences are concerned there is not the continuity which the retention of the basic corpus of the New Hymnal was able to ensure. In order to trace the whole process, we urgently need two things: an index of the manuscripts (missals, graduals) and sequences in England, such as we have from Mearns for the hymns,[42] and then a critical edition comprising the entire English tradition—this too, of course, as a contribution towards a later, definitive inventory and a comprehensive edition of the European sequence tradition as a whole.

UNIVERSITY OF MUNICH

TABLE I: THE OLD HYMNAL IN ENGLAND

At the beginning of the fifteenth century, Thomas of Elmham, a monk of St Augustine's, Canterbury, saw a manuscript (now lost) in his abbey which he described as *"Psalterium Augustini quod sibi misit idem Gregorius;"* this psalter was followed by a hymnal whose contents were listed by Thomas. There can be no doubt that this is a collection representative of the Old Hymnal in the early Anglo-Saxon period:

Mediae noctis tempus est	*pro medio noctis*
Aeterne rerum conditor	*ad gallicantum*
Splendor paternae gloriae	*ad matutinas*
Venite fratres ocius	*ad primam*
Iam surgit hora tertia	*ad tertiam*
Bis ternas horas explicans	*ad sextam*
Ter hora trina volvitur	*ad nonam*
Deus creator omnium	*ad vesperas*
Te deprecamur domine	*ad completorium*

Christe qui lux es et dies	*in quadragesima*
Rex aeterne domine	*pro die dominico*
Intende qui regis Israel	*de natali domini*
Hic est dies verus dei	*in Pascha*
Apostolorum passio	*in festo apostolorum Petri et Pauli*
Amore Christi nobilis	*de S. Iohanne Evangelista*

TABLE II: THE NEW HYMNAL IN ENGLAND

This is a comparative list of the hymns in the earliest complete English New Hymnal [B] (BM Addit. 37517, late tenth century, from Canterbury) and of the hymns according to the Use of Sarum [S], as found in liturgical manuscripts and printed books down to the sixteenth century. The list is complete but simplified; for details concerning the use of the individual hymns during particular days and hours, see *HHEM*, pp. 60–8 and 239f. (for B), and (for S) *Breviarium ad Usum Sarum*. Abbreviations used: N=Nocturns, L=Lauds, V=Vespers. Where (B) or (S) is in parentheses, a particular hymn is extant in B (or S), but is used for another day or period; a starred S* indicates that a hymn is found in a slightly different, or differently divided, form in S.

ORDINARIUM DE TEMPORE (WEEKDAYS AND SUNDAYS)

USE:		HYMN INCIPIT:	FOUND IN:
Sunday, Winter	*N*	Primo dierum omnium	BS
	L	Aeterne rerum conditor	BS
Sunday, Summer	*N*	Nocte surgentes	BS
	L	Ecce iam noctis	BS
Sunday	*V*	Lucis creator optime	BS
Daily: Prime		Iam lucis orto sidere	BS
Terce		Nunc sancte nobis spiritus	BS
Sext		Rector potens verax deus	BS
None		Rerum deus tenax vigor	BS
Compline		Te lucis ante terminum	BS
Compline (Winter)		Christe qui lux es et dies	B(S)
Monday	*N*	Somno refectis artibus	BS
	L	Splendor paternae gloriae	BS
	V	Immense caeli conditor	BS
Tuesday	*N*	Consors paterni luminis	BS
	L	Ales diei nuntius	BS
	V	Telluris ingens conditor	BS
Wednesday	*N*	Rerum creator optime	BS
	L	Nox et tenebrae et nubila	BS
	V	Caeli deus sanctissime	BS
Thursday	*N*	Nox atra rerum contegit	BS
	L	Lux ecce surgit aurea	BS
	V	Magnae deus potentiae	BS
Friday	*N*	Tu trinitatis unitas	BS
	L	Aeterna caeli gloria	BS
	V	Plasmator hominis deus	BS
Saturday	*N*	Summae deus clementiae	BS
	L	Aurora iam spargit polum	BS
Saturday, Winter	*V*	Deus creator omnium	BS
Saturday, Summer	*V*	O lux beata trinitas	BS

PROPRIUM DE TEMPORE (CHURCH FEASTS AND SPECIAL PERIODS)

USE:	HYMN INCIPIT:	FOUND IN:
Advent	Conditor alme siderum	BS
	Verbum supernum prodiens, a patre	BS
	Vox clara ecce intonat	BS
Christmas	Christe redemptor omnium, ex patre	BS
	Surgentes ad te domine	B
	Audi redemptor gentium	B
	Veni redemptor gentium	S
	A solis ortus cardine	S(B)
	Salvator mundi domine	S
Epiphany	A solis ortus cardine	B(S)
	Hostis Herodes impie	BS
	A patre unigenitus	S
	Christe redemptor omnium	S(B)
Septuagesima	Alleluia dulce carmen	B
	Alleluia piis	B
	Almum sidereae	B
Lent	Dei fide qua vivimus	B
	Meridie orandum est	B
	Perfecto trino numero	B
	Sic ter quaternis trahitur	B
	Audi benigne conditor	BS
	Ex more docti mystico	BS*
	Dicamus omnes cernui	BS*
	Iesu quadragenariae	BS
	Clarum decus ieiunii	BS
	Summe largitor praemii	S
	Ecce tempus idoneum	S
	Christe qui lux es et dies	S(B)
Passiontide	Vexilla regis prodeunt	BS*
	Arbor decora et fulgida	BS*
	Auctor salutis unicus	B
	Cultor dei memento	BS
	Pange lingua gloriosi proelium	S
	Lustra sex qui iam peracta	S
Eastertide	Ad cenam agni providi	BS
	Iesu nostra redemptio	B(S)
	Aurora lucis rutilat	BS*
	Iesu redemptor (salvator) saeculi	BS
	Chorus novae Hierusalem	S
Ascension	Hymnum canamus gloriae	B
	Optatus votis omnium	B
	Aeterne rex altissime	S*
	Iesu nostra redemptio	S(B)
Whitsuntide	Iam Christus astra ascenderat	BS
	De patris ergo lumine	BS*
	Iudaea tunc incredula	BS*
	Veni creator spiritus	BS
	Beata nobis gaudia	BS
	Anni peractis mensibus	B

USE:	HYMN INCIPIT:	FOUND IN:
	Alma chorus domini	S
All Saints	Festiva saeculis colitur	BS*
	Christe redemptor omnium, conserva	BS
	Omnium Christe	B

FEASTS OF THE VIRGIN

Purification	Quod chorus vatum	BS
	Quem terra pontus aethera	S
	O gloriosa femina	S
	Laetabundus	S
Annunciation	Quem terra pontus aethera	BS
	O gloriosa femina	BS
	Ave maris stella	BS

PROPRIUM SANCTORUM (SAINTS' DAYS)

St Andrew	Nobis ecce dies	B
St Stephen	Iam rutilat sacrata dies	B
	Sancte dei pretiose	S
St Benedict	Christe sanctorum decus atque virtus	B
St John the Baptist	Ut queant laxis	BS
	Antra deserti	BS
	O nimis felix	BS
St Peter and St Paul	Aurea luce	BS
St Laurence	Martyris Christi	B
St Michael	Mysteriorum signifer	B
	Tibi Christe splendor patris	BS
	Christe sanctorum decus angelorum	BS
St Martin	Martine confessor dei	B

COMMUNE SANCTORUM (SAINTS' DAYS WITH NO PROPER HYMNS)

Apostles	Exultet caelum laudibus	BS
	Annue Christe saeculorum domine	BS
(Verses for apostles, to be sung as stanza I of Annue Christe:)		
St Peter	Iam bone pastor Petre	BS
St Paul	Doctor egregie Paule	BS
St Andrew	Andrea pie	BS
St James the Great and St John	Bina caelestis	BS
St James the Less	Iacobe iuste	B
St Bartholomew	Bartholomaee	BS
St Matthew	Matthaee sancte	BS
St Philip	Proni rogamus	B
St Simon and St Jude	Beate Simon	BS
St Thomas	O Thoma Christi	BS
St Matthias	Matthia iuste	S
Several martyrs	Aeterna Christi munera	B
	Rex gloriose martyrum	BS
	Sanctorum meritis	BS
One martyr	Martyr dei qui unicum	BS
	Dues tuorum militum	BS

USE:	HYMN INCIPIT:	FOUND IN:
Confessors	Iste confessor	BS
	Christe splendor gloriae	B
	Iesu redemptor omnium	BS
	Summe confessor	B
Virgins	Virginis proles	BS
	Iesu corona virginum	BS

CHURCH FEASTS AND SAINTS' FEASTS INTRODUCED OR
SUPPLIED WITH HYMNS IN ENGLAND AFTER THE TENTH CENTURY

Trinity Sunday	Adesto sancta trinitas	S
	O pater sancte	S
Corpus Christi	Sacris sollemniis	S
	Pange lingua gloriosi corporis	S
	Verbum supernum prodiens nec	S
Transfiguration	Caelestis formam gloriae	S
	O sator rerum	S
	O nata lux de lumine	S
Name of Jesus	Exultet cor praecordiis	S
	Iesu dulcis memoria	S
	Iesu auctor clementiae	S
Visitation B.V.M.	Festum matris gloriosae	S
	Mundi salus affutura	S
	O salutaris fulgens stella maris	S
Assumption B.V.M.	O quam glorifica	S
	Quem terra pontus aethera	S(B)
	O gloriosa femina	S(B)
	Laetabundus	S
Nativity B.V.M. *Conception B.V.M.* }	(*as for Annunciation*)	S
St Vincent	Christi miles gloriosus	S
St Mary Magdalene	Collaudemus Magdalenae	S
	Aestimavit hortulanum	S
	O Maria noli flere	S
St Anna	Ave mater Anna	S
	In Annae puerperio	S
	Felix Anna prae aliis	S
Dedication of the Church	Urbs beata Hierusalem	S
	Angulare fundamentum	S

NOTES

[1] For the medieval *Expositio Hymnorum* cf. H. Gneuss, *Hymnar und Hymnen im englischen Mittelalter, Studien zur Überlieferung, Glossierung und Übersetzung lateinischer Hymnen in England*, Buchreihe der Anglia, 12 (Tübingen: Niemeyer, 1968) [henceforth abbreviated *HHEM*], pp. 194–206. Reviewed by Rossell Hope Robbins, *Spec.*, 47 (1972), pp. 759–61.

[2] The most comprehensive and most recent record of what has been published in the field of Latin hymnology is J. Szövérffy, *Die Annalen der lateinischen Hymnen dichtung*, 2 vols. (Berlin: Erich Schmidt, 1964–5). See also Szövérffy,

"Hymnological Notes," *Trad.*, 25 (1969), pp. 457–72, and my review of the *Annalen* in *Zeitschrift für romanische Philologie*, 83 (1967), pp. 413–18.

[3] H. A. Daniel, *Thesaurus Hymnologicus*, 2nd edn, 5 vols. (Leipzig: J. T. Löschke, 1855–6, 1st edn 1841–56); F. J. Mone, *Lateinische Hymnen des Mittelalters*, 3 vols. (1853–5; rpt. Aalen: Scientia, 1964); G. M. Dreves, C. Blume, H. M. Bannister, *Analecta Hymnica Medii Aevi*, 55 vols. (1886–1922; rpt. New York: Johnson, and Frankfurt am Main: Minerva, 1961), henceforth abbreviated *AH*.

[4] Cf. *HHEM*, p. 8 and n. 12.

[5] A. S. Walpole, *Early Latin Hymns* (1922; rpt. Hildesheim: Georg Olms, 1966). A more recent scholarly and critical edition covers only the hymns of the earliest period: W. Bulst, *Hymni Latini Antiquissimi* (Heidelberg: Kerle, 1956).

[6] See C. Blume, *Der Cursus S. Benedicti Nursini und die liturgischen Hymnen des 6.–9. Jahrhunderts*, Hymnologische Beiträge, III (Leipzig: Riesland, 1908), and *HHEM*, pp. 10–54.

[7] For details see *HHEM*, pp. 13–25. No further sources for the Old Hymnal have been found since this was published.

[8] In *AH*, Vols. L and LI, and in his *Cursus S. Benedicti*.

[9] Cf. *HHEM*, pp. 33–8.

[10] MSS Vatican Reg. lat. 11 (from north-eastern France); Paris B. N. lat. 14088 (from Corbie); B. N. lat. 528 (from St Denis); B. N. lat. 13159 (from north-eastern France or a centre to the west of this area); Oxford Bodl. Junius 25 [S. C. 5137] (from Reichenau and Murbach, with an Old High German interlinear gloss to the hymns); Zürich, Rheinau 34 (from Reichenau, or St Gall?). For contents, descriptions and references see *HHEM*, pp. 19–25.

[11] As many as three types of hymnals must have been available at Reichenau in the ninth century, as it is now clear that a MS of the Rule of St Benedict written for this monastery included a copy of the Old Hymnal; cf. *HHEM*, p. 28, n. 25.

[12] Cf. *HHEM*, pp. 24–8.

[13] The early complete hymnals of this type have between 35 and 50 hymns; there are more than 100 in the expanded versions of the same type from the later tenth century onwards. The earliest English copy (BM Addit. MS 37517) has 105 hymns, the Sarum Breviary (see below) contains 115.

[14] The Old Hymnal, however, survived in the diocese of Milan, but with many additions; this collection was later adopted by the Cistercian order, cf. *AH*, 52, pp. vi–xiii.

[15] Cf. Walpole, op. cit., p. ix; Bulst, op. cit., p. 203; Szöverffy, *Annalen*, op. cit., I, p. 216. It is obvious that all the authorities hesitate to date the anonymous hymns of the New Hymnal more or less definitely.

[16] Cf. *HHEM*, pp. 42–7, 51.

[17] I have to thank Dr Bonifatius Fischer of the Vetus Latina Institut and Mr Michael Korhammer for drawing my attention to some early MSS of the New Hymnal previously unknown to hymnologists. I am particularly grateful to Professor Bernhard Bischoff for valuable and authoritative information about date and provenance of the MSS listed above. My tentative treatment of the earliest stages of the New Hymnal (*HHEM*, pp. 47–50) was written without knowledge of some of these MSS, in particular of the Corbie MS (Düsseldorf B. 3), produced about the beginning of the ninth century. The forty-three hymns of this extremely important book have been listed by Hugo Dausend, *Das älteste Sakramentar der Münsterkirche von Essen*, Liturgische Texte und Studien (St Ludwig: Missionskolleg, 1920), pp. 32ff.

[18] This was first suggested by Ph. A. Becker, "*Vom christlichen Hymnus zum*

Minnesang," *Historisches Jahrbuch der Görres-Gesellschaft,* 52 (1932), pp. 1–39, 145–77; see especially pp. 150–61.

[19] This *Indicium regule quomodo* is found, together with other texts of Benedict of Aniane's reforms, in MS Cambridge Univ. Library Ll. 1.14 (late eleventh century; according to B. Bischoff written in England); cf. *HHEM*, p. 45, n. 14. I do not know of any other copies of the *Indicium.*

[20] For a detailed treatment of these MSS (including references to editions) see *HHEM*, pp. 55–74, 84–121. Apart from a few scattered hymns in various MSS, there is one more complete hymnal, written for use by secular clergy, unrelated to the two groups mentioned above, in MS Harley 2961 (eleventh century, used in Exeter). More evidence for different scribal and textual traditions in the two centres of reform, Canterbury and Winchester, is now accumulating. Cf. T. A. M. Bishop, *English Caroline Minuscule* (Oxford: Clarendon Press, 1971), pp. xxi–xxiii.

[21] See below n. 39.

[22] J. Mearns, *Early Latin Hymnaries, An Index of Hymns in Hymnaries before 1100, with an Appendix from Later Sources* (Cambridge: Cambridge Univ. Press, 1913). The lists of MSS and printed editions given for the individual hymns by Daniel, Mone, Walpole, in *AH* and in U. Chevalier, *Repertorium Hymnologicum,* 6 vols. (Louvain: Lefever, 1892, Polleunis & Ceuterick, 1897–1912; Brussels: Société des Bollandistes, 1920–1) are all insufficient. To be really useful, the indexes we need should be arranged according to the Church calendar (cf. *HHEM*, pp. 24, 60–8). Nearly a century ago, Henry Bradshaw spoke of "the poison of alphabetical indexes" in this field; such an alphabetical index should always be a secondary concern!

[23] An important step towards this is the publication, now in progress, of the *Corpus Consuetudinum Monasticarum,* directed by K. Hallinger (Siegburg: Franz Schmitt, 1963–); cf. A. Strittmatter in *Trad.,* 25 (1969), pp. 431–57. For earlier editions see B. Albers, *Consuetudines Monasticae,* 5 vols. (Stuttgart: Roth, 1900; Monte Cassino [Leipzig: O. Harrassowitz], 1905–12) and the Publications of the Henry Bradshaw Society.

[24] I am preparing such an edition from all English MSS written before *c.* AD 1100.

[25] On contamination within the group of early English hymnals cf. *HHEM*, pp. 125–9.

[26] For some figures of what has been lost, cf. H. Gneuss, *"Englands Bibliotheken im Mittelalter und ihr Untergang,"* in D. Riesner and H. Gneuss (eds), *Festschrift für Walter Hübner* (Berlin: Erich Schmidt, 1964), pp. 117–19.

[27] Two pioneer works in this field are R. L. Greene, *The Early English Carols* (Oxford: Clarendon Press, 1935) and R. H. Robbins, "On the Mediaeval Religious Lyric," Diss. Cambridge, England 1937; cf. also *HHEM*, pp. 211–32, and the books and articles referred to in the notes, particularly those by Carleton Brown and Rossell Hope Robbins.

[28] For the Latin and English Prymers see C. Wordsworth, *Horae Eboracenses,* Surtees Society, 132 (Durham: Andrews, 1920), pp. xv–xlvii: *HHEM*, pp. 109–11, 225–32.

[29] See the list of English Benedictine MSS and of relevant catalogues and editions in *HHEM*, pp. 249–51. To these should be added S. J. P. van Dijk, "Handlist of the Latin Liturgical Manuscripts in the Bodleian Library, Oxford," 7 vols. in 8, typescript copy in the Bodleian Library, Oxford.

[30] This development has been outlined on the basis of the evidence now available in *HHEM*, pp. 75–81. Cf. also R. W. Pfaff, *New Liturgical Feasts in Later Medieval England* (Oxford: Clarendon Press, 1970).

[31] On the Uses of Sarum and York see A. A. King, *Liturgies of the Past* (London: Longmans, 1959), esp. pp. 280–302. The Sarum and York Breviaries, including the hymns, have been edited: the first by F. Proctor and C. Wordsworth, *Breviarium ad Usum Insignis Ecclesiae Sarum*, 3 vols. (1879–86; rpt. Westmead, Farnborough, Hants: Gregg, 1970); the second by S. W. Lawley, *Breviarium ad Usum Insignis Ecclesiae Eboracensis*, Surtees Society, 71, 75 (Durham: Andrews, 1880–3). It should be noted, however, that the *Breviarium ad Usum Sarum* is essentially a reprint of a late edition printed in 1531 (Paris: C. Chevallon and F. Regnault), whereas more than fifty printed editions, issued between *c.* 1475 and 1557 (listed in *Breviarium ad Usum Sarum*, III, xliii–li) and numerous earlier MSS are still extant.

[32] For the evidence see *HHEM*, pp. 81–3.

[33] For editions of texts and literature see Szövérffy, *Annalen*, op. cit., I, p. 37, and I, p. 282, n. 1.

[34] *AH* 55, p. v.

[35] The best critical texts are those by Blume and Bannister, *AH*, vols. 53–5, but only part of the available English MSS have been used, and many of the sequences known in England do not occur here but elsewhere in various volumes of *AH*. The collections of sequences according to the uses of Sarum and York are included in the editions by W. G. Legg, *The Sarum Missal* (Oxford: Clarendon Press, 1916; rpt. 1969), and by W. G. Henderson, *Missale ad Usum Insignis Ecclesiae Eboracensis*, Surtees Society, 59, 60 (Durham: Andrews, 1874).

[36] See Szövérffy, *Annalen*, I, op. cit., pp. 283–312, and the literature quoted there. Peter Dronke has recently suggested a much earlier origin for the sequence: "The Beginnings of the Sequence," *Beiträge zur Geschichte der deutschen Sprache und Literatur* (Tübingen), 87 (1965), pp. 43–73. But see Szövérffy, "Hymnological Notes," op. cit., 25 (1969), p. 426.

[37] *AH* 53, p. xxix f.

[38] MSS CCCC 473 and Bodley 775 [S. C. 2558]. A date late in the tenth century, as usually given for Bodley 775, is too early; cf. Bishop, op. cit., p. 23, no. 27. Other early MSS, each with a few sequences or sequence incipits, are Bodley 579 [S. C. 2675] (the "Leofric Missal," tenth century, from Glastonbury?); Harley 2904 (late tenth century, from Winchester?); Harley 2961 (the "Leofric Collectar," eleventh century, used at Exeter). The famous Bodley MS 775 originally contained sixty-five sequences.

[39] Cf. *AH* 40, pp. 9, 150.

[40] The ascription of some sequences to Wulfstan, precentor of Winchester in the late tenth century, is, however, doubtful; cf. *HHEM*, p. 246.

[41] E.g. MS Cotton Caligula A. xiv, from Christ Church, Canterbury, with a collection of sequences written in the twelfth century. Cf. also the twelfth-century Durham additions on ff. 2ʳ–8ᵛ of MS Durham Univ. Library Cosin, V. v.6, a gradual from Christ Church, Canterbury.

[42] For lists of sequences in English MSS see especially J. Julian, *Dictionary of Hymnology*, 2nd edn (1907; rpt. New York: Dover Publications, 1957), pp. 1043–52; W. H. Frere (ed.), *The Winchester Troper*, Henry Bradshaw Society, 8 (London: Harrison, 1894), pp. 70–83, 124, 227–38; Proctor and Wordsworth, op. cit., III, pp. xcii–xcix (erroneously lists many pieces from the Winchester Tropers as York sequences); R. E. Messenger, "Hymns and Sequences of the Sarum Use," *Transactions and Proceedings of the American Philological Association*, 59 (1928), pp. 123–8; *AH* 53, p. 405 (by Mearns). None of these lists is comprehensive enough for the purpose outlined above.